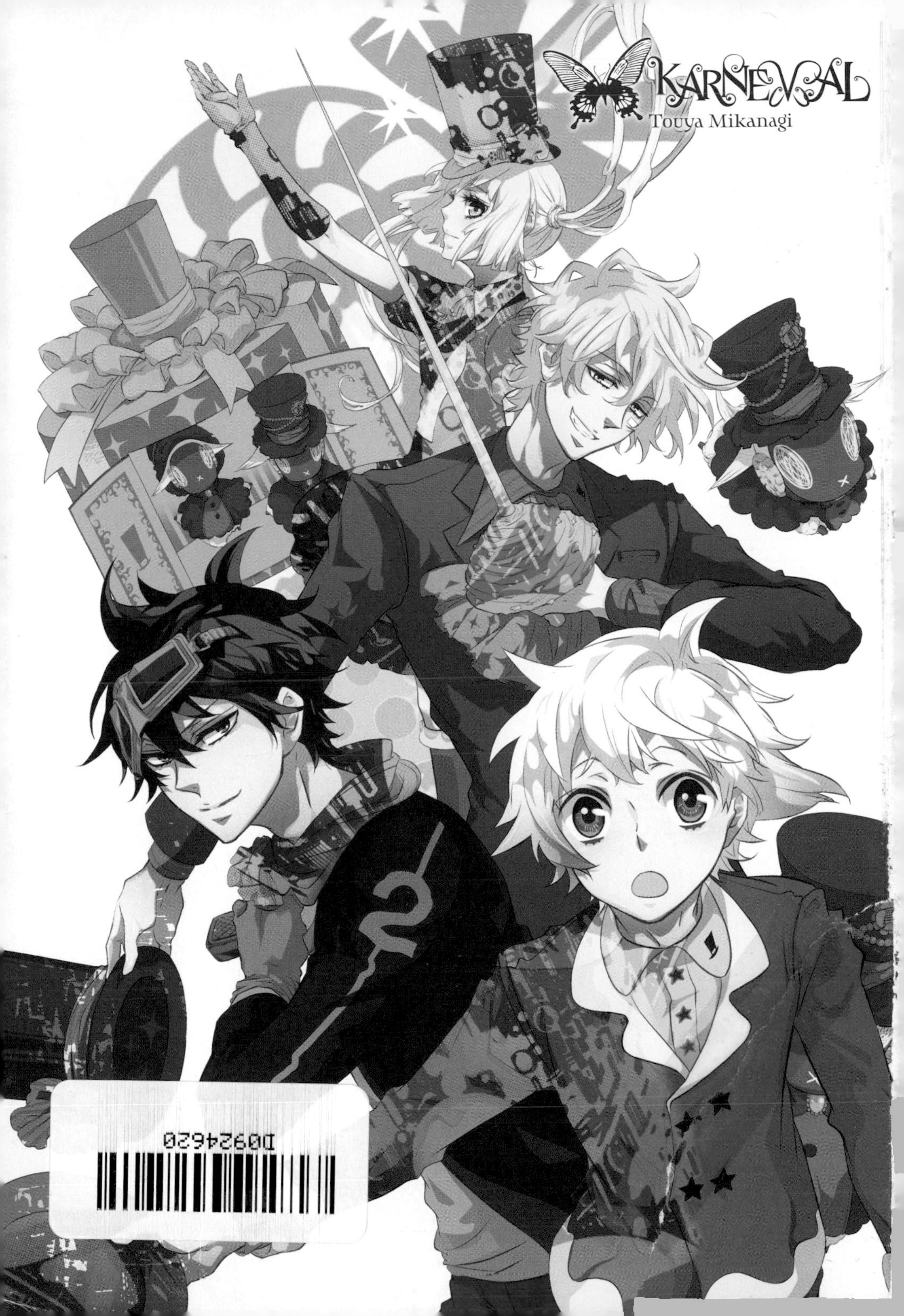
KARNEVAL
Touya Mikanagi

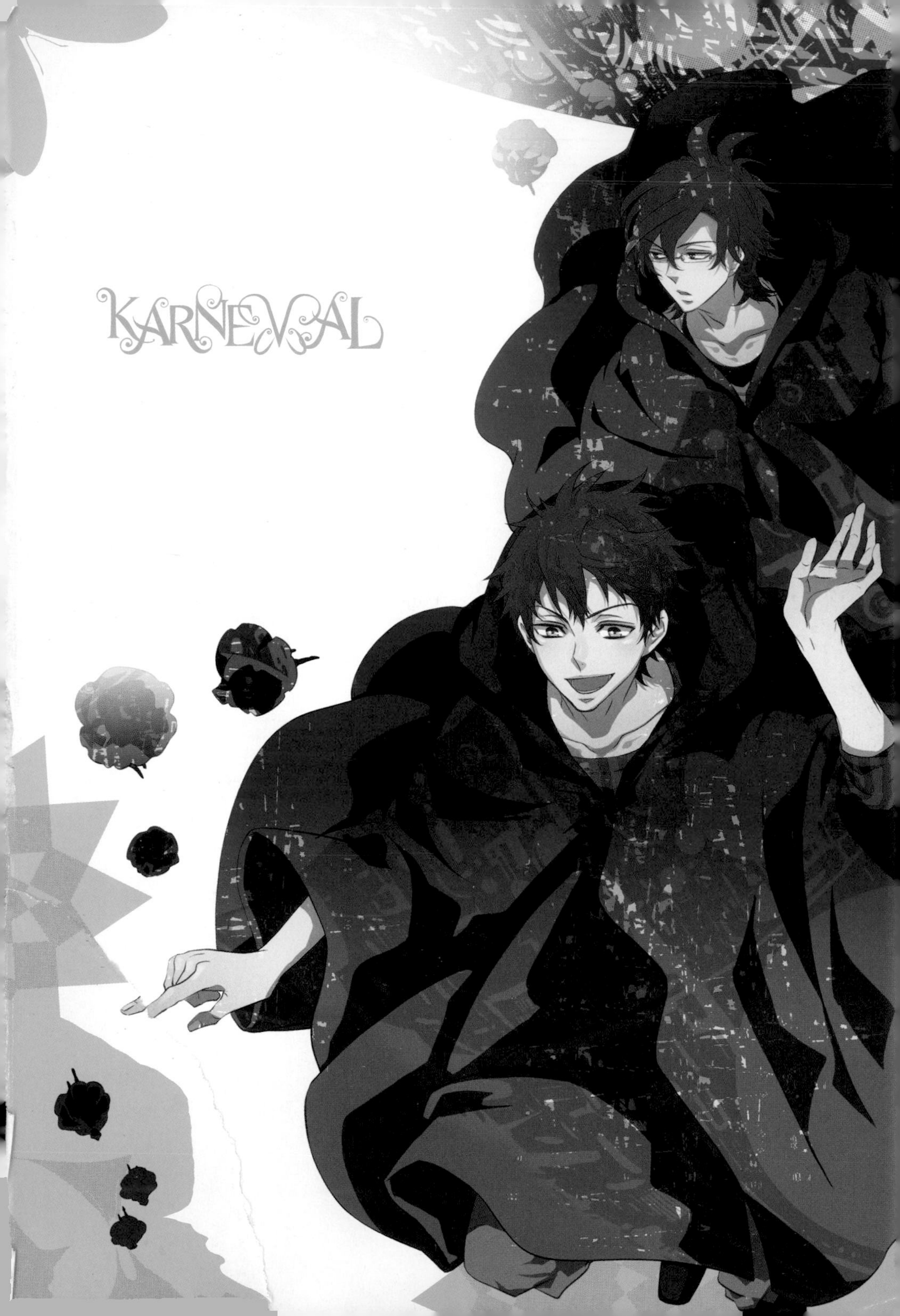
KARNEVAL

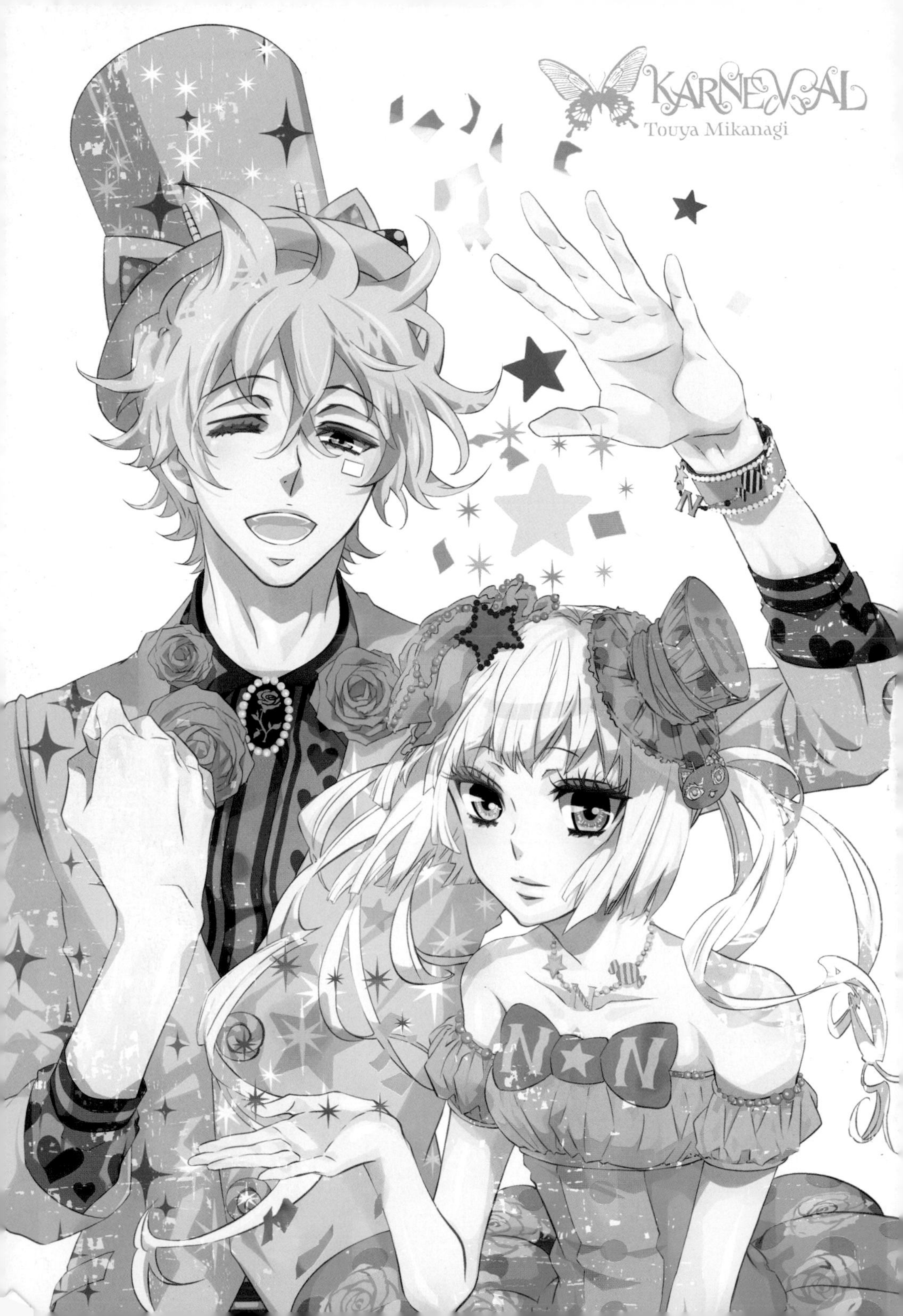
KARNEVAL
Touya Mikanagi

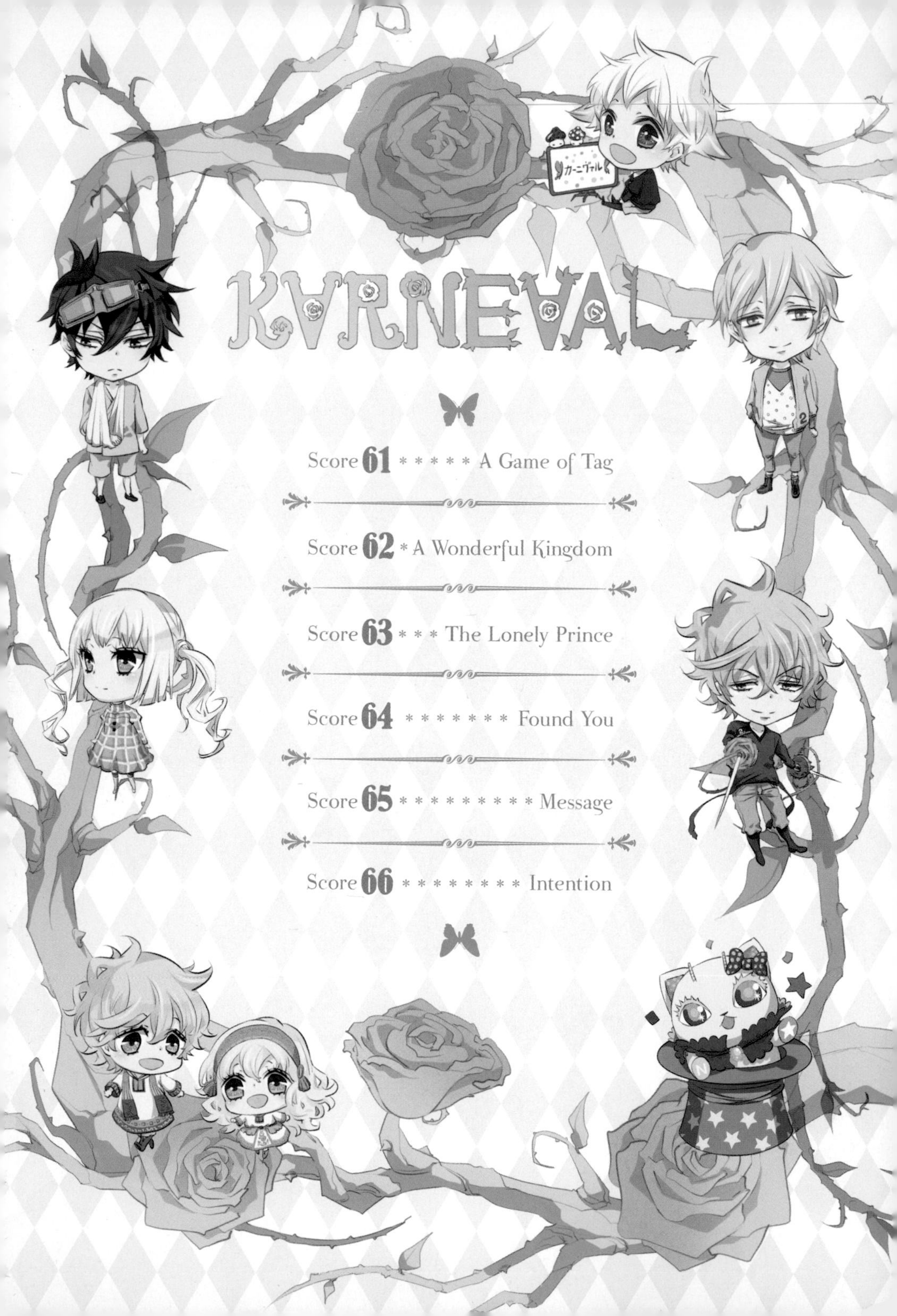
カーニヴァル

KARNEVAL

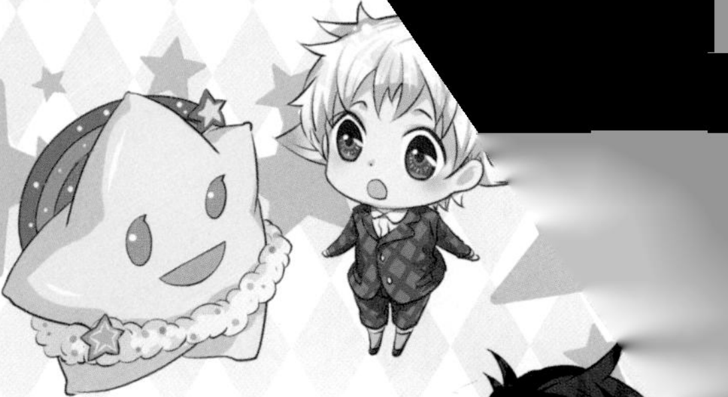

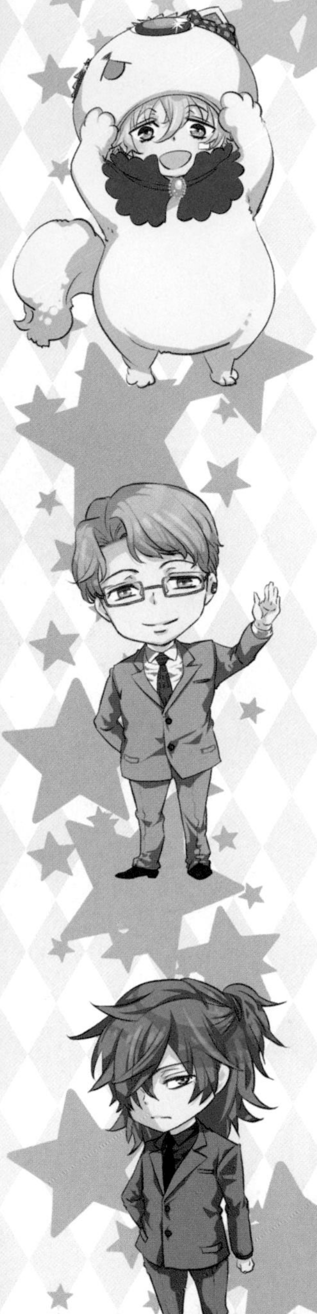

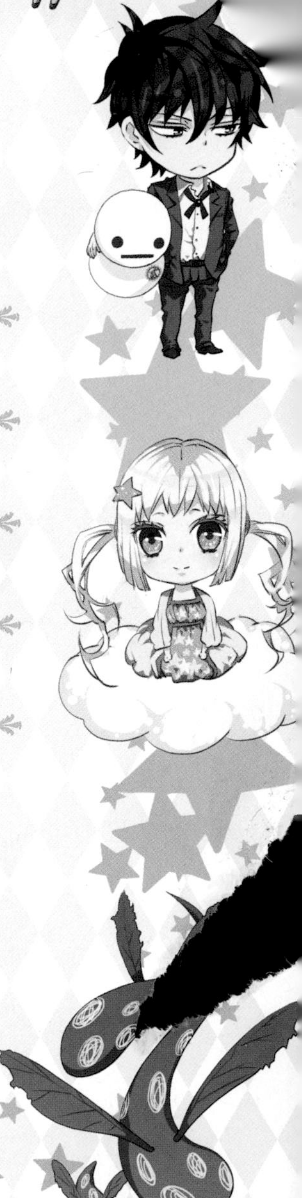

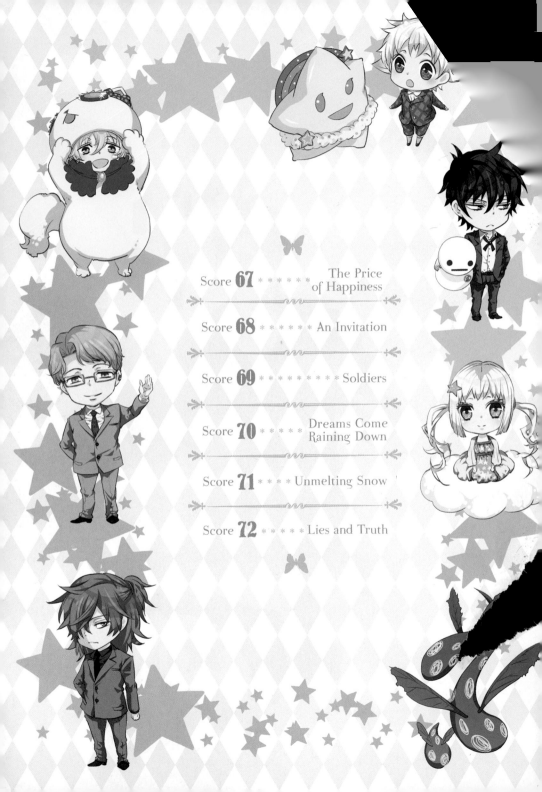

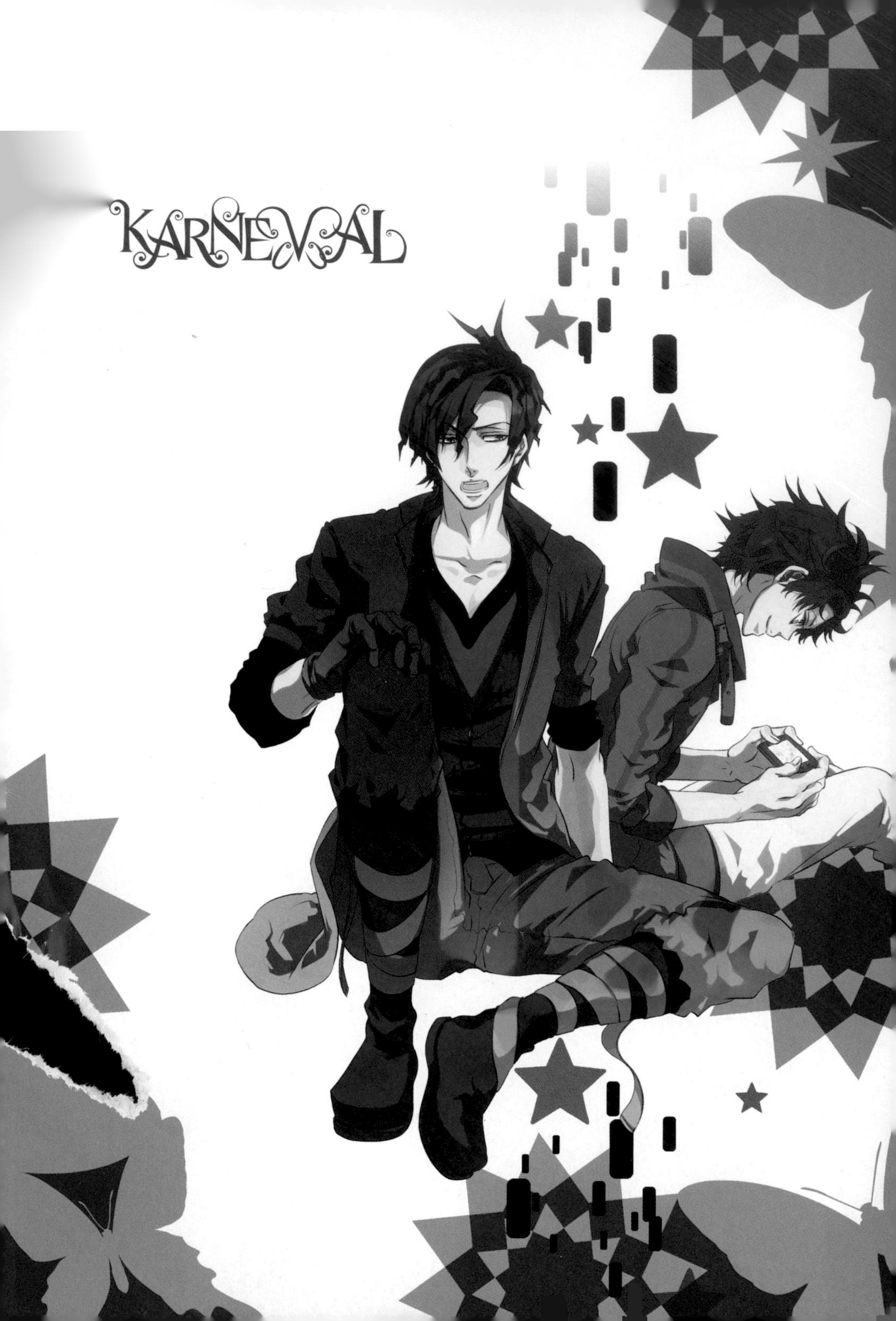
KARNEVAL

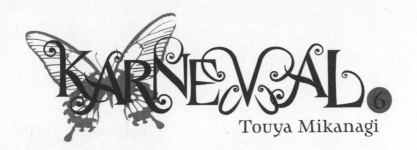

KARNEVAL 6

Touya Mikanagi

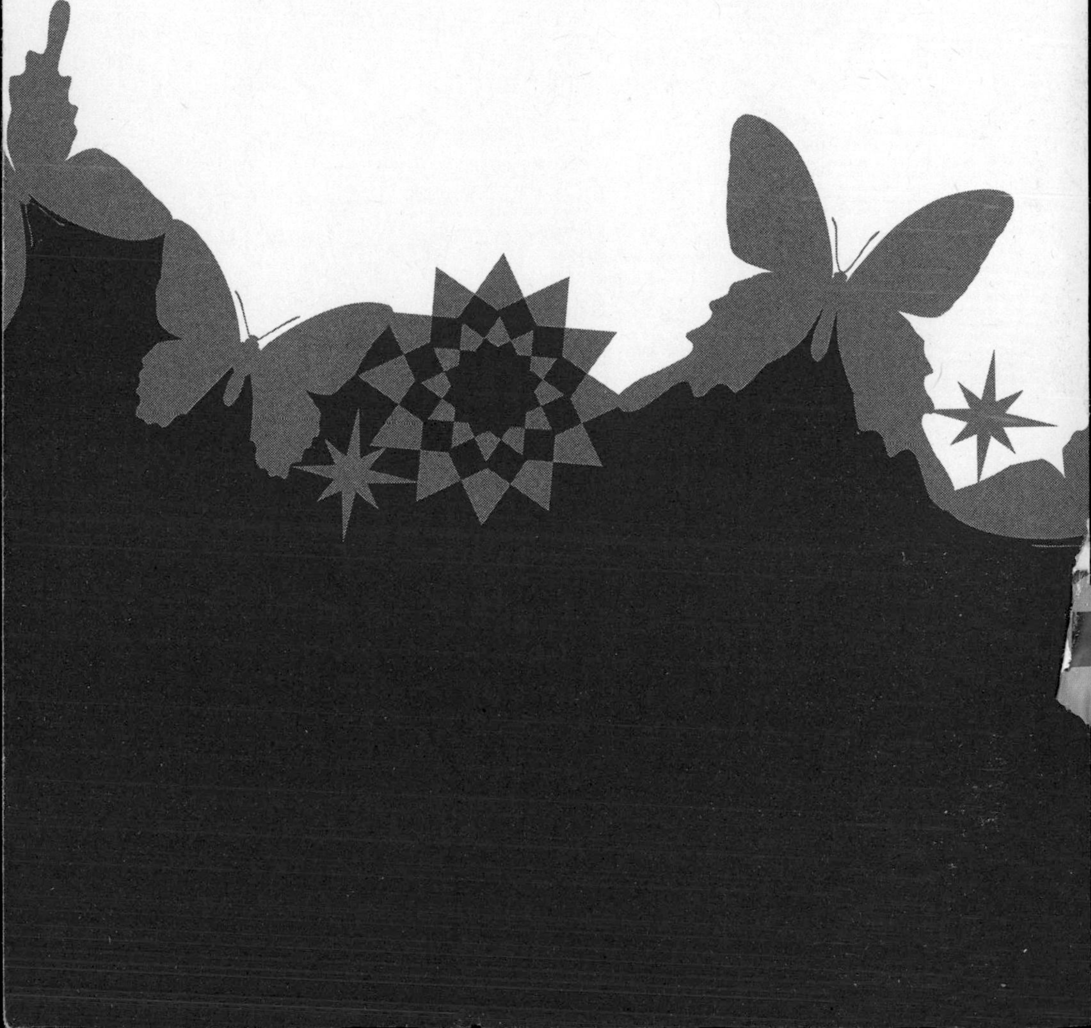

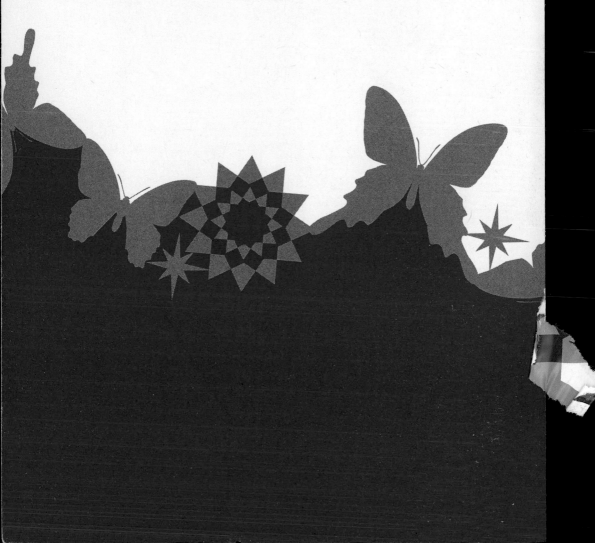

STORY

GAREKI AND FRIENDS HAVE SUCCESSFULLY RESCUED THE MISSING NAI AND KAROKU. HOWEVER, ON THEIR PATH HOME, GAREKI, YOGI, AND TSUKUMO MAKE A DETOUR TO AID DR. AKARI IN SOME FIELD RESEARCH. ALTHOUGH THEY ENCOUNTER THE MINOR MISHAP OF YOGI'S UNDERWEAR VANISHING WITHOUT A TRACE, THE RESEARCH TRIP IS SUCCESSFULLY CONCLUDED. HOWEVER, WHEN THE THREE STOP BRIEFLY IN THE NEARBY TOWN TO BUY SOUVENIRS FOR NAI, THEY ARE SUDDENLY ATTACKED BY BEAST VARUGA! EVEN FIGHTING THEIR HARDEST, YOGI AND TSUKUMO ARE SOON OVERWHELMED BY THE ENDLESS SWARM OF BEAST VARUGA—WHEN A POWERFUL HUMANOID VARUGA APPEARS AS WELL! WITH THEIR DEFENSES CRUMBLING, MORE AND MORE TOWNSPEOPLE ARE KILLED IN THE VARUGA ONSLAUGHT. JUST AS THE SITUATION SEEMS HOPELESS, DR. AKARI APPEARS BEFORE GAREKI AND OFFERS A SOLUTION—THE UNLEASHING OF YOGI'S SILVER-HAIRED "OTHER PERSONA," WHOM GAREKI HAD GLIMPSED ONCE BEFORE IN BATTLE. THANKS TO SILVER YOGI, THE ENEMY IS VANQUISHED. HOWEVER...

CHARACTERS OF KARNEVAL

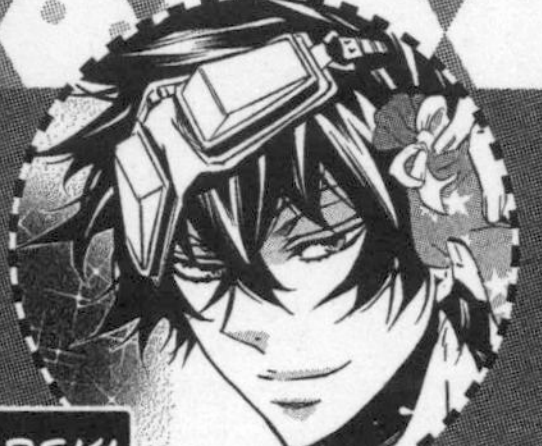

GAREKI

HE MET NAI INSIDE AN EERIE MANSION THAT HE HAD INTENDED TO BURGLARIZE. CURRENTLY ENROLLED IN THE CIRCUS PROGRAM AT THE GOVERNMENT TRAINING SCHOOL CHRONOMÉ ACADEMY.

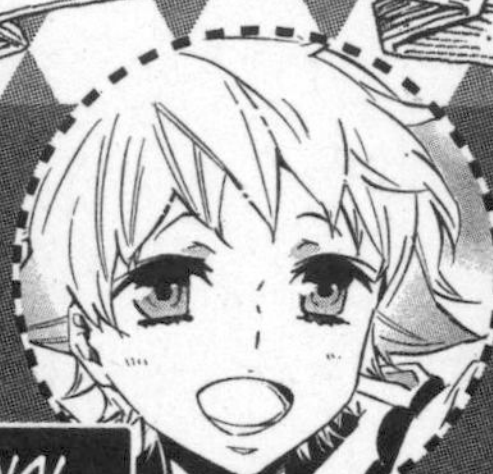

NAI

A BOY WHO POSSESSES EXTRAORDINARY HEARING AND HAS A SOMEWHAT LIMITED UNDERSTANDING OF HOW THE WORLD WORKS. HE IS CURRENTLY LIVING ABOARD CIRCUS'S 2ND SHIP ALONGSIDE KAROKU.

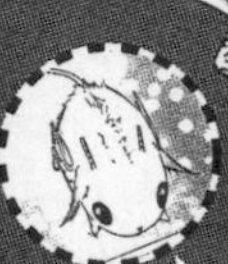

NIJI

THE ANIMAL FROM WHICH NAI WAS CREATED. THEY EXIST ONLY IN THE RAINBOW FOREST, A HIGHLY UNUSUAL ECOSYSTEM THAT ALLOWED THE NIJI TO EVOLVE AS THEY DID.

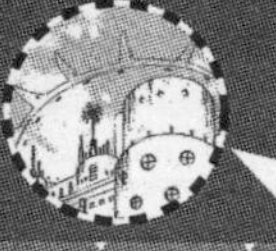

CHRONOMÉ

A VOCATIONAL SCHOOL FOR THOSE HOPING TO WORK FOR THE GOVERNMENT. ITS FOUR PROGRAMS OF STUDY ARE CIRCUS, ENGINEERING, MEDICAL & BIOLOGICAL SCIENCES, AND MANAGEMENT & INTELLIGENCE.

TAKING CARE OF

GUARDING ON SHIP

NATIONAL SUPREME DEFENSE FORCE "CIRCUS" 2ND SHIP

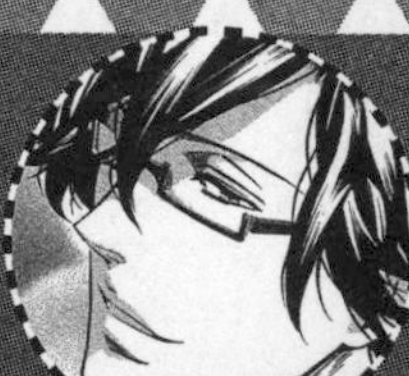

HIRATO

CAPTAIN OF CIRCUS'S 2ND SHIP. NAI (AND GAREKI), WHO BROUGHT HIM A BRACELET BELONGING TO CIRCUS, ARE CURRENTLY UNDER HIS PROTECTION.

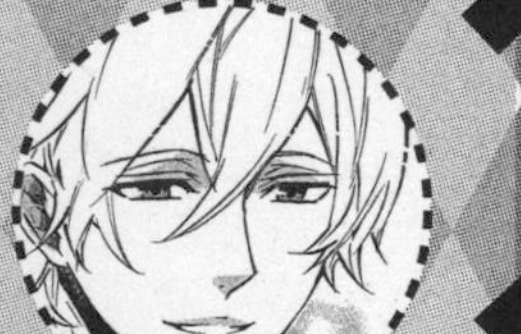

KAROKU

THE PERSON WHO CREATED NAI. TWO DIFFERENT KAROKUS WERE SEEN AT THE SMOKY MANSION, WITH NO EXPLANATION ABOUT THEM CURRENTLY KNOWN. THE KAROKU WHO WAS RESCUED FROM THE SMOKY MANSION IS CURRENTLY RECUPERATING ABOARD CIRCUS'S 2ND SHIP.

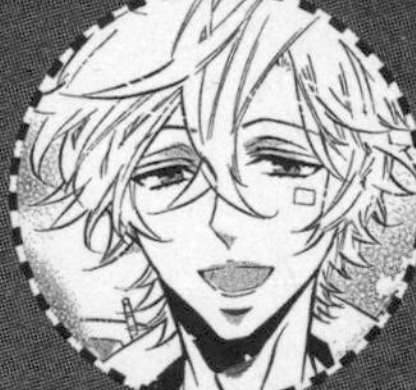

YOGI

CIRCUS'S 2ND SHIP COMBAT SPECIALIST. HE HAS A CHEERFUL, FRIENDLY PERSONALITY. WHEN THE PATCH HE WEARS ON HIS FACE RUNS OUT OF POTENCY, HIS PERSONALITY CHANGES.

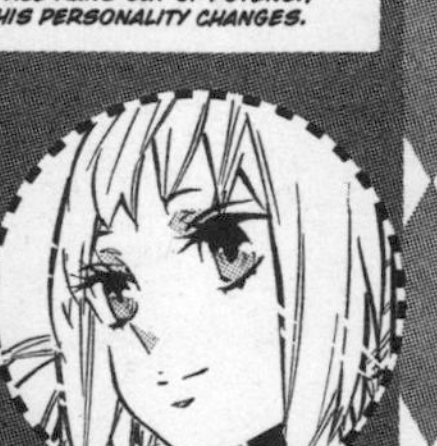

TSUKUMO

CIRCUS'S 2ND SHIP COMBAT SPECIALIST. A BEAUTIFUL GIRL WITH A COOL, SERIOUS PERSONALITY. RECENTLY, SHE SEEMS TO HAVE TAKEN UP SEWING STUFFED TOYS AS A PASTIME.

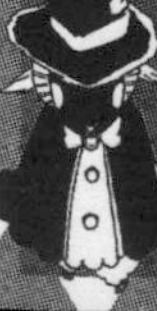

SHEEP

A CIRCUS DEFENSE SYSTEM. DESPITE THEIR CUTE APPEARANCE, THE SHEEP HAVE SOME VERY POWERFUL CAPABILITIES.

Q: WHAT IS CIRCUS?

A: THE EQUIVALENT OF THE REAL-WORLD POLICE. THEY CONDUCT THEIR LARGE-SCALE "OPERATIONS" WITHOUT FOREWARNING TO ENSURE THEIR TARGETS WILL NOT ESCAPE ARREST, UTILIZING COORDINATED, POWERFUL ATTACKS!! AFTER AN OPERATION, CIRCUS PERFORMS A "SHOW" FOR THE PEOPLE OF THE CITY AS AN APOLOGY FOR THE FEAR AND INCONVENIENCE THEIR WORK MAY HAVE CAUSED. IN SHORT, "CIRCUS" IS A CHEERFUL (?) AGENCY THAT CARRIES OUT THEIR MISSION DAY AND NIGHT TO APPREHEND EVIL AND PROTECT THE PEACE OF THE LAND.

Score 61: A Game of Tag

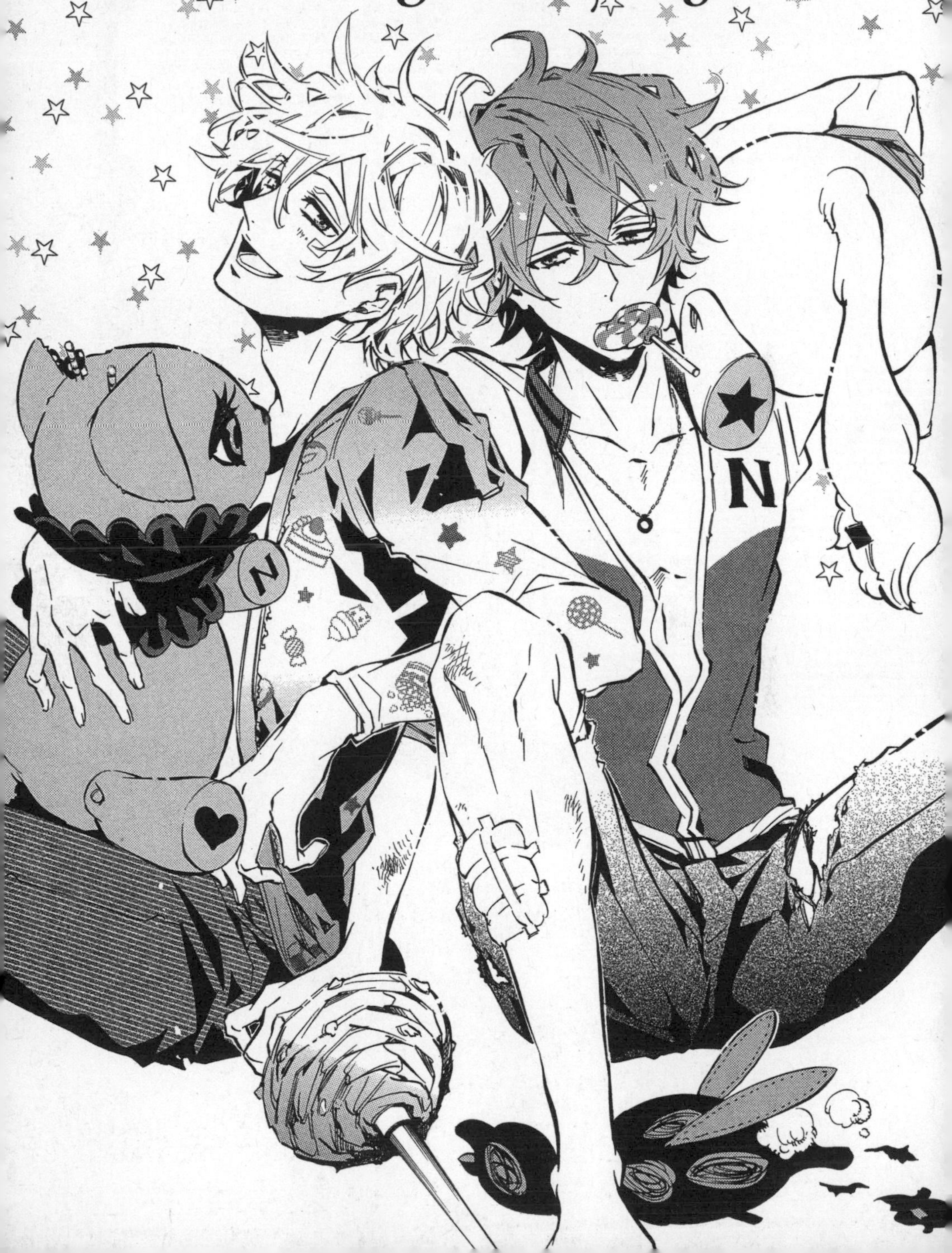

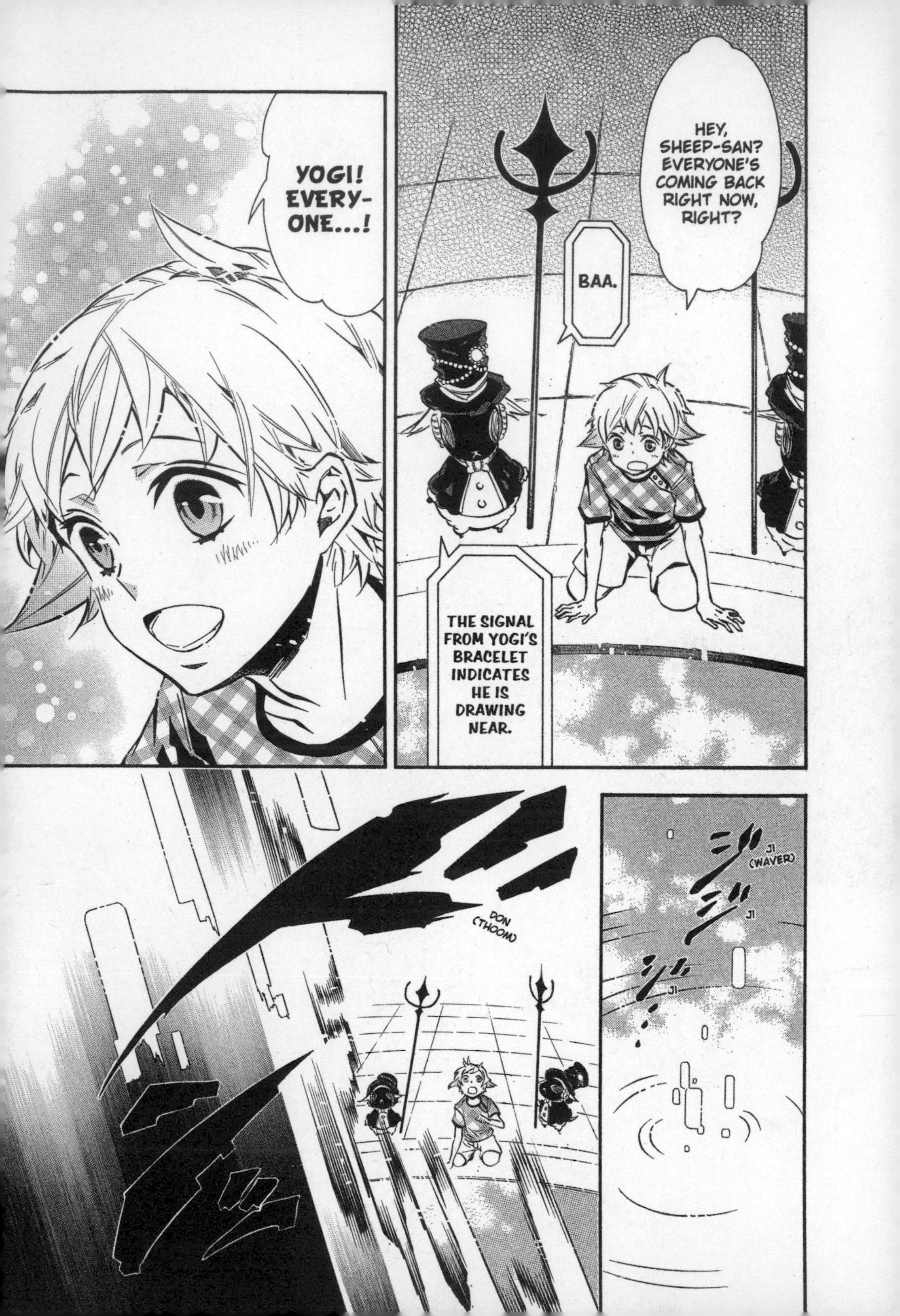
HEY, SHEEP-SAN? EVERYONE'S COMING BACK RIGHT NOW, RIGHT?
BAA.
THE SIGNAL FROM YOGI'S BRACELET INDICATES HE IS DRAWING NEAR.
YOGI! EVERY-ONE...!
JI (WAVER)
JI
JI
DON (THOOM)

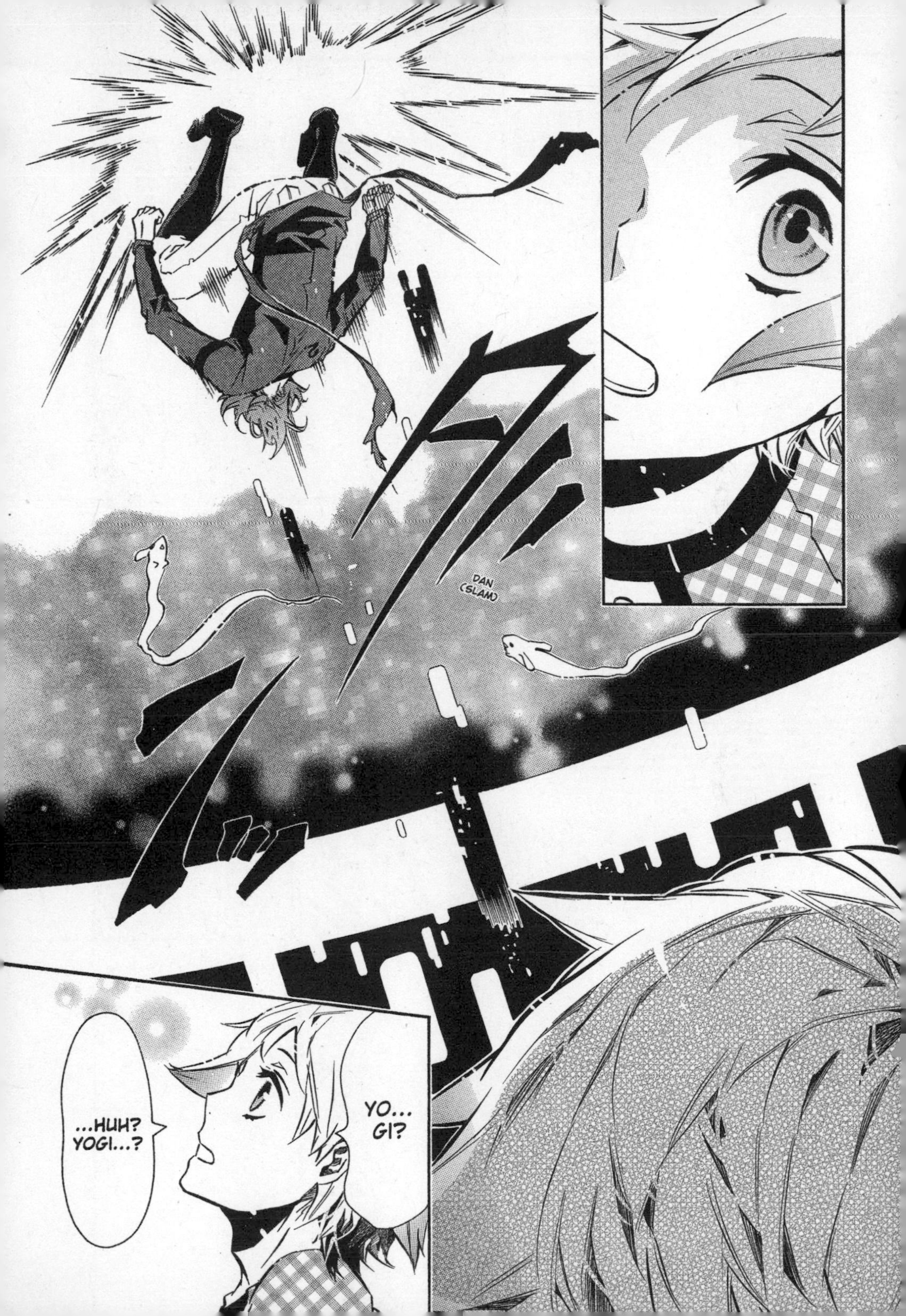
DAN
(SLAM)
YO... GI?
...HUH? YOGI...?

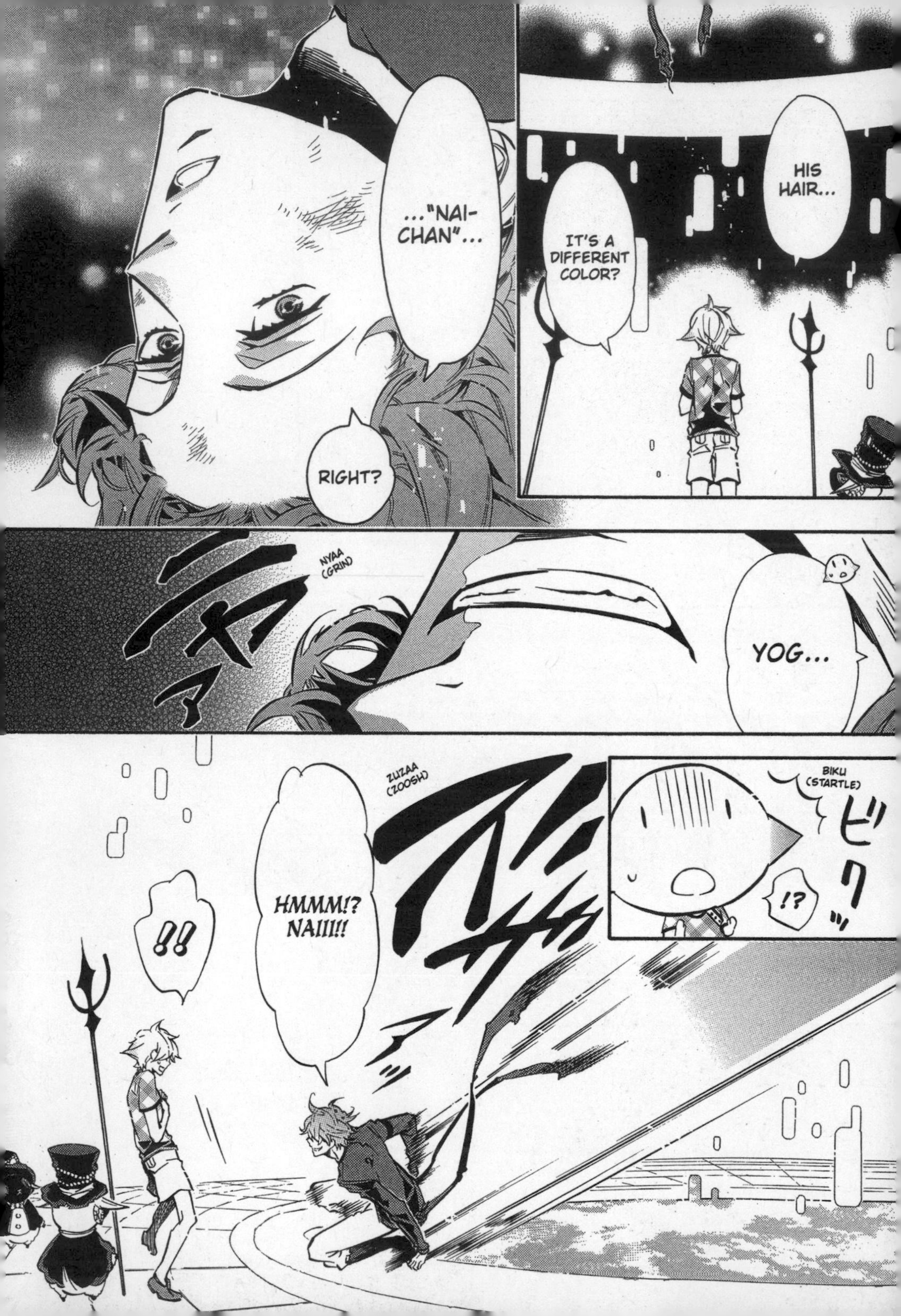
HIS HAIR...
IT'S A DIFFERENT COLOR?
..."NAI-CHAN"...
RIGHT?
YOG...
NYAA (GRIN)
BIKU (STARTLE)
!?
ZUZAA (ZOOSH)
HMMM!? NAIII!!
!!

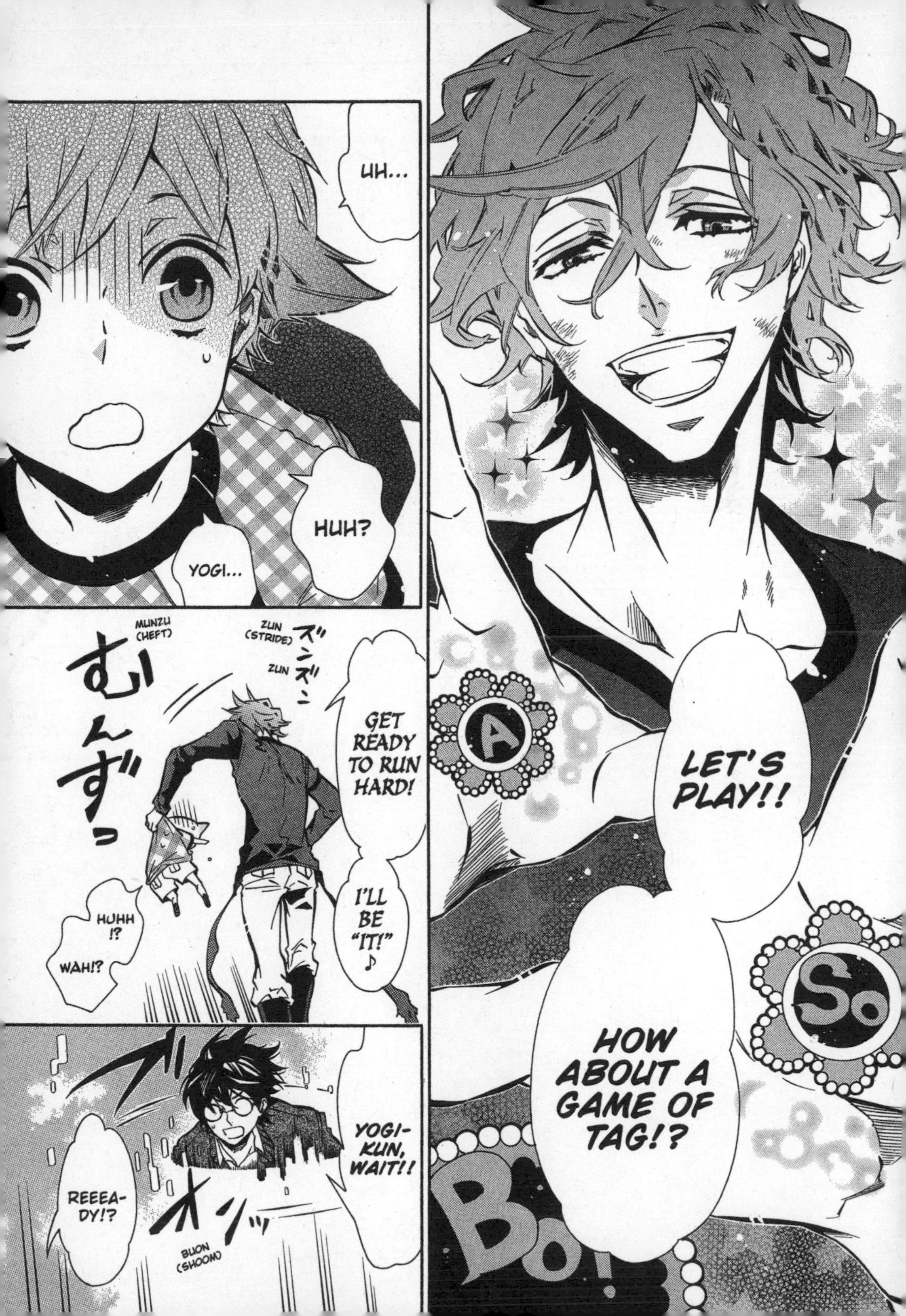
LET'S PLAY!!
So
HOW ABOUT A GAME OF TAG!?
Bo!
UH...
HUH?
YOGI...
ズンズン
ZUN (STRIDE) ZUN
GET READY TO RUN HARD!
I'LL BE "IT!" ♪
むんずっ
MUNZU (HEFT)
HUHH!?
WAH!?
YOGI-KUN, WAIT!!
ブオンッ
BUON (SHOOM)
REEEA-DY!?

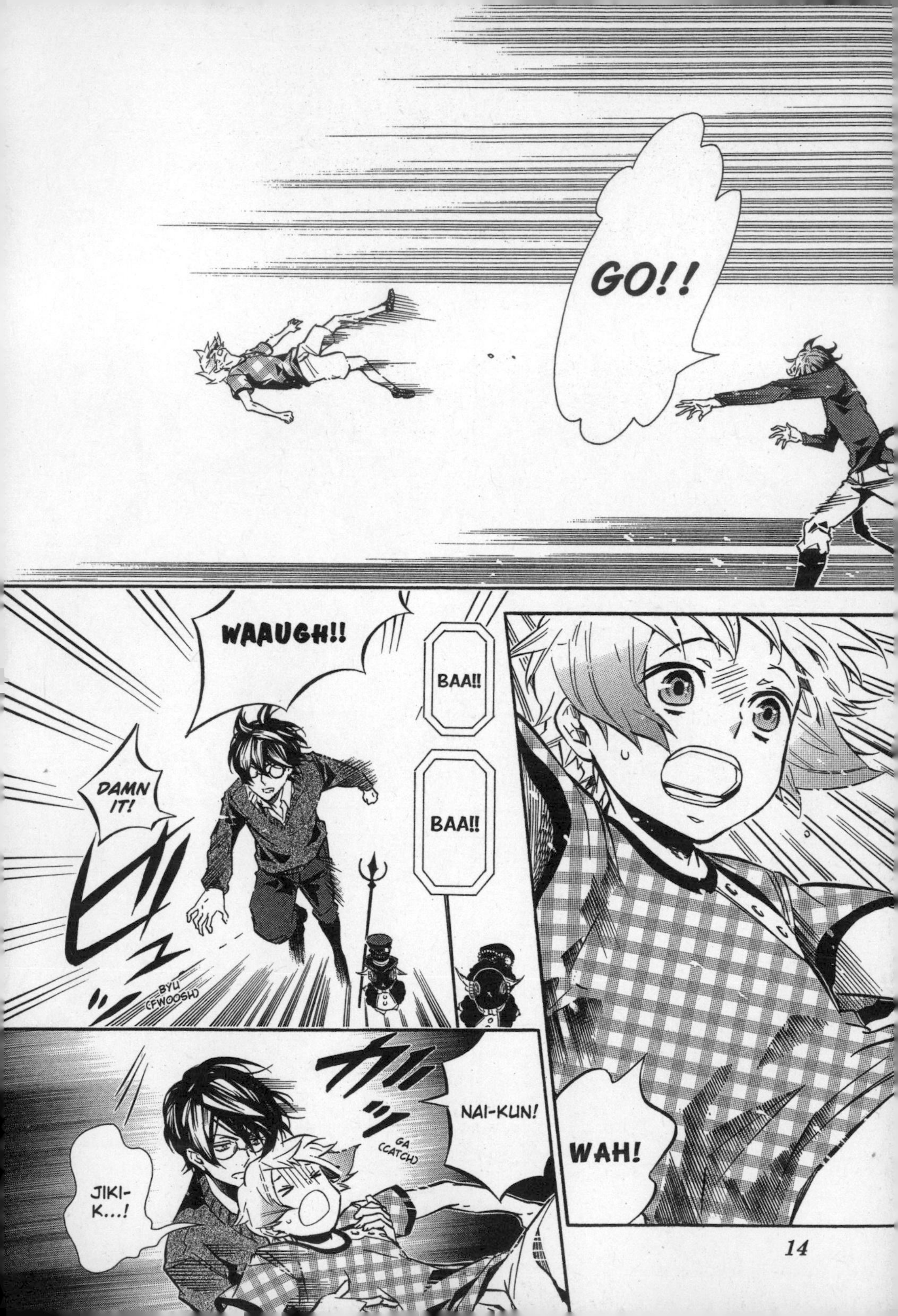
GO!!
WAH!
WAAUGH!!
BAA!!
BAA!!
DAMN IT!
BYU (FWOOSH)
NAI-KUN!
GA (CATCH)
JIKI-K...!

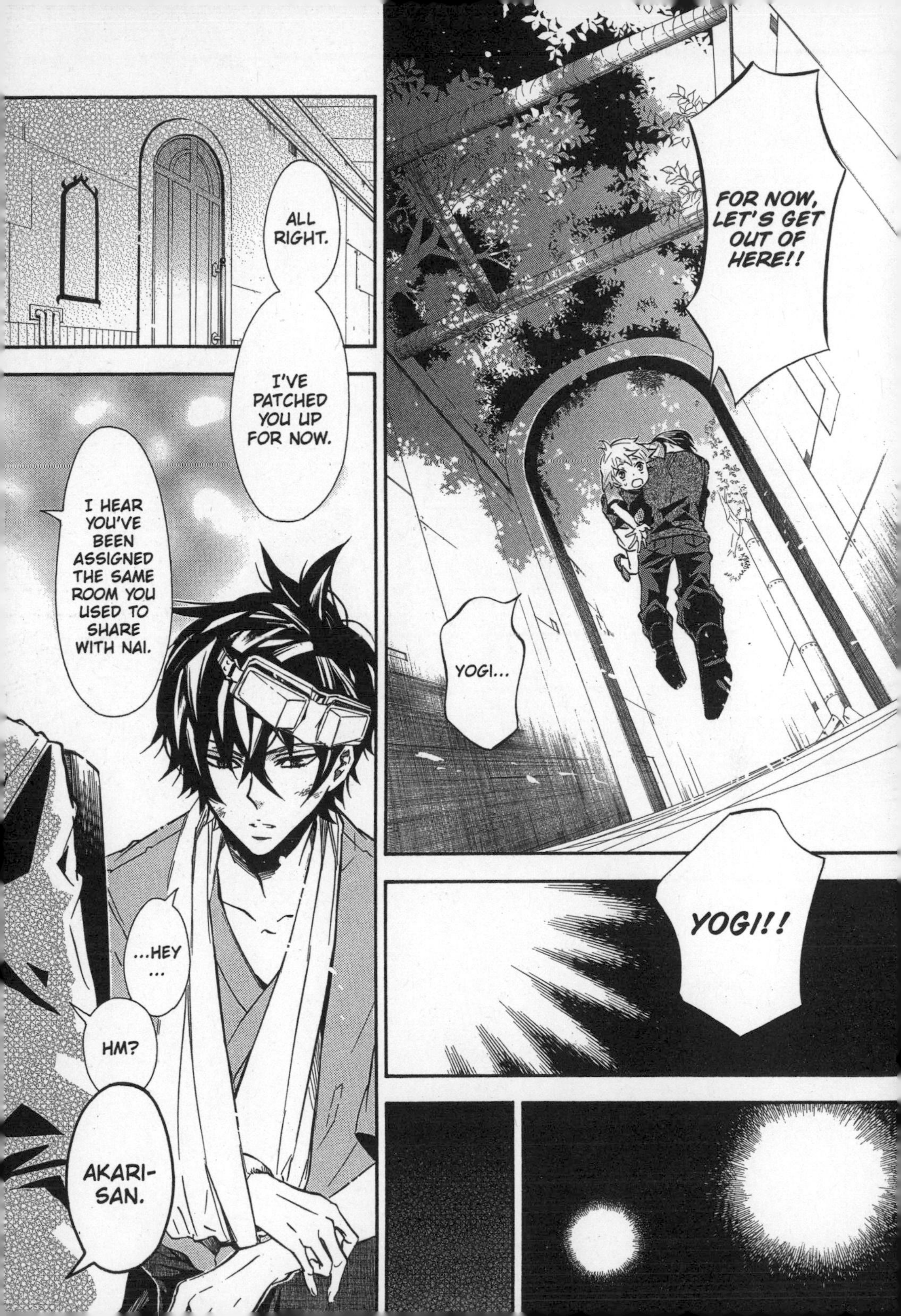
FOR NOW, LET'S GET OUT OF HERE!!
YOGI...
YOGI!!
ALL RIGHT.
I'VE PATCHED YOU UP FOR NOW.
I HEAR YOU'VE BEEN ASSIGNED THE SAME ROOM YOU USED TO SHARE WITH NAI.
...HEY ...
HM?
AKARI-SAN.

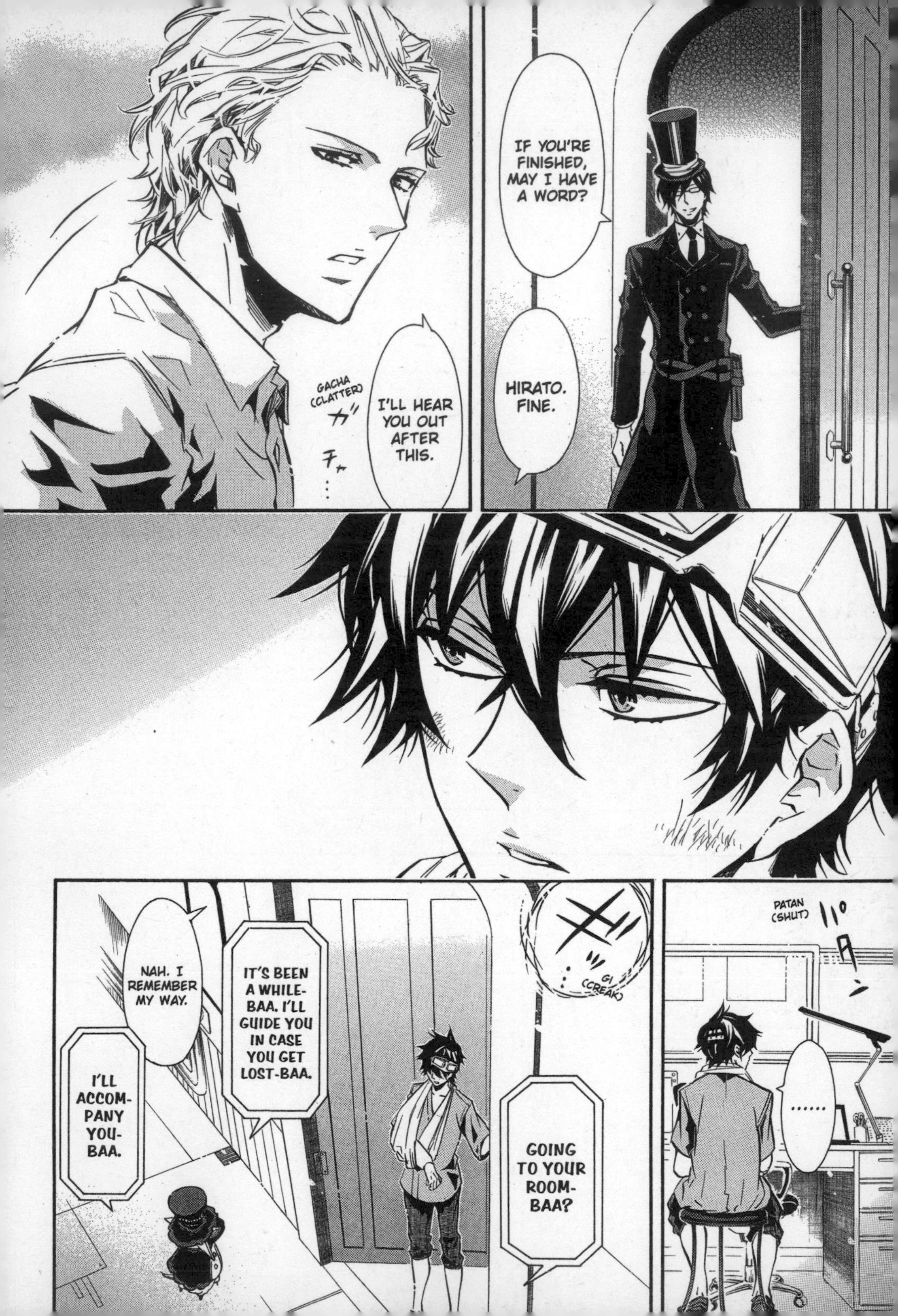
IF YOU'RE FINISHED, MAY I HAVE A WORD?
HIRATO. FINE.
GACHA (CLATTER)
I'LL HEAR YOU OUT AFTER THIS.
PATAN (SHUT)
......
GI (CREAK)
GOING TO YOUR ROOM-BAA?
IT'S BEEN A WHILE-BAA. I'LL GUIDE YOU IN CASE YOU GET LOST-BAA.
NAH. I REMEMBER MY WAY.
I'LL ACCOMPANY YOU-BAA.

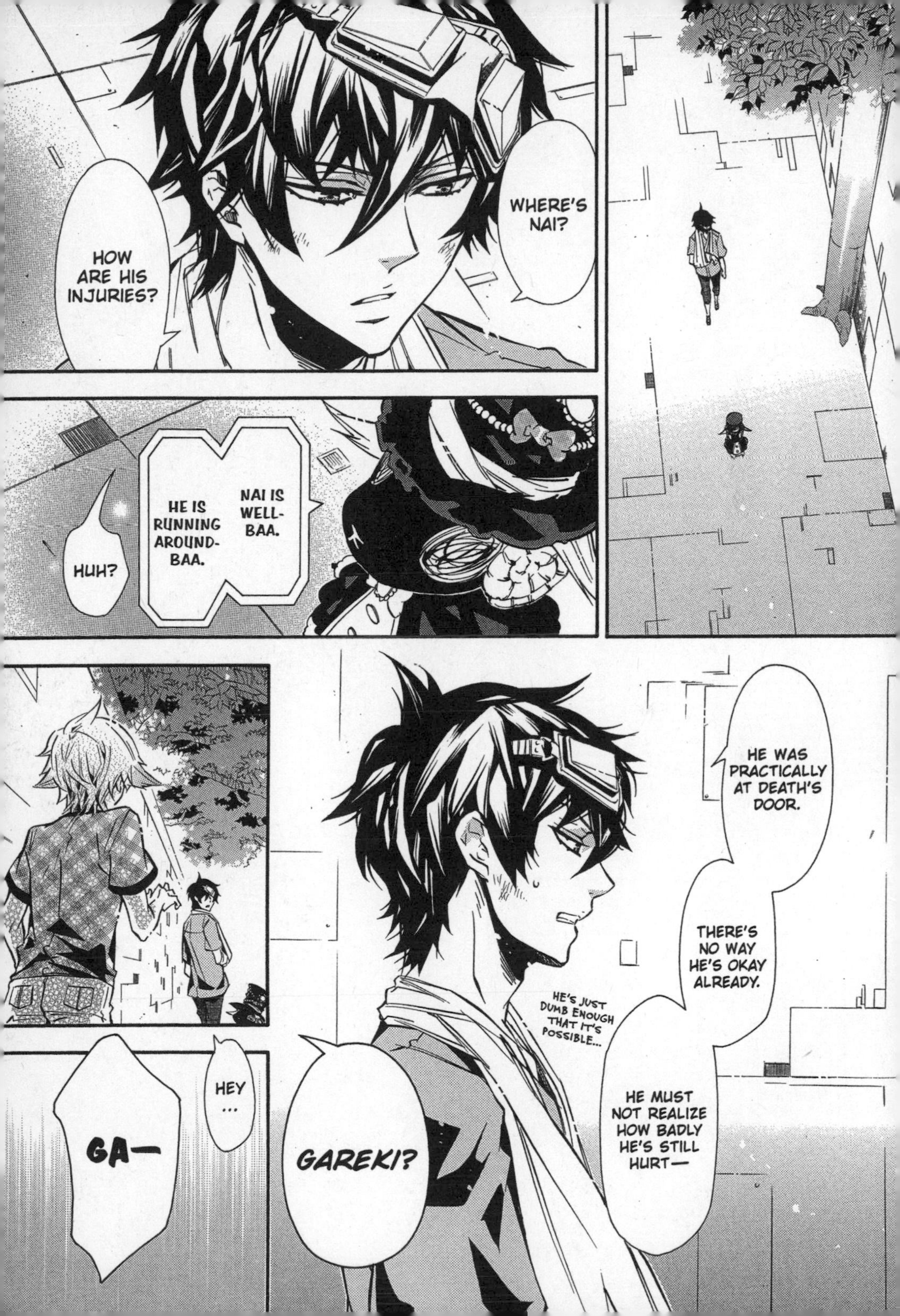

WHERE'S NAI?
HOW ARE HIS INJURIES?
NAI IS WELL-BAA.
HE IS RUNNING AROUND-BAA.
HUH?
HE WAS PRACTICALLY AT DEATH'S DOOR.
THERE'S NO WAY HE'S OKAY ALREADY.
HE'S JUST DUMB ENOUGH THAT IT'S POSSIBLE...
HE MUST NOT REALIZE HOW BADLY HE'S STILL HURT—
GAREKI?
HEY ...
GA—

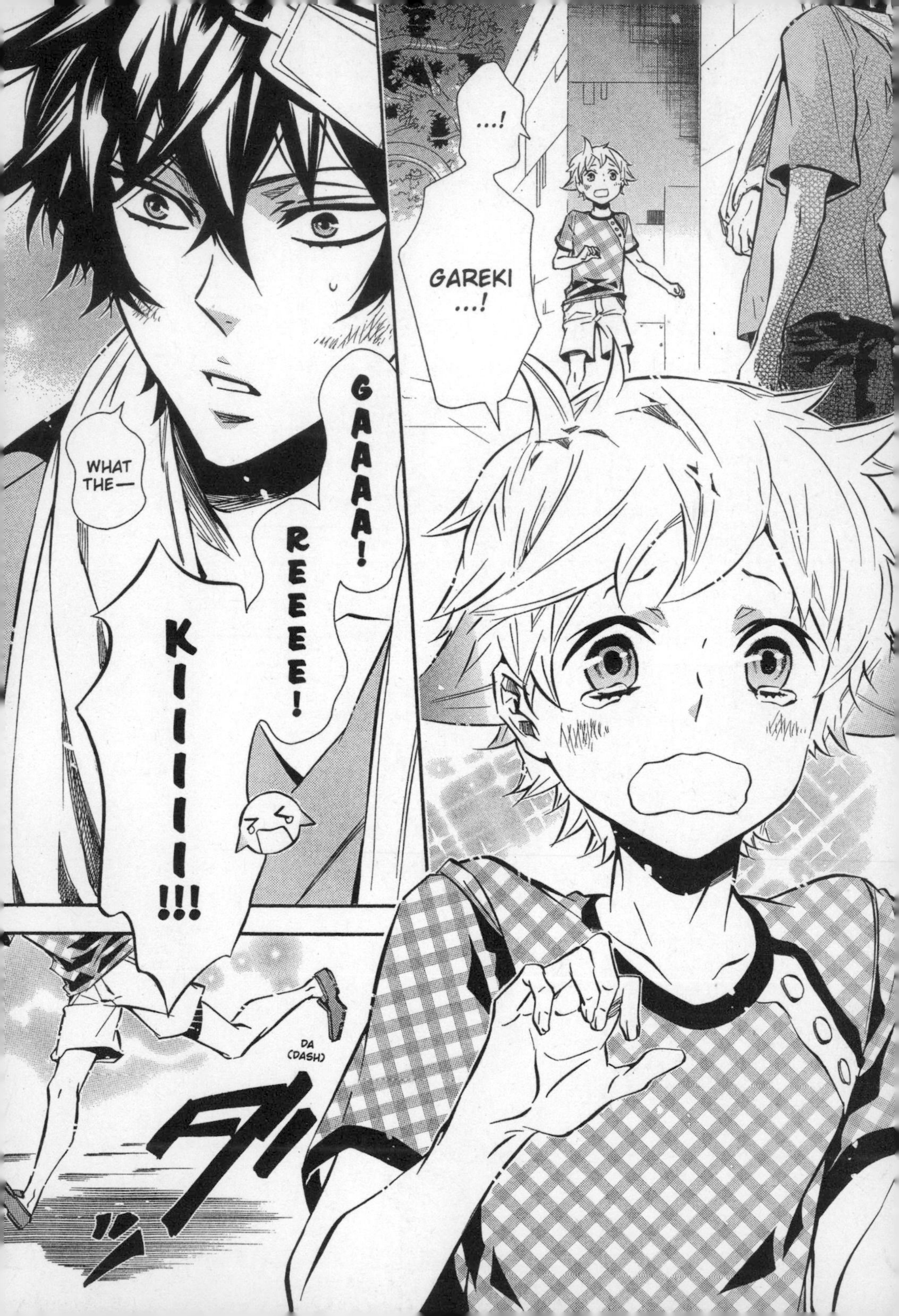

...!
GAREKI ...!
GAAAAA! REEEEE! KIIIIII!!!
WHAT THE—
DA (DASH)

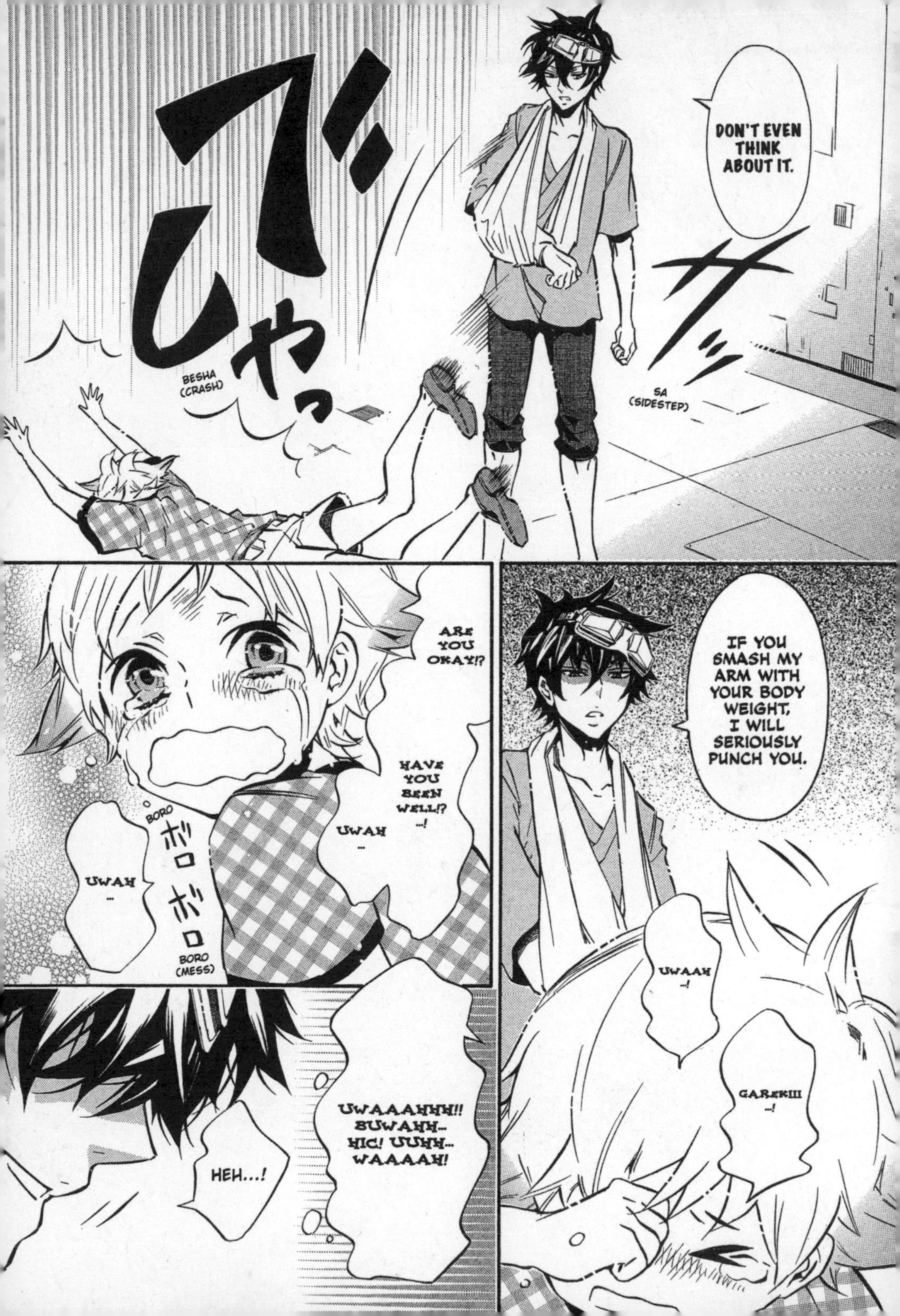
DON'T EVEN THINK ABOUT IT.
SA (SIDESTEP)
BESHA (CRASH)
IF YOU SMASH MY ARM WITH YOUR BODY WEIGHT, I WILL SERIOUSLY PUNCH YOU.
ARE YOU OKAY!?
HAVE YOU BEEN WELL!? ...!
UWAH ...
BORO
ボロ ボロ
BORO (MESS)
UWAH ...
UWAAH ...!
GAREKIII ...!
UWAAAHHH!! BUWAHH... HIC! UUHH... WAAAAH!
HEH...!

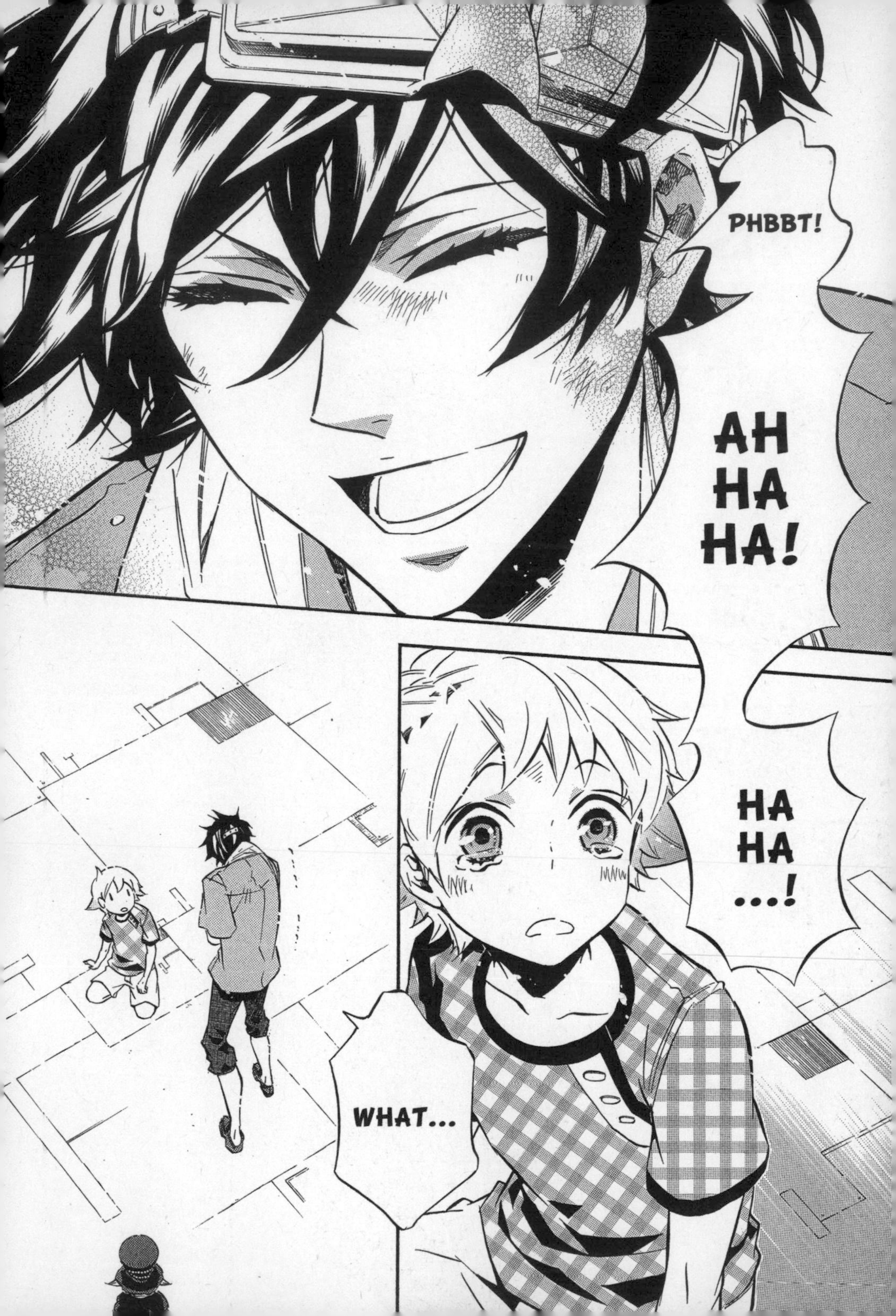
PHBBT!
AH HA HA!
HA HA ...!
WHAT...

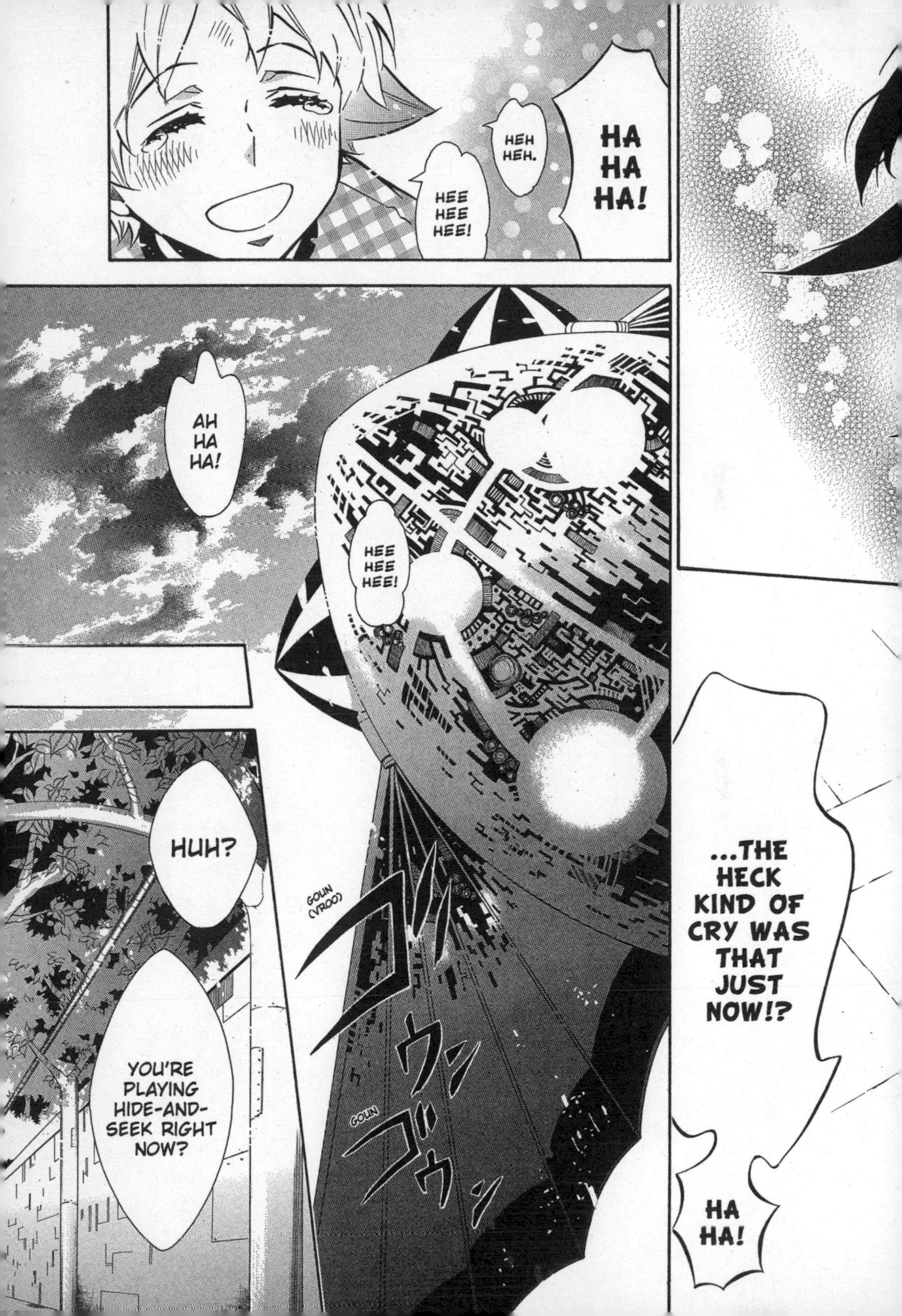
HA HA HA!
HEH HEH.
HEE HEE HEE!
AH HA HA!
HEE HEE HEE!
GOUN (VROO)
GOUN
...THE HECK KIND OF CRY WAS THAT JUST NOW!?
HA HA!
HUH?
YOU'RE PLAYING HIDE-AND-SEEK RIGHT NOW?

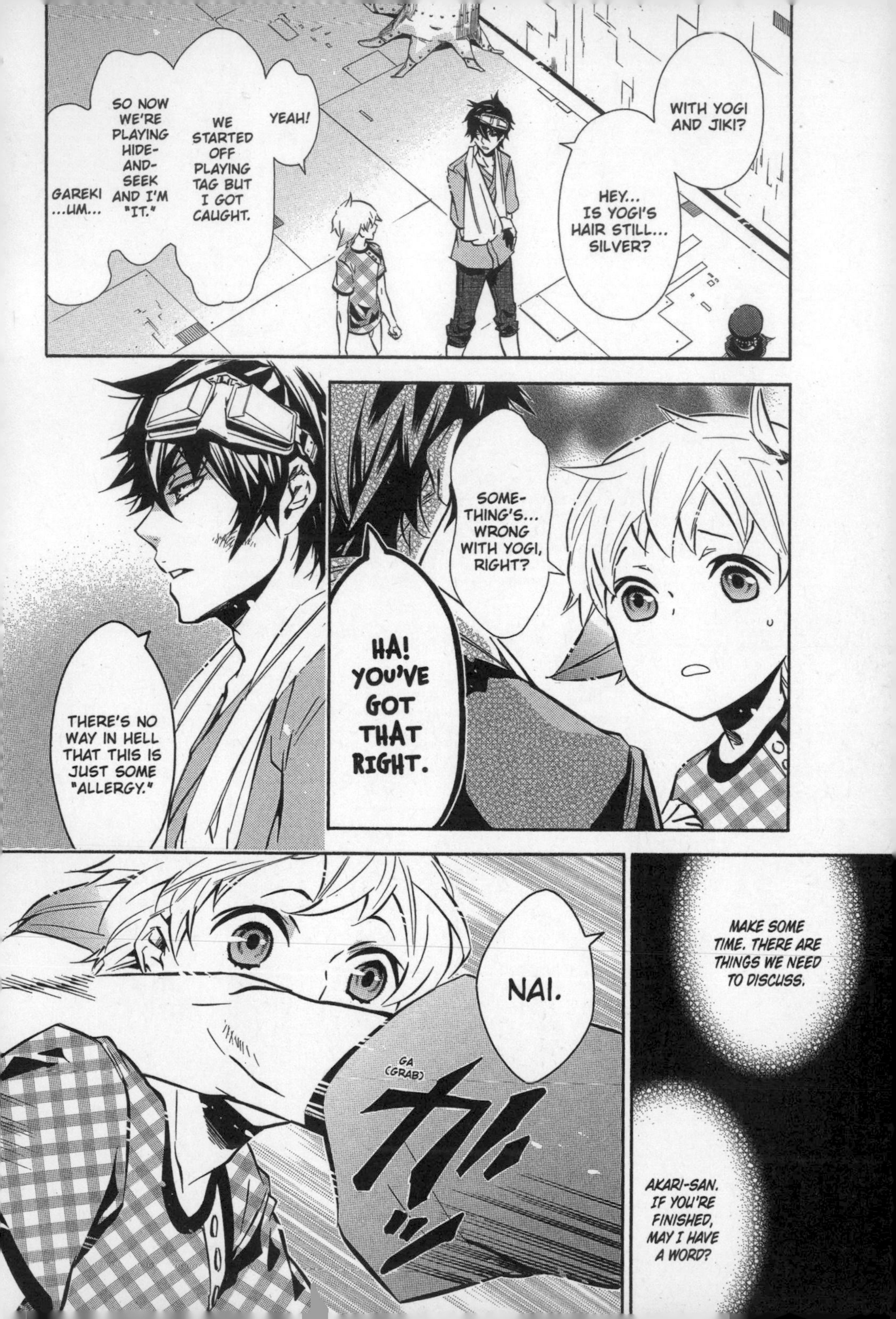
WITH YOGI AND JIKI?
HEY... IS YOGI'S HAIR STILL... SILVER?
YEAH!
WE STARTED OFF PLAYING TAG BUT I GOT CAUGHT.
SO NOW WE'RE PLAYING HIDE-AND-SEEK AND I'M "IT."
GAREKI ...UM...
SOME-THING'S... WRONG WITH YOGI, RIGHT?
HA! YOU'VE GOT THAT RIGHT.
THERE'S NO WAY IN HELL THAT THIS IS JUST SOME "ALLERGY."
MAKE SOME TIME. THERE ARE THINGS WE NEED TO DISCUSS.
AKARI-SAN. IF YOU'RE FINISHED, MAY I HAVE A WORD?
NAI.
GA (GRAB)

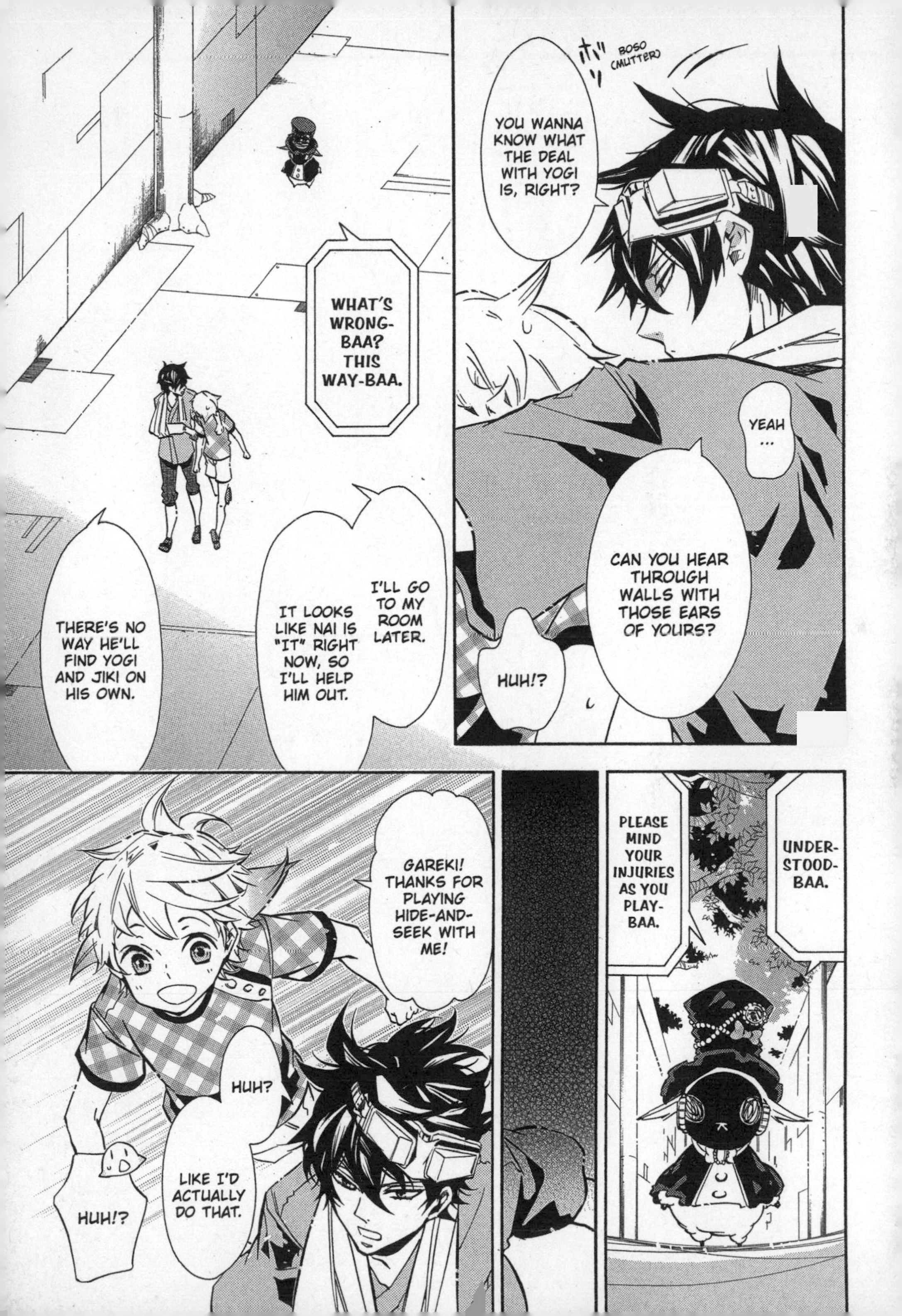
BOSO (MUTTER)
YOU WANNA KNOW WHAT THE DEAL WITH YOGI IS, RIGHT?
YEAH ...
CAN YOU HEAR THROUGH WALLS WITH THOSE EARS OF YOURS?
HUH!?
WHAT'S WRONG-BAA? THIS WAY-BAA.
I'LL GO TO MY ROOM LATER.
IT LOOKS LIKE NAI IS "IT" RIGHT NOW, SO I'LL HELP HIM OUT.
THERE'S NO WAY HE'LL FIND YOGI AND JIKI ON HIS OWN.
UNDER-STOOD-BAA.
PLEASE MIND YOUR INJURIES AS YOU PLAY-BAA.
GAREKI! THANKS FOR PLAYING HIDE-AND-SEEK WITH ME!
HUH?
LIKE I'D ACTUALLY DO THAT.
HUH!?

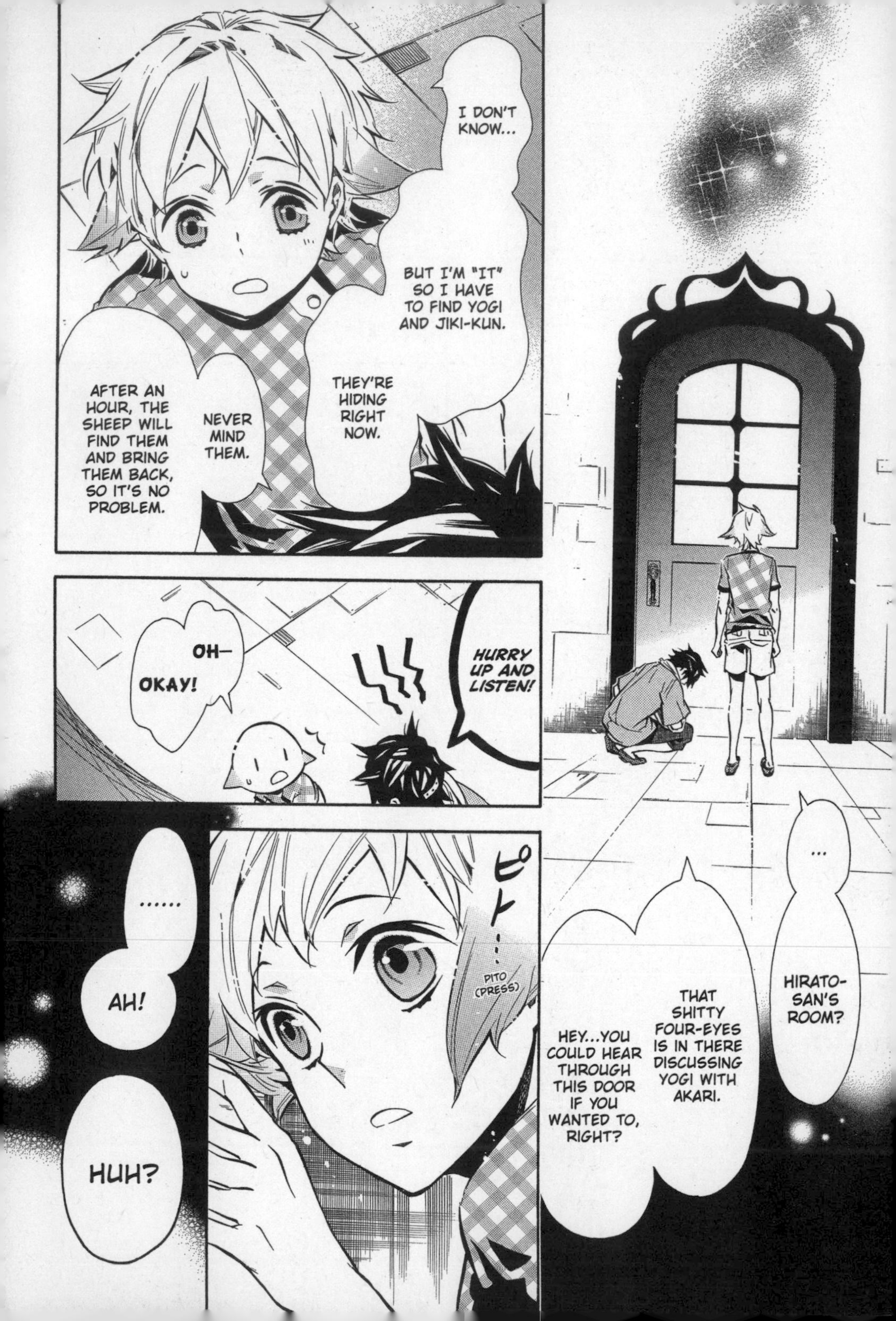
...
HIRATO-SAN'S ROOM?
THAT SHITTY FOUR-EYES IS IN THERE DISCUSSING YOGI WITH AKARI.
HEY...YOU COULD HEAR THROUGH THIS DOOR IF YOU WANTED TO, RIGHT?
I DON'T KNOW...
BUT I'M "IT" SO I HAVE TO FIND YOGI AND JIKI-KUN.
THEY'RE HIDING RIGHT NOW.
NEVER MIND THEM.
AFTER AN HOUR, THE SHEEP WILL FIND THEM AND BRING THEM BACK, SO IT'S NO PROBLEM.
HURRY UP AND LISTEN!
OH— OKAY!
ピト…
PITO (PRESS)
......
AH!
HUH?

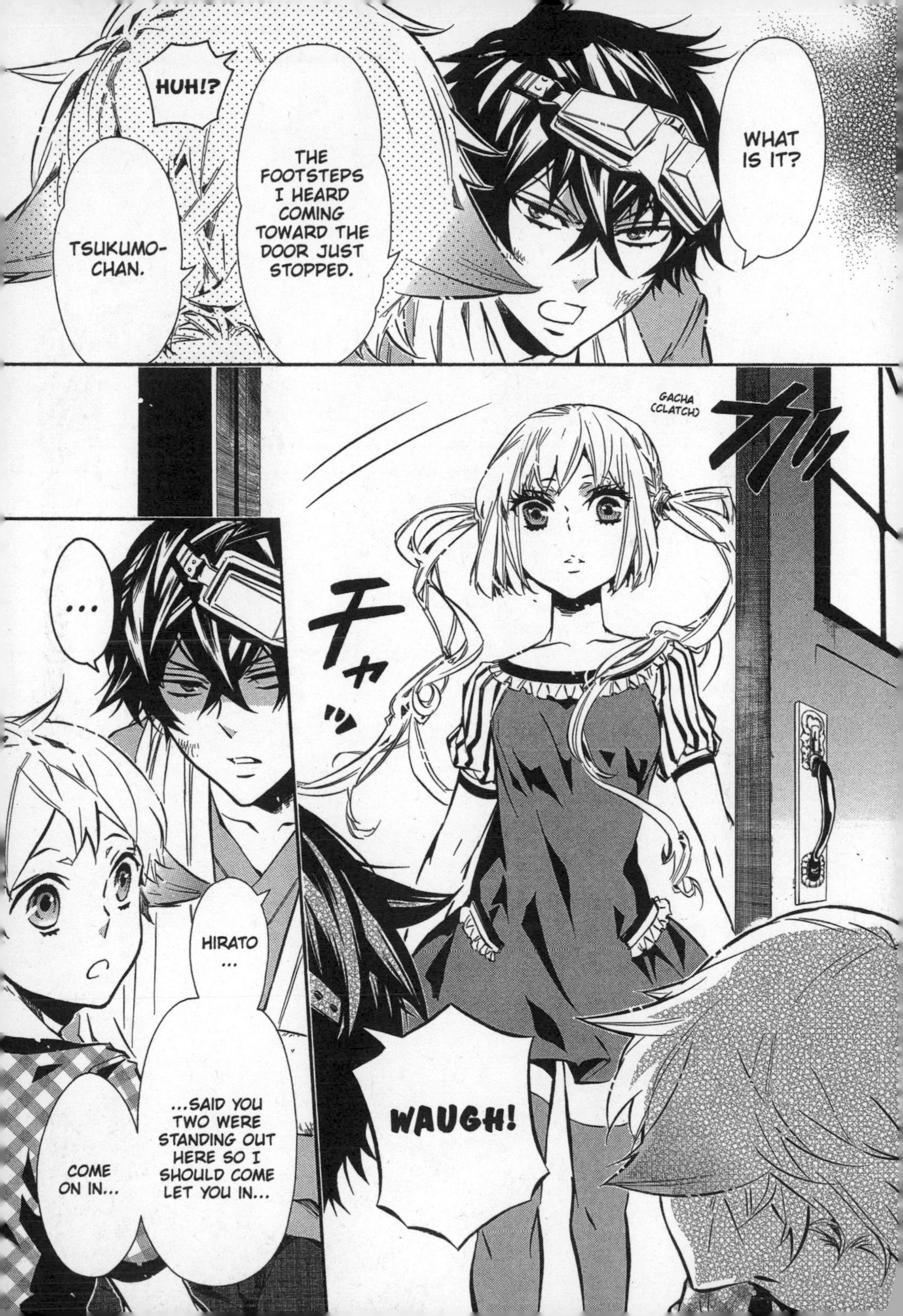
WHAT IS IT?
THE FOOTSTEPS I HEARD COMING TOWARD THE DOOR JUST STOPPED.
HUH!?
TSUKUMO-CHAN.
GACHA (CLATCH)
WAUGH!
...
HIRATO ...
...SAID YOU TWO WERE STANDING OUT HERE SO I SHOULD COME LET YOU IN...
COME ON IN...

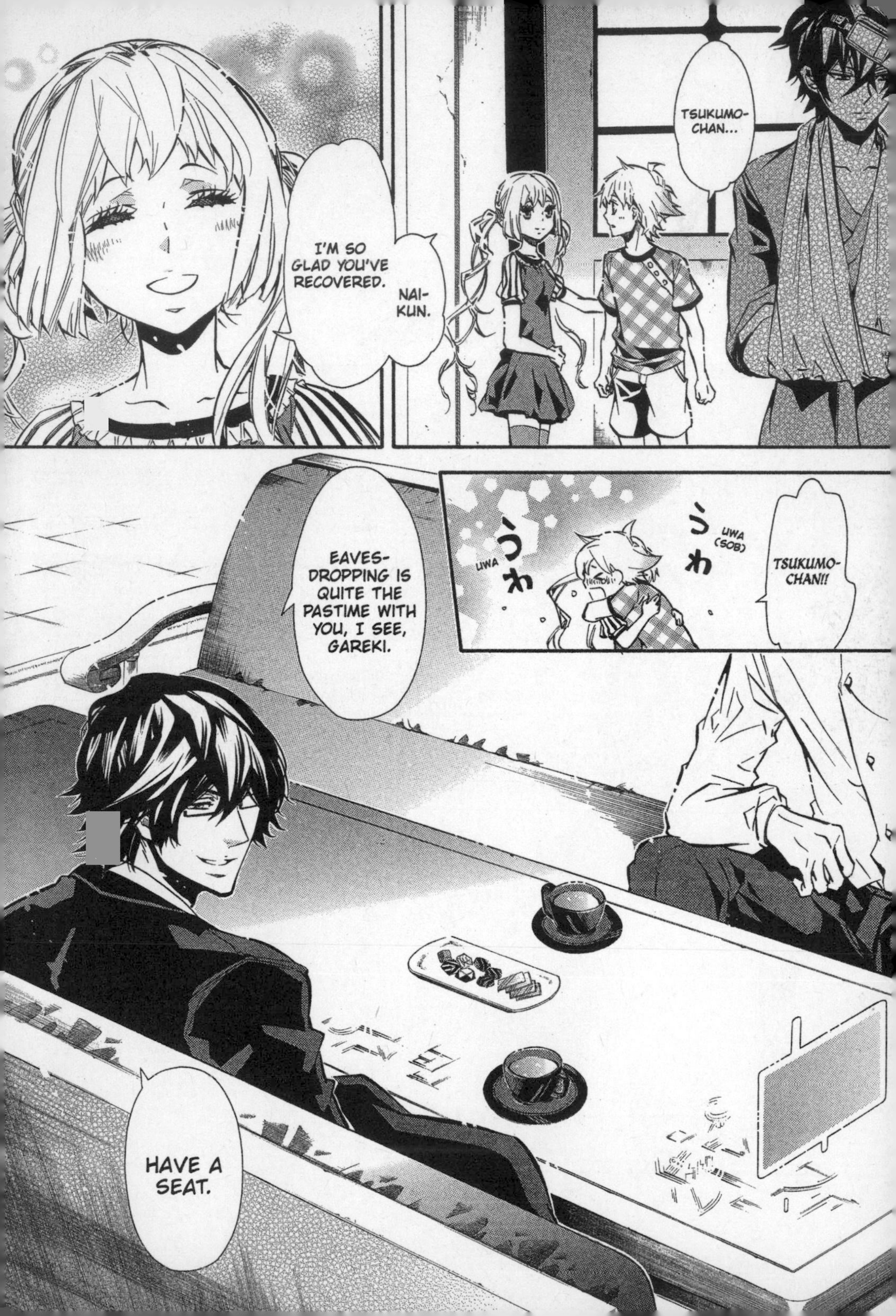
TSUKUMO-CHAN...
I'M SO GLAD YOU'VE RECOVERED.
NAI-KUN.
TSUKUMO-CHAN!!
うわ
UWA (SOB)
うわ
UWA
EAVES-DROPPING IS QUITE THE PASTIME WITH YOU, I SEE, GAREKI.
HAVE A SEAT.

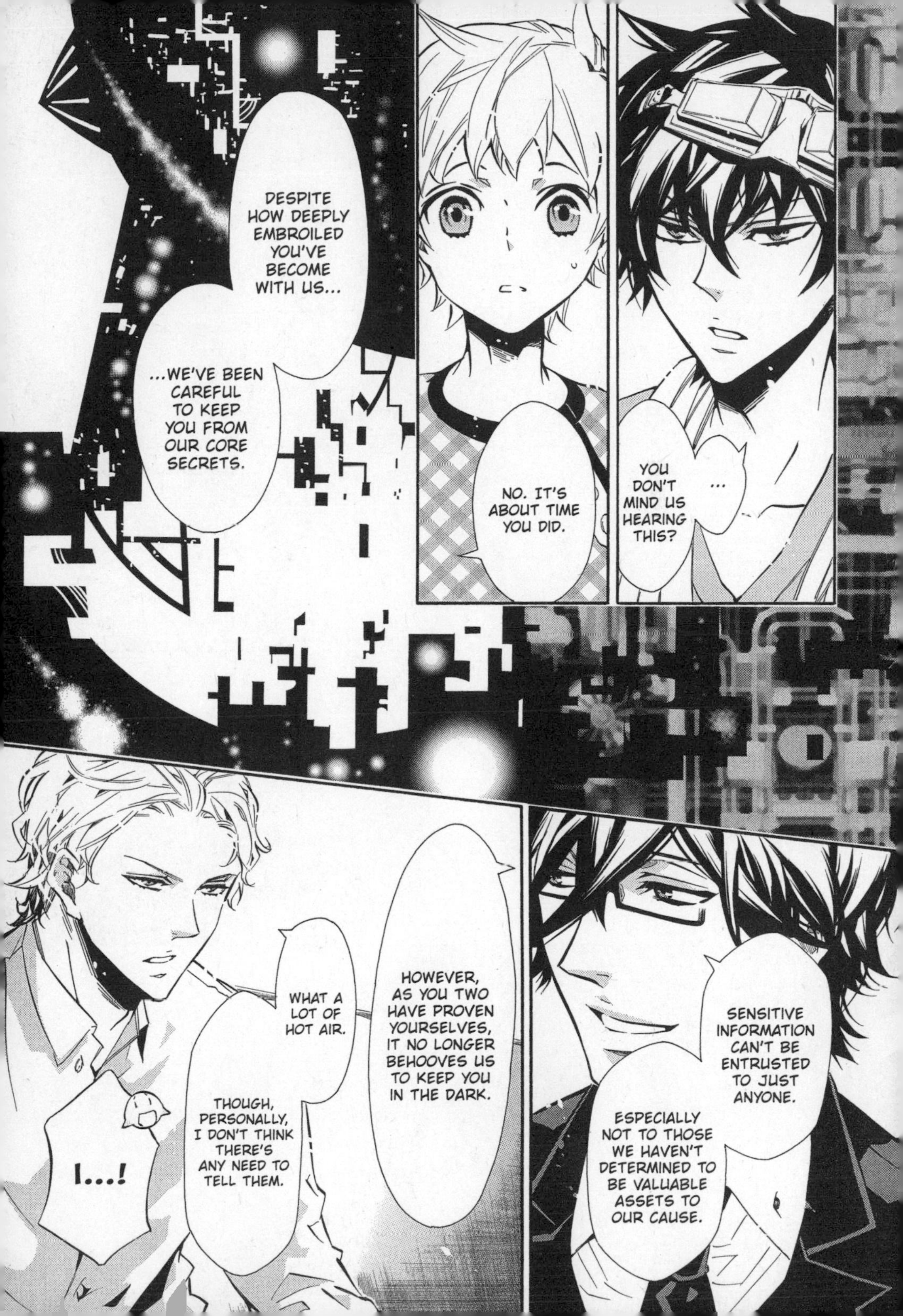
...
YOU DON'T MIND US HEARING THIS?
NO. IT'S ABOUT TIME YOU DID.
DESPITE HOW DEEPLY EMBROILED YOU'VE BECOME WITH US...
...WE'VE BEEN CAREFUL TO KEEP YOU FROM OUR CORE SECRETS.
SENSITIVE INFORMATION CAN'T BE ENTRUSTED TO JUST ANYONE.
ESPECIALLY NOT TO THOSE WE HAVEN'T DETERMINED TO BE VALUABLE ASSETS TO OUR CAUSE.
HOWEVER, AS YOU TWO HAVE PROVEN YOURSELVES, IT NO LONGER BEHOOVES US TO KEEP YOU IN THE DARK.
WHAT A LOT OF HOT AIR.
THOUGH, PERSONALLY, I DON'T THINK THERE'S ANY NEED TO TELL THEM.
I...!

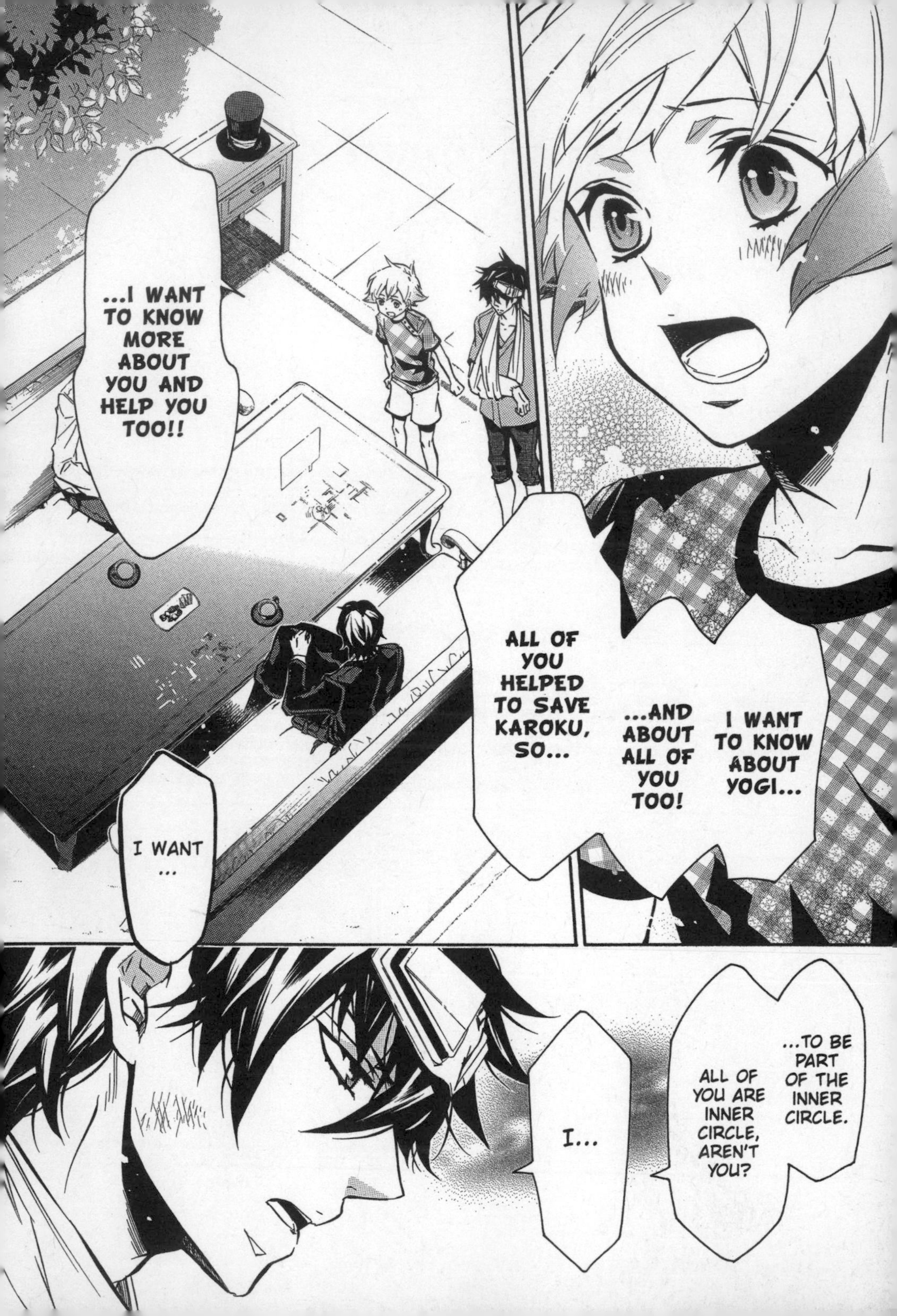
I WANT TO KNOW ABOUT YOGI...
...AND ABOUT ALL OF YOU TOO!
ALL OF YOU HELPED TO SAVE KAROKU, SO...
...I WANT TO KNOW MORE ABOUT YOU AND HELP YOU TOO!!
I WANT ...
...TO BE PART OF THE INNER CIRCLE.
ALL OF YOU ARE INNER CIRCLE, AREN'T YOU?
I...

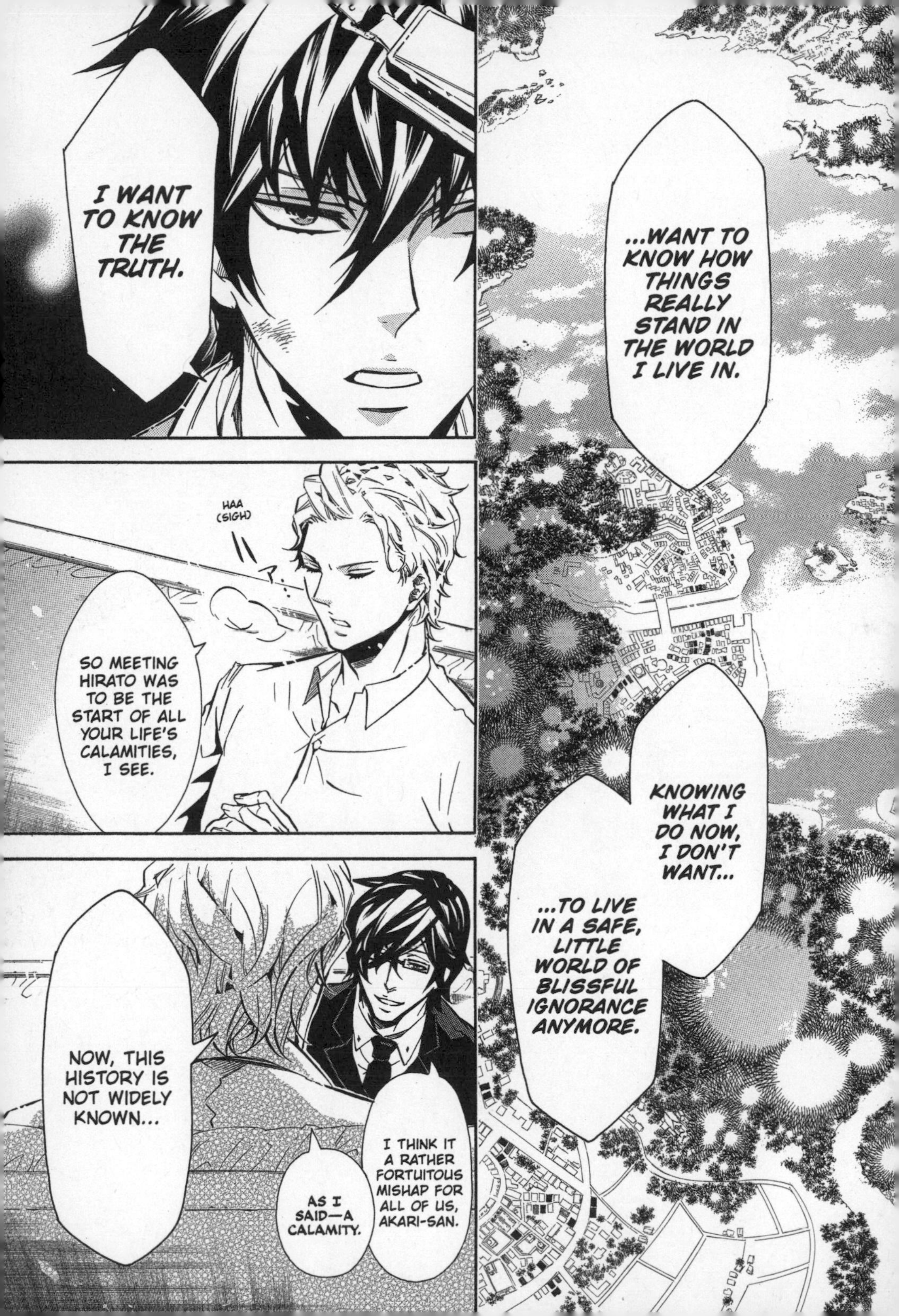
...WANT TO KNOW HOW THINGS REALLY STAND IN THE WORLD I LIVE IN.
KNOWING WHAT I DO NOW, I DON'T WANT...
...TO LIVE IN A SAFE, LITTLE WORLD OF BLISSFUL IGNORANCE ANYMORE.
I WANT TO KNOW THE TRUTH.
HAA (SIGH)
SO MEETING HIRATO WAS TO BE THE START OF ALL YOUR LIFE'S CALAMITIES, I SEE.
I THINK IT A RATHER FORTUITOUS MISHAP FOR ALL OF US, AKARI-SAN.
AS I SAID—A CALAMITY.
NOW, THIS HISTORY IS NOT WIDELY KNOWN...

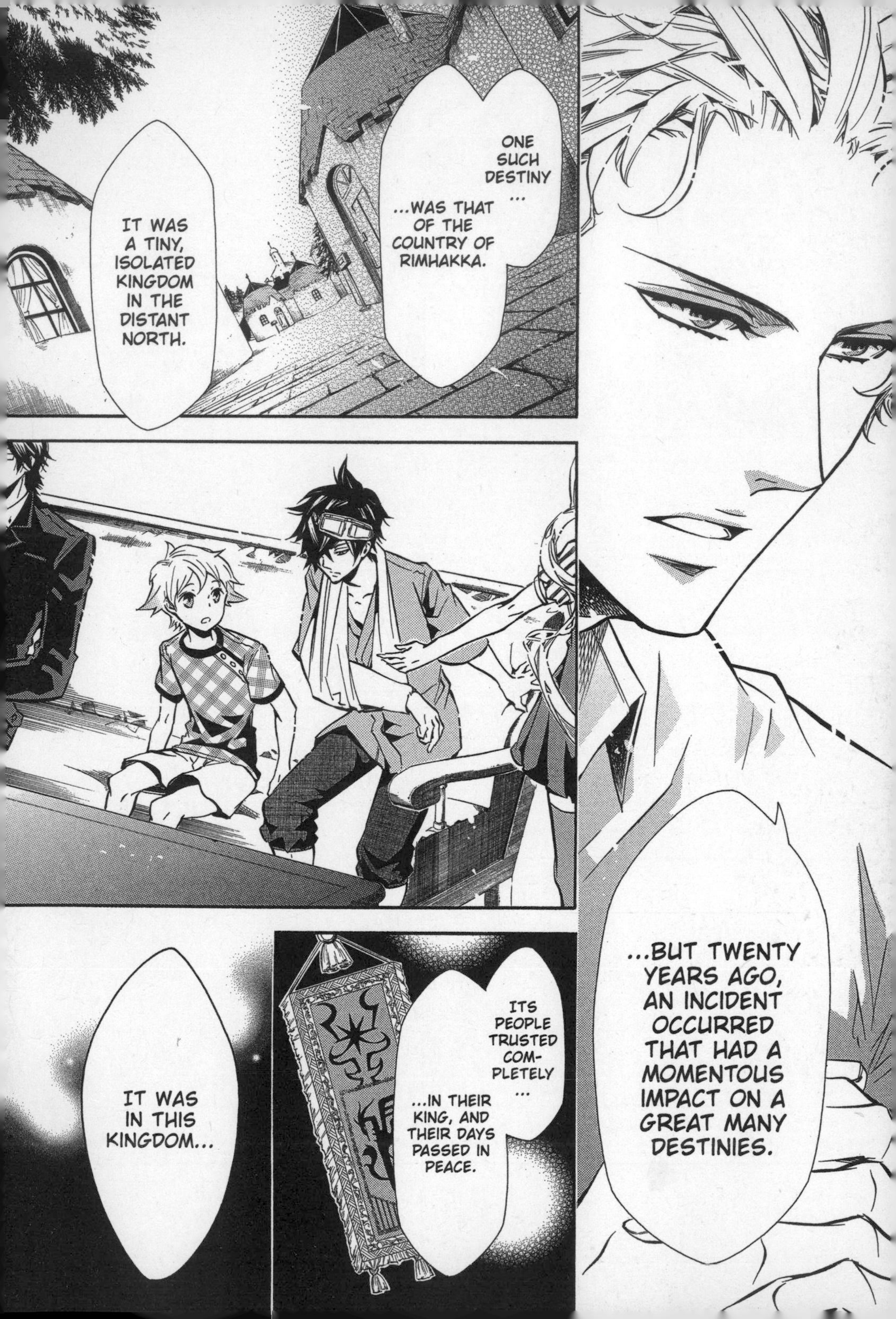
ONE SUCH DESTINY ...
...WAS THAT OF THE COUNTRY OF RIMHAKKA.
IT WAS A TINY, ISOLATED KINGDOM IN THE DISTANT NORTH.
ITS PEOPLE TRUSTED COM-PLETELY ...
...IN THEIR KING, AND THEIR DAYS PASSED IN PEACE.
IT WAS IN THIS KINGDOM...
...BUT TWENTY YEARS AGO, AN INCIDENT OCCURRED THAT HAD A MOMENTOUS IMPACT ON A GREAT MANY DESTINIES.

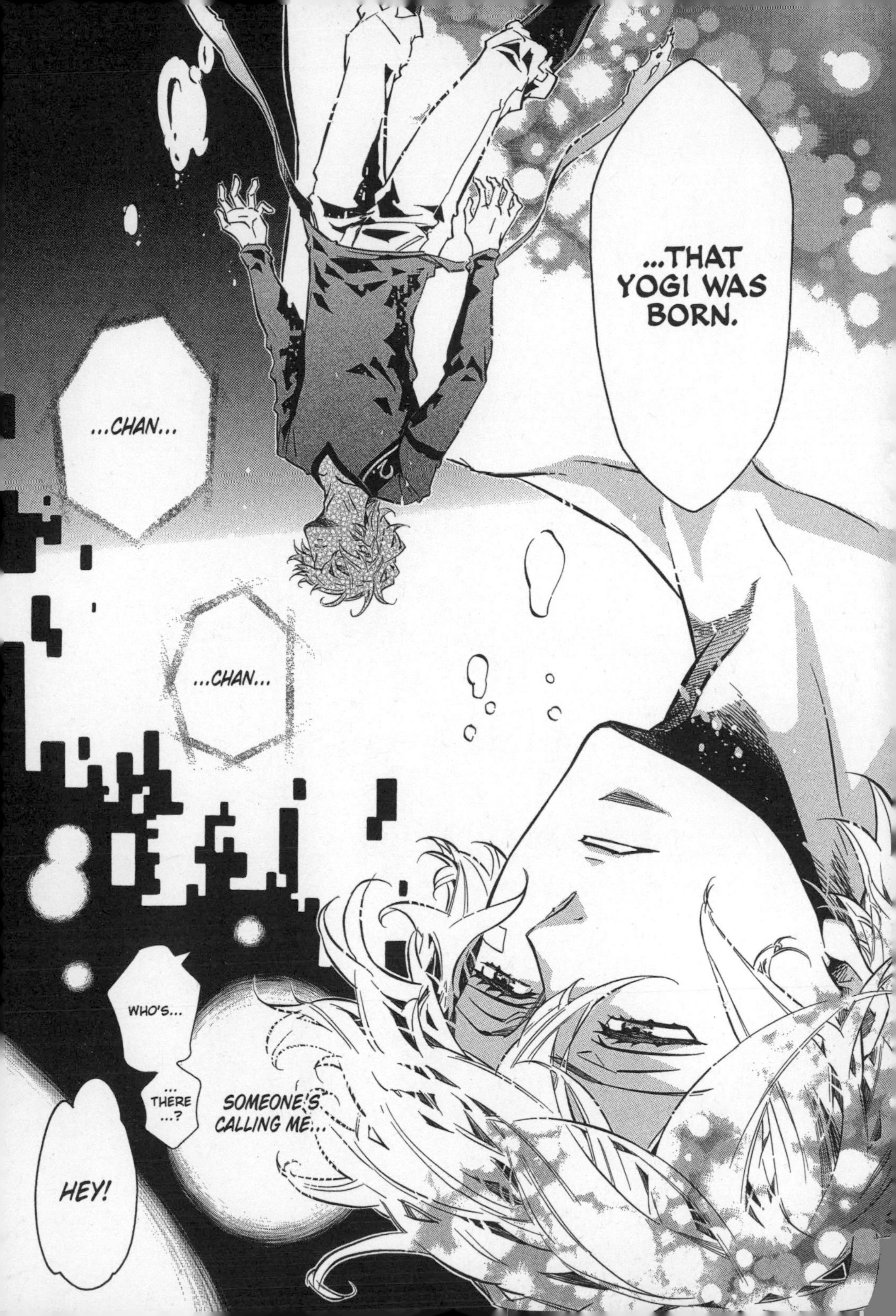
...THAT YOGI WAS BORN.
...CHAN...
...CHAN...
SOMEONE'S CALLING ME...
WHO'S...
...THERE ...?
HEY!

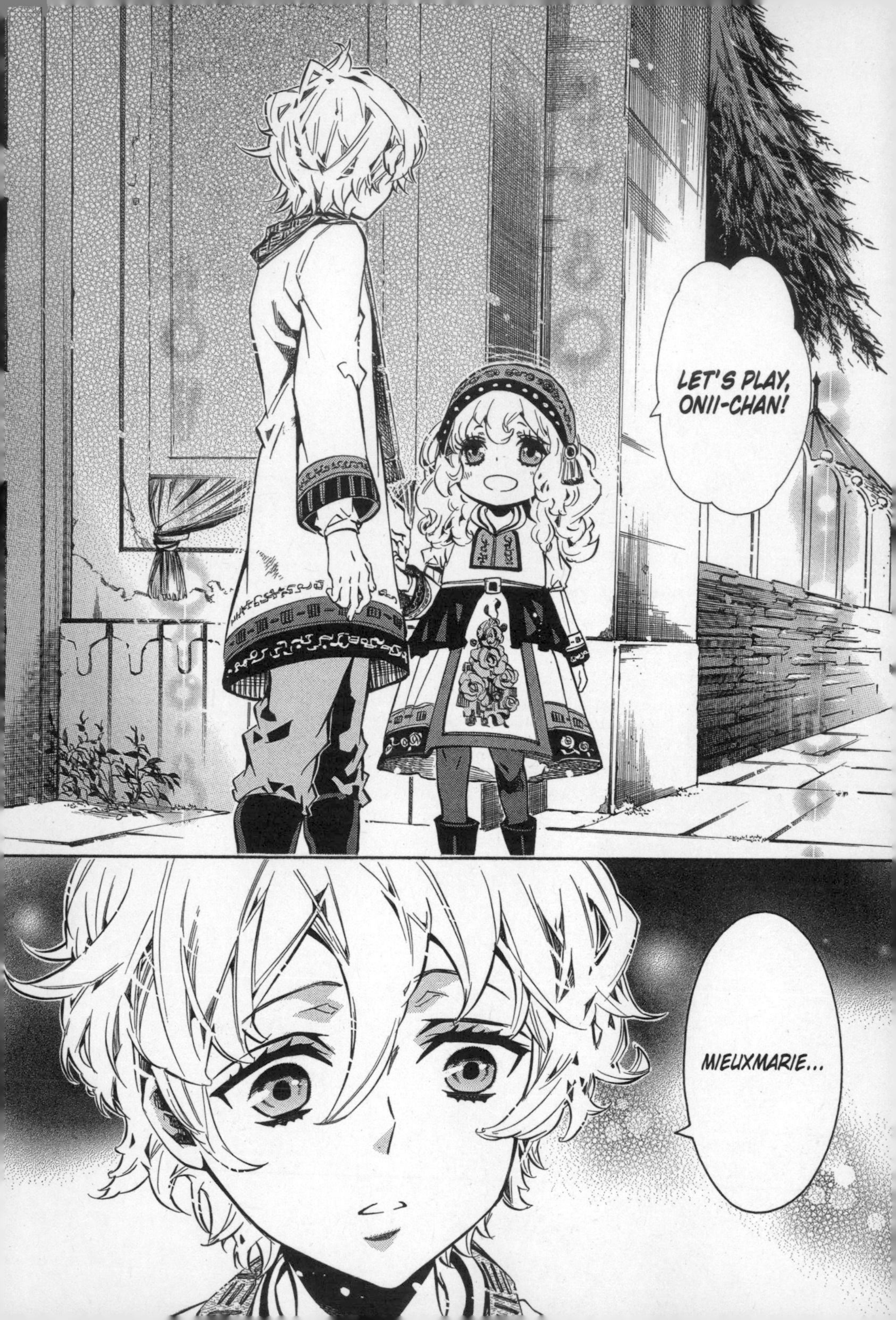
LET'S PLAY, ONII-CHAN!
MIEUXMARIE...

KARNEVAL

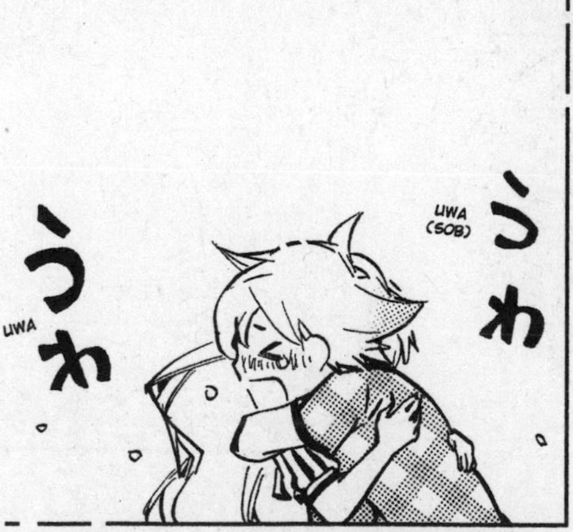
うわ
UWA
(SOB)
うわ
UWA

KARNEVAL

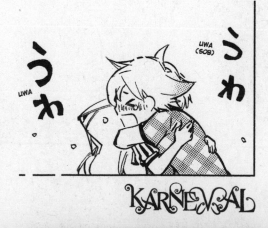

Score 62: A Wonderful Kingdom

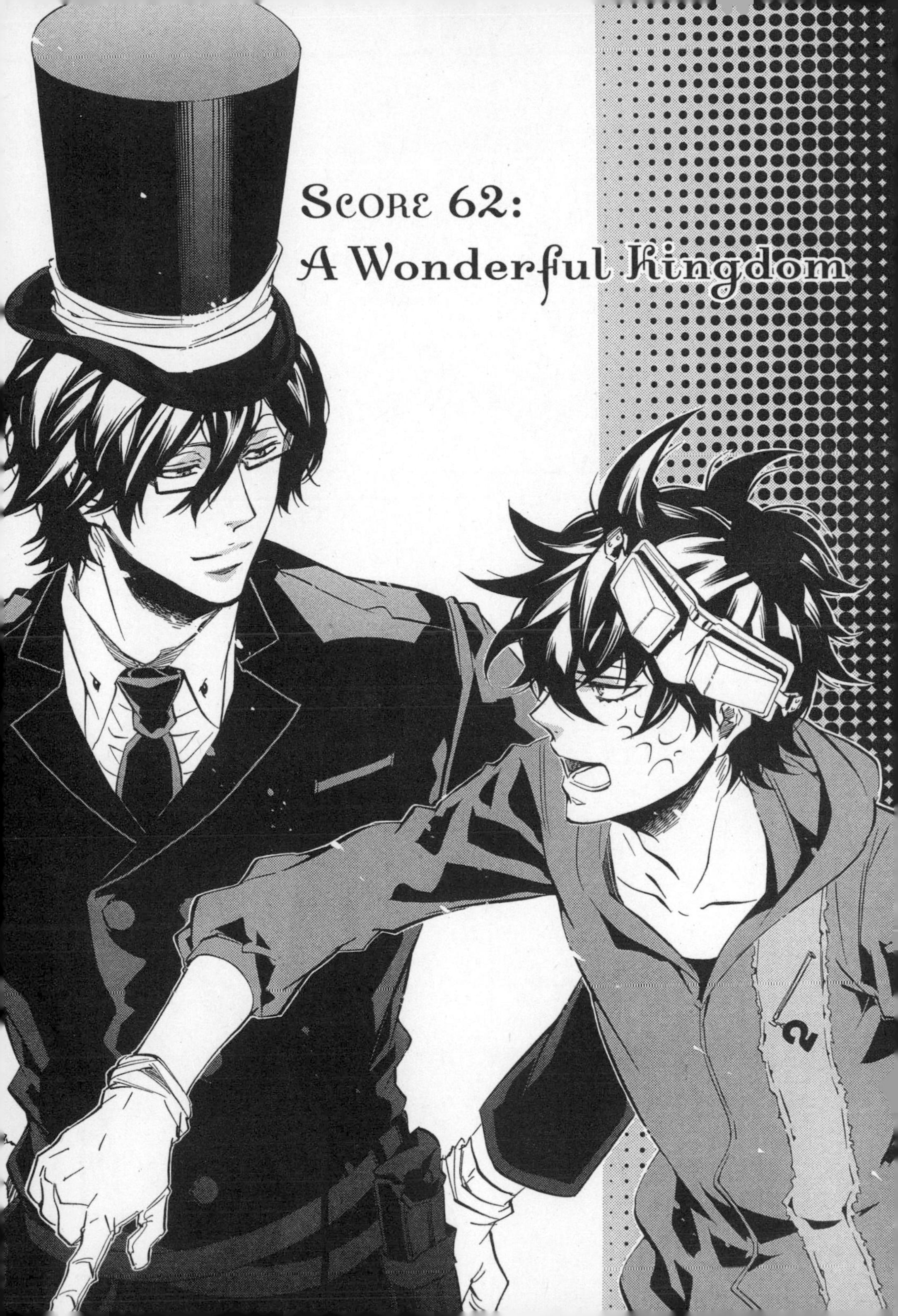

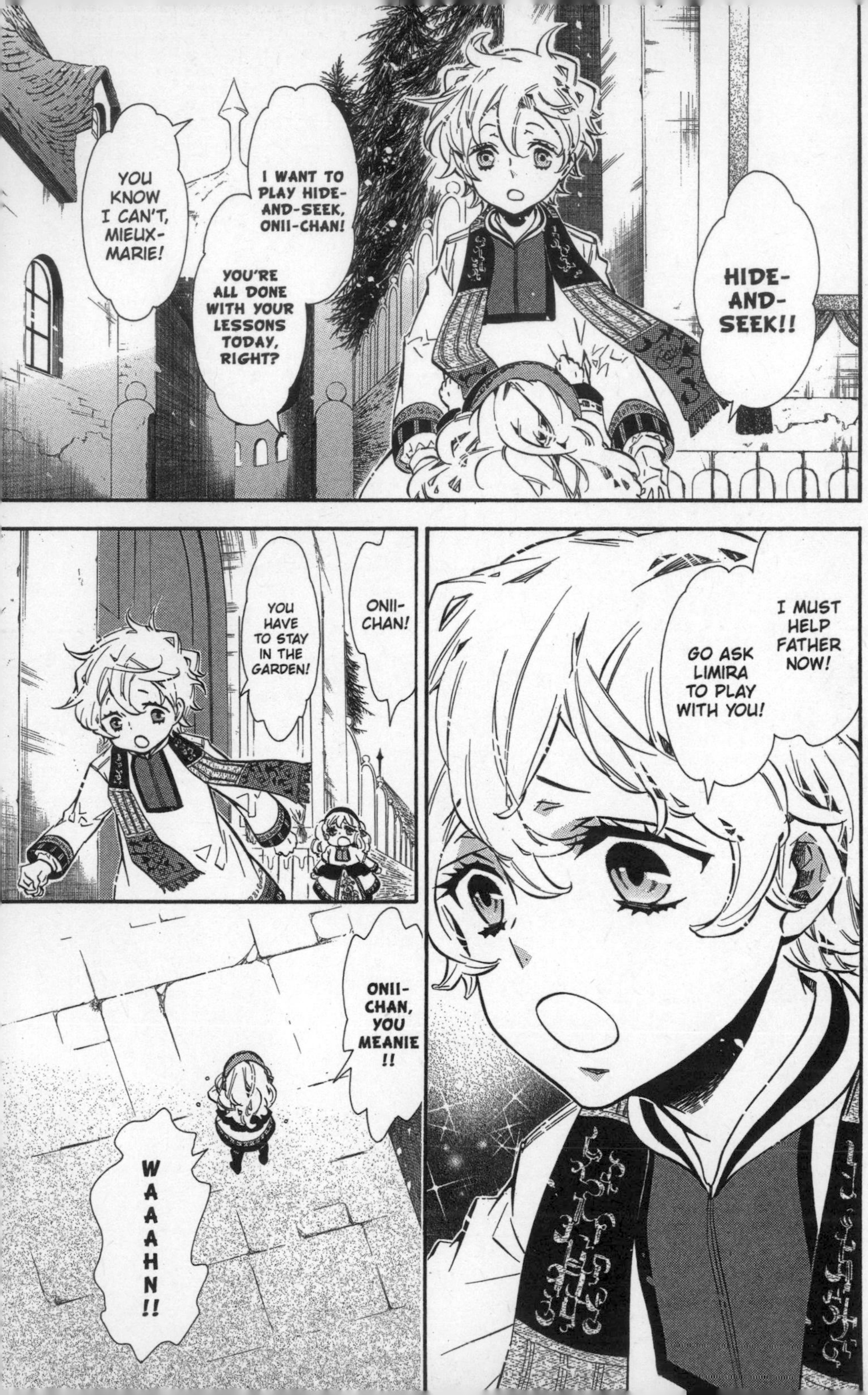
HIDE-AND-SEEK!!
I WANT TO PLAY HIDE-AND-SEEK, ONII-CHAN!
YOU'RE ALL DONE WITH YOUR LESSONS TODAY, RIGHT?
YOU KNOW I CAN'T, MIEUX-MARIE!
I MUST HELP FATHER NOW!
GO ASK LIMIRA TO PLAY WITH YOU!
ONII-CHAN!
YOU HAVE TO STAY IN THE GARDEN!
ONII-CHAN, YOU MEANIE!!
WAAAAHN!!

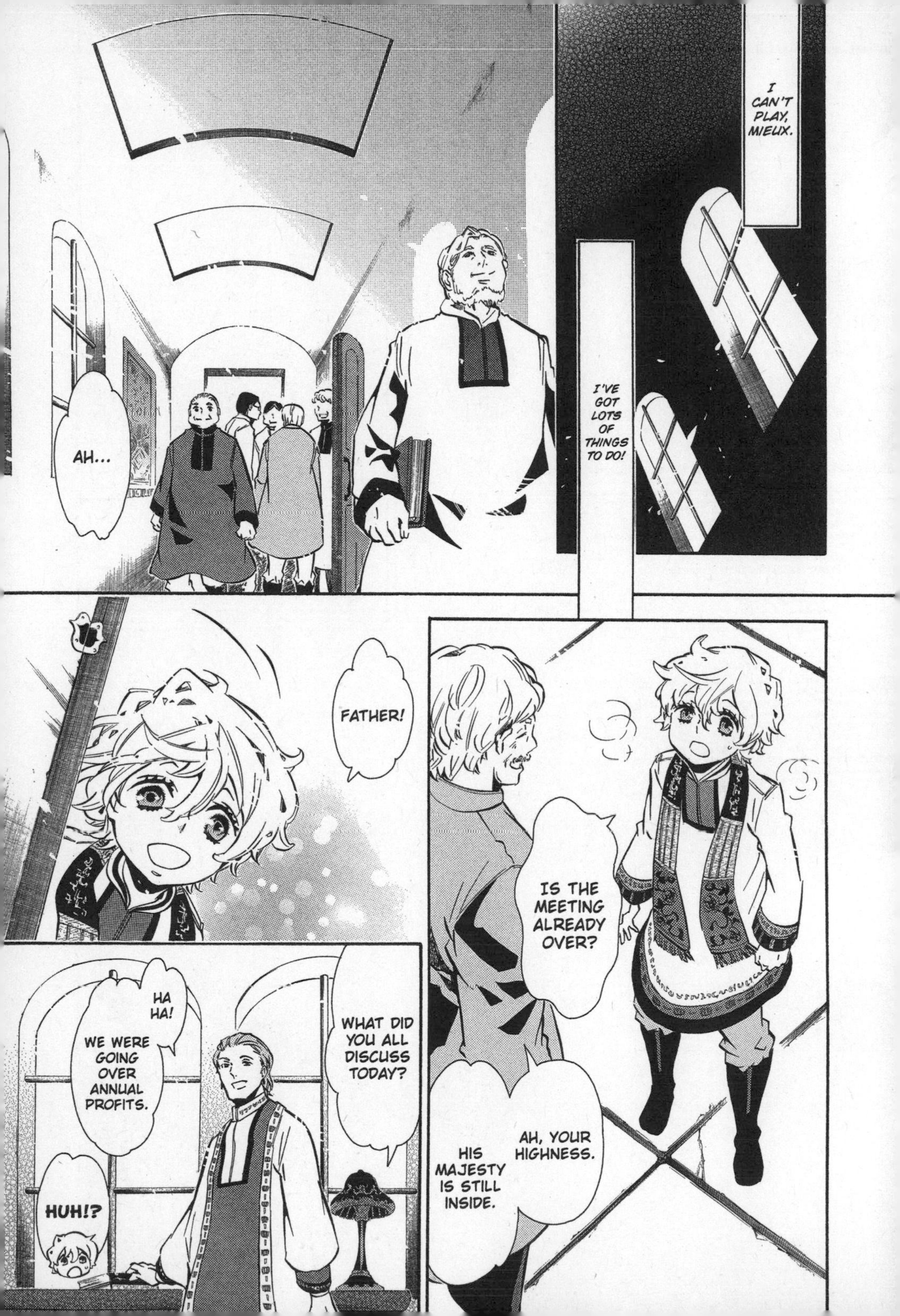
I CAN'T PLAY, MIEUX.
I'VE GOT LOTS OF THINGS TO DO!
AH...
IS THE MEETING ALREADY OVER?
AH, YOUR HIGHNESS.
HIS MAJESTY IS STILL INSIDE.
FATHER!
WHAT DID YOU ALL DISCUSS TODAY?
HA HA!
WE WERE GOING OVER ANNUAL PROFITS.
HUH!?

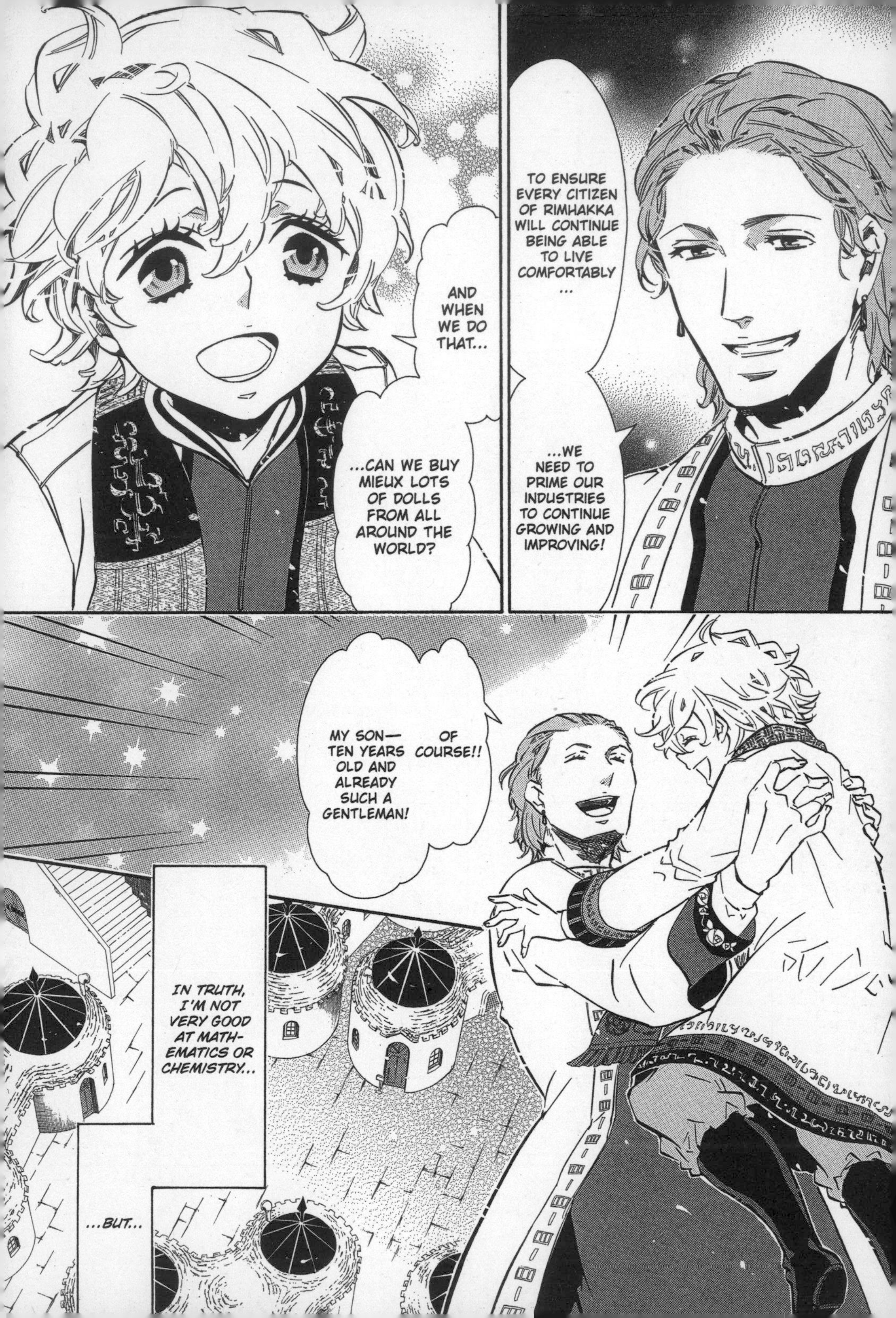
TO ENSURE EVERY CITIZEN OF RIMHAKKA WILL CONTINUE BEING ABLE TO LIVE COMFORTABLY ...
...WE NEED TO PRIME OUR INDUSTRIES TO CONTINUE GROWING AND IMPROVING!
AND WHEN WE DO THAT...
...CAN WE BUY MIEUX LOTS OF DOLLS FROM ALL AROUND THE WORLD?
OF COURSE!!
MY SON— TEN YEARS OLD AND ALREADY SUCH A GENTLEMAN!
IN TRUTH, I'M NOT VERY GOOD AT MATH-EMATICS OR CHEMISTRY...
...BUT...

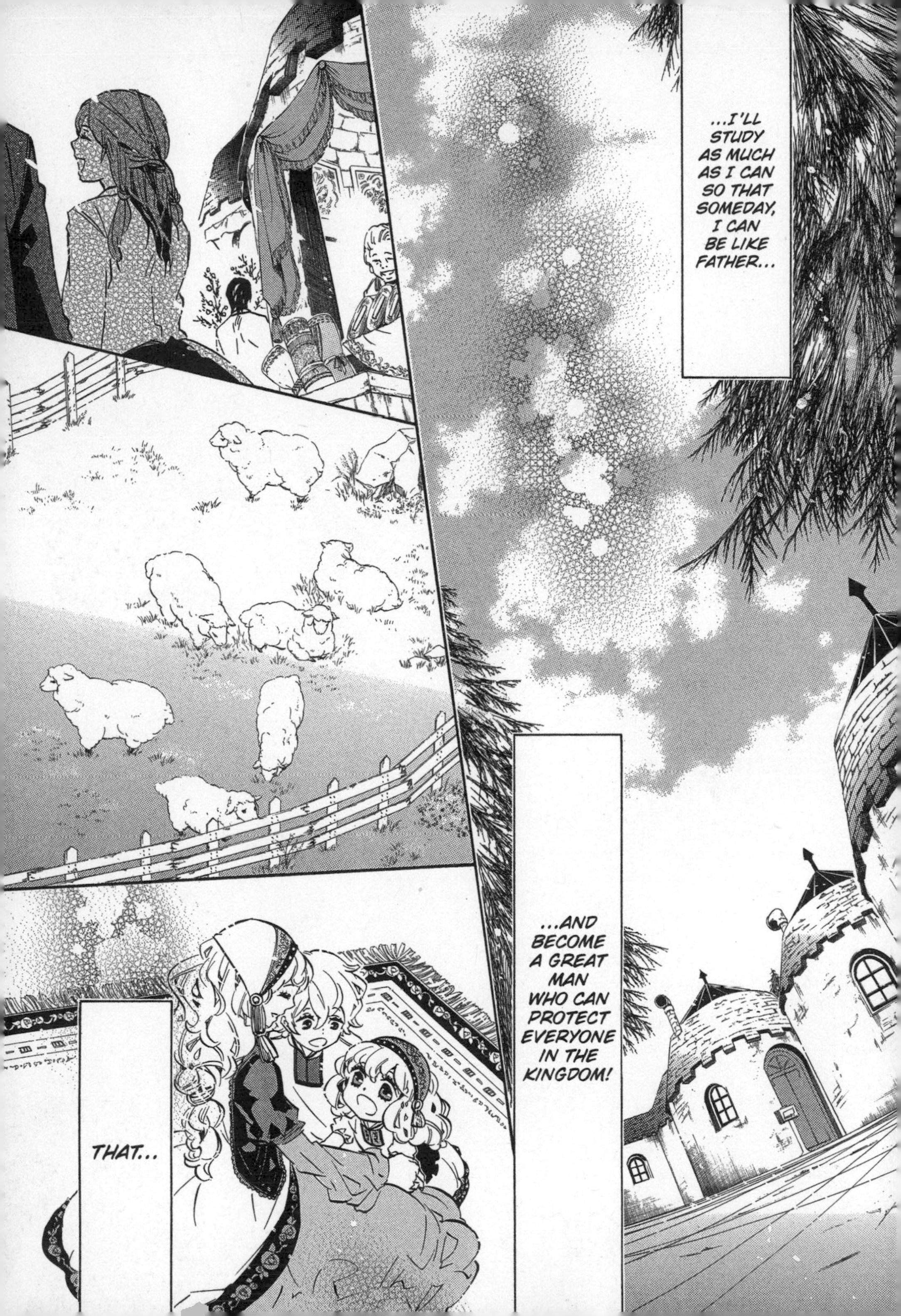
...I'LL STUDY AS MUCH AS I CAN SO THAT SOMEDAY, I CAN BE LIKE FATHER...
...AND BECOME A GREAT MAN WHO CAN PROTECT EVERYONE IN THE KINGDOM!
THAT...

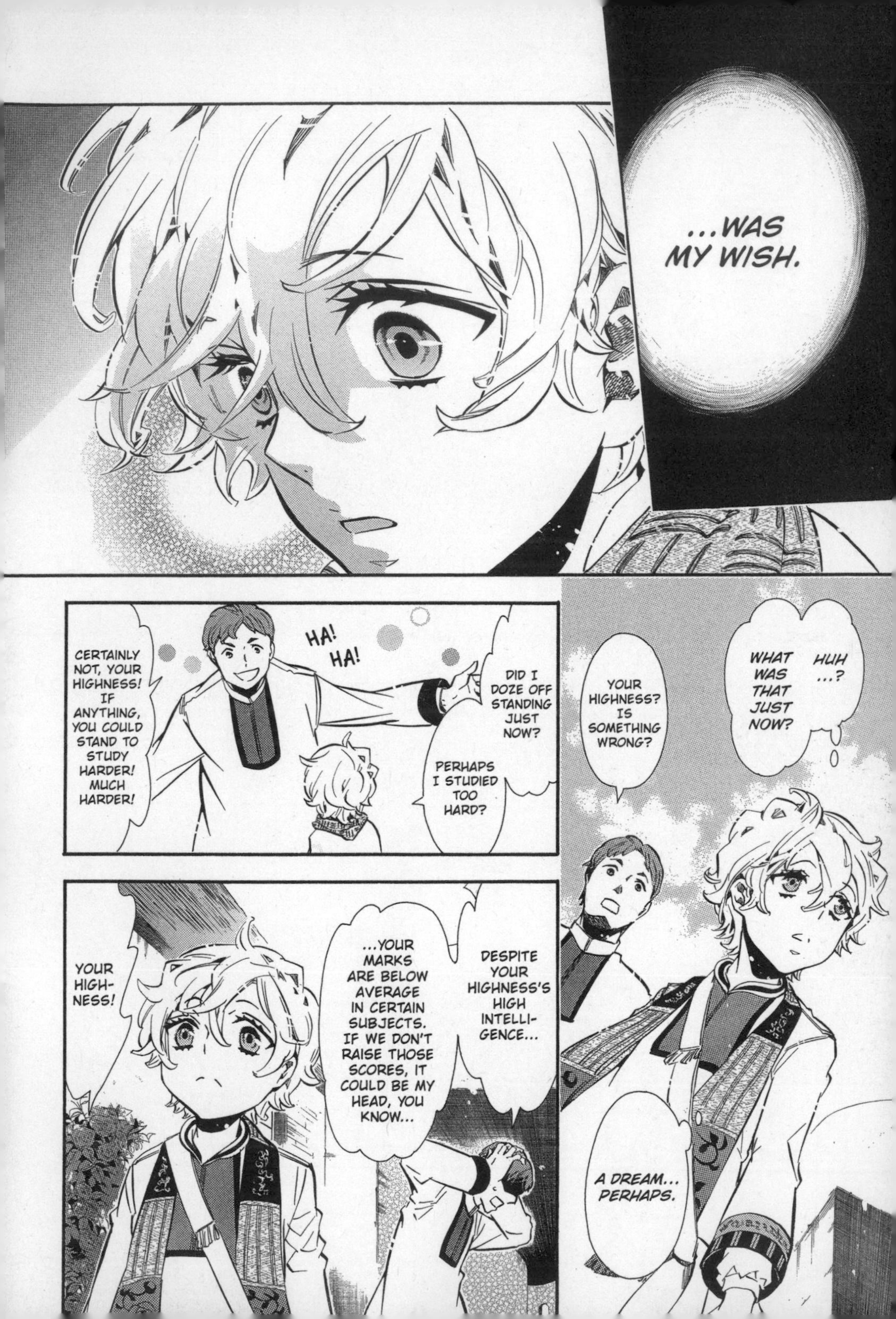
...WAS MY WISH.
HUH...?
WHAT WAS THAT JUST NOW?
YOUR HIGHNESS? IS SOMETHING WRONG?
A DREAM... PERHAPS.
DID I DOZE OFF STANDING JUST NOW?
PERHAPS I STUDIED TOO HARD?
HA! HA!
CERTAINLY NOT, YOUR HIGHNESS! IF ANYTHING, YOU COULD STAND TO STUDY HARDER! MUCH HARDER!
DESPITE YOUR HIGHNESS'S HIGH INTELLIGENCE...
...YOUR MARKS ARE BELOW AVERAGE IN CERTAIN SUBJECTS. IF WE DON'T RAISE THOSE SCORES, IT COULD BE MY HEAD, YOU KNOW...
YOUR HIGHNESS!

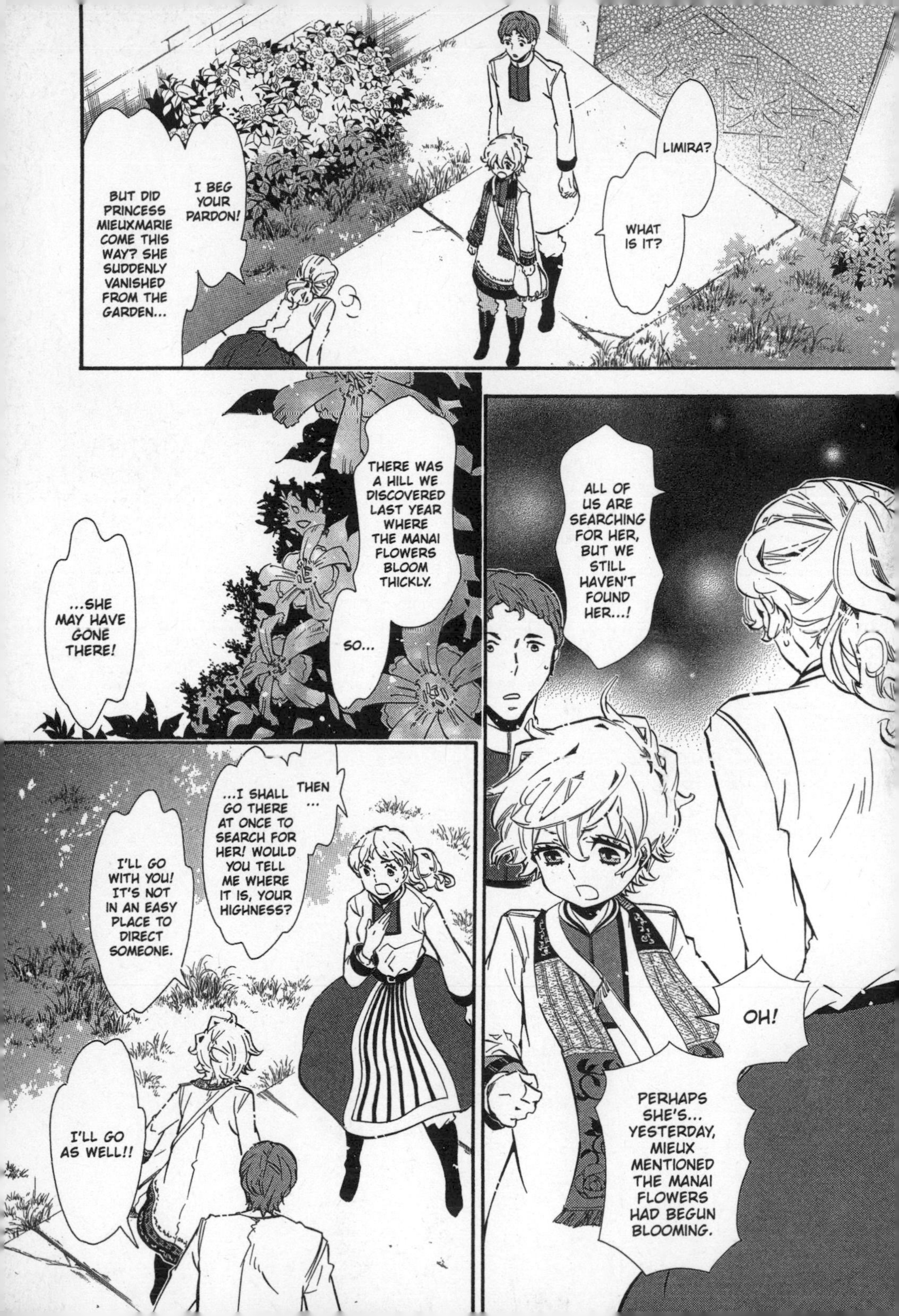
LIMIRA?
WHAT IS IT?
I BEG YOUR PARDON!
BUT DID PRINCESS MIEUXMARIE COME THIS WAY? SHE SUDDENLY VANISHED FROM THE GARDEN...
ALL OF US ARE SEARCHING FOR HER, BUT WE STILL HAVEN'T FOUND HER...!
OH!
PERHAPS SHE'S... YESTERDAY, MIEUX MENTIONED THE MANAI FLOWERS HAD BEGUN BLOOMING.
THERE WAS A HILL WE DISCOVERED LAST YEAR WHERE THE MANAI FLOWERS BLOOM THICKLY.
SO...
...SHE MAY HAVE GONE THERE!
THEN...
...I SHALL GO THERE AT ONCE TO SEARCH FOR HER! WOULD YOU TELL ME WHERE IT IS, YOUR HIGHNESS?
I'LL GO WITH YOU! IT'S NOT IN AN EASY PLACE TO DIRECT SOMEONE.
I'LL GO AS WELL!!

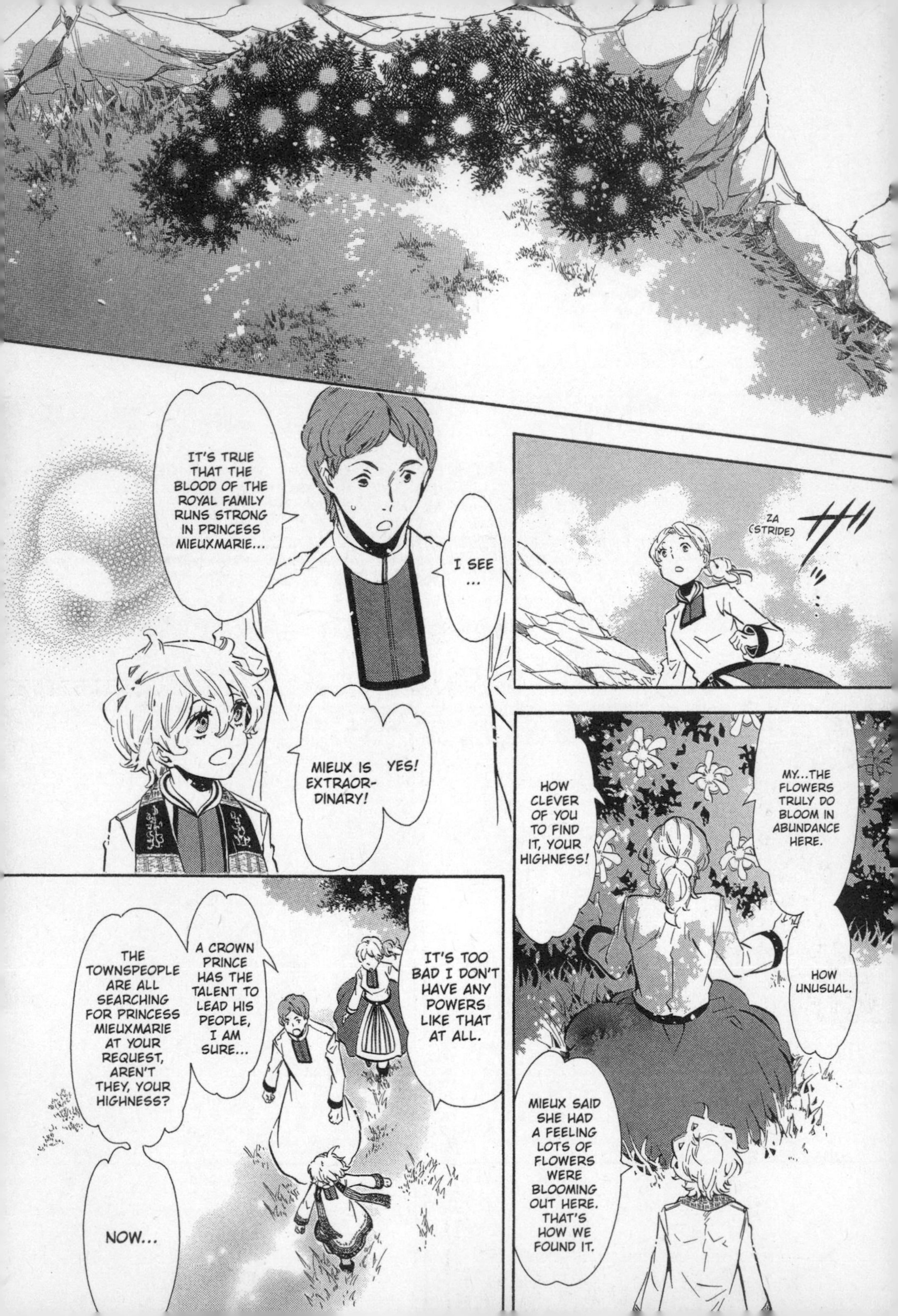
ZA (STRIDE)
MY...THE FLOWERS TRULY DO BLOOM IN ABUNDANCE HERE.
HOW CLEVER OF YOU TO FIND IT, YOUR HIGHNESS!
HOW UNUSUAL.
MIEUX SAID SHE HAD A FEELING LOTS OF FLOWERS WERE BLOOMING OUT HERE. THAT'S HOW WE FOUND IT.
I SEE ...
IT'S TRUE THAT THE BLOOD OF THE ROYAL FAMILY RUNS STRONG IN PRINCESS MIEUXMARIE...
YES! MIEUX IS EXTRAOR-DINARY!
IT'S TOO BAD I DON'T HAVE ANY POWERS LIKE THAT AT ALL.
A CROWN PRINCE HAS THE TALENT TO LEAD HIS PEOPLE, I AM SURE...
THE TOWNSPEOPLE ARE ALL SEARCHING FOR PRINCESS MIEUXMARIE AT YOUR REQUEST, AREN'T THEY, YOUR HIGHNESS?
NOW...

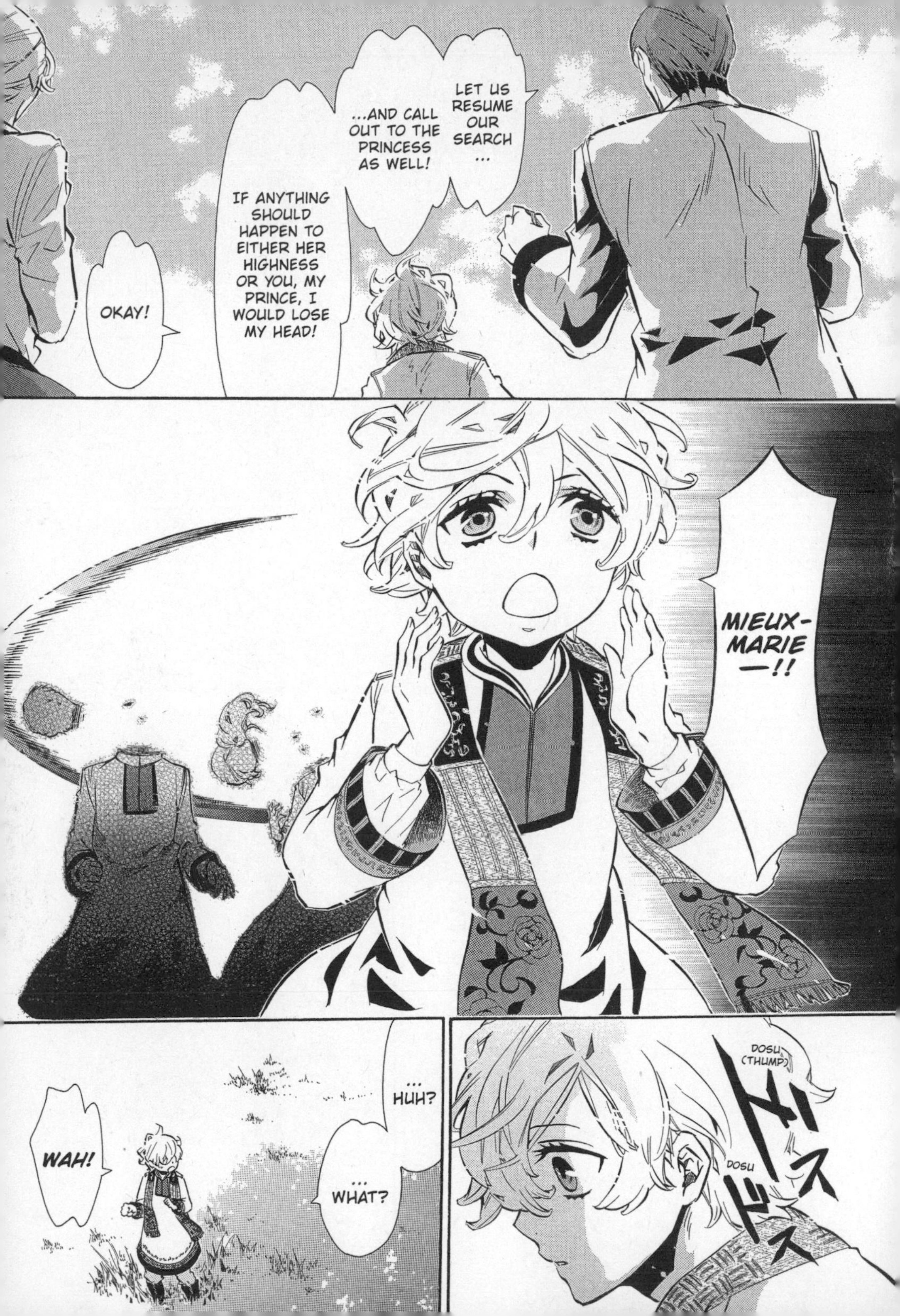
LET US RESUME OUR SEARCH ...
...AND CALL OUT TO THE PRINCESS AS WELL!
IF ANYTHING SHOULD HAPPEN TO EITHER HER HIGHNESS OR YOU, MY PRINCE, I WOULD LOSE MY HEAD!
OKAY!
MIEUX-MARIE—!!
DOSU (THUMP)
DOSU
... HUH?
... WHAT?
WAH!

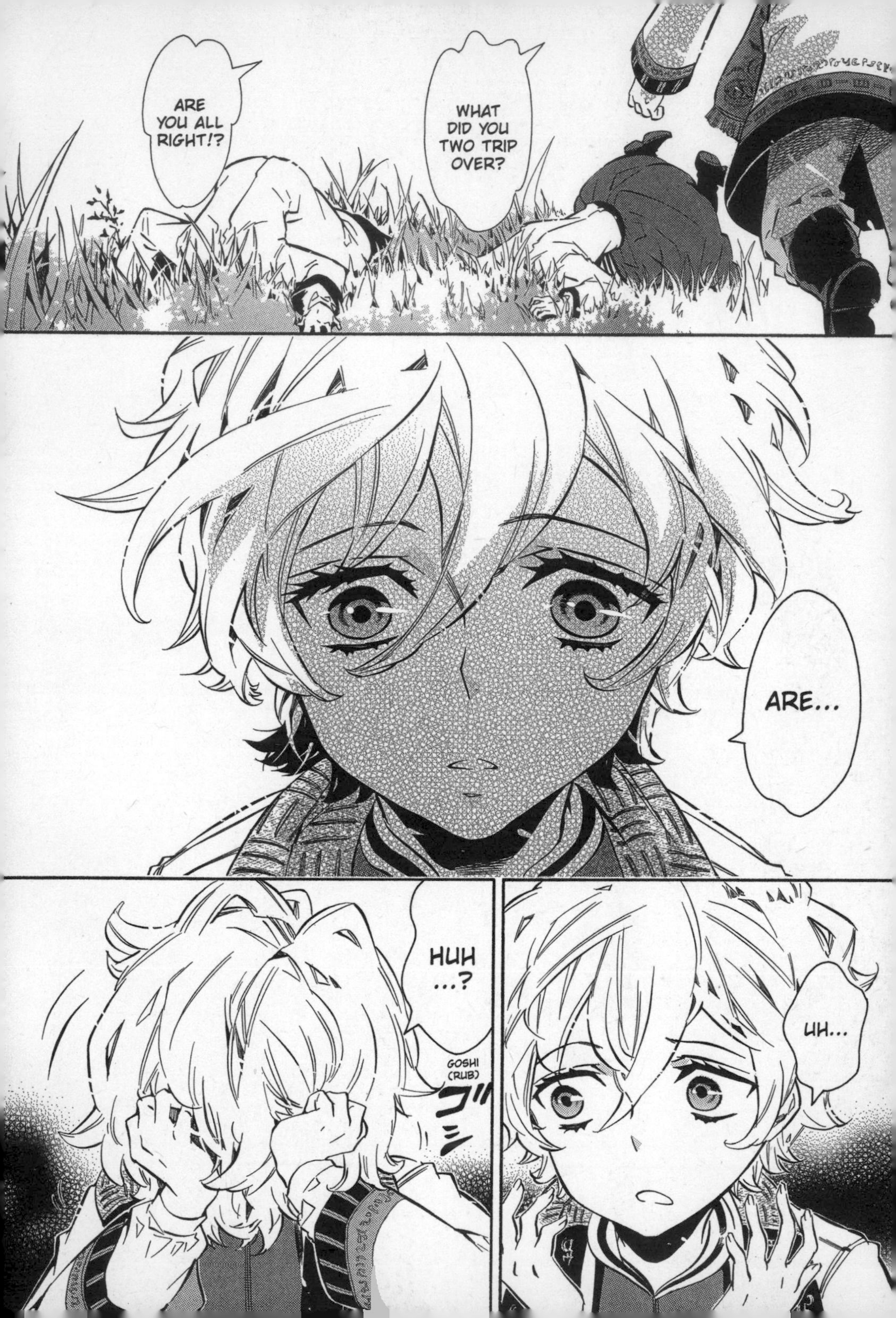
WHAT DID YOU TWO TRIP OVER?
ARE YOU ALL RIGHT!?
ARE...
UH...
HUH ...?
GOSHI (RUB)

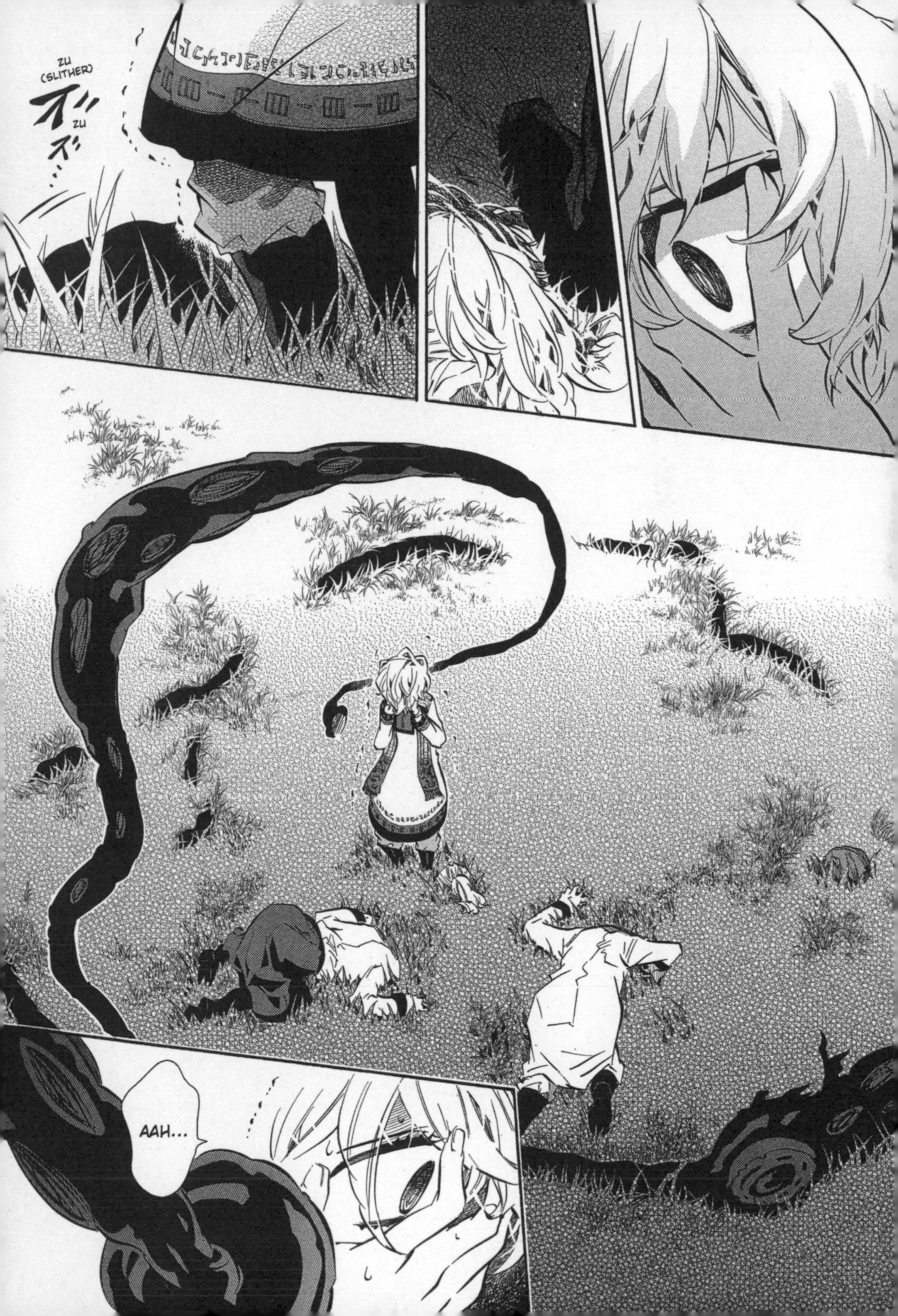
ZU (SLITHER)
ZU
AAH...
...

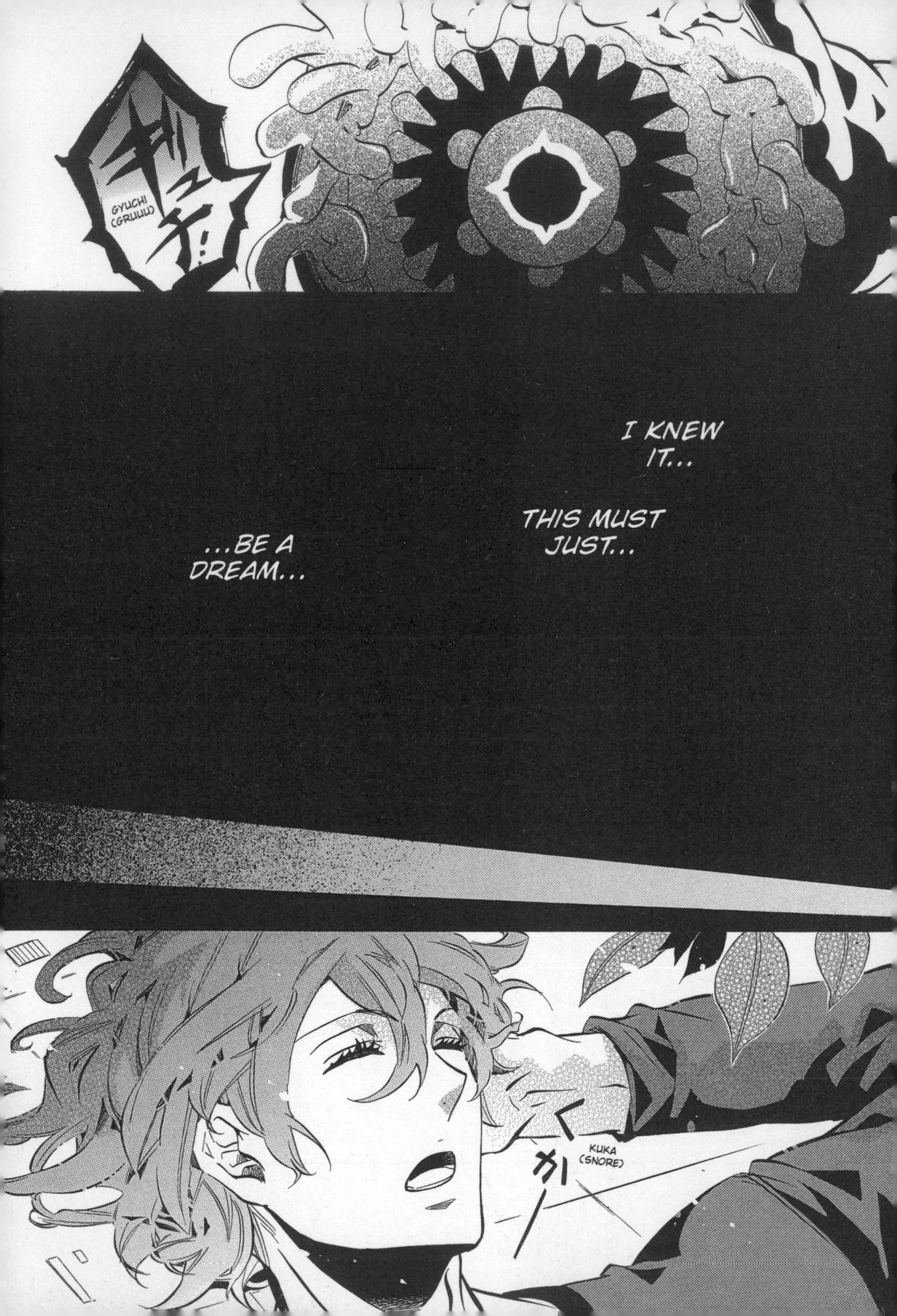
GYUCHI (GRUUU)
I KNEW IT...
THIS MUST JUST...
...BE A DREAM...
KUKA (SNORE)

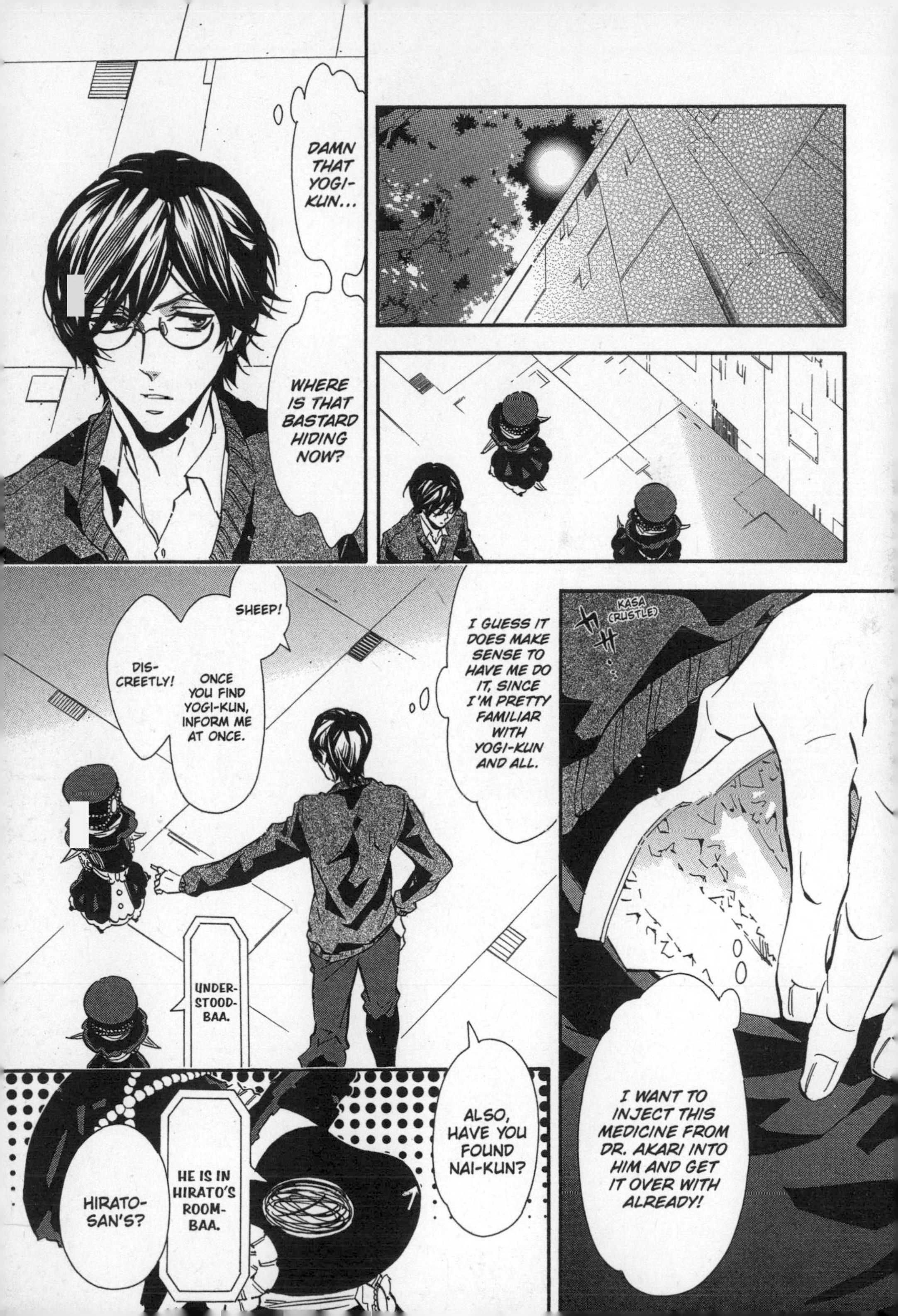
DAMN THAT YOGI-KUN...
WHERE IS THAT BASTARD HIDING NOW?
KASA (RUSTLE)
I WANT TO INJECT THIS MEDICINE FROM DR. AKARI INTO HIM AND GET IT OVER WITH ALREADY!
I GUESS IT DOES MAKE SENSE TO HAVE ME DO IT, SINCE I'M PRETTY FAMILIAR WITH YOGI-KUN AND ALL.
SHEEP!
ONCE YOU FIND YOGI-KUN, INFORM ME AT ONCE.
DIS-CREETLY!
UNDER-STOOD-BAA.
ALSO, HAVE YOU FOUND NAI-KUN?
HE IS IN HIRATO'S ROOM-BAA.
HIRATO-SAN'S?

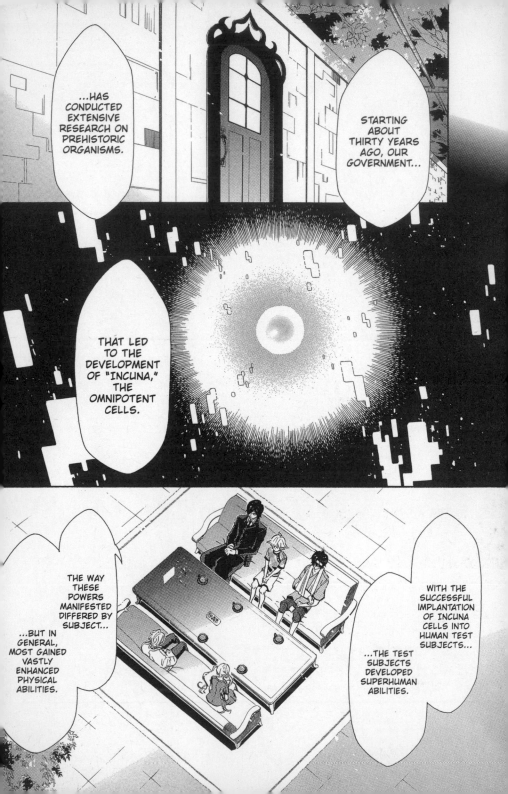

STARTING ABOUT THIRTY YEARS AGO, OUR GOVERNMENT...

...HAS CONDUCTED EXTENSIVE RESEARCH ON PREHISTORIC ORGANISMS.

THAT LED TO THE DEVELOPMENT OF "INCUNA," THE OMNIPOTENT CELLS.

WITH THE SUCCESSFUL IMPLANTATION OF INCUNA CELLS INTO HUMAN TEST SUBJECTS...

...THE TEST SUBJECTS DEVELOPED SUPERHUMAN ABILITIES.

THE WAY THESE POWERS MANIFESTED DIFFERED BY SUBJECT...

...BUT IN GENERAL, MOST GAINED VASTLY ENHANCED PHYSICAL ABILITIES.

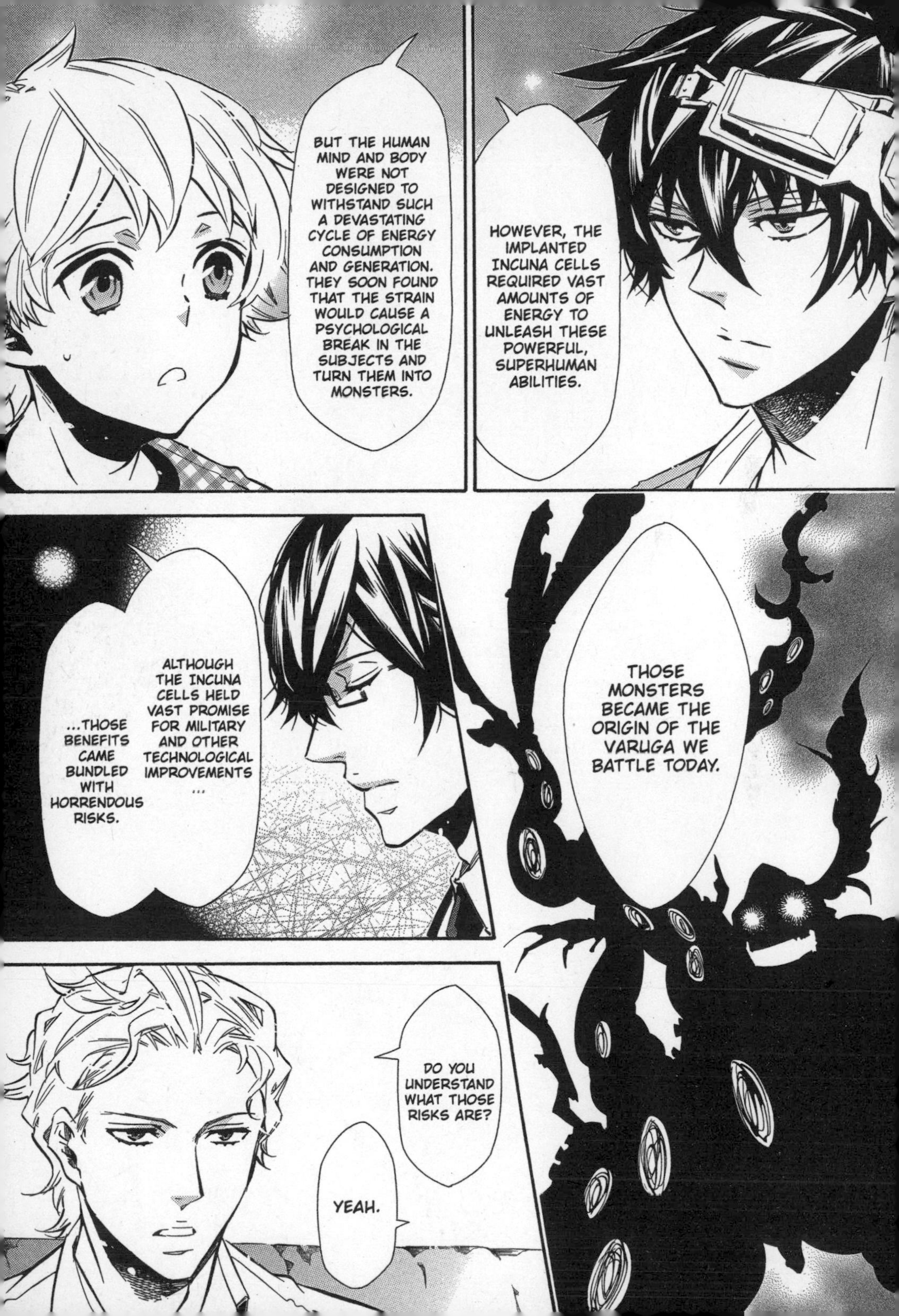
HOWEVER, THE IMPLANTED INCUNA CELLS REQUIRED VAST AMOUNTS OF ENERGY TO UNLEASH THESE POWERFUL, SUPERHUMAN ABILITIES.
BUT THE HUMAN MIND AND BODY WERE NOT DESIGNED TO WITHSTAND SUCH A DEVASTATING CYCLE OF ENERGY CONSUMPTION AND GENERATION. THEY SOON FOUND THAT THE STRAIN WOULD CAUSE A PSYCHOLOGICAL BREAK IN THE SUBJECTS AND TURN THEM INTO MONSTERS.
THOSE MONSTERS BECAME THE ORIGIN OF THE VARUGA WE BATTLE TODAY.
ALTHOUGH THE INCUNA CELLS HELD VAST PROMISE FOR MILITARY AND OTHER TECHNOLOGICAL IMPROVEMENTS...
...THOSE BENEFITS CAME BUNDLED WITH HORRENDOUS RISKS.
DO YOU UNDERSTAND WHAT THOSE RISKS ARE?
YEAH.

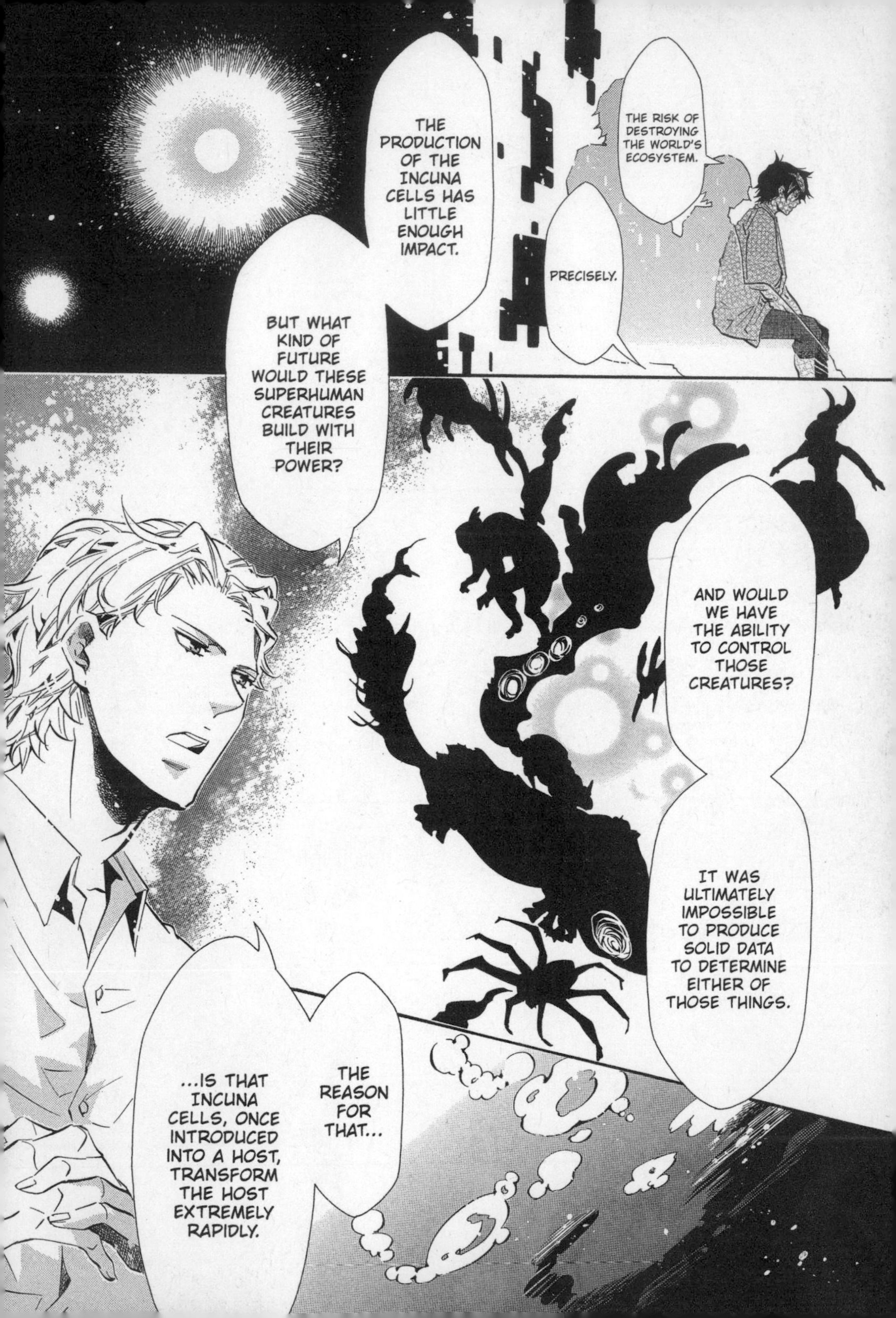
THE RISK OF DESTROYING THE WORLD'S ECOSYSTEM.
PRECISELY.
THE PRODUCTION OF THE INCUNA CELLS HAS LITTLE ENOUGH IMPACT.
BUT WHAT KIND OF FUTURE WOULD THESE SUPERHUMAN CREATURES BUILD WITH THEIR POWER?
AND WOULD WE HAVE THE ABILITY TO CONTROL THOSE CREATURES?
IT WAS ULTIMATELY IMPOSSIBLE TO PRODUCE SOLID DATA TO DETERMINE EITHER OF THOSE THINGS.
THE REASON FOR THAT...
...IS THAT INCUNA CELLS, ONCE INTRODUCED INTO A HOST, TRANSFORM THE HOST EXTREMELY RAPIDLY.

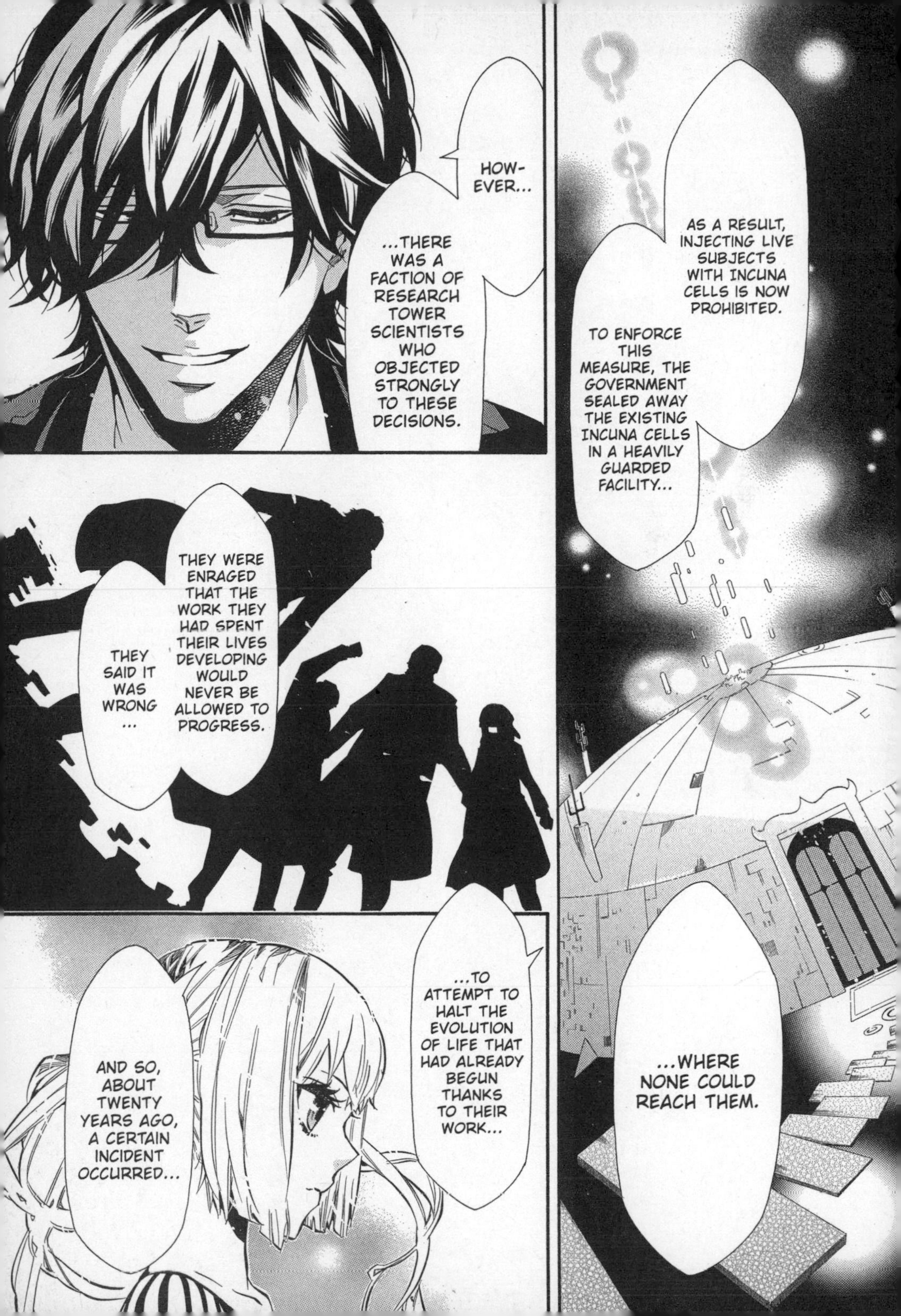
AS A RESULT, INJECTING LIVE SUBJECTS WITH INCUNA CELLS IS NOW PROHIBITED.
TO ENFORCE THIS MEASURE, THE GOVERNMENT SEALED AWAY THE EXISTING INCUNA CELLS IN A HEAVILY GUARDED FACILITY...
...WHERE NONE COULD REACH THEM.
HOW-EVER...
...THERE WAS A FACTION OF RESEARCH TOWER SCIENTISTS WHO OBJECTED STRONGLY TO THESE DECISIONS.
THEY WERE ENRAGED THAT THE WORK THEY HAD SPENT THEIR LIVES DEVELOPING WOULD NEVER BE ALLOWED TO PROGRESS.
THEY SAID IT WAS WRONG ...
...TO ATTEMPT TO HALT THE EVOLUTION OF LIFE THAT HAD ALREADY BEGUN THANKS TO THEIR WORK...
AND SO, ABOUT TWENTY YEARS AGO, A CERTAIN INCIDENT OCCURRED...

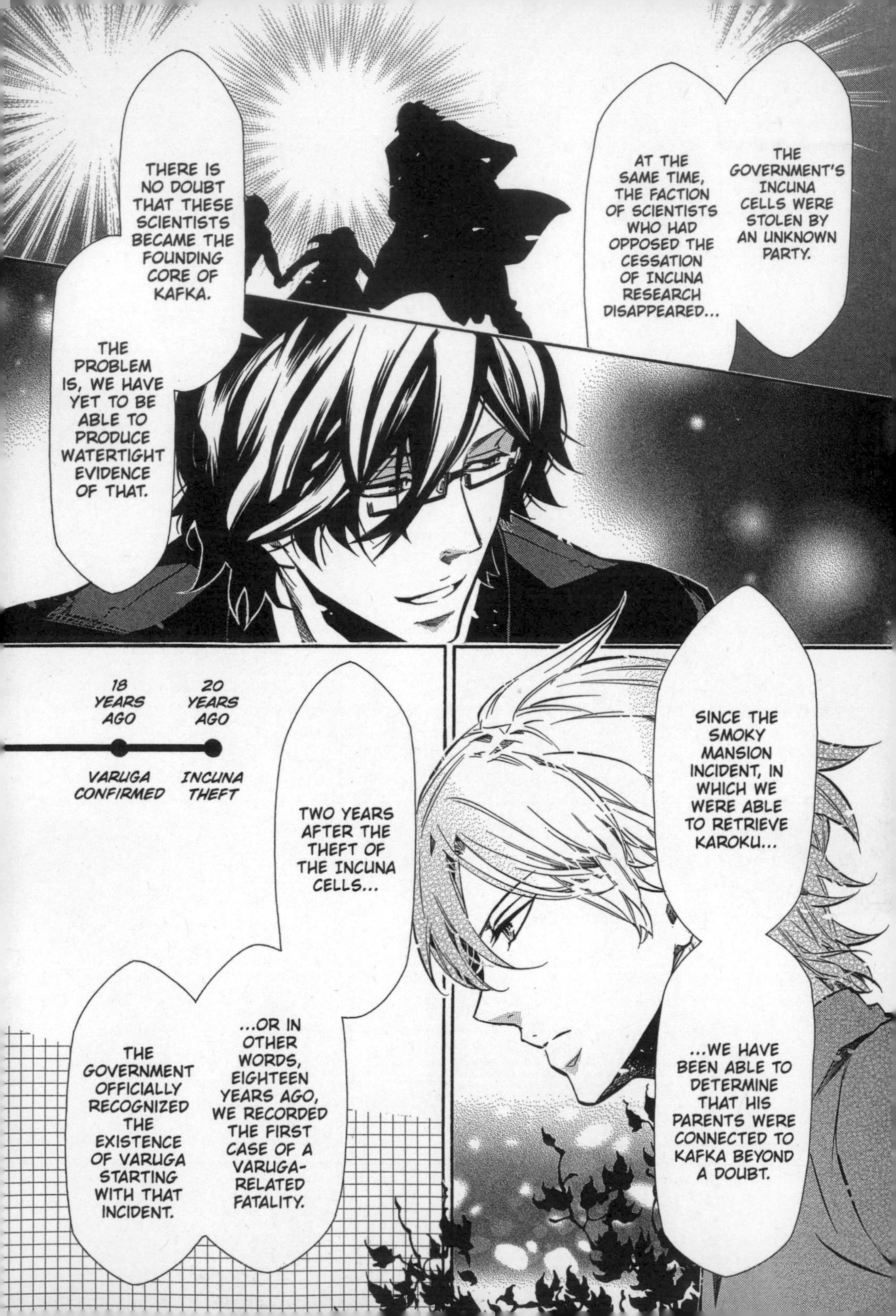
THE GOVERNMENT'S INCUNA CELLS WERE STOLEN BY AN UNKNOWN PARTY.
AT THE SAME TIME, THE FACTION OF SCIENTISTS WHO HAD OPPOSED THE CESSATION OF INCUNA RESEARCH DISAPPEARED...
THERE IS NO DOUBT THAT THESE SCIENTISTS BECAME THE FOUNDING CORE OF KAFKA.
THE PROBLEM IS, WE HAVE YET TO BE ABLE TO PRODUCE WATERTIGHT EVIDENCE OF THAT.
SINCE THE SMOKY MANSION INCIDENT, IN WHICH WE WERE ABLE TO RETRIEVE KAROKU...
...WE HAVE BEEN ABLE TO DETERMINE THAT HIS PARENTS WERE CONNECTED TO KAFKA BEYOND A DOUBT.
TWO YEARS AFTER THE THEFT OF THE INCUNA CELLS...
20 YEARS AGO
INCUNA THEFT
18 YEARS AGO
VARUGA CONFIRMED
...OR IN OTHER WORDS, EIGHTEEN YEARS AGO, WE RECORDED THE FIRST CASE OF A VARUGA-RELATED FATALITY.
THE GOVERNMENT OFFICIALLY RECOGNIZED THE EXISTENCE OF VARUGA STARTING WITH THAT INCIDENT.

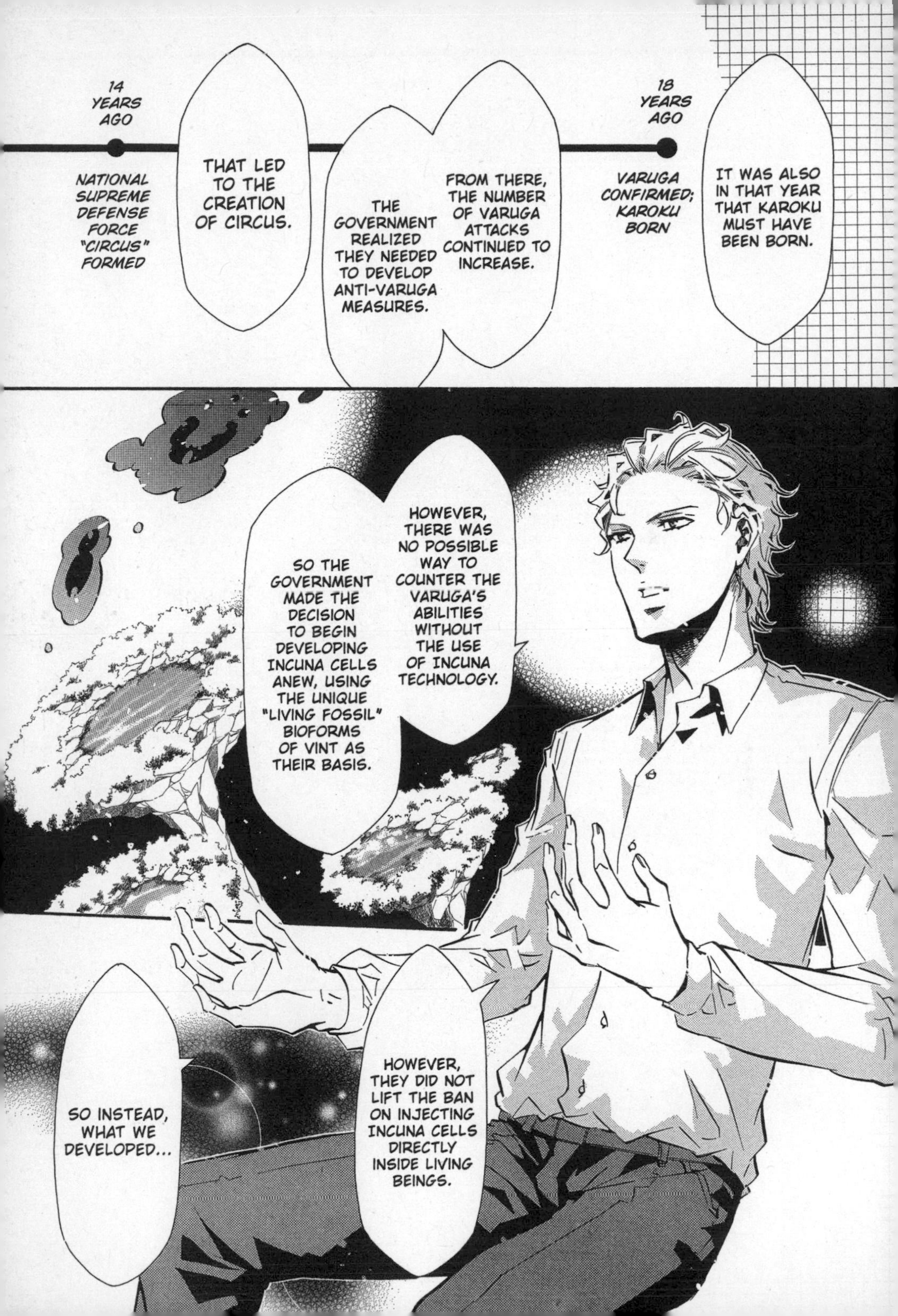
18 YEARS AGO
VARUGA CONFIRMED; KAROKU BORN
IT WAS ALSO IN THAT YEAR THAT KAROKU MUST HAVE BEEN BORN.
FROM THERE, THE NUMBER OF VARUGA ATTACKS CONTINUED TO INCREASE.
THE GOVERNMENT REALIZED THEY NEEDED TO DEVELOP ANTI-VARUGA MEASURES.
14 YEARS AGO
NATIONAL SUPREME DEFENSE FORCE "CIRCUS" FORMED
THAT LED TO THE CREATION OF CIRCUS.
HOWEVER, THERE WAS NO POSSIBLE WAY TO COUNTER THE VARUGA'S ABILITIES WITHOUT THE USE OF INCUNA TECHNOLOGY.
SO THE GOVERNMENT MADE THE DECISION TO BEGIN DEVELOPING INCUNA CELLS ANEW, USING THE UNIQUE "LIVING FOSSIL" BIOFORMS OF VINT AS THEIR BASIS.
HOWEVER, THEY DID NOT LIFT THE BAN ON INJECTING INCUNA CELLS DIRECTLY INSIDE LIVING BEINGS.
SO INSTEAD, WHAT WE DEVELOPED...

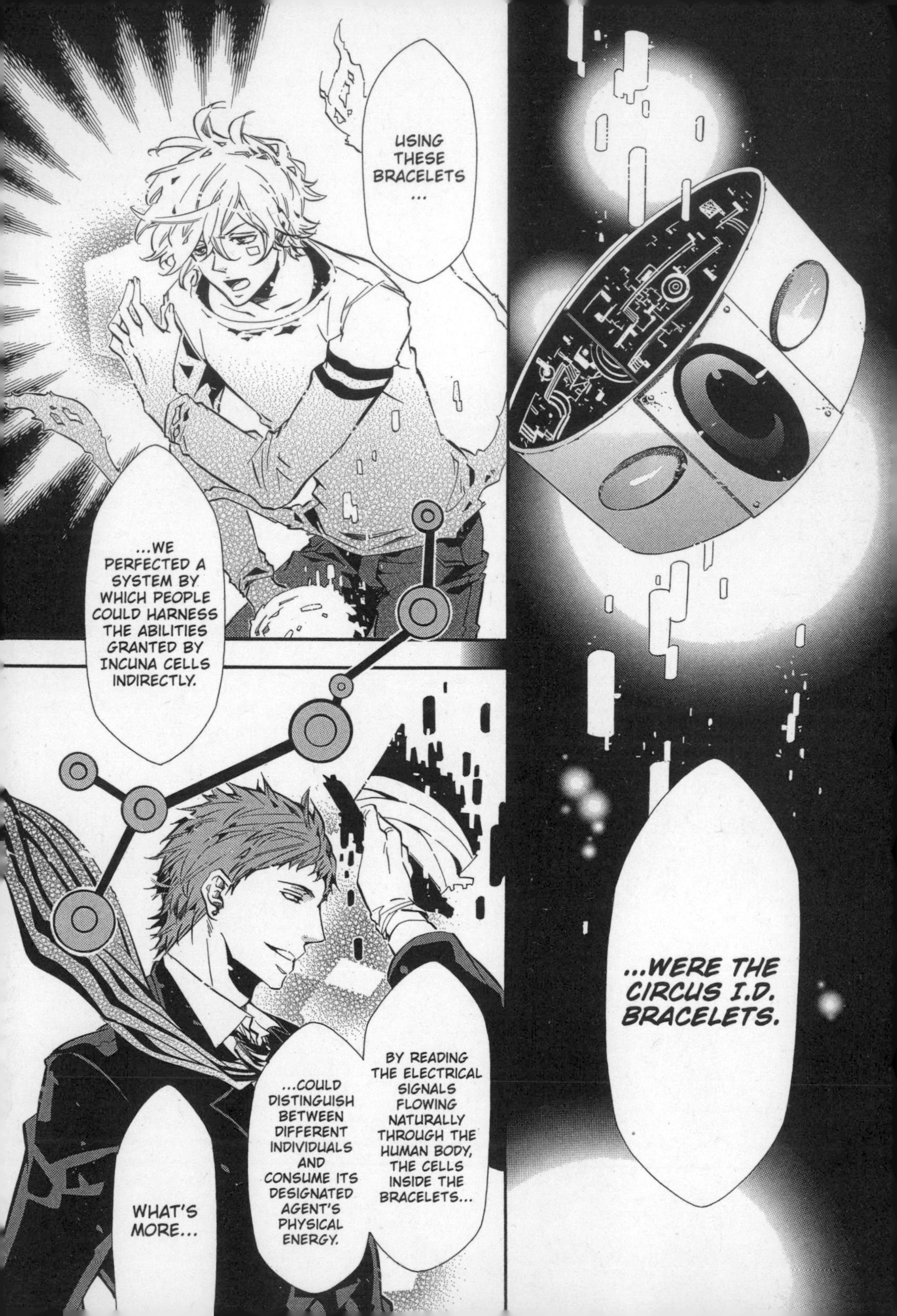
USING THESE BRACELETS ...
...WE PERFECTED A SYSTEM BY WHICH PEOPLE COULD HARNESS THE ABILITIES GRANTED BY INCUNA CELLS INDIRECTLY.
WHAT'S MORE...
BY READING THE ELECTRICAL SIGNALS FLOWING NATURALLY THROUGH THE HUMAN BODY, THE CELLS INSIDE THE BRACELETS...
...COULD DISTINGUISH BETWEEN DIFFERENT INDIVIDUALS AND CONSUME ITS DESIGNATED AGENT'S PHYSICAL ENERGY.
...WERE THE CIRCUS I.D. BRACELETS.

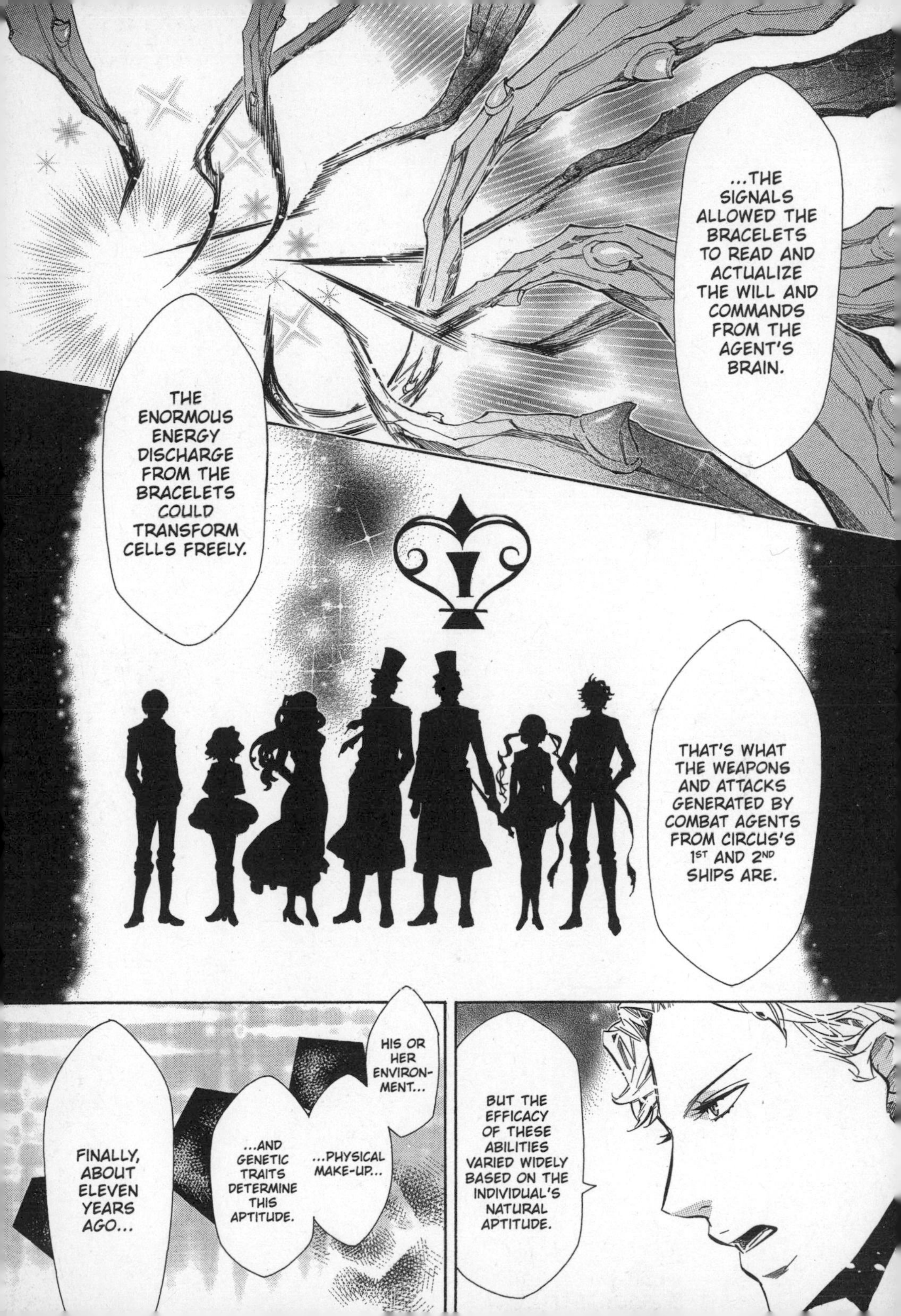
...THE SIGNALS ALLOWED THE BRACELETS TO READ AND ACTUALIZE THE WILL AND COMMANDS FROM THE AGENT'S BRAIN.
THE ENORMOUS ENERGY DISCHARGE FROM THE BRACELETS COULD TRANSFORM CELLS FREELY.
THAT'S WHAT THE WEAPONS AND ATTACKS GENERATED BY COMBAT AGENTS FROM CIRCUS'S 1st AND 2nd SHIPS ARE.
BUT THE EFFICACY OF THESE ABILITIES VARIED WIDELY BASED ON THE INDIVIDUAL'S NATURAL APTITUDE.
HIS OR HER ENVIRON-MENT...
...PHYSICAL MAKE-UP...
...AND GENETIC TRAITS DETERMINE THIS APTITUDE.
FINALLY, ABOUT ELEVEN YEARS AGO...

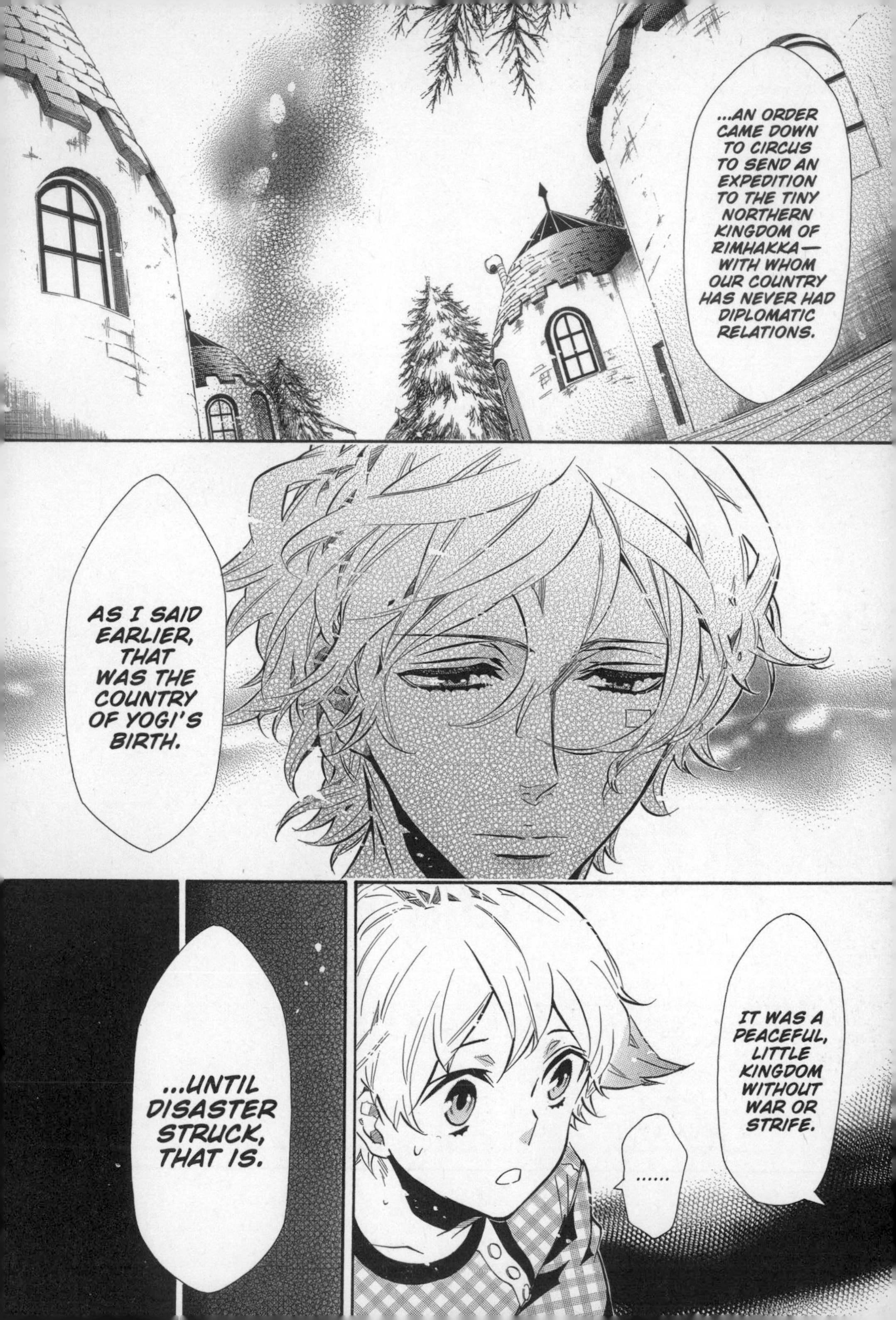
...AN ORDER CAME DOWN TO CIRCUS TO SEND AN EXPEDITION TO THE TINY NORTHERN KINGDOM OF RIMHAKKA—WITH WHOM OUR COUNTRY HAS NEVER HAD DIPLOMATIC RELATIONS.
AS I SAID EARLIER, THAT WAS THE COUNTRY OF YOGI'S BIRTH.
IT WAS A PEACEFUL, LITTLE KINGDOM WITHOUT WAR OR STRIFE.
......
...UNTIL DISASTER STRUCK, THAT IS.

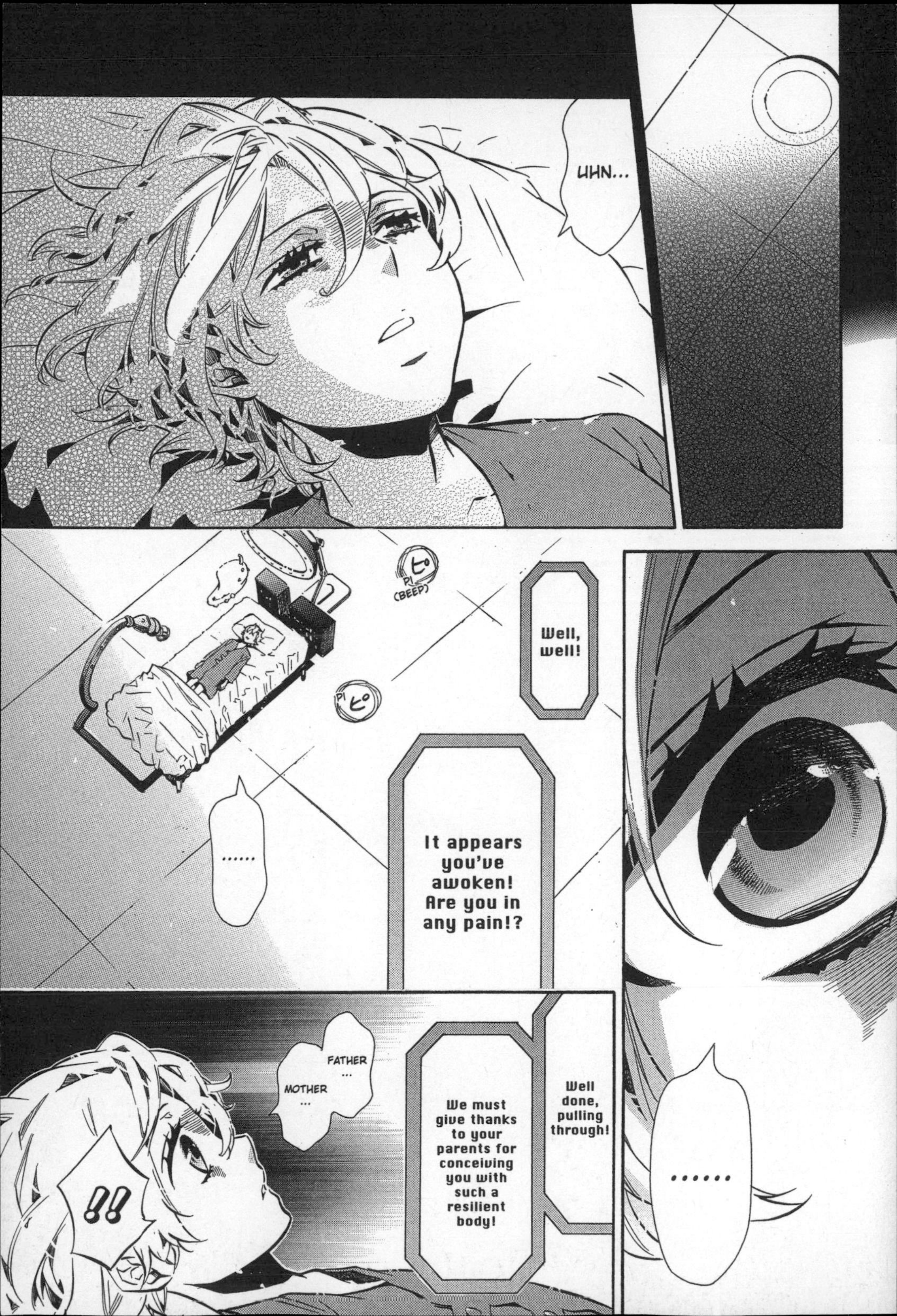

UHN...
......
Well, well!
ピ PI (BEEP)
ピ PI
It appears you've awoken! Are you in any pain!?
......
Well done, pulling through!
We must give thanks to your parents for conceiving you with such a resilient body!
FATHER ...
MOTHER ...
!!

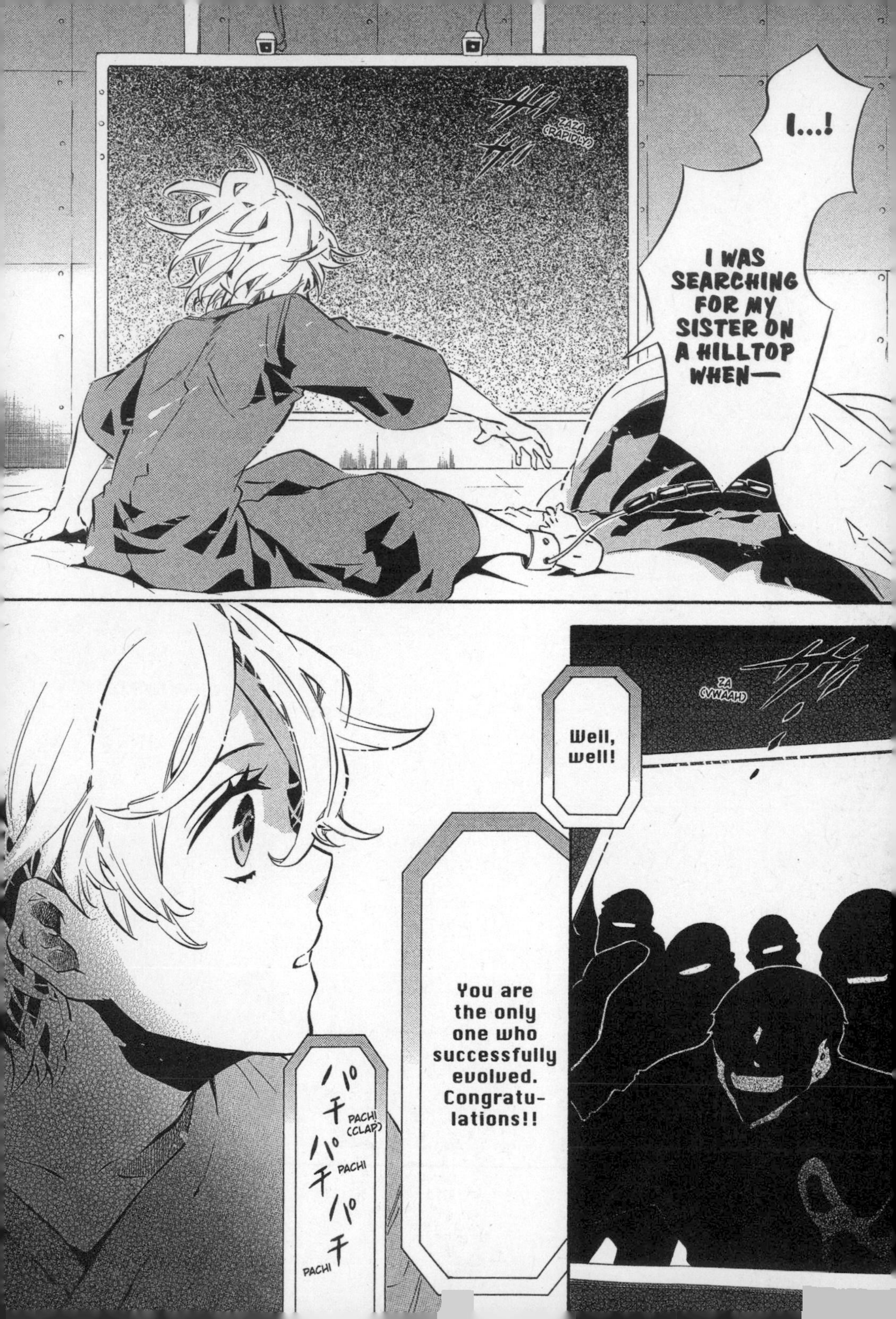
I...!
I WAS SEARCHING FOR MY SISTER ON A HILLTOP WHEN—
ZAZA (RAPIDLY)
ZA (VWAAH)
Well, well!
You are the only one who successfully evolved. Congratu-lations!!
パチパチパチ
PACHI (CLAP)
PACHI
PACHI

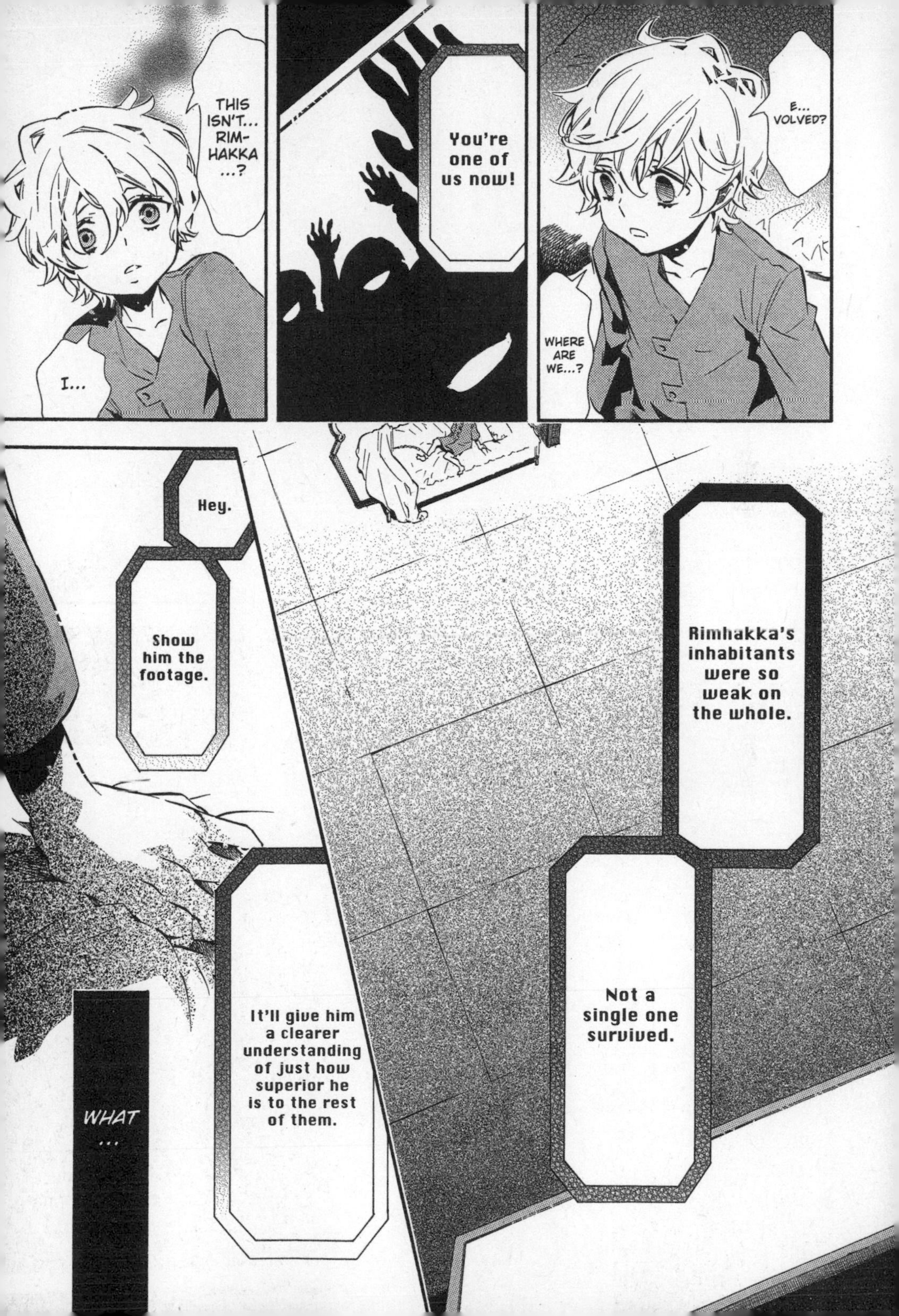
E... VOLVED?
WHERE ARE WE...?
You're one of us now!
THIS ISN'T... RIM-HAKKA ...?
I...
Rimhakka's inhabitants were so weak on the whole.
Not a single one survived.
Hey.
Show him the footage.
It'll give him a clearer understanding of just how superior he is to the rest of them.
WHAT ...

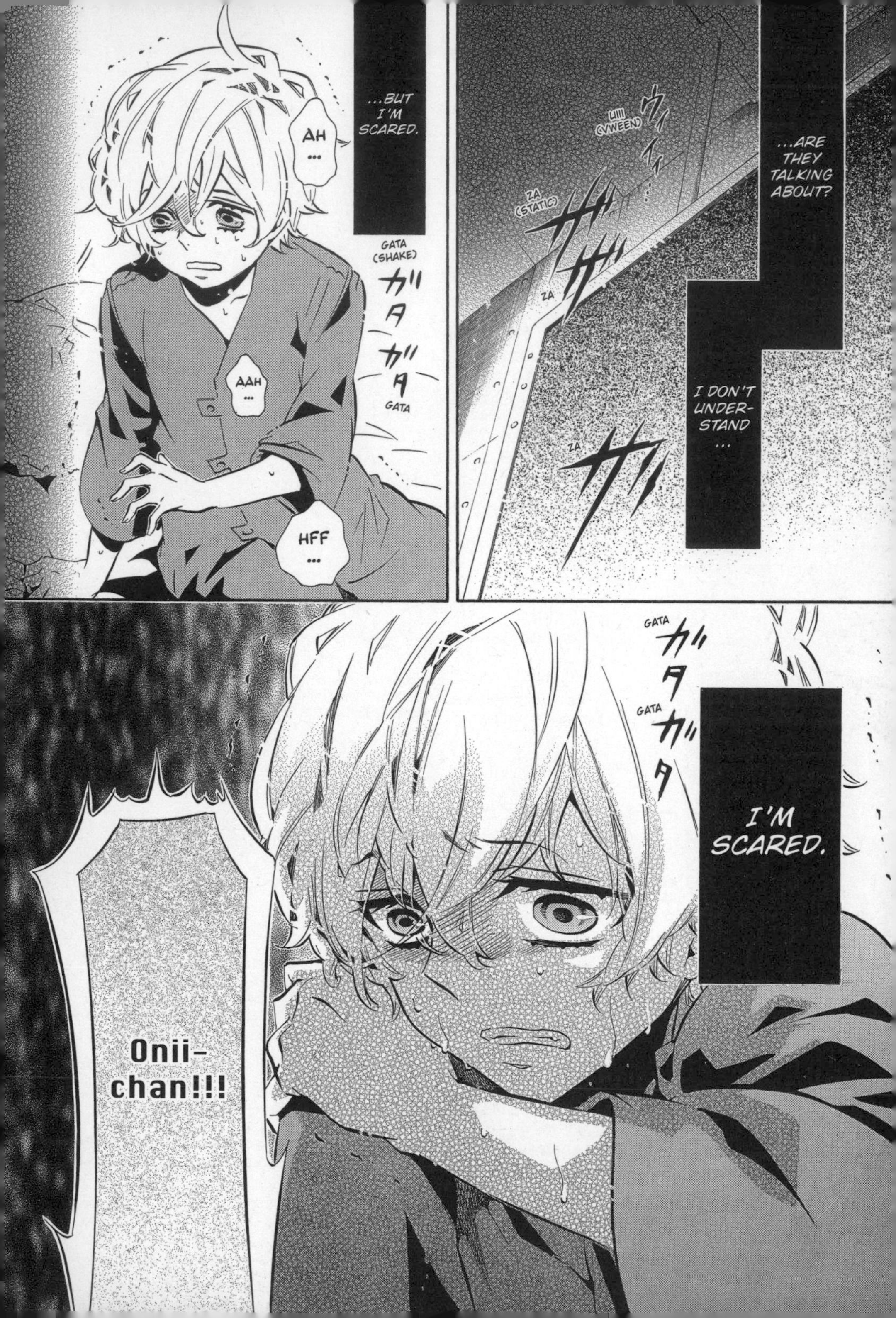
UIII (VWEEN)
...ARE THEY TALKING ABOUT?
ZA (STATIC)
ZA
I DON'T UNDER-STAND ...
ZA
...BUT I'M SCARED.
AH ...
GATA (SHAKE)
GATA
AAH ...
HFF ...
GATA
GATA
I'M SCARED.
Onii-chan!!!

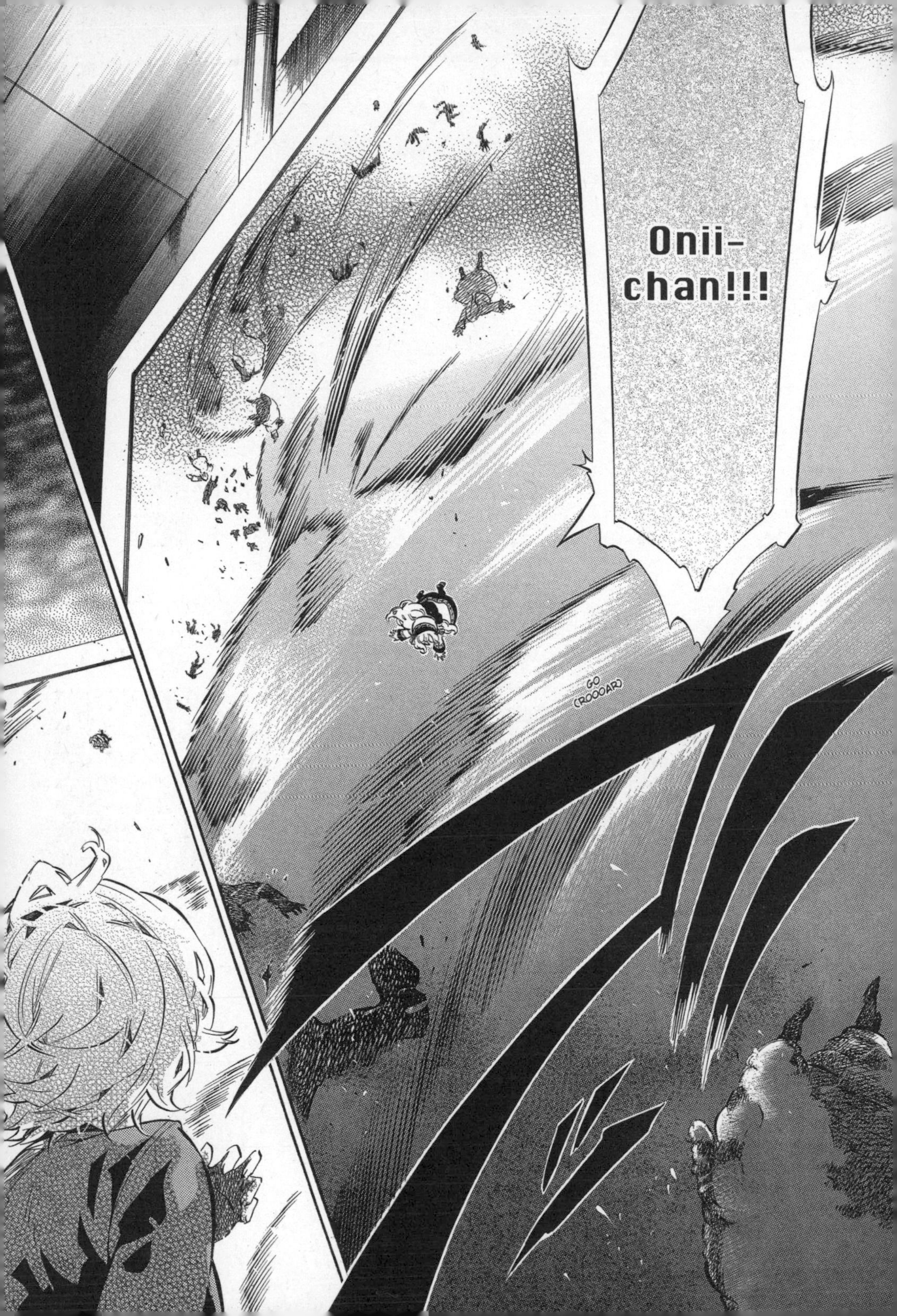
Onii-
chan!!!
GO
(ROOOAR)

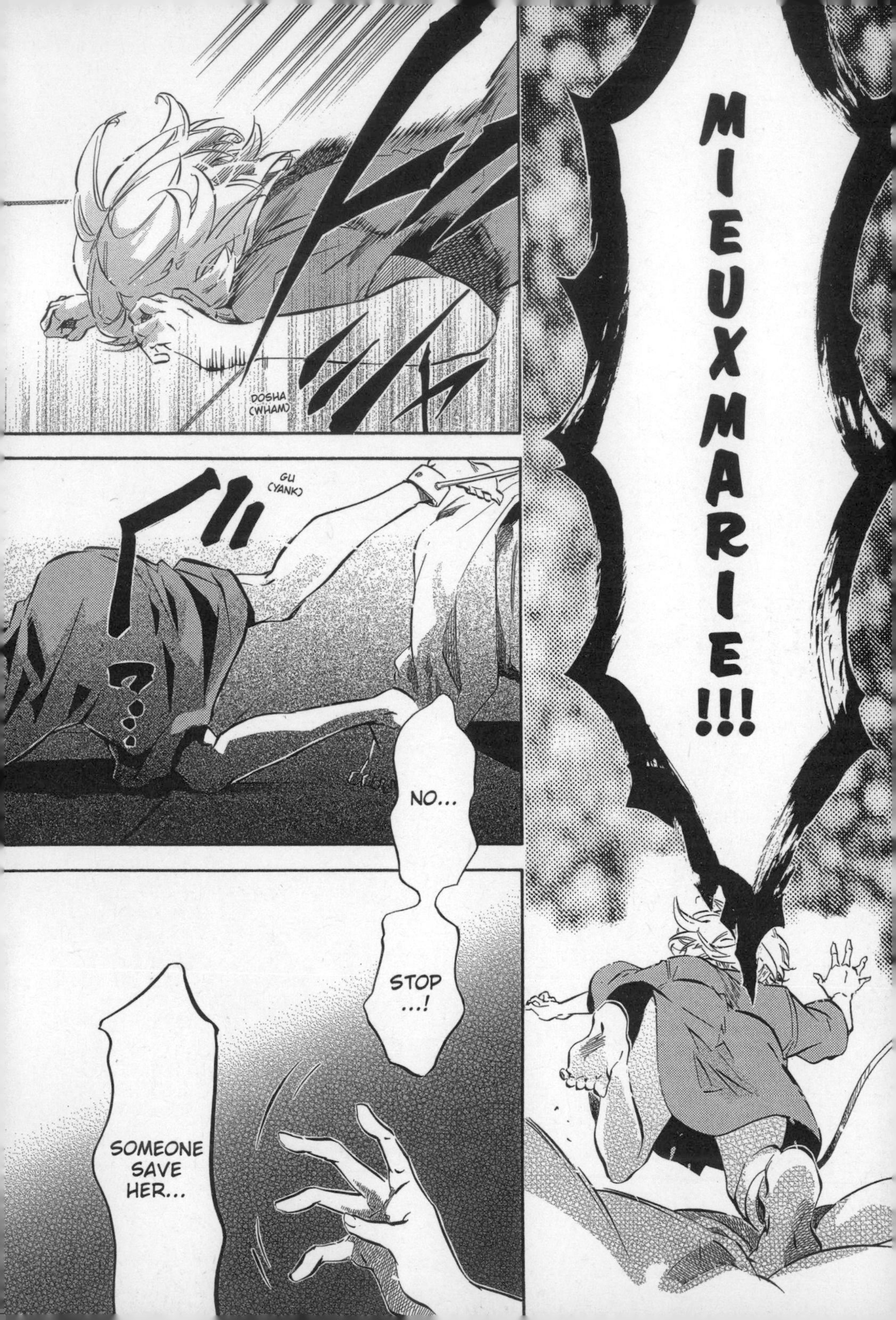
MIEUXMARIE!!!
DOSHA (WHAM)
GU (YANK)
?
NO...
STOP ...!
SOMEONE SAVE HER...

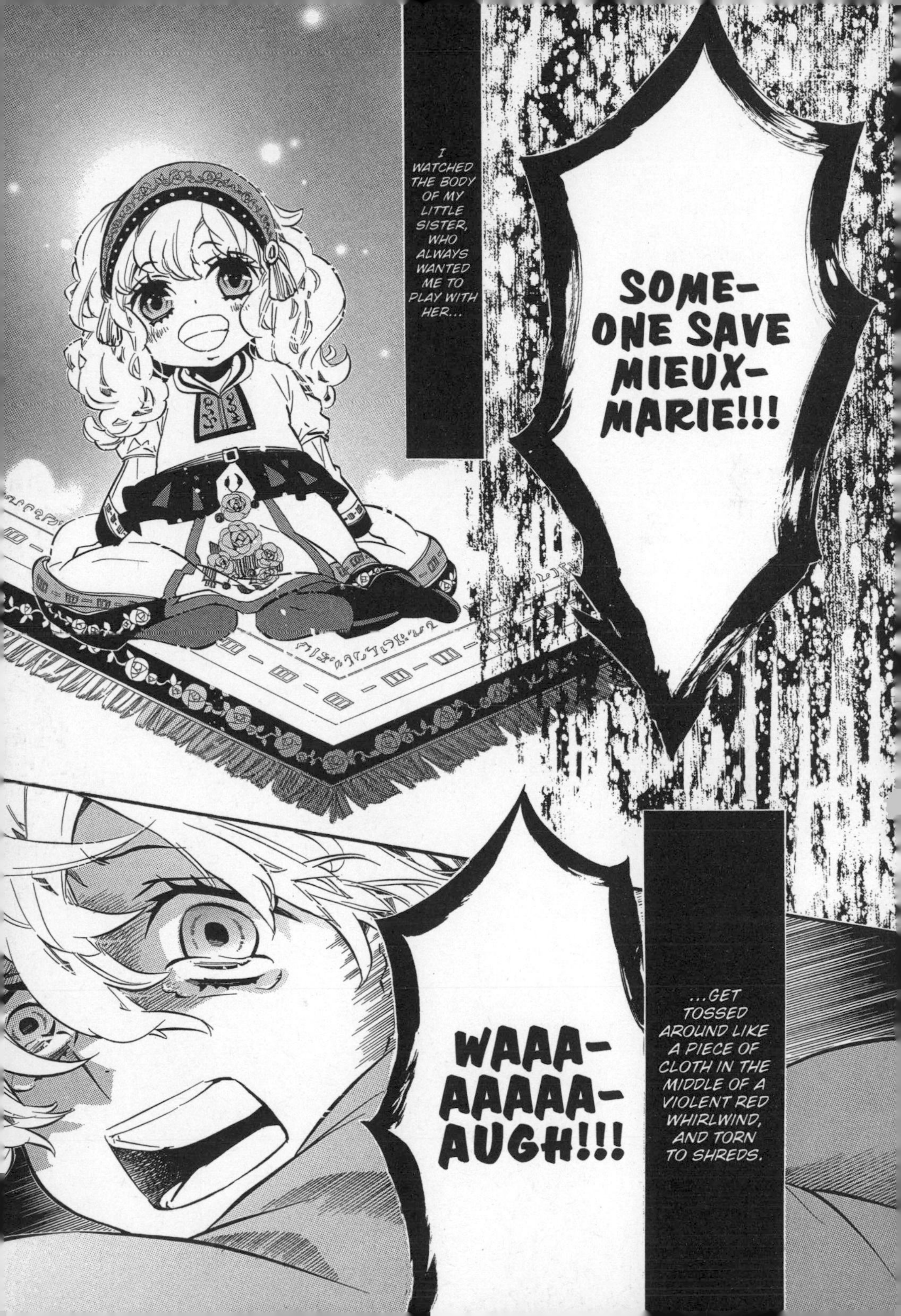
SOME-ONE SAVE MIEUX-MARIE!!!
I WATCHED THE BODY OF MY LITTLE SISTER, WHO ALWAYS WANTED ME TO PLAY WITH HER...
...GET TOSSED AROUND LIKE A PIECE OF CLOTH IN THE MIDDLE OF A VIOLENT RED WHIRLWIND, AND TORN TO SHREDS.
WAAA-AAAAA-AUGH!!!

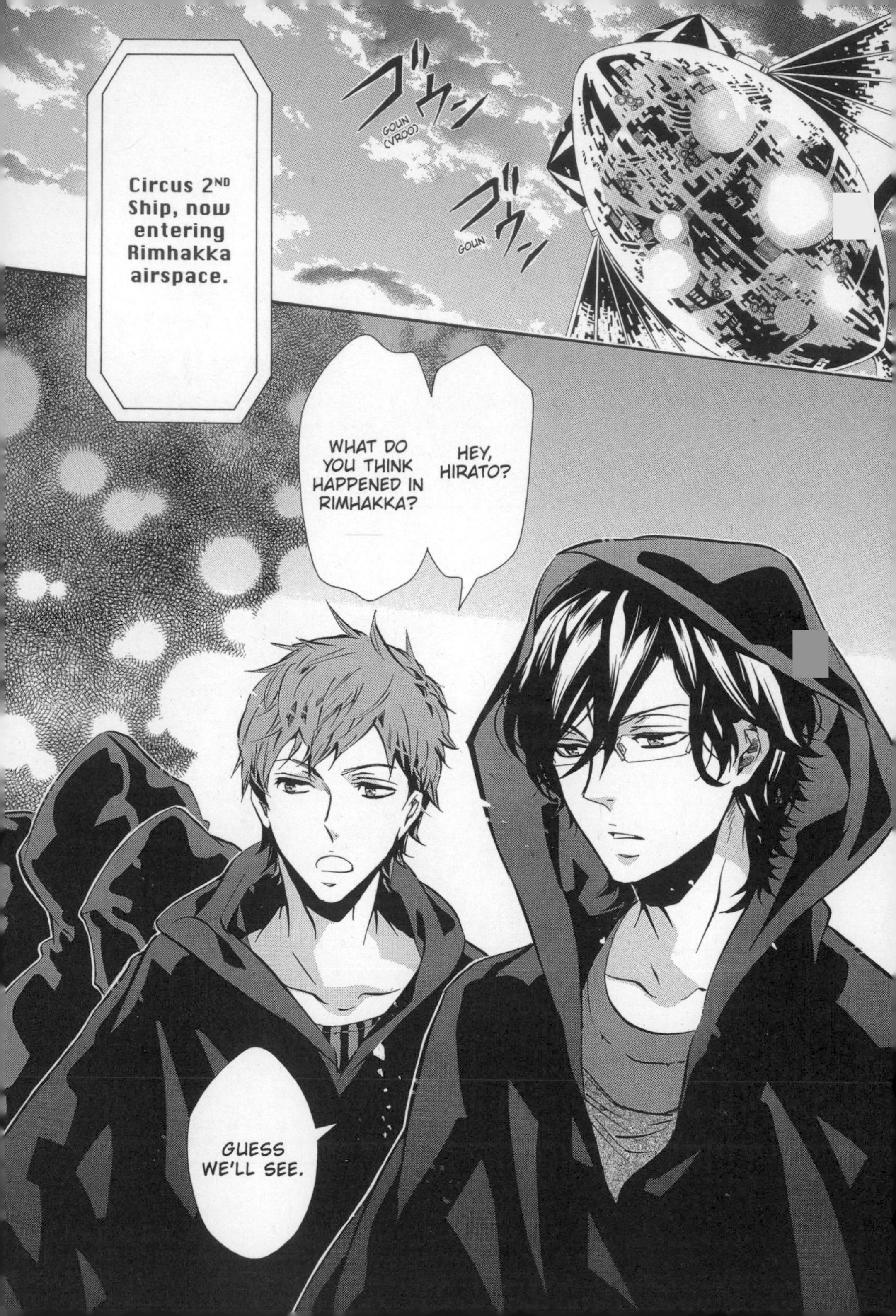
GOUN (VROO)
GOUN
Circus 2ND Ship, now entering Rimhakka airspace.
HEY, HIRATO?
WHAT DO YOU THINK HAPPENED IN RIMHAKKA?
GUESS WE'LL SEE.

KARNEVAL

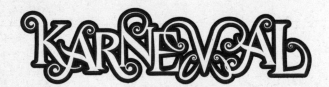

KARNEVAL

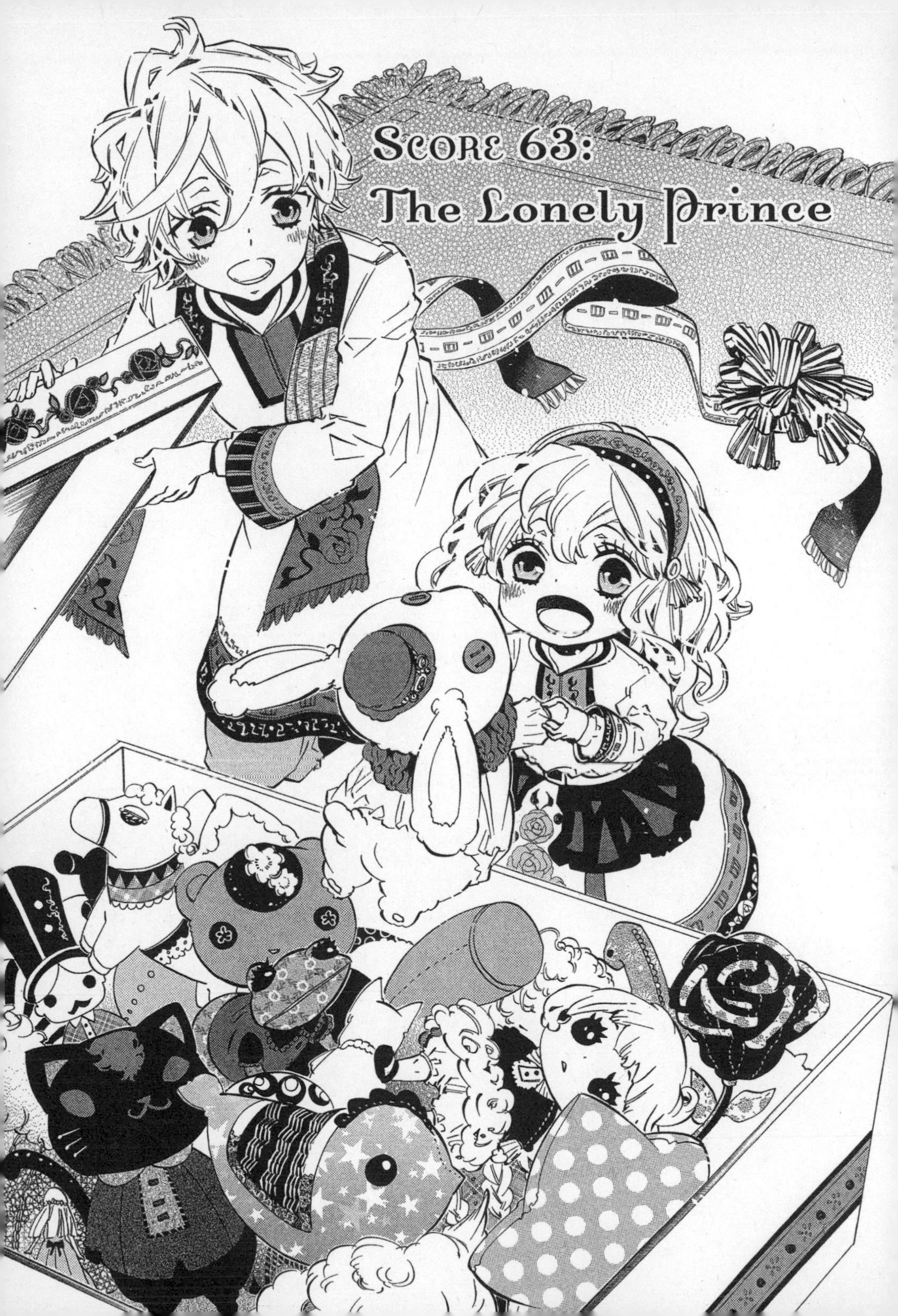
Score 63:
The Lonely Prince

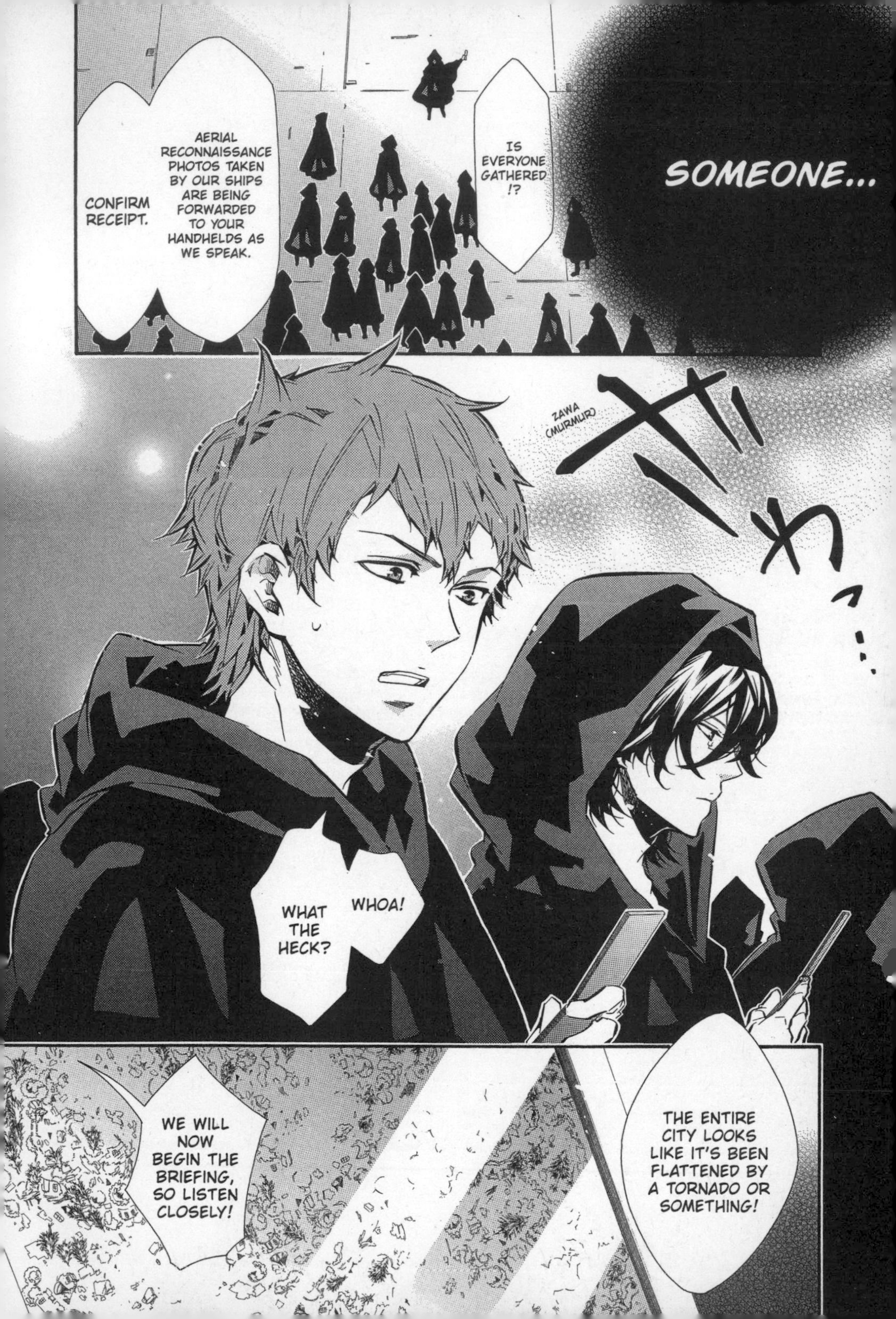
SOMEONE...
IS EVERYONE GATHERED!?
AERIAL RECONNAISSANCE PHOTOS TAKEN BY OUR SHIPS ARE BEING FORWARDED TO YOUR HANDHELDS AS WE SPEAK.
CONFIRM RECEIPT.
ZAWA (MURMUR)
WHOA!
WHAT THE HECK?
THE ENTIRE CITY LOOKS LIKE IT'S BEEN FLATTENED BY A TORNADO OR SOMETHING!
WE WILL NOW BEGIN THE BRIEFING, SO LISTEN CLOSELY!

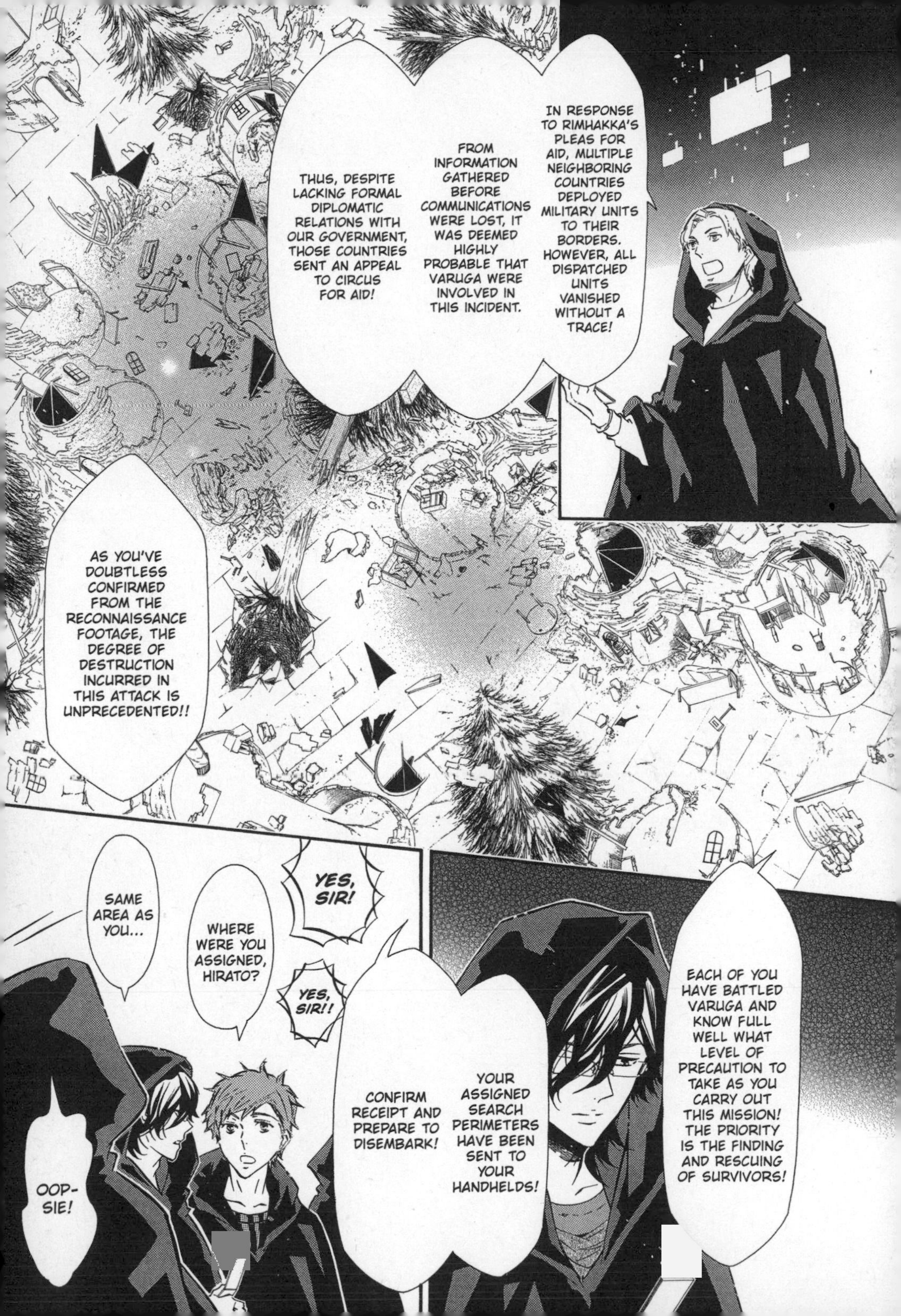

IN RESPONSE TO RIMHAKKA'S PLEAS FOR AID, MULTIPLE NEIGHBORING COUNTRIES DEPLOYED MILITARY UNITS TO THEIR BORDERS. HOWEVER, ALL DISPATCHED UNITS VANISHED WITHOUT A TRACE!
FROM INFORMATION GATHERED BEFORE COMMUNICATIONS WERE LOST, IT WAS DEEMED HIGHLY PROBABLE THAT VARUGA WERE INVOLVED IN THIS INCIDENT.
THUS, DESPITE LACKING FORMAL DIPLOMATIC RELATIONS WITH OUR GOVERNMENT, THOSE COUNTRIES SENT AN APPEAL TO CIRCUS FOR AID!
AS YOU'VE DOUBTLESS CONFIRMED FROM THE RECONNAISSANCE FOOTAGE, THE DEGREE OF DESTRUCTION INCURRED IN THIS ATTACK IS UNPRECEDENTED!!
EACH OF YOU HAVE BATTLED VARUGA AND KNOW FULL WELL WHAT LEVEL OF PRECAUTION TO TAKE AS YOU CARRY OUT THIS MISSION! THE PRIORITY IS THE FINDING AND RESCUING OF SURVIVORS!
YOUR ASSIGNED SEARCH PERIMETERS HAVE BEEN SENT TO YOUR HANDHELDS!
CONFIRM RECEIPT AND PREPARE TO DISEMBARK!
YES, SIR!
YES, SIR!!
WHERE WERE YOU ASSIGNED, HIRATO?
SAME AREA AS YOU...
OOP-SIE!

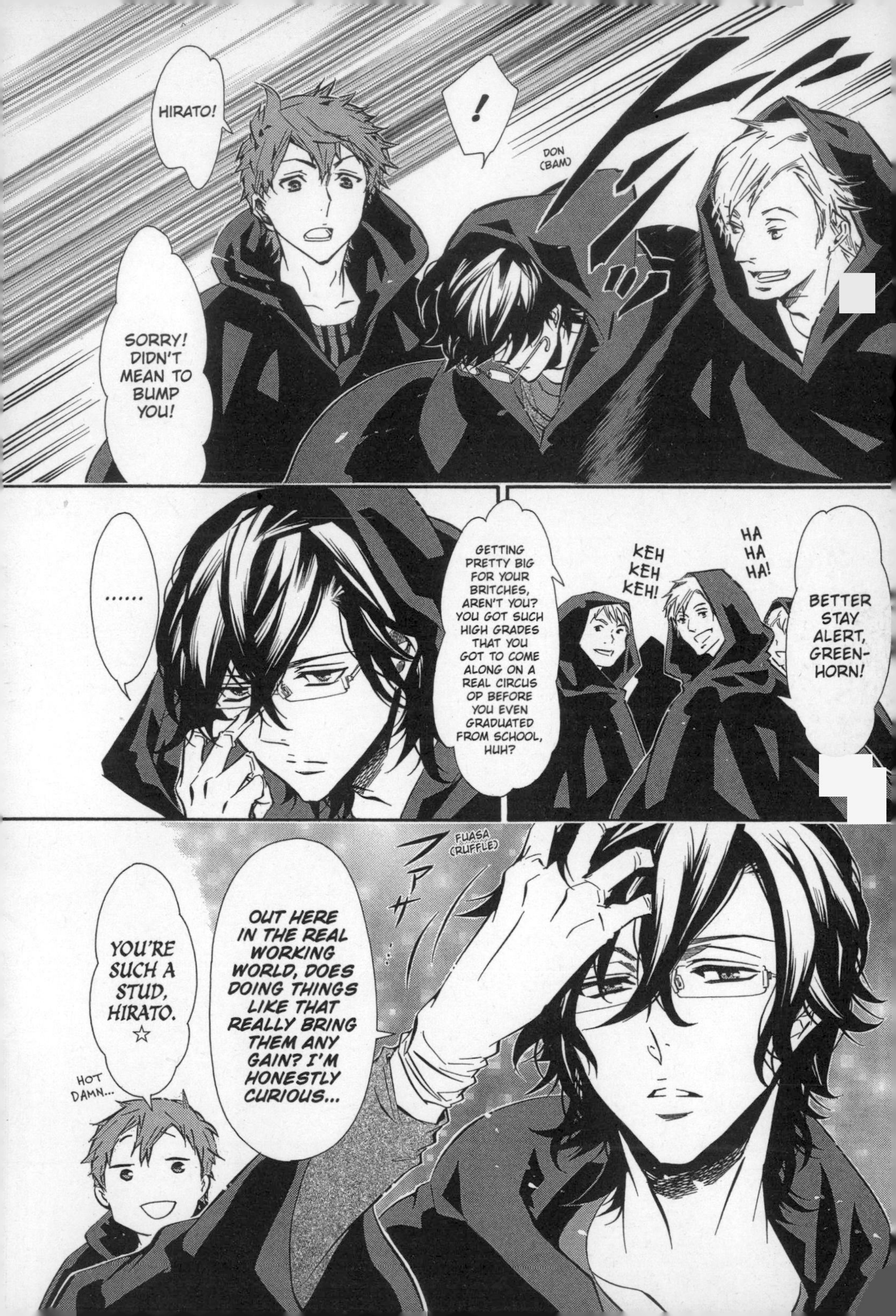
DON (BAM)
!
HIRATO!
SORRY! DIDN'T MEAN TO BUMP YOU!
BETTER STAY ALERT, GREEN-HORN!
HA HA HA!
KEH KEH KEH!
GETTING PRETTY BIG FOR YOUR BRITCHES, AREN'T YOU? YOU GOT SUCH HIGH GRADES THAT YOU GOT TO COME ALONG ON A REAL CIRCUS OP BEFORE YOU EVEN GRADUATED FROM SCHOOL, HUH?
......
FUASA (RUFFLE)
OUT HERE IN THE REAL WORKING WORLD, DOES DOING THINGS LIKE THAT REALLY BRING THEM ANY GAIN? I'M HONESTLY CURIOUS...
YOU'RE SUCH A STUD, HIRATO. ☆
HOT DAMN...

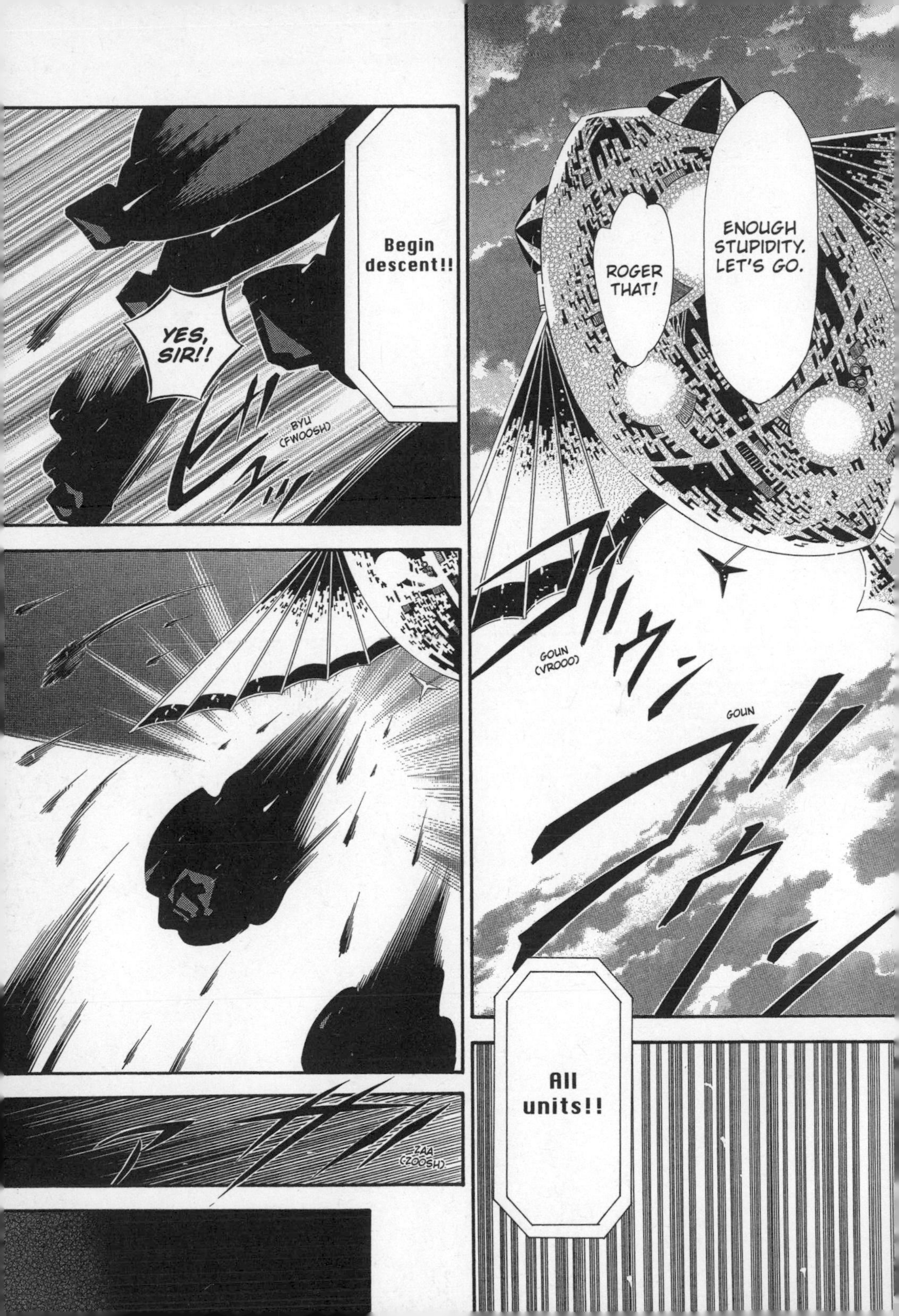
ENOUGH STUPIDITY. LET'S GO.
ROGER THAT!
GOUN (VROOO)
GOUN
Begin descent!!
YES, SIR!!
BYU (FWOOSH)
All units!!
ZAA (ZOOSH)

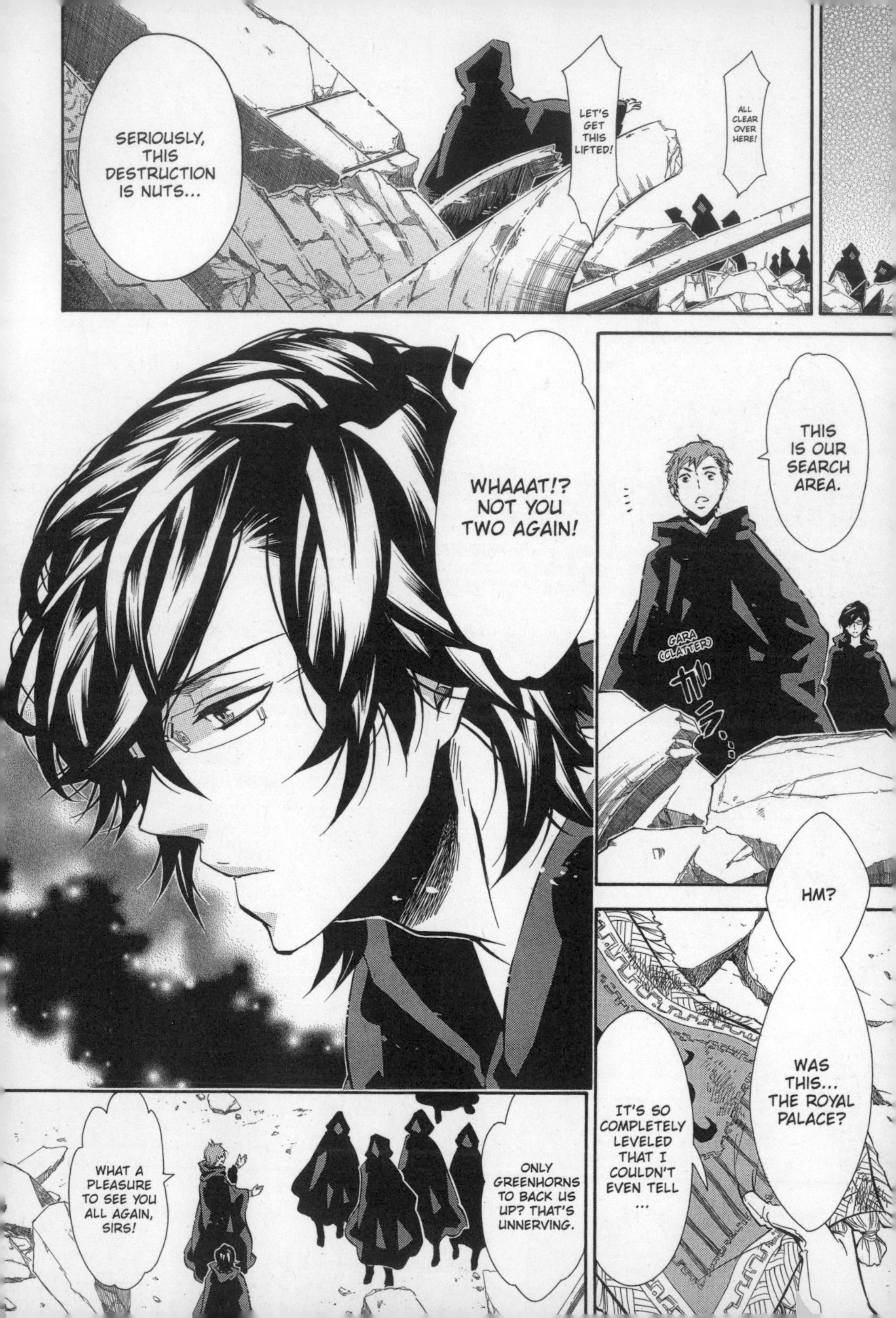
ALL CLEAR OVER HERE!
LET'S GET THIS LIFTED!
SERIOUSLY, THIS DESTRUCTION IS NUTS...
THIS IS OUR SEARCH AREA.
GARA (CLATTER)
HM?
WAS THIS... THE ROYAL PALACE?
IT'S SO COMPLETELY LEVELED THAT I COULDN'T EVEN TELL ...
WHAAAT!? NOT YOU TWO AGAIN!
ONLY GREENHORNS TO BACK US UP? THAT'S UNNERVING.
WHAT A PLEASURE TO SEE YOU ALL AGAIN, SIRS!

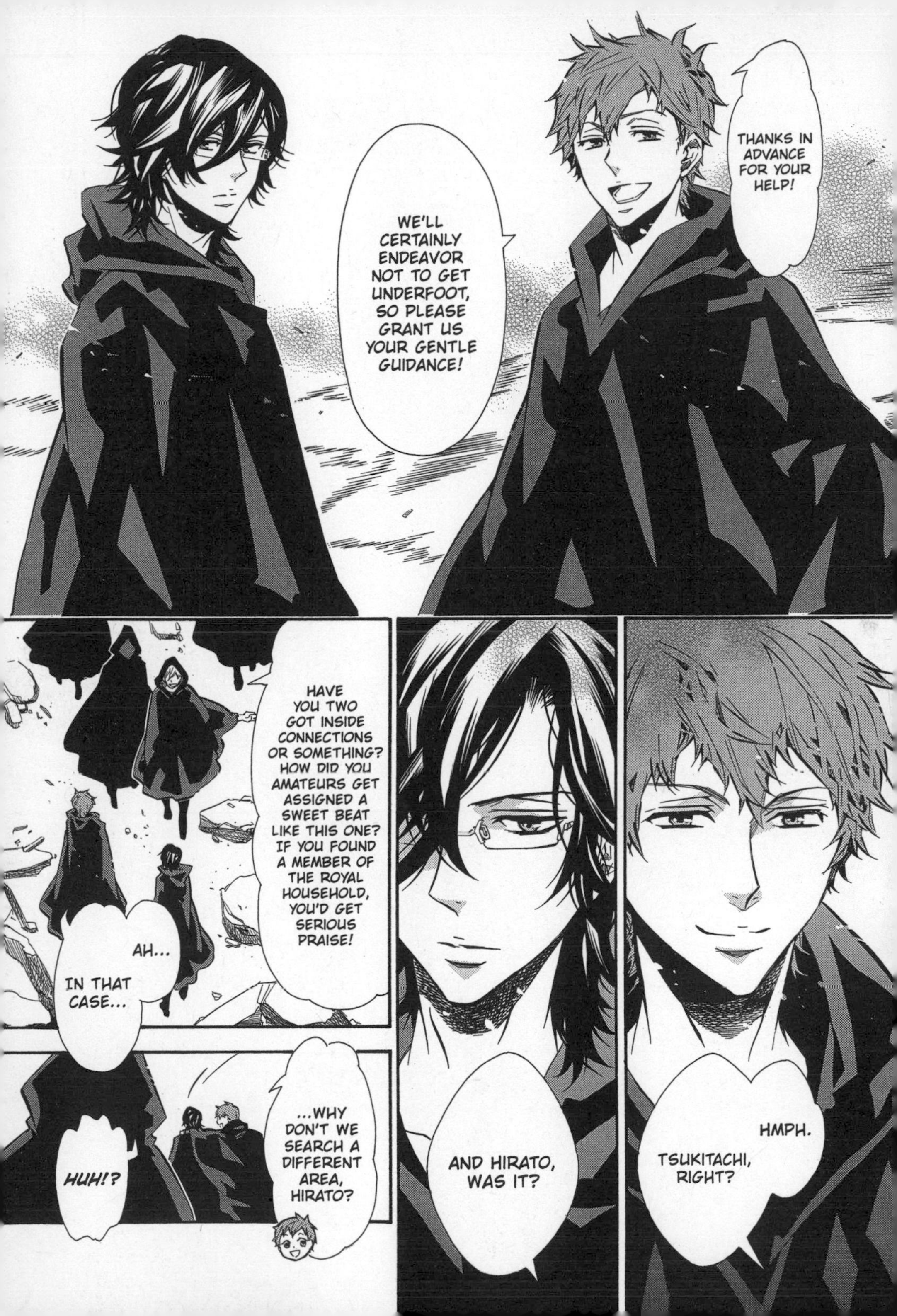
THANKS IN ADVANCE FOR YOUR HELP!
WE'LL CERTAINLY ENDEAVOR NOT TO GET UNDERFOOT, SO PLEASE GRANT US YOUR GENTLE GUIDANCE!
HMPH.
TSUKITACHI, RIGHT?
AND HIRATO, WAS IT?
HAVE YOU TWO GOT INSIDE CONNECTIONS OR SOMETHING? HOW DID YOU AMATEURS GET ASSIGNED A SWEET BEAT LIKE THIS ONE? IF YOU FOUND A MEMBER OF THE ROYAL HOUSEHOLD, YOU'D GET SERIOUS PRAISE!
AH...
IN THAT CASE...
...WHY DON'T WE SEARCH A DIFFERENT AREA, HIRATO?
HUH!?

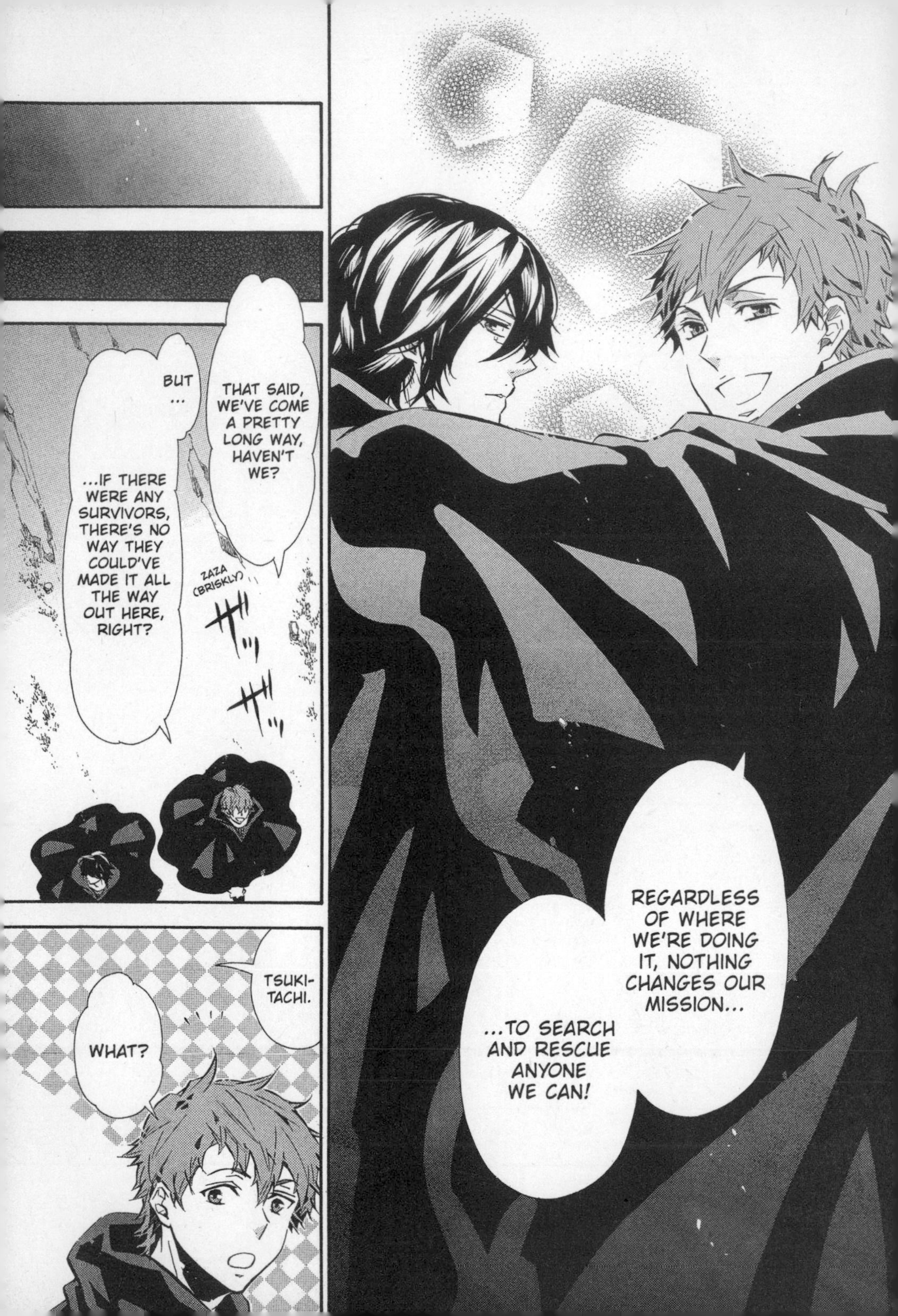
REGARDLESS OF WHERE WE'RE DOING IT, NOTHING CHANGES OUR MISSION...
...TO SEARCH AND RESCUE ANYONE WE CAN!
THAT SAID, WE'VE COME A PRETTY LONG WAY, HAVEN'T WE?
BUT ...
...IF THERE WERE ANY SURVIVORS, THERE'S NO WAY THEY COULD'VE MADE IT ALL THE WAY OUT HERE, RIGHT?
ZAZA (BRISKLY)
TSUKI-TACHI.
WHAT?

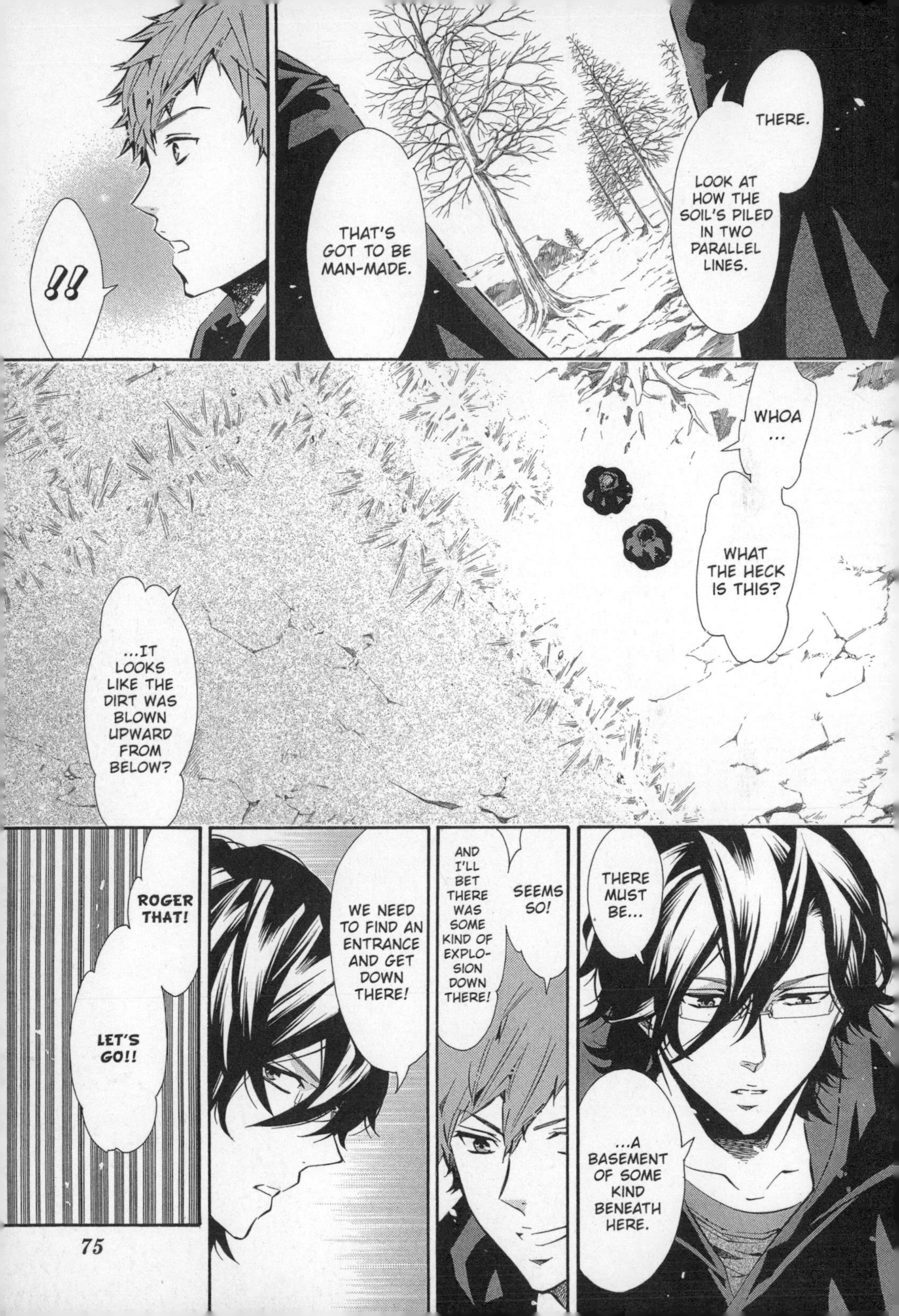
THERE.
LOOK AT HOW THE SOIL'S PILED IN TWO PARALLEL LINES.
THAT'S GOT TO BE MAN-MADE.
!!
WHOA...
WHAT THE HECK IS THIS?
...IT LOOKS LIKE THE DIRT WAS BLOWN UPWARD FROM BELOW?
THERE MUST BE...
...A BASEMENT OF SOME KIND BENEATH HERE.
SEEMS SO!
AND I'LL BET THERE WAS SOME KIND OF EXPLOSION DOWN THERE!
WE NEED TO FIND AN ENTRANCE AND GET DOWN THERE!
ROGER THAT!
LET'S GO!!

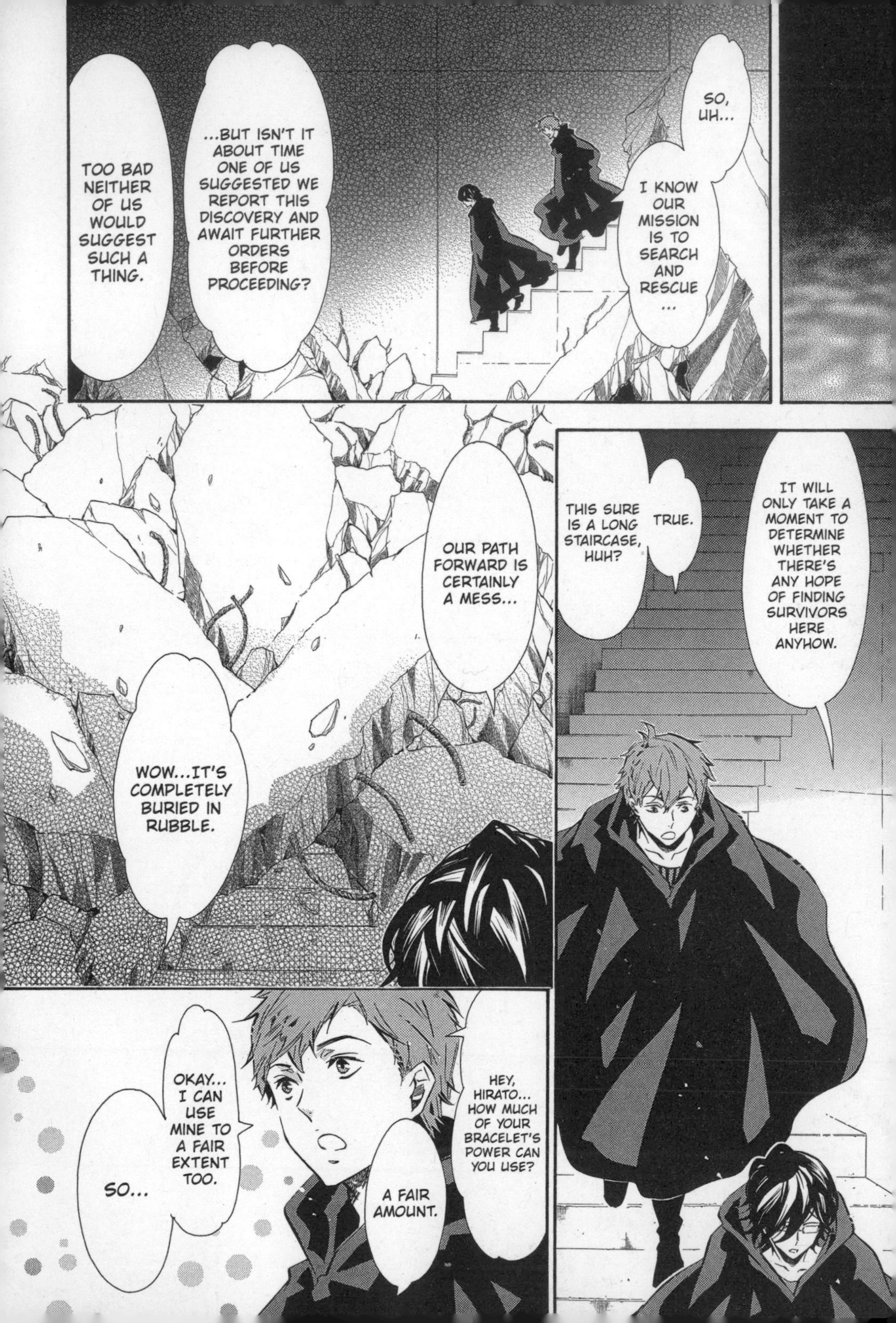
SO, UH...
I KNOW OUR MISSION IS TO SEARCH AND RESCUE...
...BUT ISN'T IT ABOUT TIME ONE OF US SUGGESTED WE REPORT THIS DISCOVERY AND AWAIT FURTHER ORDERS BEFORE PROCEEDING?
TOO BAD NEITHER OF US WOULD SUGGEST SUCH A THING.
IT WILL ONLY TAKE A MOMENT TO DETERMINE WHETHER THERE'S ANY HOPE OF FINDING SURVIVORS HERE ANYHOW.
TRUE.
THIS SURE IS A LONG STAIRCASE, HUH?
OUR PATH FORWARD IS CERTAINLY A MESS...
WOW...IT'S COMPLETELY BURIED IN RUBBLE.
HEY, HIRATO... HOW MUCH OF YOUR BRACELET'S POWER CAN YOU USE?
A FAIR AMOUNT.
OKAY... I CAN USE MINE TO A FAIR EXTENT TOO.
SO...

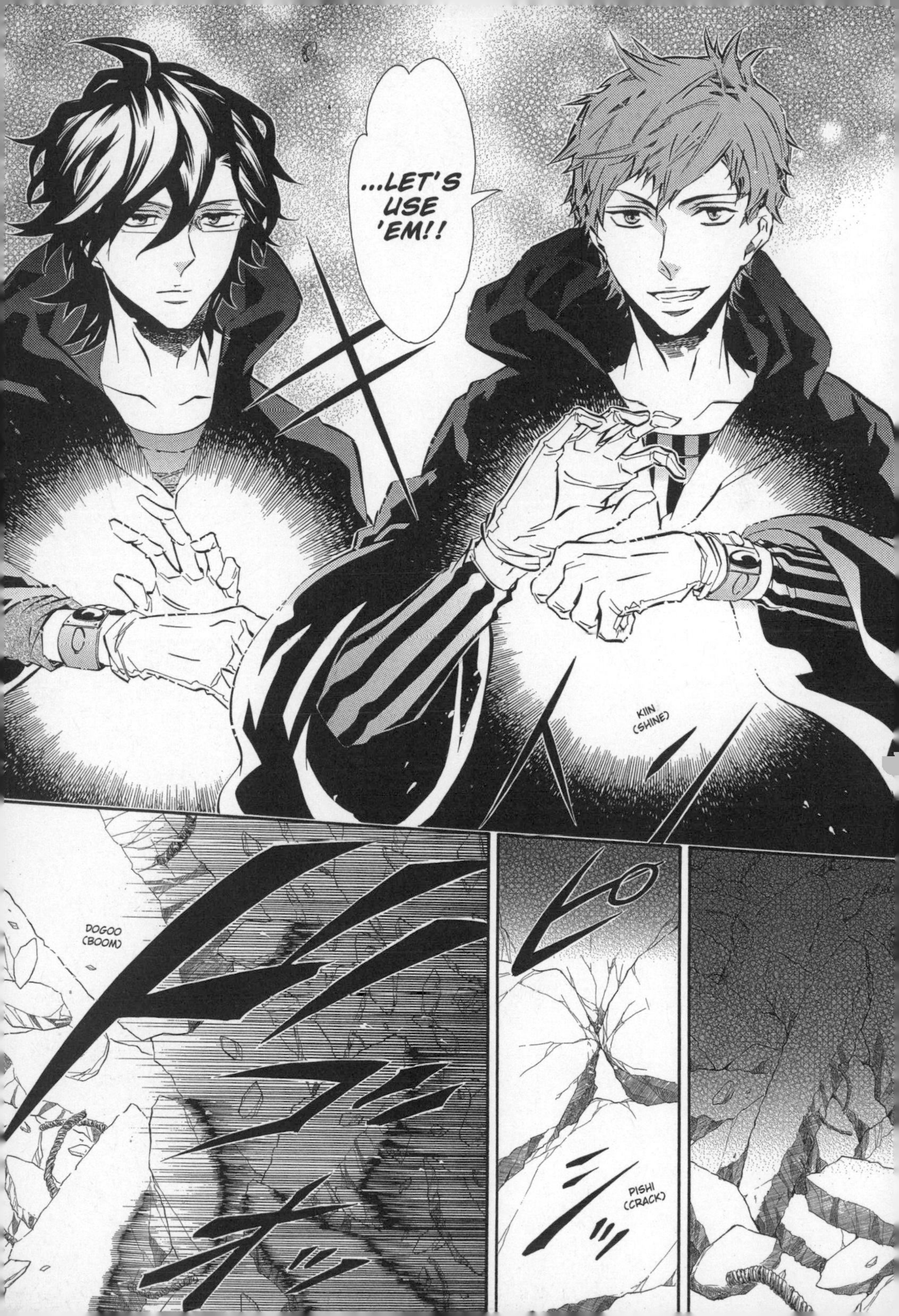
...LET'S USE 'EM!!
KIIN (SHINE)
PISHI (CRACK)
DOGOO (BOOM)

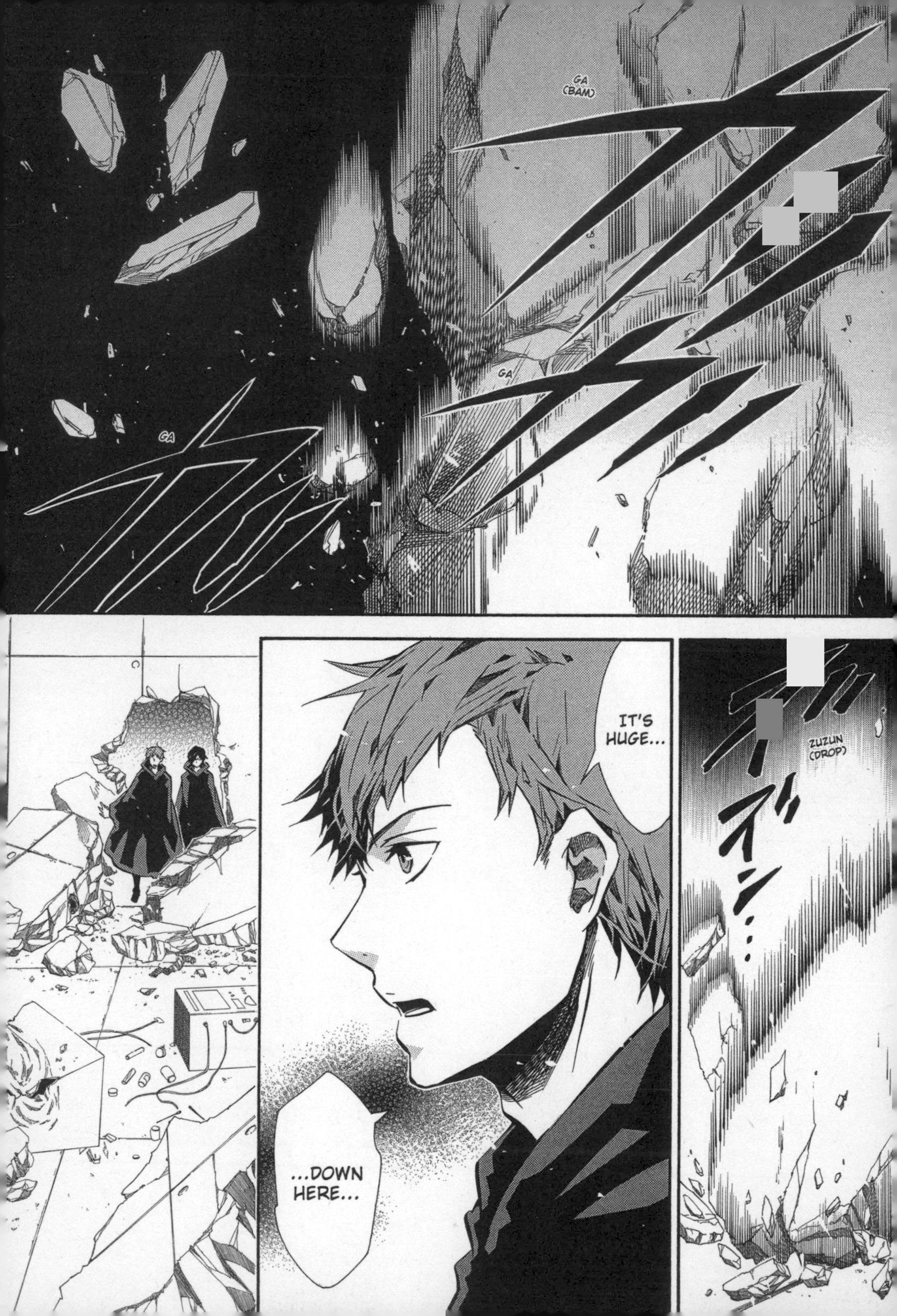
GA
(BAM)
GA
GA
ZUZUN
(DROP)
IT'S HUGE...
...DOWN HERE...

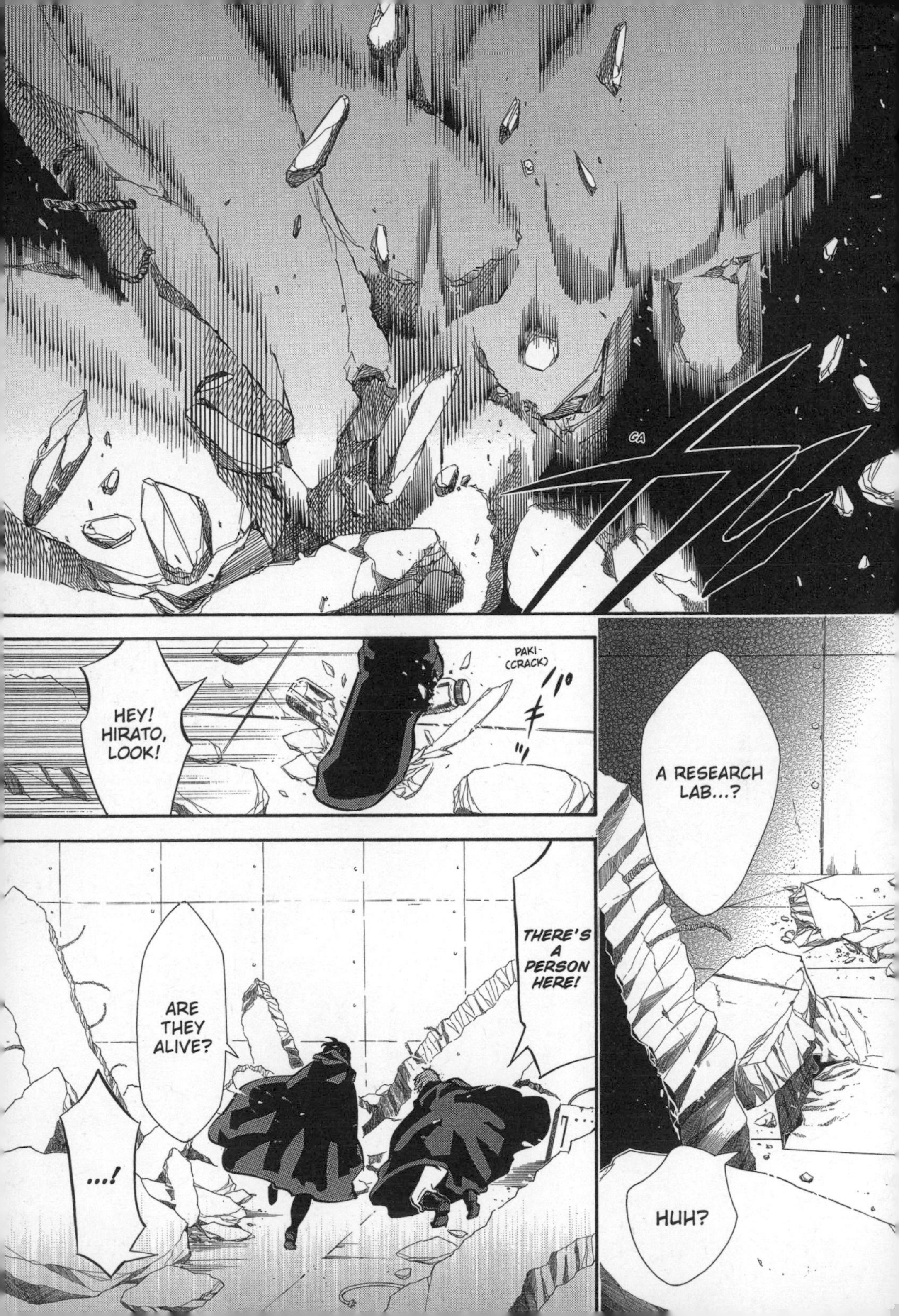
GA
A RESEARCH LAB...?
HUH?
PAKI (CRACK)
HEY! HIRATO, LOOK!
THERE'S A PERSON HERE!
ARE THEY ALIVE?
...!

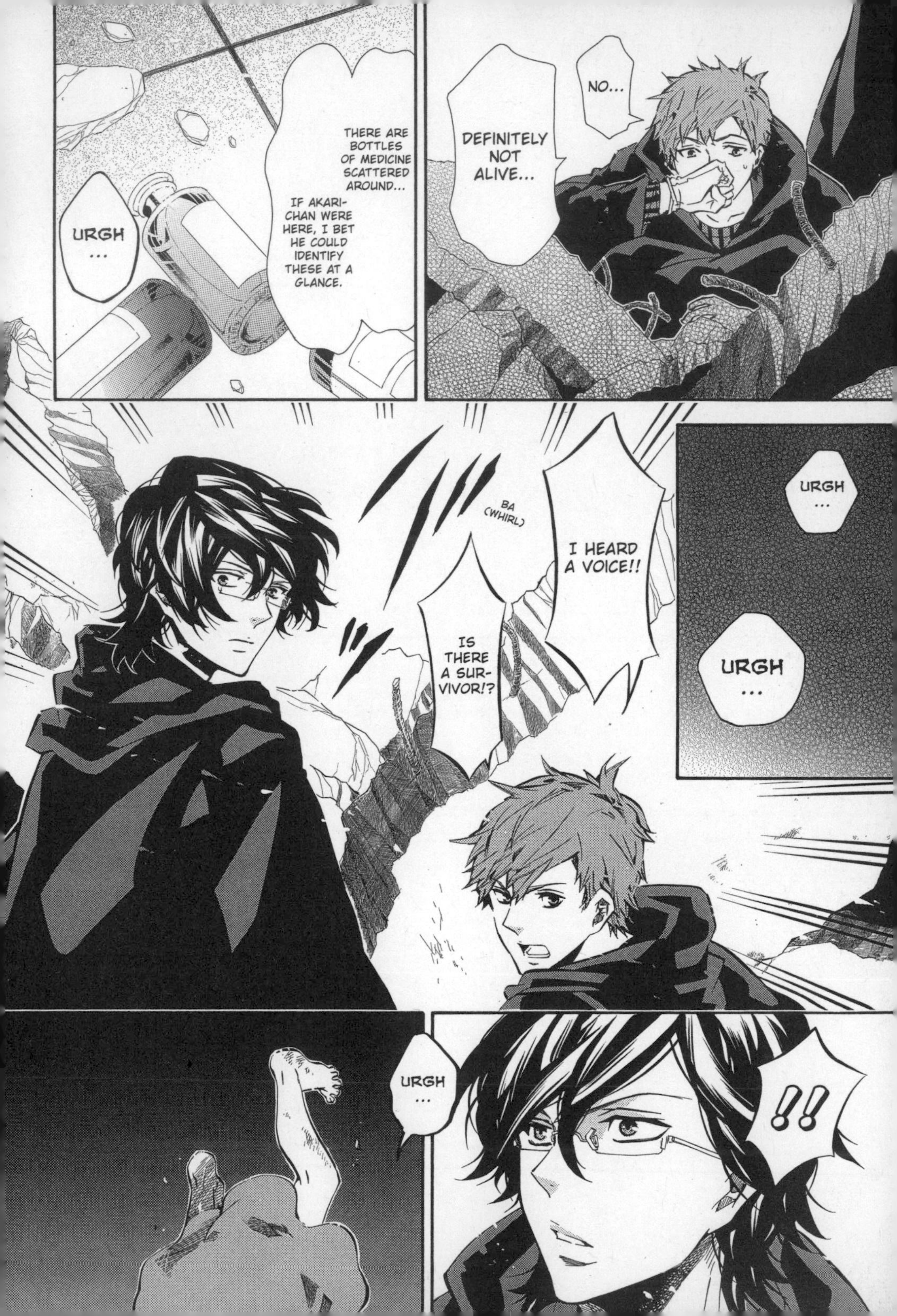
NO...
DEFINITELY NOT ALIVE...
THERE ARE BOTTLES OF MEDICINE SCATTERED AROUND...
IF AKARI-CHAN WERE HERE, I BET HE COULD IDENTIFY THESE AT A GLANCE.
URGH...
URGH...
URGH...
BA (WHIRL)
I HEARD A VOICE!!
IS THERE A SUR-VIVOR!?
!!
URGH...

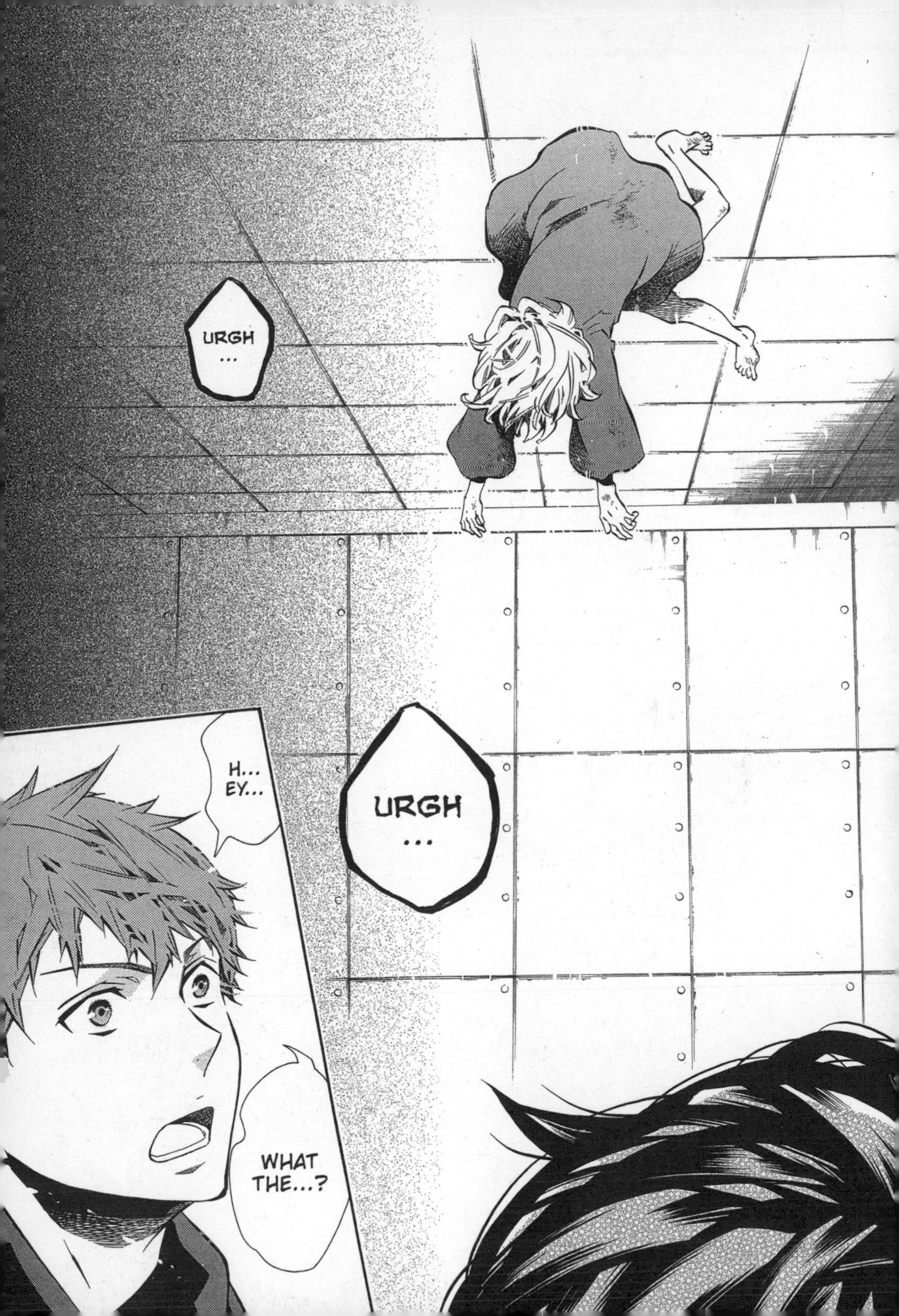
URGH ...
URGH ...
H... EY...
WHAT THE...?

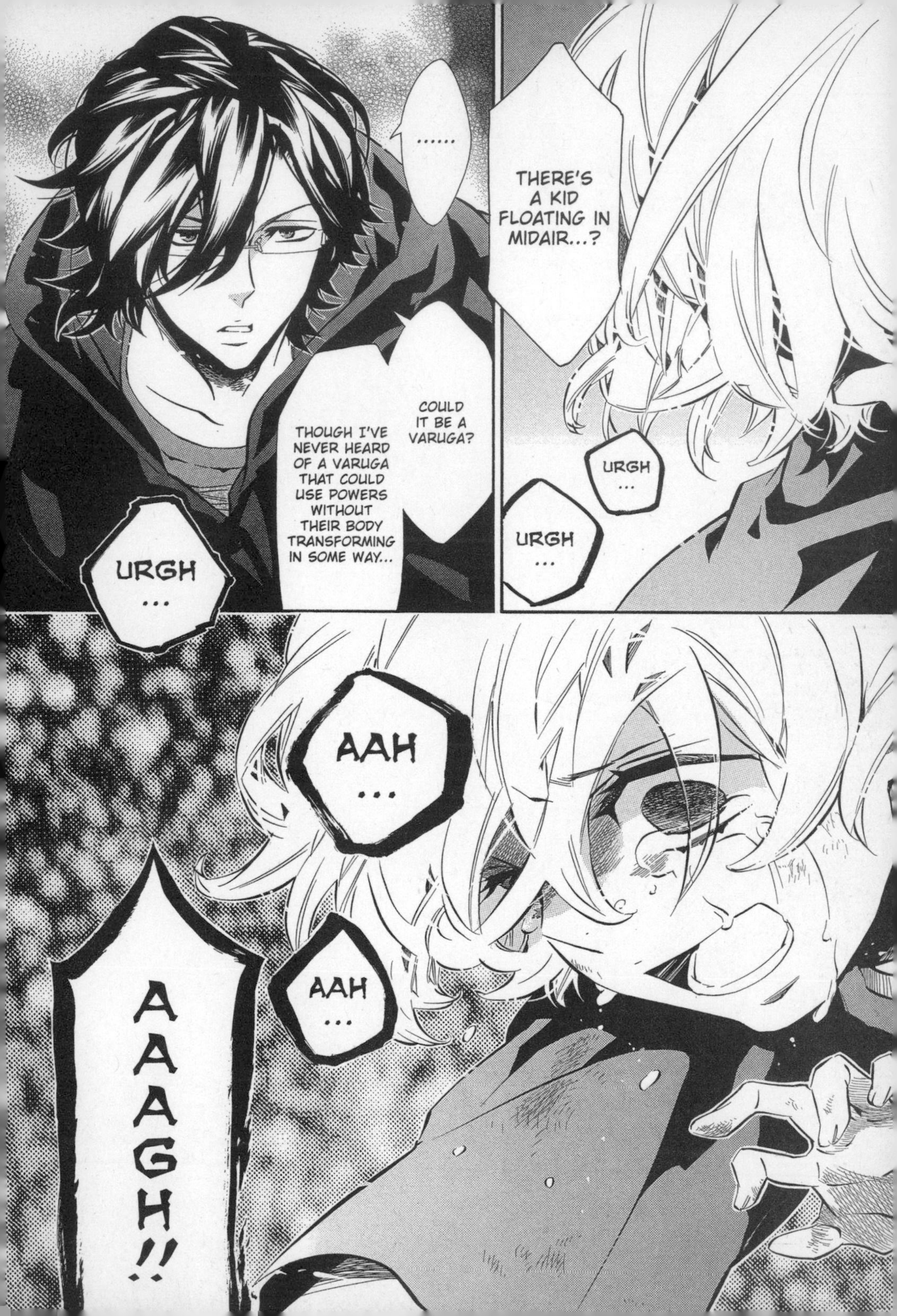
THERE'S A KID FLOATING IN MIDAIR...?
URGH ...
URGH ...
......
COULD IT BE A VARUGA?
THOUGH I'VE NEVER HEARD OF A VARUGA THAT COULD USE POWERS WITHOUT THEIR BODY TRANSFORMING IN SOME WAY...
URGH ...
AAH ...
AAH ...
AAAAGH!!

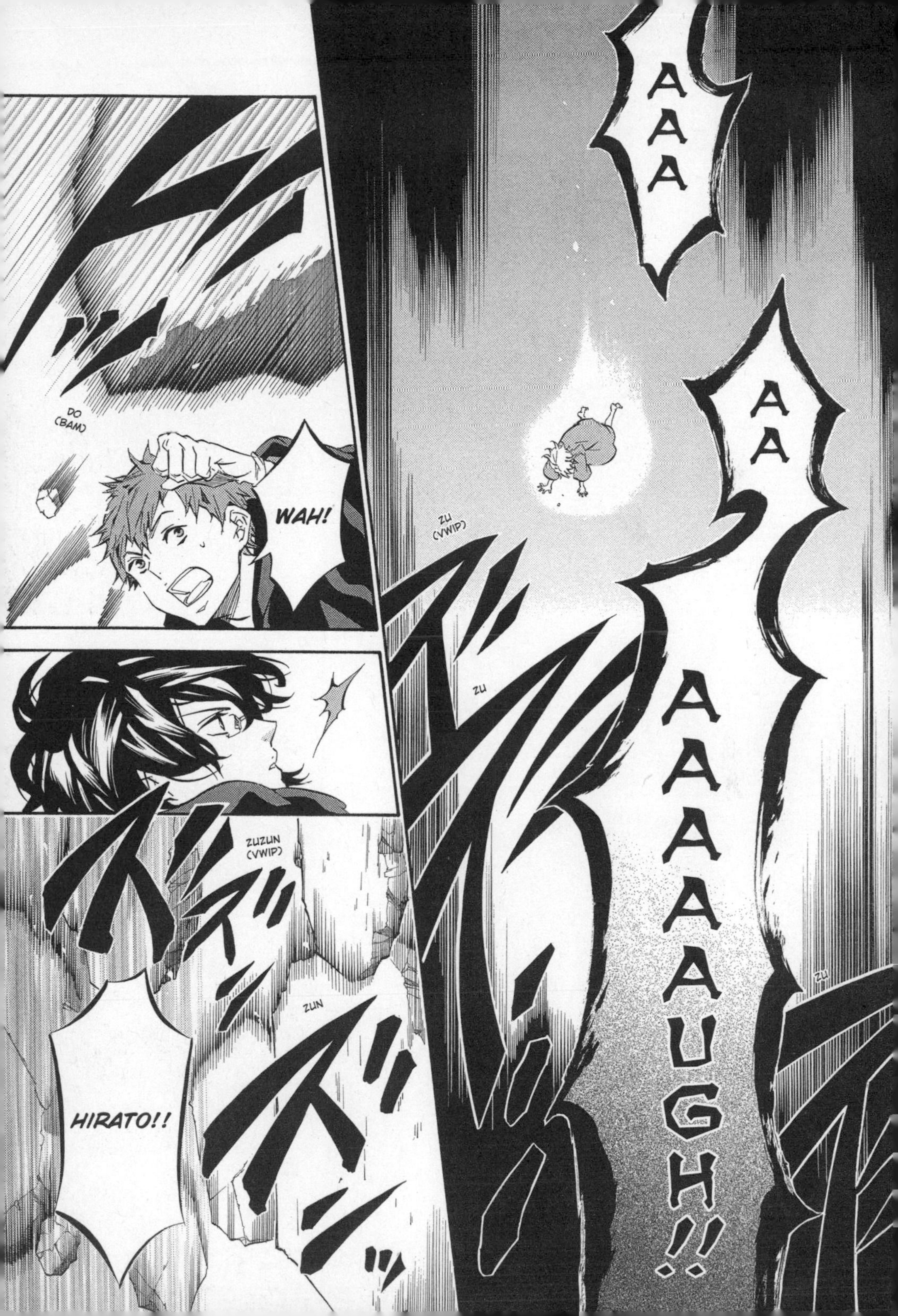
AAA
AA
AAAAAUGH!!
ZU (VWIP)
ZU
ZU
DO (BAM)
WAH!
ZUZUN (VWIP)
ZUN
HIRATO!!

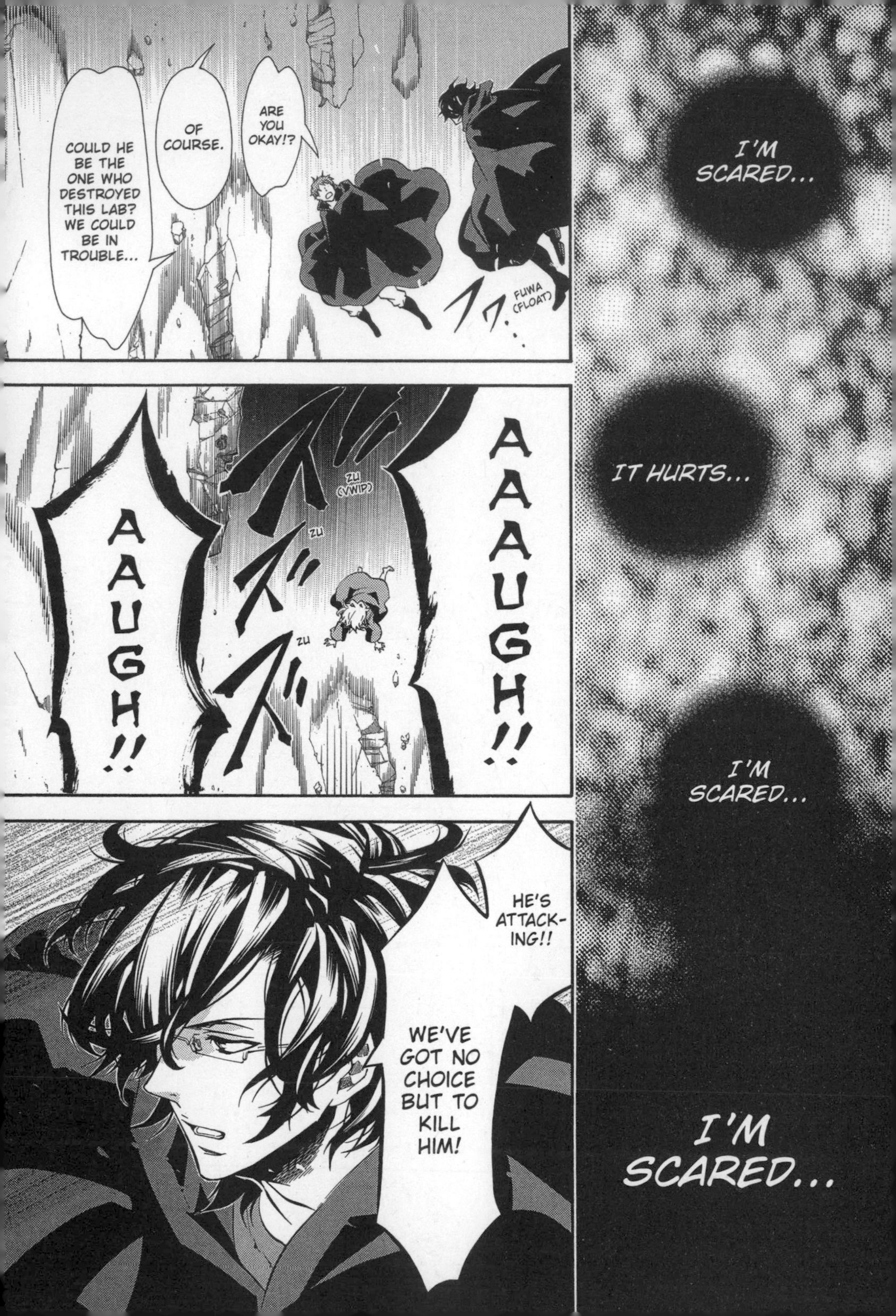
I'M SCARED...
IT HURTS...
I'M SCARED...
I'M SCARED...
ARE YOU OKAY!?
OF COURSE.
COULD HE BE THE ONE WHO DESTROYED THIS LAB? WE COULD BE IN TROUBLE...
FUWA (FLOAT)
AAAUGH!!
ZU (VWIP)
ZU
ZU
AAUGH!!
HE'S ATTACKING!!
WE'VE GOT NO CHOICE BUT TO KILL HIM!

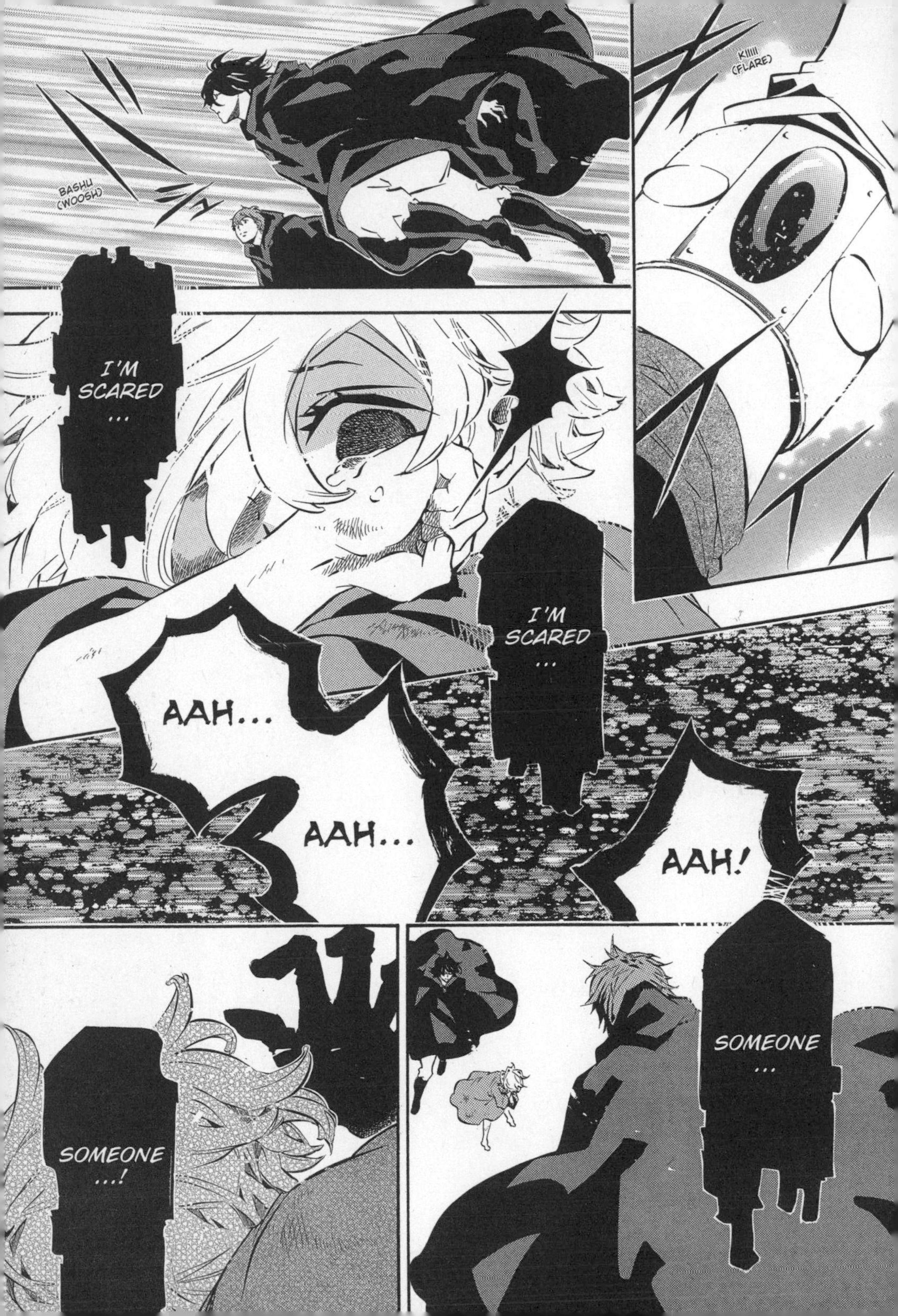
KIIIII (FLARE)
BASHU (WOOSH)
I'M SCARED ...
I'M SCARED ...
AAH...
AAH...
AAH!
SOMEONE ...
SOMEONE ...!

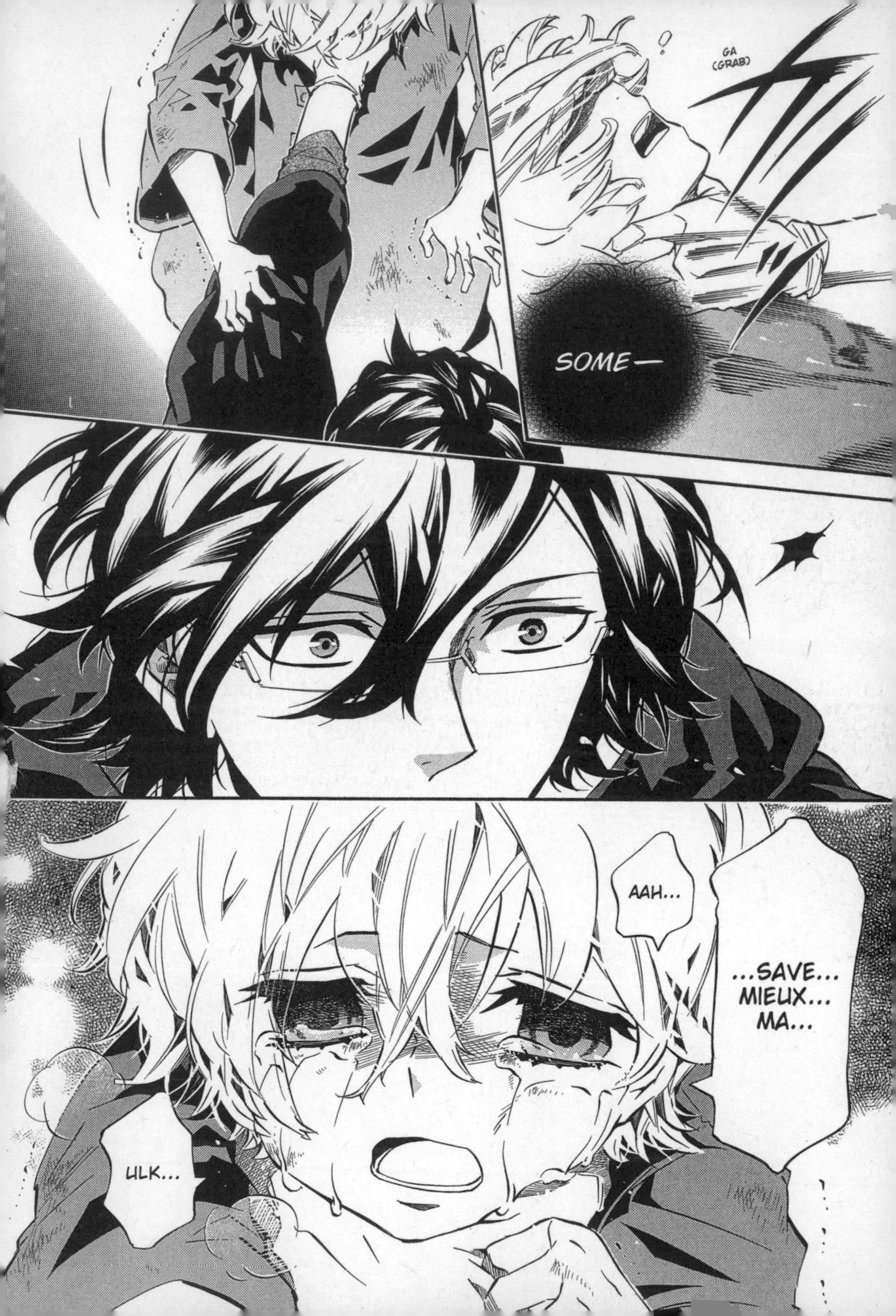
!
GA
(GRAB)
SOME—
...SAVE... MIEUX... MA...
AAH...
ULK...

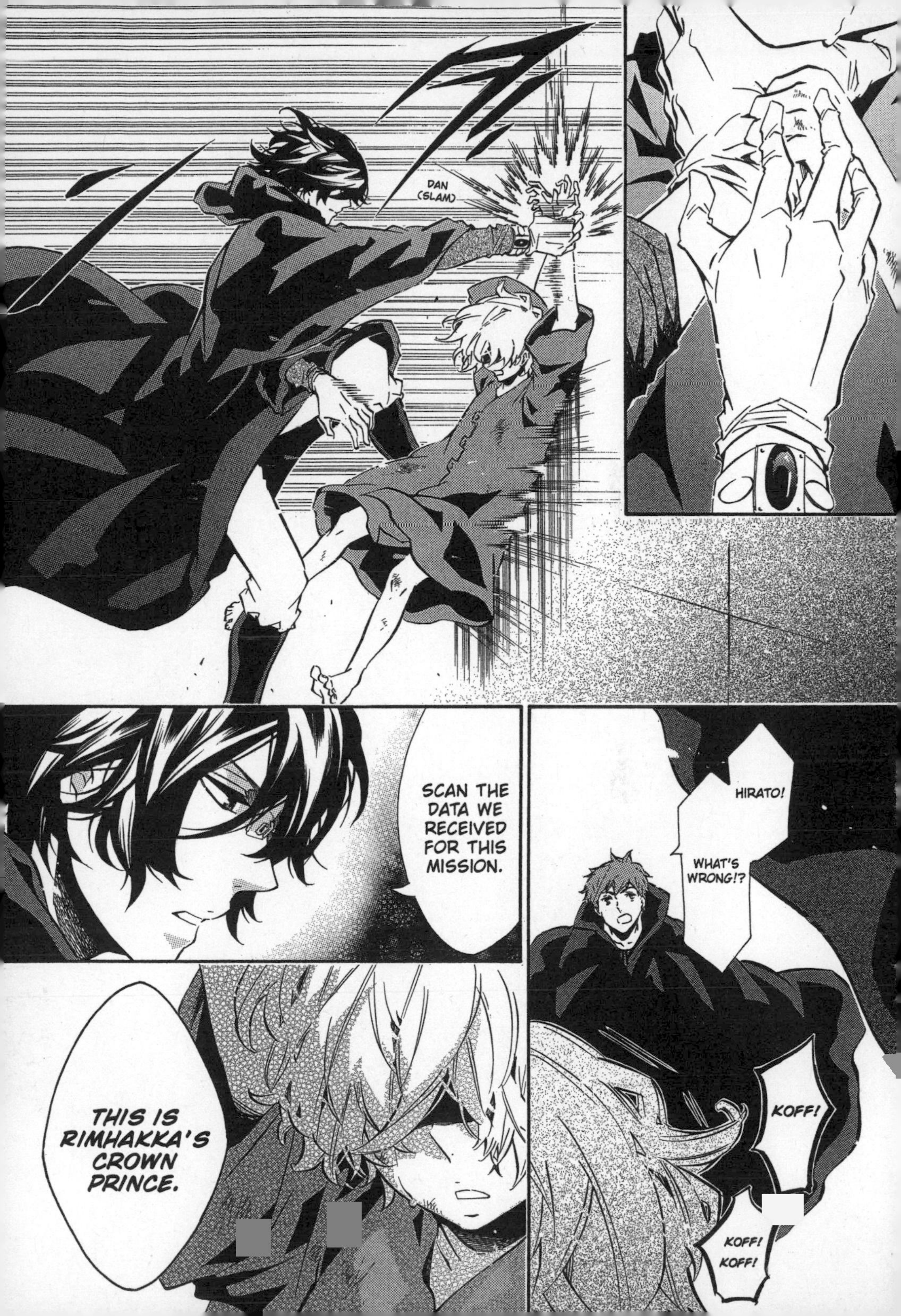
DAN (SLAM)
HIRATO!
WHAT'S WRONG!?
KOFF!
KOFF! KOFF!
SCAN THE DATA WE RECEIVED FOR THIS MISSION.
THIS IS RIMHAKKA'S CROWN PRINCE.

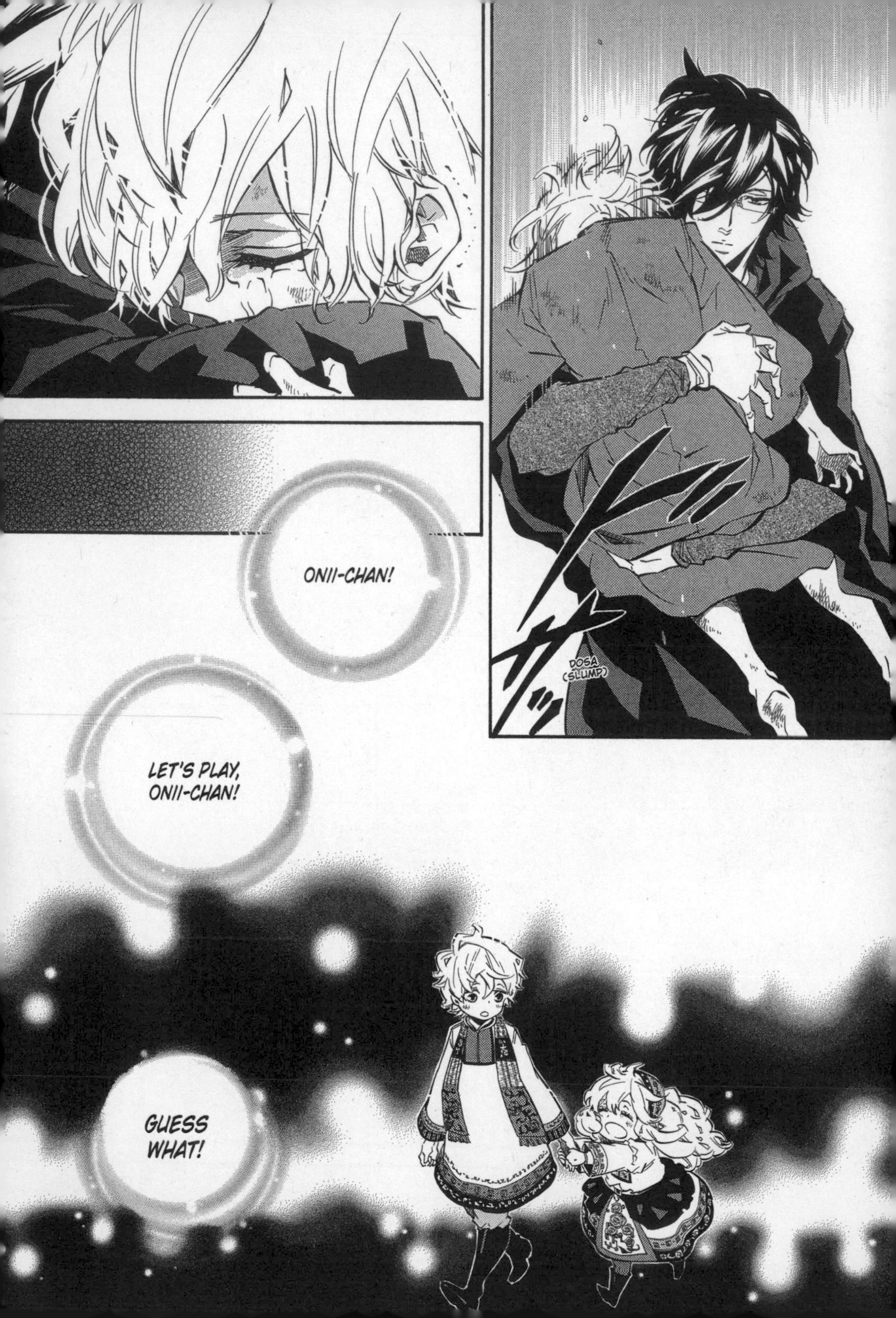
DOSA (SLUMP)
ONII-CHAN!
LET'S PLAY, ONII-CHAN!
GUESS WHAT!

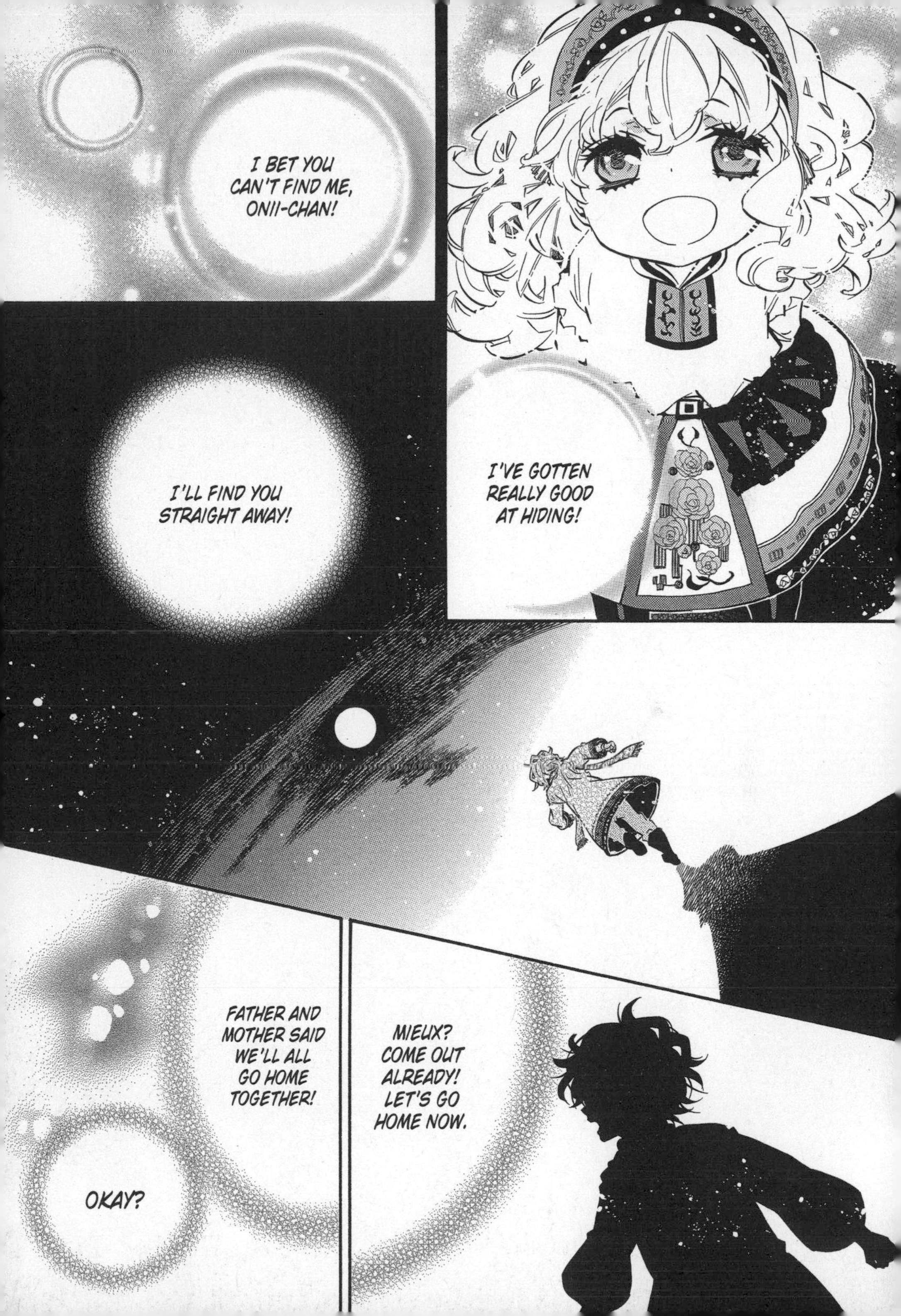
I'VE GOTTEN REALLY GOOD AT HIDING!
I BET YOU CAN'T FIND ME, ONII-CHAN!
I'LL FIND YOU STRAIGHT AWAY!
MIEUX? COME OUT ALREADY! LET'S GO HOME NOW.
FATHER AND MOTHER SAID WE'LL ALL GO HOME TOGETHER!
OKAY?

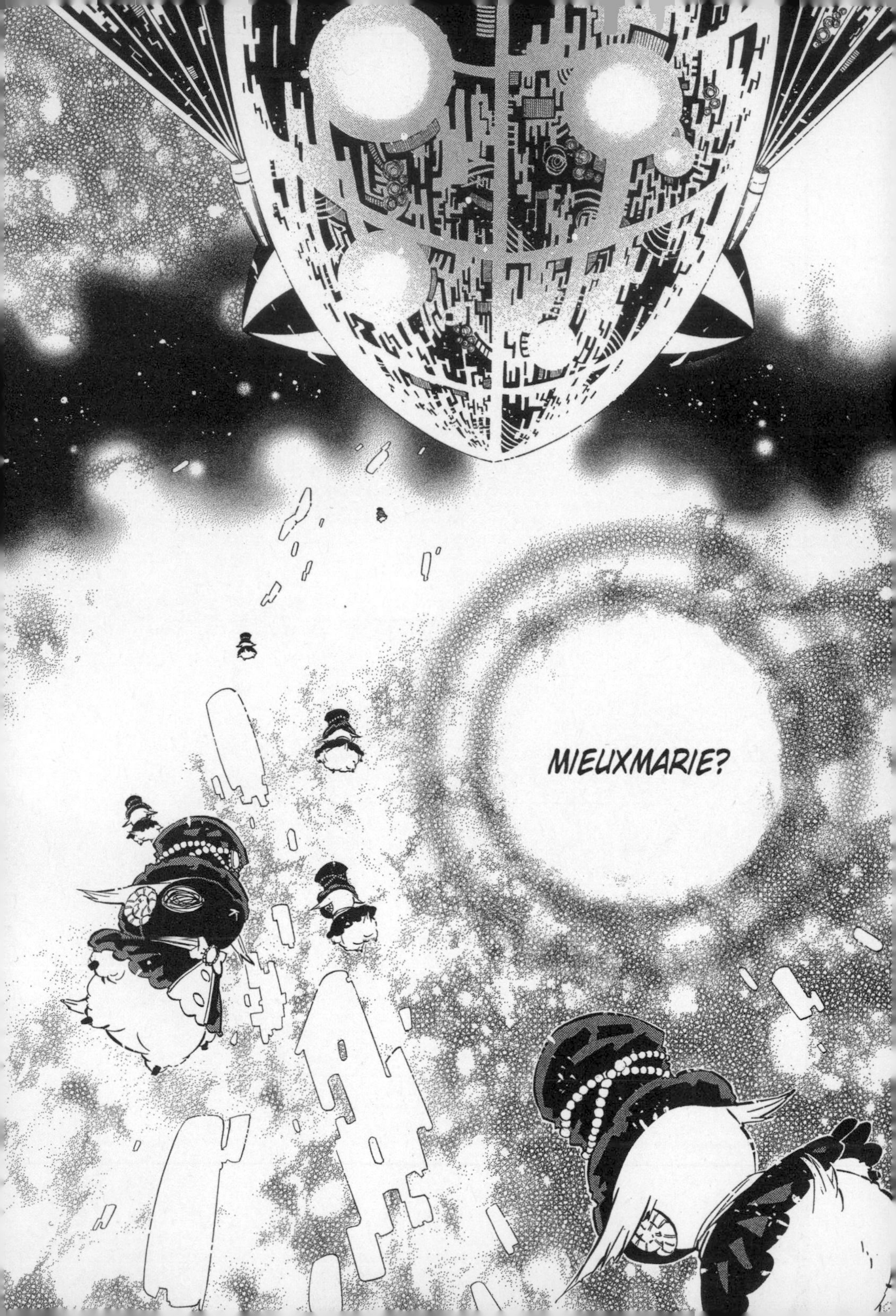
MIEUXMARIE?

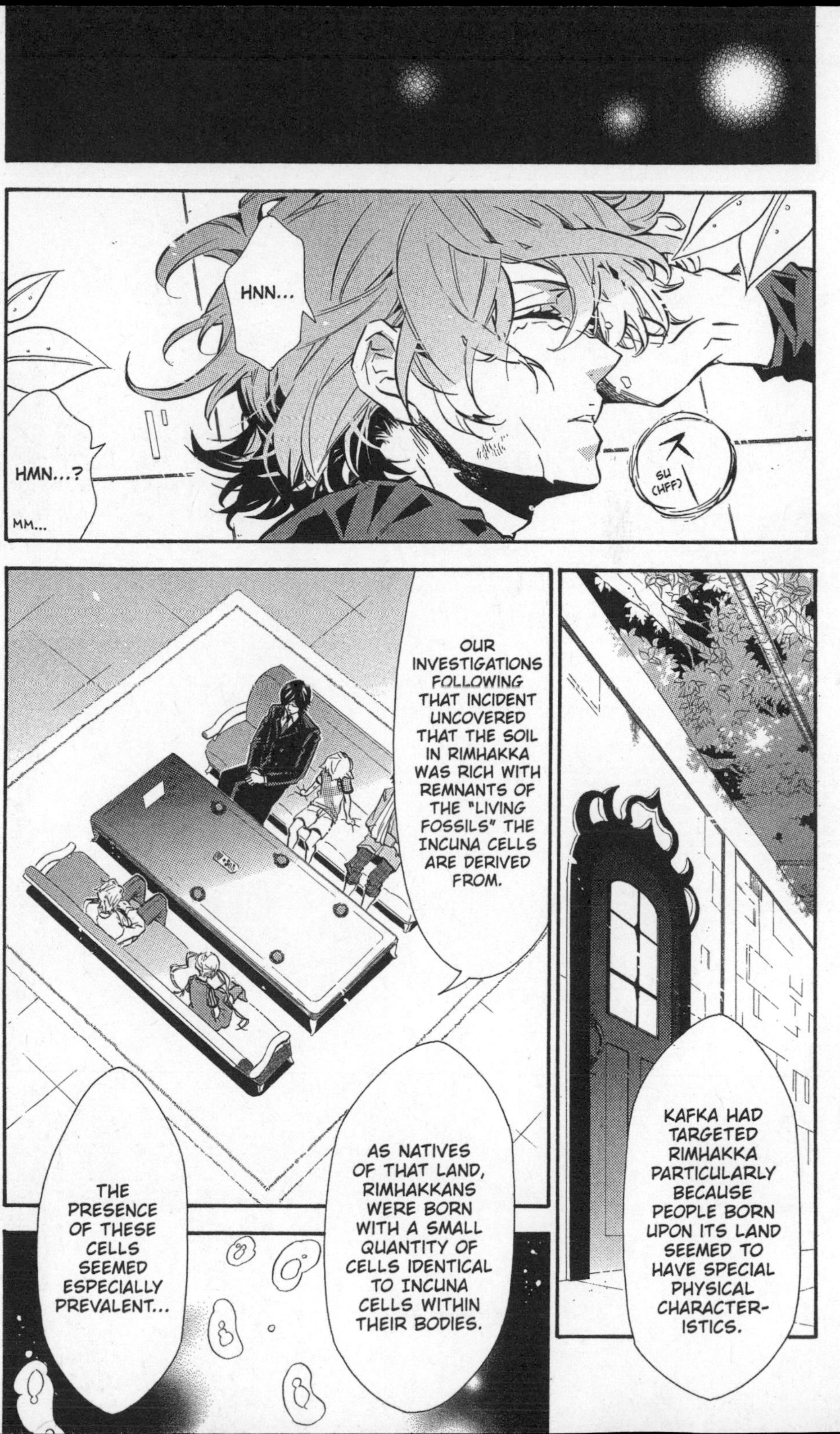
HNN...
SU (HFF)
HMN...?
MM...
KAFKA HAD TARGETED RIMHAKKA PARTICULARLY BECAUSE PEOPLE BORN UPON ITS LAND SEEMED TO HAVE SPECIAL PHYSICAL CHARACTER-ISTICS.
OUR INVESTIGATIONS FOLLOWING THAT INCIDENT UNCOVERED THAT THE SOIL IN RIMHAKKA WAS RICH WITH REMNANTS OF THE "LIVING FOSSILS" THE INCUNA CELLS ARE DERIVED FROM.
AS NATIVES OF THAT LAND, RIMHAKKANS WERE BORN WITH A SMALL QUANTITY OF CELLS IDENTICAL TO INCUNA CELLS WITHIN THEIR BODIES.
THE PRESENCE OF THESE CELLS SEEMED ESPECIALLY PREVALENT...

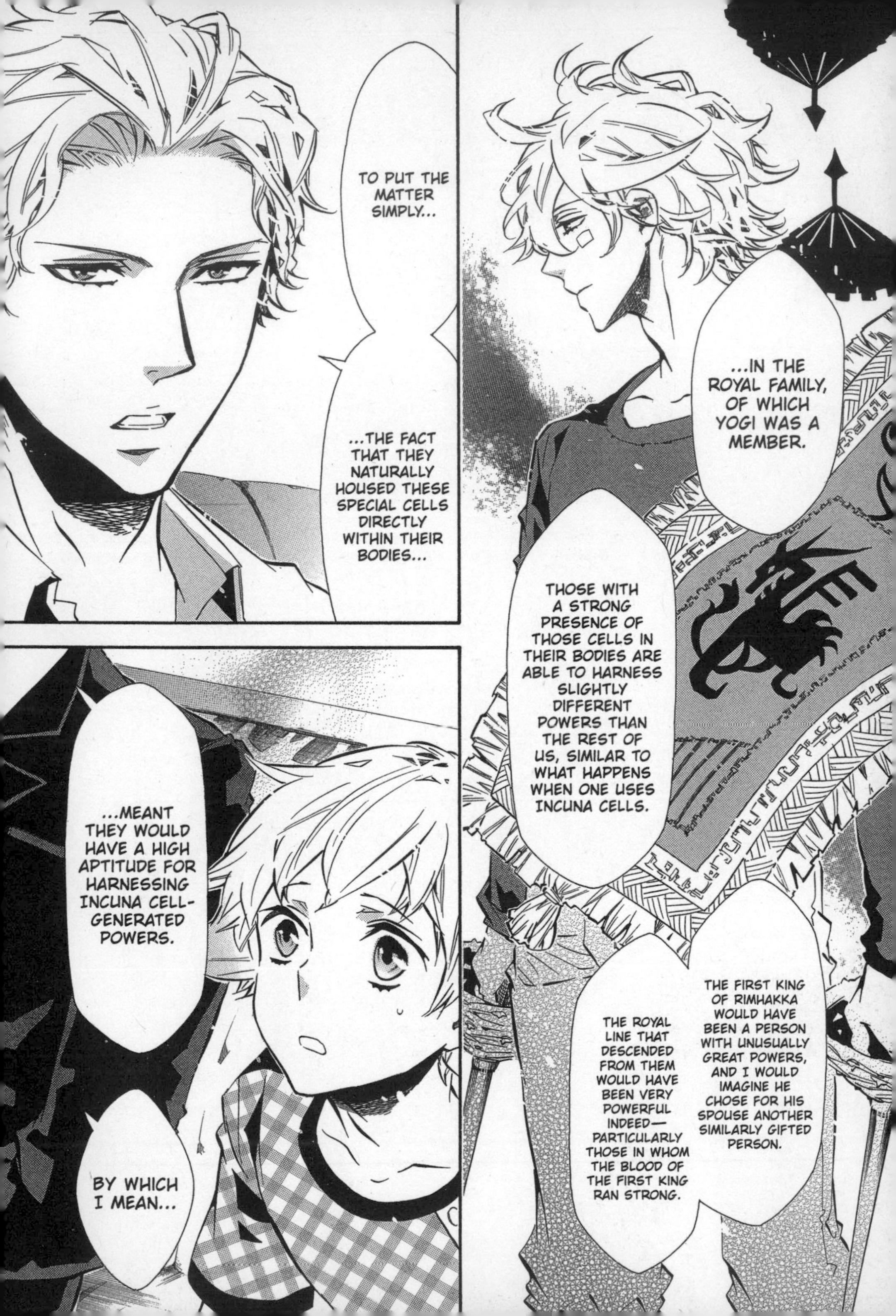

...IN THE ROYAL FAMILY, OF WHICH YOGI WAS A MEMBER.
THOSE WITH A STRONG PRESENCE OF THOSE CELLS IN THEIR BODIES ARE ABLE TO HARNESS SLIGHTLY DIFFERENT POWERS THAN THE REST OF US, SIMILAR TO WHAT HAPPENS WHEN ONE USES INCUNA CELLS.
THE FIRST KING OF RIMHAKKA WOULD HAVE BEEN A PERSON WITH UNUSUALLY GREAT POWERS, AND I WOULD IMAGINE HE CHOSE FOR HIS SPOUSE ANOTHER SIMILARLY GIFTED PERSON.
THE ROYAL LINE THAT DESCENDED FROM THEM WOULD HAVE BEEN VERY POWERFUL INDEED—PARTICULARLY THOSE IN WHOM THE BLOOD OF THE FIRST KING RAN STRONG.
TO PUT THE MATTER SIMPLY...
...THE FACT THAT THEY NATURALLY HOUSED THESE SPECIAL CELLS DIRECTLY WITHIN THEIR BODIES...
...MEANT THEY WOULD HAVE A HIGH APTITUDE FOR HARNESSING INCUNA CELL-GENERATED POWERS.
BY WHICH I MEAN...

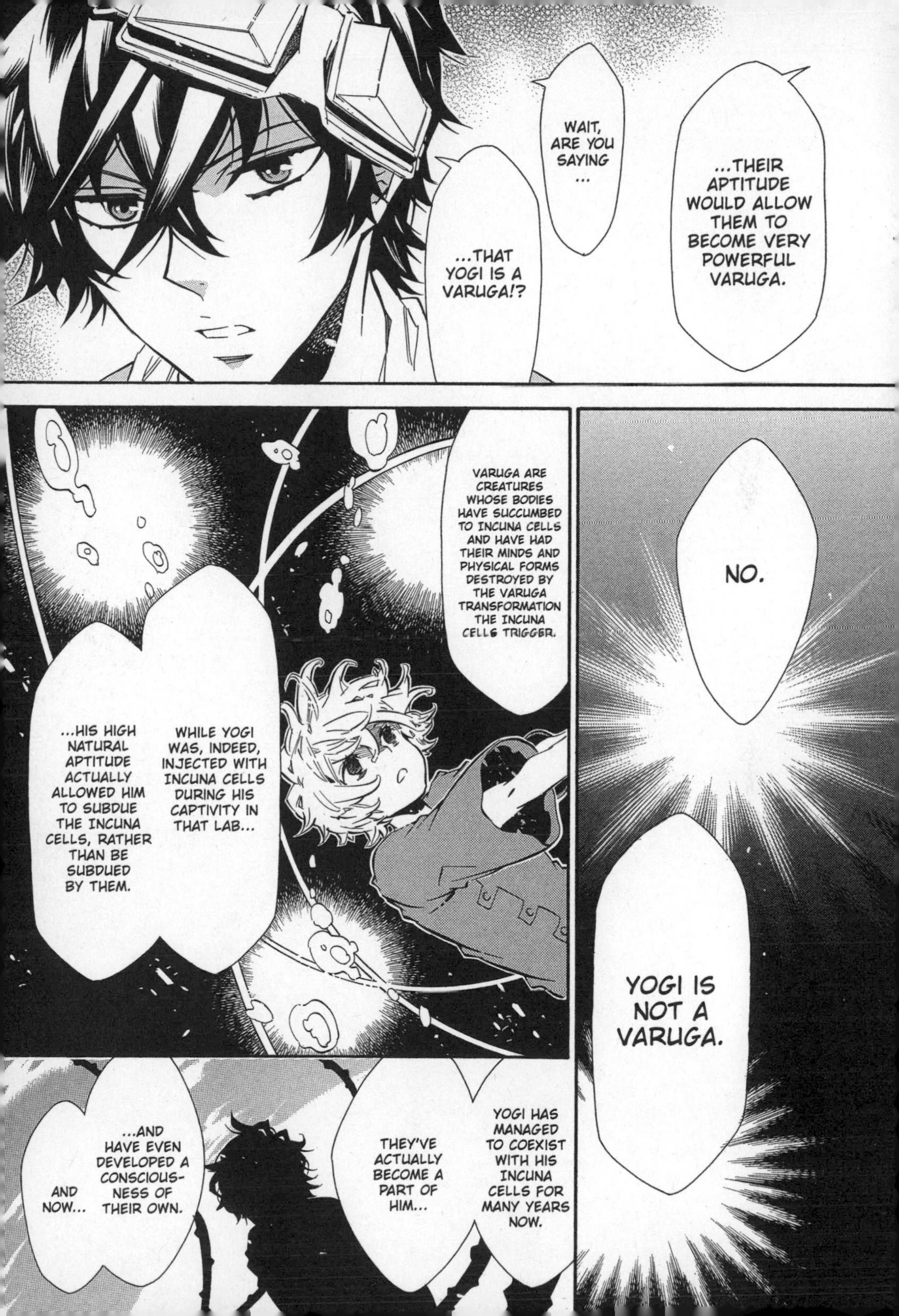
...THEIR APTITUDE WOULD ALLOW THEM TO BECOME VERY POWERFUL VARUGA.
WAIT, ARE YOU SAYING ...
...THAT YOGI IS A VARUGA!?
NO.
YOGI IS NOT A VARUGA.
VARUGA ARE CREATURES WHOSE BODIES HAVE SUCCUMBED TO INCUNA CELLS AND HAVE HAD THEIR MINDS AND PHYSICAL FORMS DESTROYED BY THE VARUGA TRANSFORMATION THE INCUNA CELLS TRIGGER.
WHILE YOGI WAS, INDEED, INJECTED WITH INCUNA CELLS DURING HIS CAPTIVITY IN THAT LAB...
...HIS HIGH NATURAL APTITUDE ACTUALLY ALLOWED HIM TO SUBDUE THE INCUNA CELLS, RATHER THAN BE SUBDUED BY THEM.
YOGI HAS MANAGED TO COEXIST WITH HIS INCUNA CELLS FOR MANY YEARS NOW.
THEY'VE ACTUALLY BECOME A PART OF HIM...
...AND HAVE EVEN DEVELOPED A CONSCIOUS-NESS OF THEIR OWN.
AND NOW...

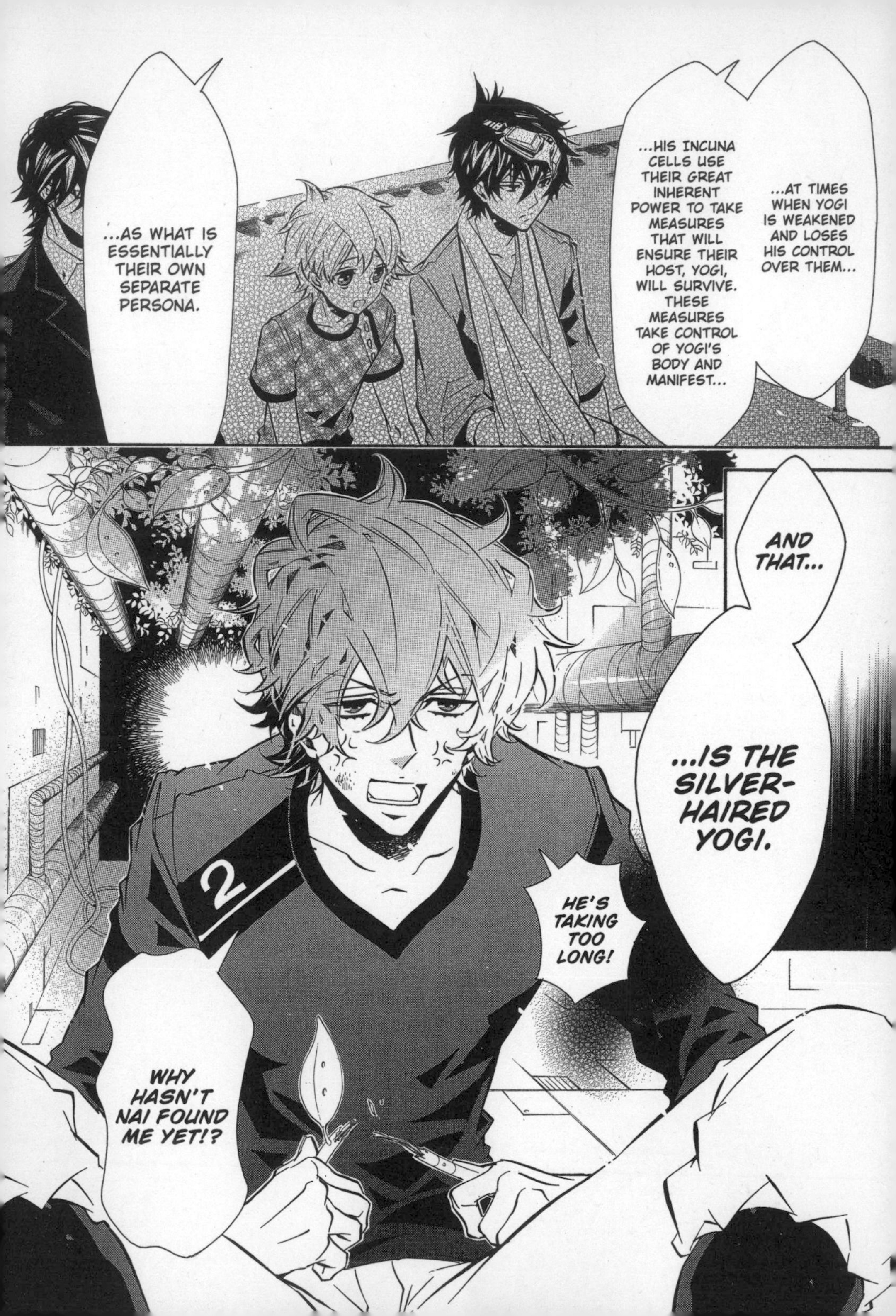
...AT TIMES WHEN YOGI IS WEAKENED AND LOSES HIS CONTROL OVER THEM...
...HIS INCUNA CELLS USE THEIR GREAT INHERENT POWER TO TAKE MEASURES THAT WILL ENSURE THEIR HOST, YOGI, WILL SURVIVE. THESE MEASURES TAKE CONTROL OF YOGI'S BODY AND MANIFEST...
...AS WHAT IS ESSENTIALLY THEIR OWN SEPARATE PERSONA.
AND THAT...
...IS THE SILVER-HAIRED YOGI.
HE'S TAKING TOO LONG!
WHY HASN'T NAI FOUND ME YET!?

KARNEVAL

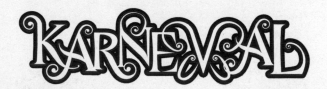

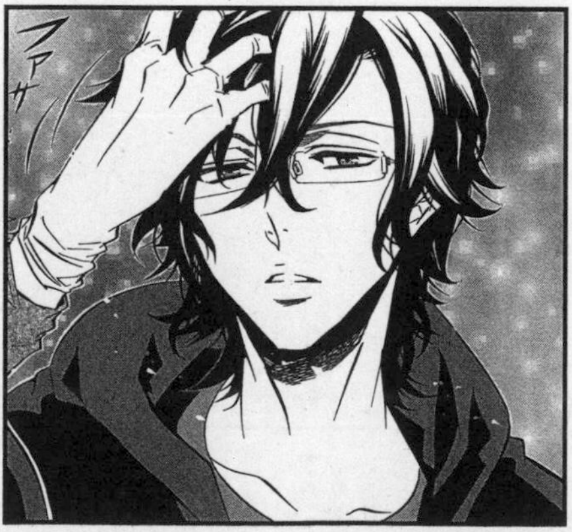
ファサ

KARNEVAL

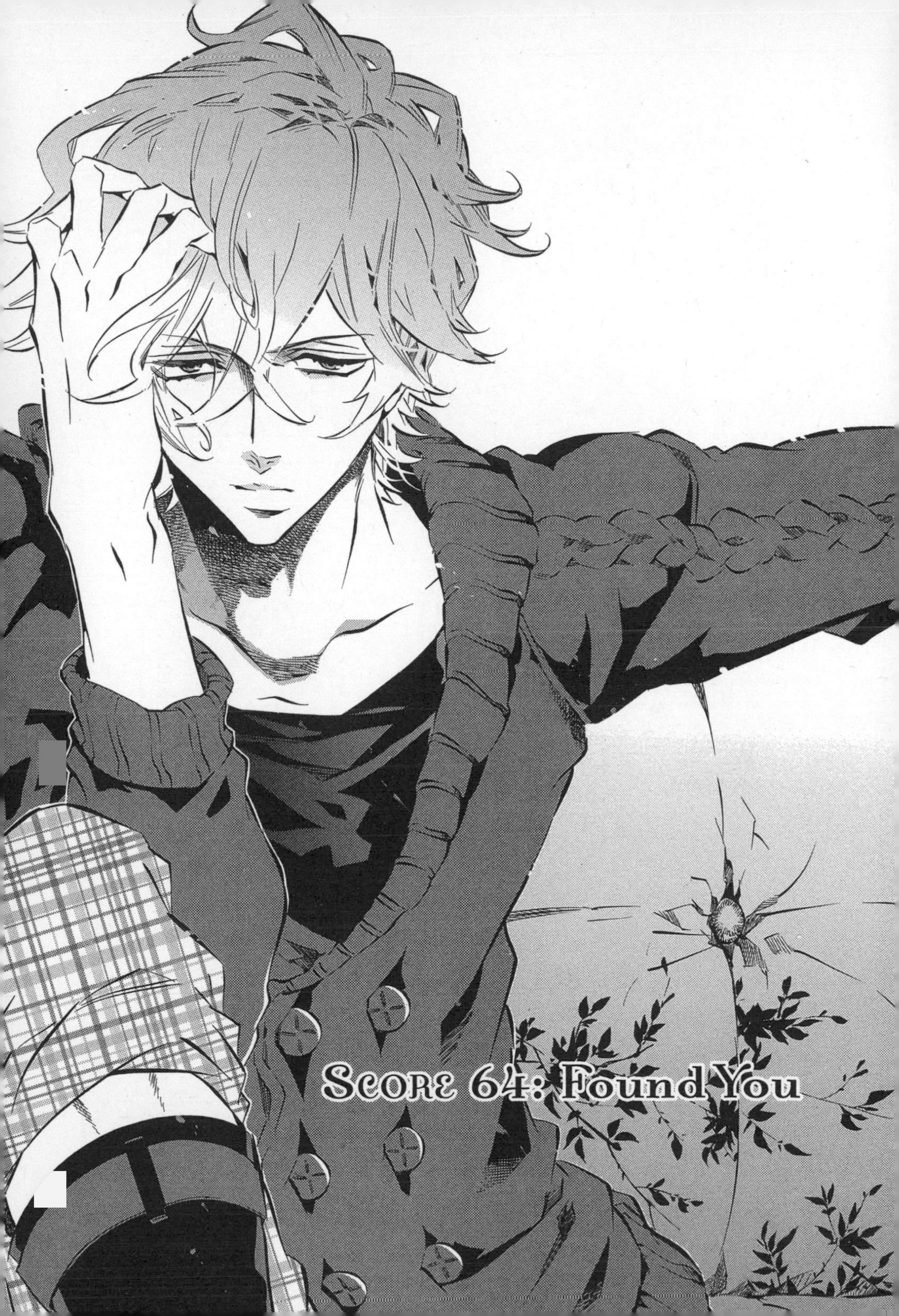
Score 64: Found You

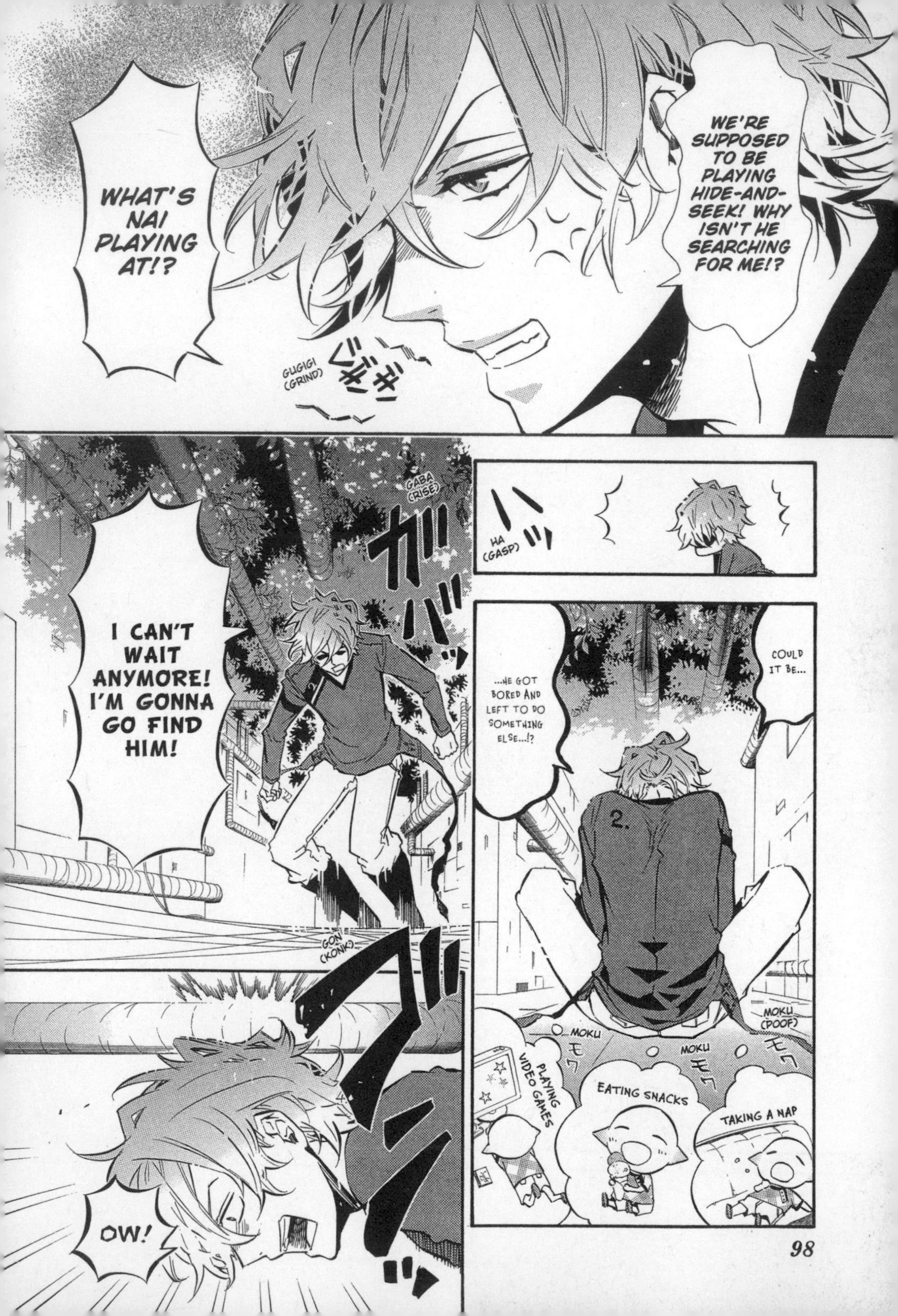
WE'RE SUPPOSED TO BE PLAYING HIDE-AND-SEEK! WHY ISN'T HE SEARCHING FOR ME!?
WHAT'S NAI PLAYING AT!?
GUGIGI (GRIND)
HA (GASP)
COULD IT BE...
...HE GOT BORED AND LEFT TO DO SOMETHING ELSE...!?
MOKU (POOF)
MOKU
MOKU
PLAYING VIDEO GAMES
EATING SNACKS
TAKING A NAP
GABA (RISE)
I CAN'T WAIT ANYMORE! I'M GONNA GO FIND HIM!
GON (KONK)
OW!

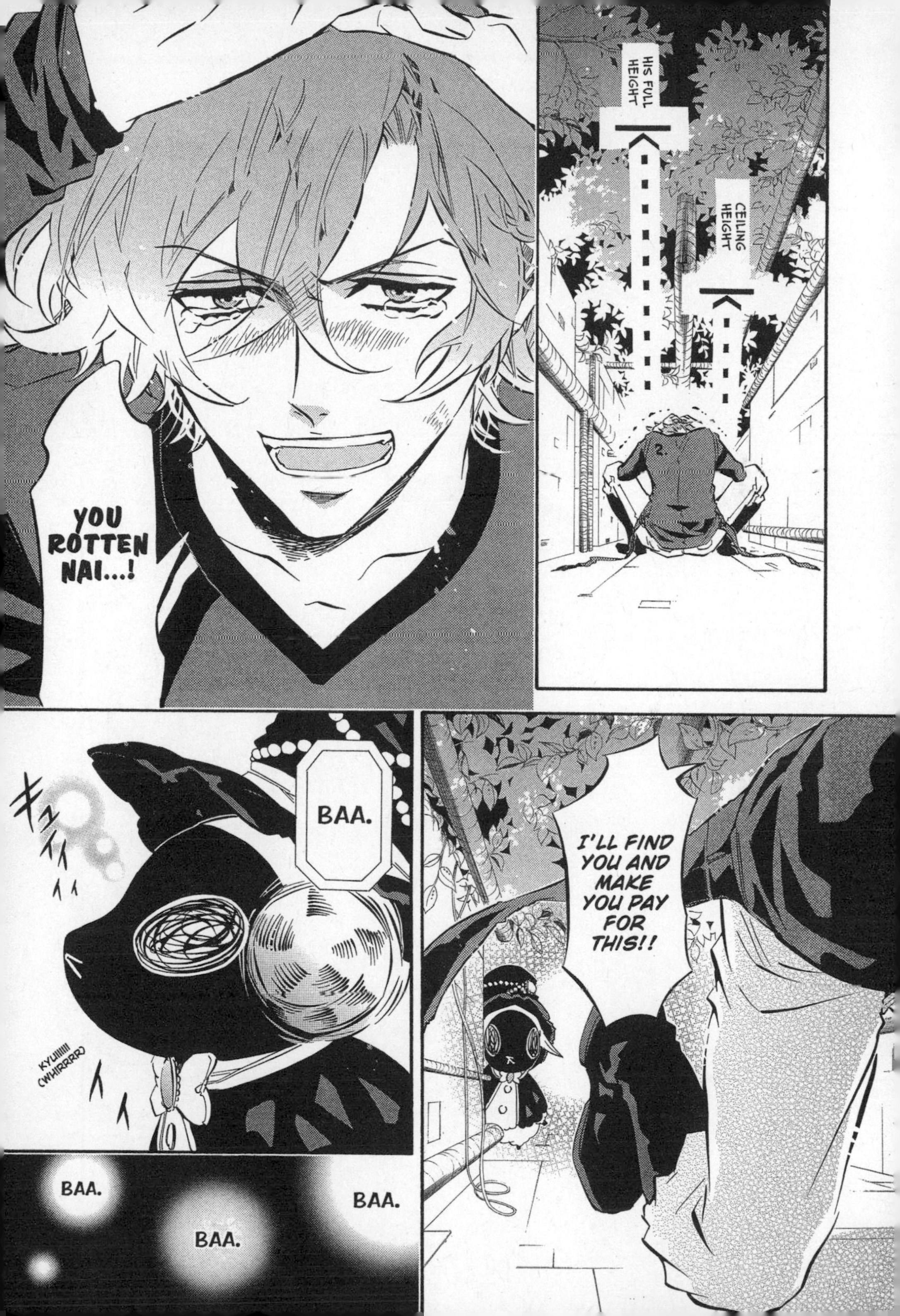
HIS FULL HEIGHT
CEILING HEIGHT
YOU ROTTEN NAI...!
I'LL FIND YOU AND MAKE YOU PAY FOR THIS!!
BAA.
KYUIIIIII (WHIRRRR)
BAA.
BAA.
BAA.

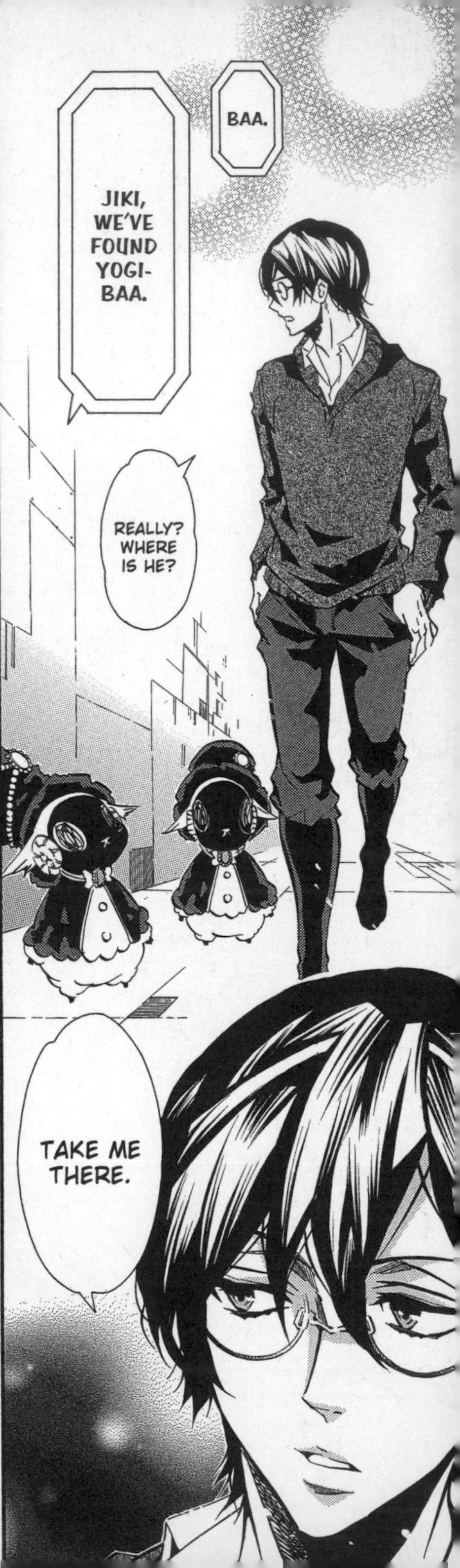
BAA.
JIKI, WE'VE FOUND YOGI-BAA.
REALLY? WHERE IS HE?
TAKE ME THERE.

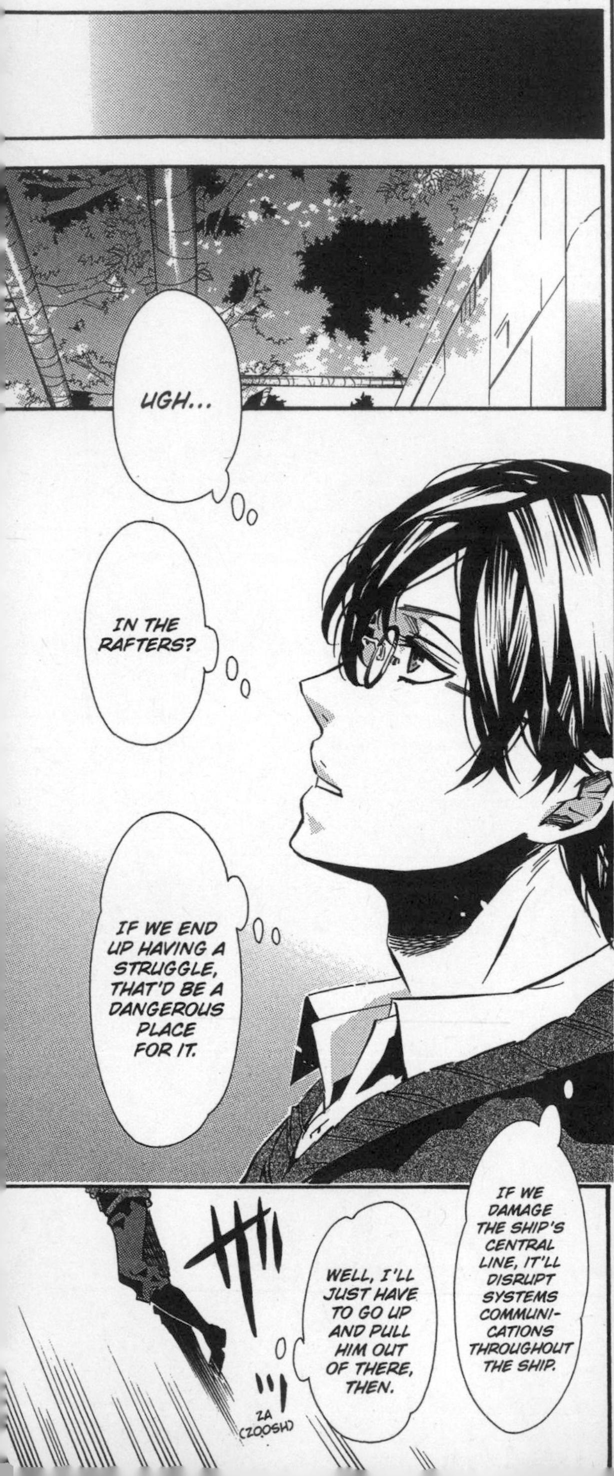
UGH...
IN THE RAFTERS?
IF WE END UP HAVING A STRUGGLE, THAT'D BE A DANGEROUS PLACE FOR IT.
IF WE DAMAGE THE SHIP'S CENTRAL LINE, IT'LL DISRUPT SYSTEMS COMMUNICATIONS THROUGHOUT THE SHIP.
WELL, I'LL JUST HAVE TO GO UP AND PULL HIM OUT OF THERE, THEN.
ZA (ZOOSH)

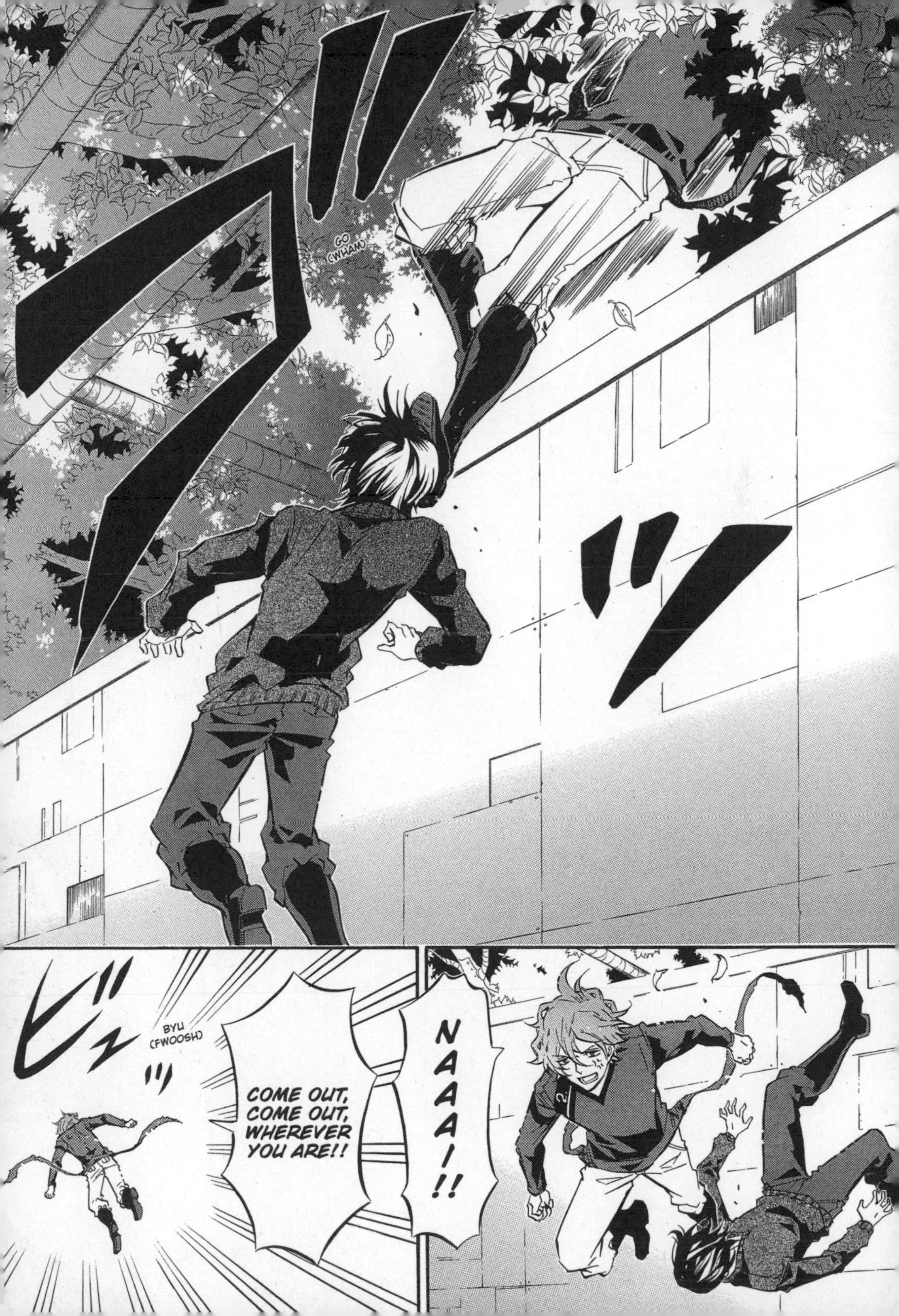

GO (WHAM)
NAAA!!!
BYU (FWOOSH)
COME OUT, COME OUT, WHEREVER YOU ARE!!

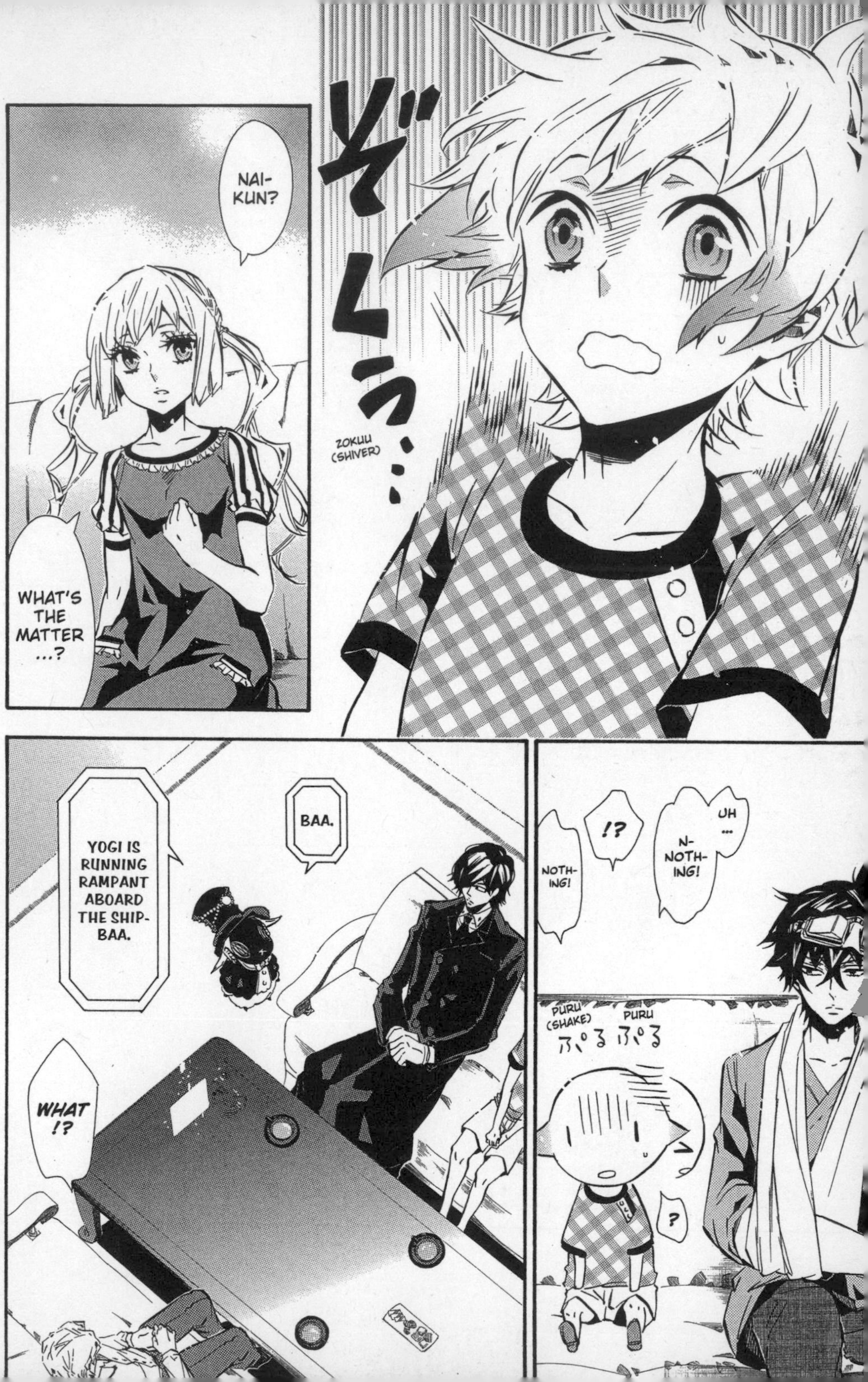
ぞくぅ…
ZOKUU (SHIVER)
NAI-KUN?
WHAT'S THE MATTER ...?
UH ...
N-NOTHING!
!?
NOTHING!
PURU (SHAKE) PURU
ぷるぷる
?
BAA.
YOGI IS RUNNING RAMPANT ABOARD THE SHIP-BAA.
WHAT!?

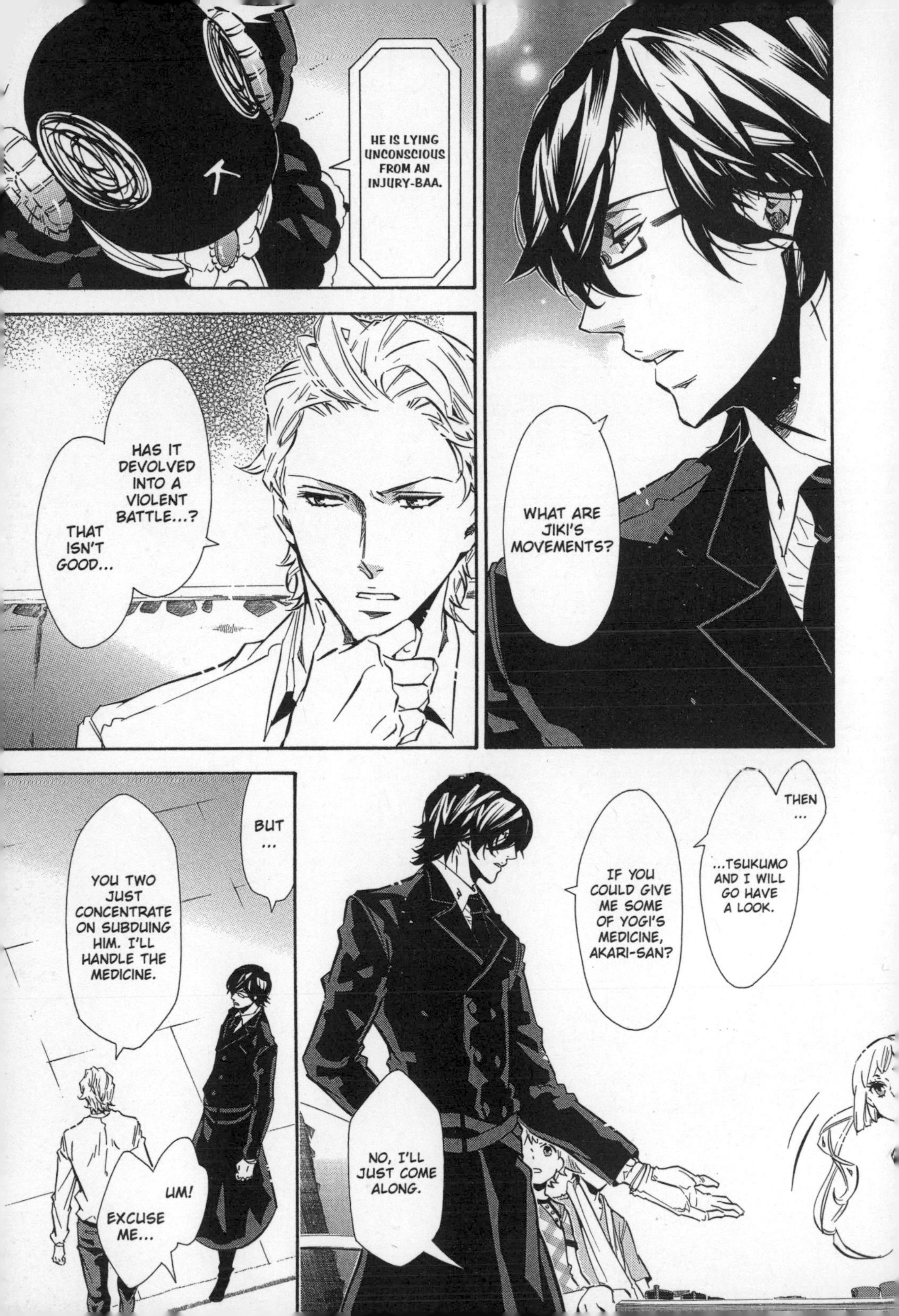
WHAT ARE JIKI'S MOVEMENTS?
HE IS LYING UNCONSCIOUS FROM AN INJURY-BAA.
HAS IT DEVOLVED INTO A VIOLENT BATTLE...?
THAT ISN'T GOOD...
THEN...
...TSUKUMO AND I WILL GO HAVE A LOOK.
IF YOU COULD GIVE ME SOME OF YOGI'S MEDICINE, AKARI-SAN?
NO, I'LL JUST COME ALONG.
BUT...
YOU TWO JUST CONCENTRATE ON SUBDUING HIM. I'LL HANDLE THE MEDICINE.
UM! EXCUSE ME...

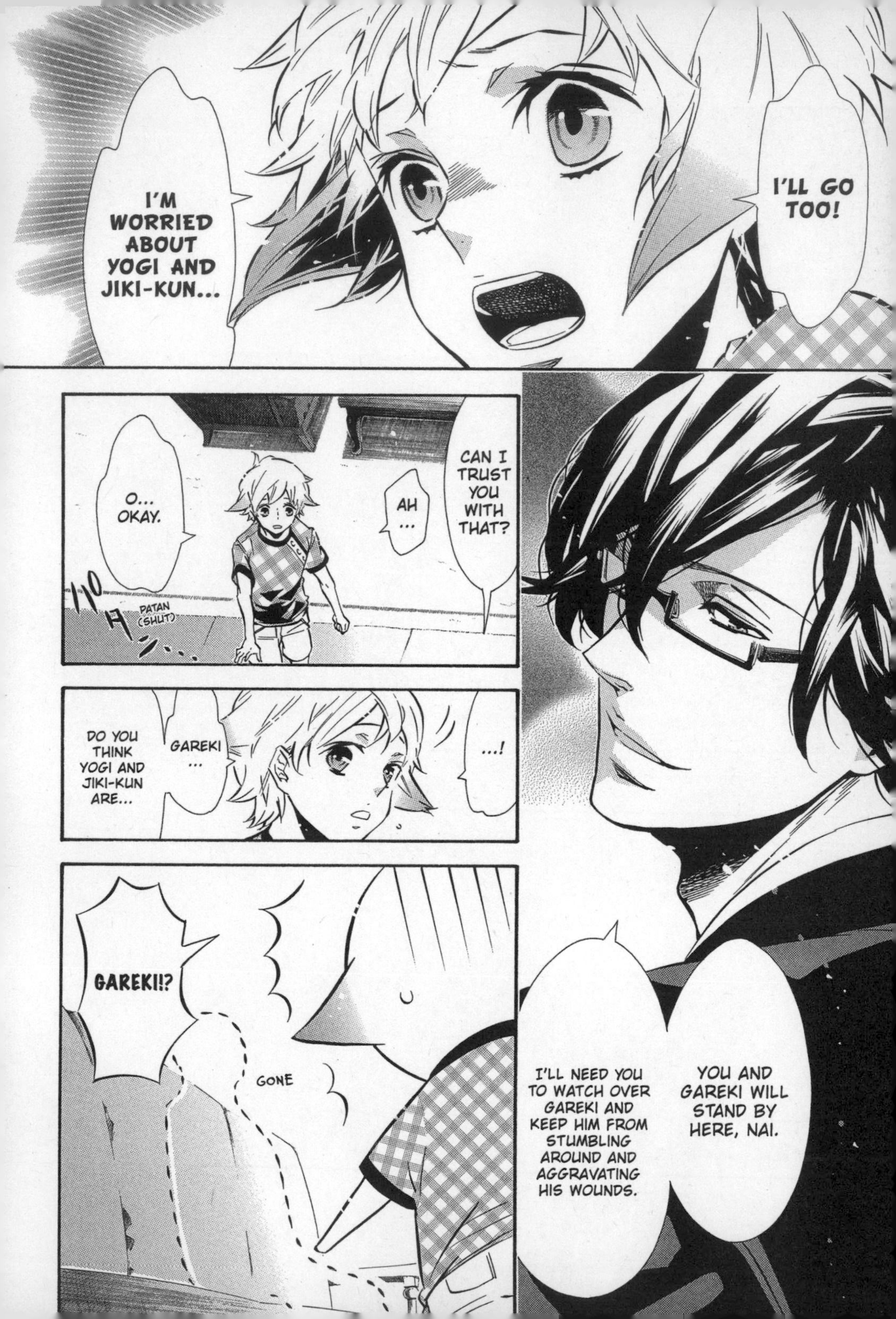
I'LL GO TOO!
I'M WORRIED ABOUT YOGI AND JIKI-KUN...
YOU AND GAREKI WILL STAND BY HERE, NAI.
I'LL NEED YOU TO WATCH OVER GAREKI AND KEEP HIM FROM STUMBLING AROUND AND AGGRAVATING HIS WOUNDS.
CAN I TRUST YOU WITH THAT?
AH ...
O... OKAY.
PATAN (SHUT)
...!
GAREKI ...
DO YOU THINK YOGI AND JIKI-KUN ARE...
GAREKI!?
GONE

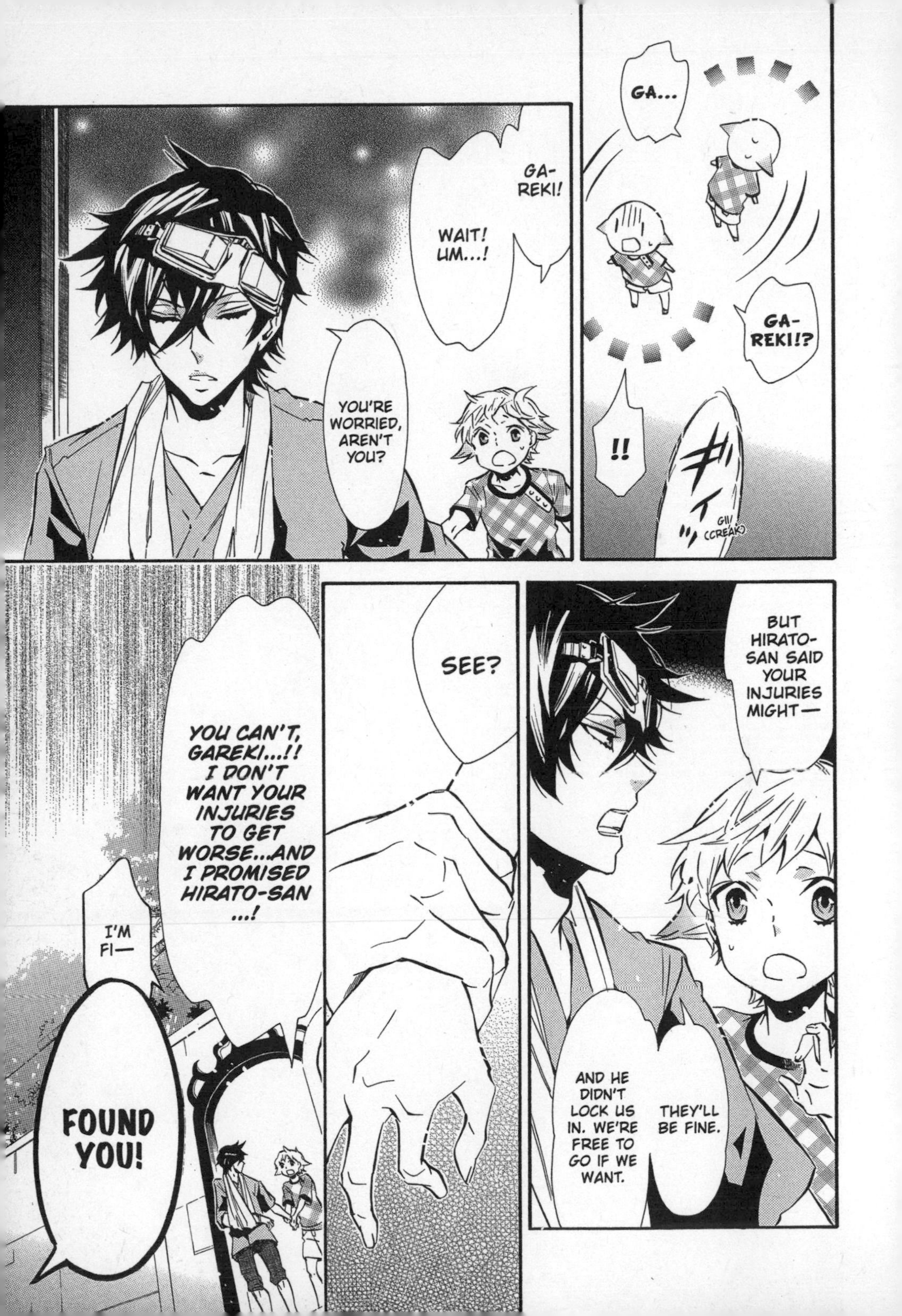
GA...
GA-REKI!?
!!
GII (CREAK)
GA-REKI!
WAIT! UM...!
YOU'RE WORRIED, AREN'T YOU?
BUT HIRATO-SAN SAID YOUR INJURIES MIGHT—
THEY'LL BE FINE.
AND HE DIDN'T LOCK US IN. WE'RE FREE TO GO IF WE WANT.
SEE?
YOU CAN'T, GAREKI...!! I DON'T WANT YOUR INJURIES TO GET WORSE...AND I PROMISED HIRATO-SAN...!
I'M FI—
FOUND YOU!

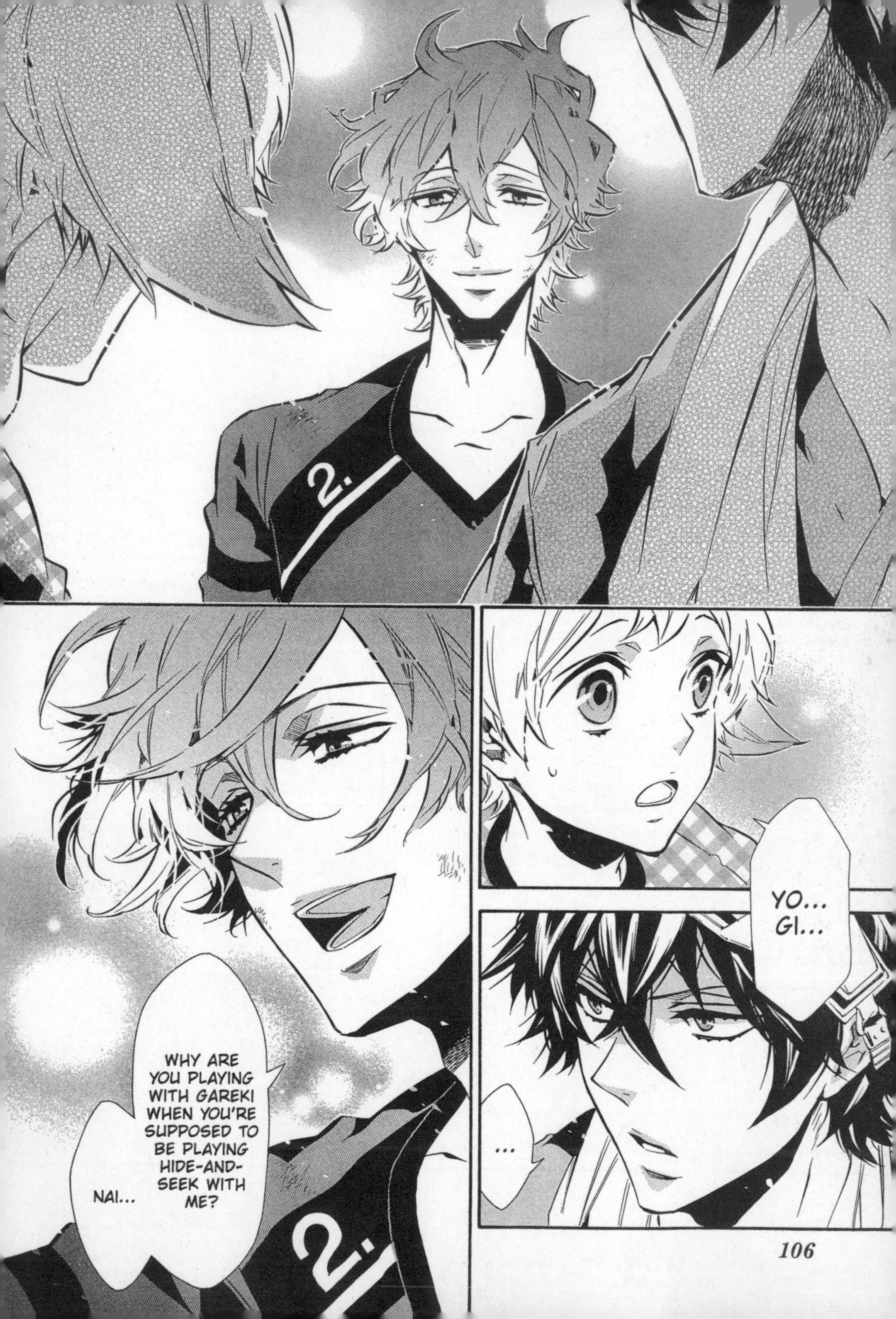
YO... GI...
...
WHY ARE YOU PLAYING WITH GAREKI WHEN YOU'RE SUPPOSED TO BE PLAYING HIDE-AND-SEEK WITH ME?
NAI...

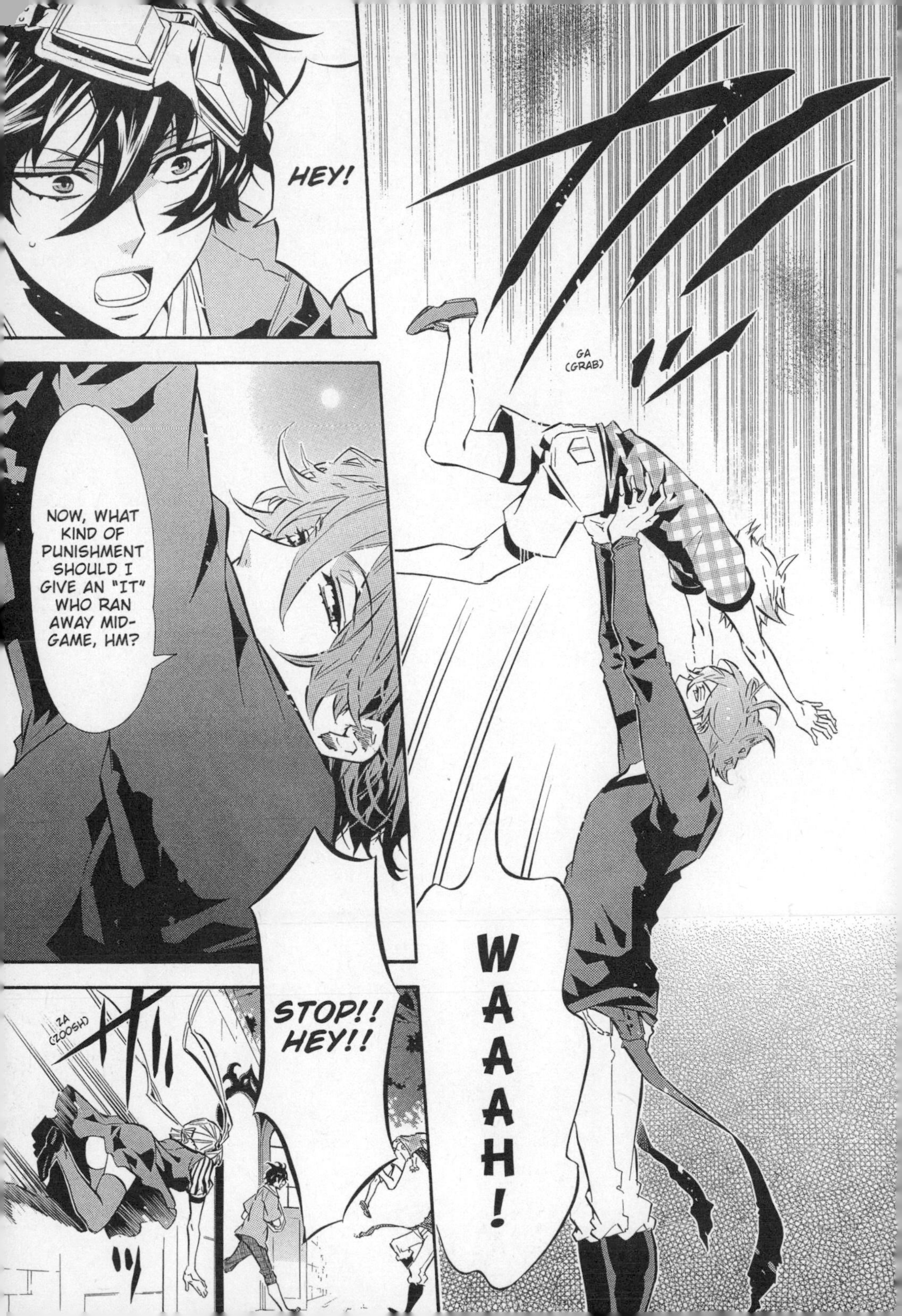
GA
(GRAB)
WAAAH!
HEY!
NOW, WHAT KIND OF PUNISHMENT SHOULD I GIVE AN "IT" WHO RAN AWAY MID-GAME, HM?
STOP!! HEY!!
ZA
(ZOOSH)

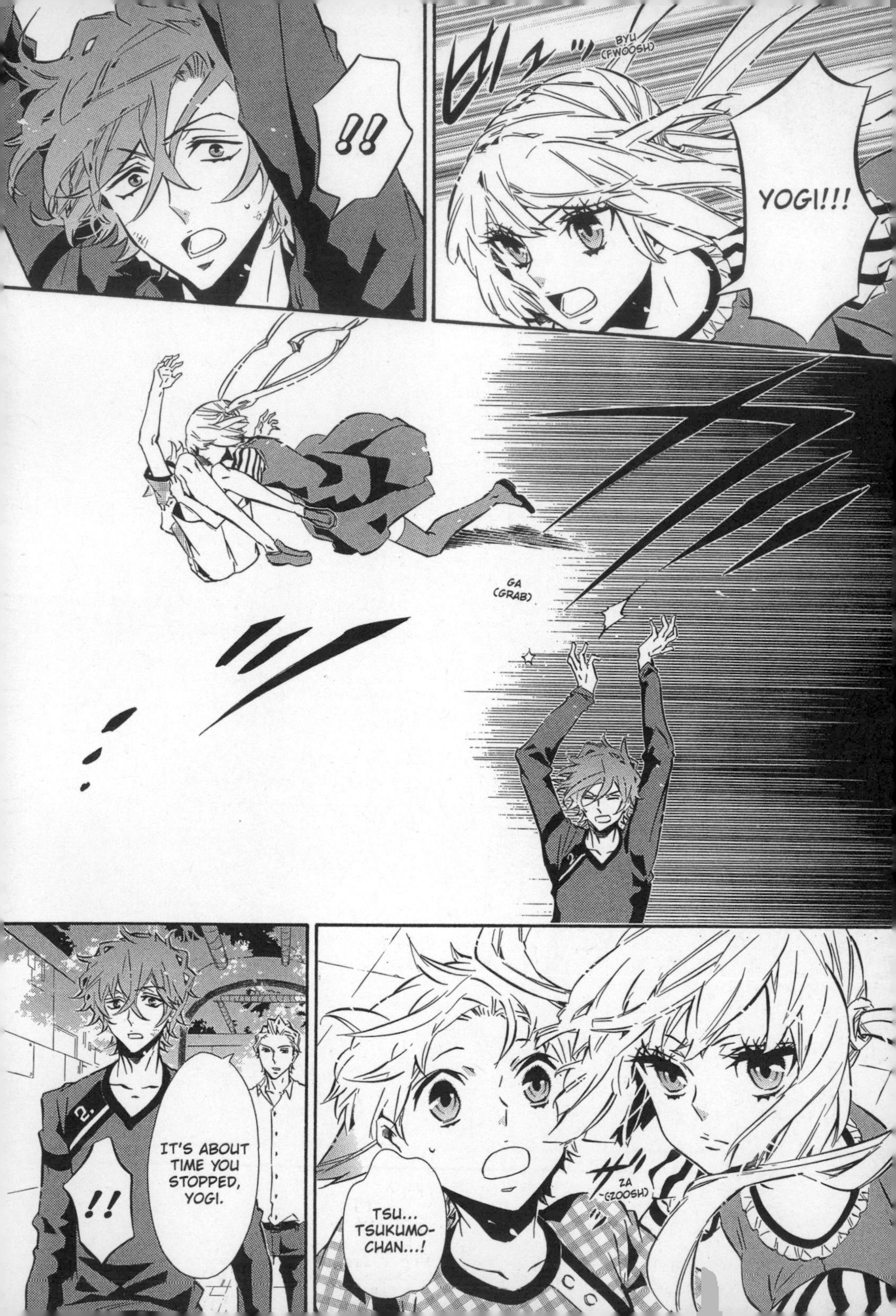
BYU (FWOOSH)
YOGI!!!
!!
GA (GRAB)
ZA (ZOOSH)
TSU... TSUKUMO-CHAN...!
IT'S ABOUT TIME YOU STOPPED, YOGI.
!!

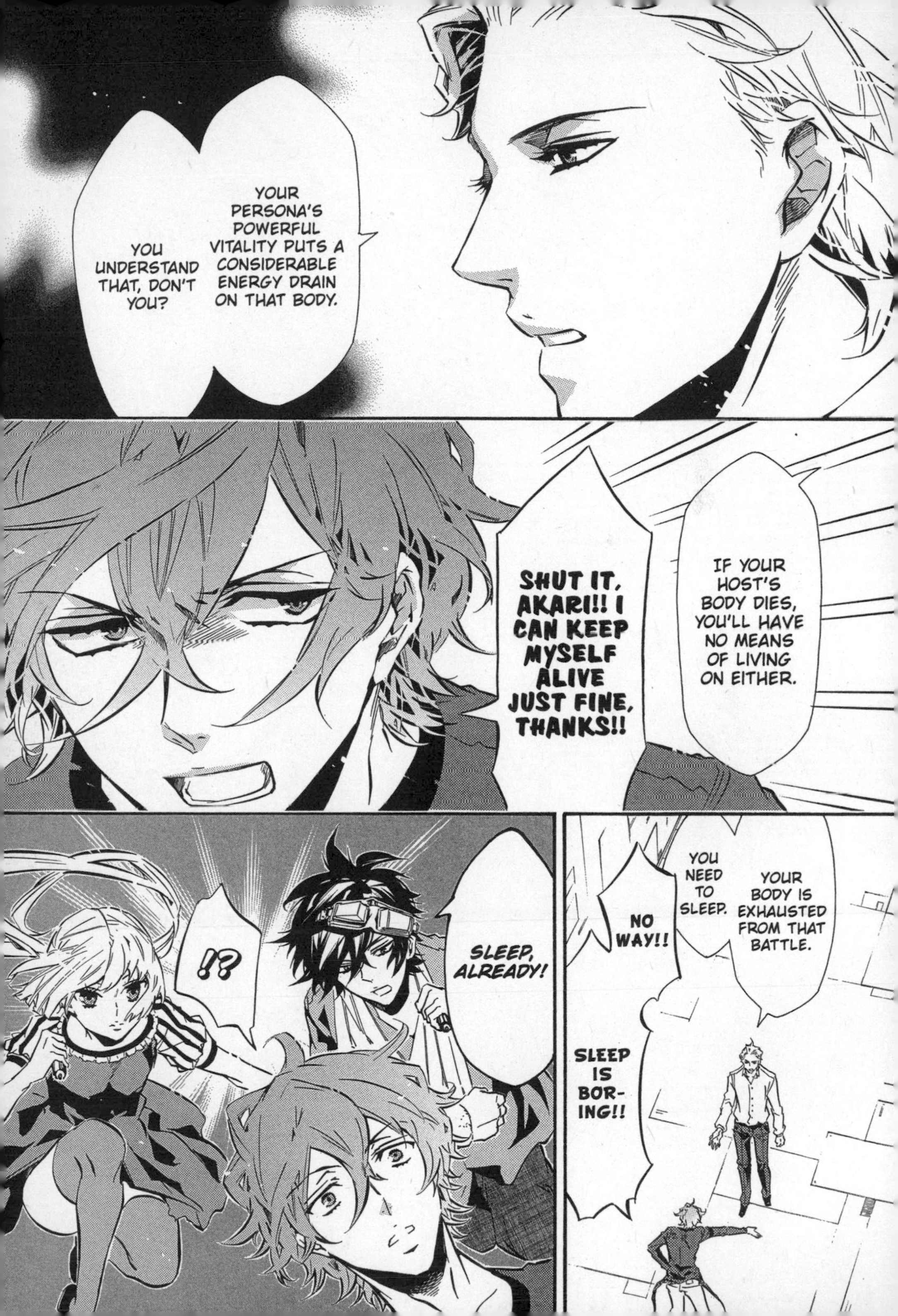
YOUR PERSONA'S POWERFUL VITALITY PUTS A CONSIDERABLE ENERGY DRAIN ON THAT BODY.
YOU UNDERSTAND THAT, DON'T YOU?
IF YOUR HOST'S BODY DIES, YOU'LL HAVE NO MEANS OF LIVING ON EITHER.
SHUT IT, AKARI!! I CAN KEEP MYSELF ALIVE JUST FINE, THANKS!!
YOUR BODY IS EXHAUSTED FROM THAT BATTLE.
YOU NEED TO SLEEP.
NO WAY!!
SLEEP IS BOR-ING!!
SLEEP, ALREADY!
!?

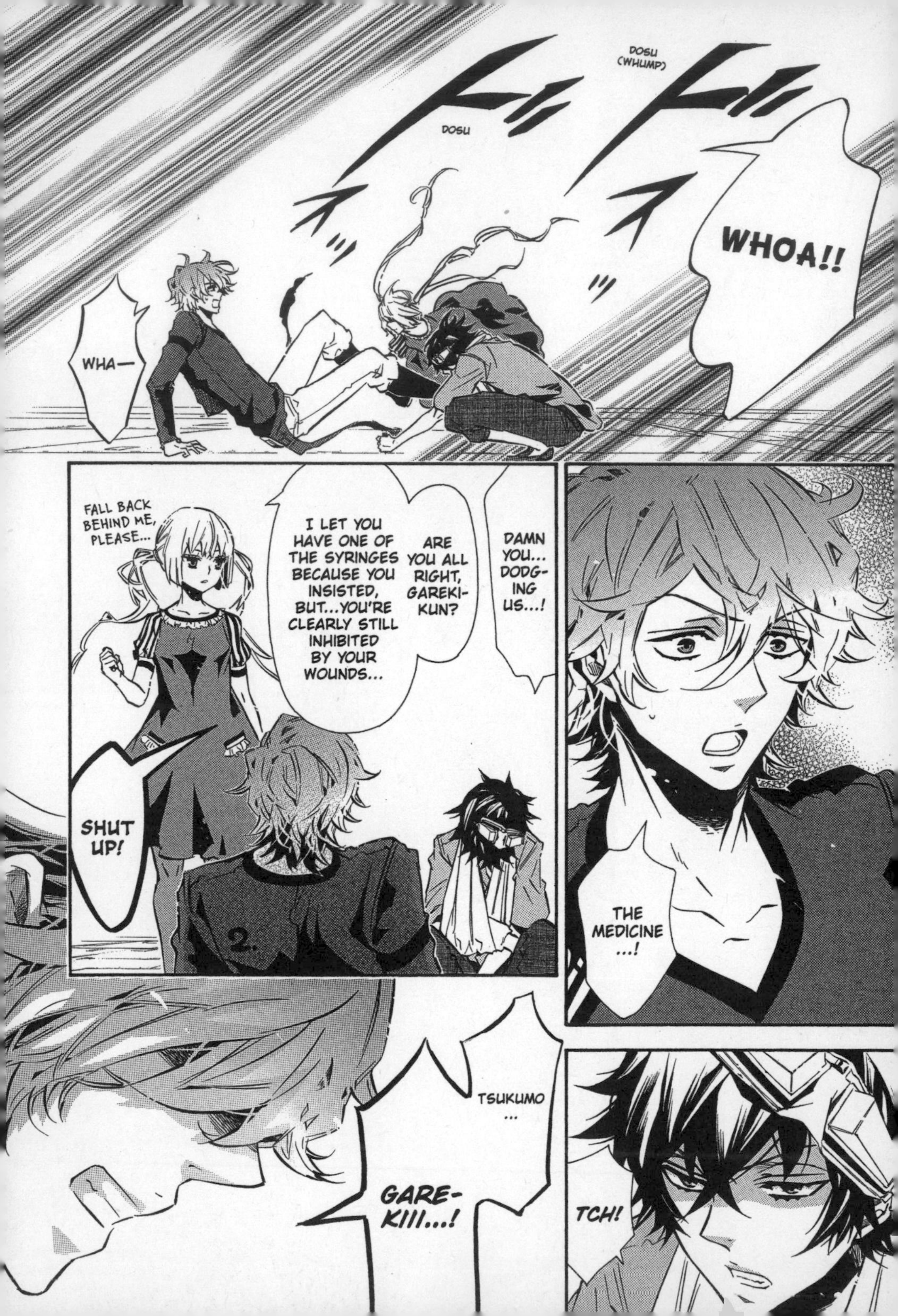
DOSU (WHUMP)
DOSU
WHOA!!
WHA—
THE MEDICINE ...!
DAMN YOU... DODGING US...!
ARE YOU ALL RIGHT, GAREKI-KUN?
I LET YOU HAVE ONE OF THE SYRINGES BECAUSE YOU INSISTED, BUT...YOU'RE CLEARLY STILL INHIBITED BY YOUR WOUNDS...
FALL BACK BEHIND ME, PLEASE...
SHUT UP!
TCH!
TSUKUMO ...
GARE-KIII...!

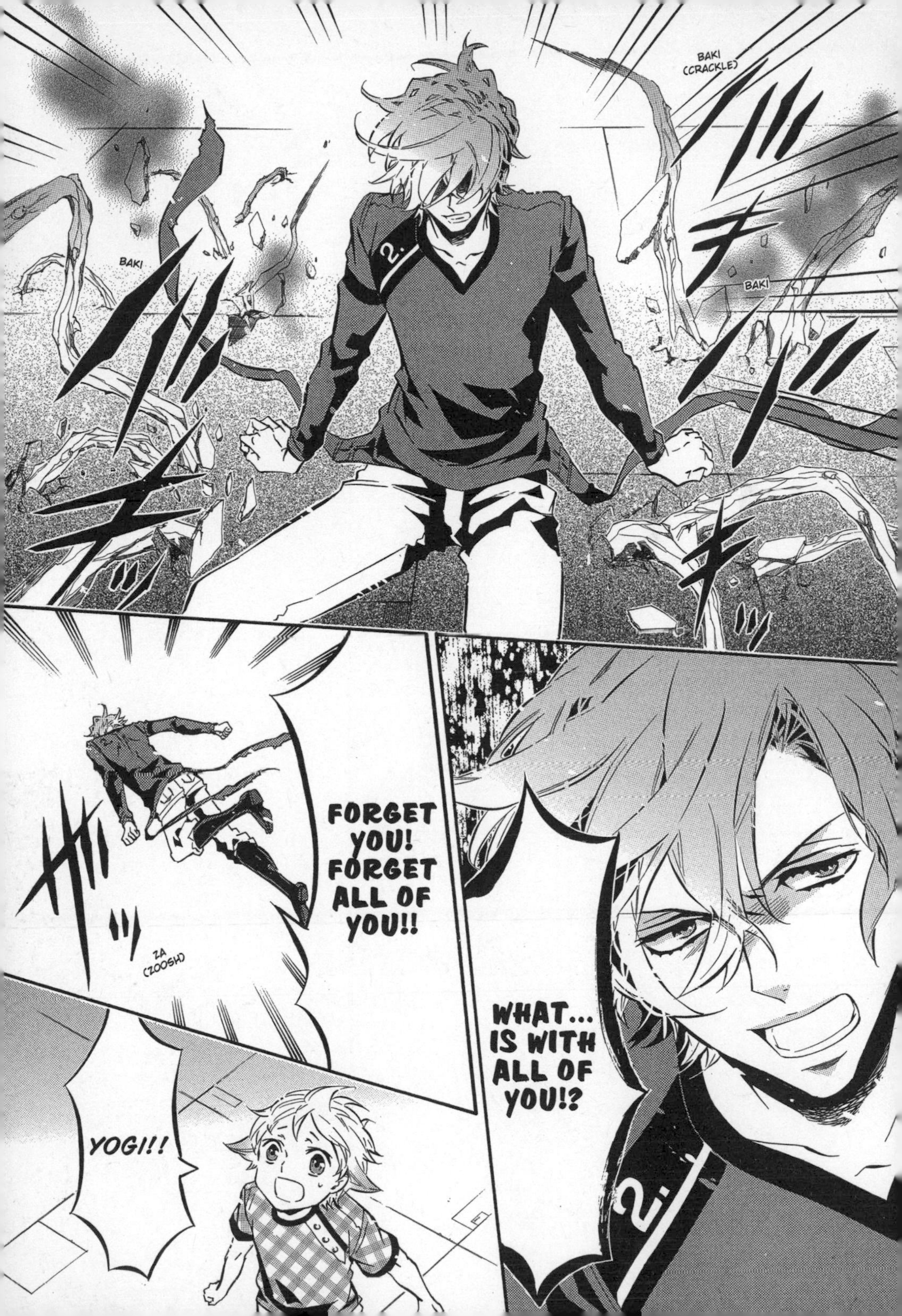
BAKI (CRACKLE)
BAKI
BAKI
WHAT... IS WITH ALL OF YOU!?
FORGET YOU! FORGET ALL OF YOU!!
ZA (ZOOSH)
YOGI!!

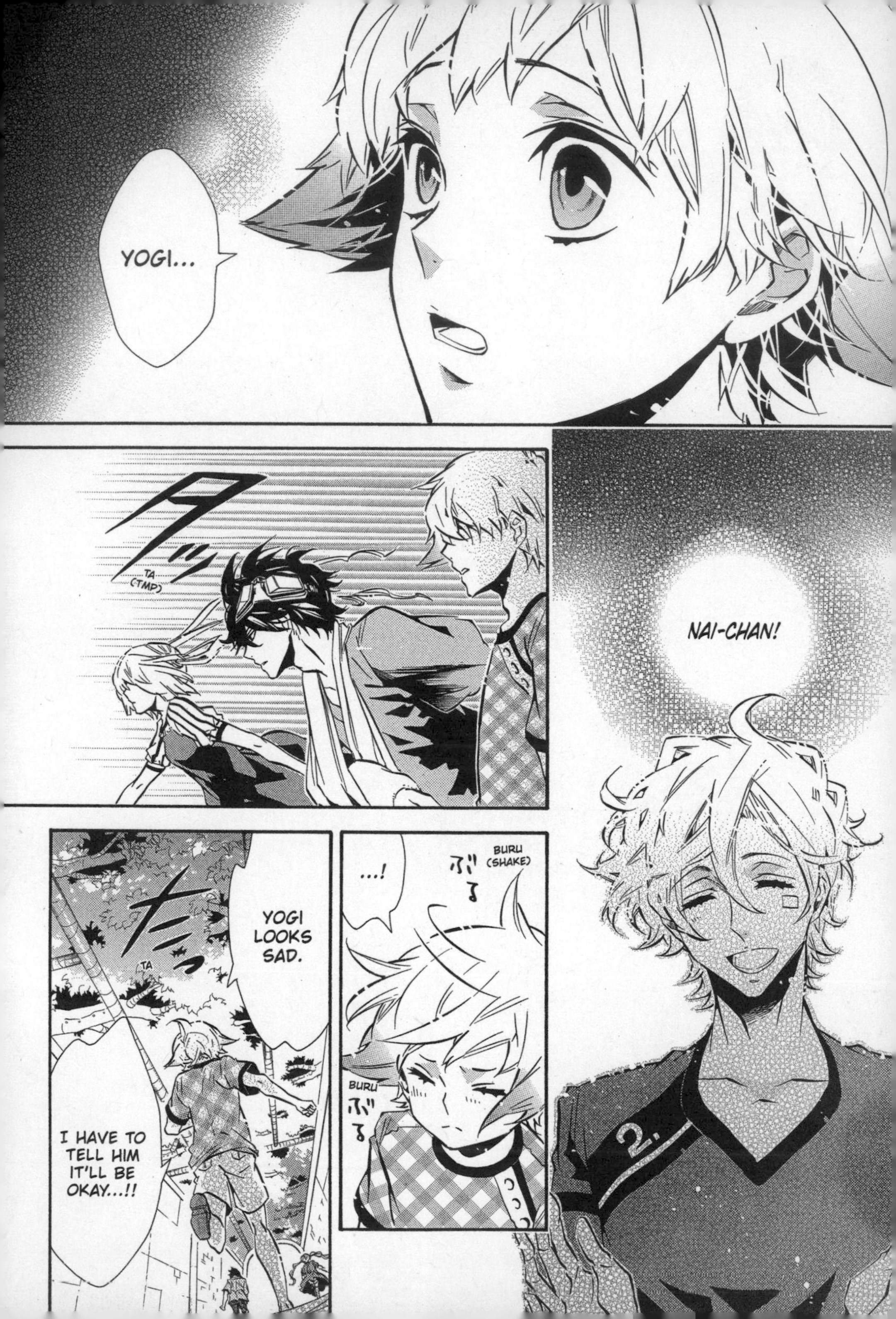
YOGI...
NAI-CHAN!
TA (TMP)
...!
BURU (SHAKE)
ぶる
BURU
ぶる
YOGI LOOKS SAD.
TA
I HAVE TO TELL HIM IT'LL BE OKAY...!!

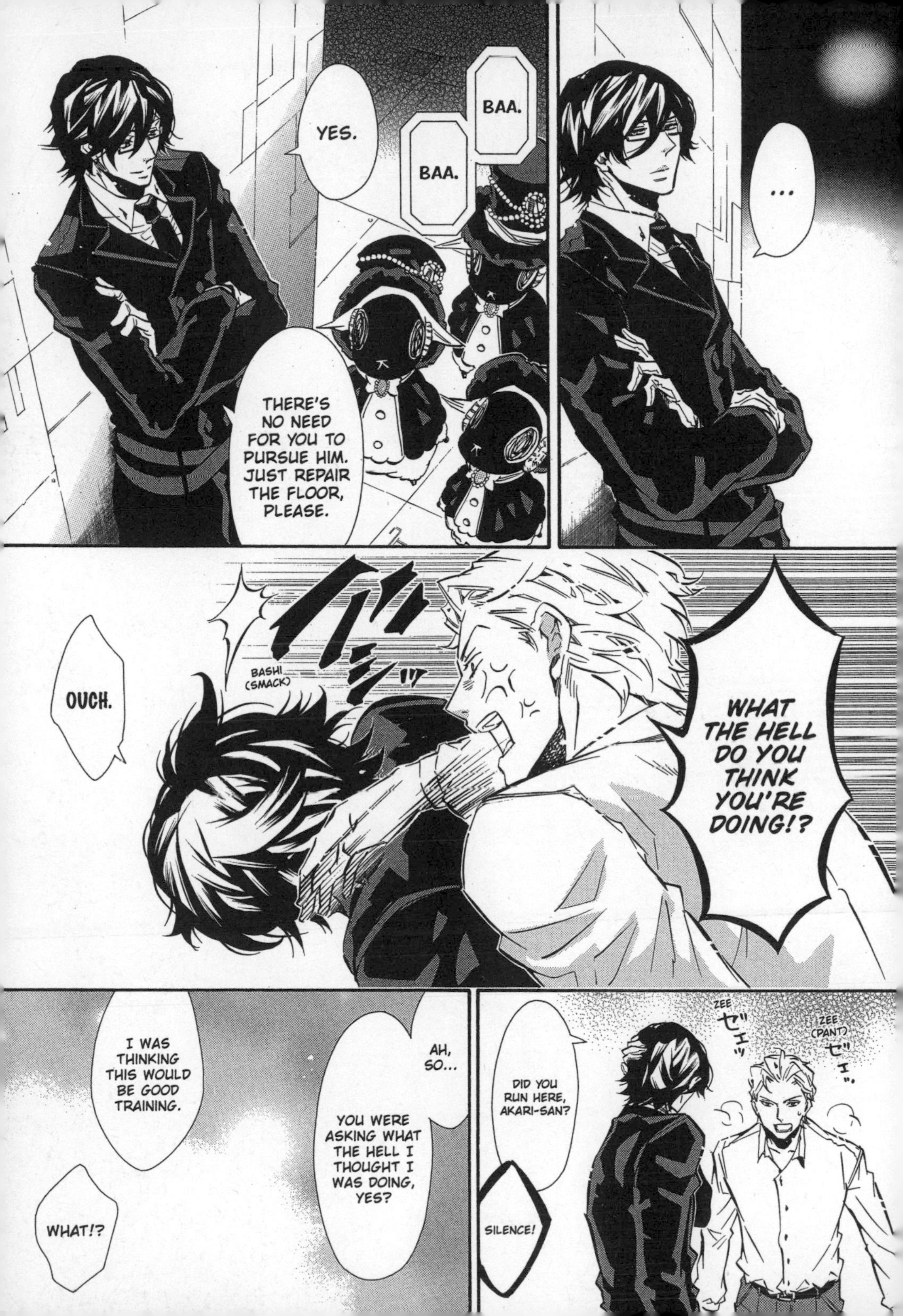
...
BAA.
BAA.
YES.
THERE'S NO NEED FOR YOU TO PURSUE HIM. JUST REPAIR THE FLOOR, PLEASE.
WHAT THE HELL DO YOU THINK YOU'RE DOING!?
BASHI (SMACK)
OUCH.
ZEE (PANT)
ゼェ
ZEE
ゼェッ
DID YOU RUN HERE, AKARI-SAN?
SILENCE!
AH, SO...
YOU WERE ASKING WHAT THE HELL I THOUGHT I WAS DOING, YES?
I WAS THINKING THIS WOULD BE GOOD TRAINING.
WHAT!?

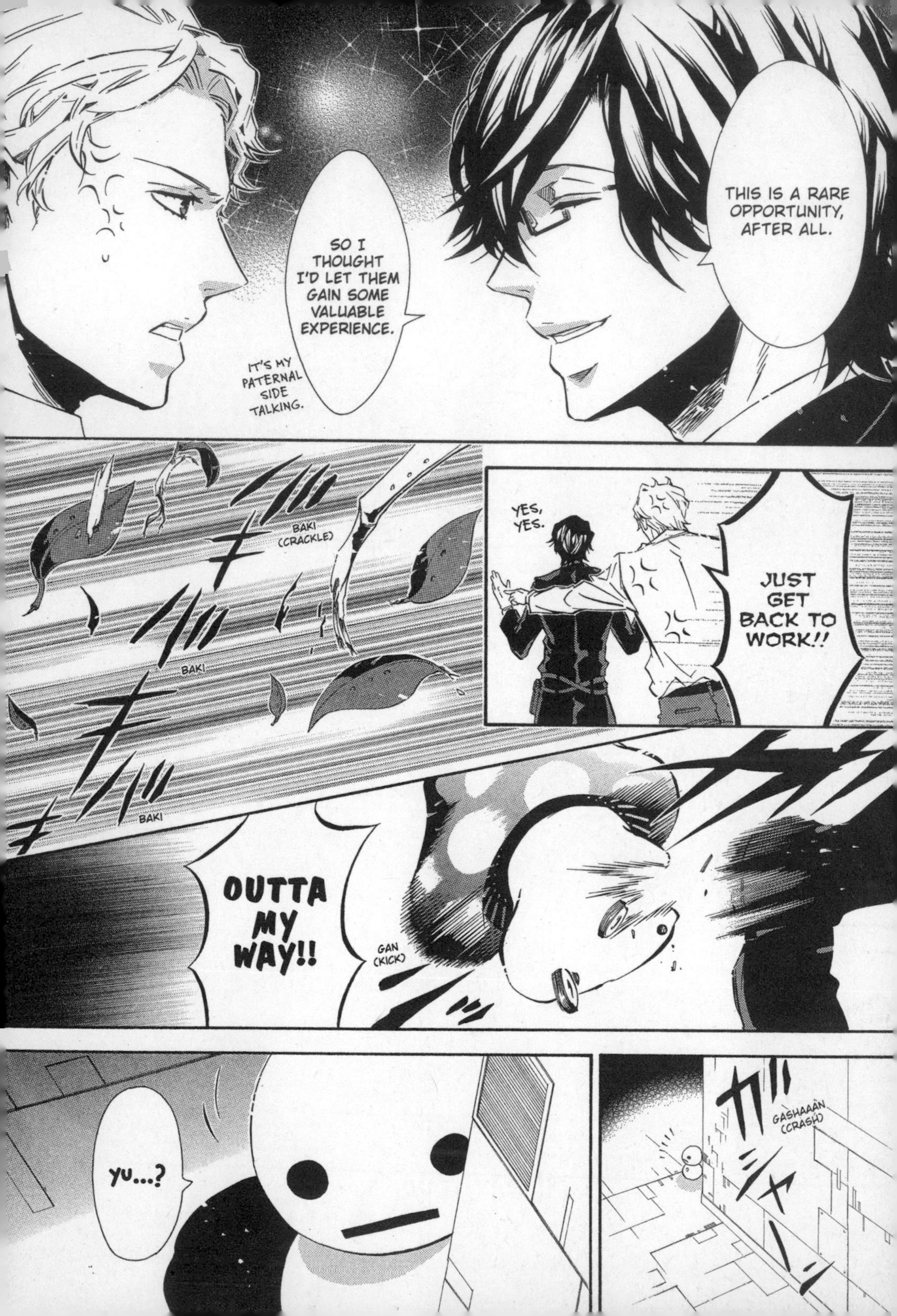
THIS IS A RARE OPPORTUNITY, AFTER ALL.
SO I THOUGHT I'D LET THEM GAIN SOME VALUABLE EXPERIENCE.
IT'S MY PATERNAL SIDE TALKING.
JUST GET BACK TO WORK!!
YES, YES.
BAKI (CRACKLE)
BAKI
BAKI
GAN (KICK)
OUTTA MY WAY!!
GASHAAAN (CRASH)
yu...?

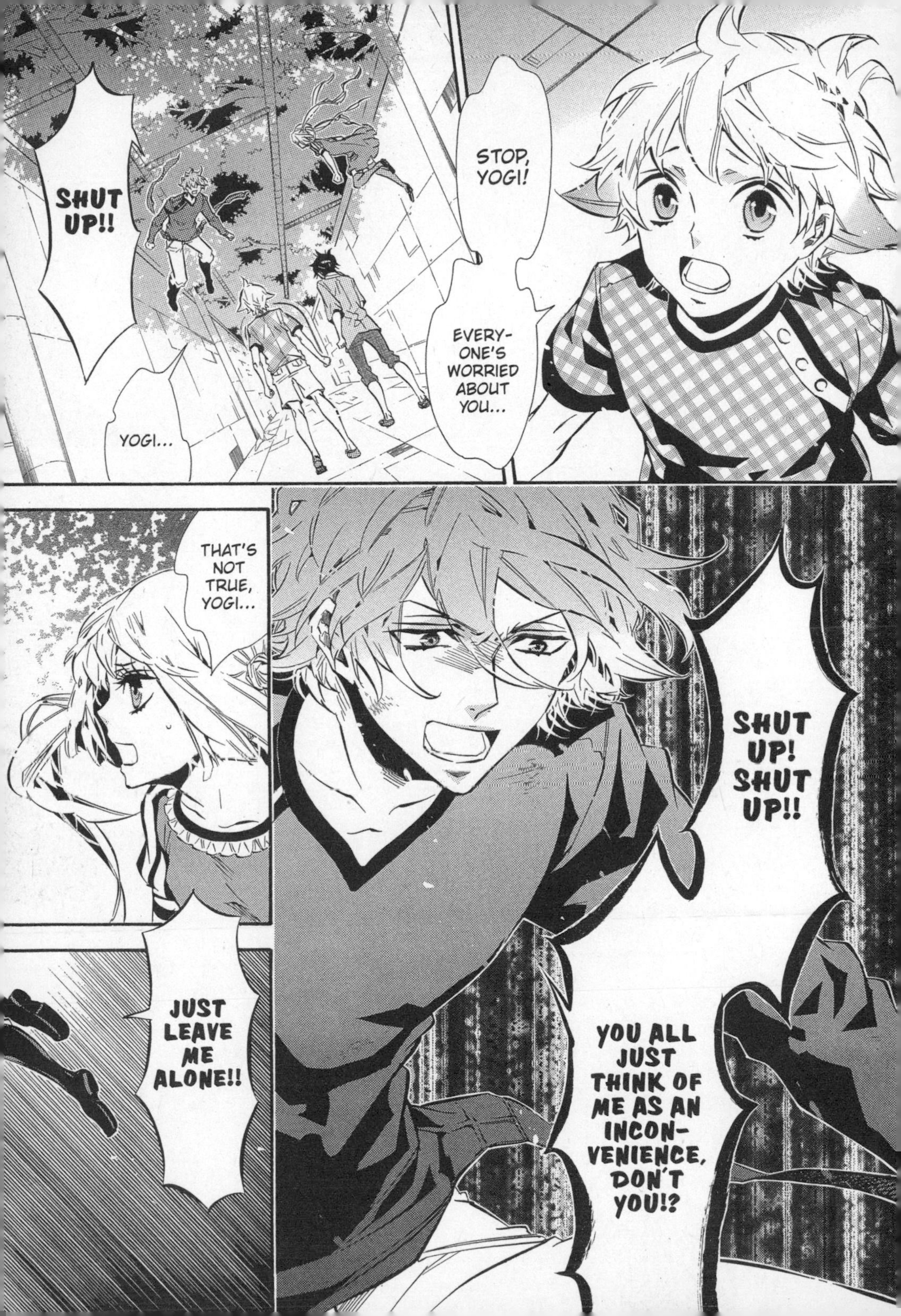
STOP, YOGI!
EVERY-ONE'S WORRIED ABOUT YOU...
SHUT UP!!
YOGI...
SHUT UP! SHUT UP!!
YOU ALL JUST THINK OF ME AS AN INCON-VENIENCE, DON'T YOU!?
THAT'S NOT TRUE, YOGI...
JUST LEAVE ME ALONE!!

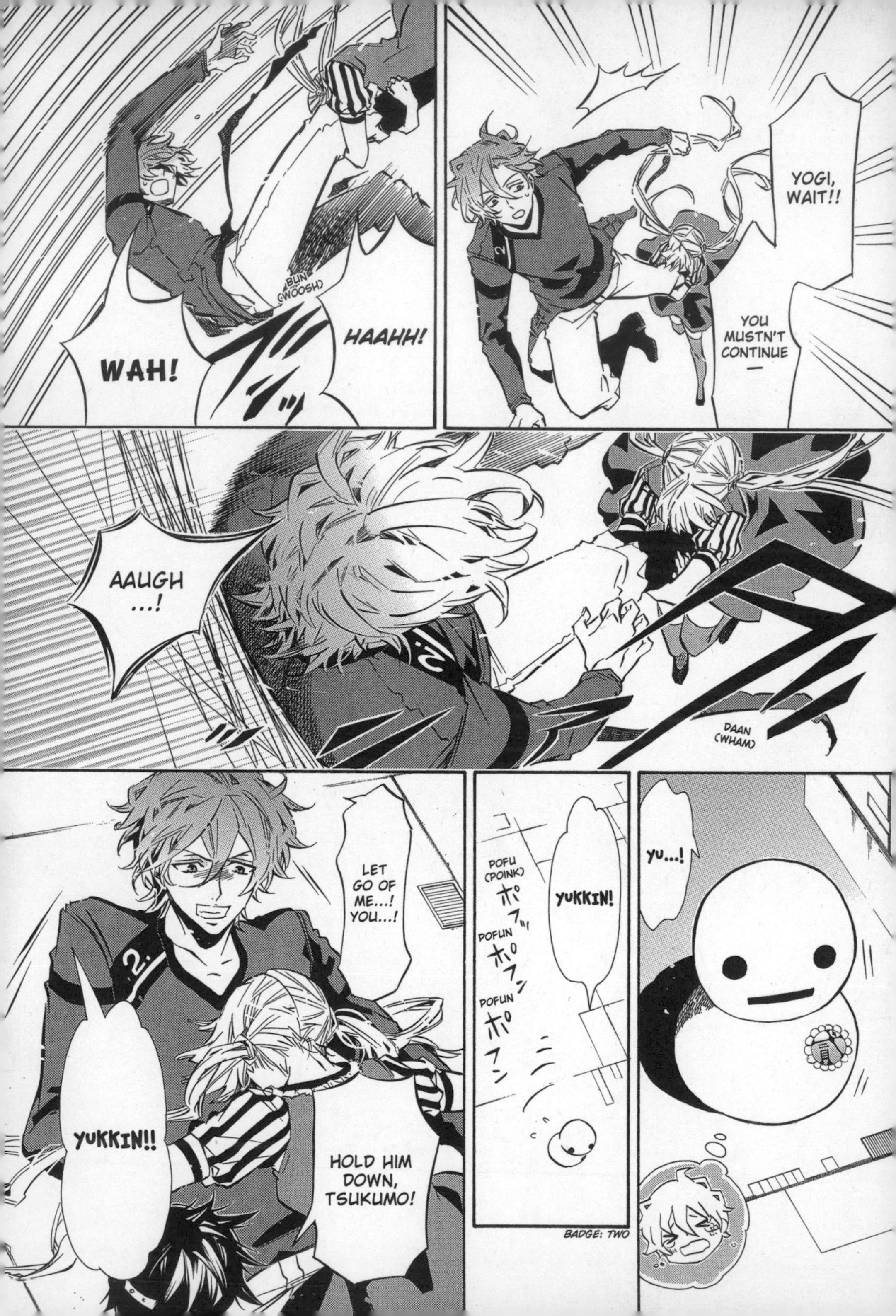

YOGI, WAIT!!
YOU MUSTN'T CONTINUE —
BUN (WOOSH)
HAAHH!
WAH!
AAUGH ...!
DAAN (WHAM)
YU...!
BADGE: TWO
YUKKIN!
POFU (POINK)
ポフ
POFUN
ポフン
POFUN
ポフン
LET GO OF ME...! YOU...!
YUKKIN!!
HOLD HIM DOWN, TSUKUMO!

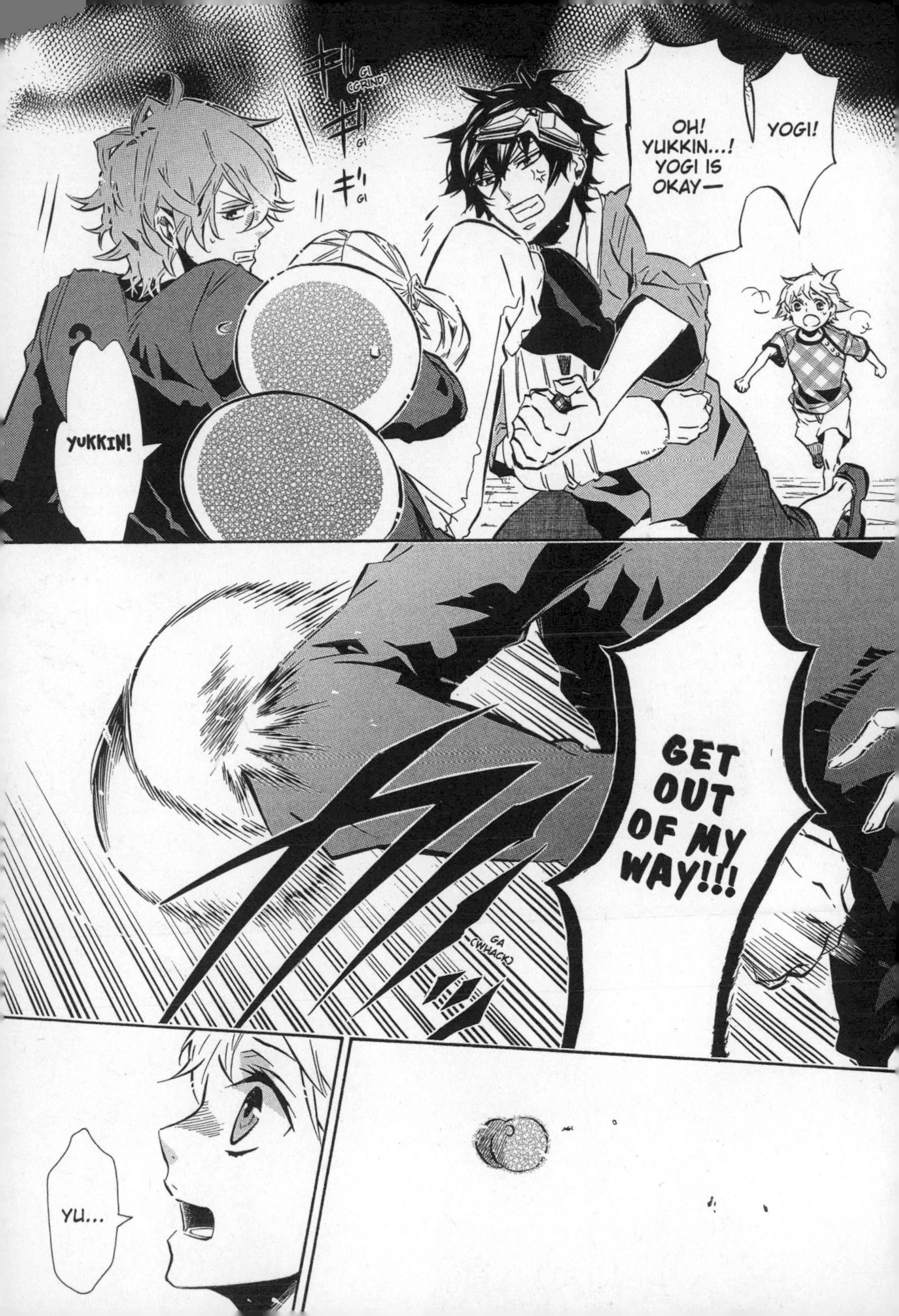
YOGI!
OH! YUKKIN...! YOGI IS OKAY—
GI (GRIND)
GI
GI
YUKKIN!
GET OUT OF MY WAY!!!
GA (WHACK)
YU...

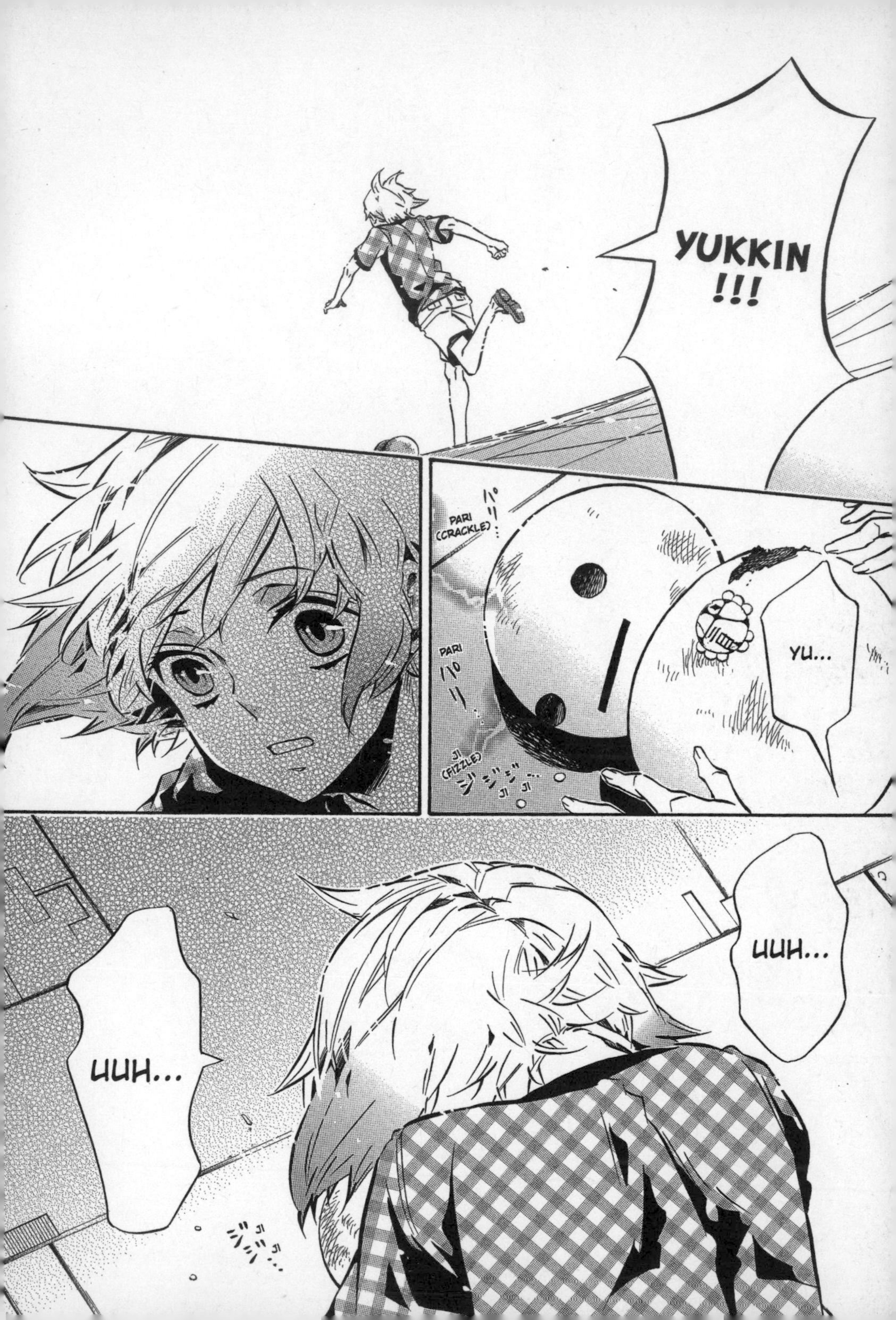
YUKKIN !!!
PARI (CRACKLE)
PARI
JI (FIZZLE)
JI JI
YU...
UUH...
UUH...
JI JI JI

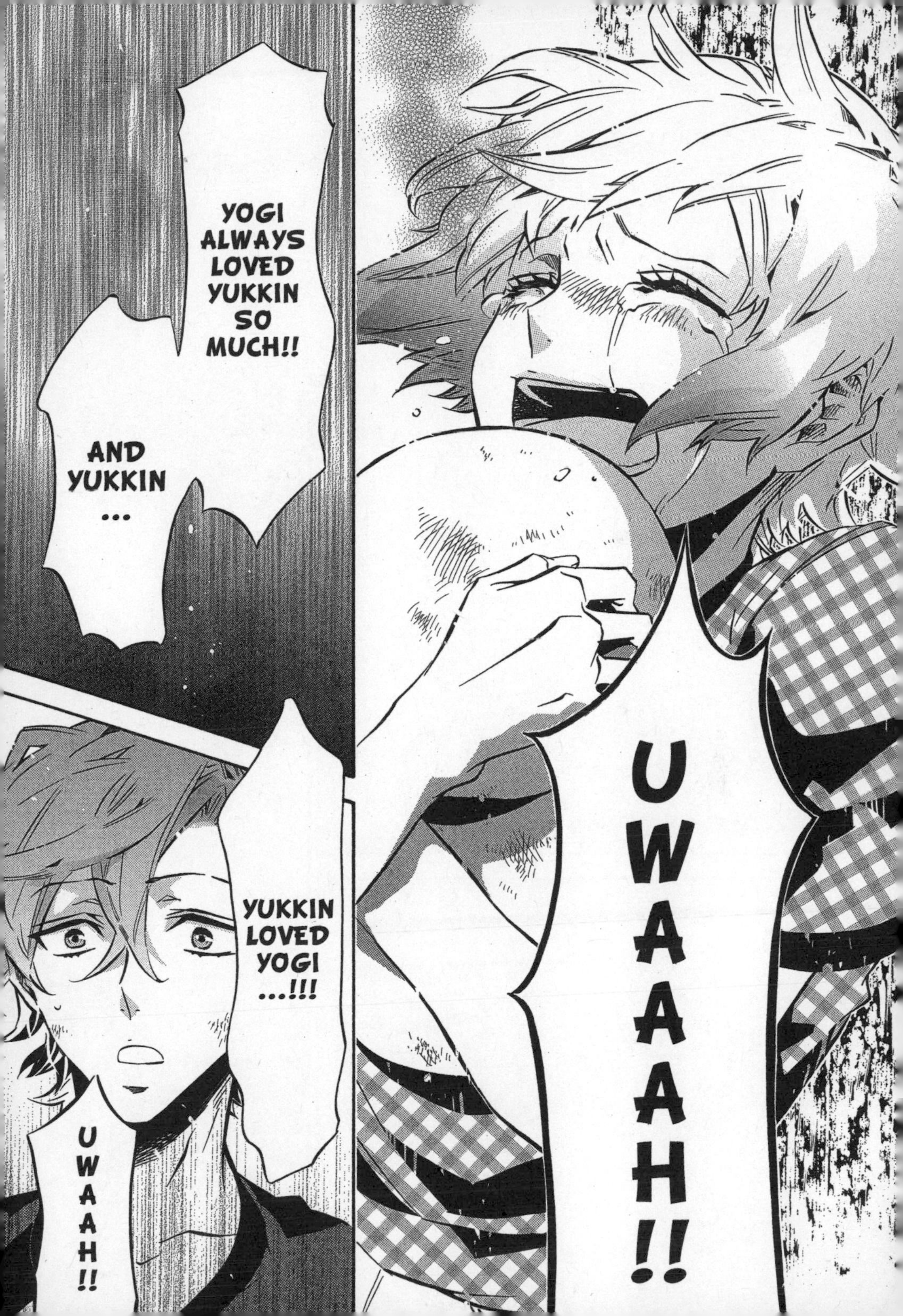
UWAAAH!!
YOGI ALWAYS LOVED YUKKIN SO MUCH!!
AND YUKKIN...
YUKKIN LOVED YOGI...!!!
UWAAH!!

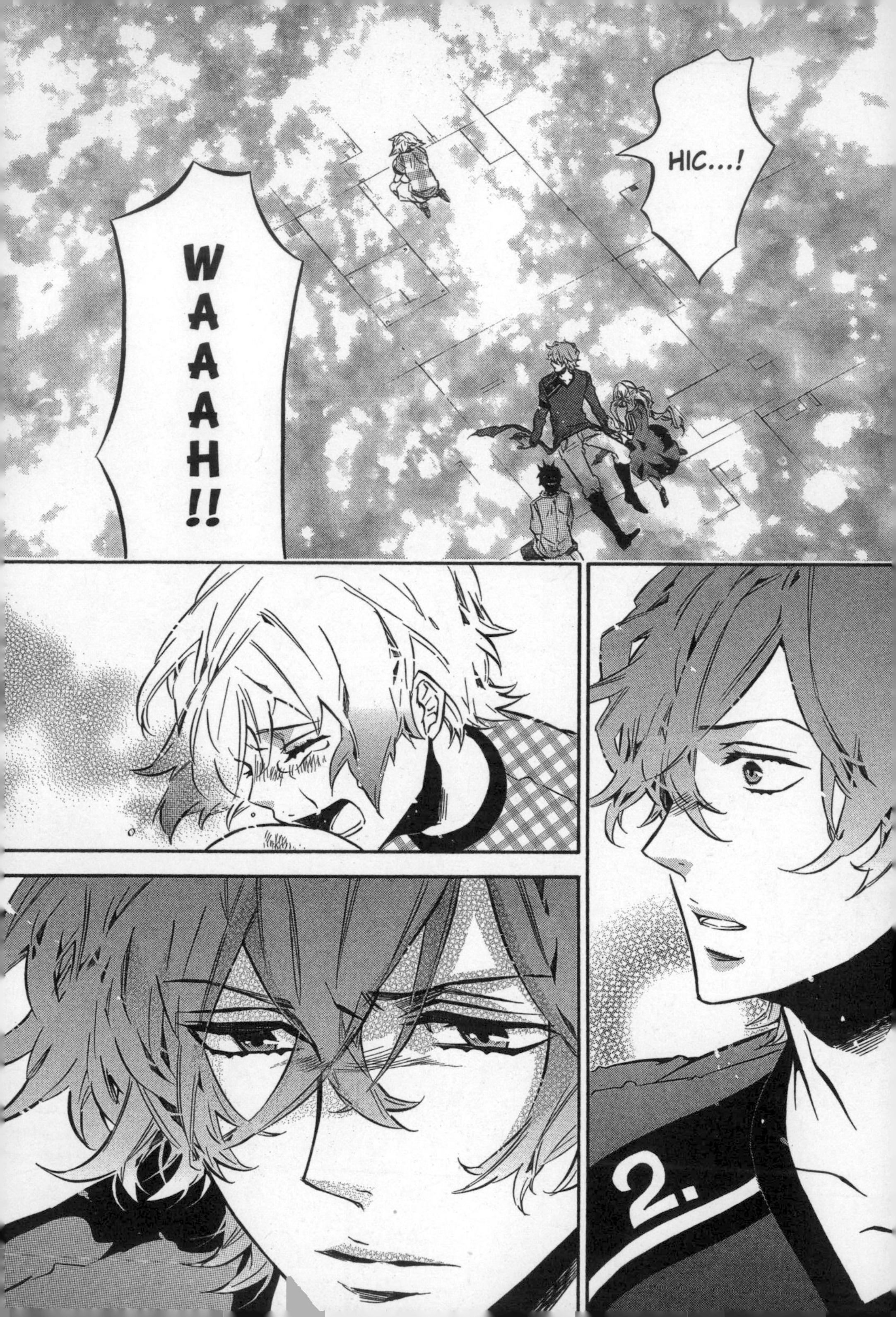
HIC...!
WAAAAH!!

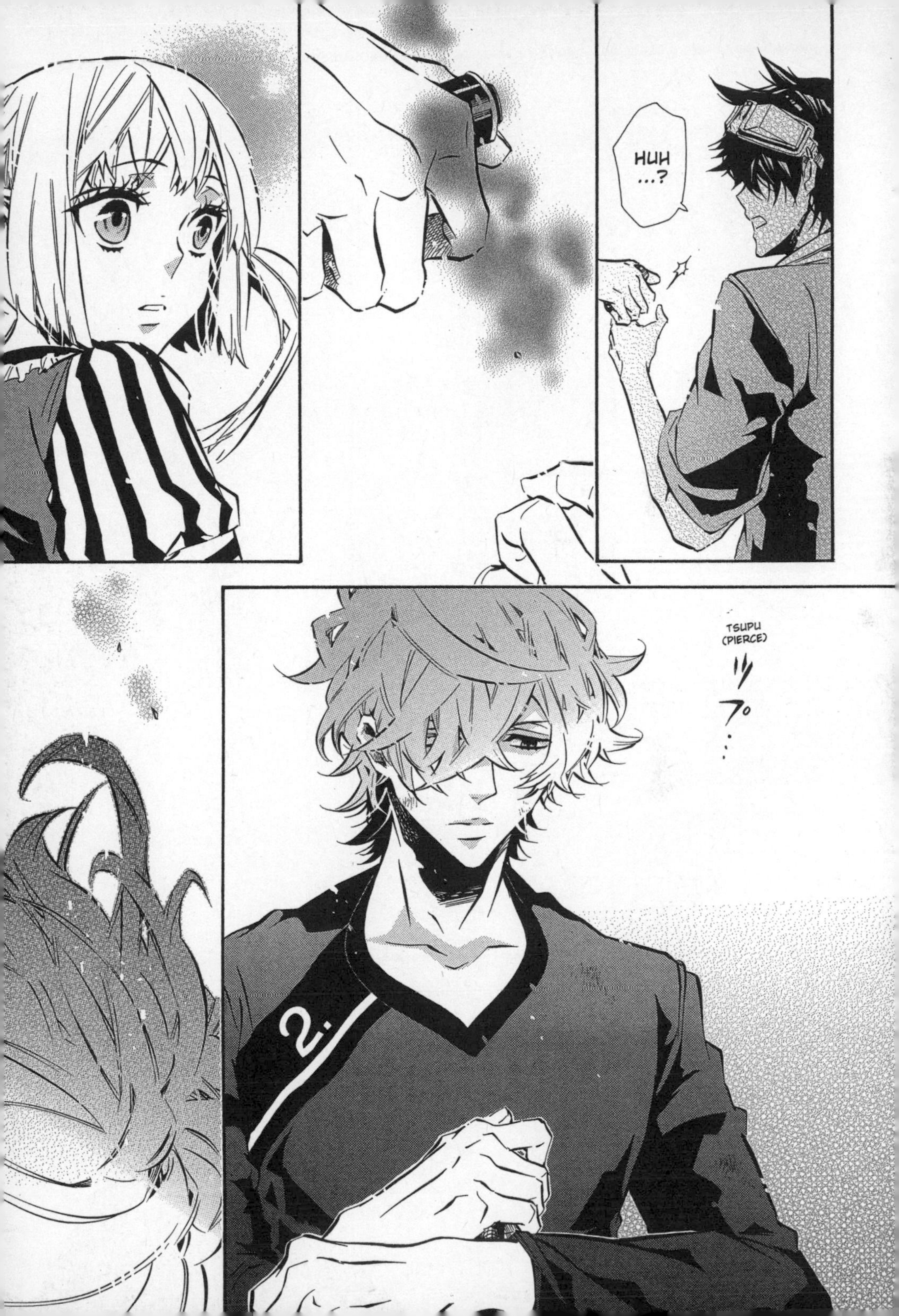
HUH ...?
TSUPU (PIERCE)
ツプ…

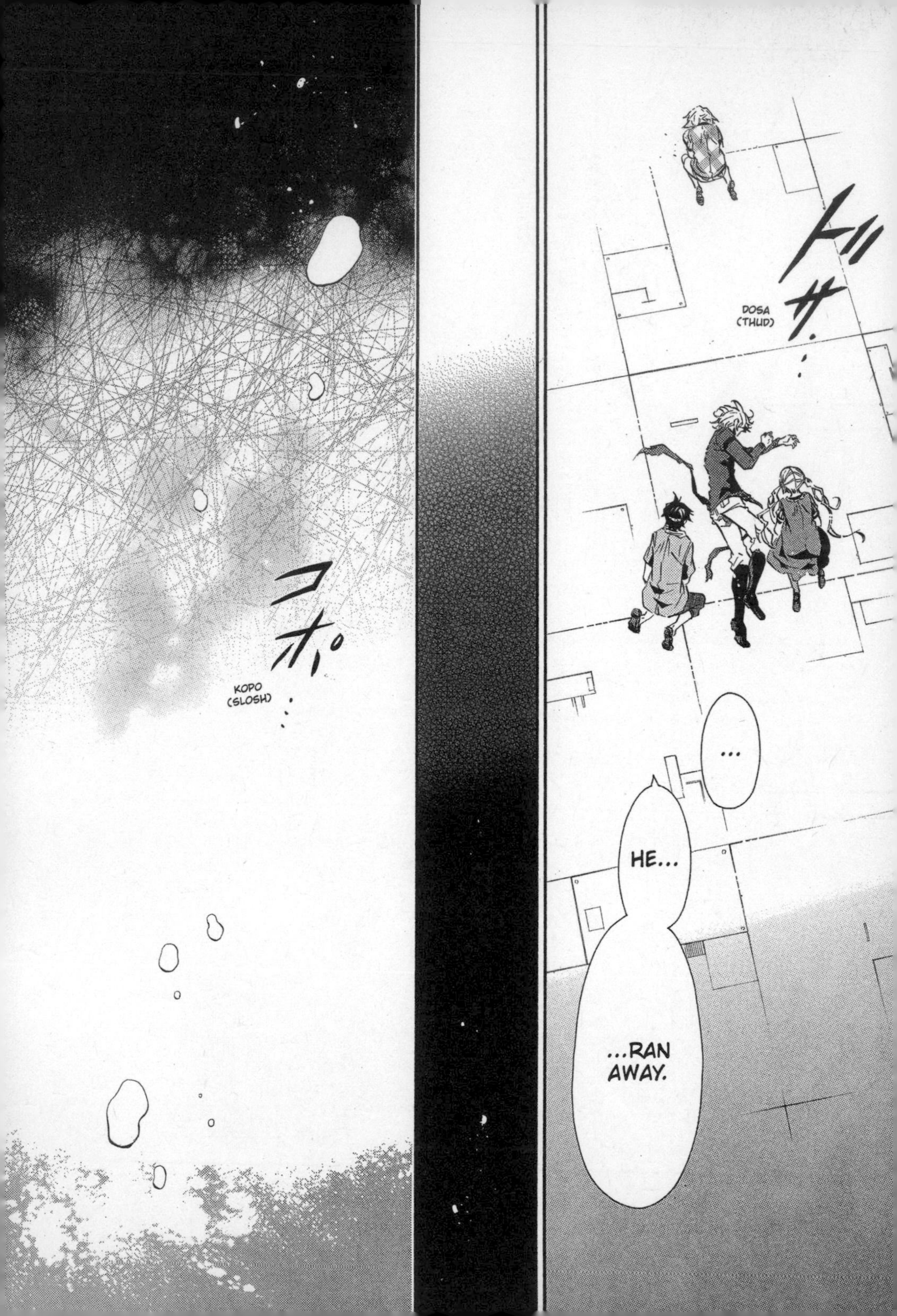
ドサ
DOSA
(THUD)
...
HE...
...RAN AWAY.
コポ
KOPO
(SLOSH)

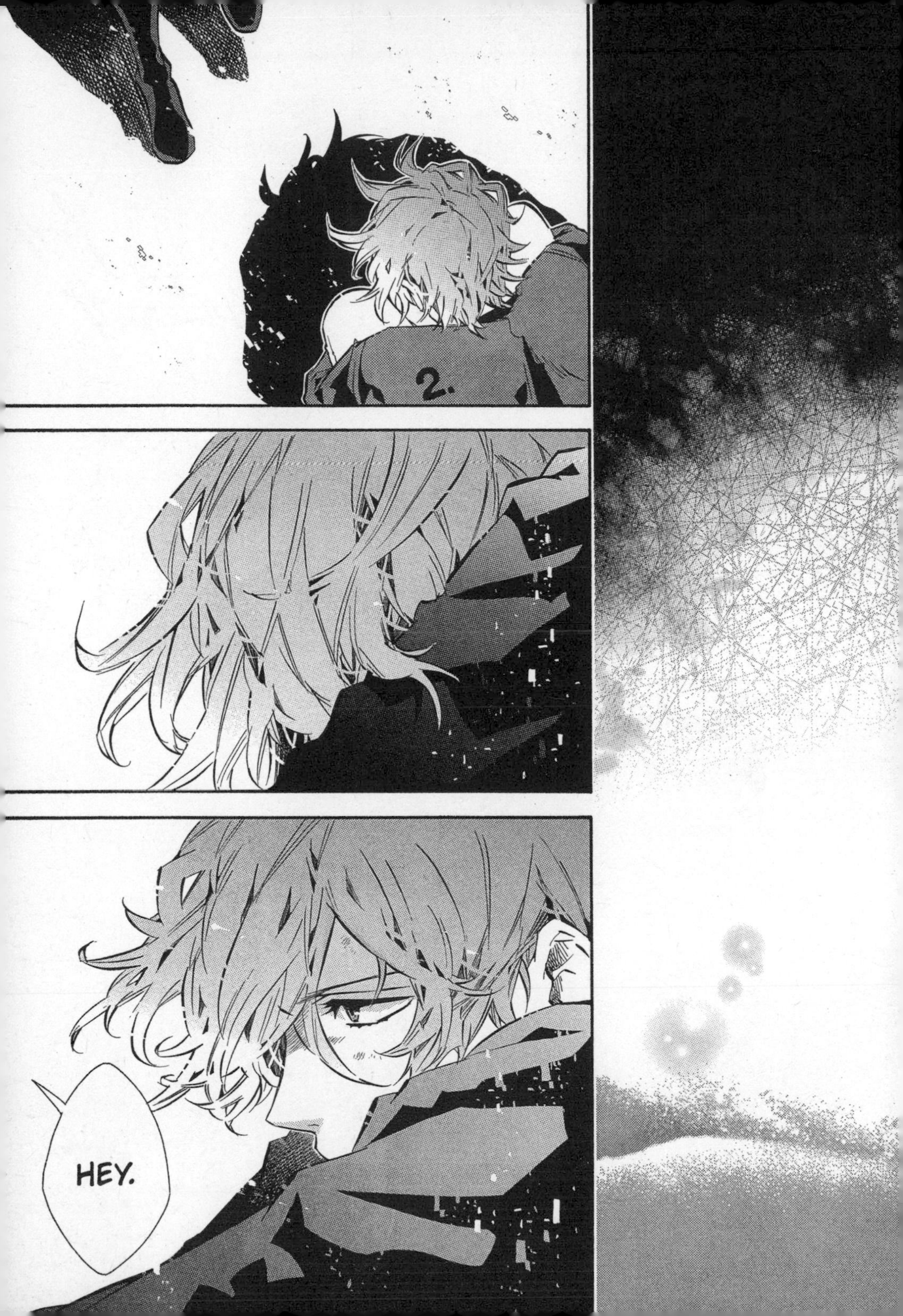
2.
HEY.

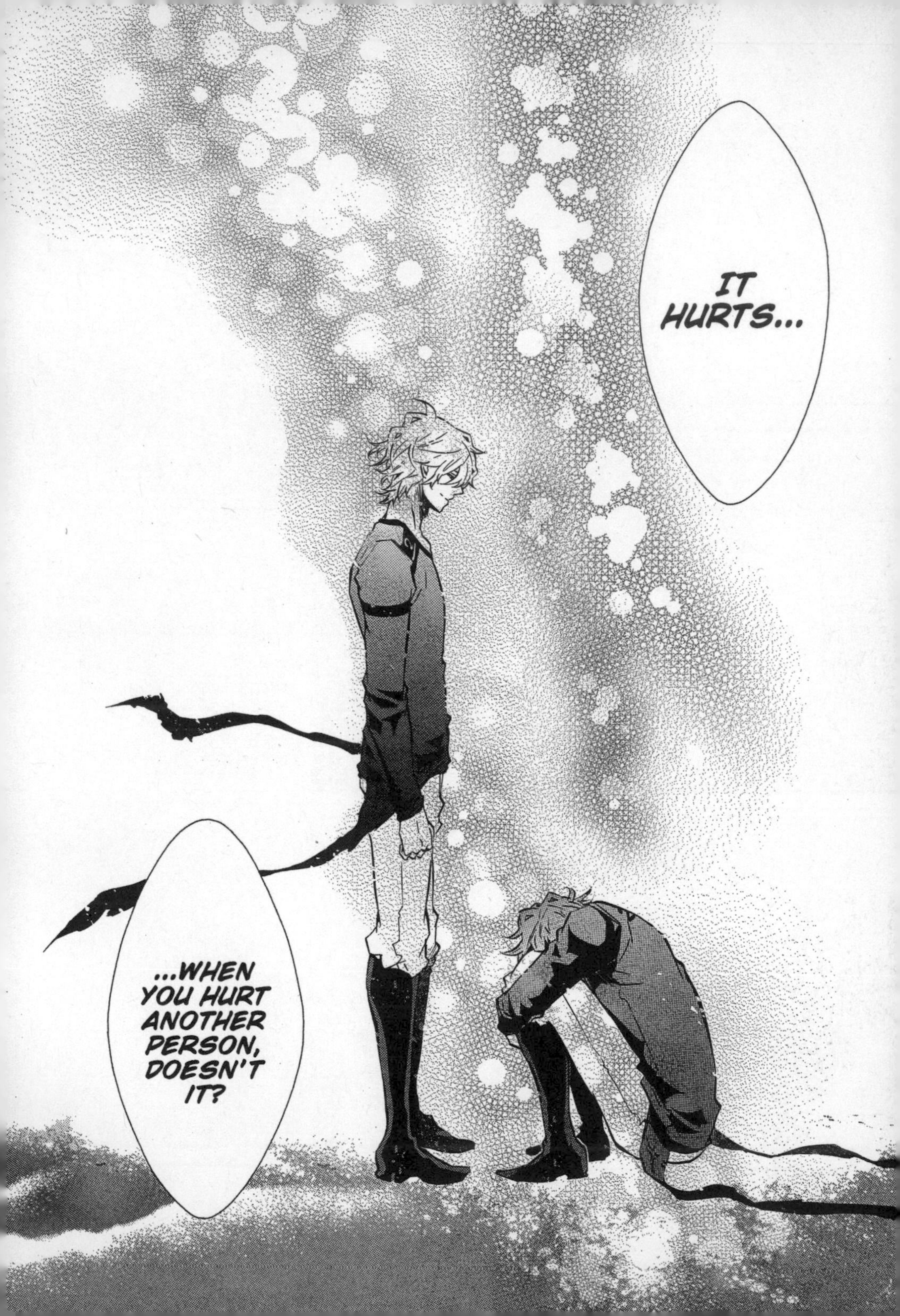
IT HURTS...
...WHEN YOU HURT ANOTHER PERSON, DOESN'T IT?

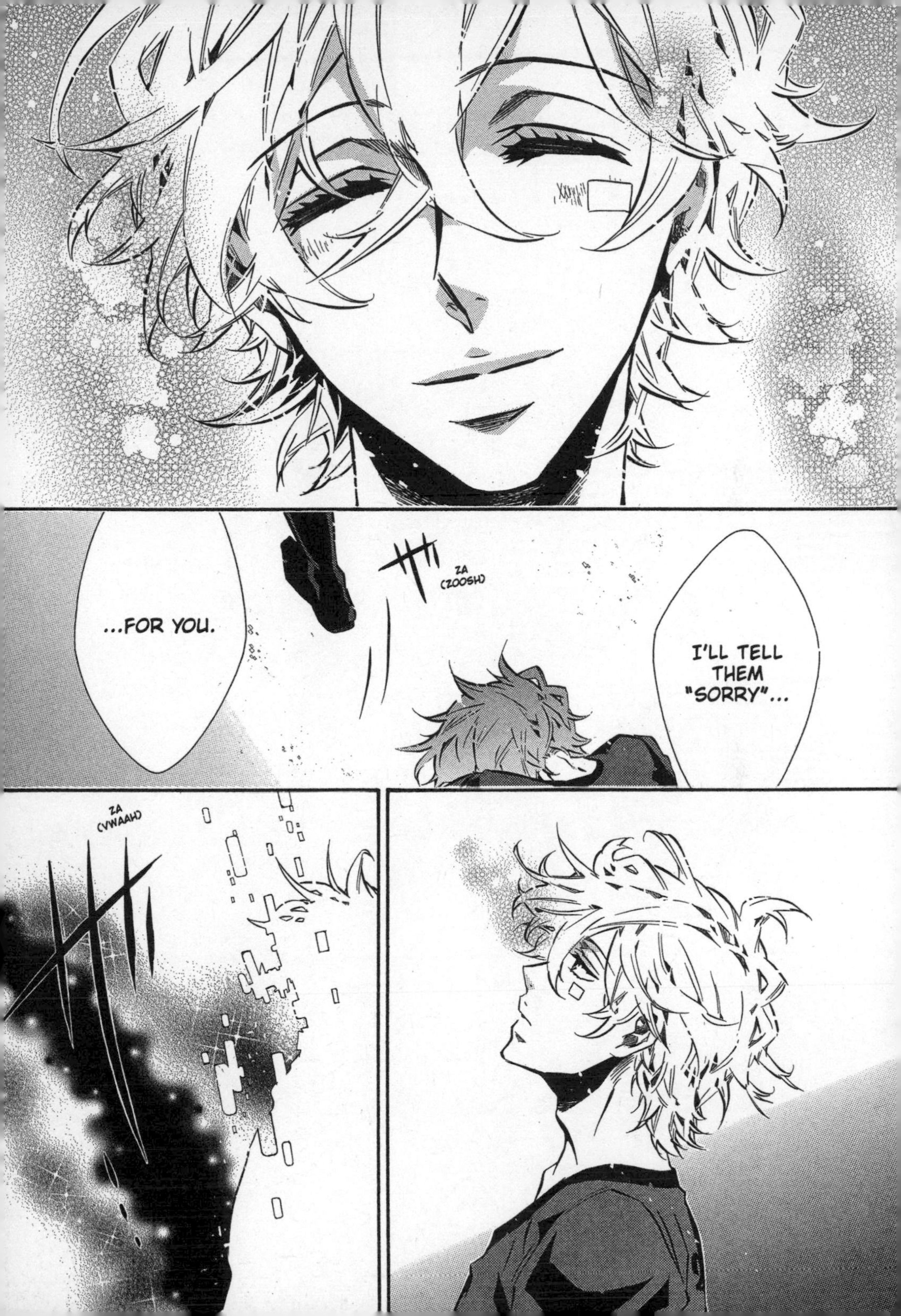
I'LL TELL THEM "SORRY"...
ZA (ZOOSH)
...FOR YOU.
ZA (VWAAH)

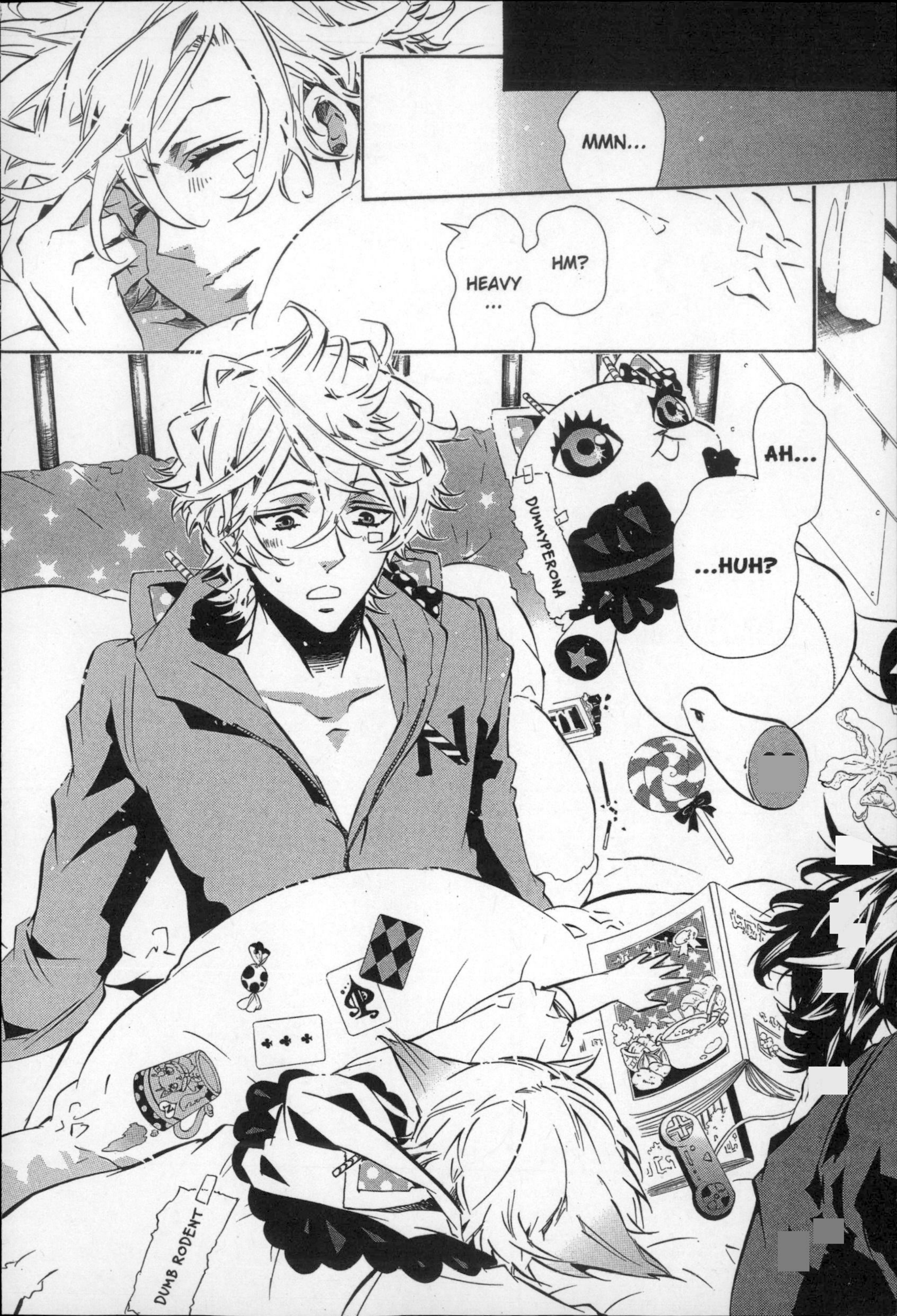
MMN...
HM?
HEAVY ...
AH...
...HUH?
DUMMYPERONA
DUMB RODENT

KARNEVAL

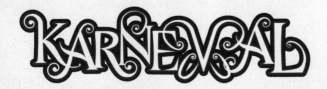

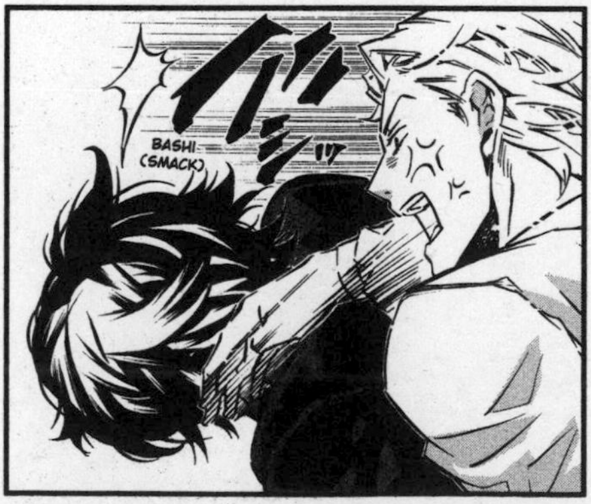
BASHI
(SMACK)
!?

KARNEVAL

Score 65: Message

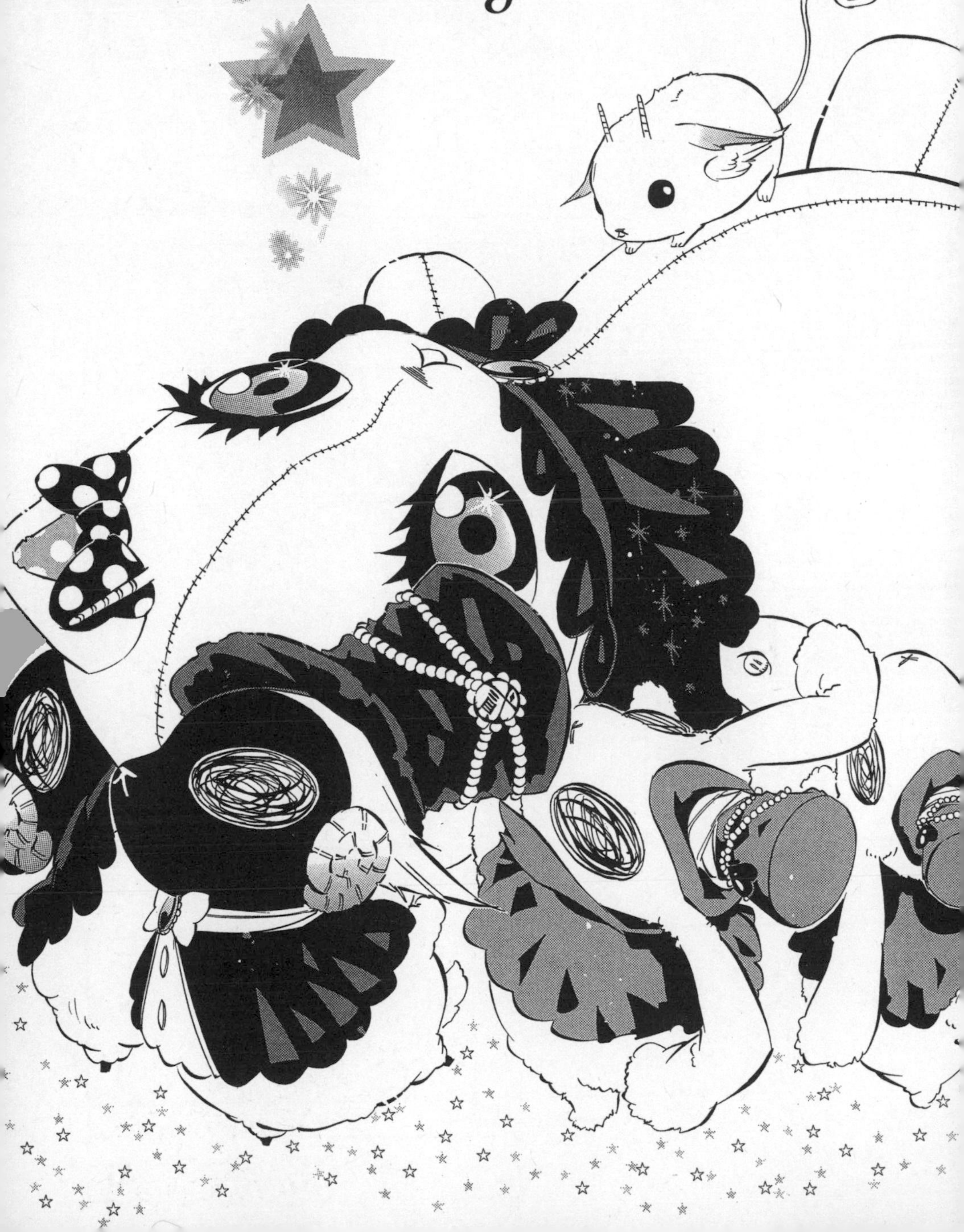

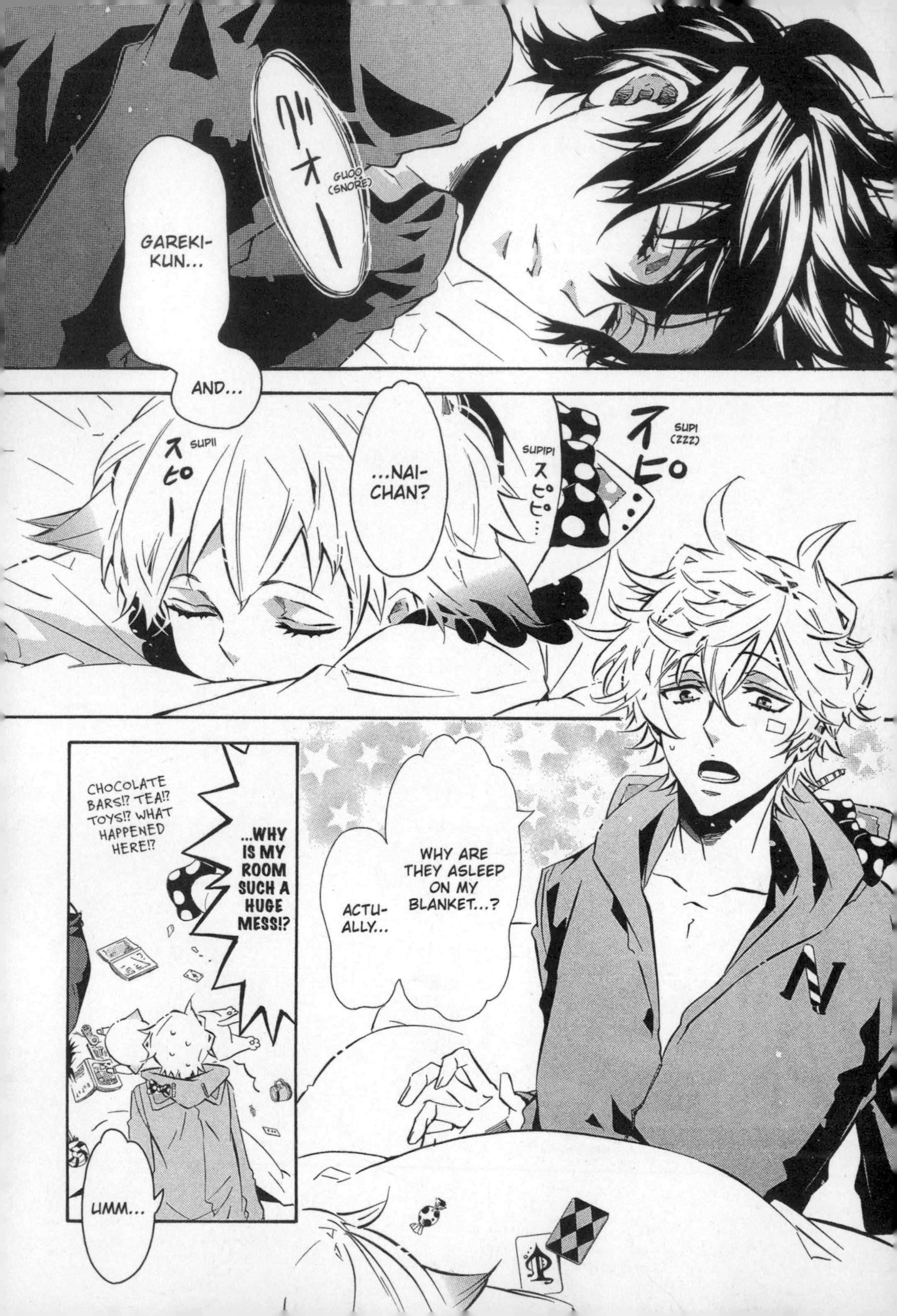

グォー
GUOO (SNORE)
GAREKI-KUN...
AND...
スピ
SUPI (ZZZ)
スピピ...
SUPIPI
...NAI-CHAN?
スピー
SUPII
WHY ARE THEY ASLEEP ON MY BLANKET...?
ACTU-ALLY...
...WHY IS MY ROOM SUCH A HUGE MESS!?
CHOCOLATE BARS!? TEA!? TOYS!? WHAT HAPPENED HERE!?
UMM...

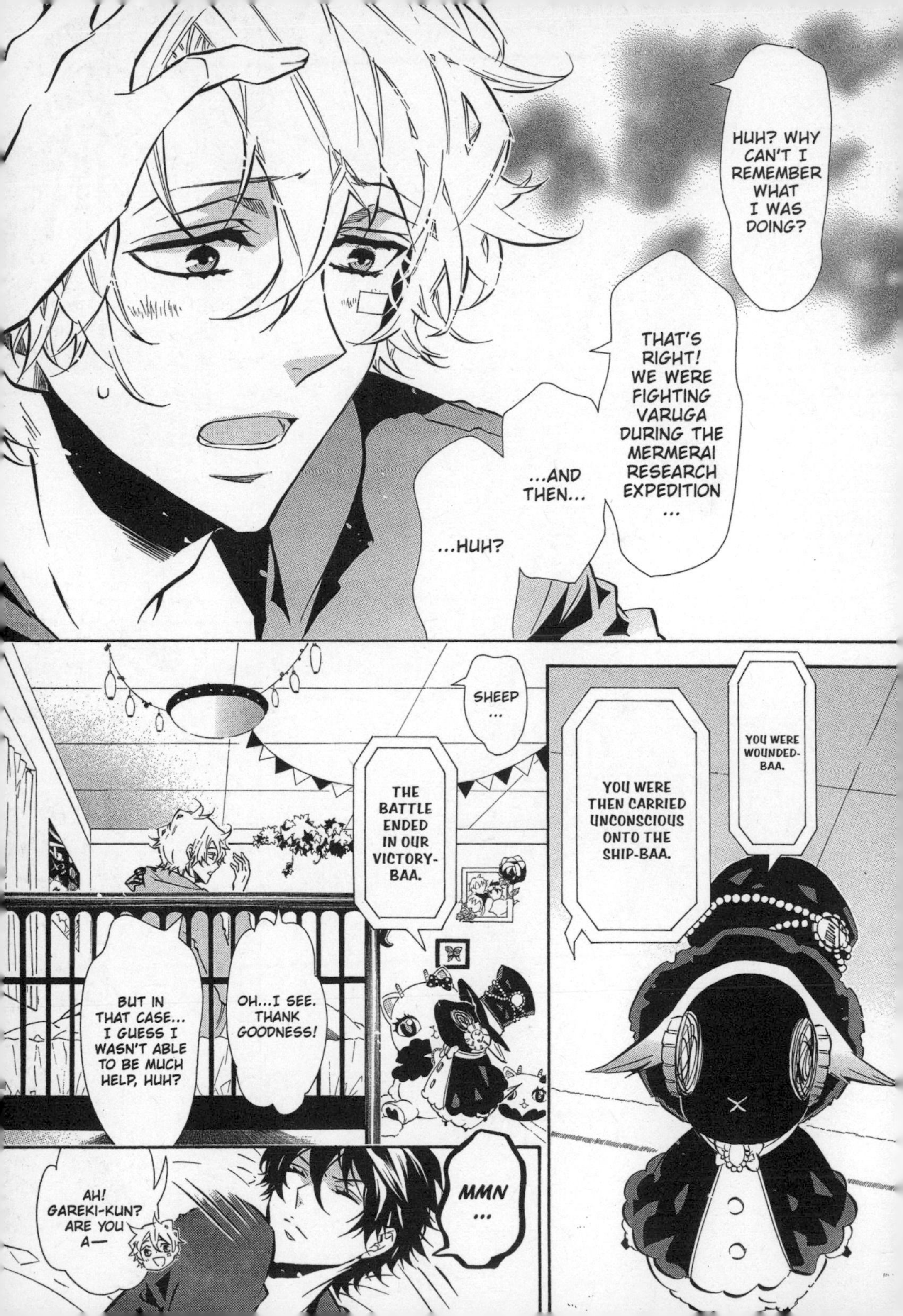
HUH? WHY CAN'T I REMEMBER WHAT I WAS DOING?
THAT'S RIGHT! WE WERE FIGHTING VARUGA DURING THE MERMERAI RESEARCH EXPEDITION...
...AND THEN...
...HUH?
YOU WERE WOUNDED-BAA.
YOU WERE THEN CARRIED UNCONSCIOUS ONTO THE SHIP-BAA.
SHEEP...
THE BATTLE ENDED IN OUR VICTORY-BAA.
OH...I SEE. THANK GOODNESS!
BUT IN THAT CASE... I GUESS I WASN'T ABLE TO BE MUCH HELP, HUH?
MMN...
AH! GAREKI-KUN? ARE YOU A—

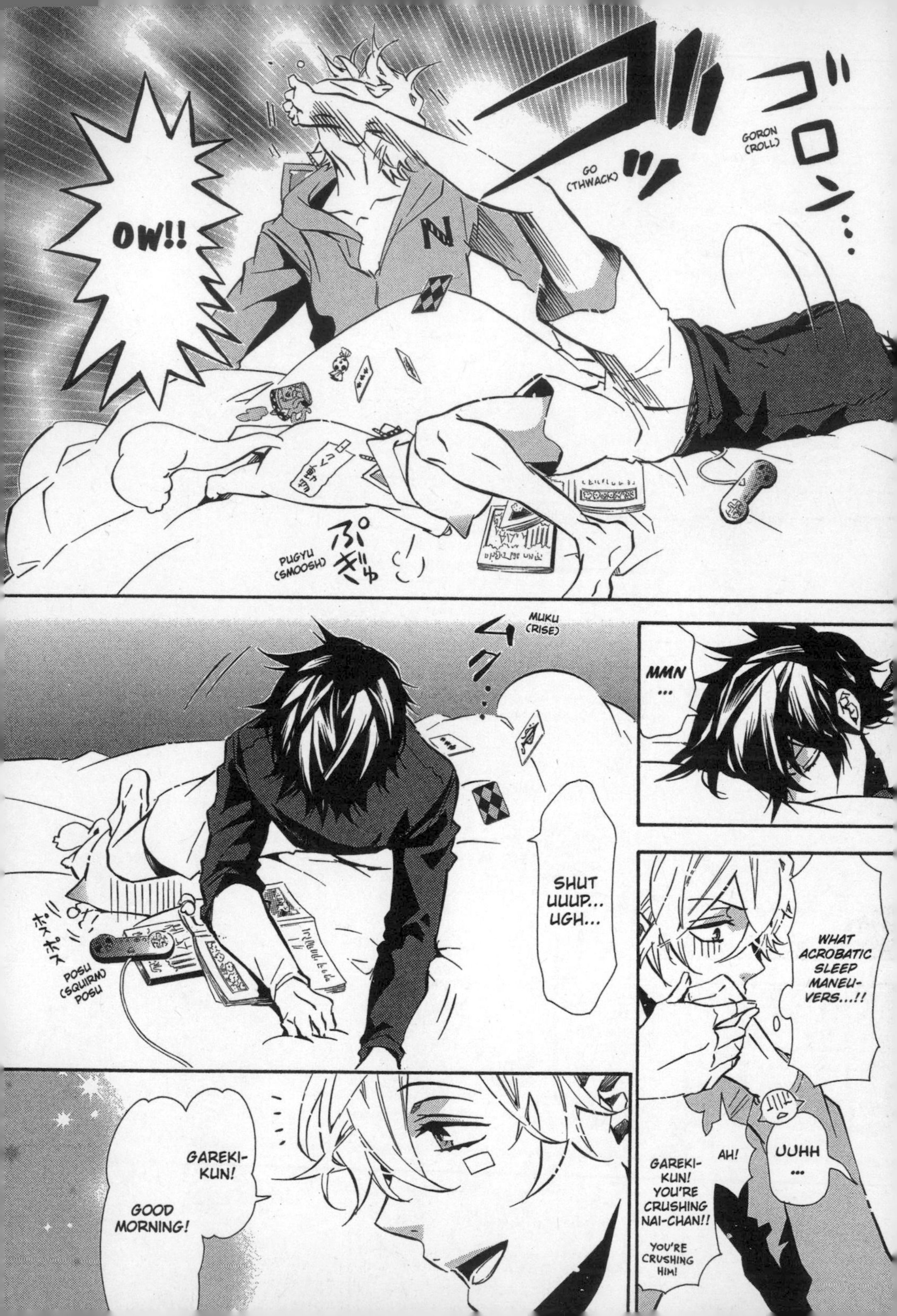
ゴロン…
GORON (ROLL)
ゴッ
GO (THWACK)
OW!!
ぷぎゅ
PUGYU (SMOOSH)
MMN …
ムク…
MUKU (RISE)
SHUT UUUP… UGH…
ポスポス
POSU (SQUIRM) POSU
WHAT ACROBATIC SLEEP MANEU- VERS…!!
UUHH …
AH!
GAREKI- KUN! YOU'RE CRUSHING NAI-CHAN!!
YOU'RE CRUSHING HIM!
GAREKI- KUN!
GOOD MORNING!

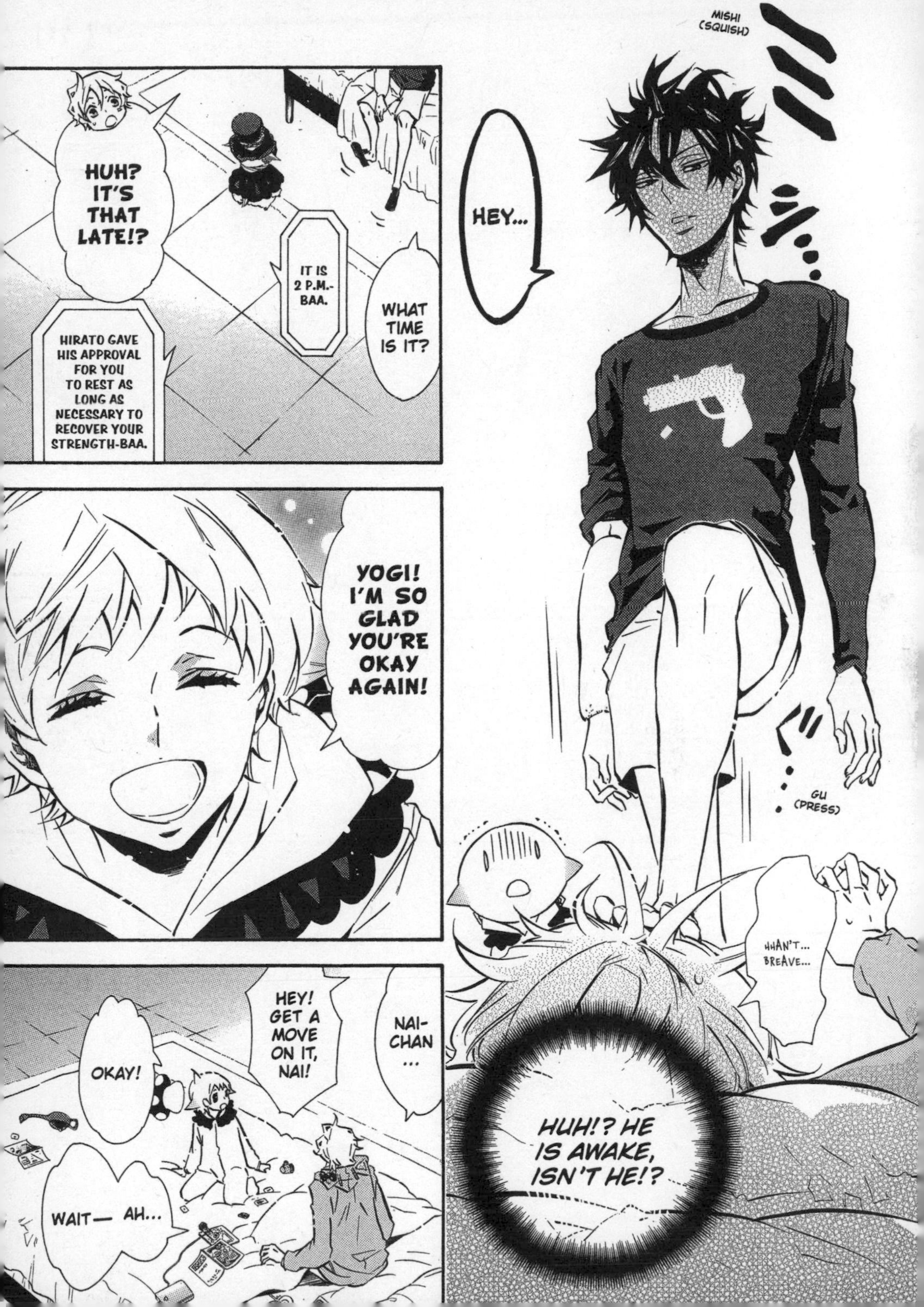
MISHI (SQUISH)
HEY...
GU (PRESS)
HHAN'T... BREAVE...
HUH!? HE IS AWAKE, ISN'T HE!?
WHAT TIME IS IT?
IT IS 2 P.M.-BAA.
HUH? IT'S THAT LATE!?
HIRATO GAVE HIS APPROVAL FOR YOU TO REST AS LONG AS NECESSARY TO RECOVER YOUR STRENGTH-BAA.
YOGI! I'M SO GLAD YOU'RE OKAY AGAIN!
NAI-CHAN...
HEY! GET A MOVE ON IT, NAI!
OKAY!
WAIT— AH...

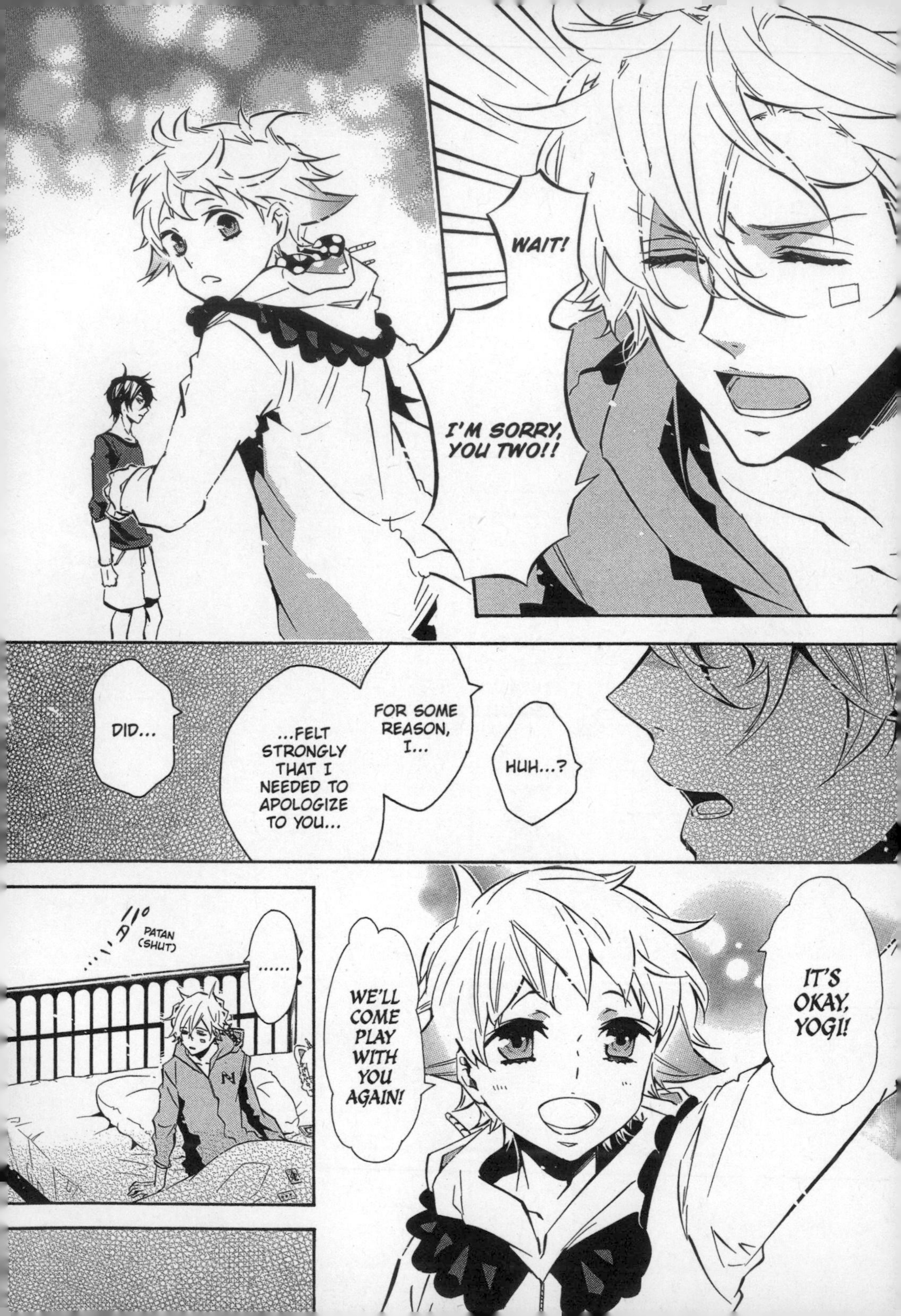
WAIT!
I'M SORRY, YOU TWO!!
HUH...?
FOR SOME REASON, I...
...FELT STRONGLY THAT I NEEDED TO APOLOGIZE TO YOU...
DID...
IT'S OKAY, YOGI!
WE'LL COME PLAY WITH YOU AGAIN!
......
PATAN (SHUT)

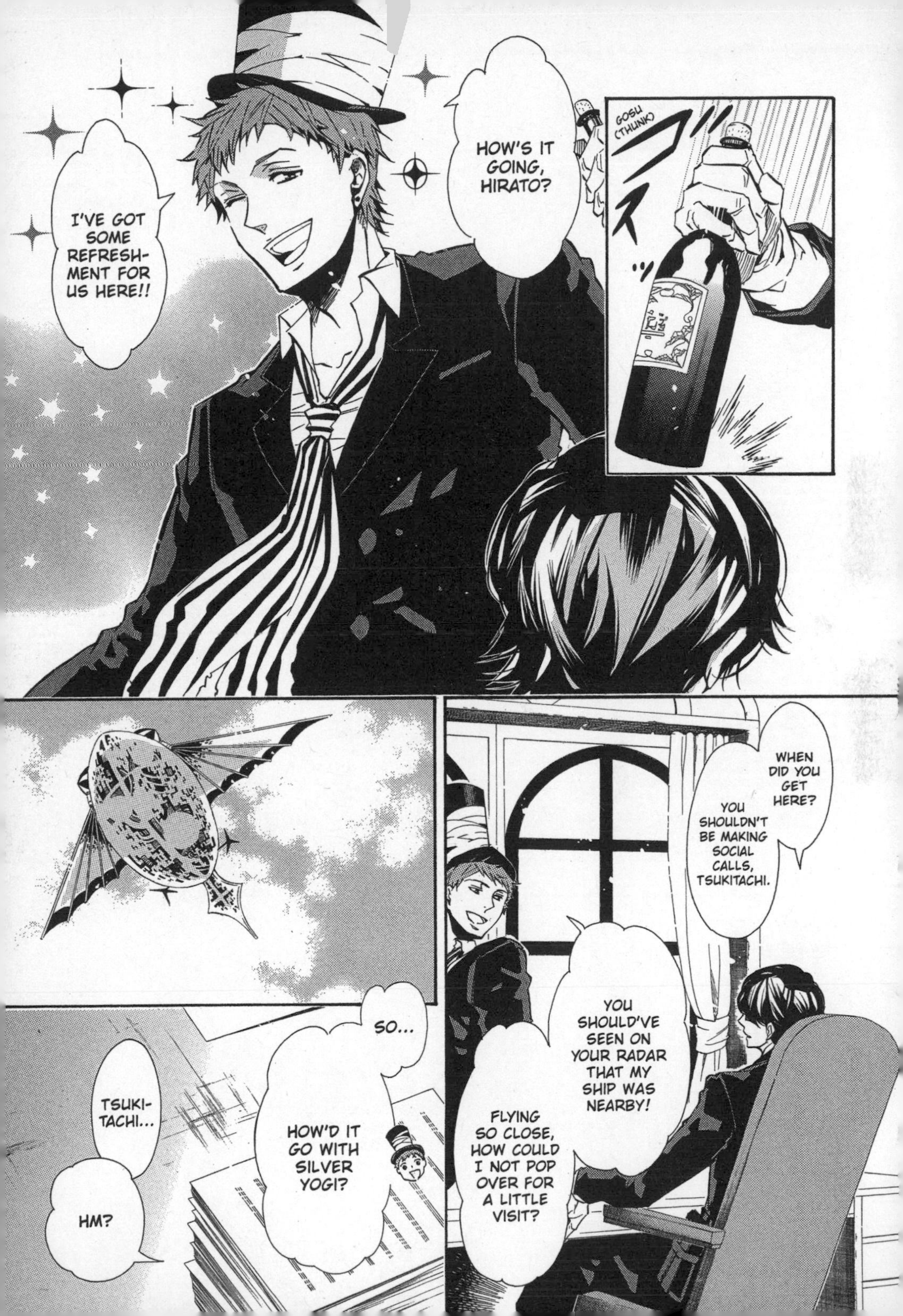
GOSU (THUNK)
HOW'S IT GOING, HIRATO?
I'VE GOT SOME REFRESH-MENT FOR US HERE!!
WHEN DID YOU GET HERE?
YOU SHOULDN'T BE MAKING SOCIAL CALLS, TSUKITACHI.
YOU SHOULD'VE SEEN ON YOUR RADAR THAT MY SHIP WAS NEARBY!
FLYING SO CLOSE, HOW COULD I NOT POP OVER FOR A LITTLE VISIT?
SO...
HOW'D IT GO WITH SILVER YOGI?
TSUKI-TACHI...
HM?

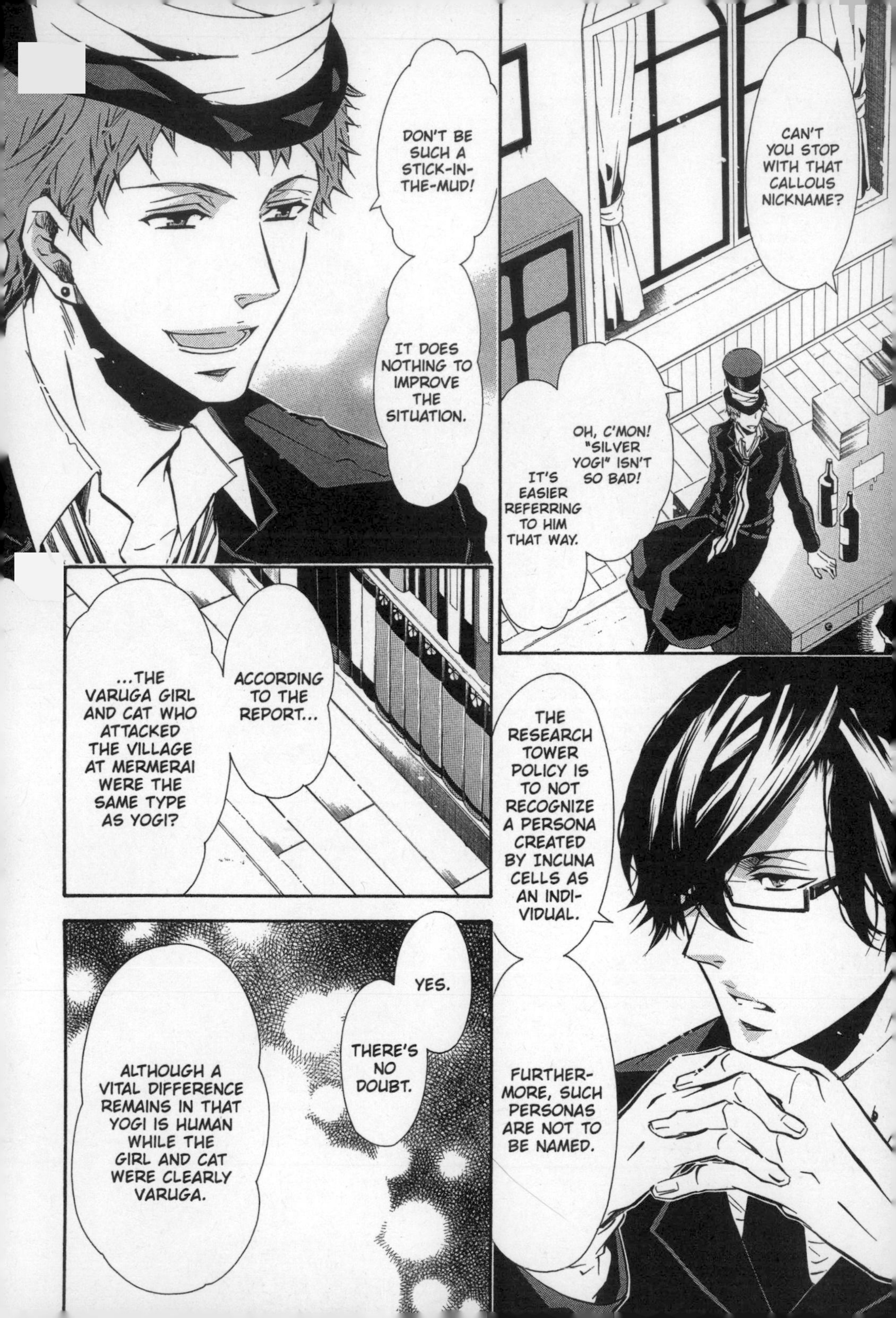
CAN'T YOU STOP WITH THAT CALLOUS NICKNAME?
OH, C'MON! "SILVER YOGI" ISN'T SO BAD!
IT'S EASIER REFERRING TO HIM THAT WAY.
DON'T BE SUCH A STICK-IN-THE-MUD!
IT DOES NOTHING TO IMPROVE THE SITUATION.
THE RESEARCH TOWER POLICY IS TO NOT RECOGNIZE A PERSONA CREATED BY INCUNA CELLS AS AN INDI-VIDUAL.
FURTHER-MORE, SUCH PERSONAS ARE NOT TO BE NAMED.
ACCORDING TO THE REPORT...
...THE VARUGA GIRL AND CAT WHO ATTACKED THE VILLAGE AT MERMERAI WERE THE SAME TYPE AS YOGI?
YES.
THERE'S NO DOUBT.
ALTHOUGH A VITAL DIFFERENCE REMAINS IN THAT YOGI IS HUMAN WHILE THE GIRL AND CAT WERE CLEARLY VARUGA.

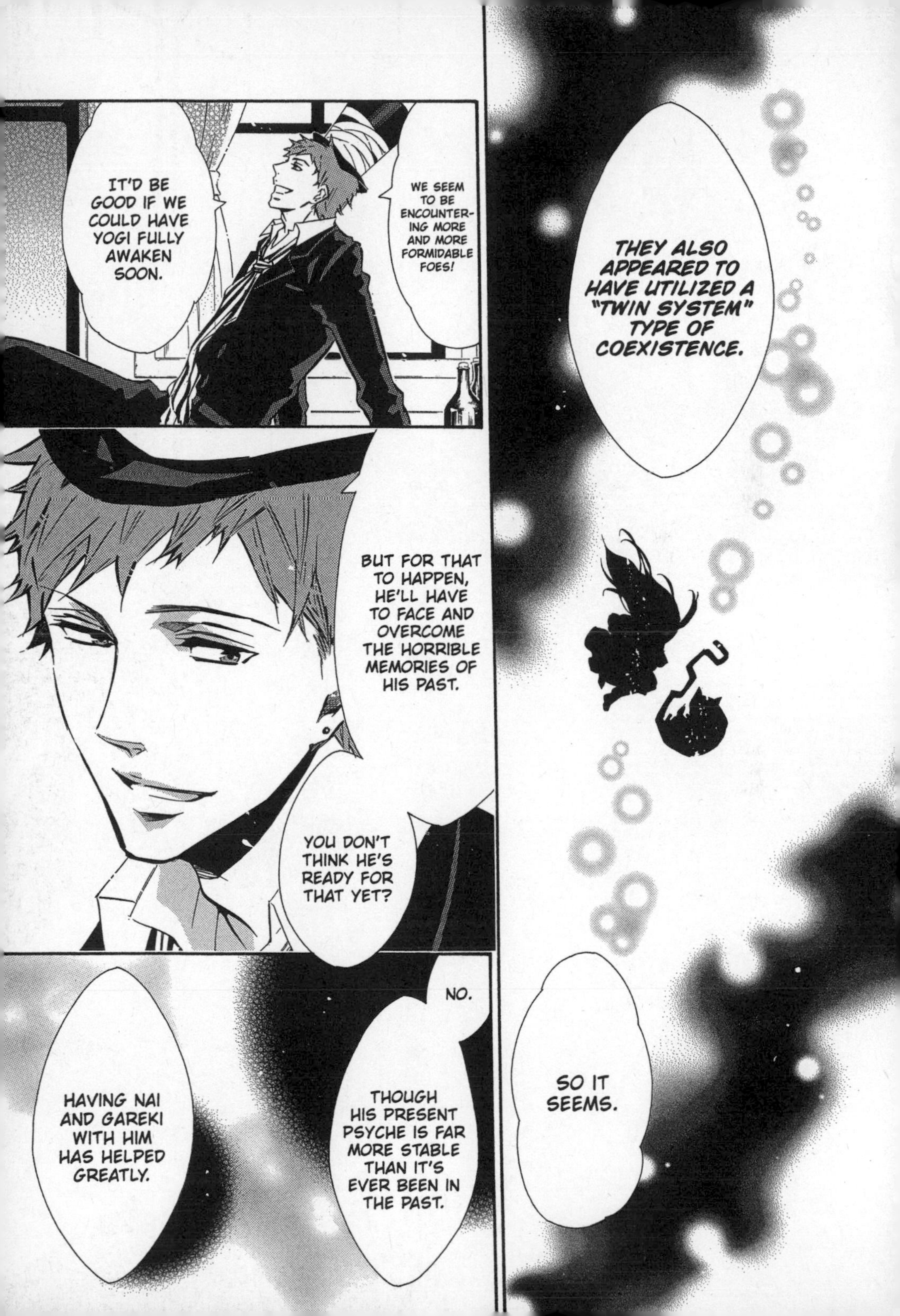
THEY ALSO APPEARED TO HAVE UTILIZED A "TWIN SYSTEM" TYPE OF COEXISTENCE.
SO IT SEEMS.
WE SEEM TO BE ENCOUNTERING MORE AND MORE FORMIDABLE FOES!
IT'D BE GOOD IF WE COULD HAVE YOGI FULLY AWAKEN SOON.
BUT FOR THAT TO HAPPEN, HE'LL HAVE TO FACE AND OVERCOME THE HORRIBLE MEMORIES OF HIS PAST.
YOU DON'T THINK HE'S READY FOR THAT YET?
NO.
THOUGH HIS PRESENT PSYCHE IS FAR MORE STABLE THAN IT'S EVER BEEN IN THE PAST.
HAVING NAI AND GAREKI WITH HIM HAS HELPED GREATLY.

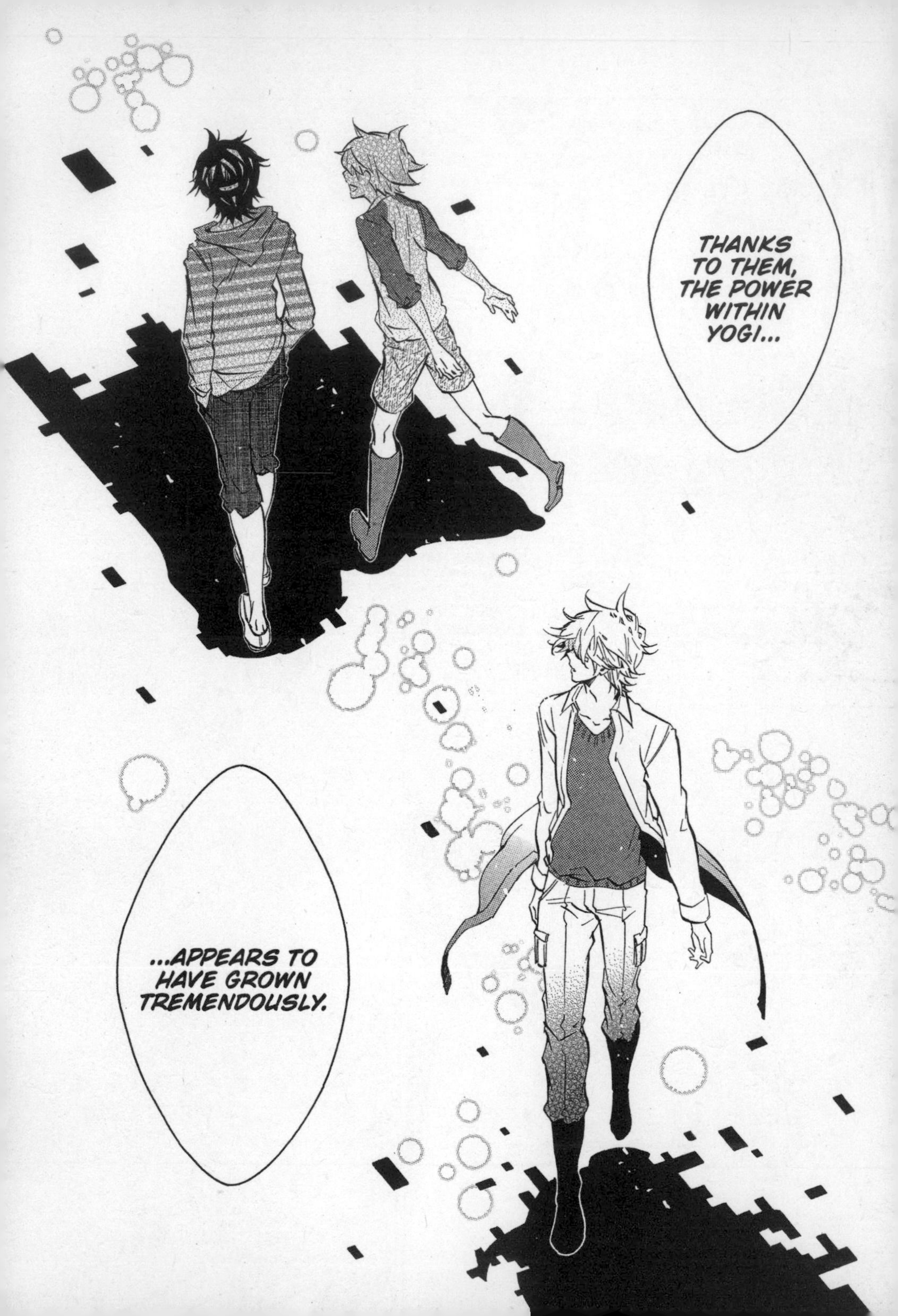
THANKS TO THEM, THE POWER WITHIN YOGI...
...APPEARS TO HAVE GROWN TREMENDOUSLY.

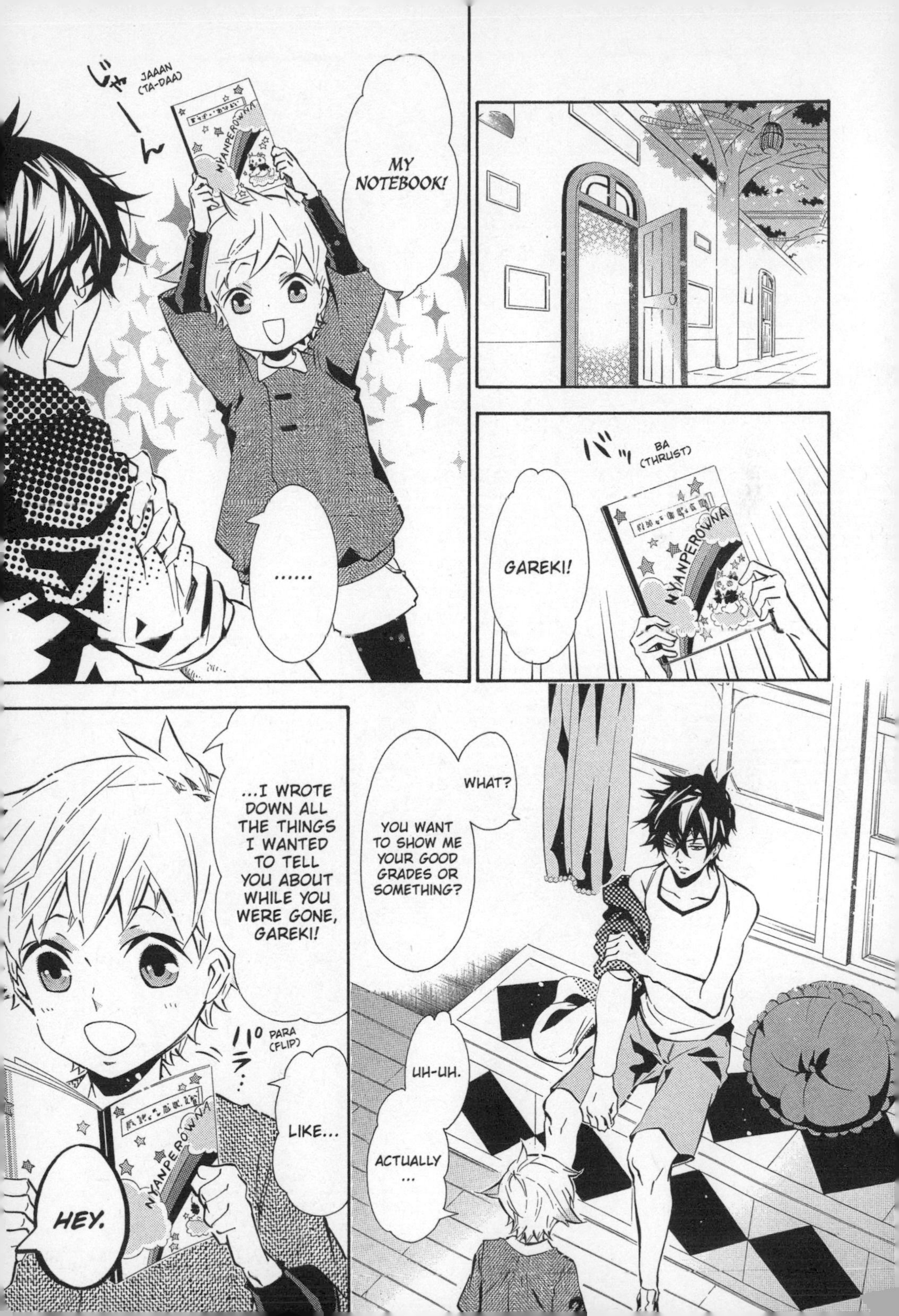
バッ
BA (THRUST)
GAREKI!
NYANPEROWNA
じゃーん
JAAAN (TA-DAA)
MY NOTEBOOK!
NYANPEROWNA
......
WHAT?
YOU WANT TO SHOW ME YOUR GOOD GRADES OR SOMETHING?
UH-UH.
ACTUALLY ...
...I WROTE DOWN ALL THE THINGS I WANTED TO TELL YOU ABOUT WHILE YOU WERE GONE, GAREKI!
パラ
PARA (FLIP)
LIKE...
NYANPEROWNA
HEY.

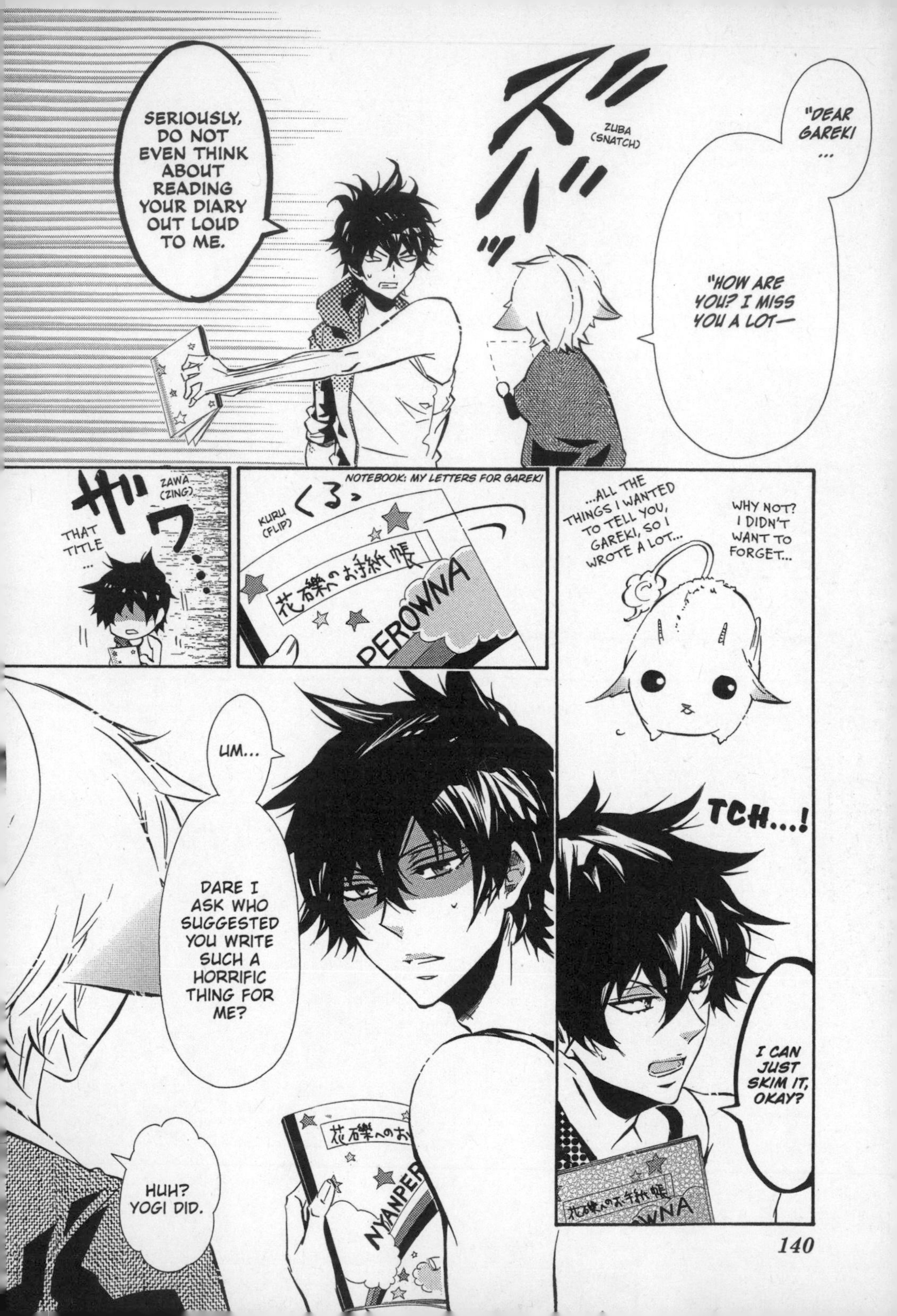
"DEAR GAREKI...
"HOW ARE YOU? I MISS YOU A LOT—
ZUBA (SNATCH)
SERIOUSLY, DO NOT EVEN THINK ABOUT READING YOUR DIARY OUT LOUD TO ME.
WHY NOT? I DIDN'T WANT TO FORGET...
...ALL THE THINGS I WANTED TO TELL YOU, GAREKI, SO I WROTE A LOT...
TCH...!
I CAN JUST SKIM IT, OKAY?
NOTEBOOK: MY LETTERS FOR GAREKI
KURU (FLIP)
くるっ
花礫へのお手紙帳
PEROWNA
ZAWA (ZING)
ザワ
THAT TITLE...
UM...
DARE I ASK WHO SUGGESTED YOU WRITE SUCH A HORRIFIC THING FOR ME?
HUH? YOGI DID.
NYANPER

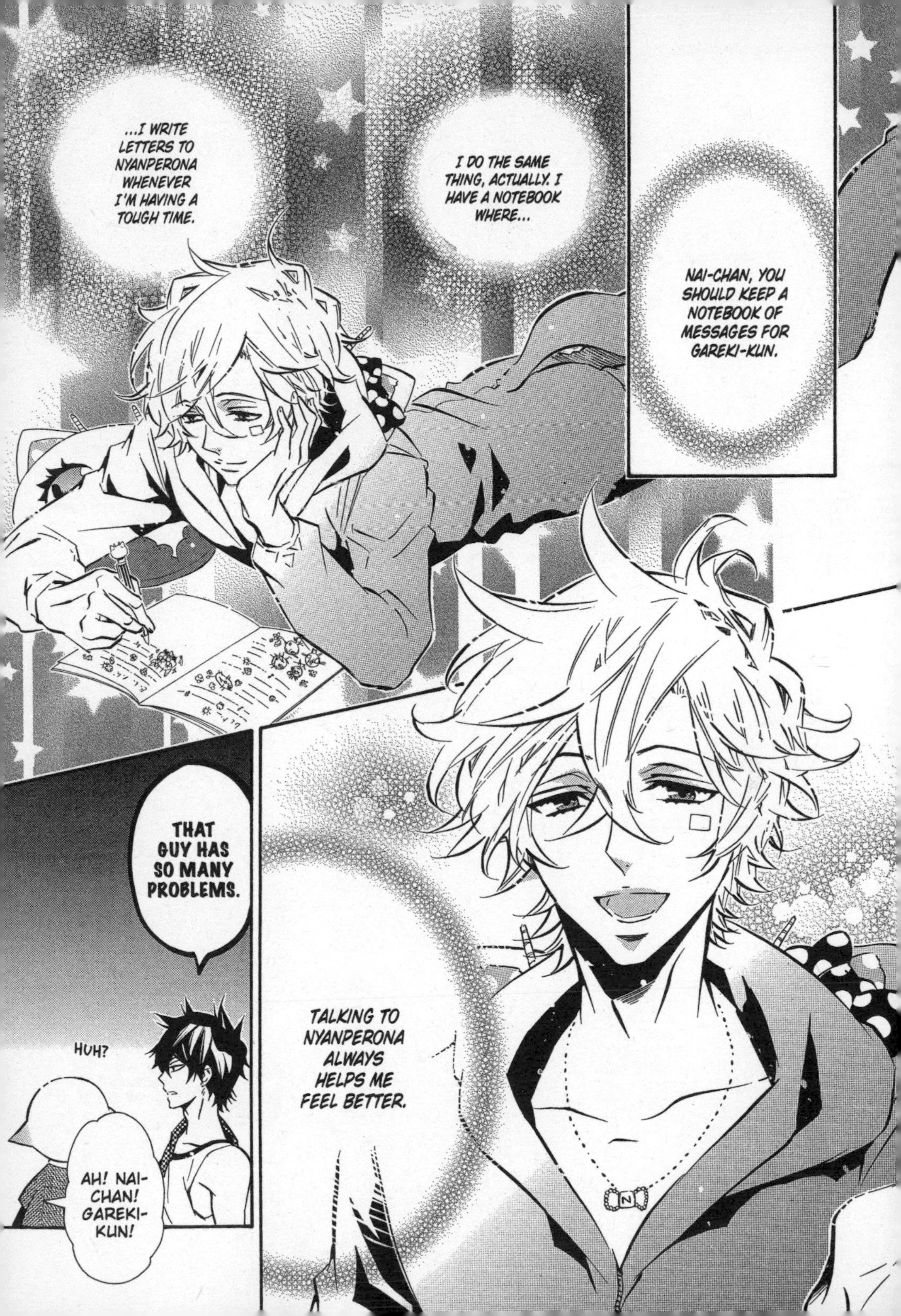
...I WRITE LETTERS TO NYANPERONA WHENEVER I'M HAVING A TOUGH TIME.
I DO THE SAME THING, ACTUALLY. I HAVE A NOTEBOOK WHERE...
NAI-CHAN, YOU SHOULD KEEP A NOTEBOOK OF MESSAGES FOR GAREKI-KUN.
TALKING TO NYANPERONA ALWAYS HELPS ME FEEL BETTER.
THAT GUY HAS SO MANY PROBLEMS.
HUH?
AH! NAI-CHAN! GAREKI-KUN!

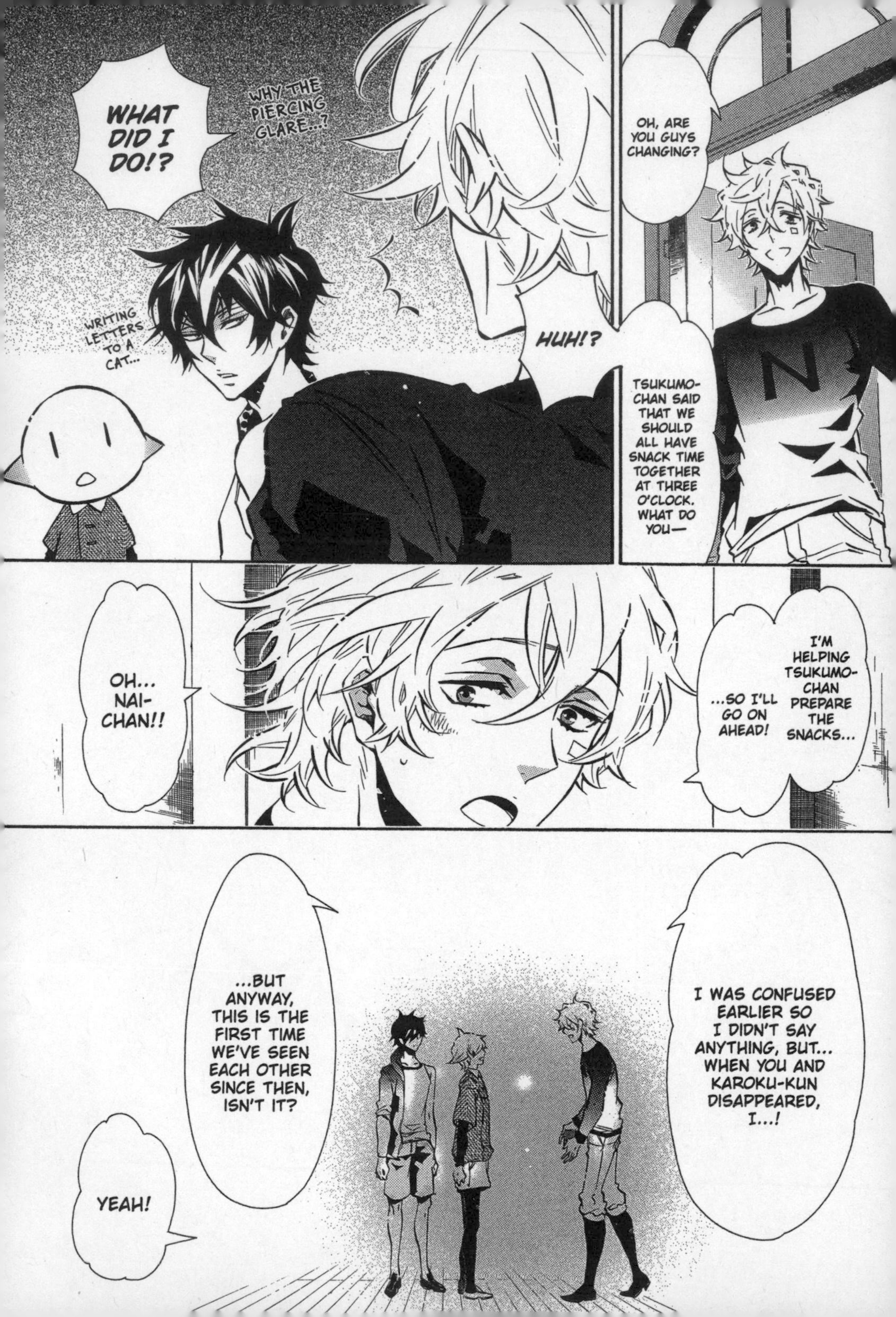
OH, ARE YOU GUYS CHANGING?
TSUKUMO-CHAN SAID THAT WE SHOULD ALL HAVE SNACK TIME TOGETHER AT THREE O'CLOCK. WHAT DO YOU—
HUH!?
WHY THE PIERCING GLARE...?
WHAT DID I DO!?
WRITING LETTERS TO A CAT...
I'M HELPING TSUKUMO-CHAN PREPARE THE SNACKS...
...SO I'LL GO ON AHEAD!
OH... NAI-CHAN!!
I WAS CONFUSED EARLIER SO I DIDN'T SAY ANYTHING, BUT... WHEN YOU AND KAROKU-KUN DISAPPEARED, I...!
...BUT ANYWAY, THIS IS THE FIRST TIME WE'VE SEEN EACH OTHER SINCE THEN, ISN'T IT?
YEAH!

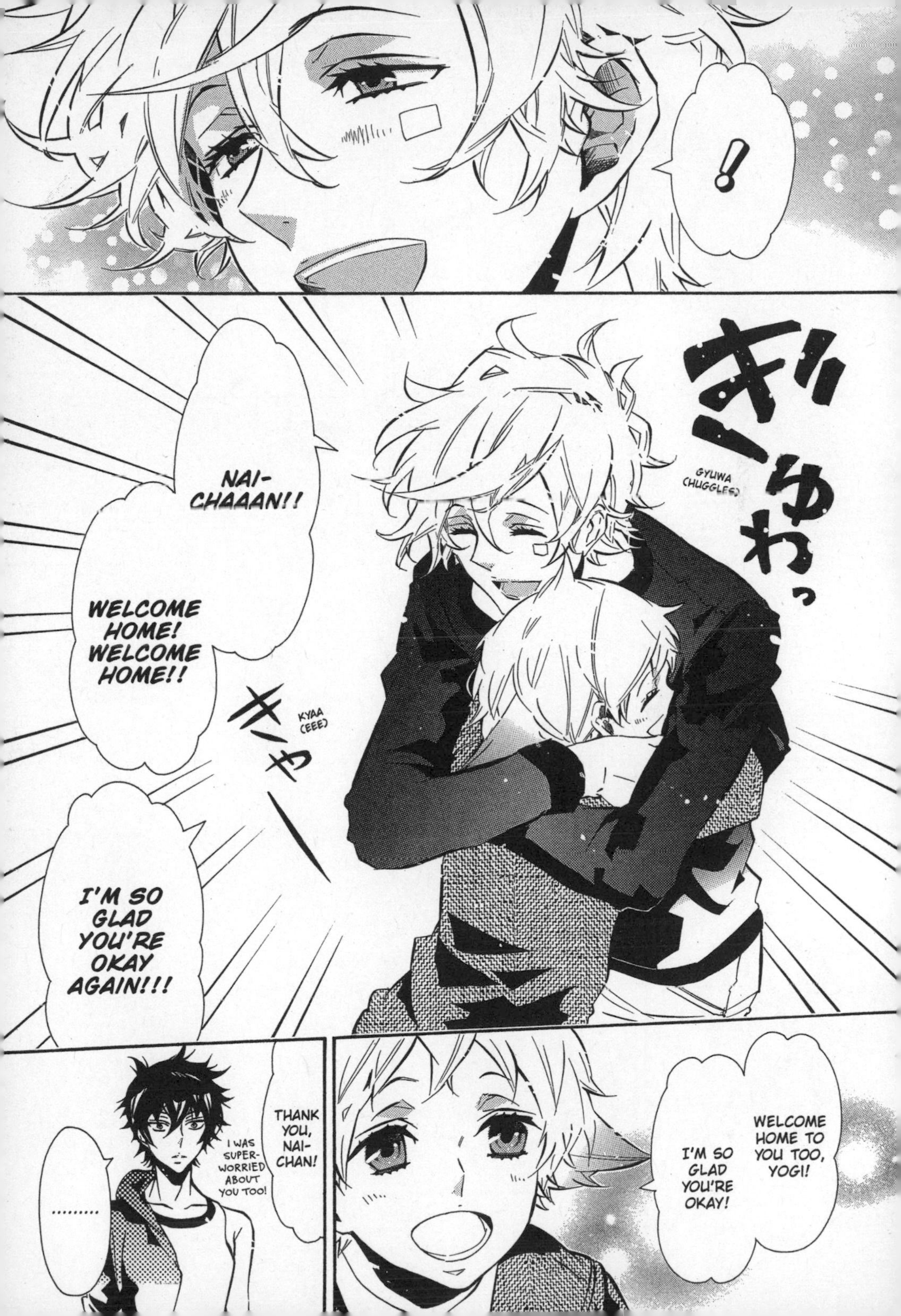
!
ぎゅわっ
GYUWA (HUGGLES)
NAI-CHAAAN!!
WELCOME HOME! WELCOME HOME!!
キャ
KYAA (EEE)
I'M SO GLAD YOU'RE OKAY AGAIN!!!
WELCOME HOME TO YOU TOO, YOGI!
I'M SO GLAD YOU'RE OKAY!
THANK YOU, NAI-CHAN!
I WAS SUPER-WORRIED ABOUT YOU TOO!
....

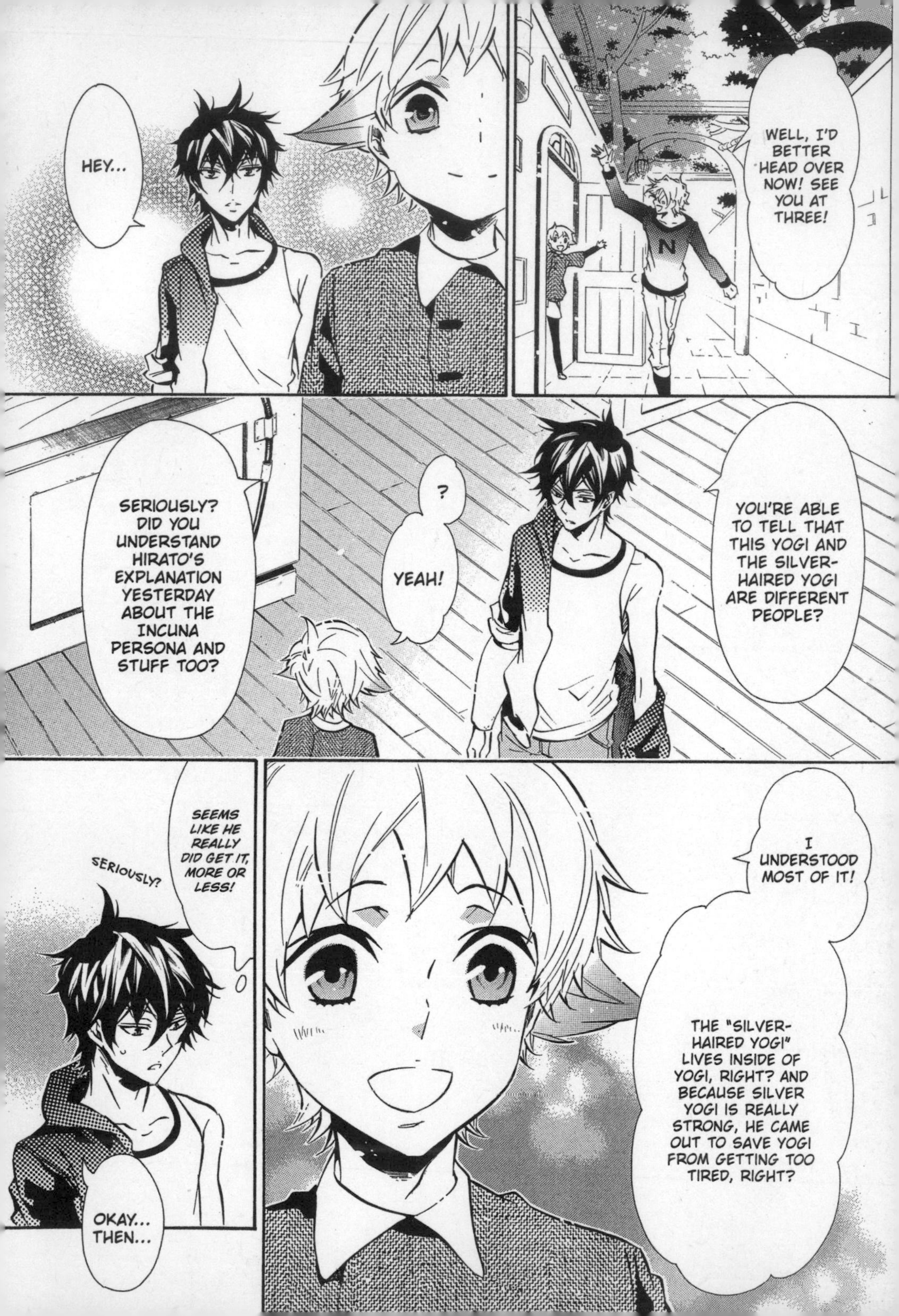
WELL, I'D BETTER HEAD OVER NOW! SEE YOU AT THREE!
HEY...
YOU'RE ABLE TO TELL THAT THIS YOGI AND THE SILVER-HAIRED YOGI ARE DIFFERENT PEOPLE?
?
YEAH!
SERIOUSLY? DID YOU UNDERSTAND HIRATO'S EXPLANATION YESTERDAY ABOUT THE INCUNA PERSONA AND STUFF TOO?
I UNDERSTOOD MOST OF IT!
THE "SILVER-HAIRED YOGI" LIVES INSIDE OF YOGI, RIGHT? AND BECAUSE SILVER YOGI IS REALLY STRONG, HE CAME OUT TO SAVE YOGI FROM GETTING TOO TIRED, RIGHT?
SEEMS LIKE HE REALLY DID GET IT, MORE OR LESS!
SERIOUSLY?
OKAY... THEN...

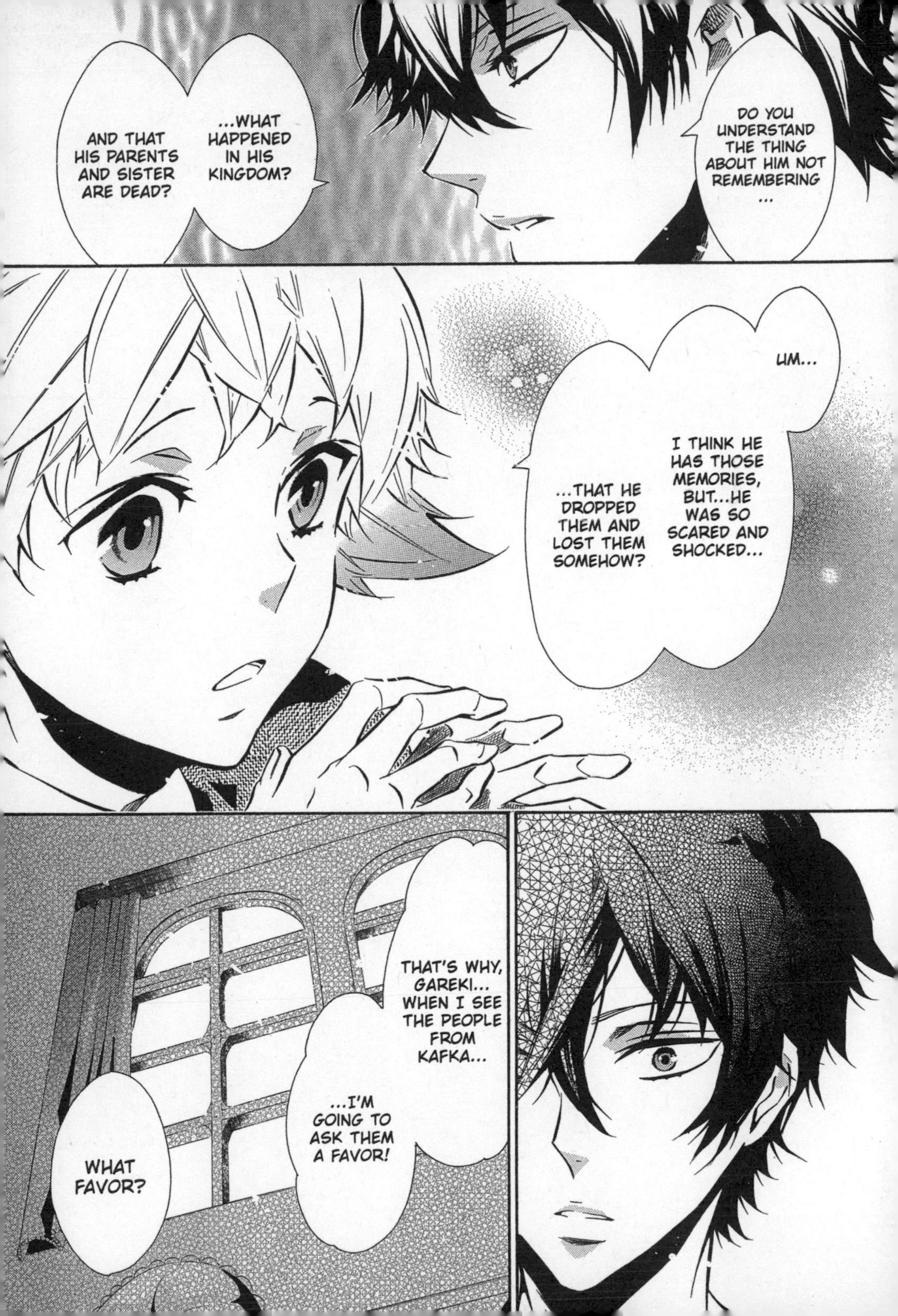
DO YOU UNDERSTAND THE THING ABOUT HIM NOT REMEMBERING ...
...WHAT HAPPENED IN HIS KINGDOM?
AND THAT HIS PARENTS AND SISTER ARE DEAD?
UM...
I THINK HE HAS THOSE MEMORIES, BUT...HE WAS SO SCARED AND SHOCKED...
...THAT HE DROPPED THEM AND LOST THEM SOMEHOW?
THAT'S WHY, GAREKI... WHEN I SEE THE PEOPLE FROM KAFKA...
...I'M GOING TO ASK THEM A FAVOR!
WHAT FAVOR?

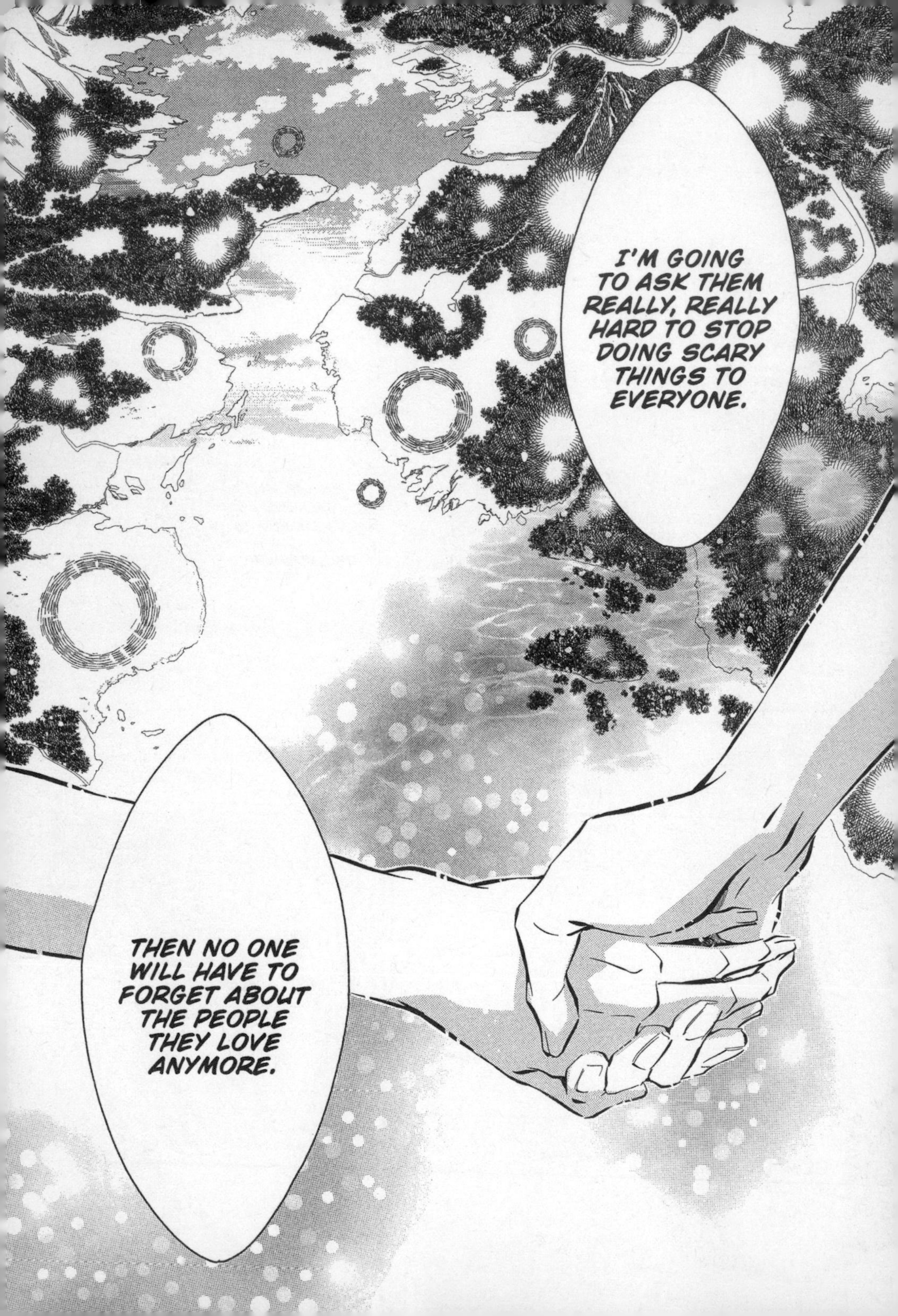
I'M GOING TO ASK THEM REALLY, REALLY HARD TO STOP DOING SCARY THINGS TO EVERYONE.
THEN NO ONE WILL HAVE TO FORGET ABOUT THE PEOPLE THEY LOVE ANYMORE.

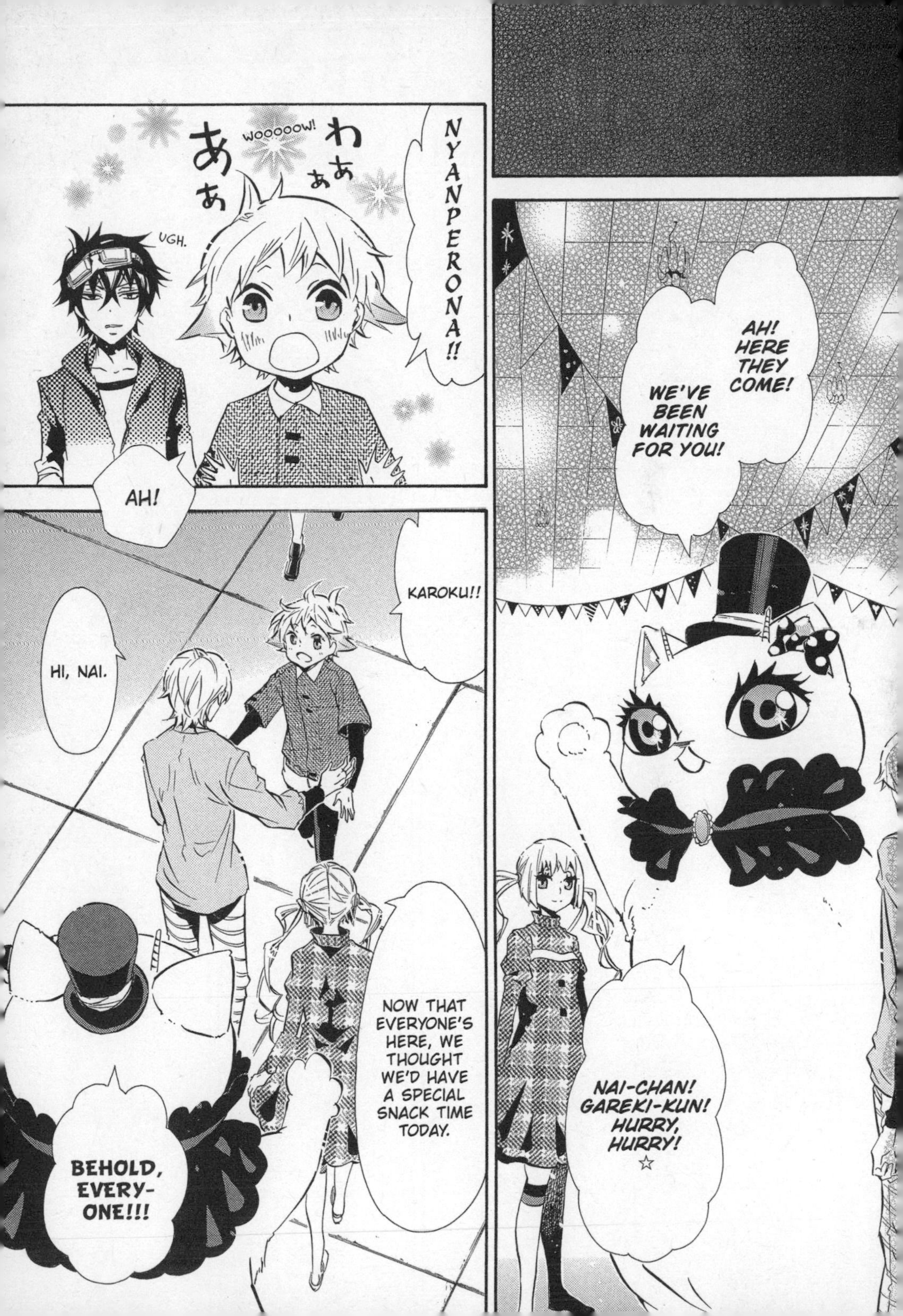
AH! HERE THEY COME!
WE'VE BEEN WAITING FOR YOU!
NAI-CHAN! GAREKI-KUN! HURRY, HURRY! ☆
NYANPERONA!!
わぁぁ
WOOOOOW!
あぁ
UGH.
AH!
KAROKU!!
HI, NAI.
NOW THAT EVERYONE'S HERE, WE THOUGHT WE'D HAVE A SPECIAL SNACK TIME TODAY.
BEHOLD, EVERY-ONE!!!

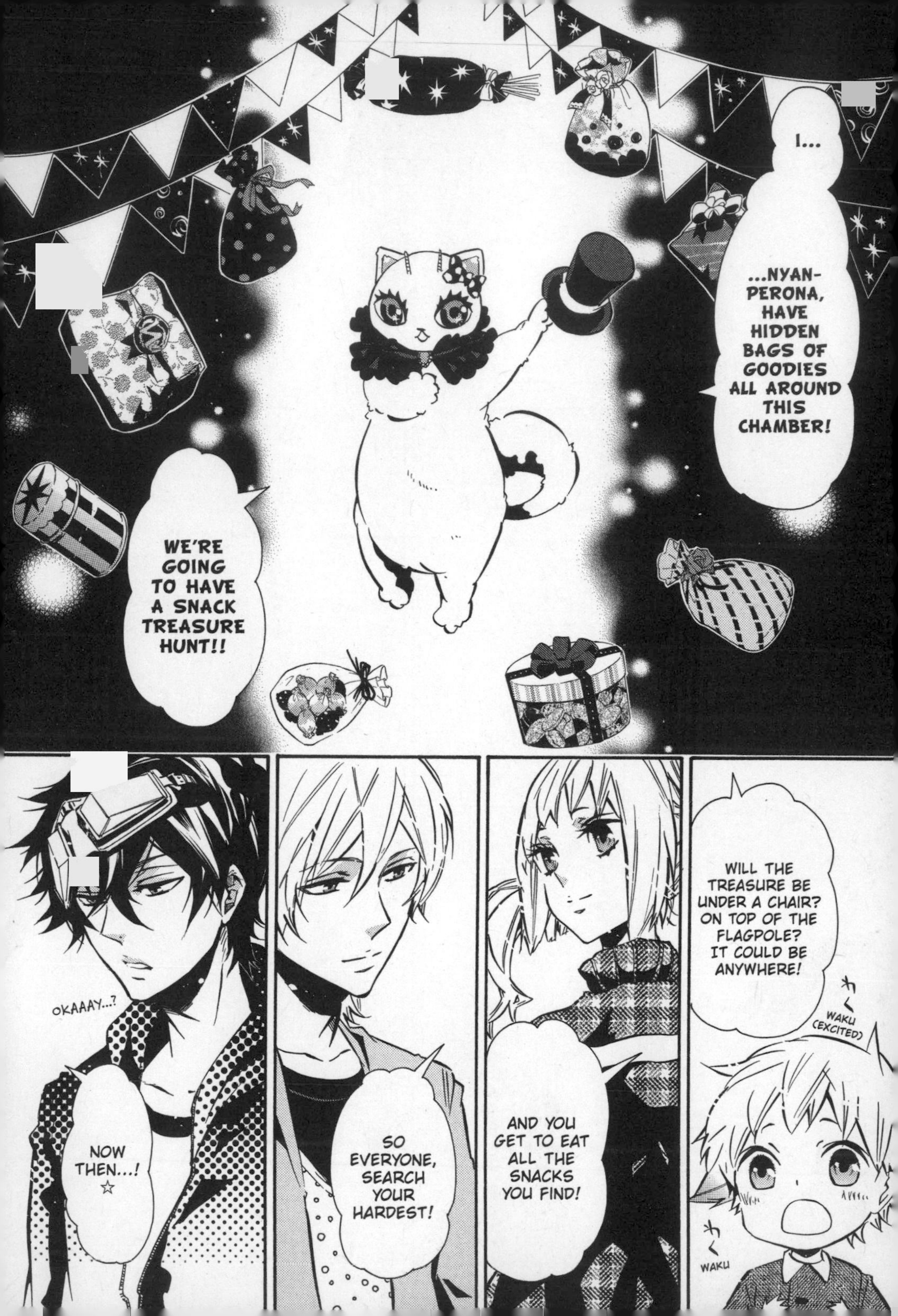
I...
...NYAN-PERONA, HAVE HIDDEN BAGS OF GOODIES ALL AROUND THIS CHAMBER!
WE'RE GOING TO HAVE A SNACK TREASURE HUNT!!
WILL THE TREASURE BE UNDER A CHAIR? ON TOP OF THE FLAGPOLE? IT COULD BE ANYWHERE!
WAKU (EXCITED)
WAKU
AND YOU GET TO EAT ALL THE SNACKS YOU FIND!
SO EVERYONE, SEARCH YOUR HARDEST!
OKAAAY...?
NOW THEN...! ☆

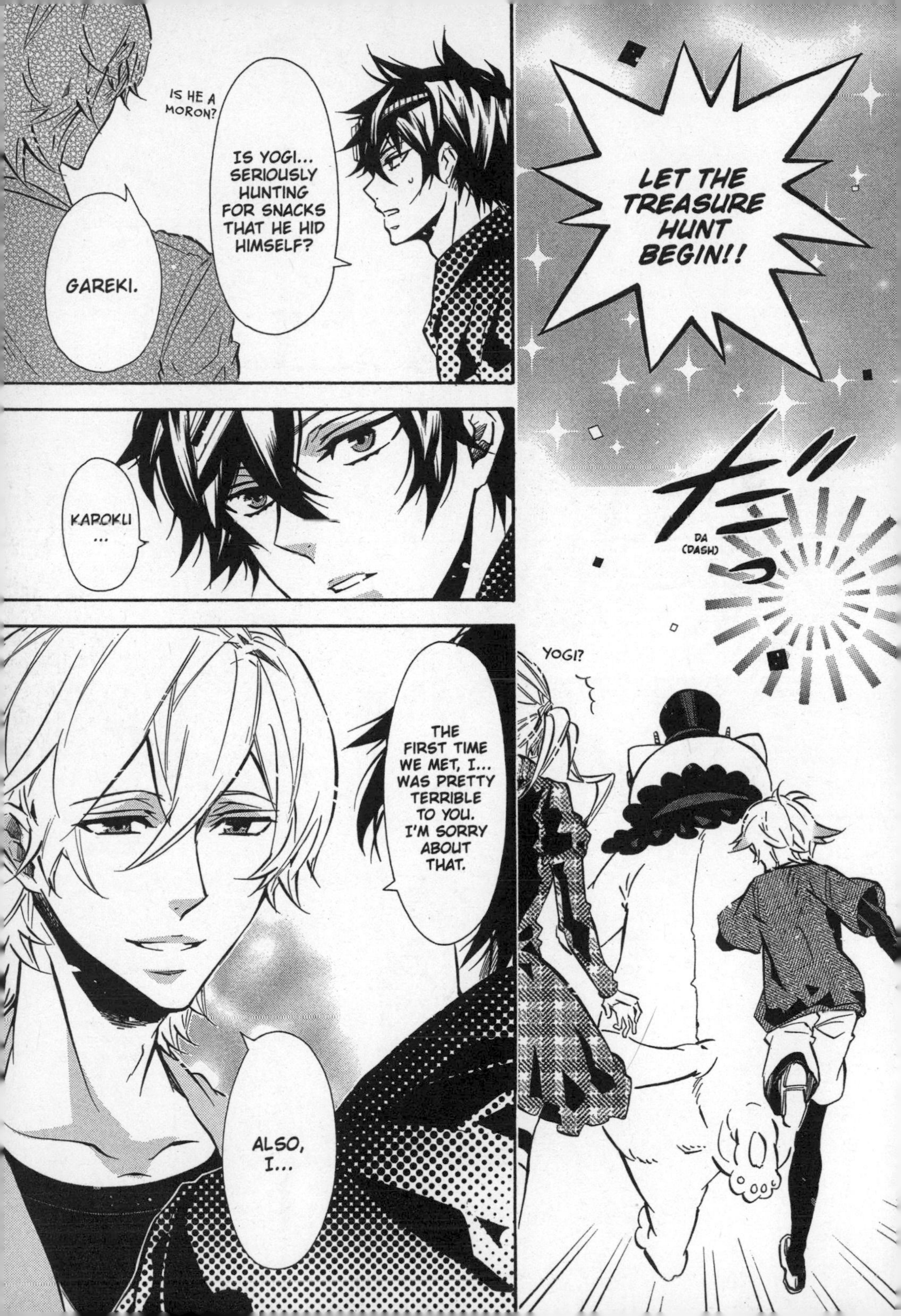
LET THE TREASURE HUNT BEGIN!!
DA (DASH)
YOGI?
IS YOGI... SERIOUSLY HUNTING FOR SNACKS THAT HE HID HIMSELF?
IS HE A MORON?
GAREKI.
KAROKU ...
THE FIRST TIME WE MET, I... WAS PRETTY TERRIBLE TO YOU. I'M SORRY ABOUT THAT.
ALSO, I...

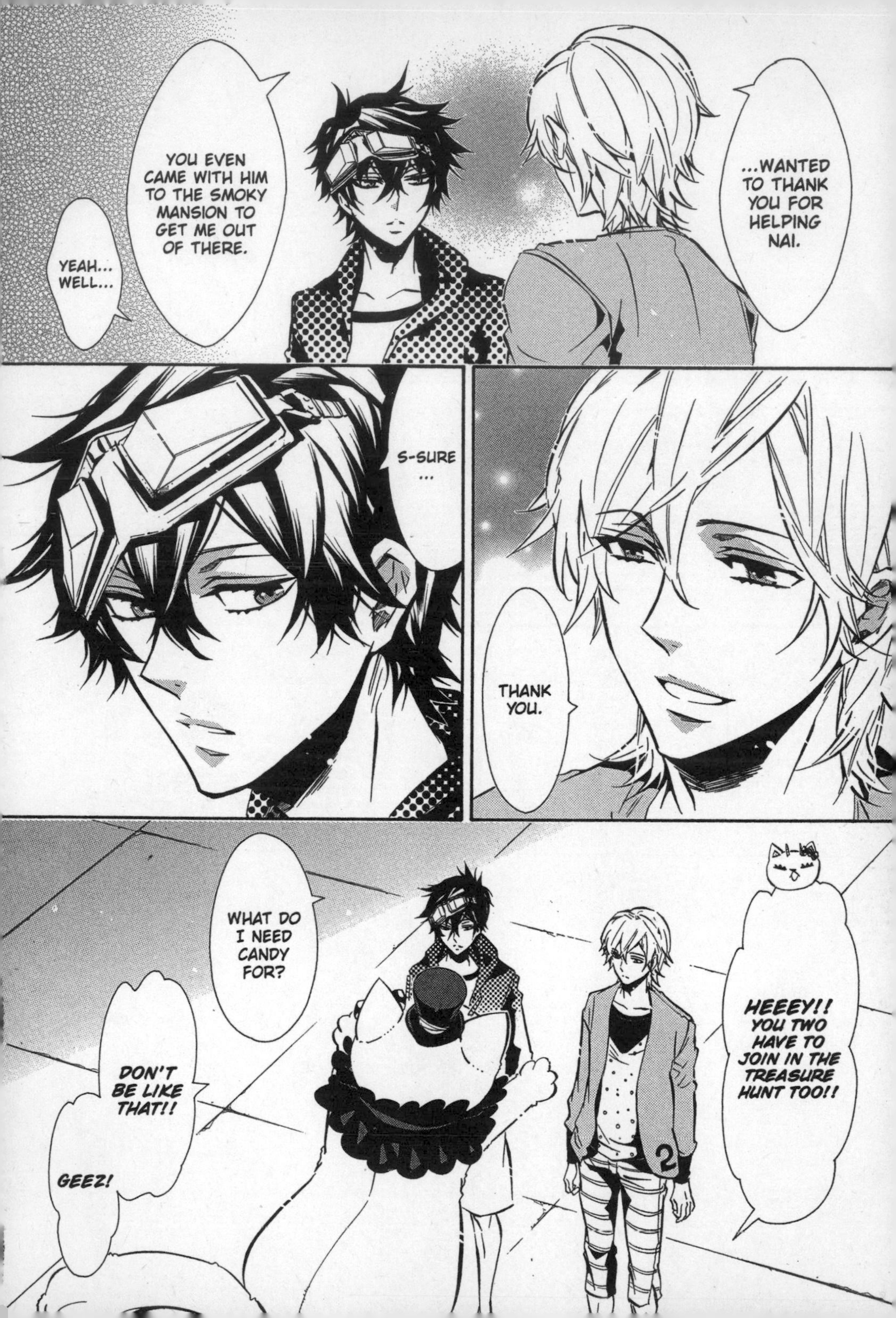
...WANTED TO THANK YOU FOR HELPING NAI.
YOU EVEN CAME WITH HIM TO THE SMOKY MANSION TO GET ME OUT OF THERE.
YEAH... WELL...
THANK YOU.
S-SURE ...
HEEEY!! YOU TWO HAVE TO JOIN IN THE TREASURE HUNT TOO!!
WHAT DO I NEED CANDY FOR?
DON'T BE LIKE THAT!!
GEEZ!

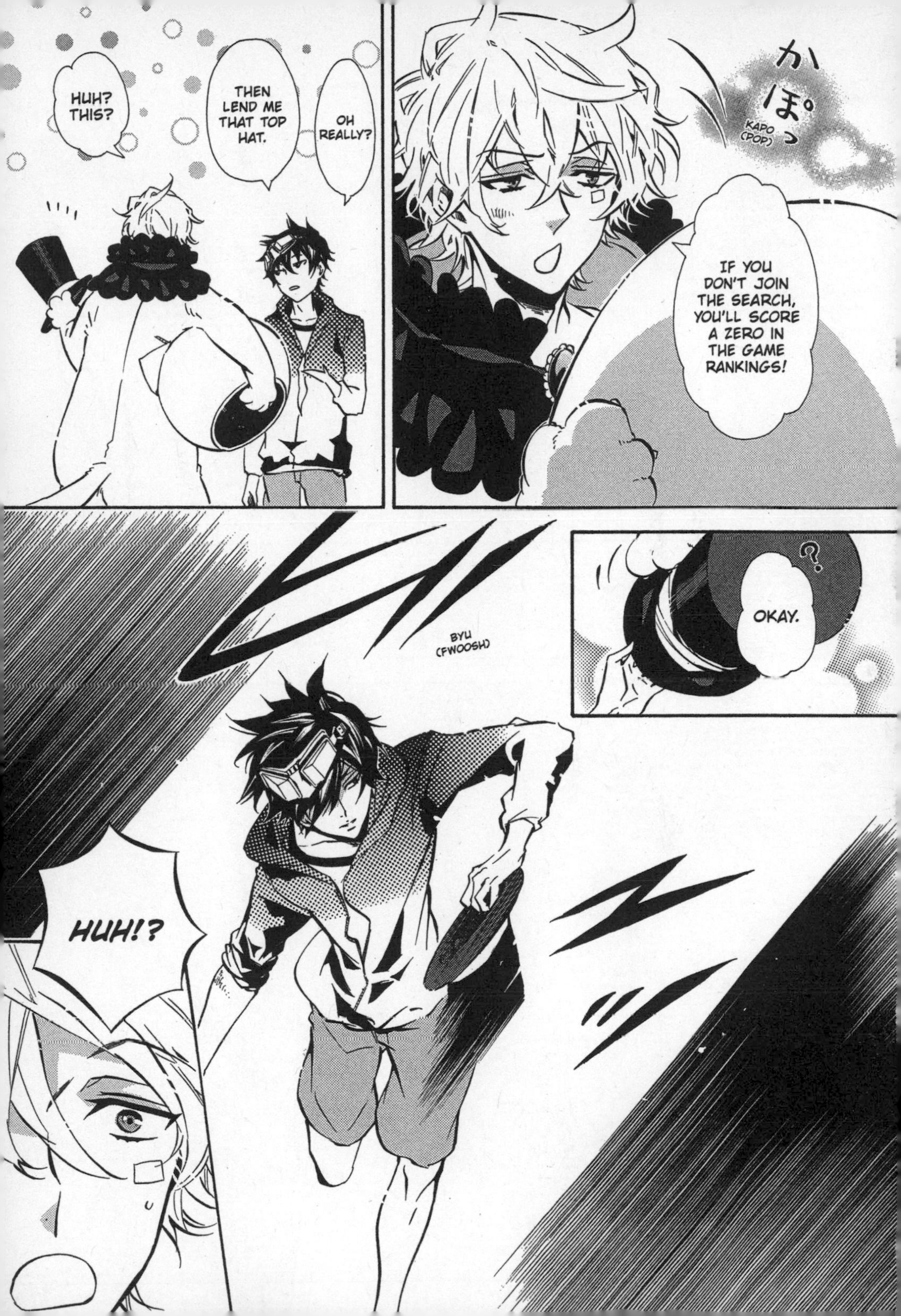
かぽっ
KAPO (POP)
IF YOU DON'T JOIN THE SEARCH, YOU'LL SCORE A ZERO IN THE GAME RANKINGS!
OH REALLY?
THEN LEND ME THAT TOP HAT.
HUH? THIS?
?
OKAY.
BYU (FWOOSH)
HUH!?

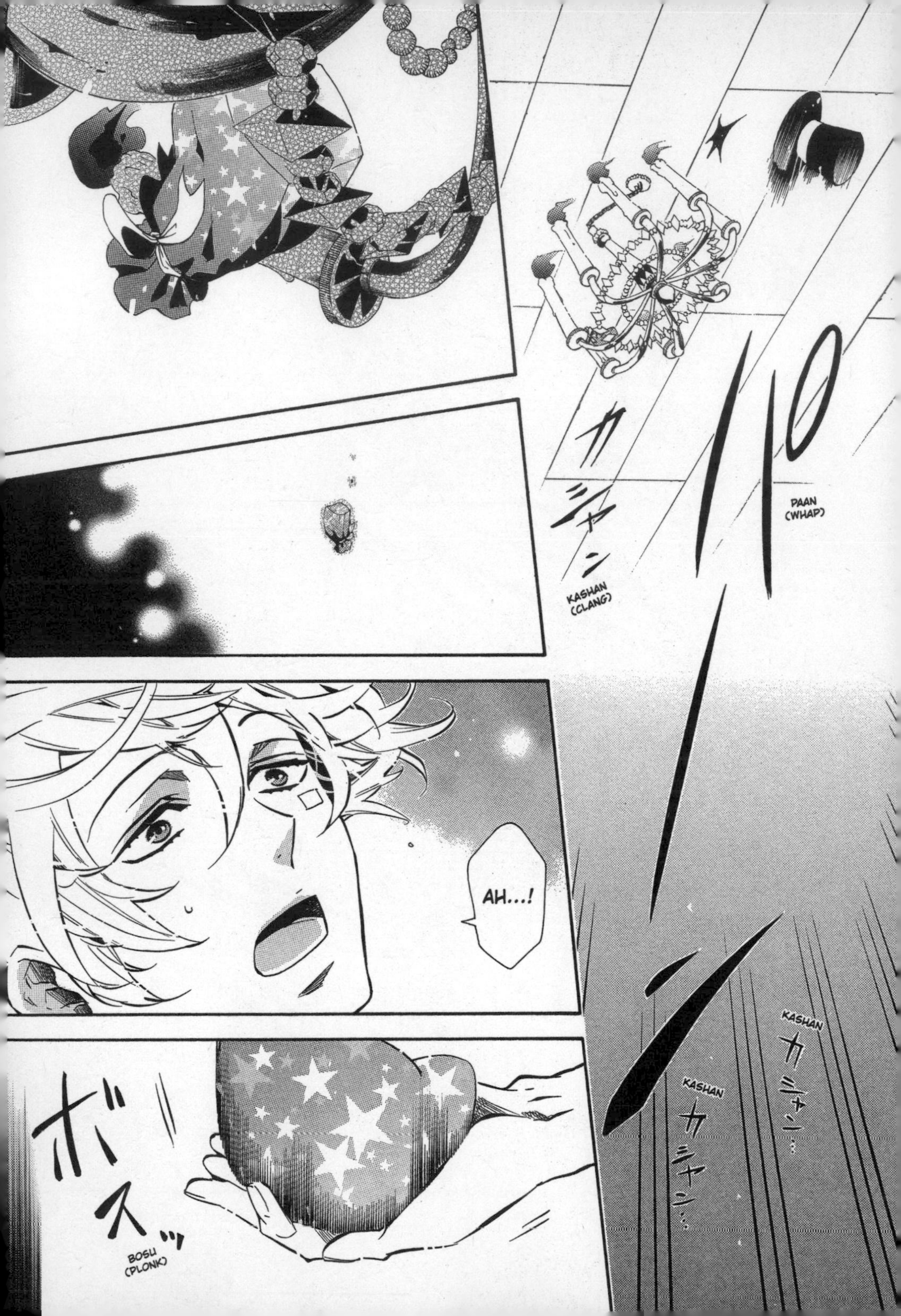
PAAN
(WHAP)
カシャン
KASHAN
(CLANG)
KASHAN
カシャン…
KASHAN
カシャン…
AH…!
ボスッ
BOSU
(PLONK)

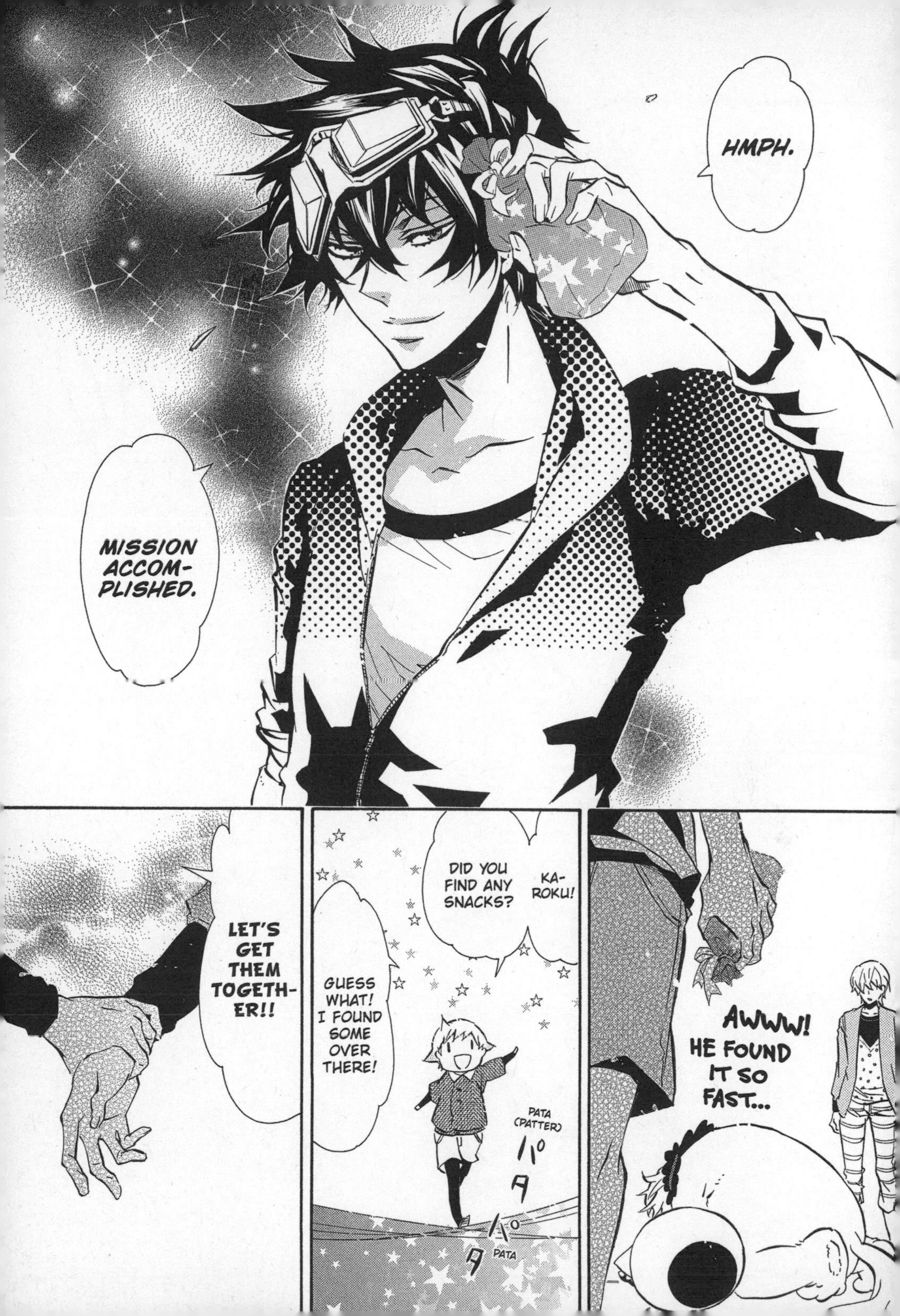
HMPH.
MISSION ACCOM-PLISHED.
AWWW! HE FOUND IT SO FAST...
KA-ROKU!
DID YOU FIND ANY SNACKS?
GUESS WHAT! I FOUND SOME OVER THERE!
PATA (PATTER)
PATA
LET'S GET THEM TOGETH-ER!!

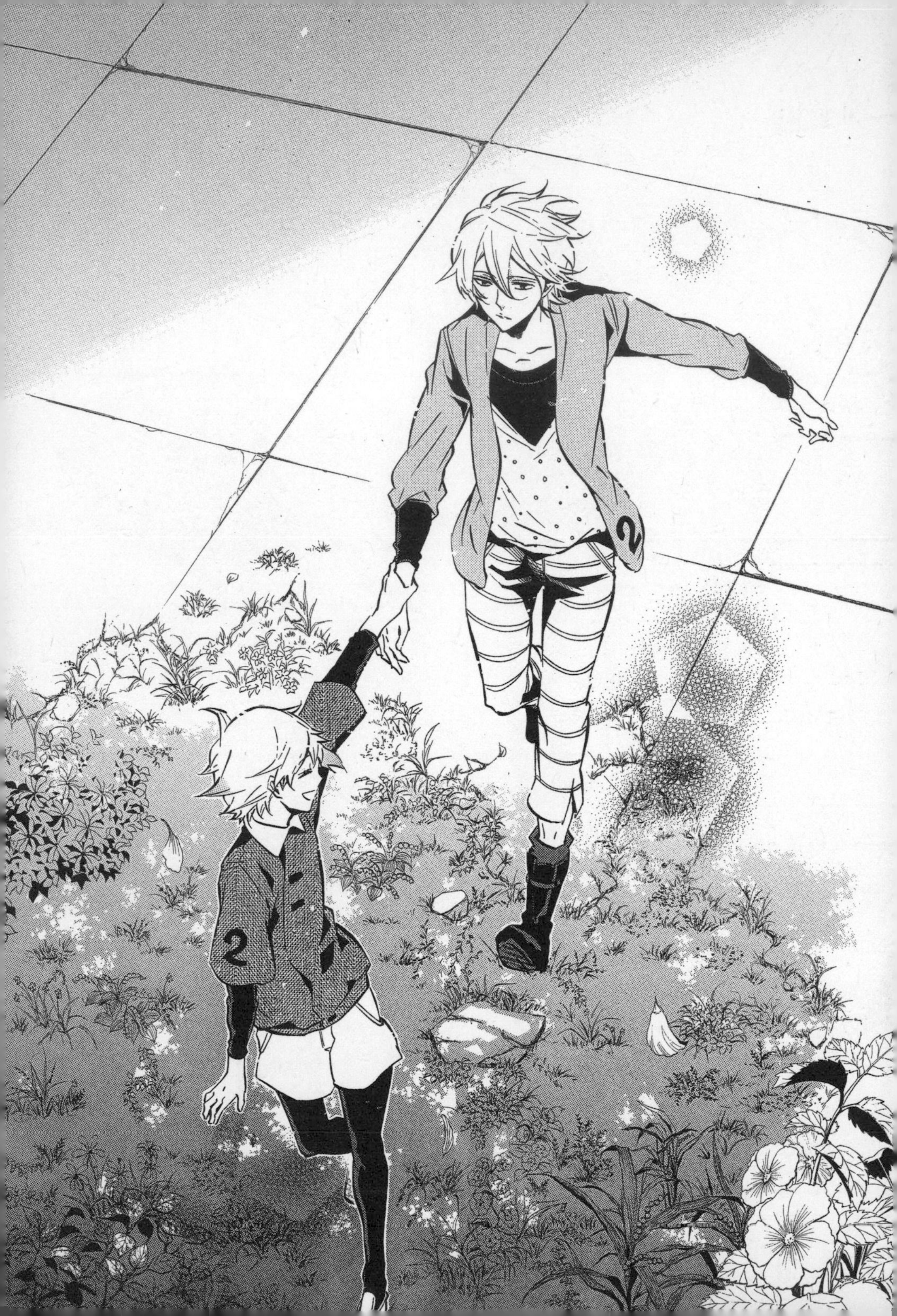

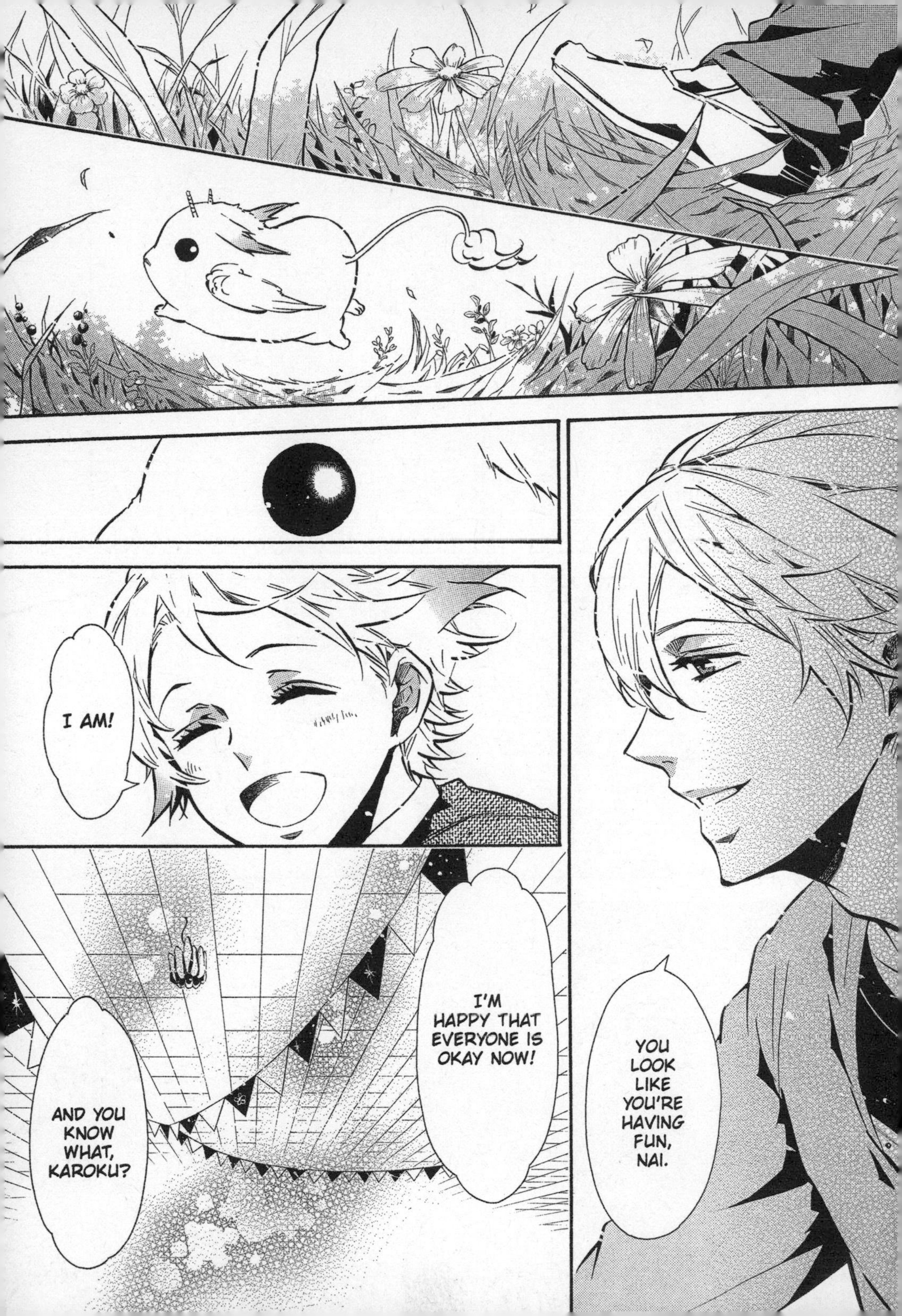
YOU LOOK LIKE YOU'RE HAVING FUN, NAI.
I AM!
I'M HAPPY THAT EVERYONE IS OKAY NOW!
AND YOU KNOW WHAT, KAROKU?

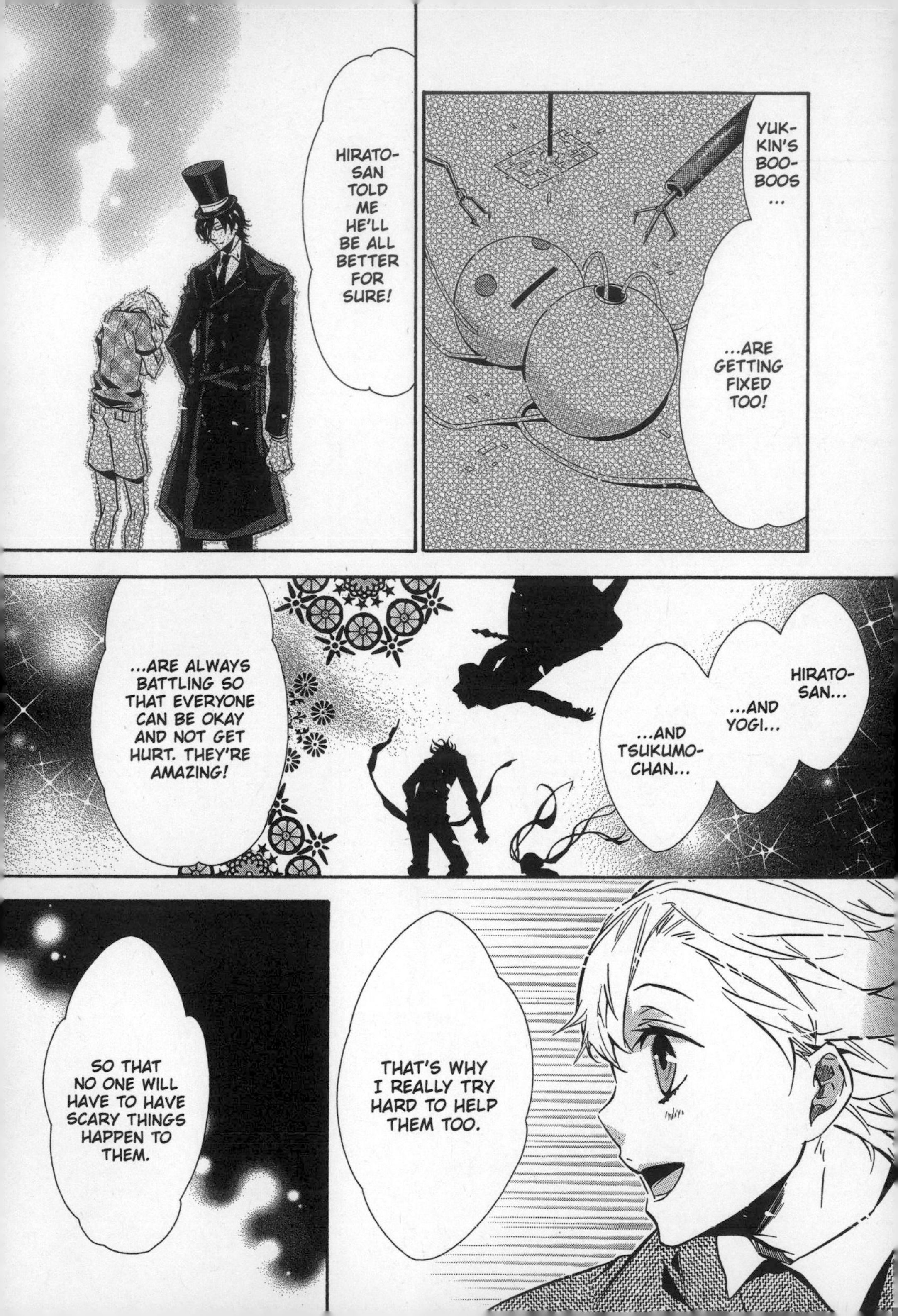
YUK-KIN'S BOO-BOOS...
...ARE GETTING FIXED TOO!
HIRATO-SAN TOLD ME HE'LL BE ALL BETTER FOR SURE!
HIRATO-SAN...
...AND YOGI...
...AND TSUKUMO-CHAN...
...ARE ALWAYS BATTLING SO THAT EVERYONE CAN BE OKAY AND NOT GET HURT. THEY'RE AMAZING!
THAT'S WHY I REALLY TRY HARD TO HELP THEM TOO.
SO THAT NO ONE WILL HAVE TO HAVE SCARY THINGS HAPPEN TO THEM.

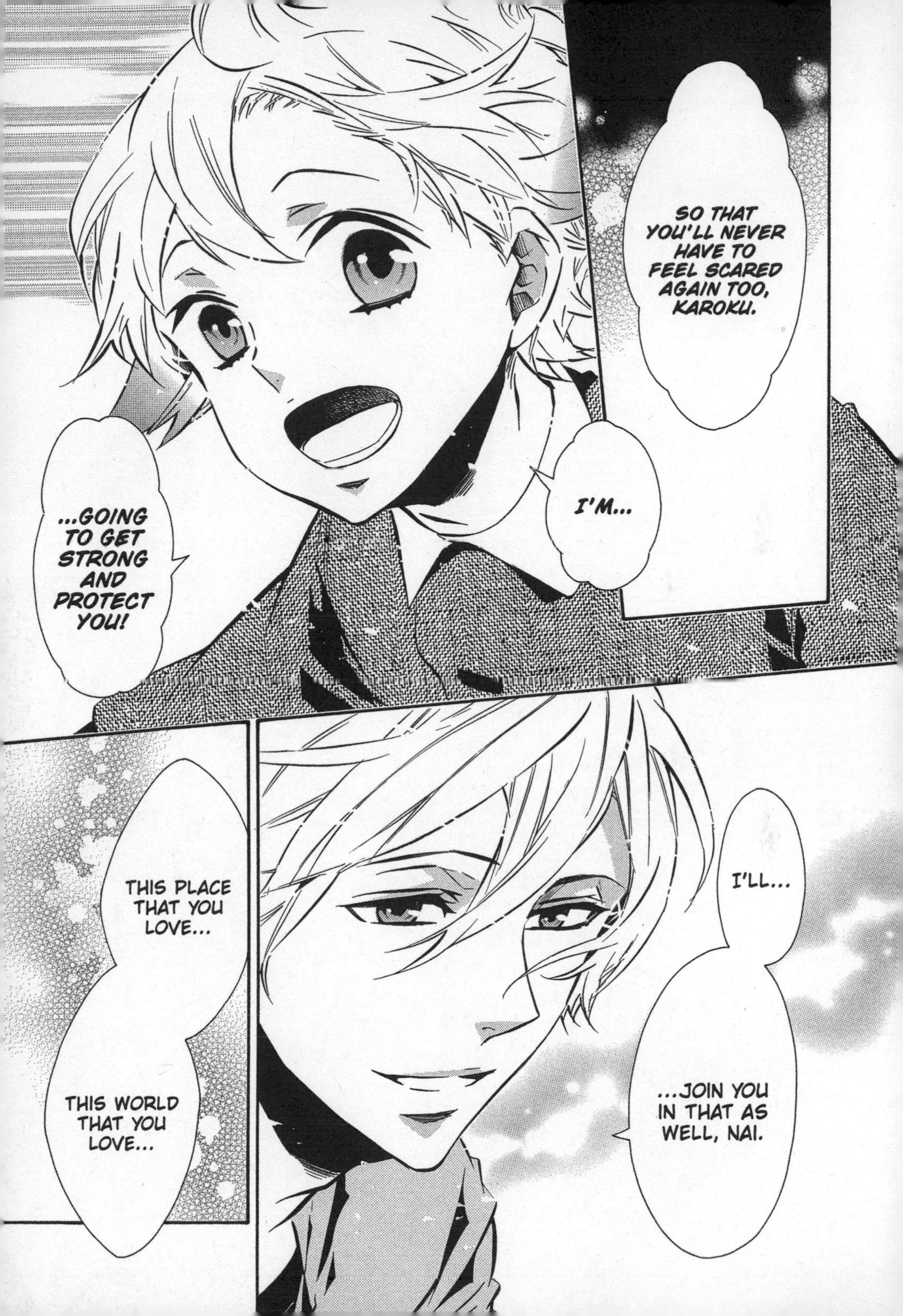
SO THAT YOU'LL NEVER HAVE TO FEEL SCARED AGAIN TOO, KAROKU.
I'M...
...GOING TO GET STRONG AND PROTECT YOU!
I'LL...
...JOIN YOU IN THAT AS WELL, NAI.
THIS PLACE THAT YOU LOVE...
THIS WORLD THAT YOU LOVE...

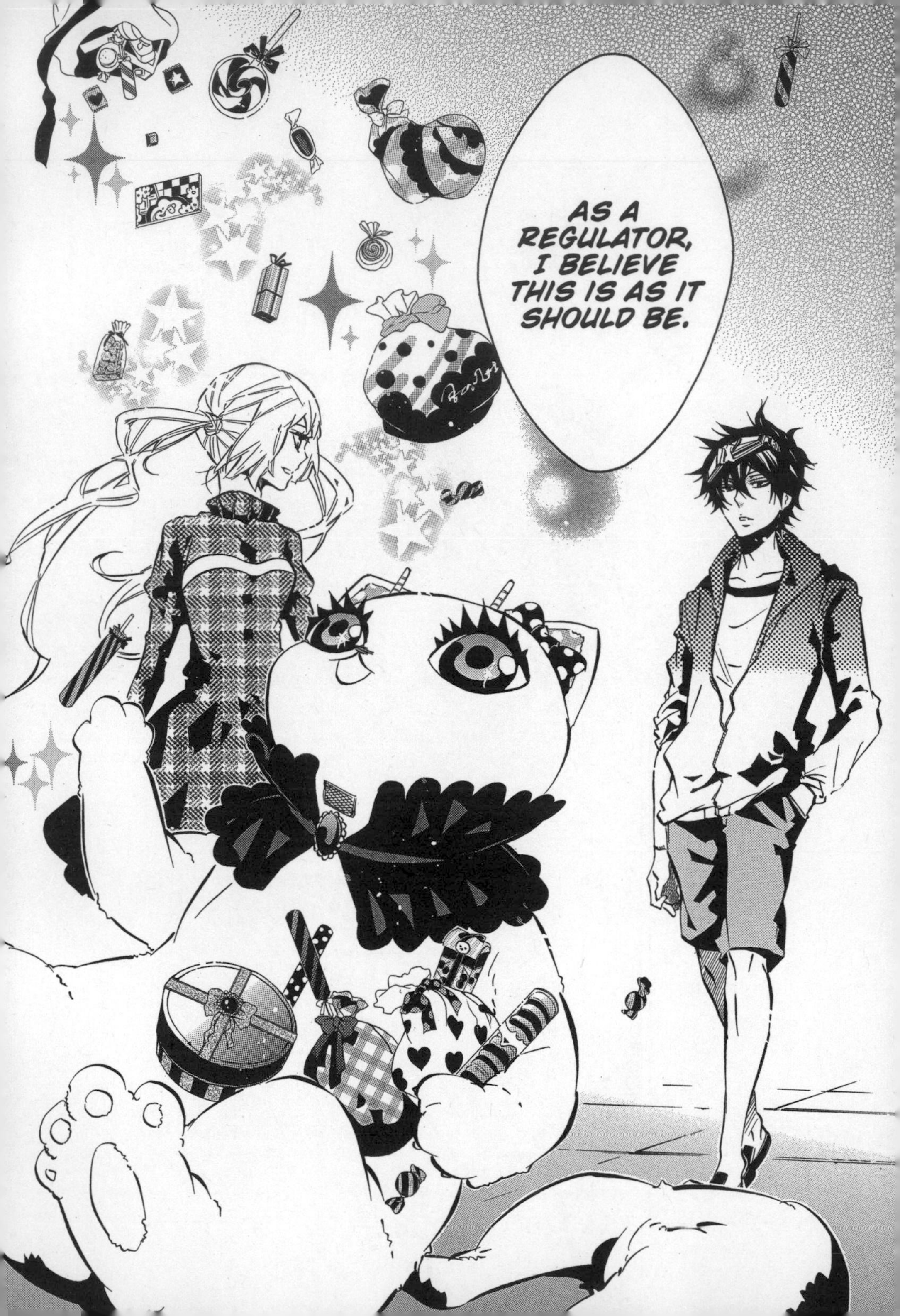
AS A REGULATOR, I BELIEVE THIS IS AS IT SHOULD BE.

KARNEVAL

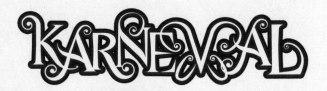

ズバッ
ZUBA (SNATCH)

KARNEVAL

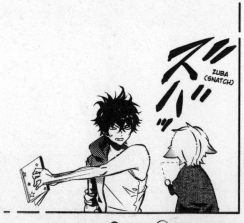

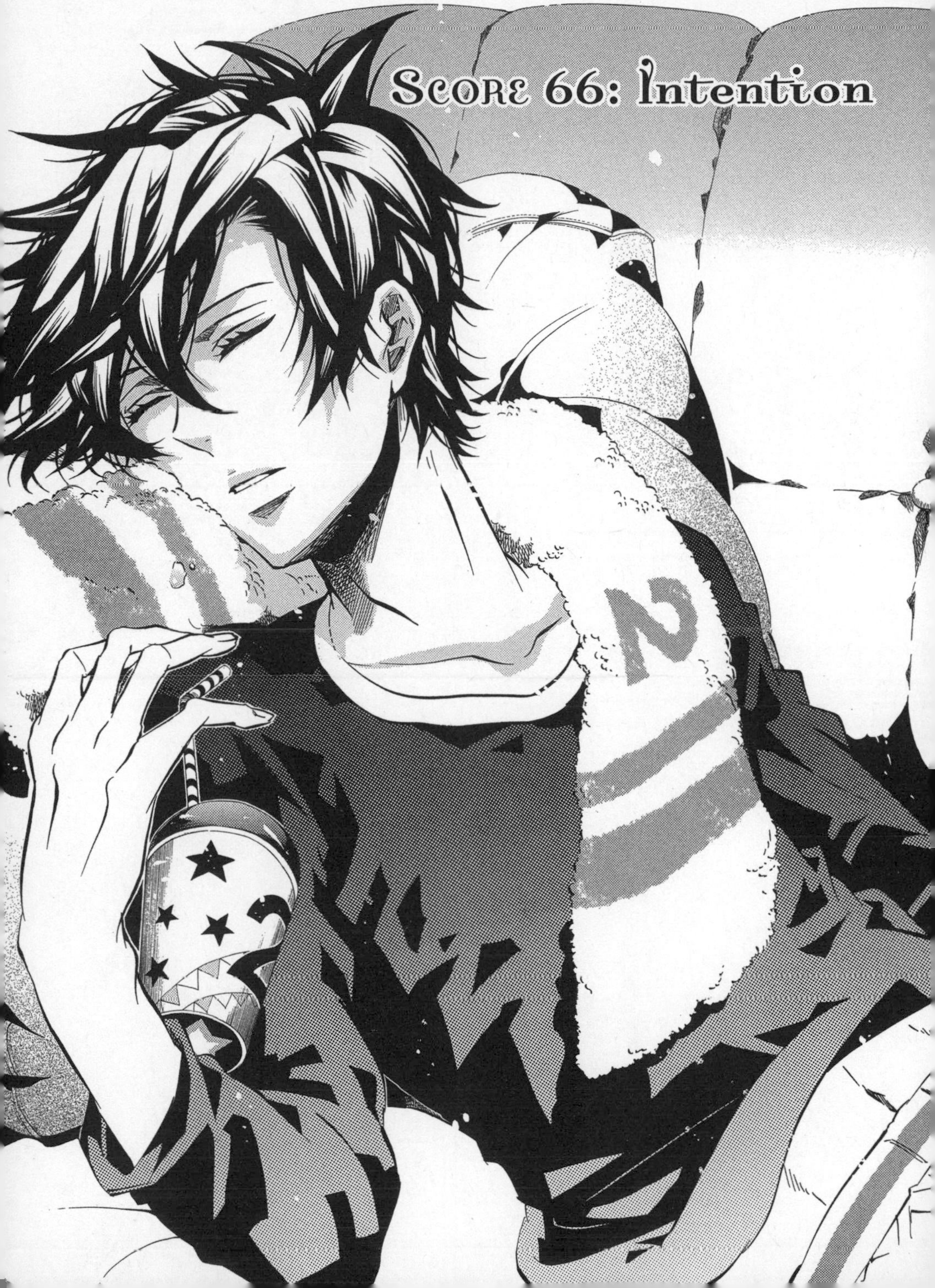
Score 66: Intention

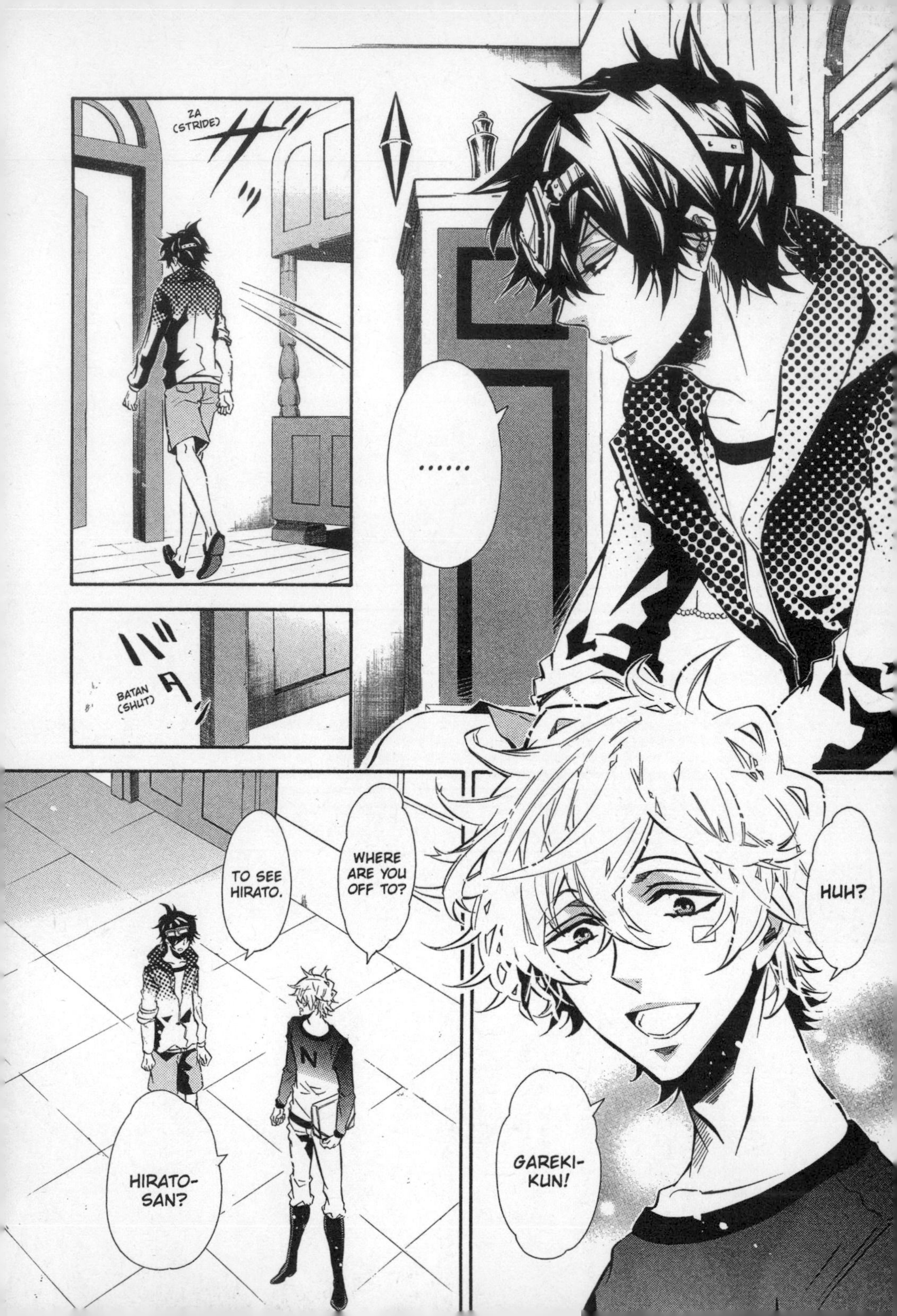
......
ZA (STRIDE)
BATAN (SHUT)
HUH?
GAREKI-KUN!
WHERE ARE YOU OFF TO?
TO SEE HIRATO.
HIRATO-SAN?

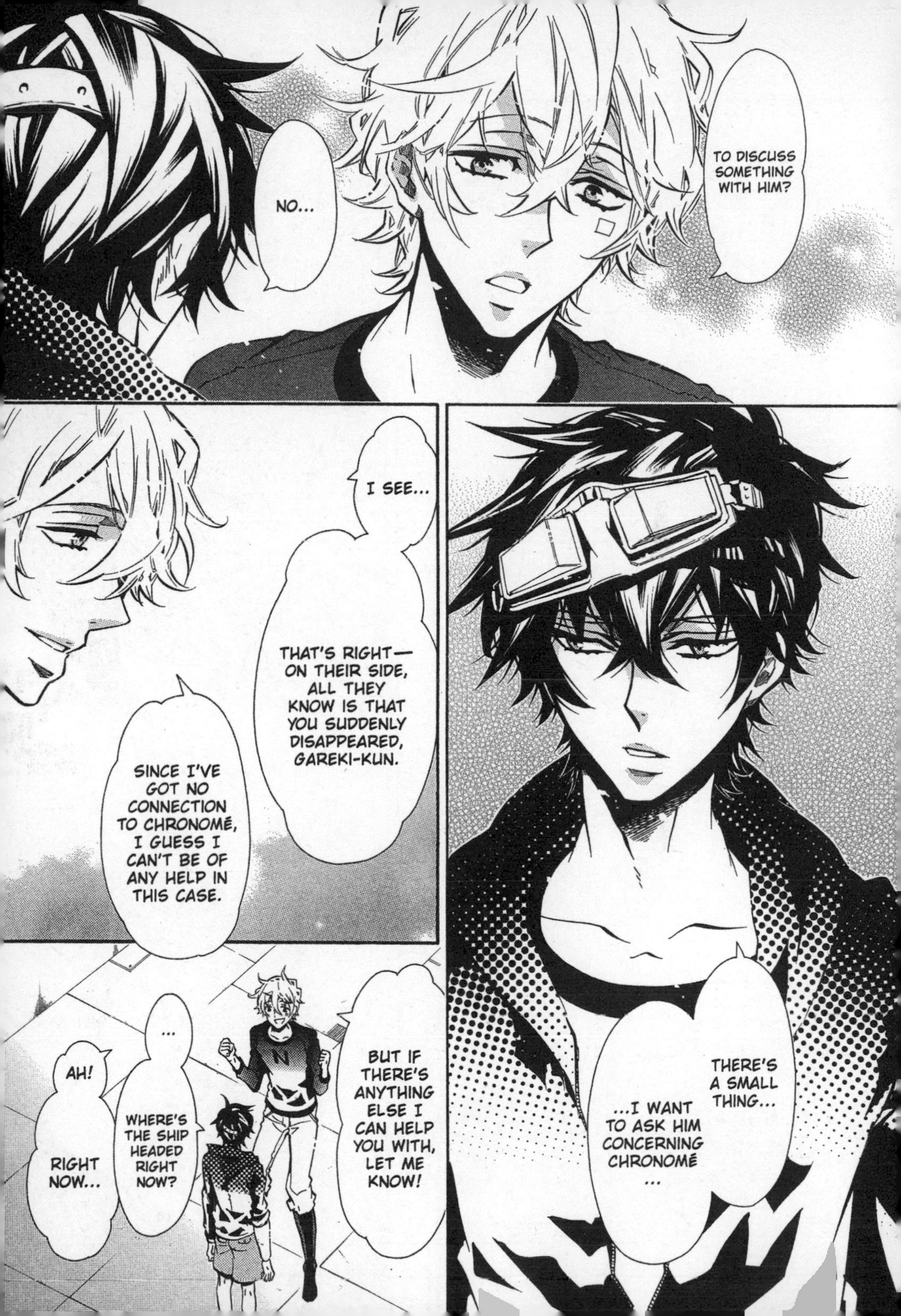
TO DISCUSS SOMETHING WITH HIM?
NO...
I SEE...
THAT'S RIGHT— ON THEIR SIDE, ALL THEY KNOW IS THAT YOU SUDDENLY DISAPPEARED, GAREKI-KUN.
SINCE I'VE GOT NO CONNECTION TO CHRONOMÉ, I GUESS I CAN'T BE OF ANY HELP IN THIS CASE.
BUT IF THERE'S ANYTHING ELSE I CAN HELP YOU WITH, LET ME KNOW!
THERE'S A SMALL THING...
...I WANT TO ASK HIM CONCERNING CHRONOMÉ ...
...
WHERE'S THE SHIP HEADED RIGHT NOW?
AH!
RIGHT NOW...

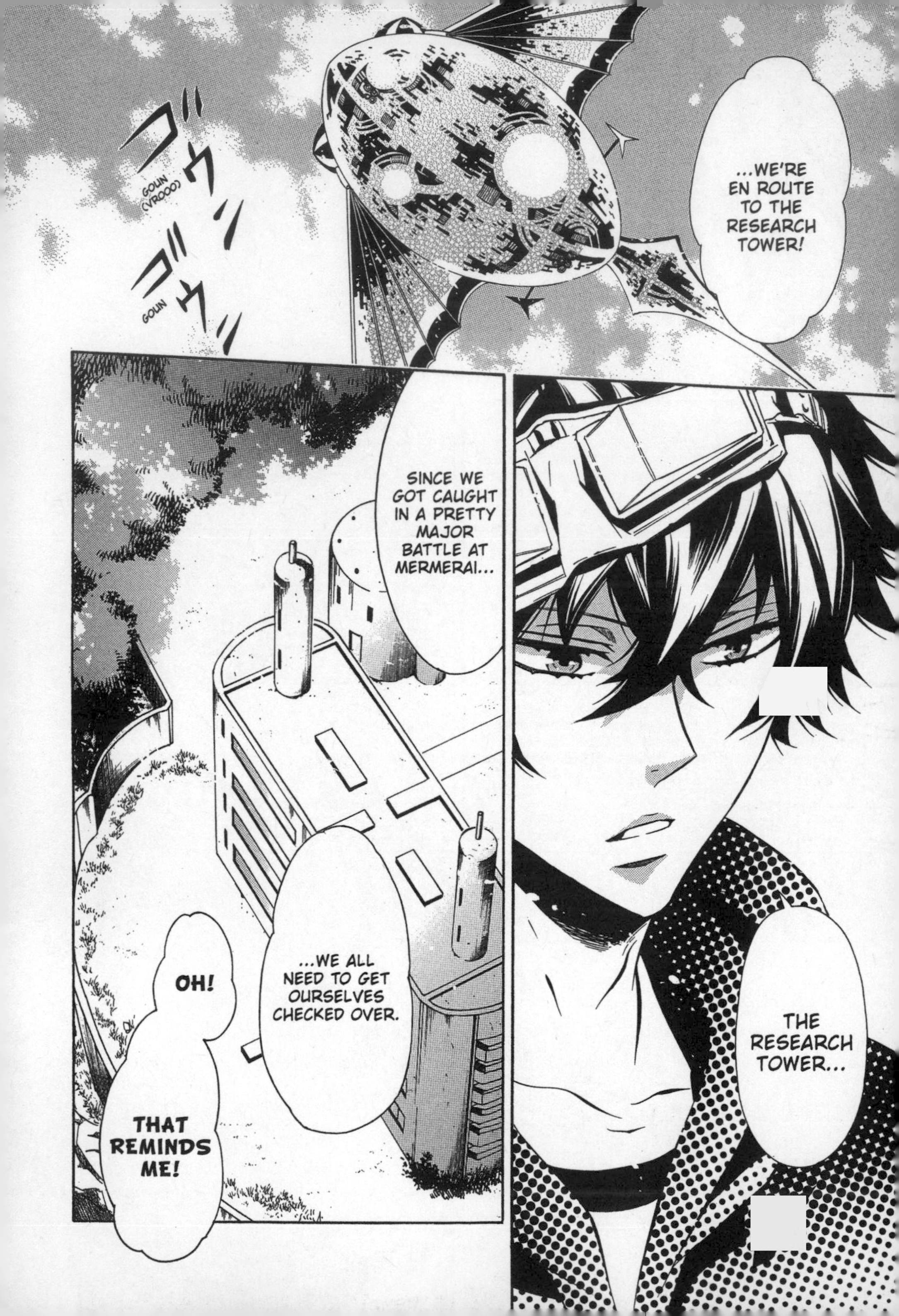
...WE'RE EN ROUTE TO THE RESEARCH TOWER!
ゴウン
GOUN (VROOO)
ゴウン
GOUN
THE RESEARCH TOWER...
SINCE WE GOT CAUGHT IN A PRETTY MAJOR BATTLE AT MERMERAI...
...WE ALL NEED TO GET OURSELVES CHECKED OVER.
OH!
THAT REMINDS ME!

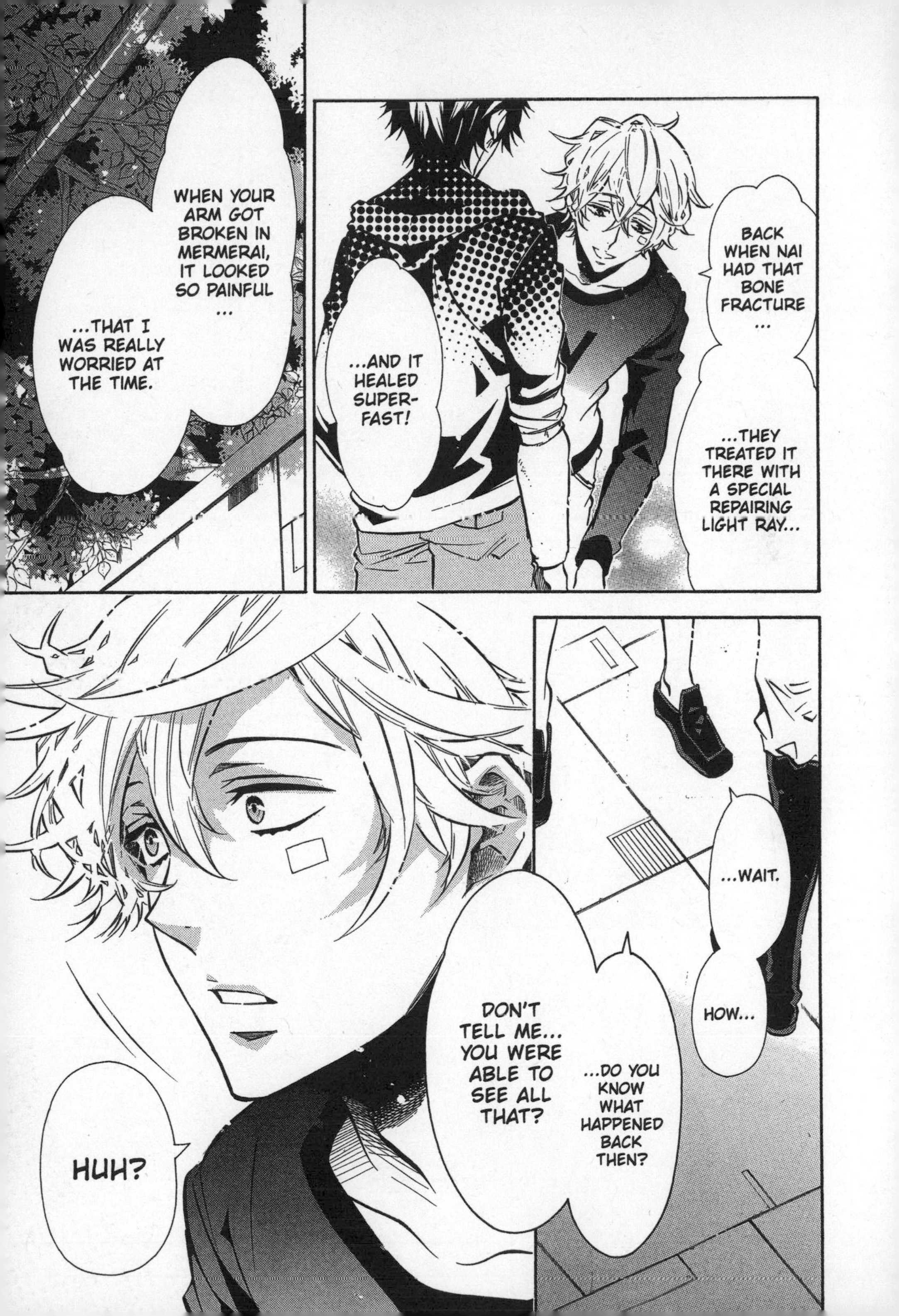
BACK WHEN NAI HAD THAT BONE FRACTURE...
...THEY TREATED IT THERE WITH A SPECIAL REPAIRING LIGHT RAY...
...AND IT HEALED SUPER-FAST!
WHEN YOUR ARM GOT BROKEN IN MERMERAI, IT LOOKED SO PAINFUL...
...THAT I WAS REALLY WORRIED AT THE TIME.
...WAIT.
HOW...
...DO YOU KNOW WHAT HAPPENED BACK THEN?
DON'T TELL ME... YOU WERE ABLE TO SEE ALL THAT?
HUH?

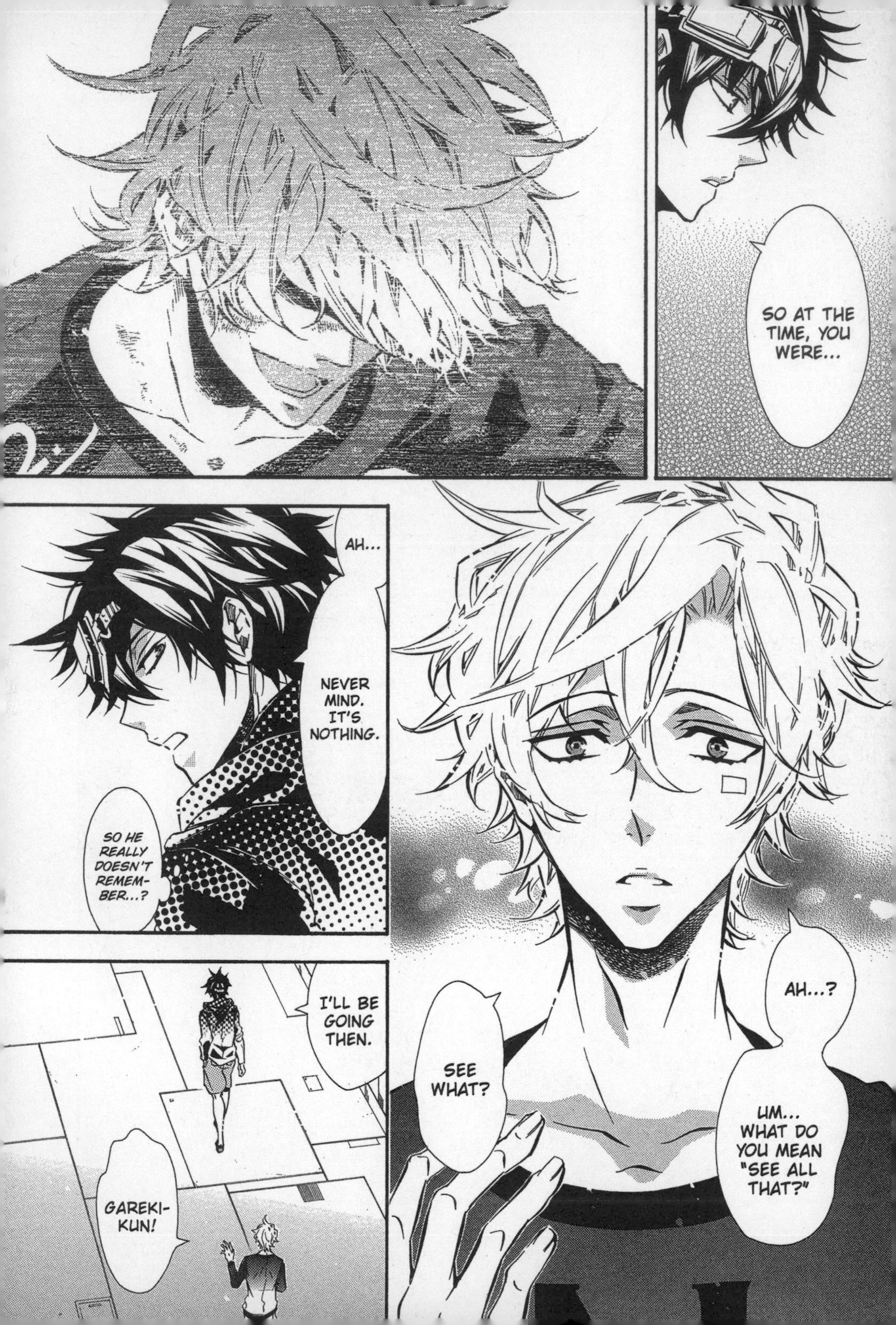
SO AT THE TIME, YOU WERE...
AH...?
UM... WHAT DO YOU MEAN "SEE ALL THAT?"
SEE WHAT?
AH...
NEVER MIND. IT'S NOTHING.
SO HE REALLY DOESN'T REMEMBER...?
I'LL BE GOING THEN.
GAREKI-KUN!

NOW THAT YOU MENTION IT...HOW DID YOU BREAK YOUR ARM?

I DON'T KNOW, BUT...I COULD SWEAR I SAW YOU IN PAIN...

HUH...?

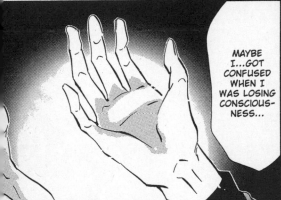

MAYBE I...GOT CONFUSED WHEN I WAS LOSING CONSCIOUS-NESS...

C'MON, YOGI!!

...PULL MYSELF TOGETH-ER!

I'VE GOTTA...

バチン
(SLAP)

167

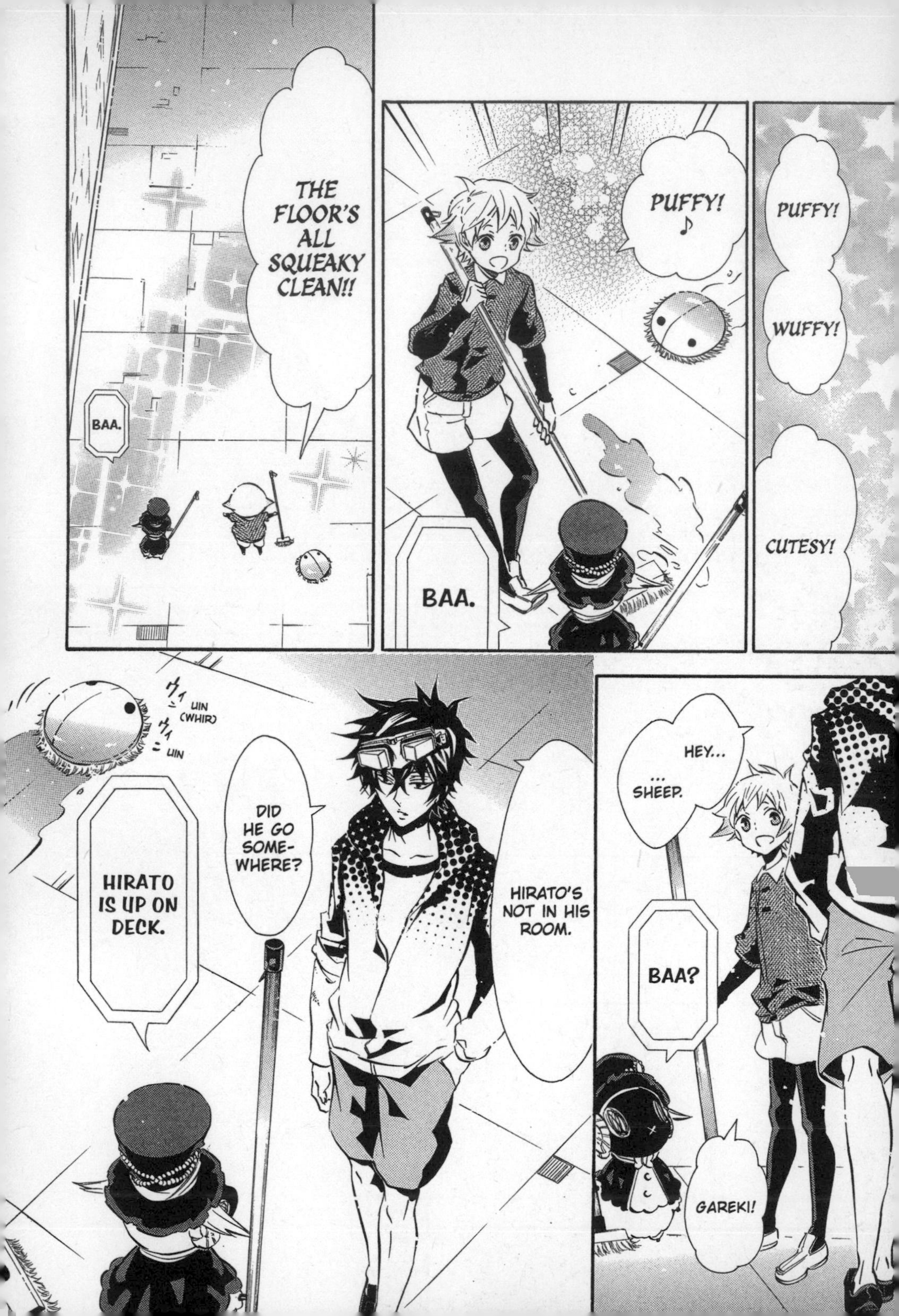
PUFFY!
WUFFY!
CUTESY!
PUFFY! ♪
BAA.
THE FLOOR'S ALL SQUEAKY CLEAN!!
BAA.
HEY... ...SHEEP.
BAA?
GAREKI!
HIRATO'S NOT IN HIS ROOM.
DID HE GO SOMEWHERE?
ウィン UIN (WHIR)
ウィン UIN
HIRATO IS UP ON DECK.

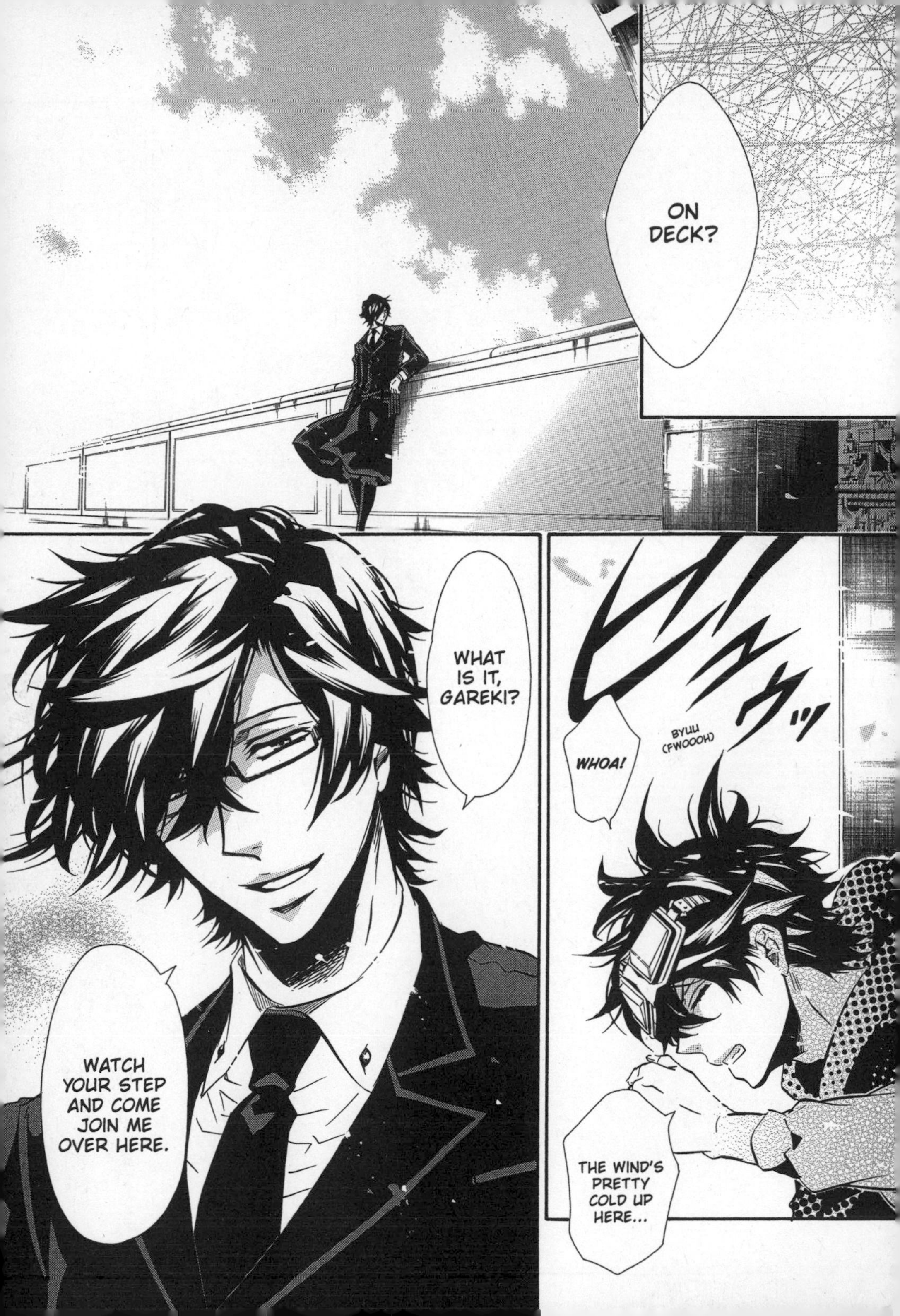
ON DECK?
BYUU (FWOOOH)
WHOA!
THE WIND'S PRETTY COLD UP HERE...
WHAT IS IT, GAREKI?
WATCH YOUR STEP AND COME JOIN ME OVER HERE.

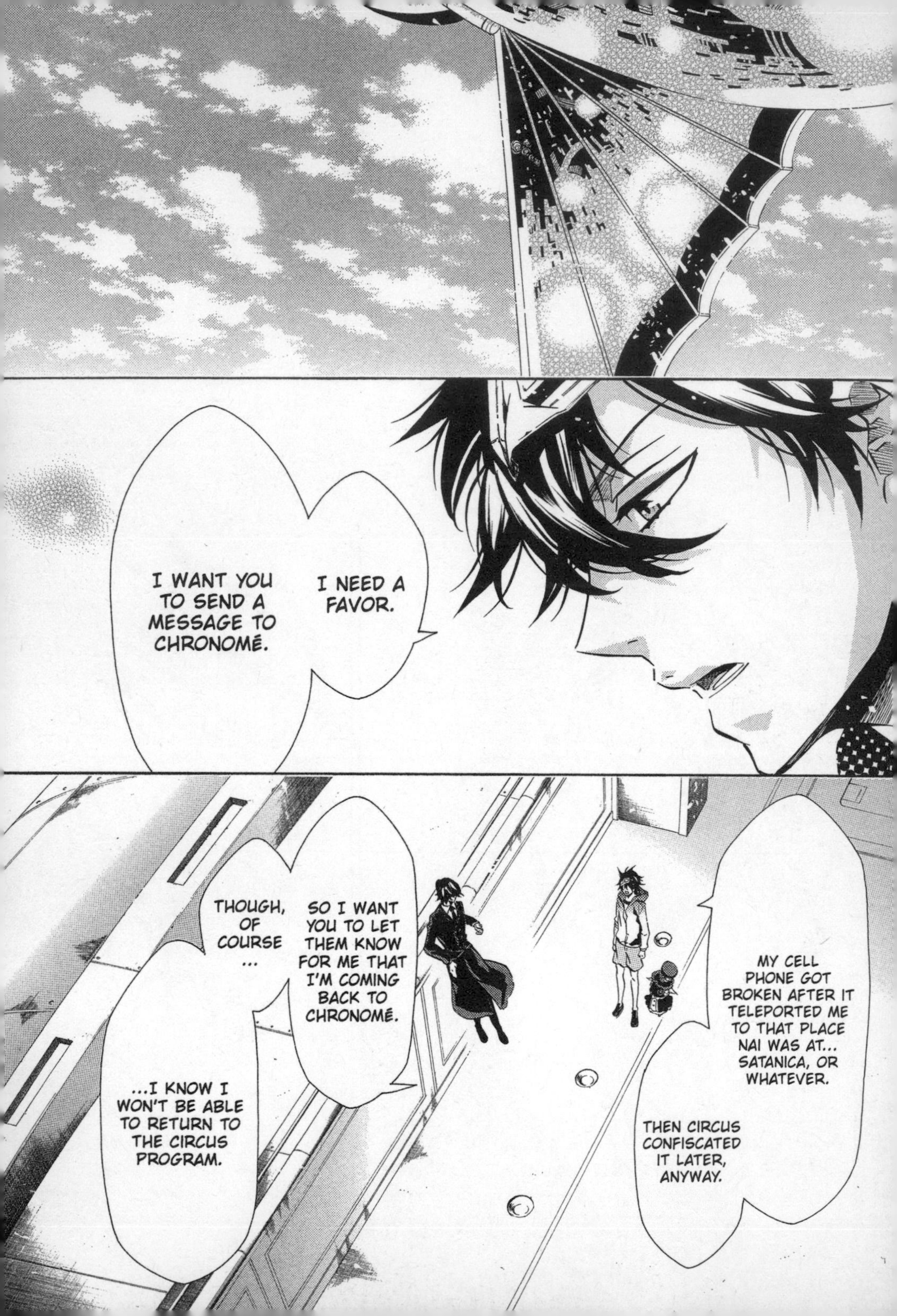
I NEED A FAVOR.
I WANT YOU TO SEND A MESSAGE TO CHRONOMÉ.
MY CELL PHONE GOT BROKEN AFTER IT TELEPORTED ME TO THAT PLACE NAI WAS AT... SATANICA, OR WHATEVER.
THEN CIRCUS CONFISCATED IT LATER, ANYWAY.
SO I WANT YOU TO LET THEM KNOW FOR ME THAT I'M COMING BACK TO CHRONOMÉ.
THOUGH, OF COURSE...
...I KNOW I WON'T BE ABLE TO RETURN TO THE CIRCUS PROGRAM.

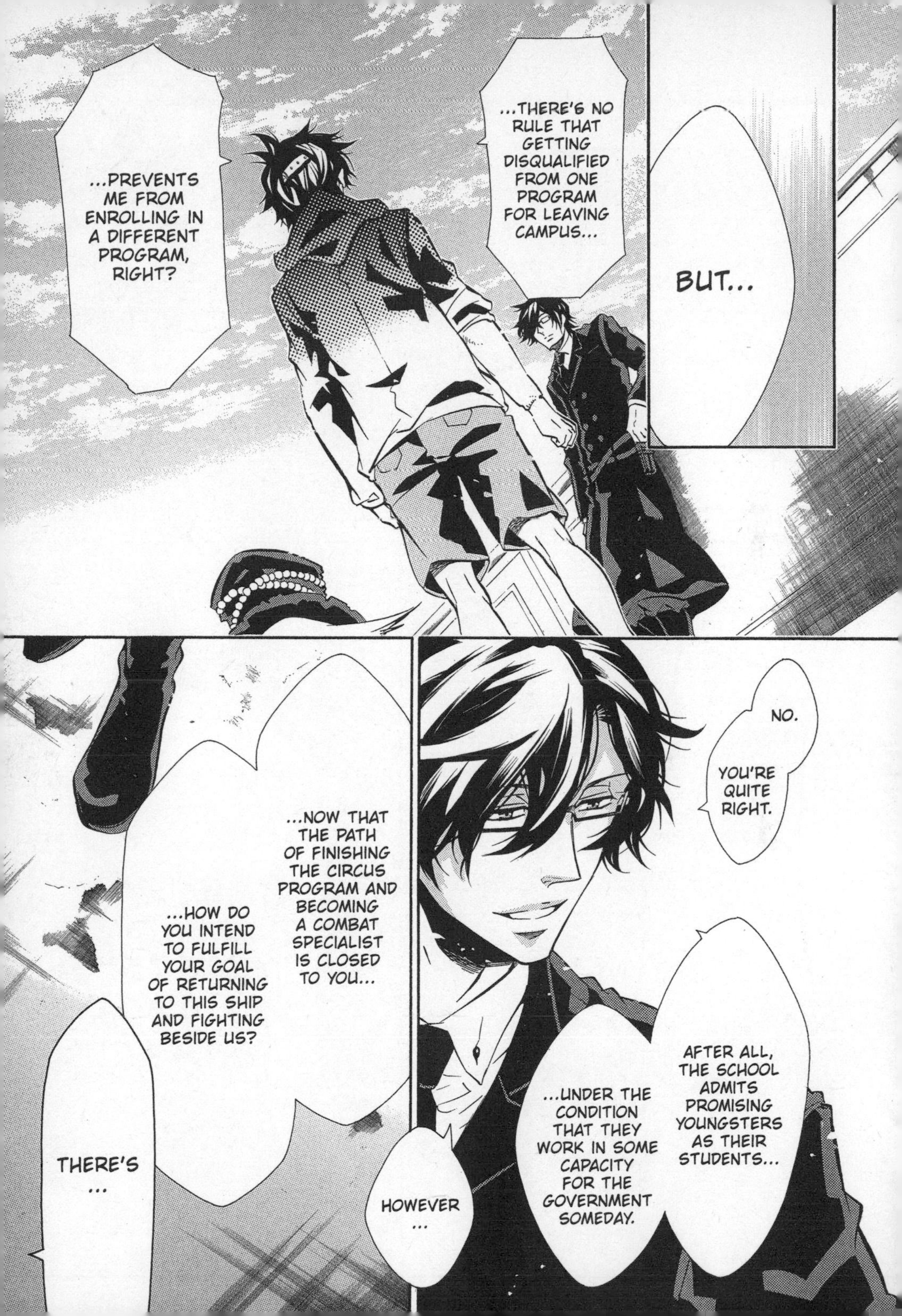
BUT...
...THERE'S NO RULE THAT GETTING DISQUALIFIED FROM ONE PROGRAM FOR LEAVING CAMPUS...
...PREVENTS ME FROM ENROLLING IN A DIFFERENT PROGRAM, RIGHT?
NO.
YOU'RE QUITE RIGHT.
AFTER ALL, THE SCHOOL ADMITS PROMISING YOUNGSTERS AS THEIR STUDENTS...
...UNDER THE CONDITION THAT THEY WORK IN SOME CAPACITY FOR THE GOVERNMENT SOMEDAY.
HOWEVER ...
...NOW THAT THE PATH OF FINISHING THE CIRCUS PROGRAM AND BECOMING A COMBAT SPECIALIST IS CLOSED TO YOU...
...HOW DO YOU INTEND TO FULFILL YOUR GOAL OF RETURNING TO THIS SHIP AND FIGHTING BESIDE US?
THERE'S ...

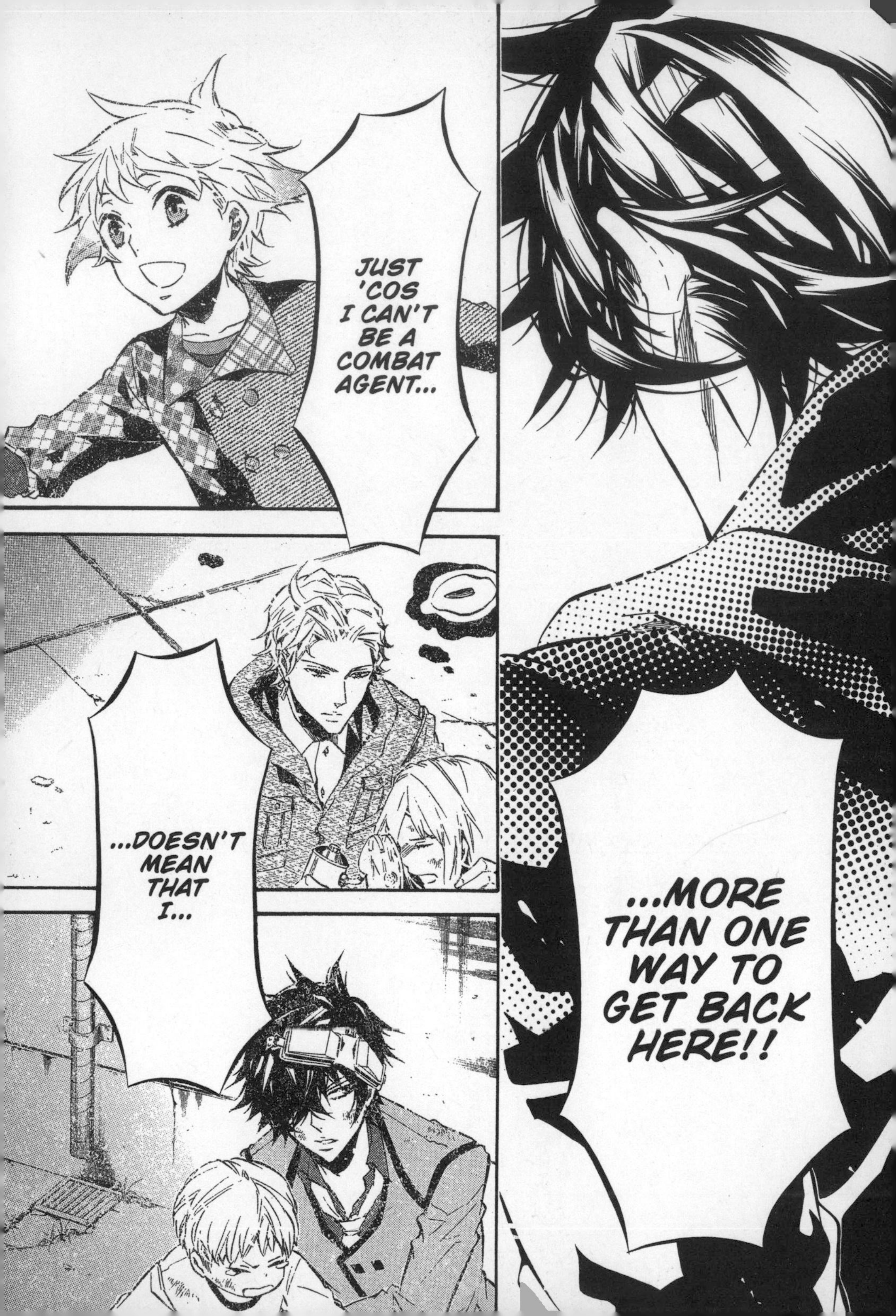
...MORE THAN ONE WAY TO GET BACK HERE!!
JUST 'COS I CAN'T BE A COMBAT AGENT...
...DOESN'T MEAN THAT I...

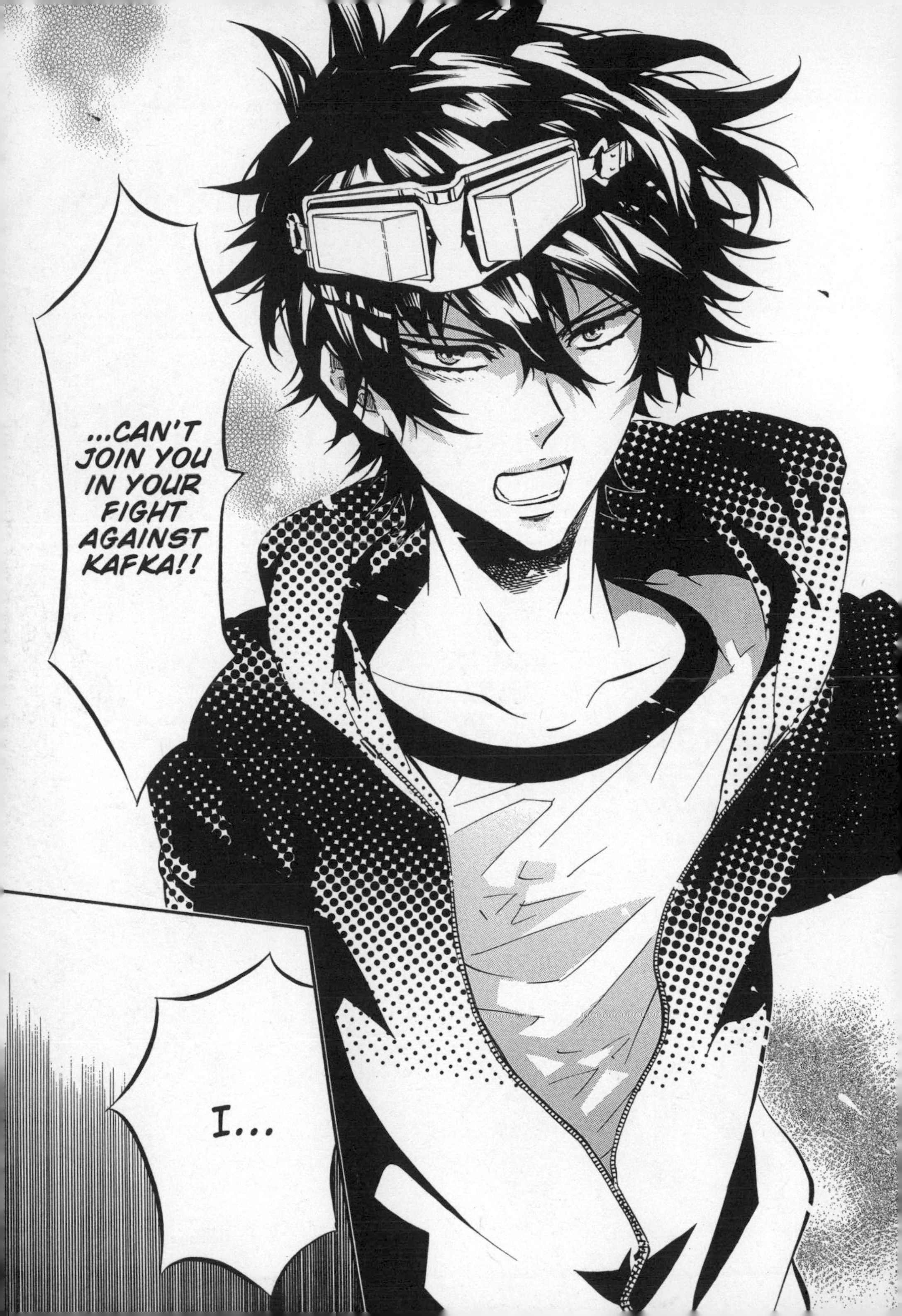
I...
...CAN'T JOIN YOU IN YOUR FIGHT AGAINST KAFKA!!

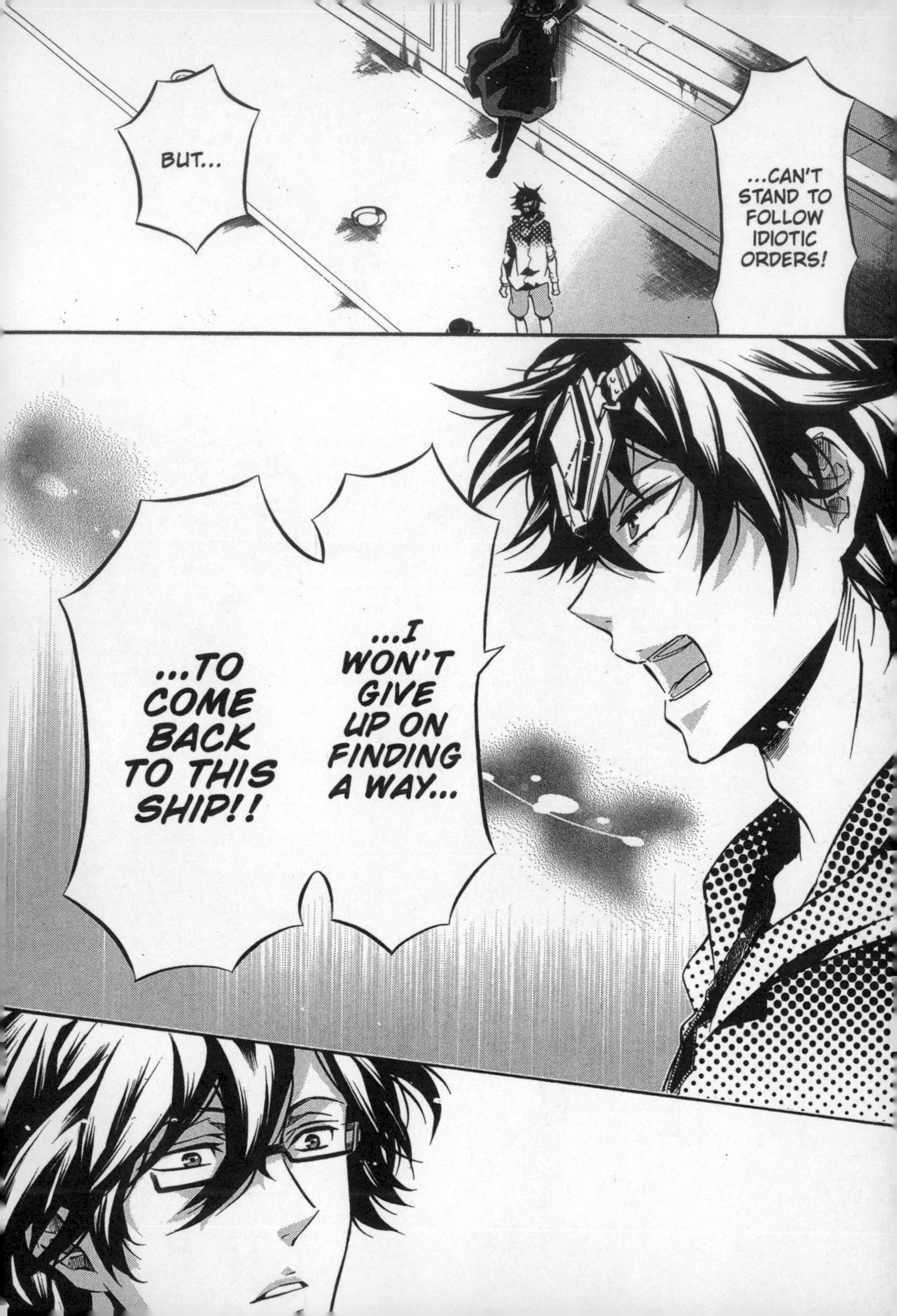
...CAN'T STAND TO FOLLOW IDIOTIC ORDERS!
BUT...
...I WON'T GIVE UP ON FINDING A WAY...
...TO COME BACK TO THIS SHIP!!

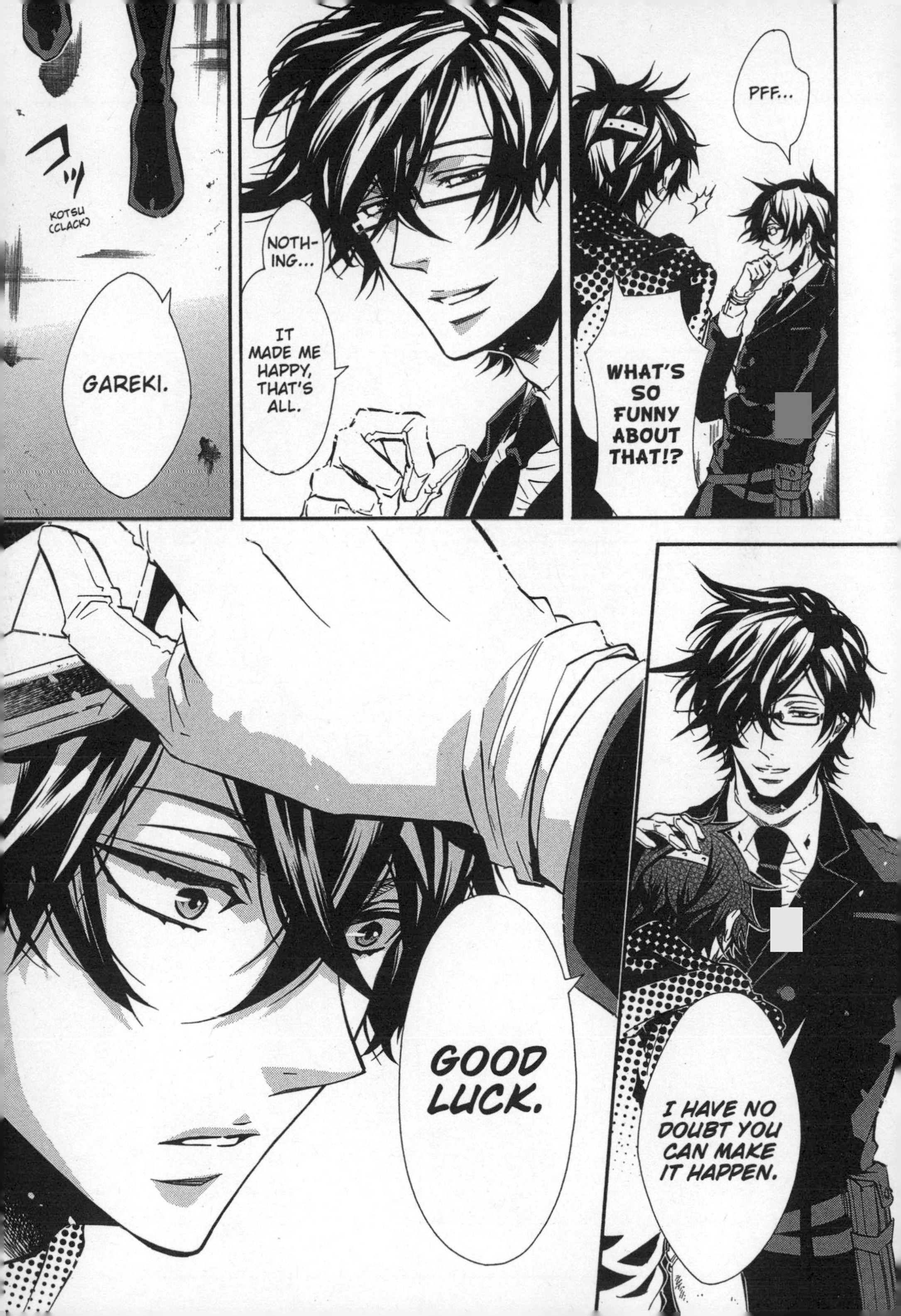
PFF...
WHAT'S SO FUNNY ABOUT THAT!?
NOTH-ING...
IT MADE ME HAPPY, THAT'S ALL.
コッ
KOTSU (CLACK)
GAREKI.
I HAVE NO DOUBT YOU CAN MAKE IT HAPPEN.
GOOD LUCK.

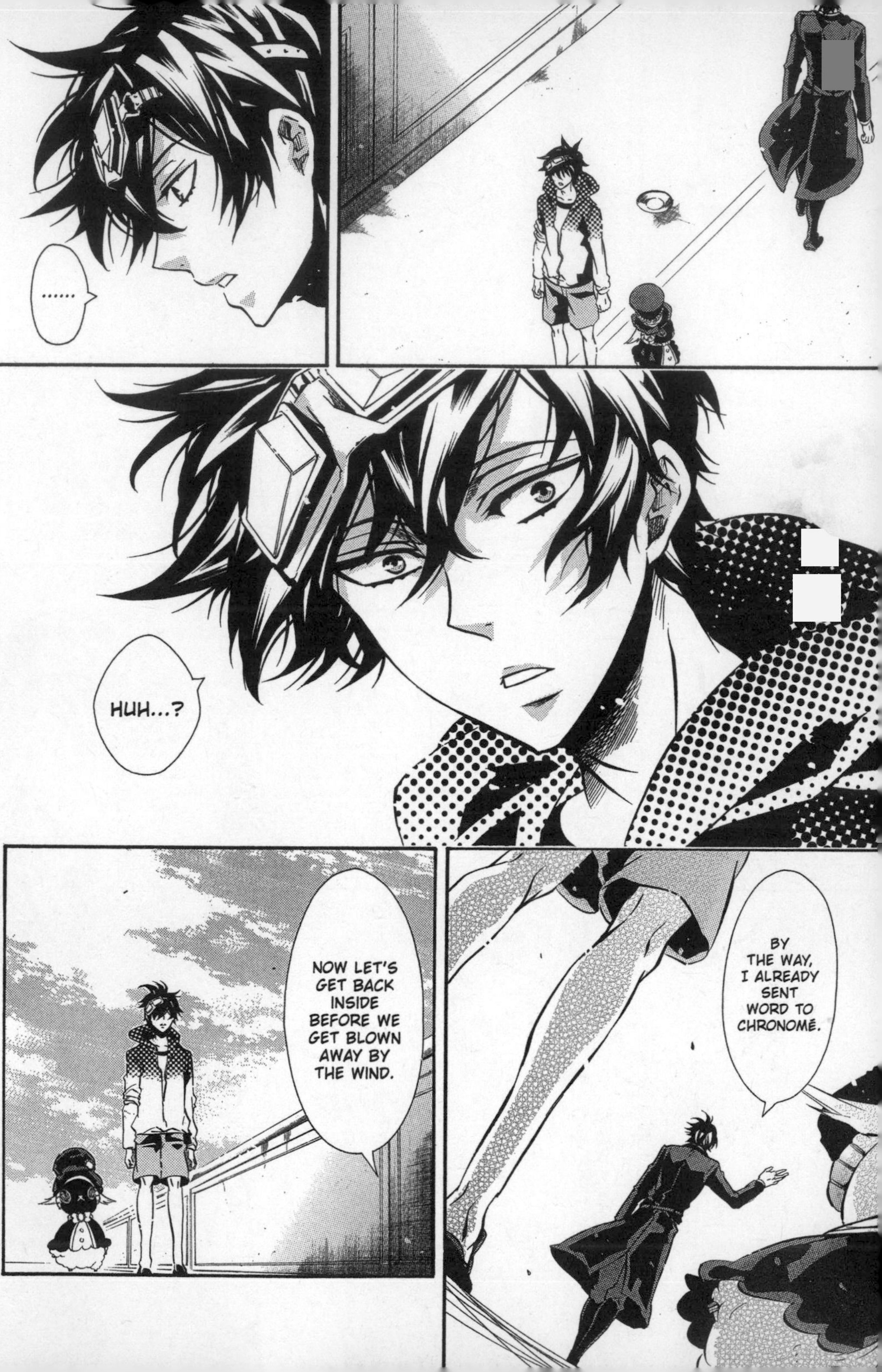
......
HUH...?
BY THE WAY, I ALREADY SENT WORD TO CHRONOMÉ.
NOW LET'S GET BACK INSIDE BEFORE WE GET BLOWN AWAY BY THE WIND.

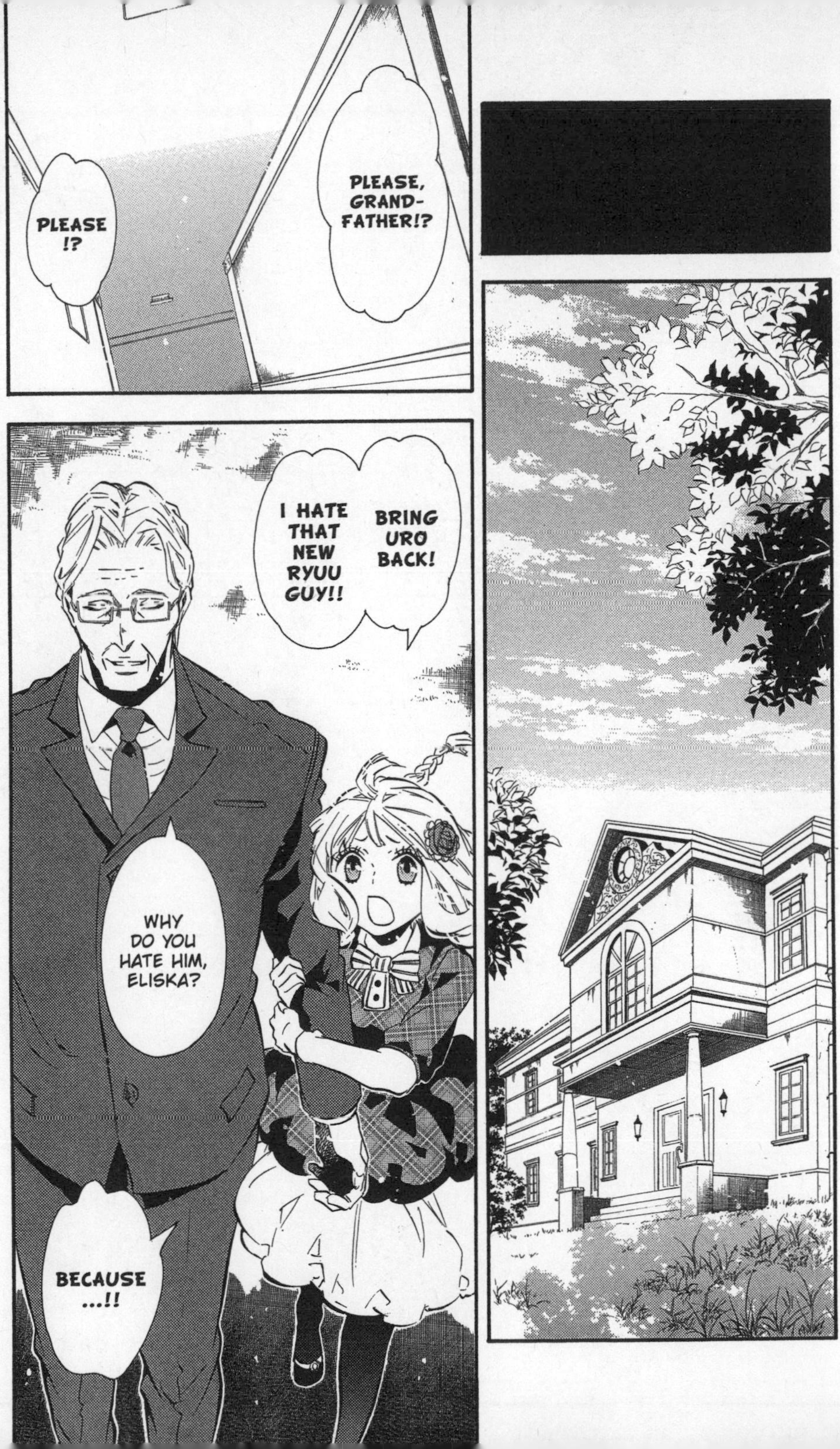
PLEASE, GRAND-FATHER!?
PLEASE!?
BRING URO BACK!
I HATE THAT NEW RYUU GUY!!
WHY DO YOU HATE HIM, ELISKA?
BECAUSE...!!

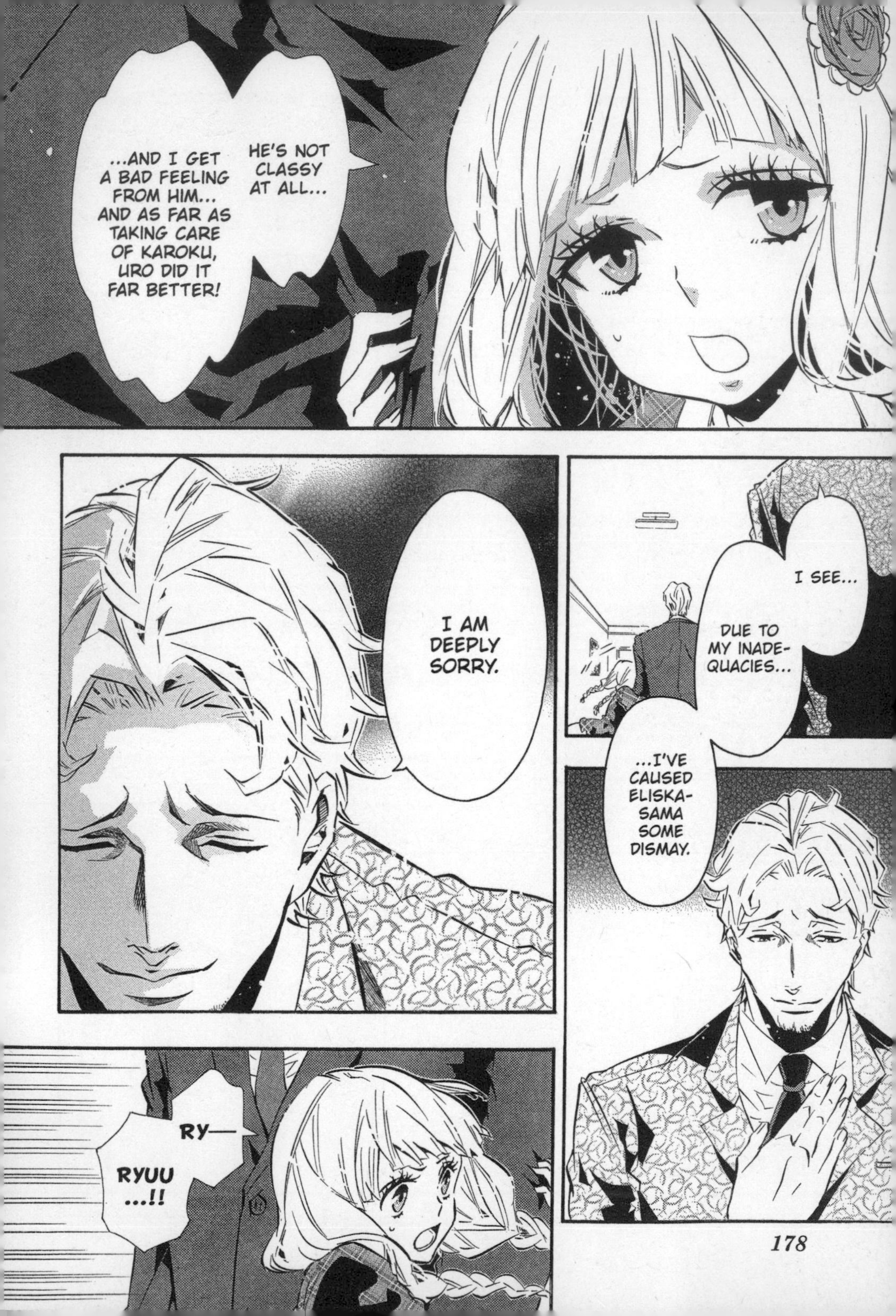
HE'S NOT CLASSY AT ALL...
...AND I GET A BAD FEELING FROM HIM... AND AS FAR AS TAKING CARE OF KAROKU, URO DID IT FAR BETTER!
I SEE...
DUE TO MY INADE-QUACIES...
...I'VE CAUSED ELISKA-SAMA SOME DISMAY.
I AM DEEPLY SORRY.
RY—
RYUU ...!!

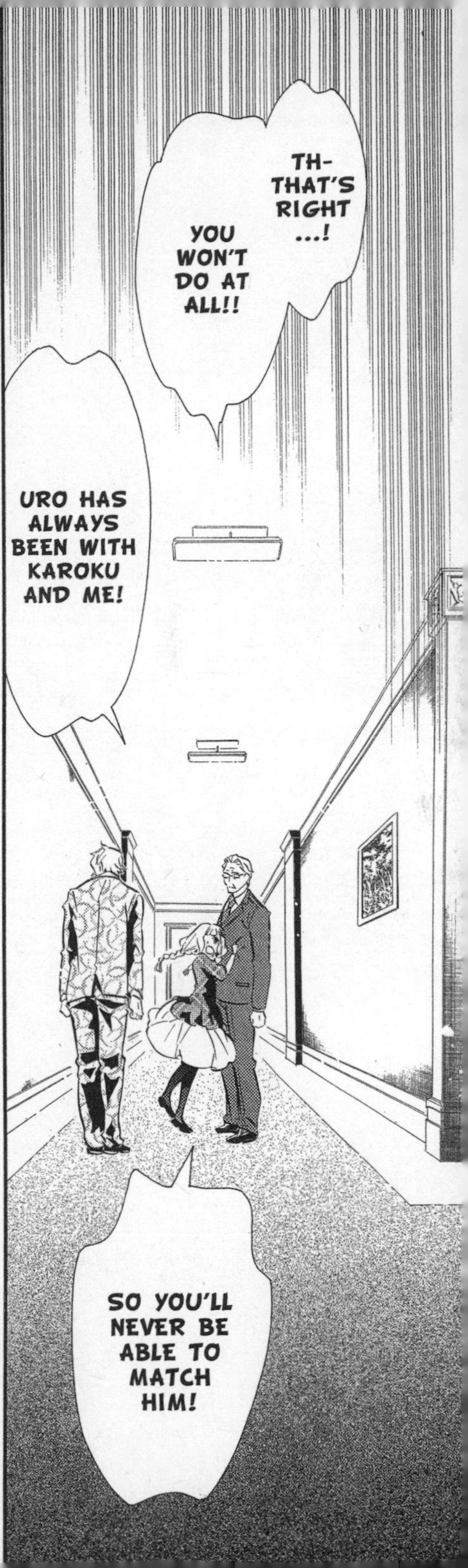
TH-THAT'S RIGHT...!
YOU WON'T DO AT ALL!!
URO HAS ALWAYS BEEN WITH KAROKU AND ME!
SO YOU'LL NEVER BE ABLE TO MATCH HIM!

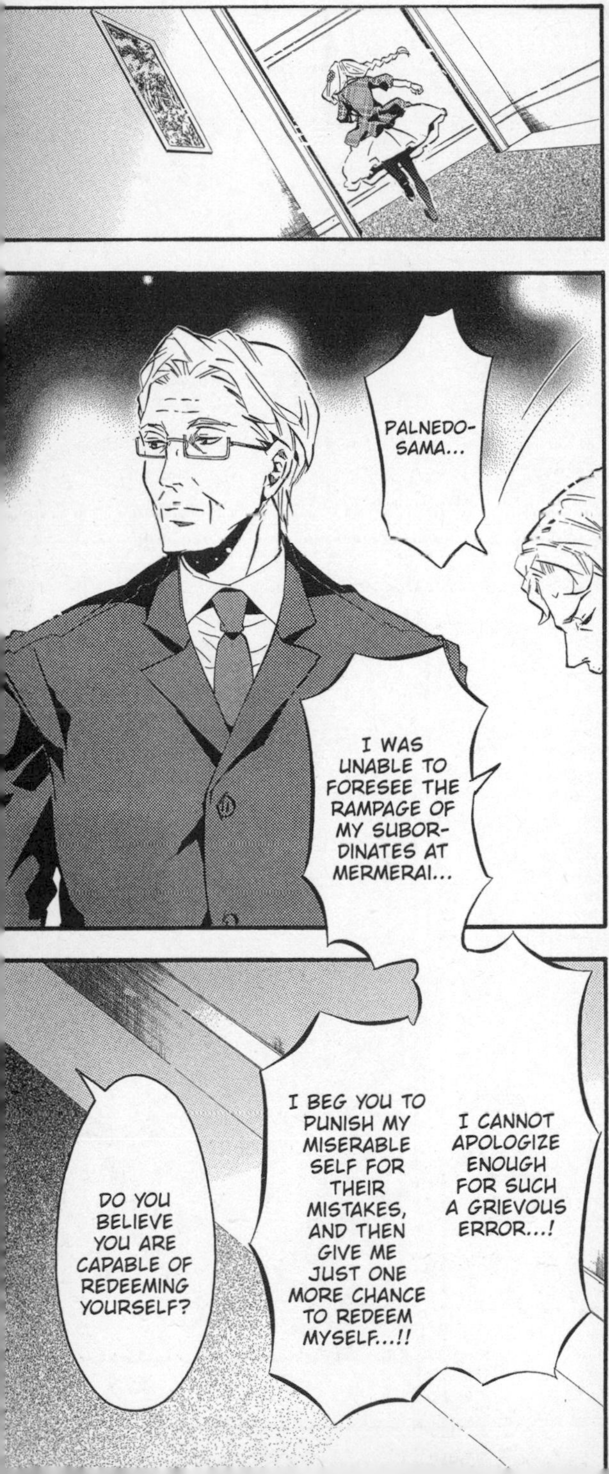
PALNEDO-SAMA...
I WAS UNABLE TO FORESEE THE RAMPAGE OF MY SUBORDINATES AT MERMERAI...
I CANNOT APOLOGIZE ENOUGH FOR SUCH A GRIEVOUS ERROR...!
I BEG YOU TO PUNISH MY MISERABLE SELF FOR THEIR MISTAKES, AND THEN GIVE ME JUST ONE MORE CHANCE TO REDEEM MYSELF...!!
DO YOU BELIEVE YOU ARE CAPABLE OF REDEEMING YOURSELF?

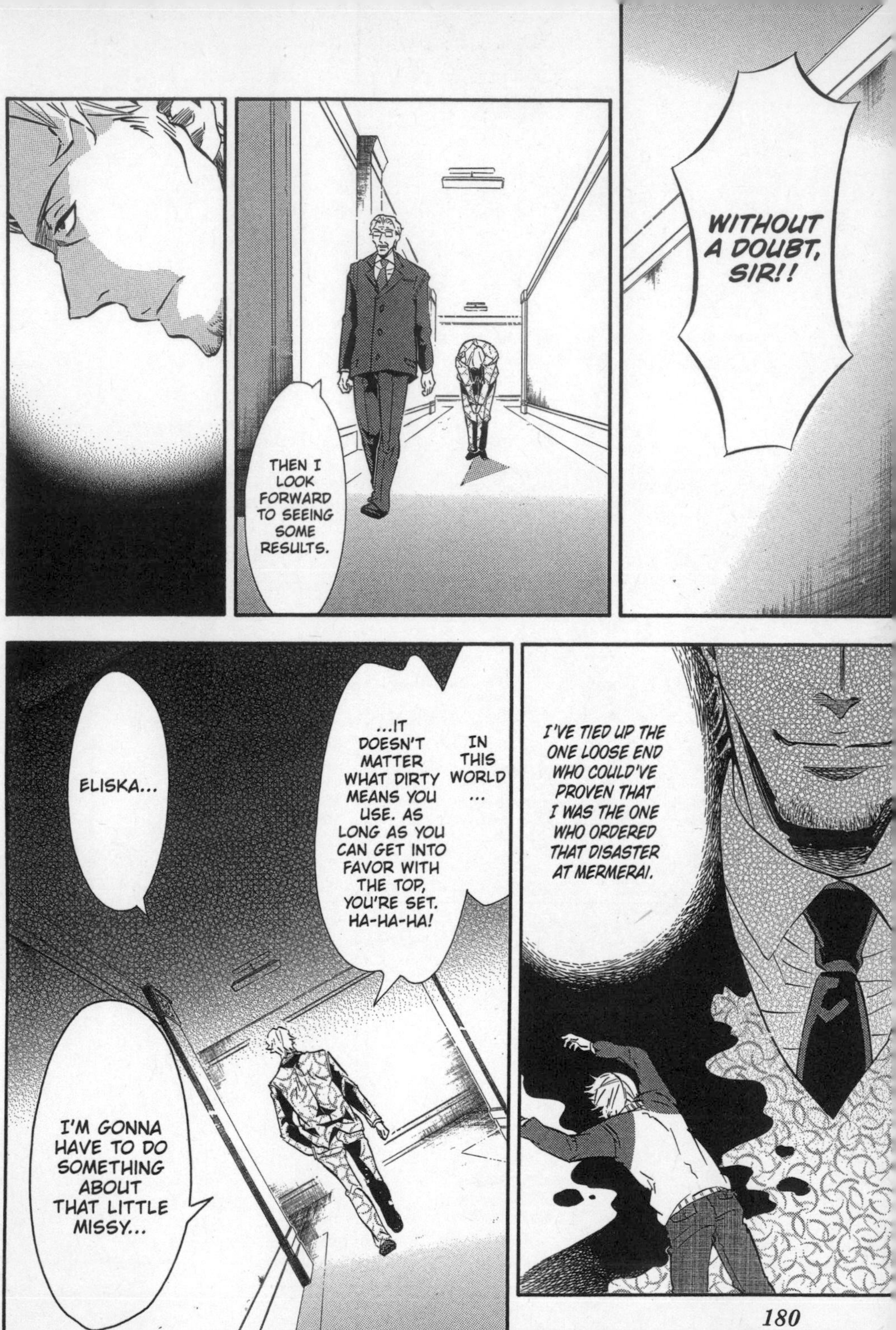
WITHOUT A DOUBT, SIR!!
THEN I LOOK FORWARD TO SEEING SOME RESULTS.
I'VE TIED UP THE ONE LOOSE END WHO COULD'VE PROVEN THAT I WAS THE ONE WHO ORDERED THAT DISASTER AT MERMERAI.
IN THIS WORLD...
...IT DOESN'T MATTER WHAT DIRTY MEANS YOU USE. AS LONG AS YOU CAN GET INTO FAVOR WITH THE TOP, YOU'RE SET. HA-HA-HA!
ELISKA...
I'M GONNA HAVE TO DO SOMETHING ABOUT THAT LITTLE MISSY...

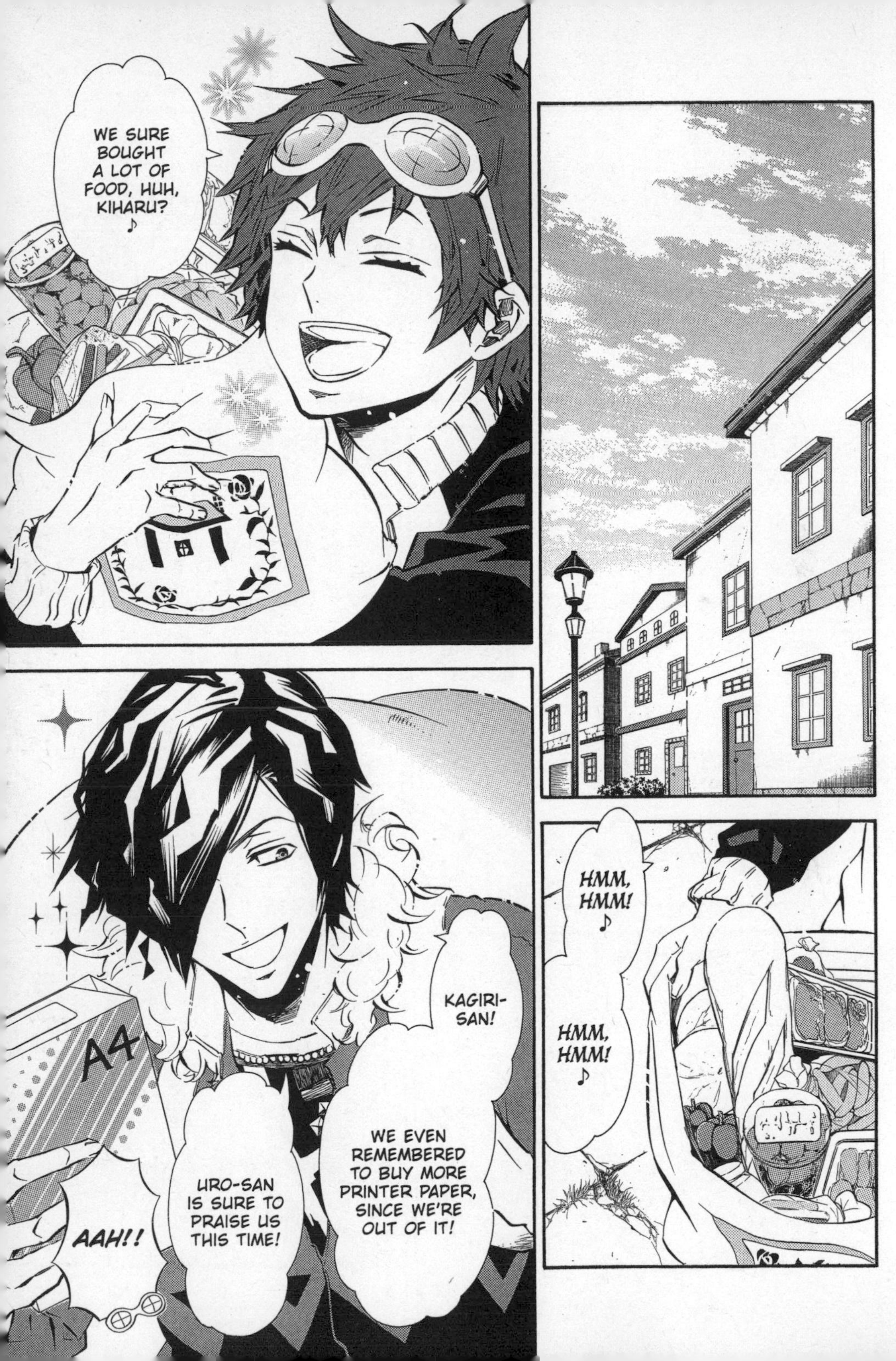
HMM, HMM! ♪
HMM, HMM! ♪
WE SURE BOUGHT A LOT OF FOOD, HUH, KIHARU? ♪
KAGIRI-SAN!
WE EVEN REMEMBERED TO BUY MORE PRINTER PAPER, SINCE WE'RE OUT OF IT!
URO-SAN IS SURE TO PRAISE US THIS TIME!
AAH!!
A4

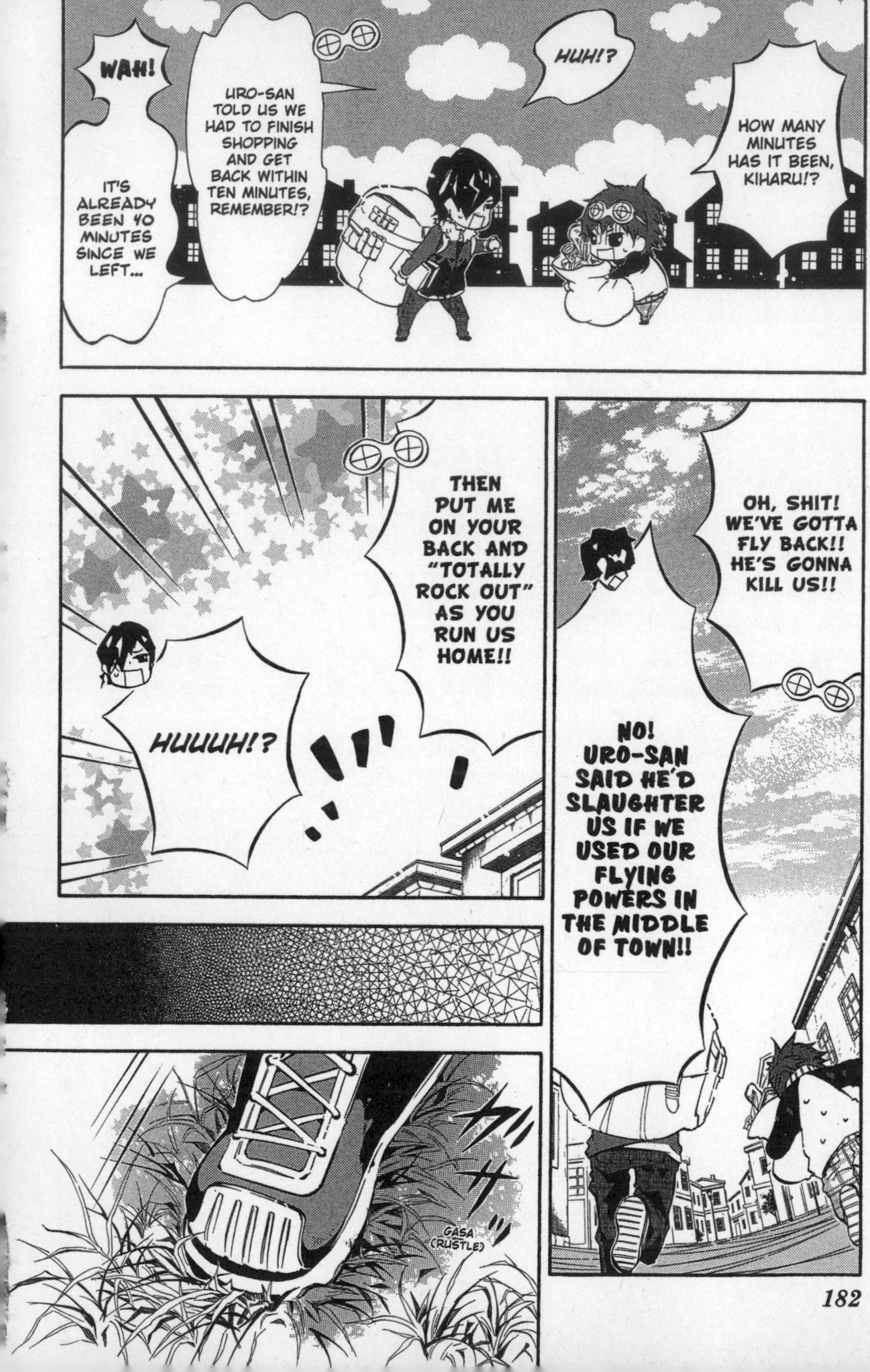
HOW MANY MINUTES HAS IT BEEN, KIHARU!?
HUH!?
URO-SAN TOLD US WE HAD TO FINISH SHOPPING AND GET BACK WITHIN TEN MINUTES, REMEMBER!?
WAH!
IT'S ALREADY BEEN 40 MINUTES SINCE WE LEFT...
OH, SHIT! WE'VE GOTTA FLY BACK!! HE'S GONNA KILL US!!
NO! URO-SAN SAID HE'D SLAUGHTER US IF WE USED OUR FLYING POWERS IN THE MIDDLE OF TOWN!!
THEN PUT ME ON YOUR BACK AND "TOTALLY ROCK OUT" AS YOU RUN US HOME!!
HUUUH!?
GASA (RUSTLE)

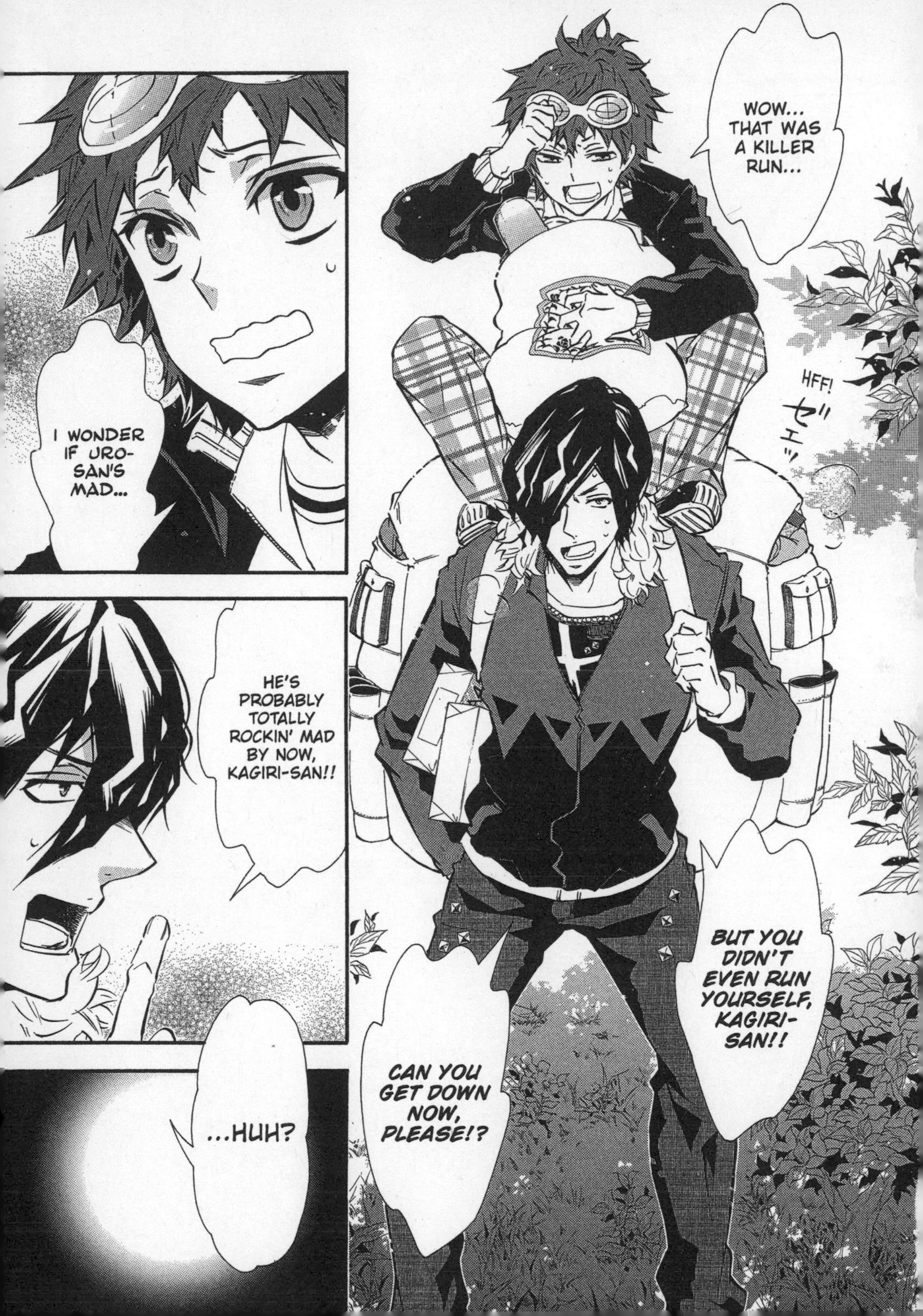
WOW... THAT WAS A KILLER RUN...
HFF!
ゼェッ
BUT YOU DIDN'T EVEN RUN YOURSELF, KAGIRI-SAN!!
CAN YOU GET DOWN NOW, PLEASE!?
I WONDER IF URO-SAN'S MAD...
HE'S PROBABLY TOTALLY ROCKIN' MAD BY NOW, KAGIRI-SAN!!
...HUH?

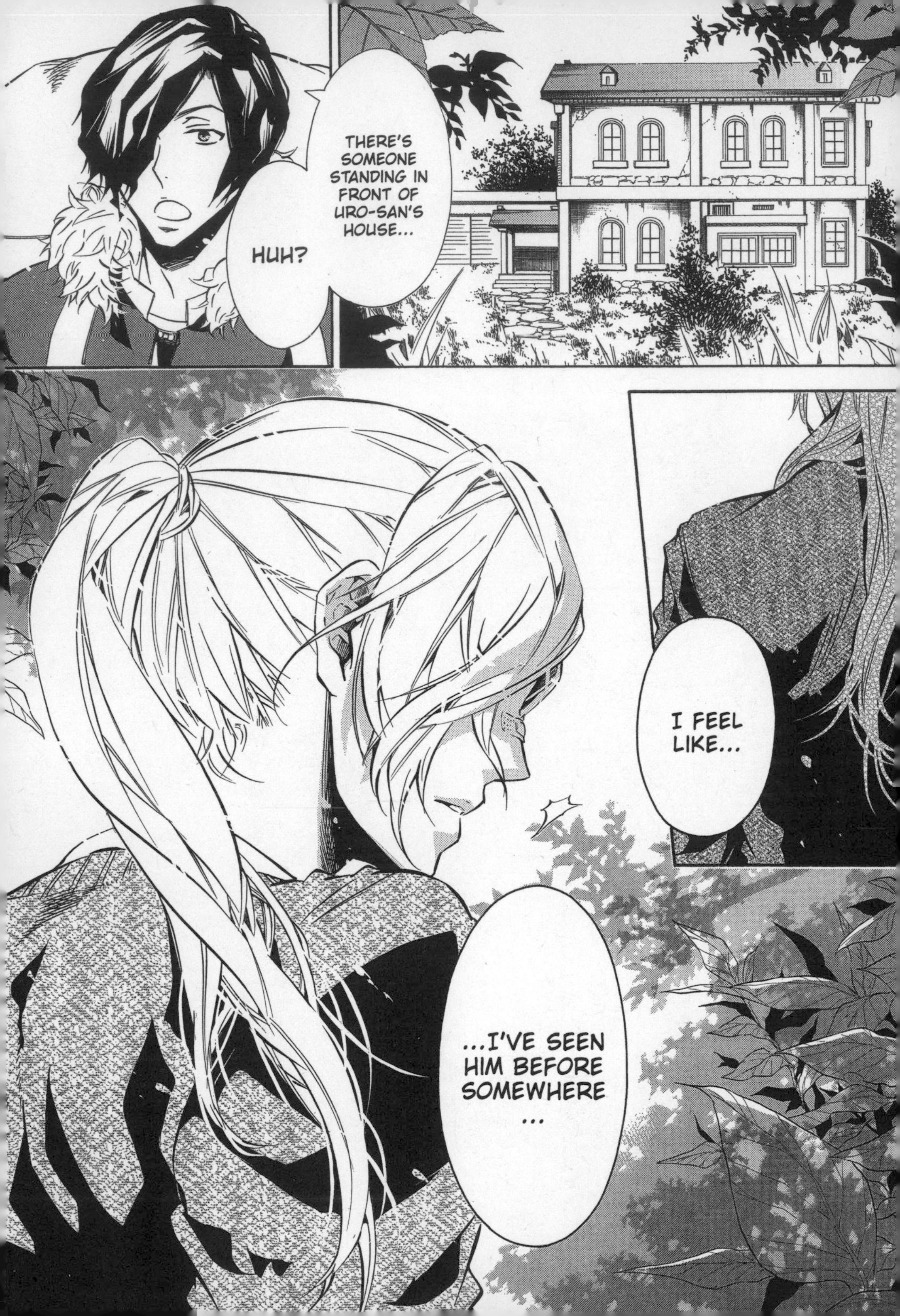
THERE'S SOMEONE STANDING IN FRONT OF URO-SAN'S HOUSE...
HUH?
I FEEL LIKE...
...I'VE SEEN HIM BEFORE SOMEWHERE ...

KARNEVAL

KARNEVAL

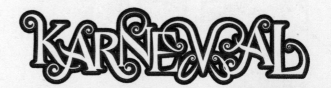

KARNEVAL

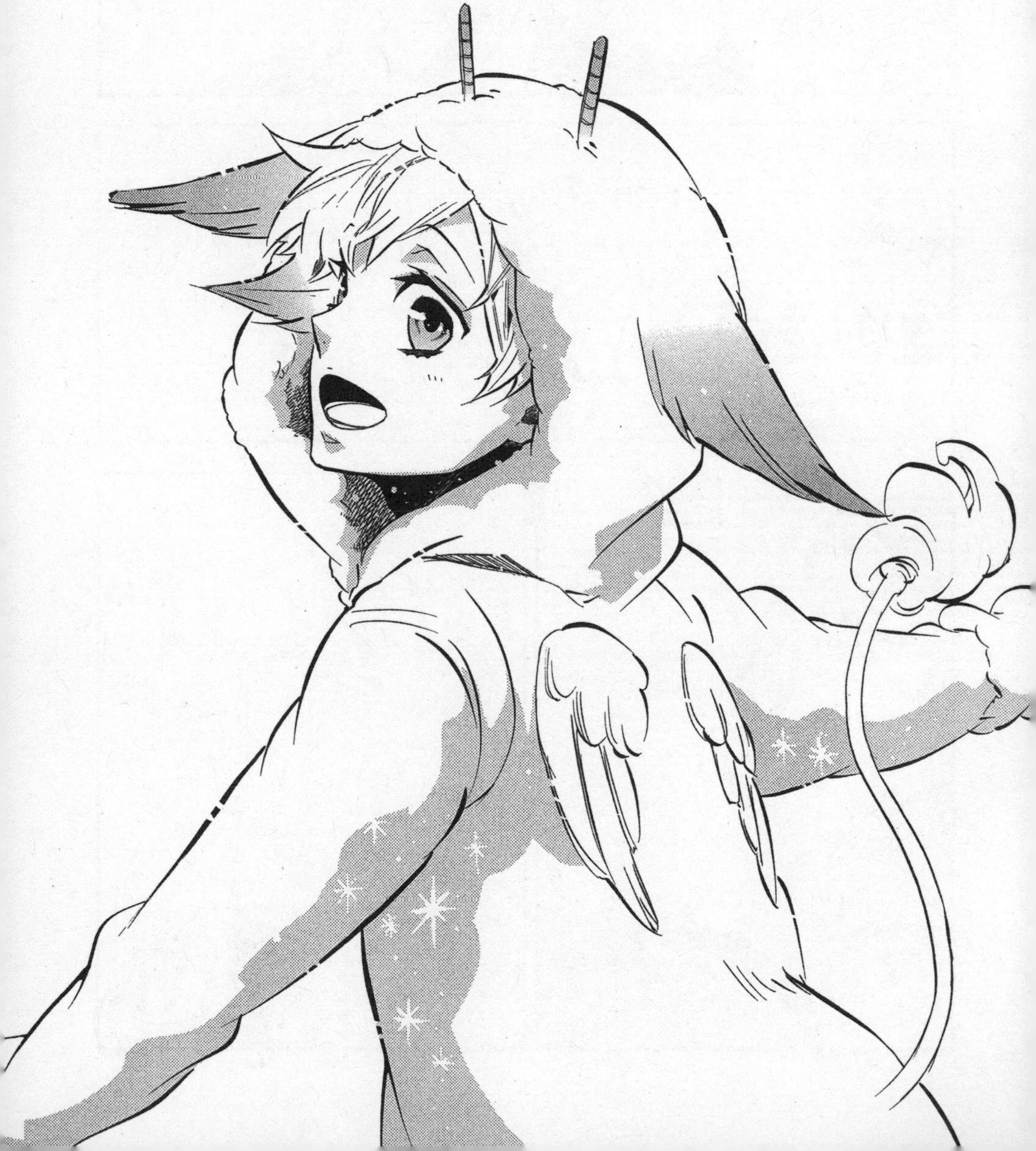

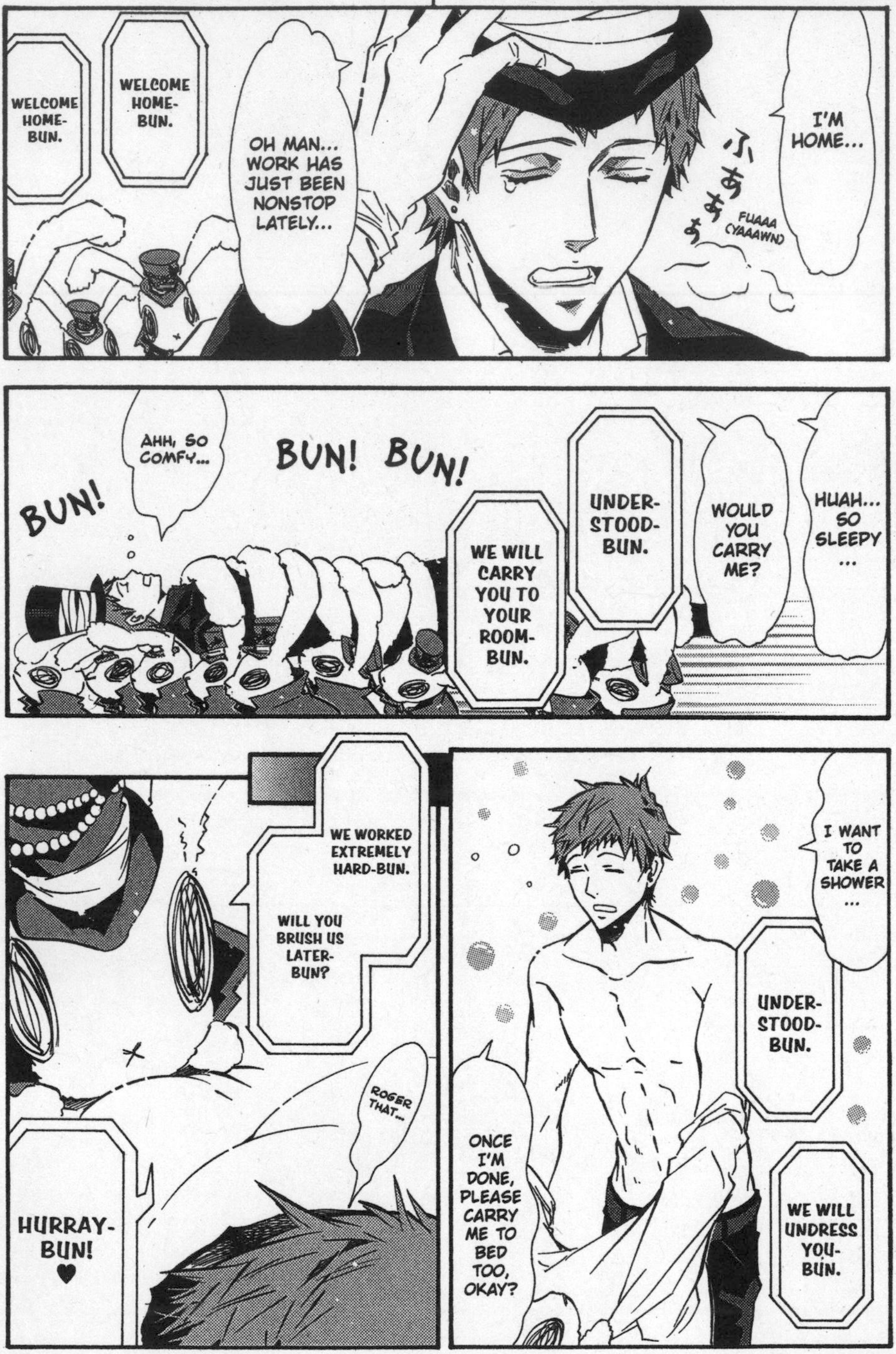
I'M HOME...
ふあぁぁ FUAAA (YAAAWN)
OH MAN... WORK HAS JUST BEEN NONSTOP LATELY...
WELCOME HOME-BUN.
WELCOME HOME-BUN.
HUAH... SO SLEEPY...
WOULD YOU CARRY ME?
UNDER-STOOD-BUN.
WE WILL CARRY YOU TO YOUR ROOM-BUN.
BUN! BUN!
AHH, SO COMFY...
BUN!
I WANT TO TAKE A SHOWER...
UNDER-STOOD-BUN.
WE WILL UNDRESS YOU-BUN.
ONCE I'M DONE, PLEASE CARRY ME TO BED TOO, OKAY?
WE WORKED EXTREMELY HARD-BUN.
WILL YOU BRUSH US LATER-BUN?
ROGER THAT...
HURRAY-BUN! ♥

Bonus Comic 2 - Don't You Just Want to Chase Around Small Animals?

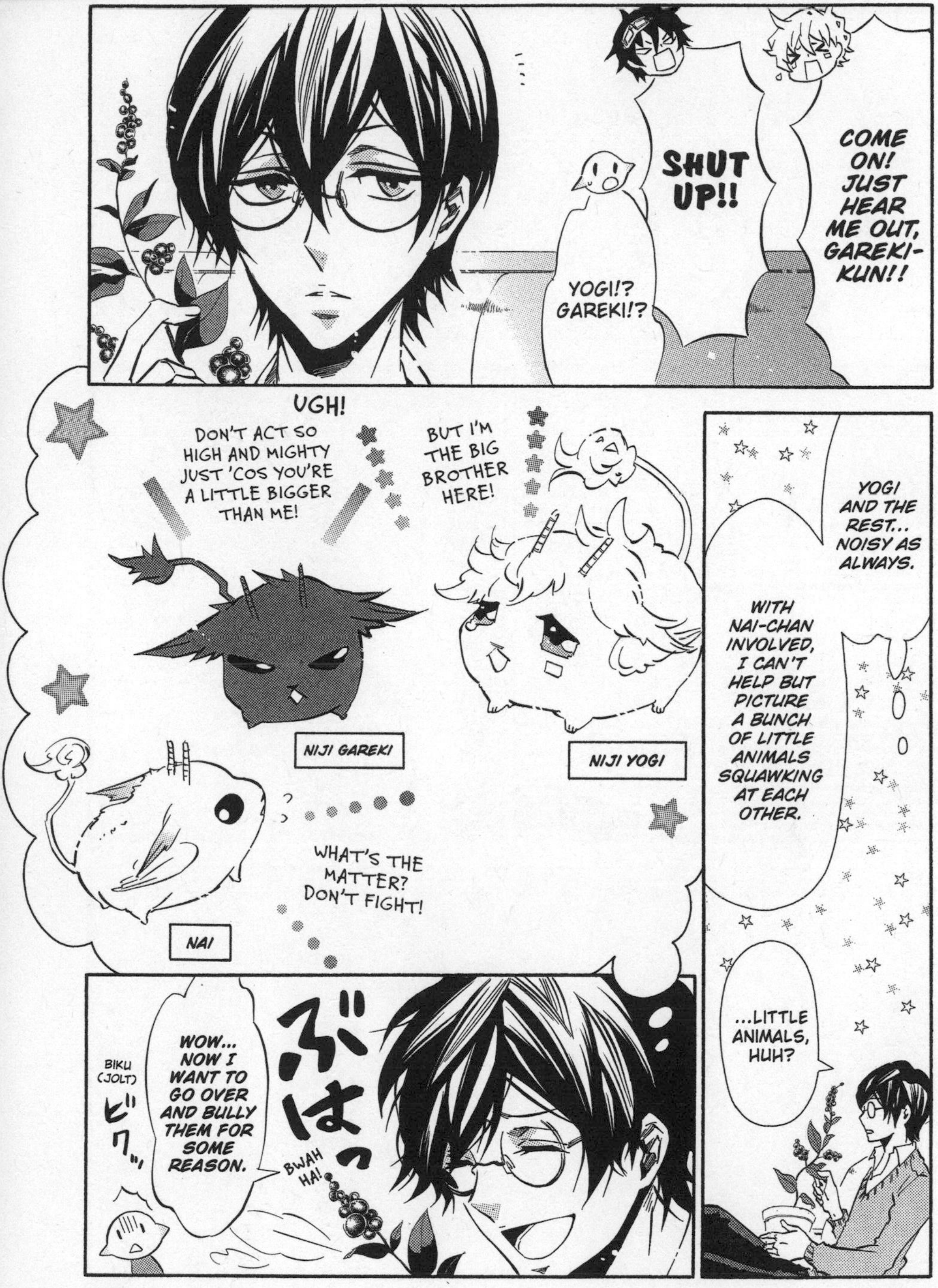

COME ON! JUST HEAR ME OUT, GAREKI-KUN!!
SHUT UP!!
YOGI!? GAREKI!?
YOGI AND THE REST... NOISY AS ALWAYS.
WITH NAI-CHAN INVOLVED, I CAN'T HELP BUT PICTURE A BUNCH OF LITTLE ANIMALS SQUAWKING AT EACH OTHER.
...LITTLE ANIMALS, HUH?
BUT I'M THE BIG BROTHER HERE!
UGH! DON'T ACT SO HIGH AND MIGHTY JUST 'COS YOU'RE A LITTLE BIGGER THAN ME!
NIJI YOGI
NIJI GAREKI
WHAT'S THE MATTER? DON'T FIGHT!
NAI
ぶはっ
BWAH HA!
WOW... NOW I WANT TO GO OVER AND BULLY THEM FOR SOME REASON.
BIKU (JOLT)
ビクッ

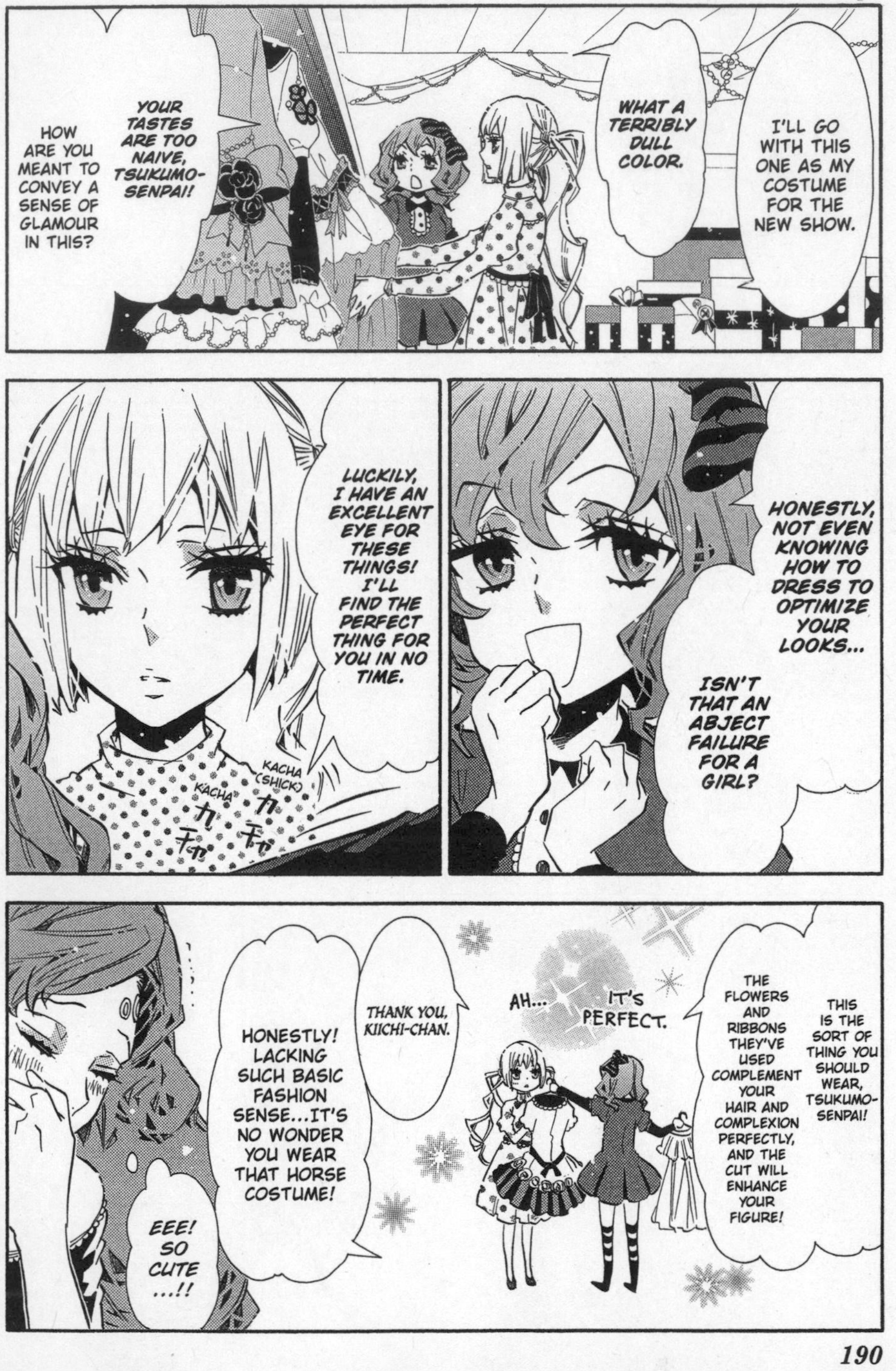
I'LL GO WITH THIS ONE AS MY COSTUME FOR THE NEW SHOW.
WHAT A TERRIBLY DULL COLOR.
YOUR TASTES ARE TOO NAIVE, TSUKUMO-SENPAI!
HOW ARE YOU MEANT TO CONVEY A SENSE OF GLAMOUR IN THIS?
HONESTLY, NOT EVEN KNOWING HOW TO DRESS TO OPTIMIZE YOUR LOOKS...
ISN'T THAT AN ABJECT FAILURE FOR A GIRL?
LUCKILY, I HAVE AN EXCELLENT EYE FOR THESE THINGS! I'LL FIND THE PERFECT THING FOR YOU IN NO TIME.
KACHA (SHICK)
カチャ
KACHA
カチャ
THIS IS THE SORT OF THING YOU SHOULD WEAR, TSUKUMO-SENPAI!
THE FLOWERS AND RIBBONS THEY'VE USED COMPLEMENT YOUR HAIR AND COMPLEXION PERFECTLY, AND THE CUT WILL ENHANCE YOUR FIGURE!
AH... IT'S PERFECT.
THANK YOU, KIICHI-CHAN.
HONESTLY! LACKING SUCH BASIC FASHION SENSE...IT'S NO WONDER YOU WEAR THAT HORSE COSTUME!
EEE! SO CUTE ...!!

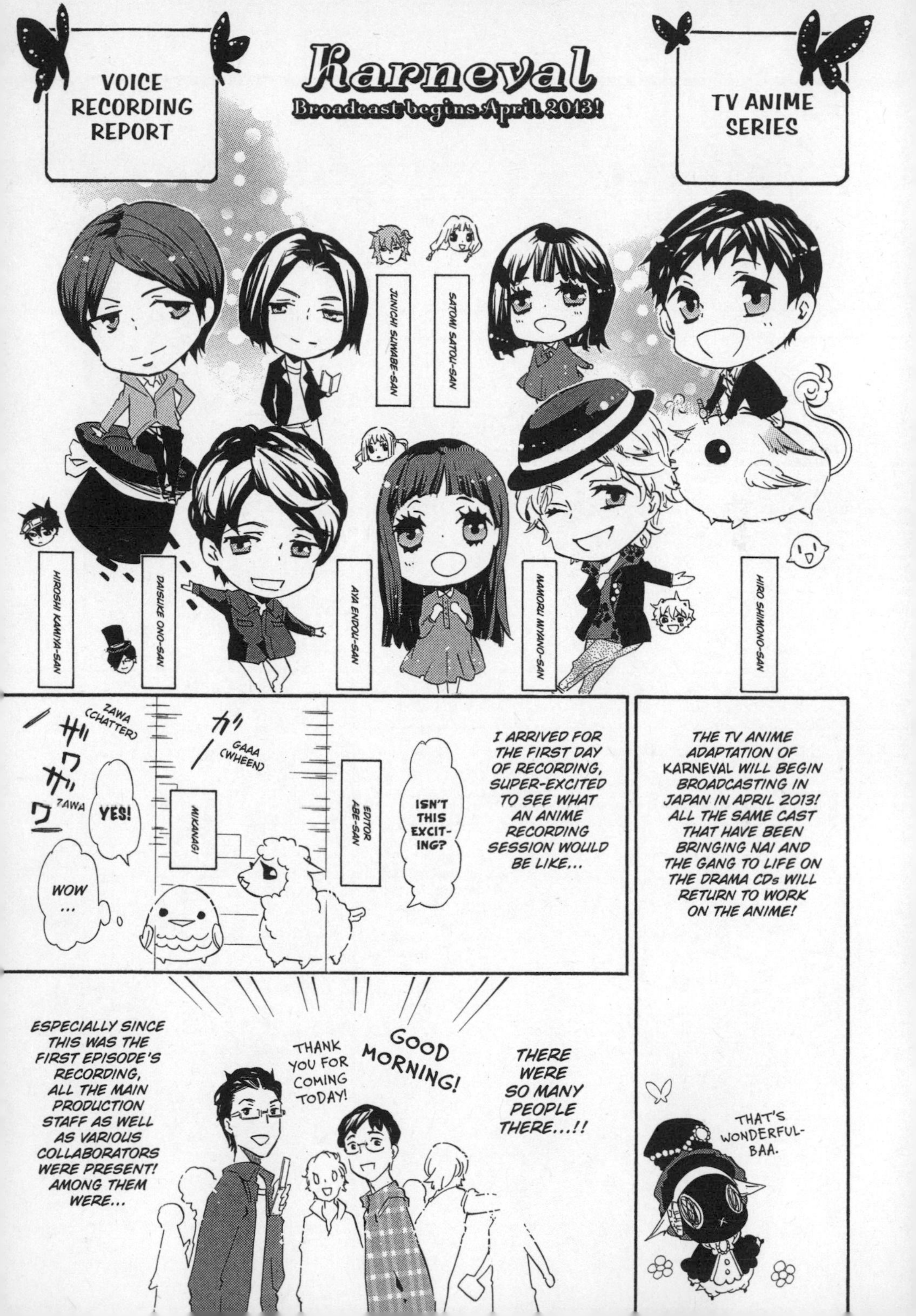
Karneval
Broadcast begins April 2013!
TV ANIME SERIES
VOICE RECORDING REPORT
SATOMI SATOU-SAN
JUNICHI SUWABE-SAN
HIRO SHIMONO-SAN
MAMORU MIYANO-SAN
AYA ENDOU-SAN
DAISUKE ONO-SAN
HIROSHI KAMIYA-SAN
THE TV ANIME ADAPTATION OF KARNEVAL WILL BEGIN BROADCASTING IN JAPAN IN APRIL 2013! ALL THE SAME CAST THAT HAVE BEEN BRINGING NAI AND THE GANG TO LIFE ON THE DRAMA CDS WILL RETURN TO WORK ON THE ANIME!
THAT'S WONDERFUL-BAA.
I ARRIVED FOR THE FIRST DAY OF RECORDING, SUPER-EXCITED TO SEE WHAT AN ANIME RECORDING SESSION WOULD BE LIKE...
ISN'T THIS EXCIT-ING?
EDITOR ABE-SAN
MIKANAGI
GAAA (WHEEN)
YES!
ZAWA (CHATTER)
ZAWA
WOW...
THERE WERE SO MANY PEOPLE THERE...!!
GOOD MORNING!
THANK YOU FOR COMING TODAY!
ESPECIALLY SINCE THIS WAS THE FIRST EPISODE'S RECORDING, ALL THE MAIN PRODUCTION STAFF AS WELL AS VARIOUS COLLABORATORS WERE PRESENT! AMONG THEM WERE...

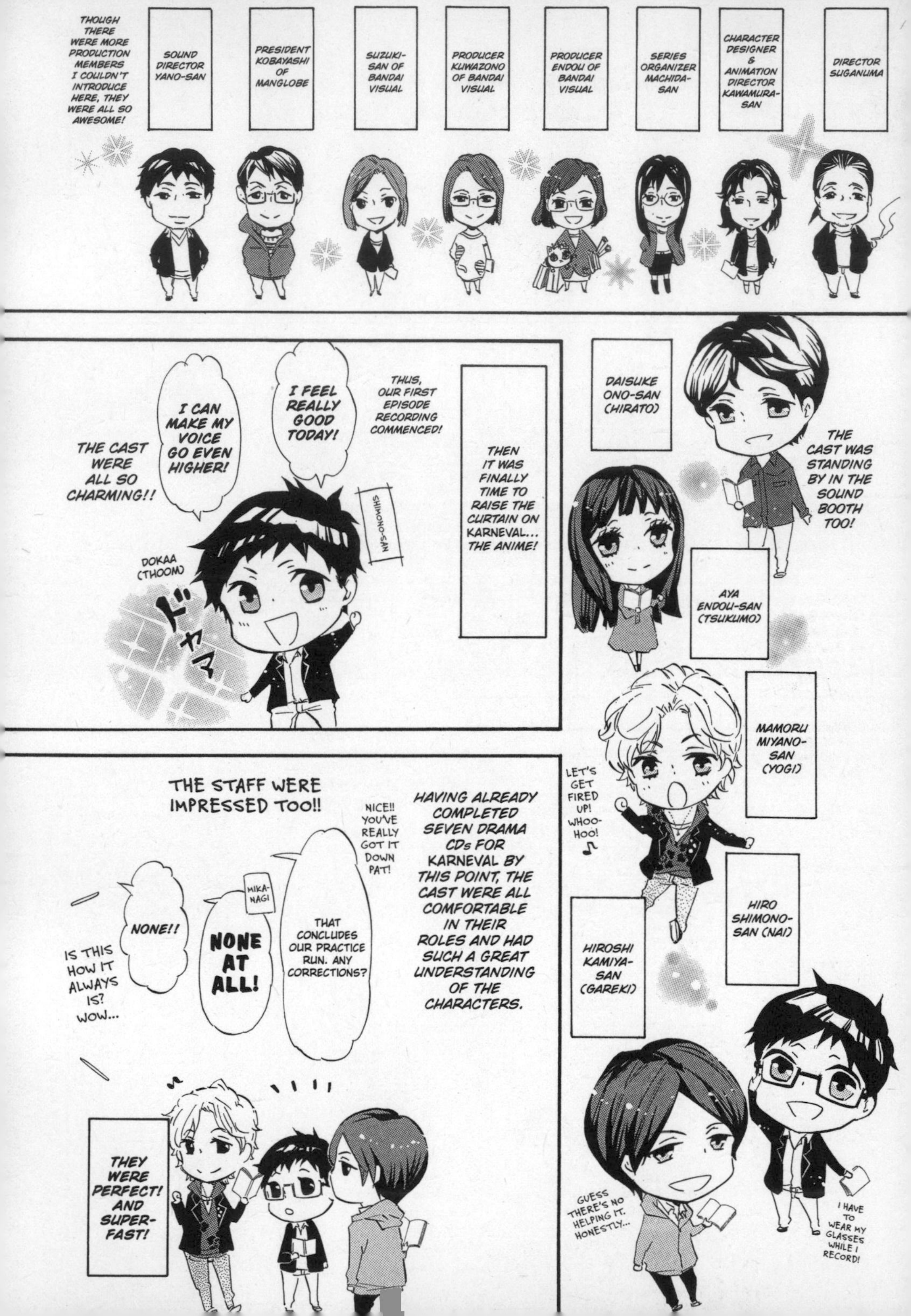
DIRECTOR SUGANUMA
CHARACTER DESIGNER & ANIMATION DIRECTOR KAWAMURA-SAN
SERIES ORGANIZER MACHIDA-SAN
PRODUCER ENDOU OF BANDAI VISUAL
PRODUCER KUWAZONO OF BANDAI VISUAL
SUZUKI-SAN OF BANDAI VISUAL
PRESIDENT KOBAYASHI OF MANGLOBE
SOUND DIRECTOR YANO-SAN
THOUGH THERE WERE MORE PRODUCTION MEMBERS I COULDN'T INTRODUCE HERE, THEY WERE ALL SO AWESOME!
DAISUKE ONO-SAN (HIRATO)
THE CAST WAS STANDING BY IN THE SOUND BOOTH TOO!
AYA ENDOU-SAN (TSUKUMO)
MAMORU MIYANO-SAN (YOGI)
LET'S GET FIRED UP! WHOO-HOO!
HIRO SHIMONO-SAN (NAI)
HIROSHI KAMIYA-SAN (GAREKI)
I HAVE TO WEAR MY GLASSES WHILE I RECORD!
GUESS THERE'S NO HELPING IT. HONESTLY...
THEN IT WAS FINALLY TIME TO RAISE THE CURTAIN ON KARNEVAL... THE ANIME!
THUS, OUR FIRST EPISODE RECORDING COMMENCED!
I FEEL REALLY GOOD TODAY!
I CAN MAKE MY VOICE GO EVEN HIGHER!
THE CAST WERE ALL SO CHARMING!!
SHIMONO-SAN
DOKAA (THOOM)
HAVING ALREADY COMPLETED SEVEN DRAMA CDs FOR KARNEVAL BY THIS POINT, THE CAST WERE ALL COMFORTABLE IN THEIR ROLES AND HAD SUCH A GREAT UNDERSTANDING OF THE CHARACTERS.
THE STAFF WERE IMPRESSED TOO!!
NICE!! YOU'VE REALLY GOT IT DOWN PAT!
THAT CONCLUDES OUR PRACTICE RUN. ANY CORRECTIONS?
MIKA-NAGI
NONE AT ALL!
NONE!!
IS THIS HOW IT ALWAYS IS? WOW...
THEY WERE PERFECT! AND SUPER-FAST!

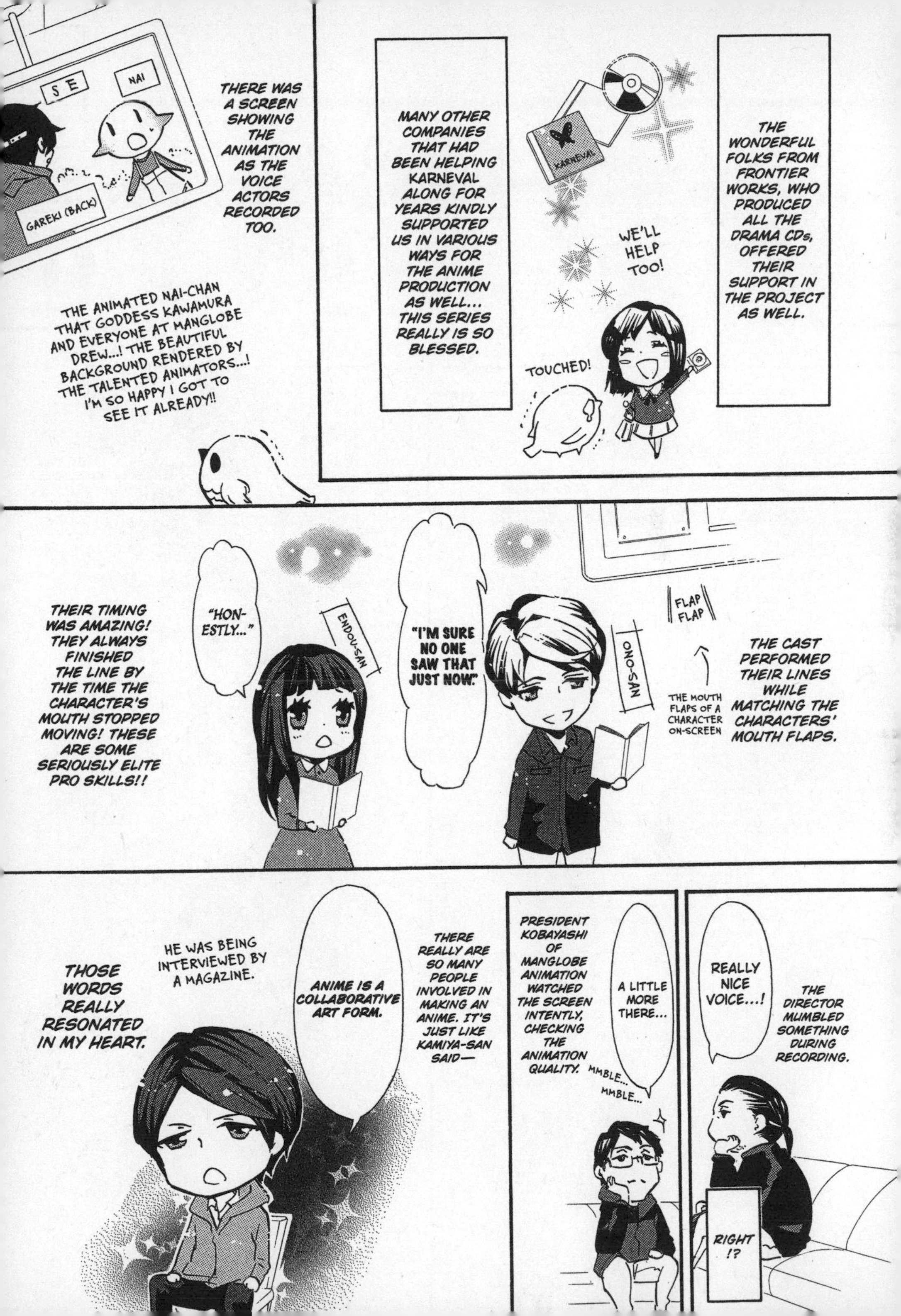
THE WONDERFUL FOLKS FROM FRONTIER WORKS, WHO PRODUCED ALL THE DRAMA CDs, OFFERED THEIR SUPPORT IN THE PROJECT AS WELL.
WE'LL HELP TOO!
MANY OTHER COMPANIES THAT HAD BEEN HELPING KARNEVAL ALONG FOR YEARS KINDLY SUPPORTED US IN VARIOUS WAYS FOR THE ANIME PRODUCTION AS WELL... THIS SERIES REALLY IS SO BLESSED.
KARNEVAL
TOUCHED!
THERE WAS A SCREEN SHOWING THE ANIMATION AS THE VOICE ACTORS RECORDED TOO.
NAI
S E
GAREKI (BACK)
THE ANIMATED NAI-CHAN THAT GODDESS KAWAMURA AND EVERYONE AT MANGLOBE DREW...! THE BEAUTIFUL BACKGROUND RENDERED BY THE TALENTED ANIMATORS...! I'M SO HAPPY I GOT TO SEE IT ALREADY!!
THE CAST PERFORMED THEIR LINES WHILE MATCHING THE CHARACTERS' MOUTH FLAPS.
FLAP FLAP
THE MOUTH FLAPS OF A CHARACTER ON-SCREEN
ONO-SAN
"I'M SURE NO ONE SAW THAT JUST NOW."
ENDOU-SAN
"HON-ESTLY..."
THEIR TIMING WAS AMAZING! THEY ALWAYS FINISHED THE LINE BY THE TIME THE CHARACTER'S MOUTH STOPPED MOVING! THESE ARE SOME SERIOUSLY ELITE PRO SKILLS!!
THE DIRECTOR MUMBLED SOMETHING DURING RECORDING.
REALLY NICE VOICE...!
RIGHT!?
A LITTLE MORE THERE...
PRESIDENT KOBAYASHI OF MANGLOBE ANIMATION WATCHED THE SCREEN INTENTLY, CHECKING THE ANIMATION QUALITY.
MMBLE... MMBLE...
THERE REALLY ARE SO MANY PEOPLE INVOLVED IN MAKING AN ANIME. IT'S JUST LIKE KAMIYA-SAN SAID—
ANIME IS A COLLABORATIVE ART FORM.
HE WAS BEING INTERVIEWED BY A MAGAZINE.
THOSE WORDS REALLY RESONATED IN MY HEART.

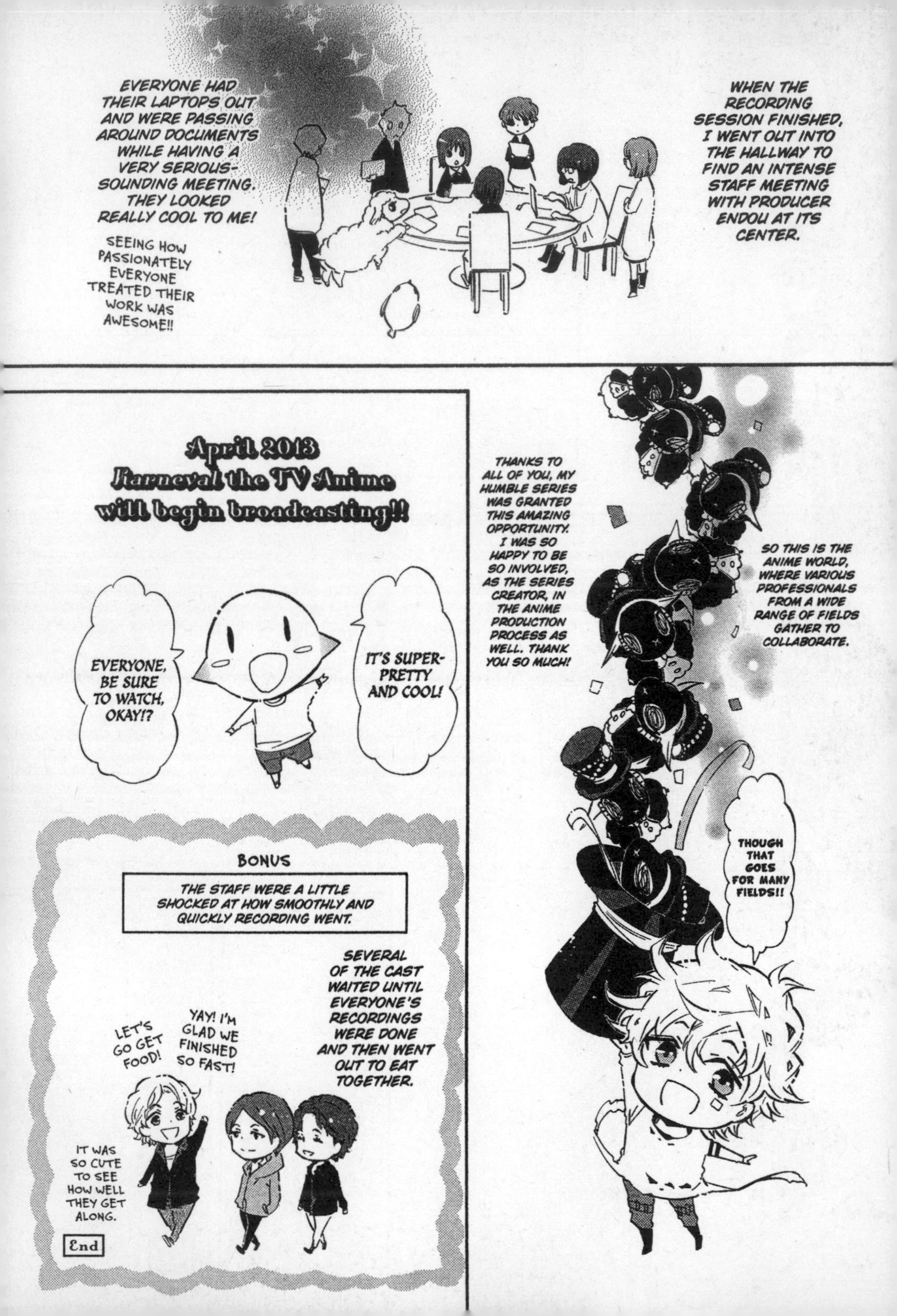
WHEN THE RECORDING SESSION FINISHED, I WENT OUT INTO THE HALLWAY TO FIND AN INTENSE STAFF MEETING WITH PRODUCER ENDOU AT ITS CENTER.
EVERYONE HAD THEIR LAPTOPS OUT AND WERE PASSING AROUND DOCUMENTS WHILE HAVING A VERY SERIOUS-SOUNDING MEETING. THEY LOOKED REALLY COOL TO ME!
SEEING HOW PASSIONATELY EVERYONE TREATED THEIR WORK WAS AWESOME!!
THANKS TO ALL OF YOU, MY HUMBLE SERIES WAS GRANTED THIS AMAZING OPPORTUNITY. I WAS SO HAPPY TO BE SO INVOLVED, AS THE SERIES CREATOR, IN THE ANIME PRODUCTION PROCESS AS WELL.. THANK YOU SO MUCH!
SO THIS IS THE ANIME WORLD, WHERE VARIOUS PROFESSIONALS FROM A WIDE RANGE OF FIELDS GATHER TO COLLABORATE.
THOUGH THAT GOES FOR MANY FIELDS!!
April 2013
Karneval the TV Anime
will begin broadcasting!!
IT'S SUPER-PRETTY AND COOL!
EVERYONE, BE SURE TO WATCH, OKAY!?
BONUS
THE STAFF WERE A LITTLE SHOCKED AT HOW SMOOTHLY AND QUICKLY RECORDING WENT.
SEVERAL OF THE CAST WAITED UNTIL EVERYONE'S RECORDINGS WERE DONE AND THEN WENT OUT TO EAT TOGETHER.
YAY! I'M GLAD WE FINISHED SO FAST!
LET'S GO GET FOOD!
IT WAS SO CUTE TO SEE HOW WELL THEY GET ALONG.
End

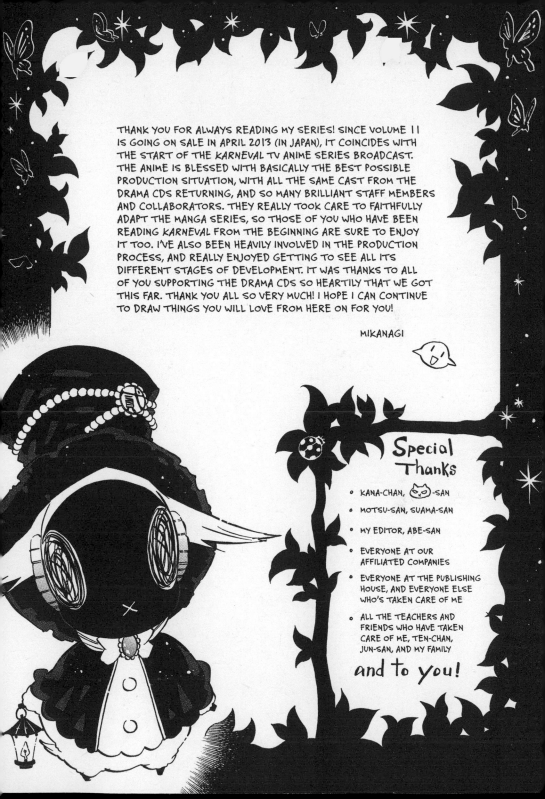

THANK YOU FOR ALWAYS READING MY SERIES! SINCE VOLUME 11 IS GOING ON SALE IN APRIL 2013 (IN JAPAN), IT COINCIDES WITH THE START OF THE *KARNEVAL* TV ANIME SERIES BROADCAST. THE ANIME IS BLESSED WITH BASICALLY THE BEST POSSIBLE PRODUCTION SITUATION, WITH ALL THE SAME CAST FROM THE DRAMA CDS RETURNING, AND SO MANY BRILLIANT STAFF MEMBERS AND COLLABORATORS. THEY REALLY TOOK CARE TO FAITHFULLY ADAPT THE MANGA SERIES, SO THOSE OF YOU WHO HAVE BEEN READING *KARNEVAL* FROM THE BEGINNING ARE SURE TO ENJOY IT TOO. I'VE ALSO BEEN HEAVILY INVOLVED IN THE PRODUCTION PROCESS, AND REALLY ENJOYED GETTING TO SEE ALL ITS DIFFERENT STAGES OF DEVELOPMENT. IT WAS THANKS TO ALL OF YOU SUPPORTING THE DRAMA CDS SO HEARTILY THAT WE GOT THIS FAR. THANK YOU ALL SO VERY MUCH! I HOPE I CAN CONTINUE TO DRAW THINGS YOU WILL LOVE FROM HERE ON FOR YOU!

MIKANAGI

Special Thanks

- KANA-CHAN, [cat]-SAN
- MOTSU-SAN, SUAMA-SAN
- MY EDITOR, ABE-SAN
- EVERYONE AT OUR AFFILIATED COMPANIES
- EVERYONE AT THE PUBLISHING HOUSE, AND EVERYONE ELSE WHO'S TAKEN CARE OF ME
- ALL THE TEACHERS AND FRIENDS WHO HAVE TAKEN CARE OF ME, TEN-CHAN, JUN-SAN, AND MY FAMILY

and to you!

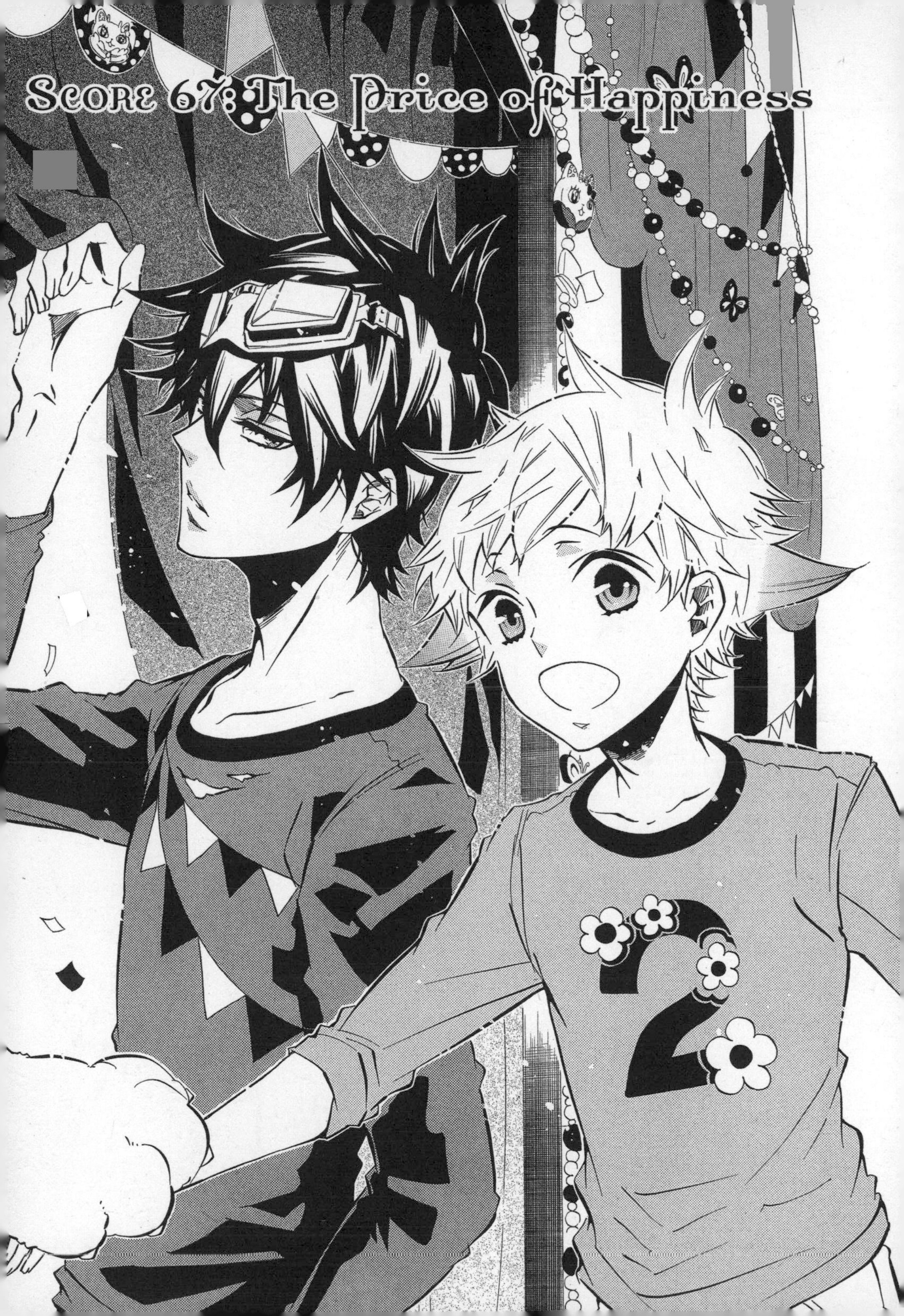
Score 67: The Price of Happiness

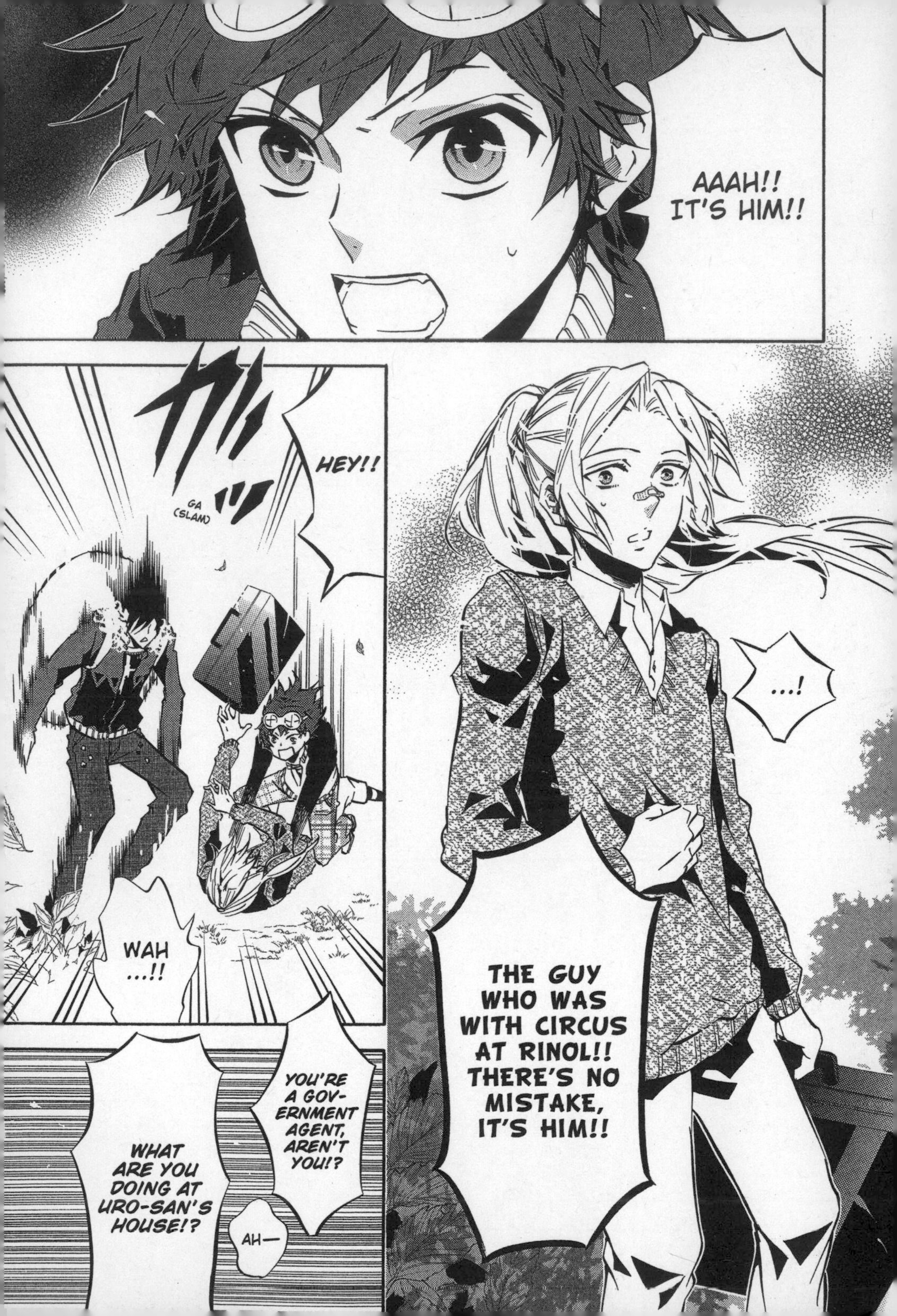
AAAH!! IT'S HIM!!
...!
THE GUY WHO WAS WITH CIRCUS AT RINOL!! THERE'S NO MISTAKE, IT'S HIM!!
HEY!!
GA (SLAM)
WAH ...!!
YOU'RE A GOVERNMENT AGENT, AREN'T YOU!?
WHAT ARE YOU DOING AT URO-SAN'S HOUSE!?
AH—

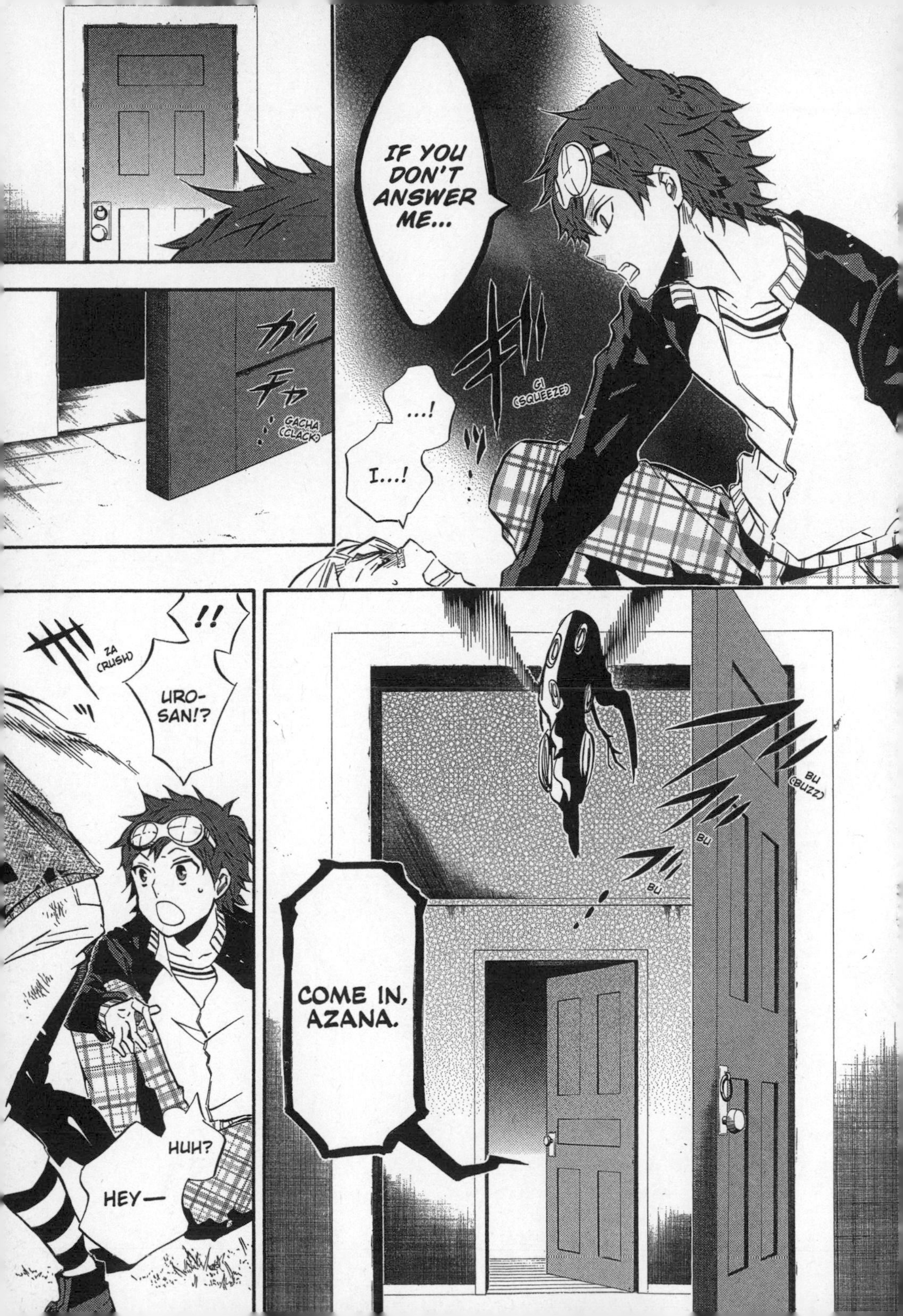
IF YOU DON'T ANSWER ME...
ギ
GI (SQUEEZE)
...!
I...!
ガチャ
GACHA (CLACK)
ブ
BU (BUZZ)
BU
BU
COME IN, AZANA.
!!
ザ
ZA (RUSH)
URO-SAN!?
HUH?
HEY—

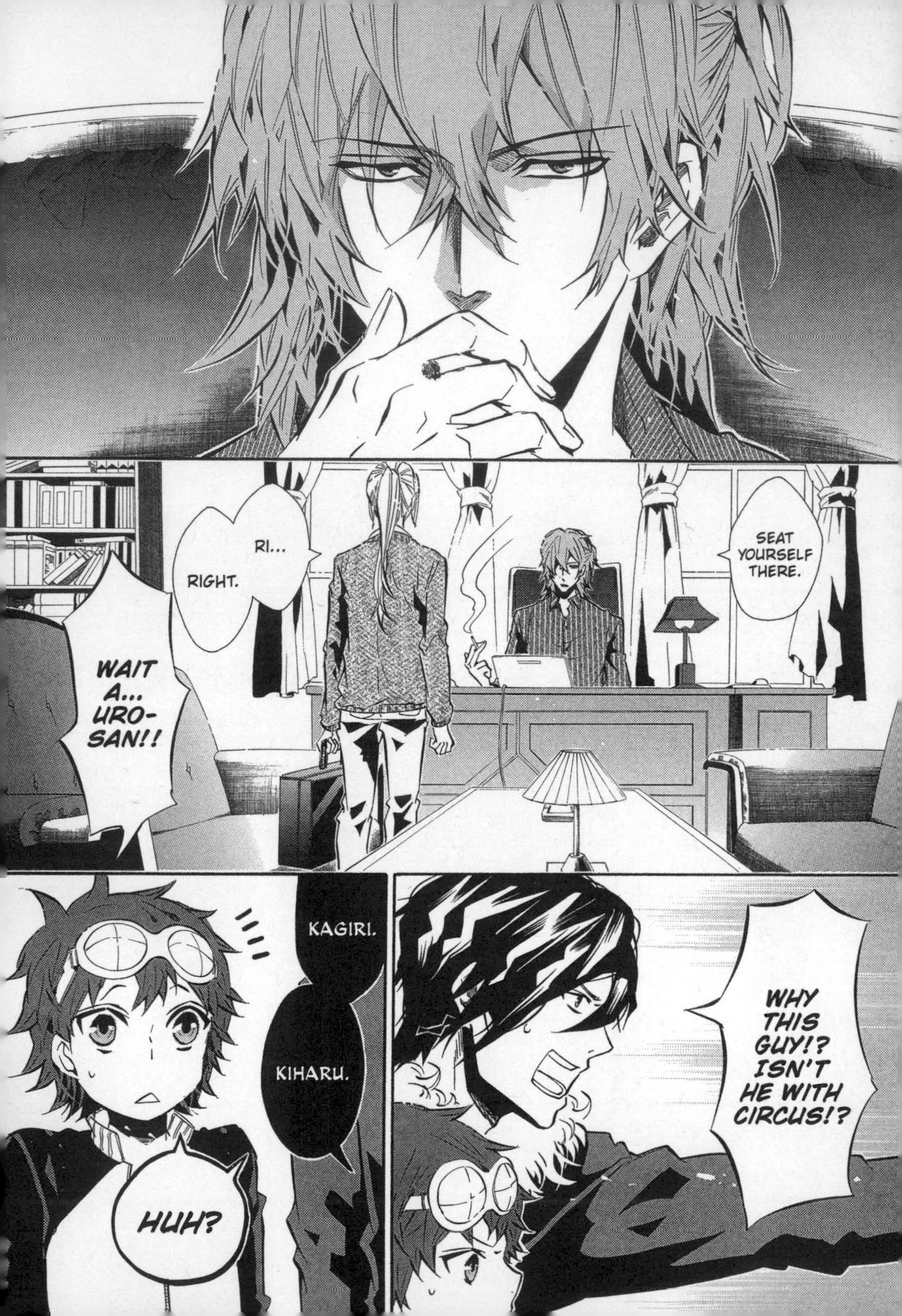
SEAT YOURSELF THERE.
RI... RIGHT.
WAIT A... URO-SAN!!
WHY THIS GUY!? ISN'T HE WITH CIRCUS!?
KAGIRI.
KIHARU.
HUH?

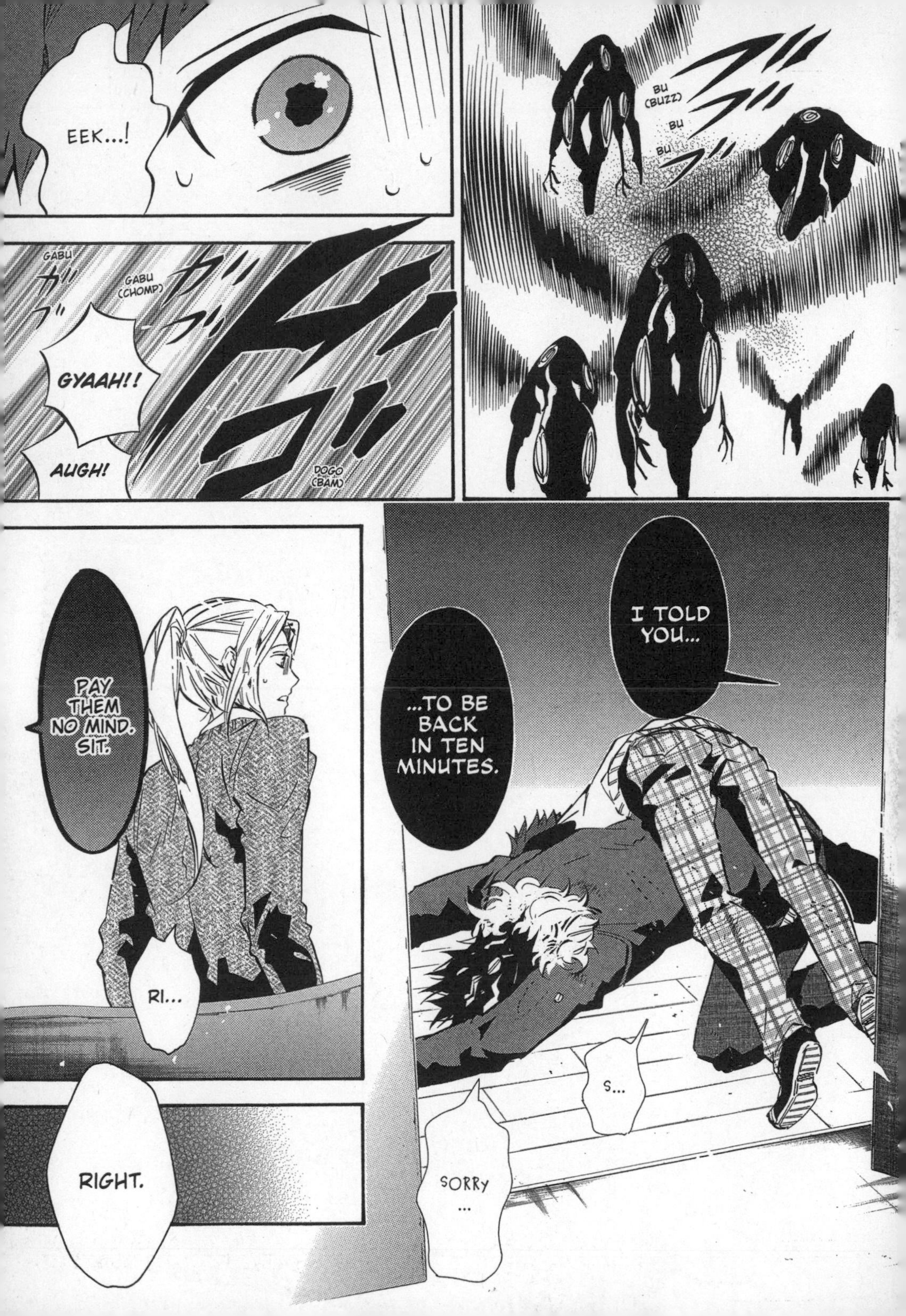
BU (BUZZ)
BU
BU
EEK...!
GABU
GABU (CHOMP)
GYAAH!!
AUGH!
DOGO (BAM)
I TOLD YOU...
...TO BE BACK IN TEN MINUTES.
S...
SORRY ...
PAY THEM NO MIND. SIT.
RI...
RIGHT.

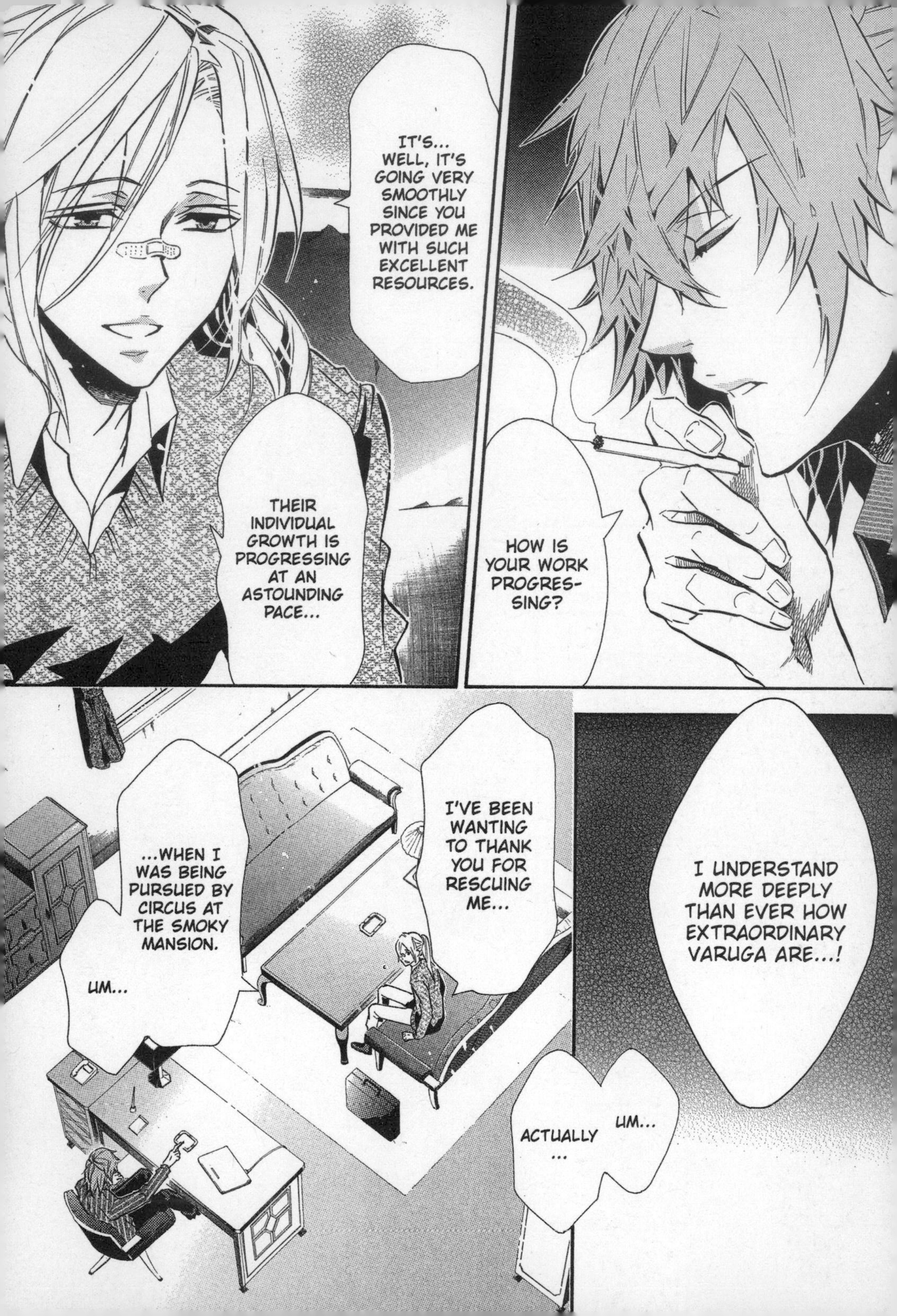
HOW IS YOUR WORK PROGRES-SING?
IT'S... WELL, IT'S GOING VERY SMOOTHLY SINCE YOU PROVIDED ME WITH SUCH EXCELLENT RESOURCES.
THEIR INDIVIDUAL GROWTH IS PROGRESSING AT AN ASTOUNDING PACE...
I UNDERSTAND MORE DEEPLY THAN EVER HOW EXTRAORDINARY VARUGA ARE...!
UM...
ACTUALLY ...
I'VE BEEN WANTING TO THANK YOU FOR RESCUING ME...
...WHEN I WAS BEING PURSUED BY CIRCUS AT THE SMOKY MANSION.
UM...

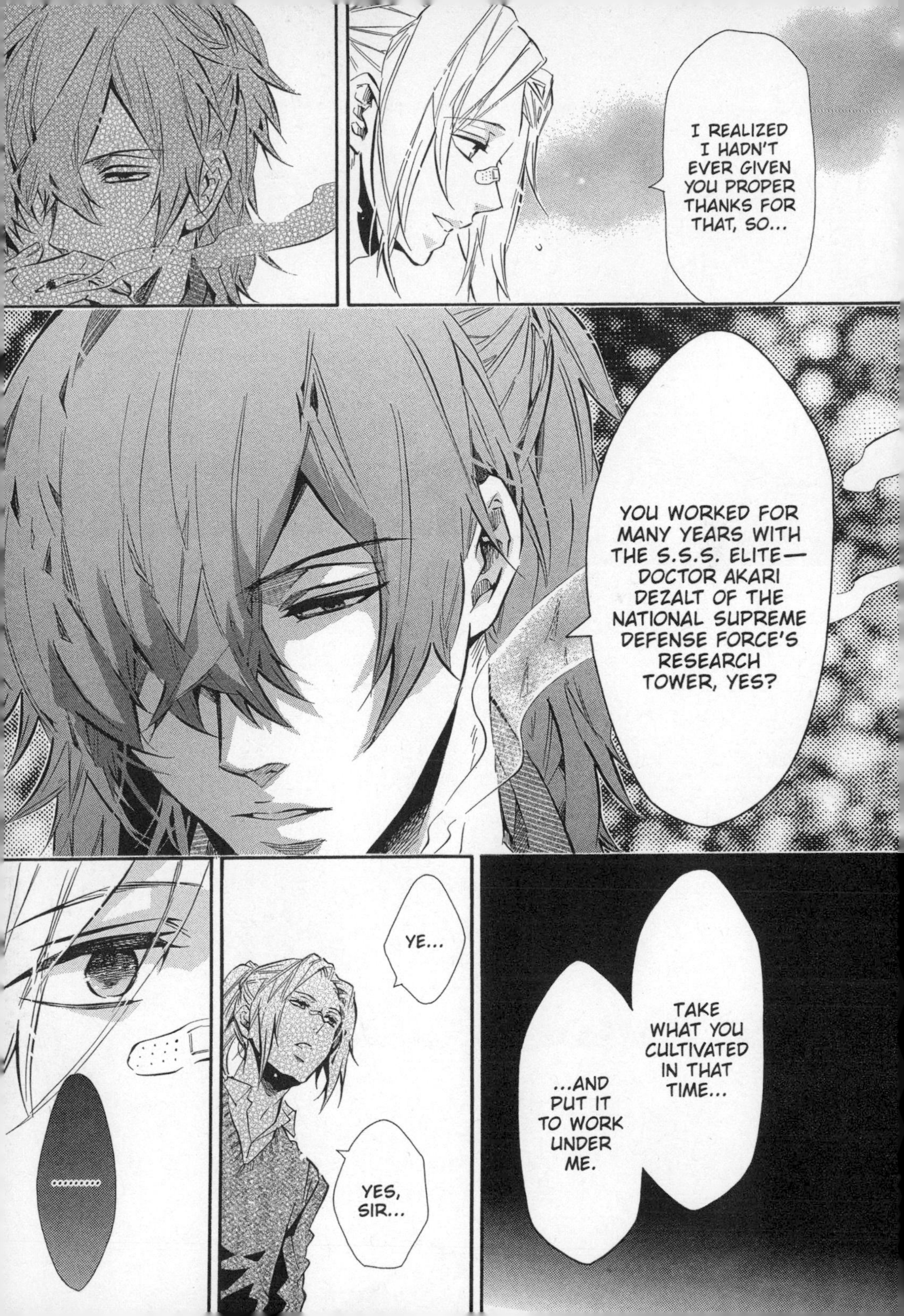
I REALIZED I HADN'T EVER GIVEN YOU PROPER THANKS FOR THAT, SO...
YOU WORKED FOR MANY YEARS WITH THE S.S.S. ELITE—DOCTOR AKARI DEZALT OF THE NATIONAL SUPREME DEFENSE FORCE'S RESEARCH TOWER, YES?
TAKE WHAT YOU CULTIVATED IN THAT TIME...
...AND PUT IT TO WORK UNDER ME.
YE...
YES, SIR...
....

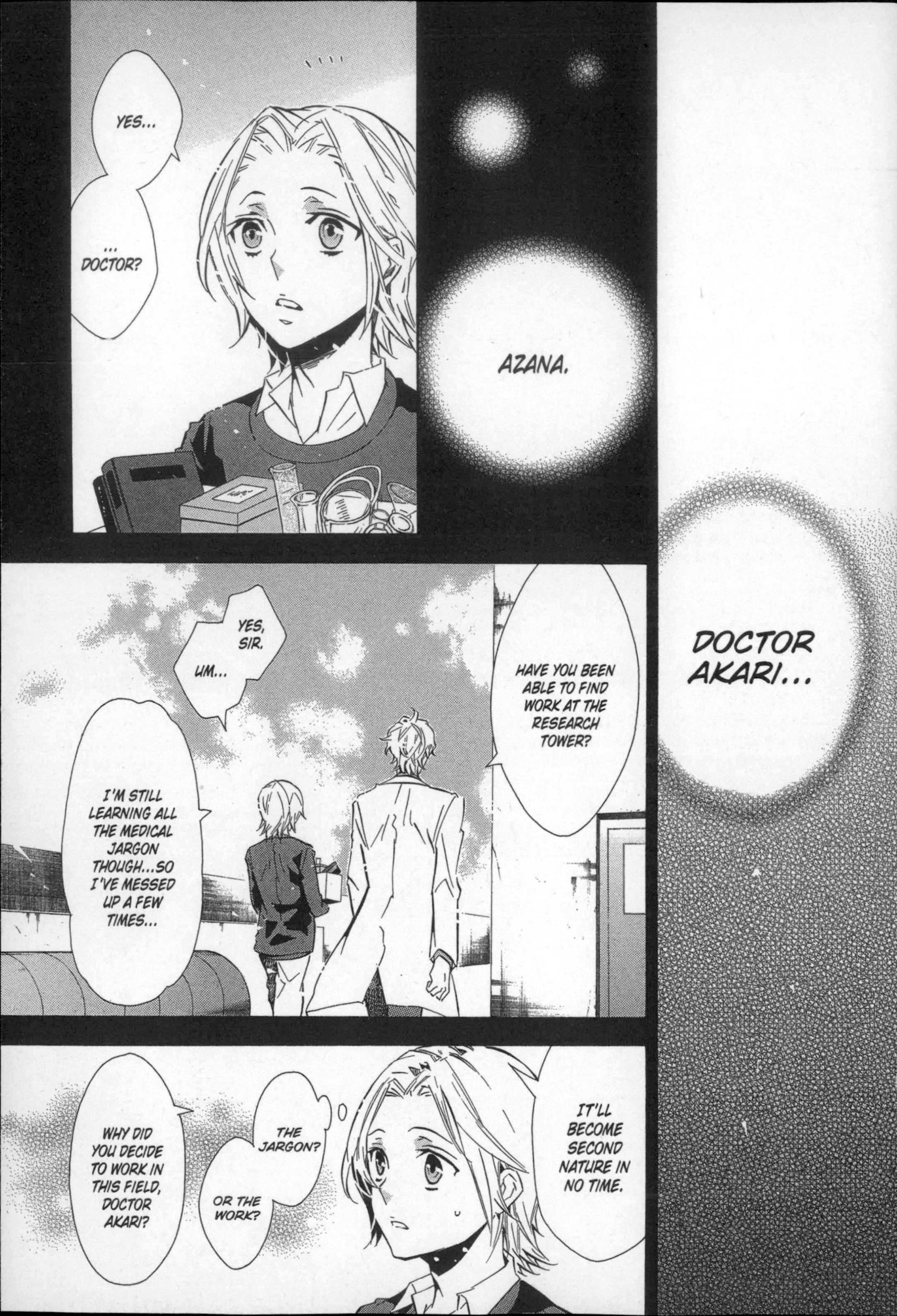
DOCTOR AKARI...
AZANA.
YES...
... DOCTOR?
HAVE YOU BEEN ABLE TO FIND WORK AT THE RESEARCH TOWER?
YES, SIR.
UM...
I'M STILL LEARNING ALL THE MEDICAL JARGON THOUGH...SO I'VE MESSED UP A FEW TIMES...
IT'LL BECOME SECOND NATURE IN NO TIME.
THE JARGON?
OR THE WORK?
WHY DID YOU DECIDE TO WORK IN THIS FIELD, DOCTOR AKARI?

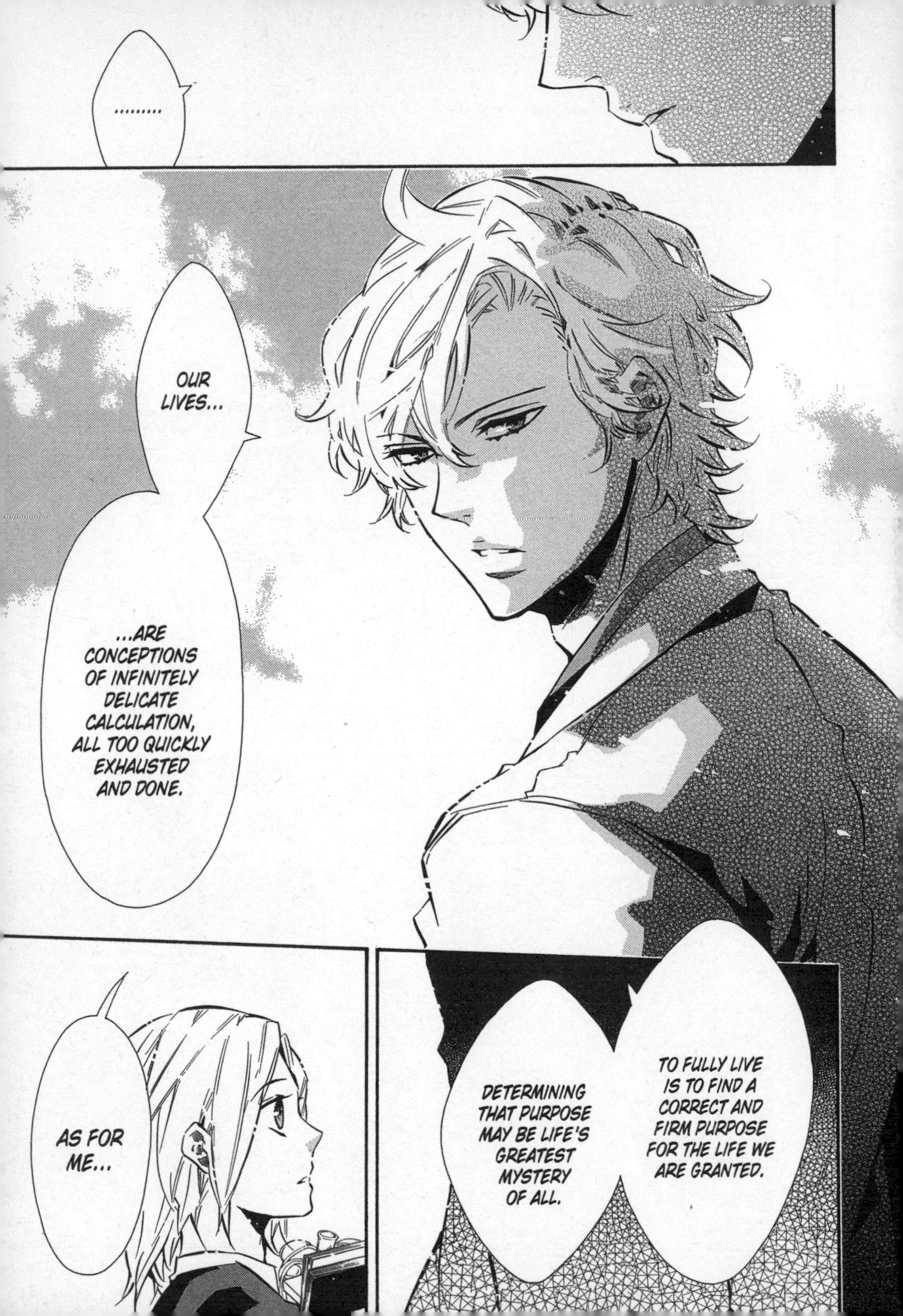
....
OUR LIVES...
...ARE CONCEPTIONS OF INFINITELY DELICATE CALCULATION, ALL TOO QUICKLY EXHAUSTED AND DONE.
TO FULLY LIVE IS TO FIND A CORRECT AND FIRM PURPOSE FOR THE LIFE WE ARE GRANTED.
DETERMINING THAT PURPOSE MAY BE LIFE'S GREATEST MYSTERY OF ALL.
AS FOR ME...

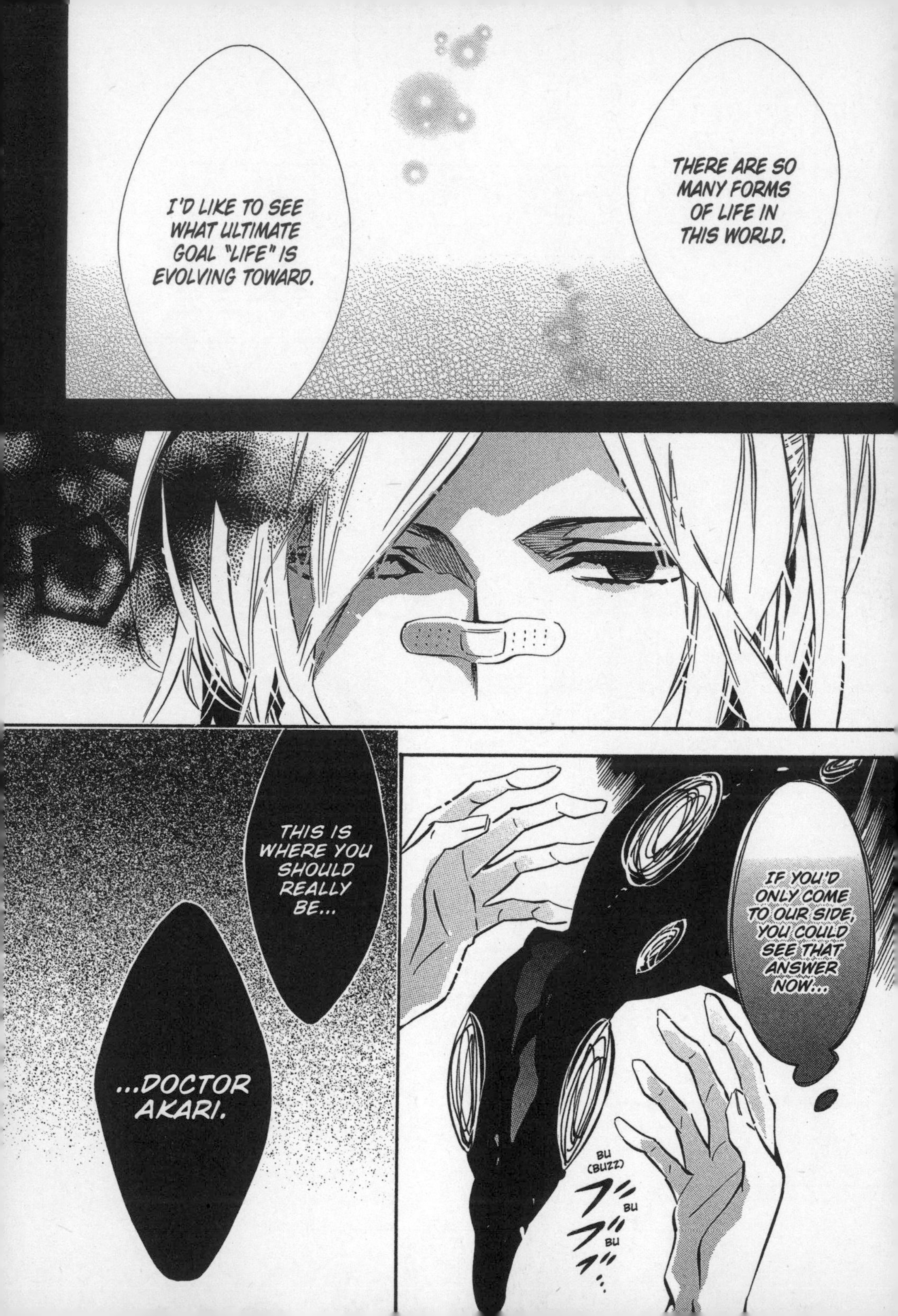
THERE ARE SO MANY FORMS OF LIFE IN THIS WORLD.
I'D LIKE TO SEE WHAT ULTIMATE GOAL "LIFE" IS EVOLVING TOWARD.
IF YOU'D ONLY COME TO OUR SIDE, YOU COULD SEE THAT ANSWER NOW...
BU (BUZZ)
BU
BU
THIS IS WHERE YOU SHOULD REALLY BE...
...DOCTOR AKARI.

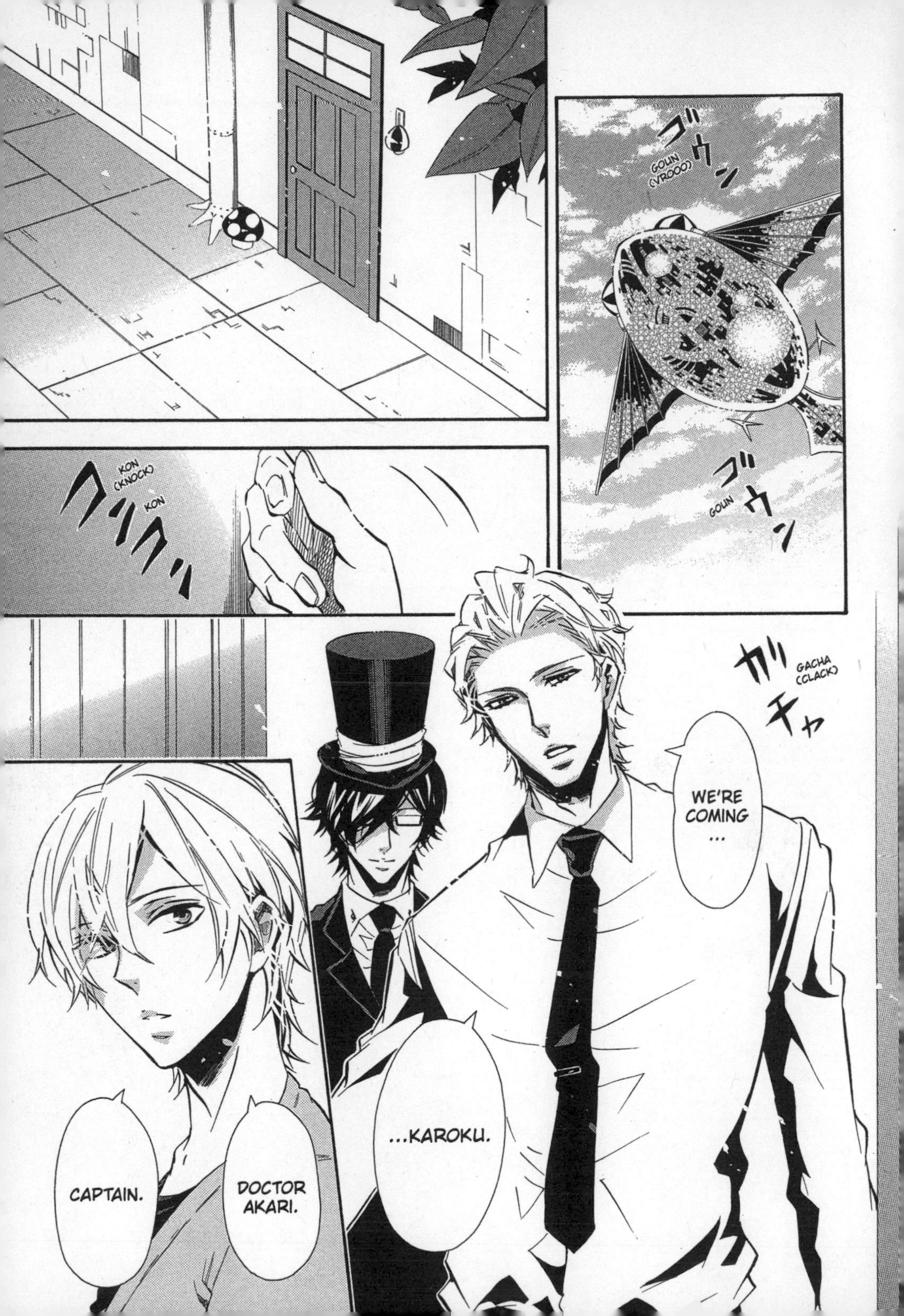
GOUN (VROOO)
GOUN
KON (KNOCK)
KON
GACHA (CLACK)
WE'RE COMING ...
...KAROKU.
DOCTOR AKARI.
CAPTAIN.

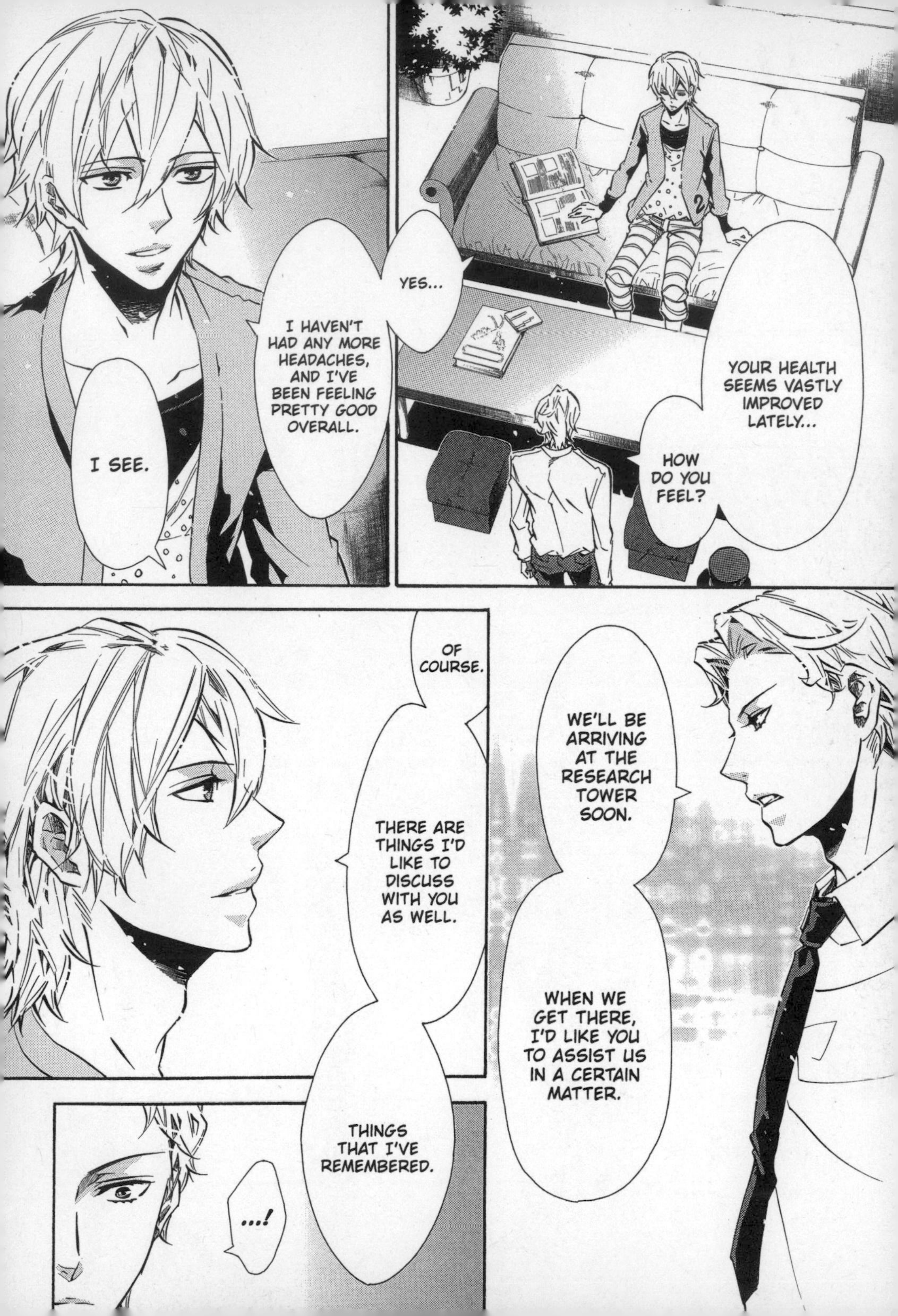
YOUR HEALTH SEEMS VASTLY IMPROVED LATELY...
HOW DO YOU FEEL?
YES...
I HAVEN'T HAD ANY MORE HEADACHES, AND I'VE BEEN FEELING PRETTY GOOD OVERALL.
I SEE.
WE'LL BE ARRIVING AT THE RESEARCH TOWER SOON.
WHEN WE GET THERE, I'D LIKE YOU TO ASSIST US IN A CERTAIN MATTER.
OF COURSE.
THERE ARE THINGS I'D LIKE TO DISCUSS WITH YOU AS WELL.
THINGS THAT I'VE REMEMBERED.
...!

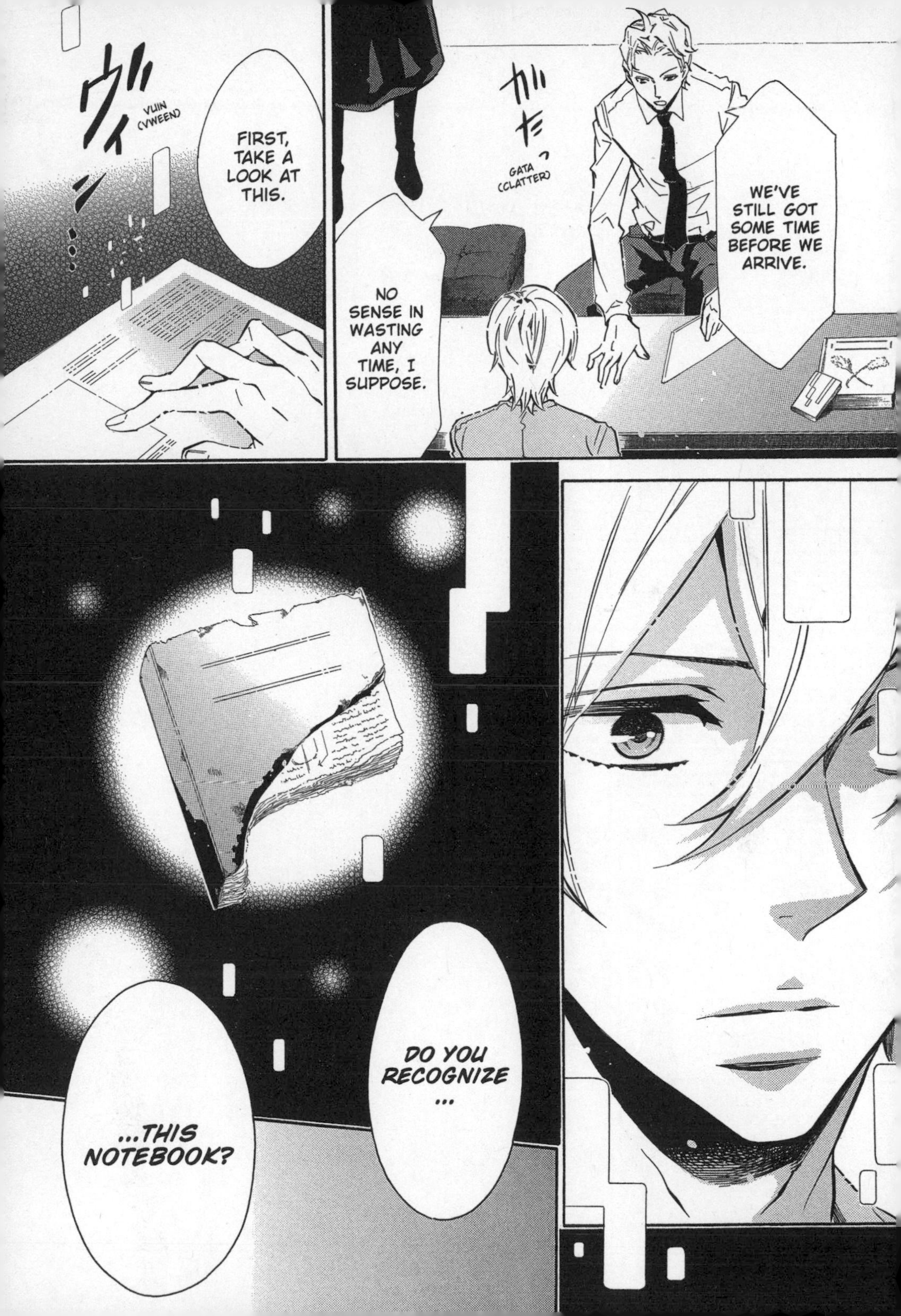
WE'VE STILL GOT SOME TIME BEFORE WE ARRIVE.
GATA (CLATTER)
NO SENSE IN WASTING ANY TIME, I SUPPOSE.
VUIN (VWEEN)
FIRST, TAKE A LOOK AT THIS.
DO YOU RECOGNIZE...
...THIS NOTEBOOK?

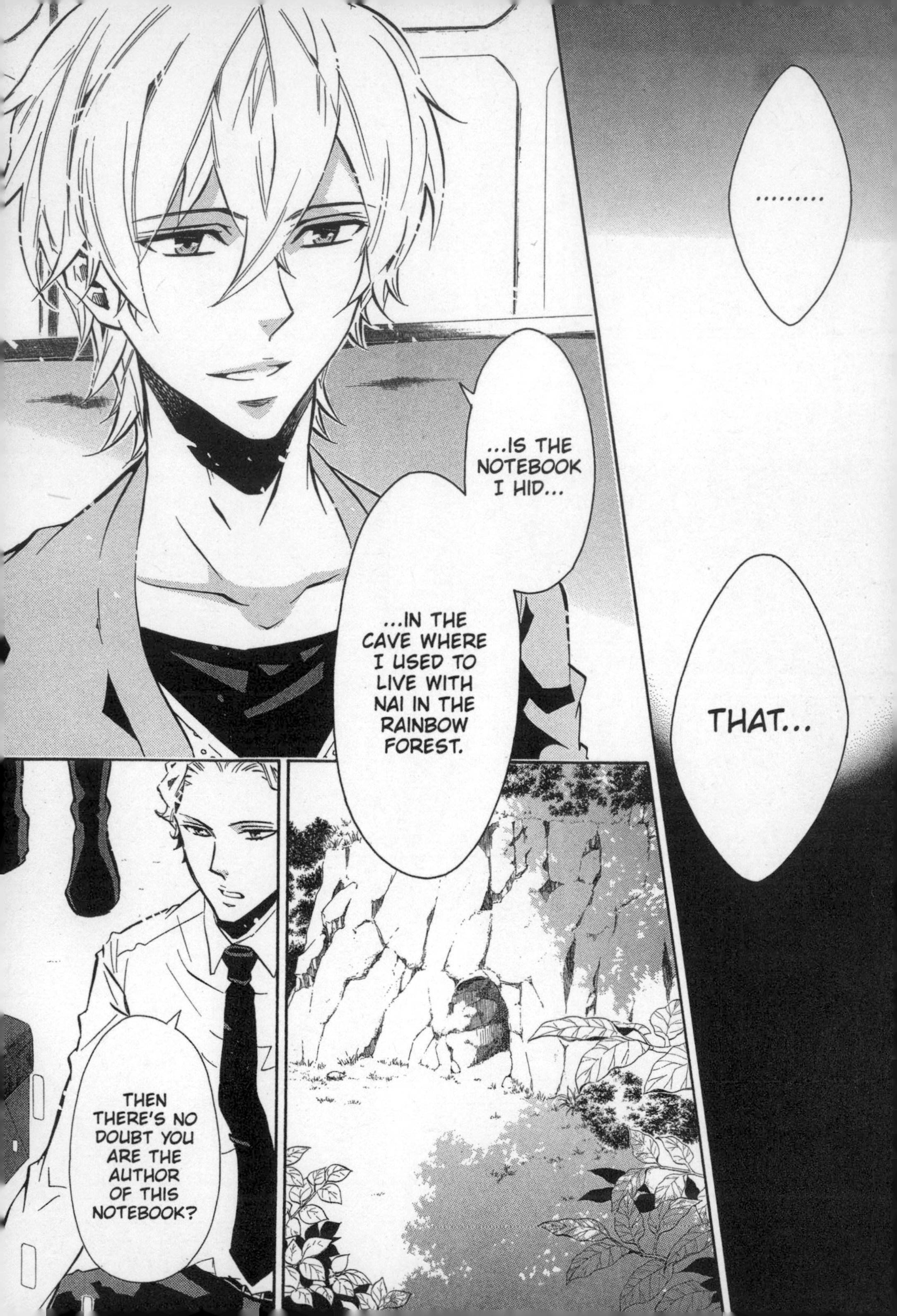
....
THAT...
...IS THE NOTEBOOK I HID...
...IN THE CAVE WHERE I USED TO LIVE WITH NAI IN THE RAINBOW FOREST.
THEN THERE'S NO DOUBT YOU ARE THE AUTHOR OF THIS NOTEBOOK?

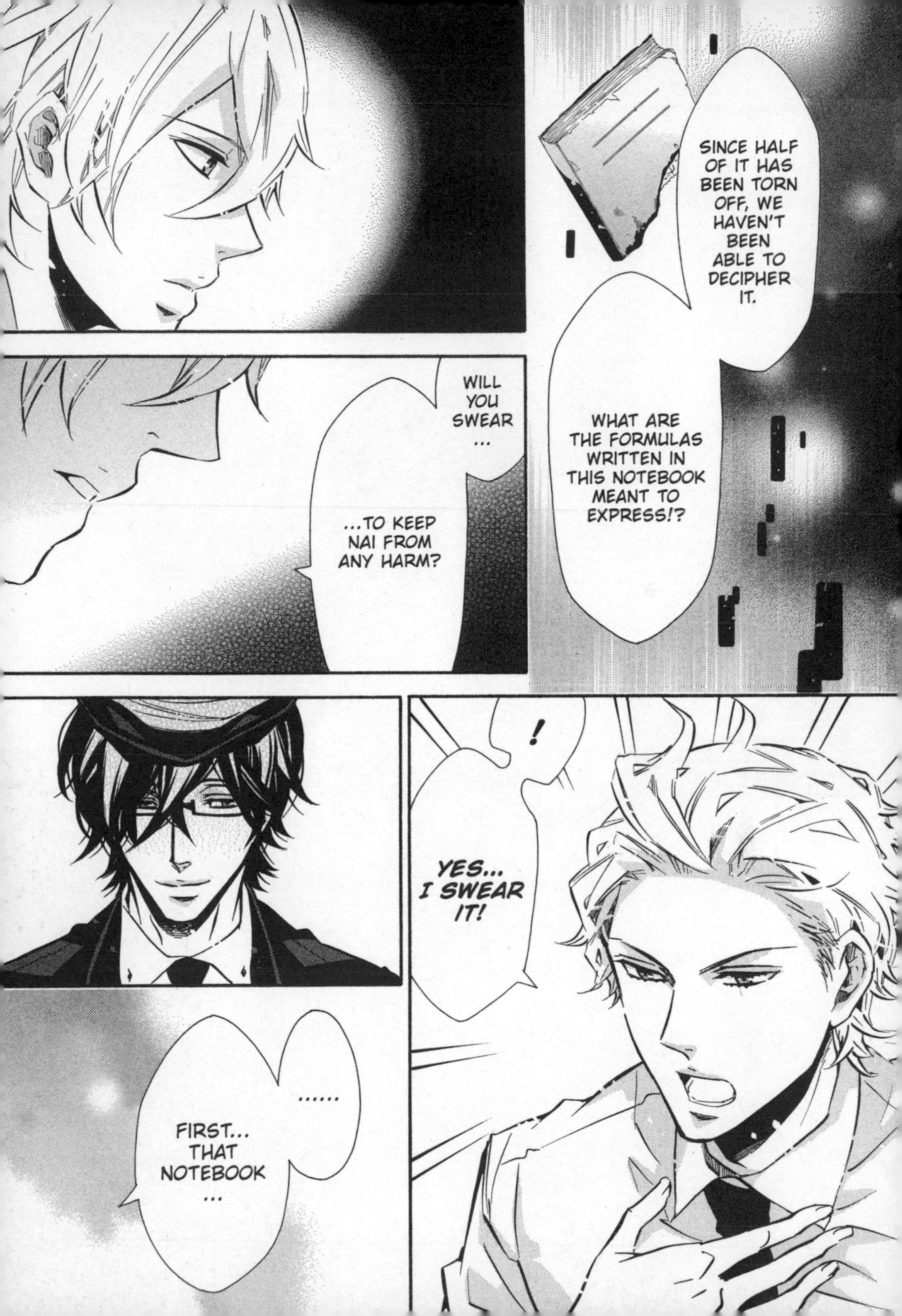
SINCE HALF OF IT HAS BEEN TORN OFF, WE HAVEN'T BEEN ABLE TO DECIPHER IT.
WHAT ARE THE FORMULAS WRITTEN IN THIS NOTEBOOK MEANT TO EXPRESS!?
WILL YOU SWEAR ...
...TO KEEP NAI FROM ANY HARM?
!
YES... I SWEAR IT!
......
FIRST... THAT NOTEBOOK ...

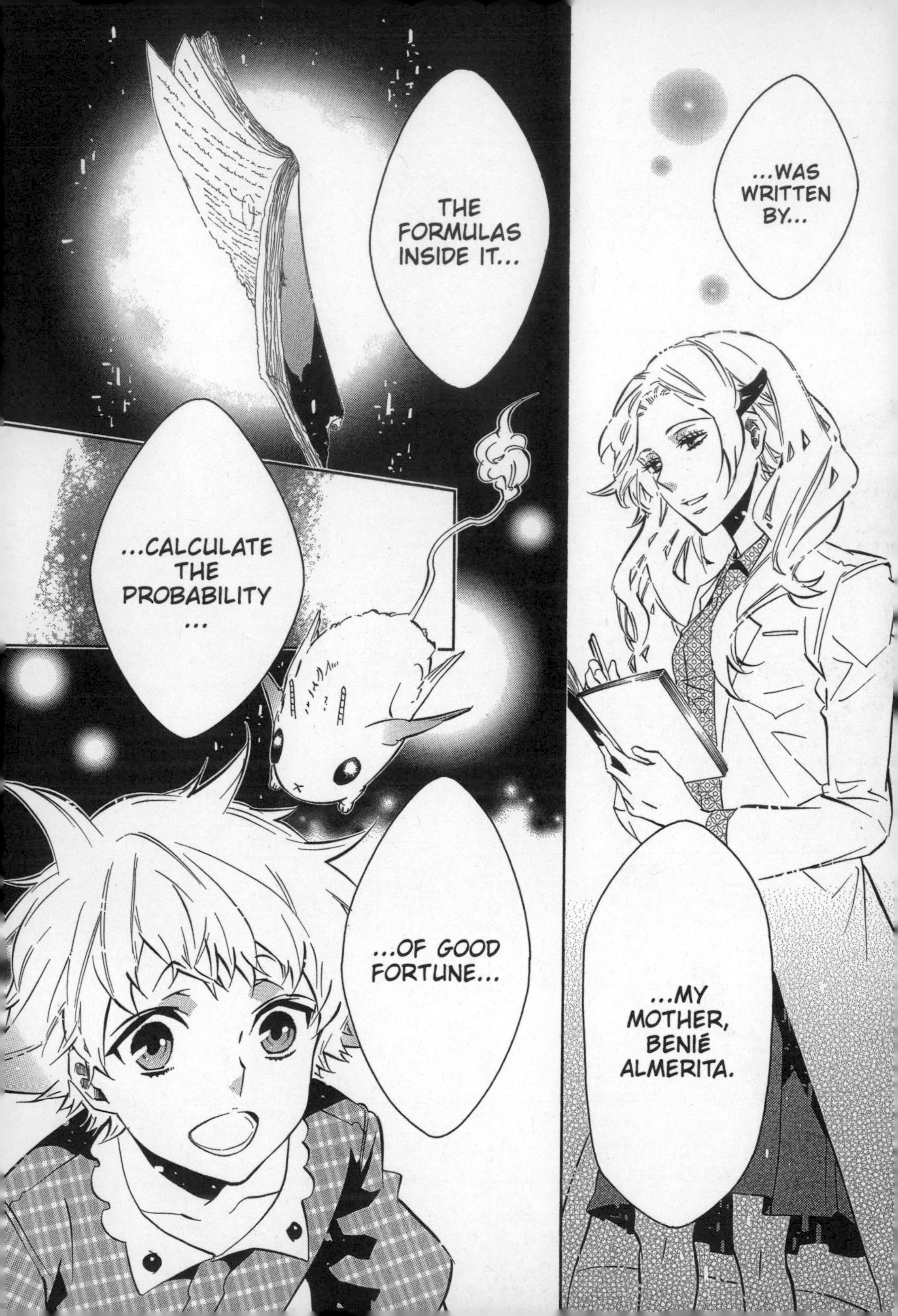
THE FORMULAS INSIDE IT...
...CALCULATE THE PROBABILITY...
...OF GOOD FORTUNE...
...WAS WRITTEN BY...
...MY MOTHER, BENIÉ ALMERITA.

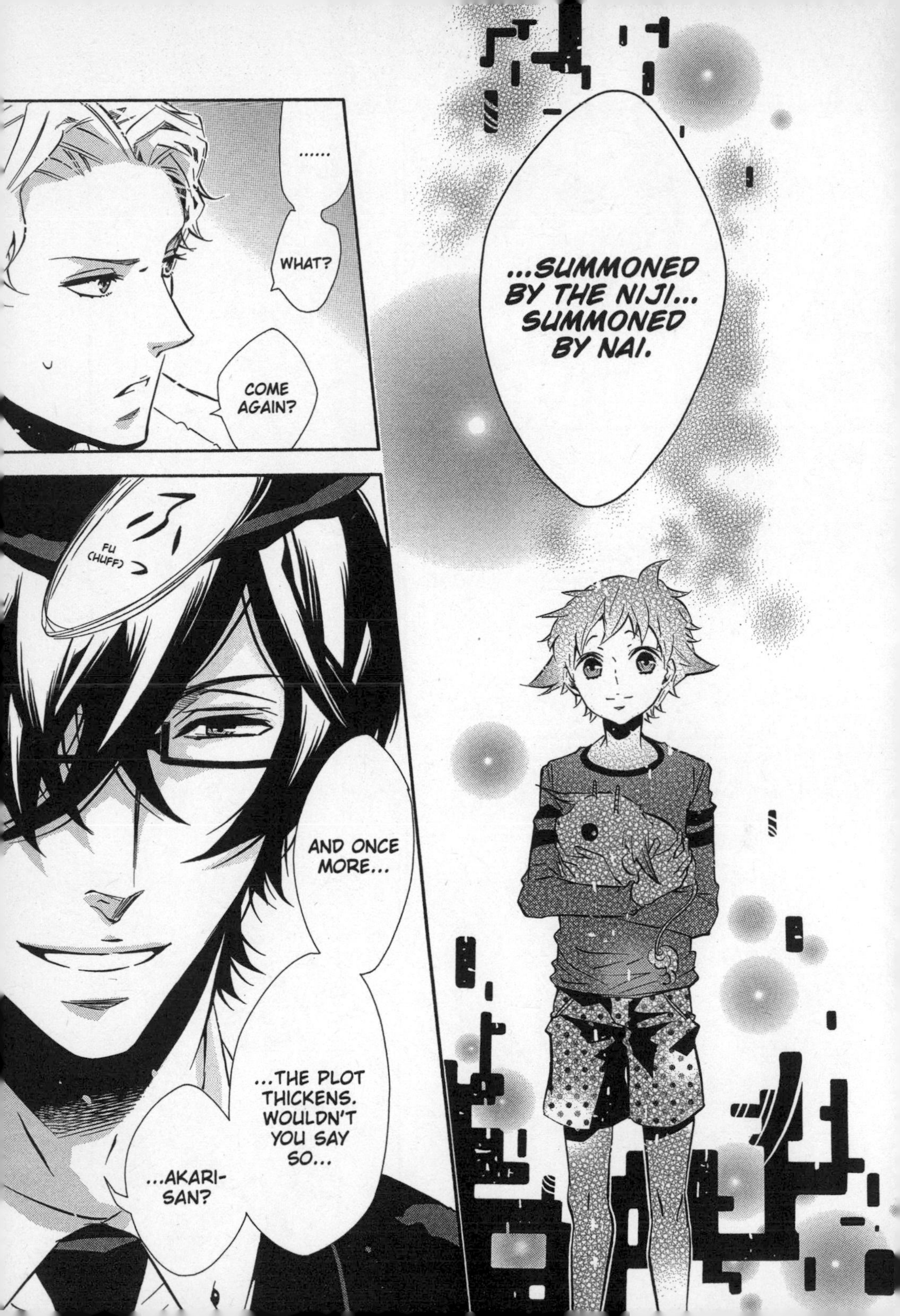
...SUMMONED BY THE NIJI... SUMMONED BY NAI.
......
WHAT?
COME AGAIN?
FU (HUFF)
AND ONCE MORE...
...THE PLOT THICKENS. WOULDN'T YOU SAY SO...
...AKARI-SAN?

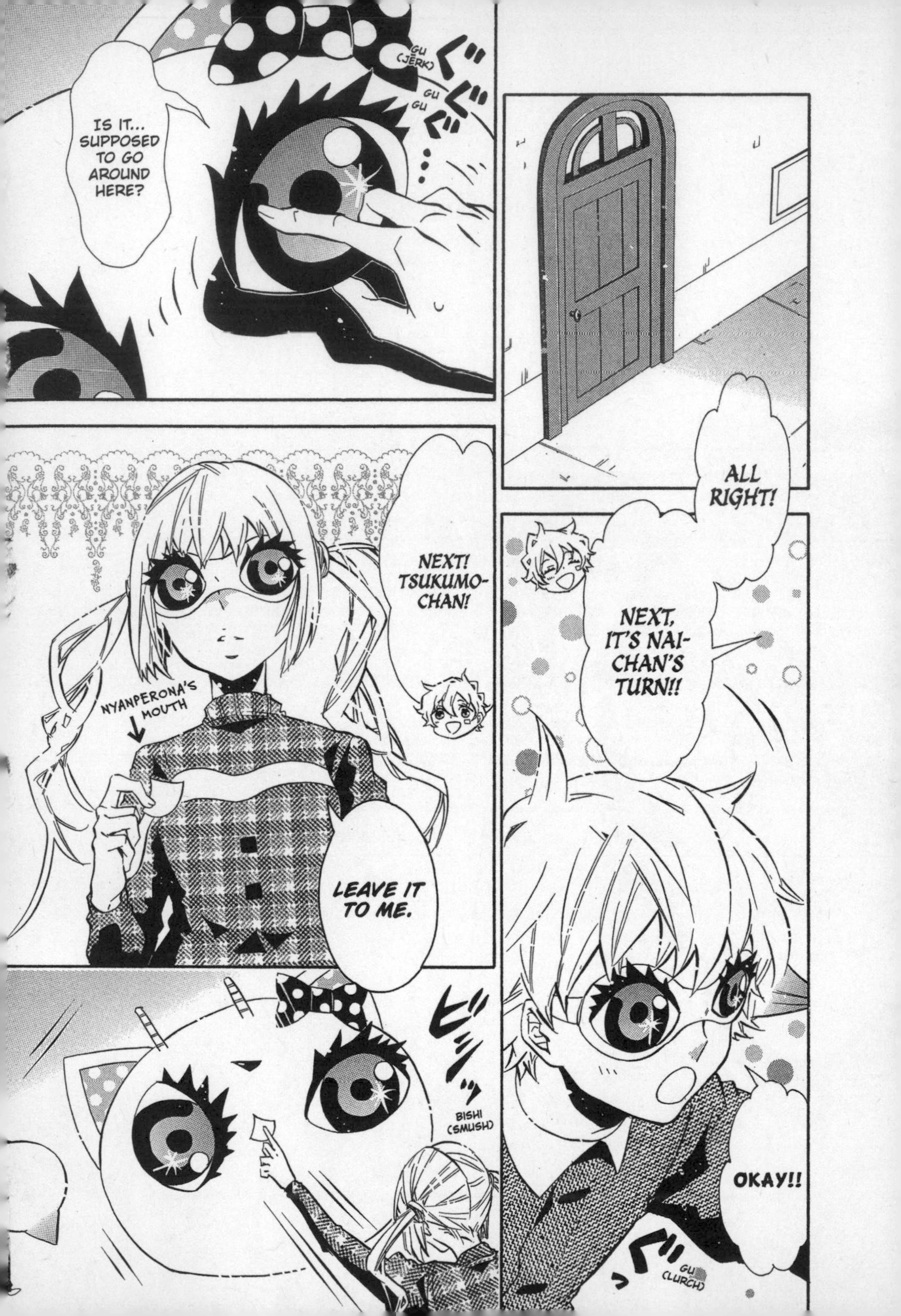
GU (JERK)
GU
GU
IS IT... SUPPOSED TO GO AROUND HERE?
ALL RIGHT!
NEXT, IT'S NAI-CHAN'S TURN!!
OKAY!!
GU (LURCH)
NEXT! TSUKUMO-CHAN!
NYANPERONA'S MOUTH
LEAVE IT TO ME.
BISHI (SMUSH)

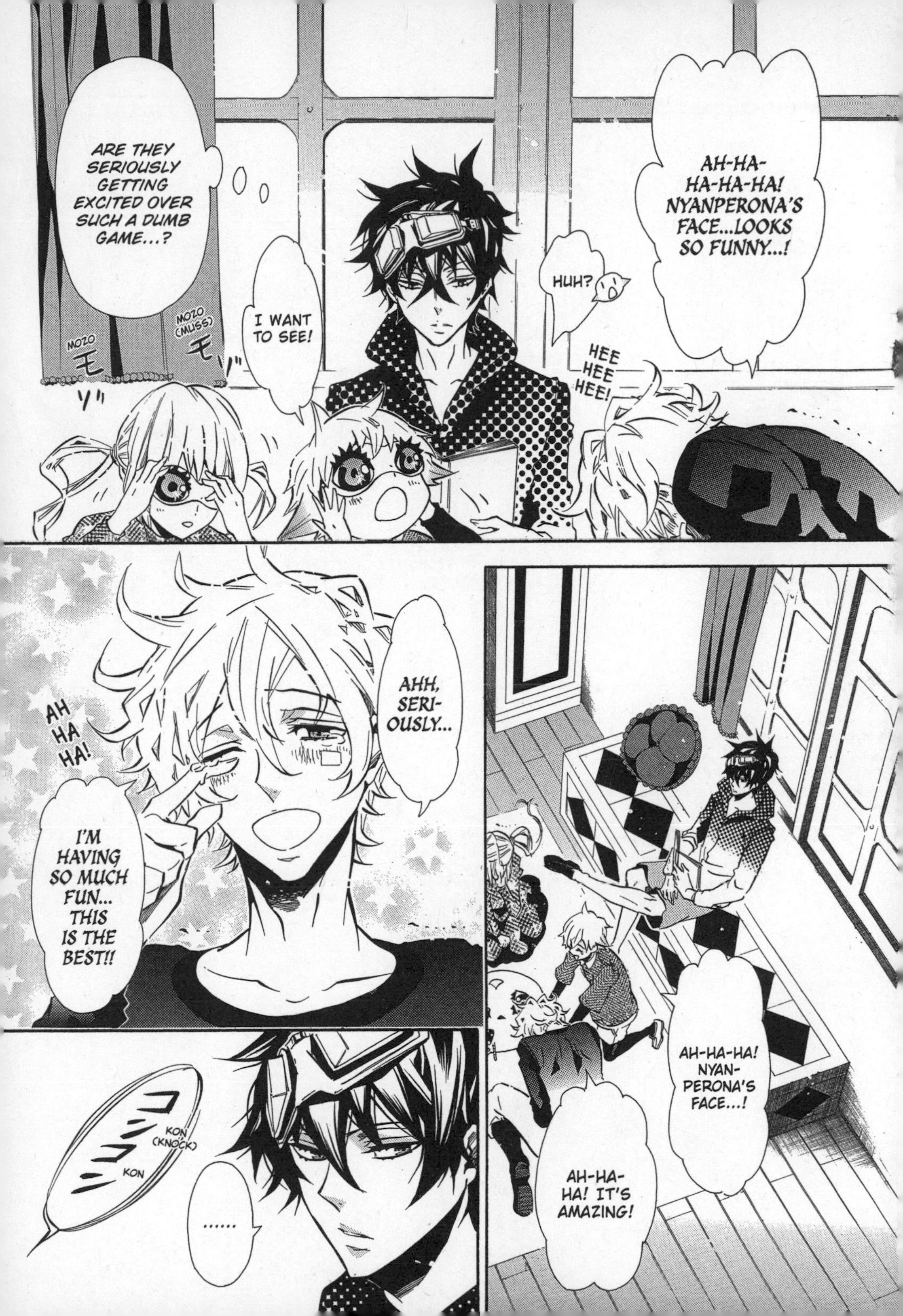
AH-HA-HA-HA-HA! NYANPERONA'S FACE...LOOKS SO FUNNY...!
HEE HEE HEE!
HUH?
I WANT TO SEE!
ARE THEY SERIOUSLY GETTING EXCITED OVER SUCH A DUMB GAME...?
MOZO (MUSS)
MOZO
AH-HA-HA! NYAN-PERONA'S FACE...!
AH-HA-HA! IT'S AMAZING!
AHH, SERI-OUSLY...
AH HA HA!
I'M HAVING SO MUCH FUN... THIS IS THE BEST!!
KON (KNOCK)
KON
......

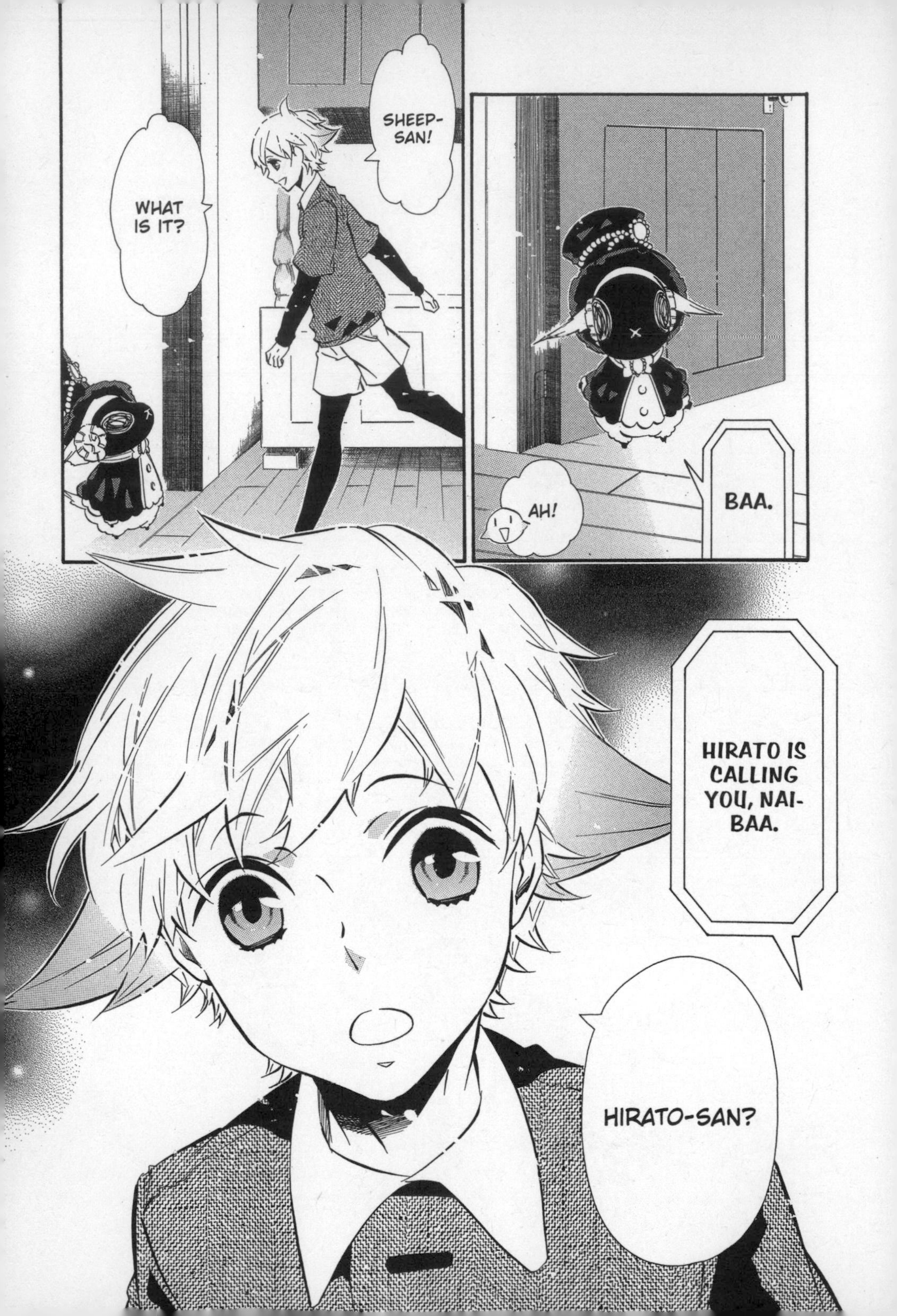
BAA.
AH!
SHEEP-SAN!
WHAT IS IT?
HIRATO IS CALLING YOU, NAI-BAA.
HIRATO-SAN?

KARNEVAL

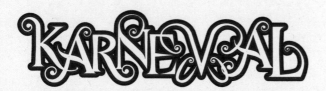

NYANPERONA'S MOUTH

KARNEVAL

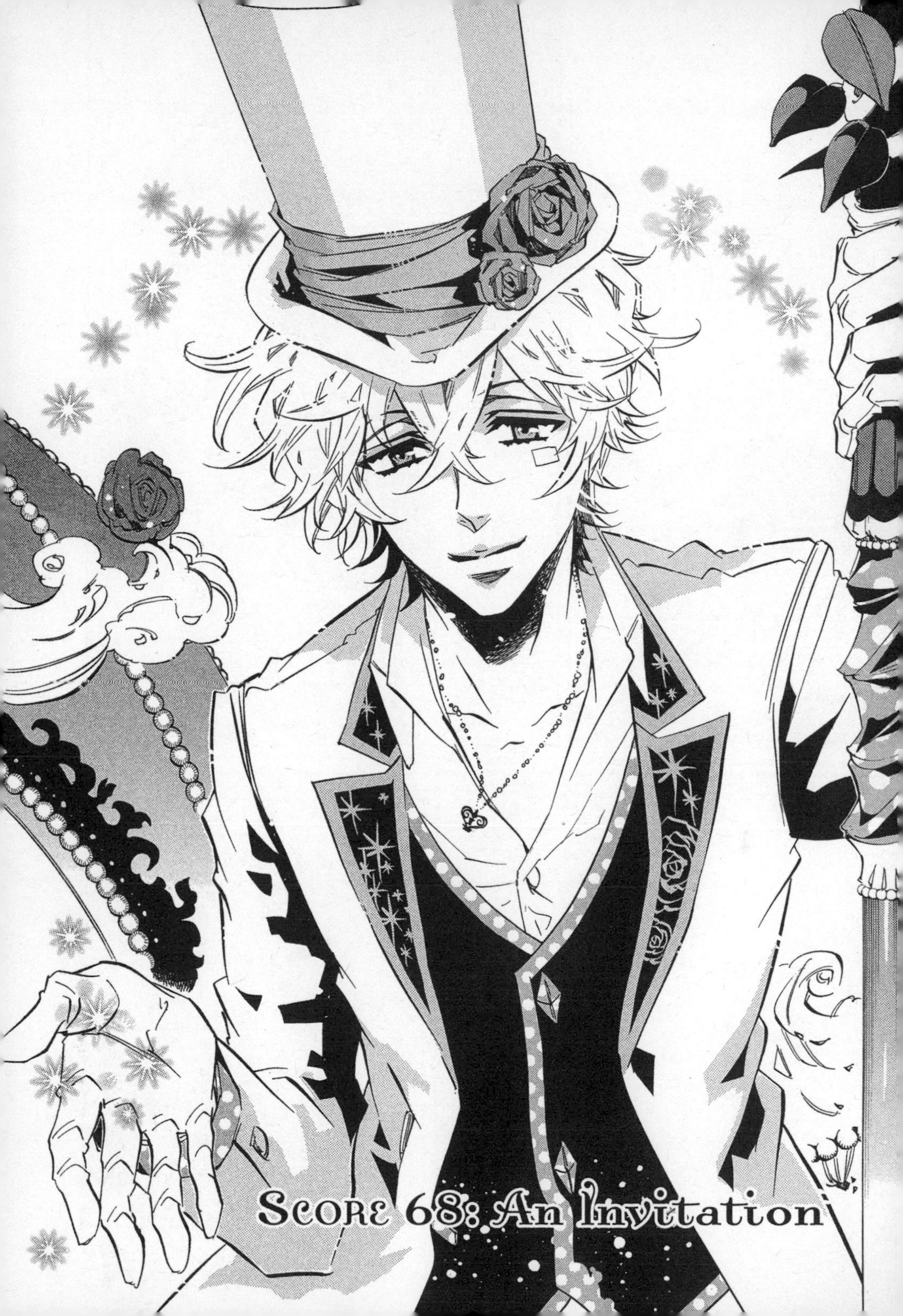
Score 68: An Invitation

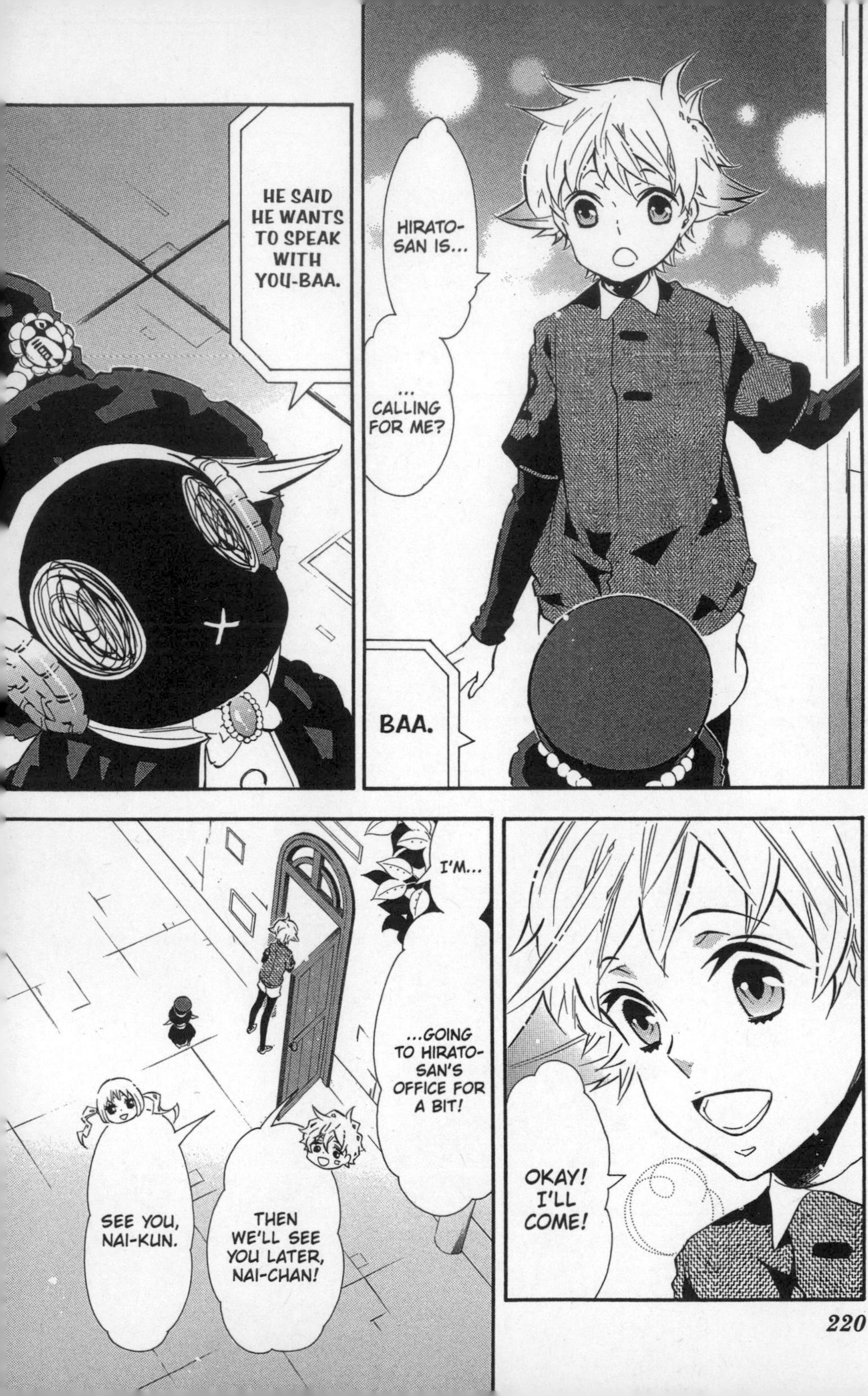
HIRATO-SAN IS...
...CALLING FOR ME?
BAA.
HE SAID HE WANTS TO SPEAK WITH YOU-BAA.
OKAY! I'LL COME!
I'M...
...GOING TO HIRATO-SAN'S OFFICE FOR A BIT!
THEN WE'LL SEE YOU LATER, NAI-CHAN!
SEE YOU, NAI-KUN.

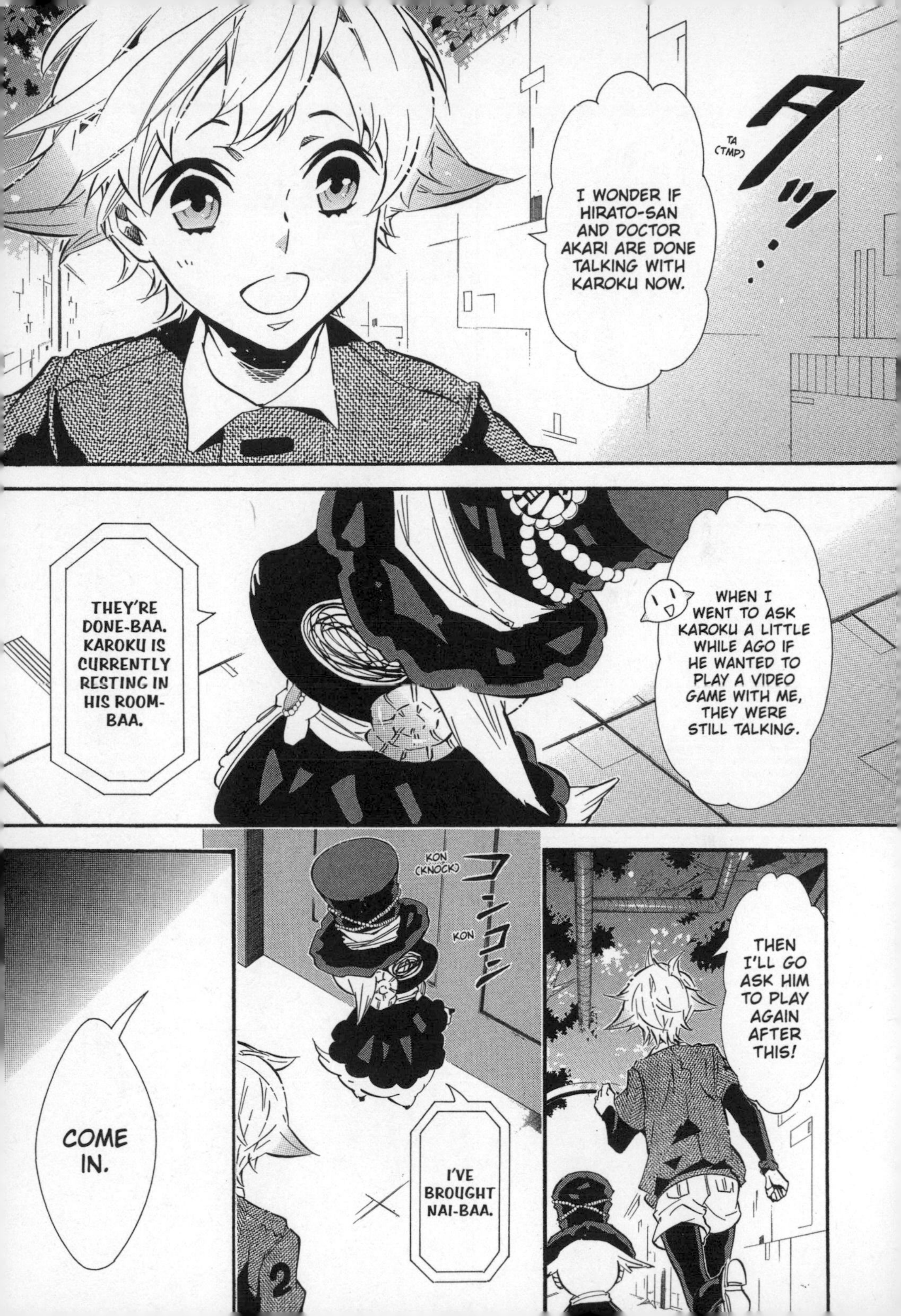
TA (TMP)
I WONDER IF HIRATO-SAN AND DOCTOR AKARI ARE DONE TALKING WITH KAROKU NOW.
WHEN I WENT TO ASK KAROKU A LITTLE WHILE AGO IF HE WANTED TO PLAY A VIDEO GAME WITH ME, THEY WERE STILL TALKING.
THEY'RE DONE-BAA. KAROKU IS CURRENTLY RESTING IN HIS ROOM-BAA.
THEN I'LL GO ASK HIM TO PLAY AGAIN AFTER THIS!
KON (KNOCK)
KON
I'VE BROUGHT NAI-BAA.
COME IN.

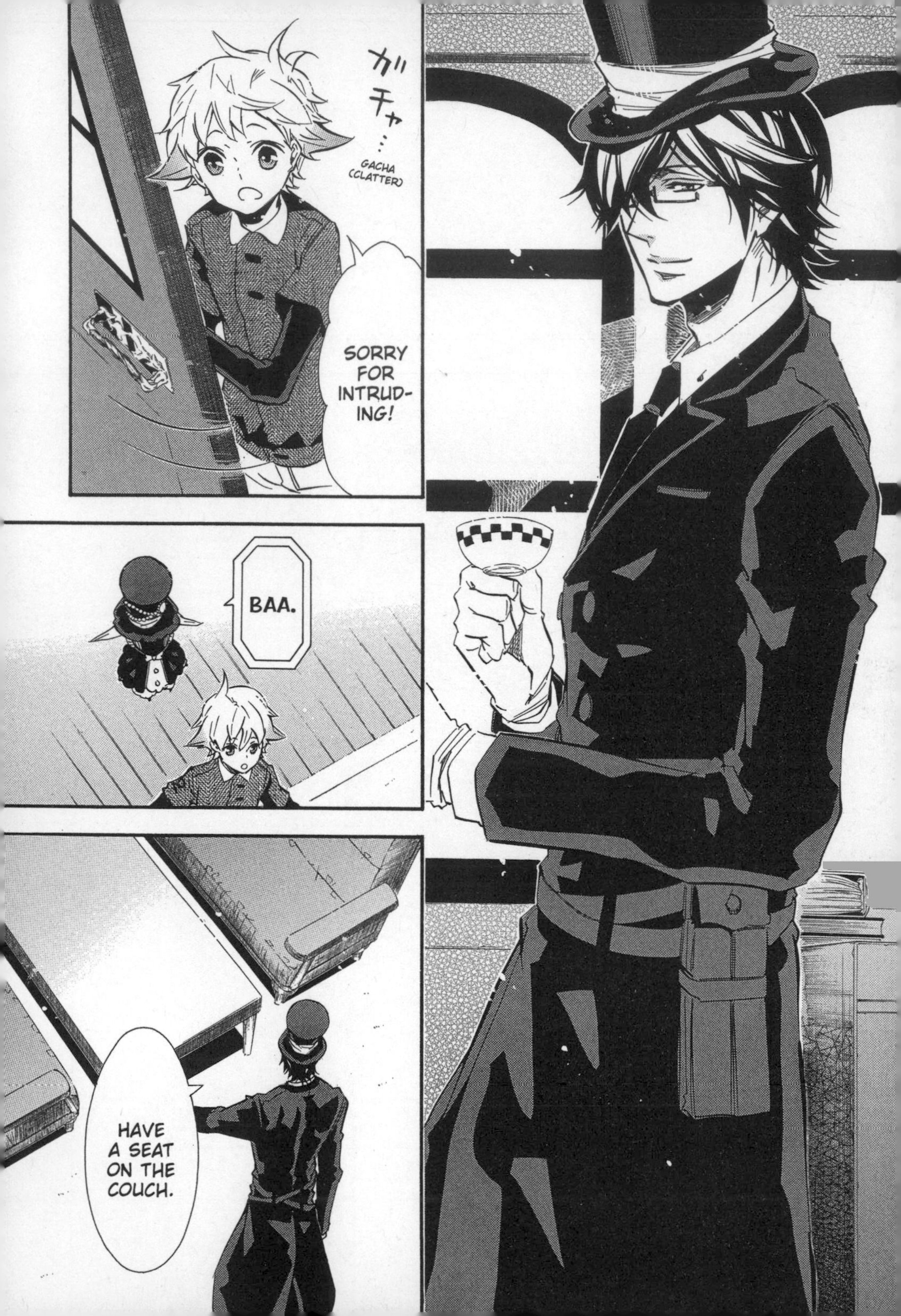
ガチャ…
GACHA (CLATTER)
SORRY FOR INTRUD-ING!
BAA.
HAVE A SEAT ON THE COUCH.

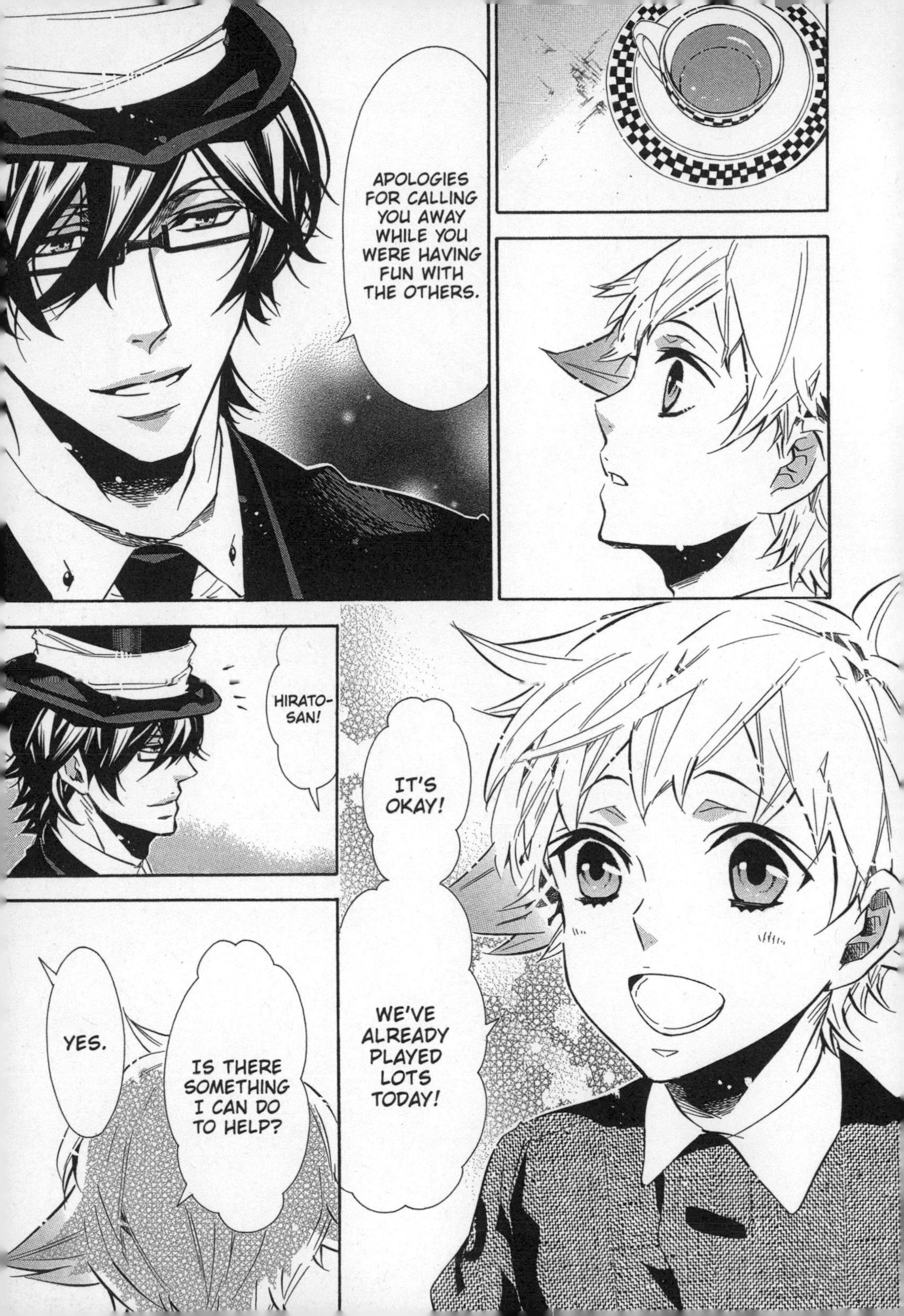
APOLOGIES FOR CALLING YOU AWAY WHILE YOU WERE HAVING FUN WITH THE OTHERS.
IT'S OKAY!
WE'VE ALREADY PLAYED LOTS TODAY!
HIRATO-SAN!
YES.
IS THERE SOMETHING I CAN DO TO HELP?

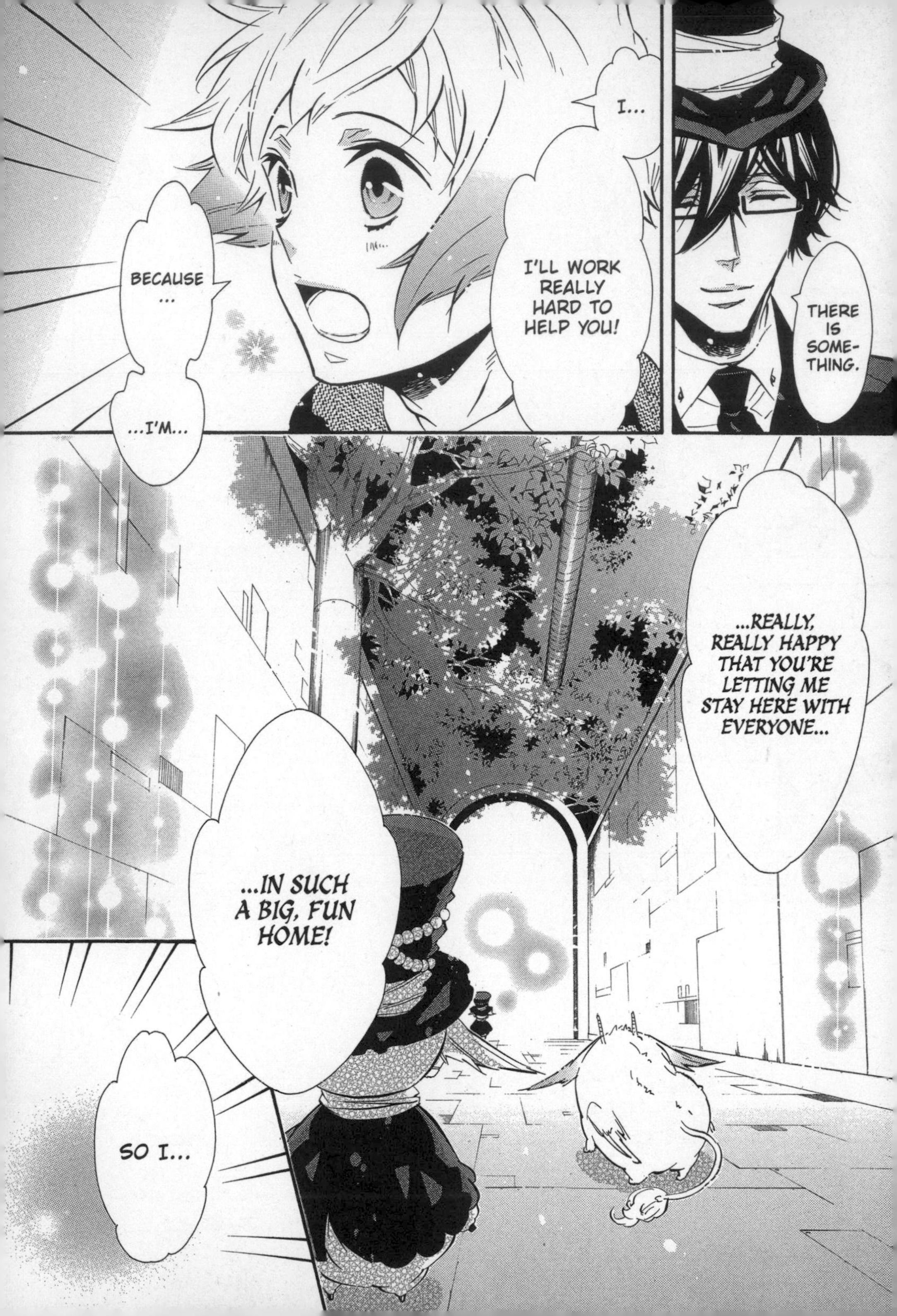
THERE IS SOME-THING.
I...
I'LL WORK REALLY HARD TO HELP YOU!
BECAUSE ...
...I'M...
...REALLY, REALLY HAPPY THAT YOU'RE LETTING ME STAY HERE WITH EVERYONE...
...IN SUCH A BIG, FUN HOME!
SO I...

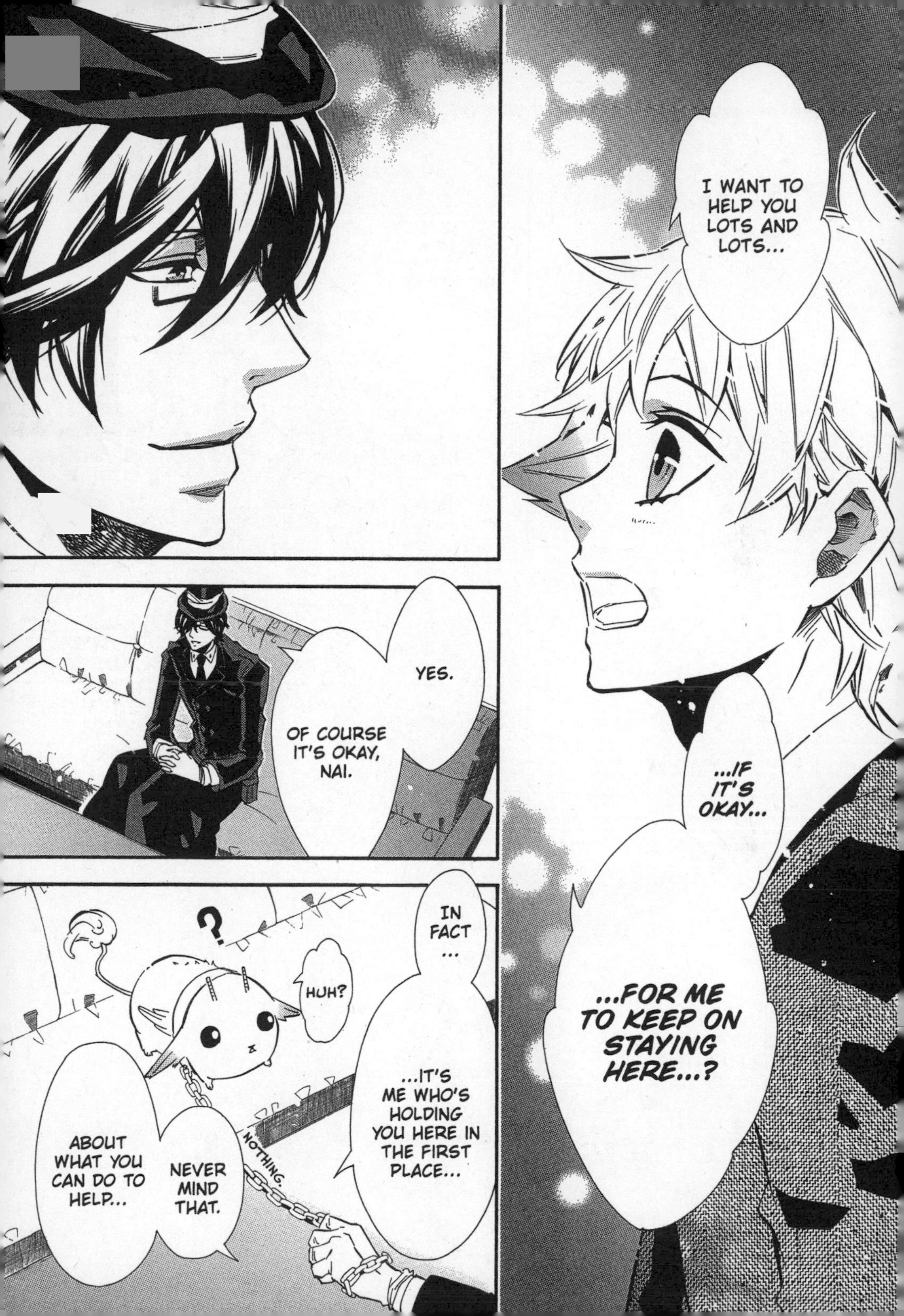
I WANT TO HELP YOU LOTS AND LOTS...
...IF IT'S OKAY...
...FOR ME TO KEEP ON STAYING HERE...?
YES.
OF COURSE IT'S OKAY, NAI.
IN FACT ...
...IT'S ME WHO'S HOLDING YOU HERE IN THE FIRST PLACE...
HUH?
?
NOTHING.
NEVER MIND THAT.
ABOUT WHAT YOU CAN DO TO HELP...

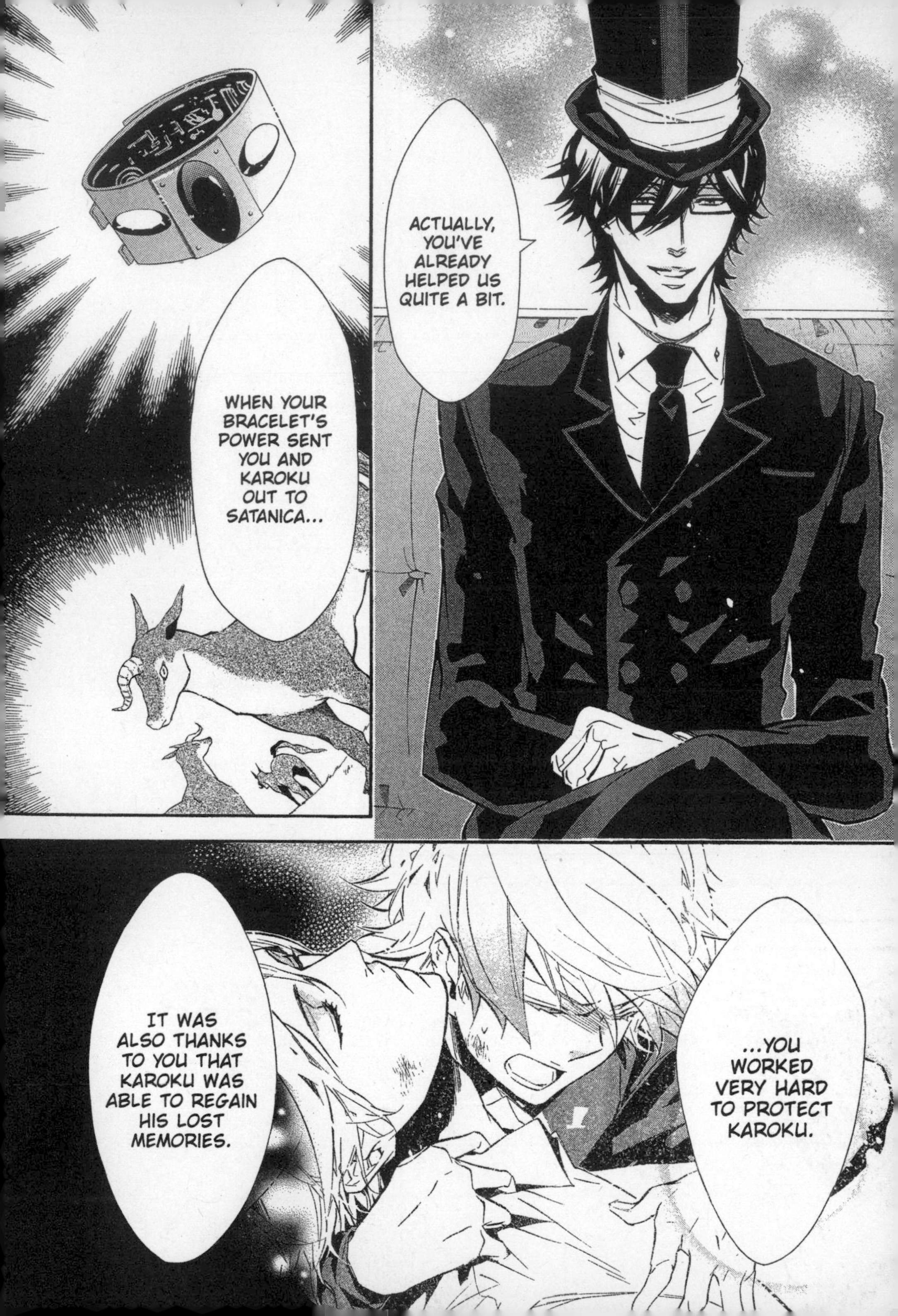
ACTUALLY, YOU'VE ALREADY HELPED US QUITE A BIT.
WHEN YOUR BRACELET'S POWER SENT YOU AND KAROKU OUT TO SATANICA...
...YOU WORKED VERY HARD TO PROTECT KAROKU.
IT WAS ALSO THANKS TO YOU THAT KAROKU WAS ABLE TO REGAIN HIS LOST MEMORIES.

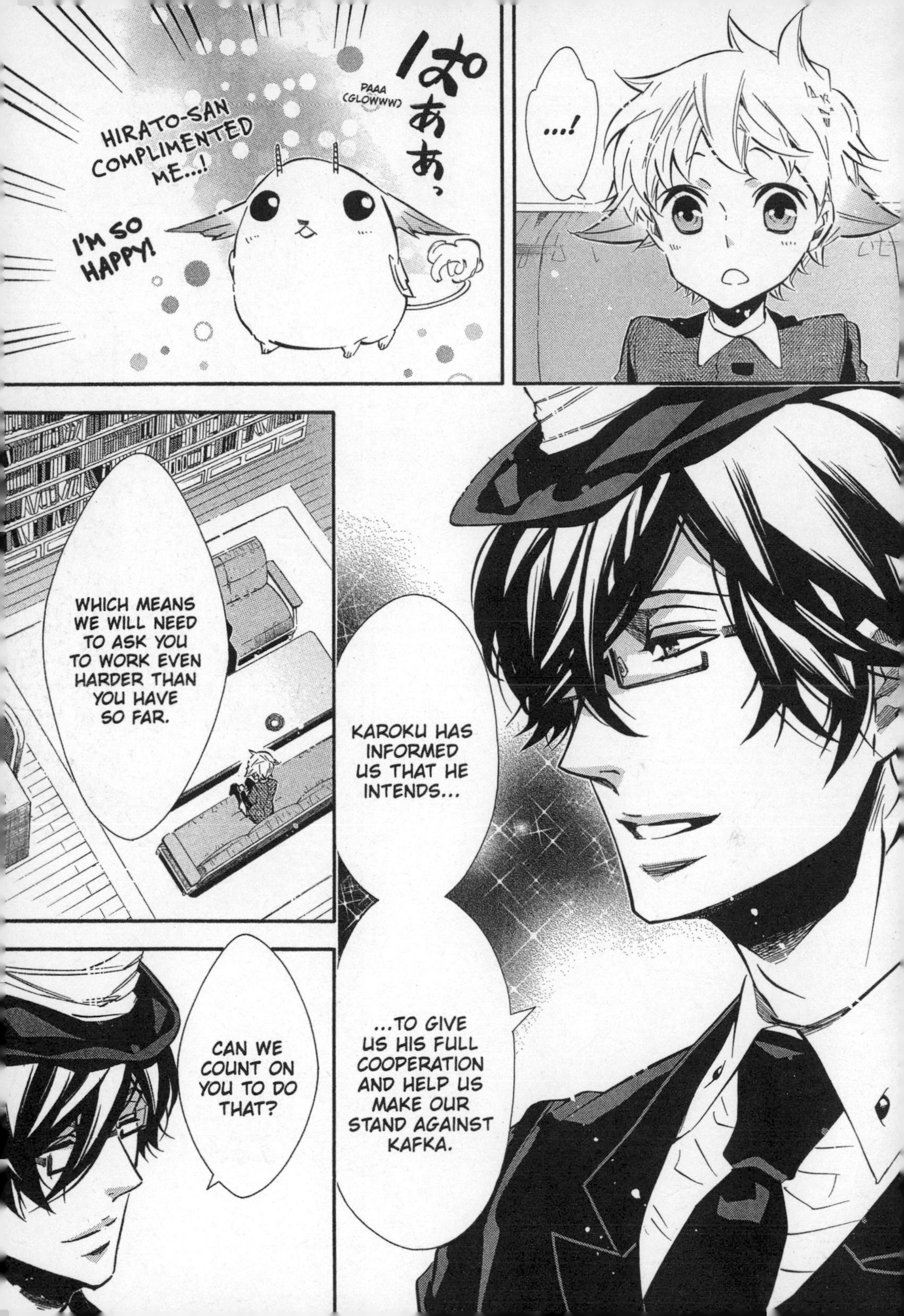
...!
ぱあぁっ
PAAA (GLOWWW)
HIRATO-SAN COMPLIMENTED ME...!
I'M SO HAPPY!
KAROKU HAS INFORMED US THAT HE INTENDS...
...TO GIVE US HIS FULL COOPERATION AND HELP US MAKE OUR STAND AGAINST KAFKA.
WHICH MEANS WE WILL NEED TO ASK YOU TO WORK EVEN HARDER THAN YOU HAVE SO FAR.
CAN WE COUNT ON YOU TO DO THAT?

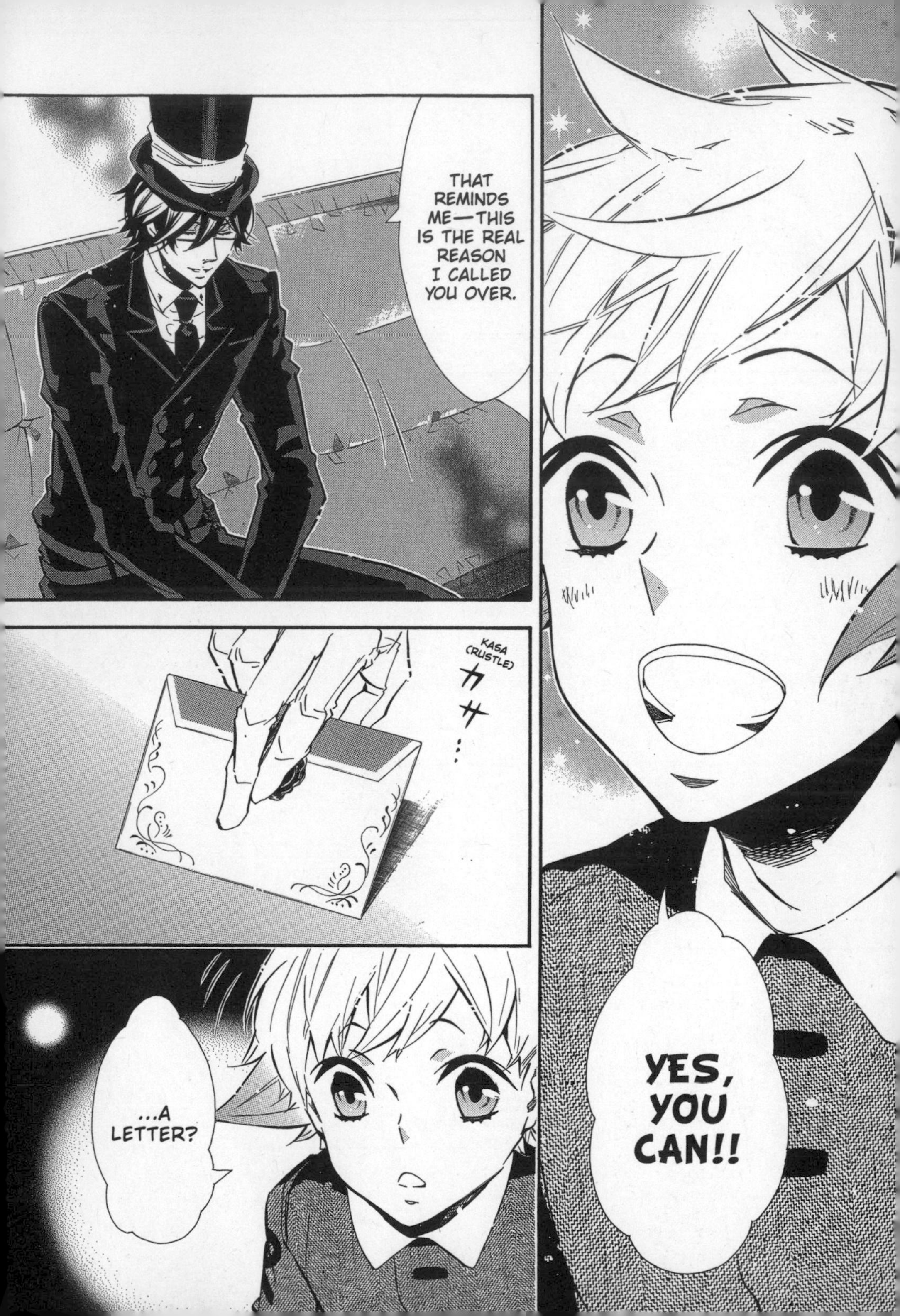
YES, YOU CAN!!
THAT REMINDS ME—THIS IS THE REAL REASON I CALLED YOU OVER.
KASA (RUSTLE)
カサ…
...A LETTER?

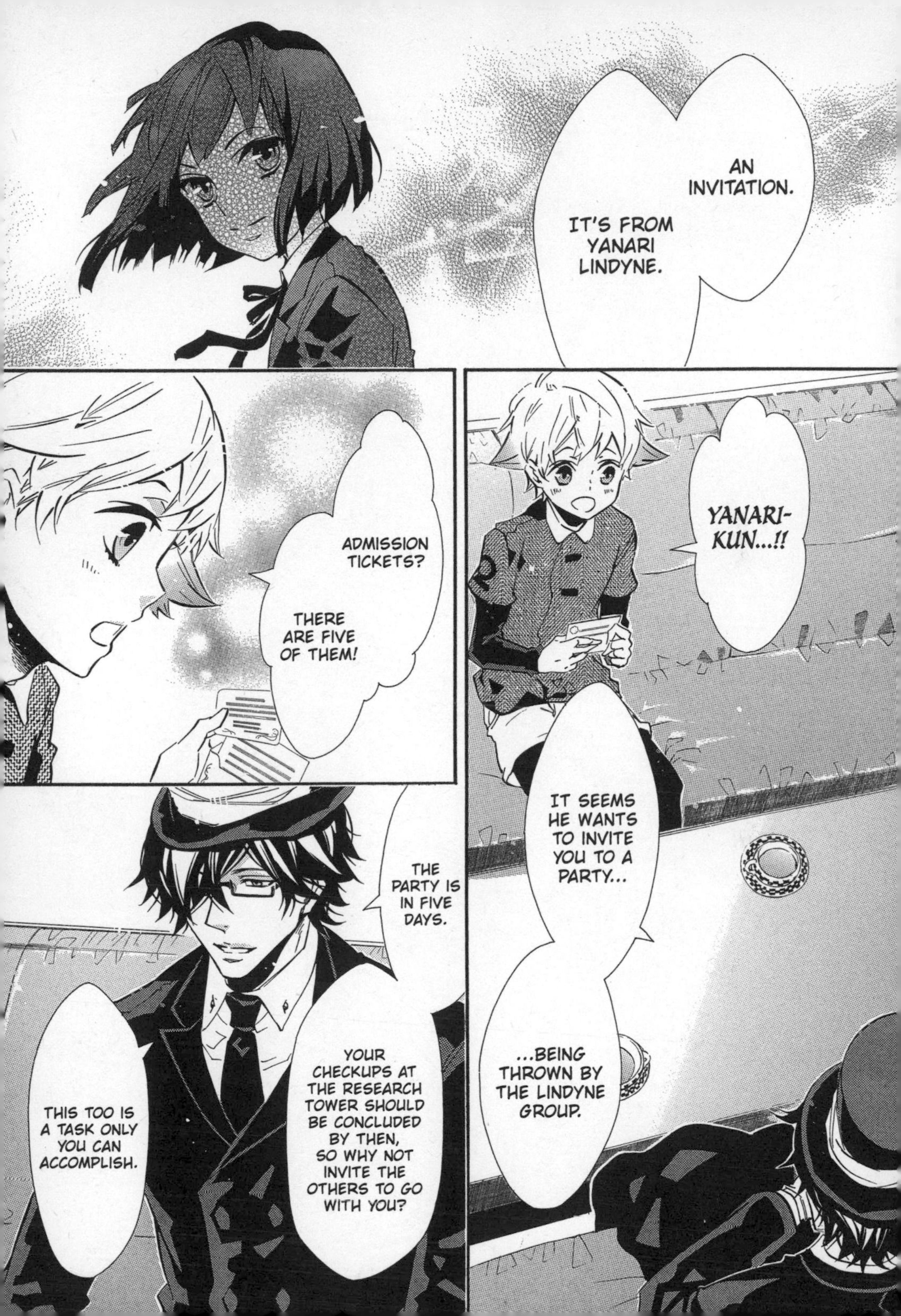
AN INVITATION.
IT'S FROM YANARI LINDYNE.
YANARI-KUN...!!
IT SEEMS HE WANTS TO INVITE YOU TO A PARTY...
...BEING THROWN BY THE LINDYNE GROUP.
ADMISSION TICKETS?
THERE ARE FIVE OF THEM!
THE PARTY IS IN FIVE DAYS.
YOUR CHECKUPS AT THE RESEARCH TOWER SHOULD BE CONCLUDED BY THEN, SO WHY NOT INVITE THE OTHERS TO GO WITH YOU?
THIS TOO IS A TASK ONLY YOU CAN ACCOMPLISH.

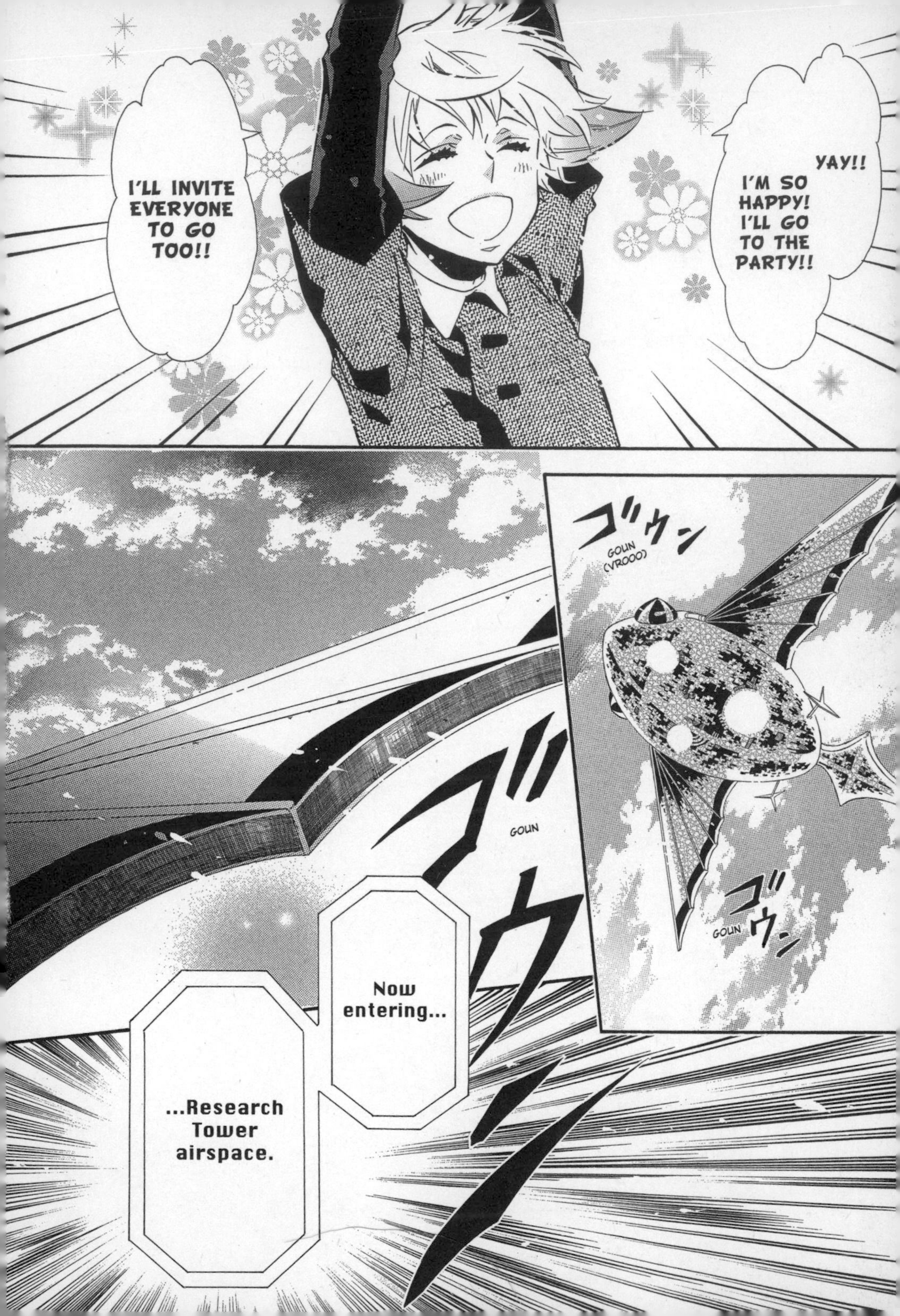
YAY!! I'M SO HAPPY! I'LL GO TO THE PARTY!!
I'LL INVITE EVERYONE TO GO TOO!!
ゴウン
GOUN (VROOO)
ゴウン
GOUN
ゴウン
GOUN
Now entering...
...Research Tower airspace.

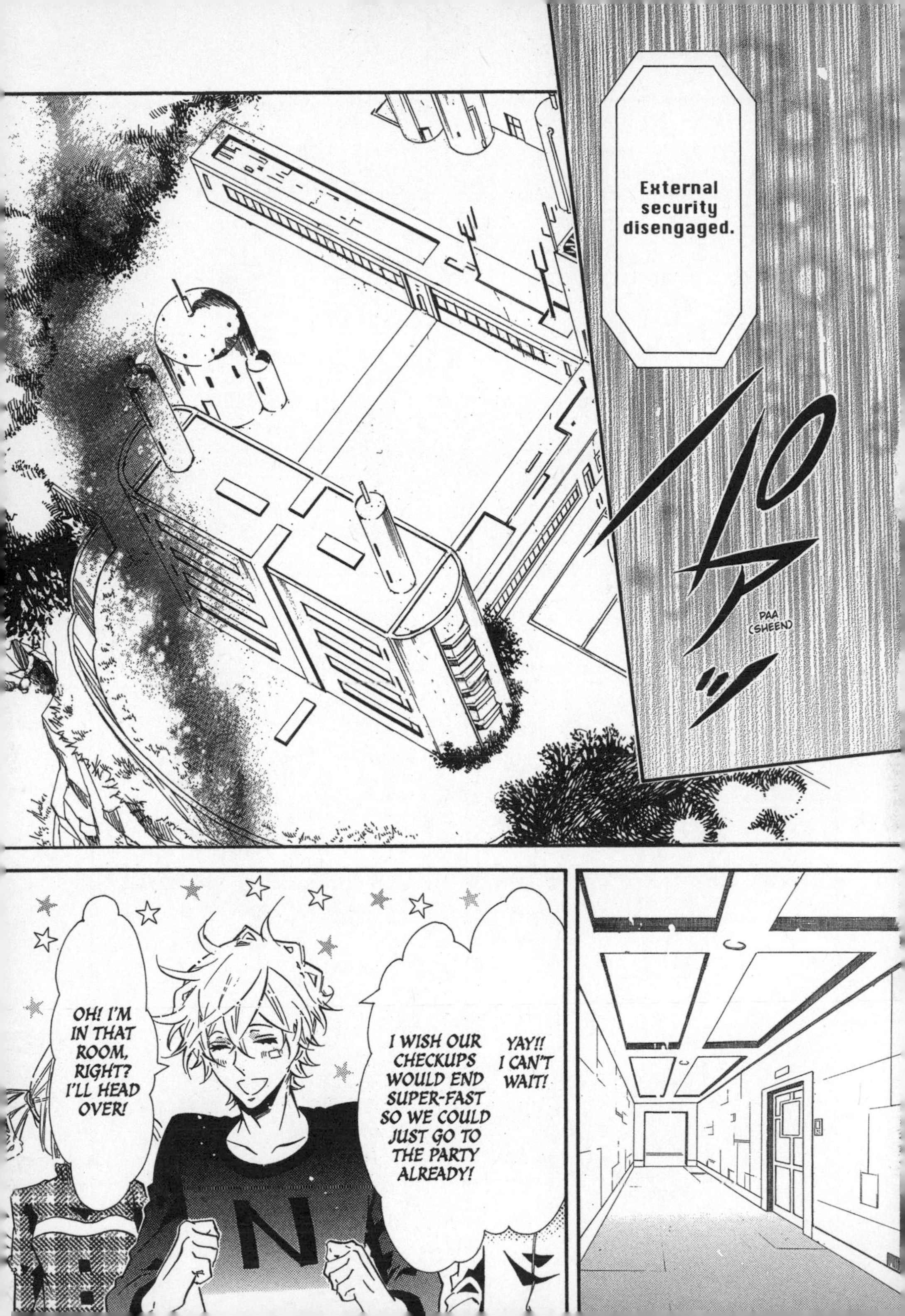
External security disengaged.
PAA (SHEEN)
YAY!! I CAN'T WAIT!
I WISH OUR CHECKUPS WOULD END SUPER-FAST SO WE COULD JUST GO TO THE PARTY ALREADY!
OH! I'M IN THAT ROOM, RIGHT? I'LL HEAD OVER!

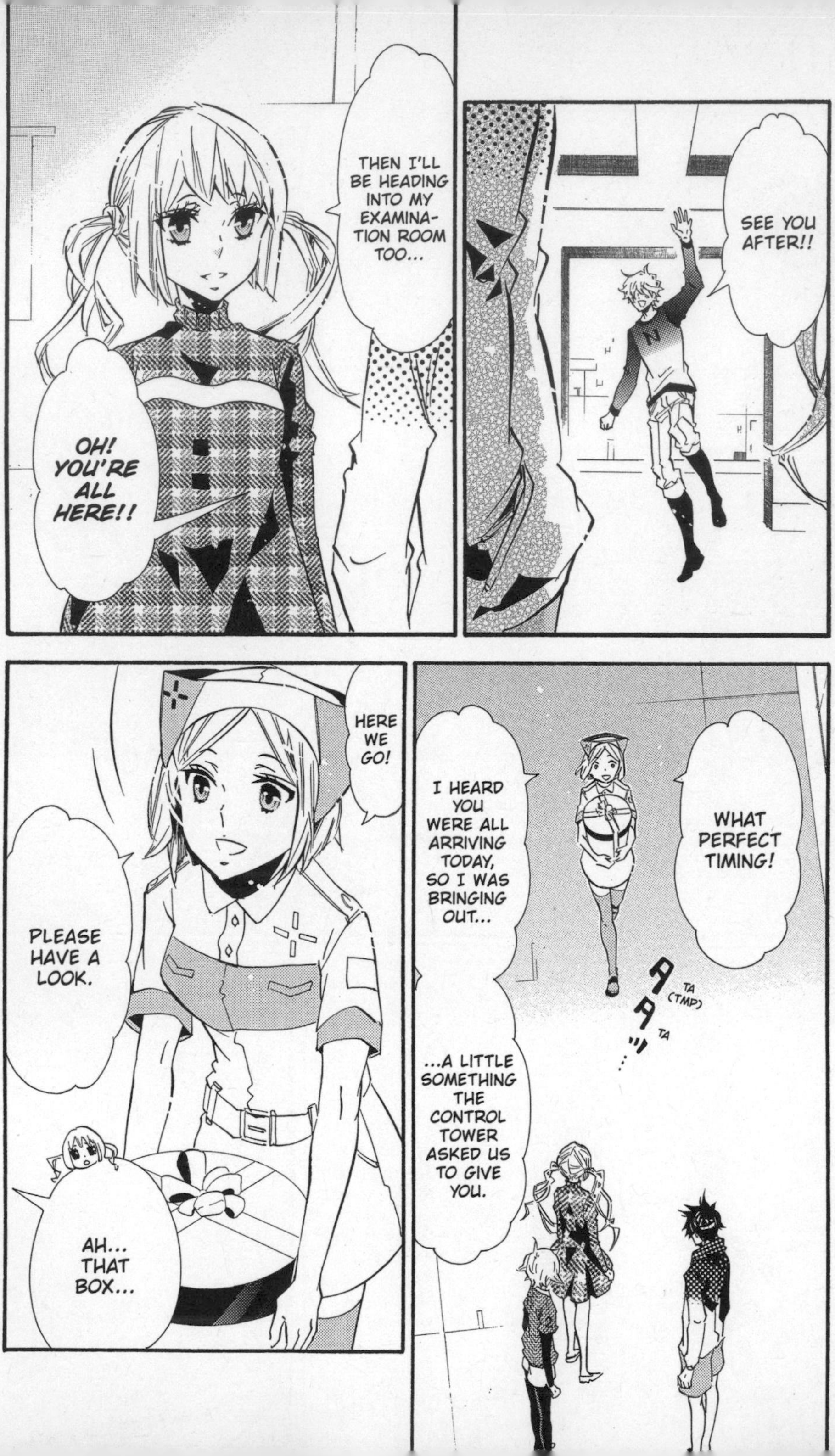
SEE YOU AFTER!!
THEN I'LL BE HEADING INTO MY EXAMINATION ROOM TOO...
OH! YOU'RE ALL HERE!!
WHAT PERFECT TIMING!
I HEARD YOU WERE ALL ARRIVING TODAY, SO I WAS BRINGING OUT...
TA (TMP) TA
...A LITTLE SOMETHING THE CONTROL TOWER ASKED US TO GIVE YOU.
HERE WE GO!
PLEASE HAVE A LOOK.
AH... THAT BOX...

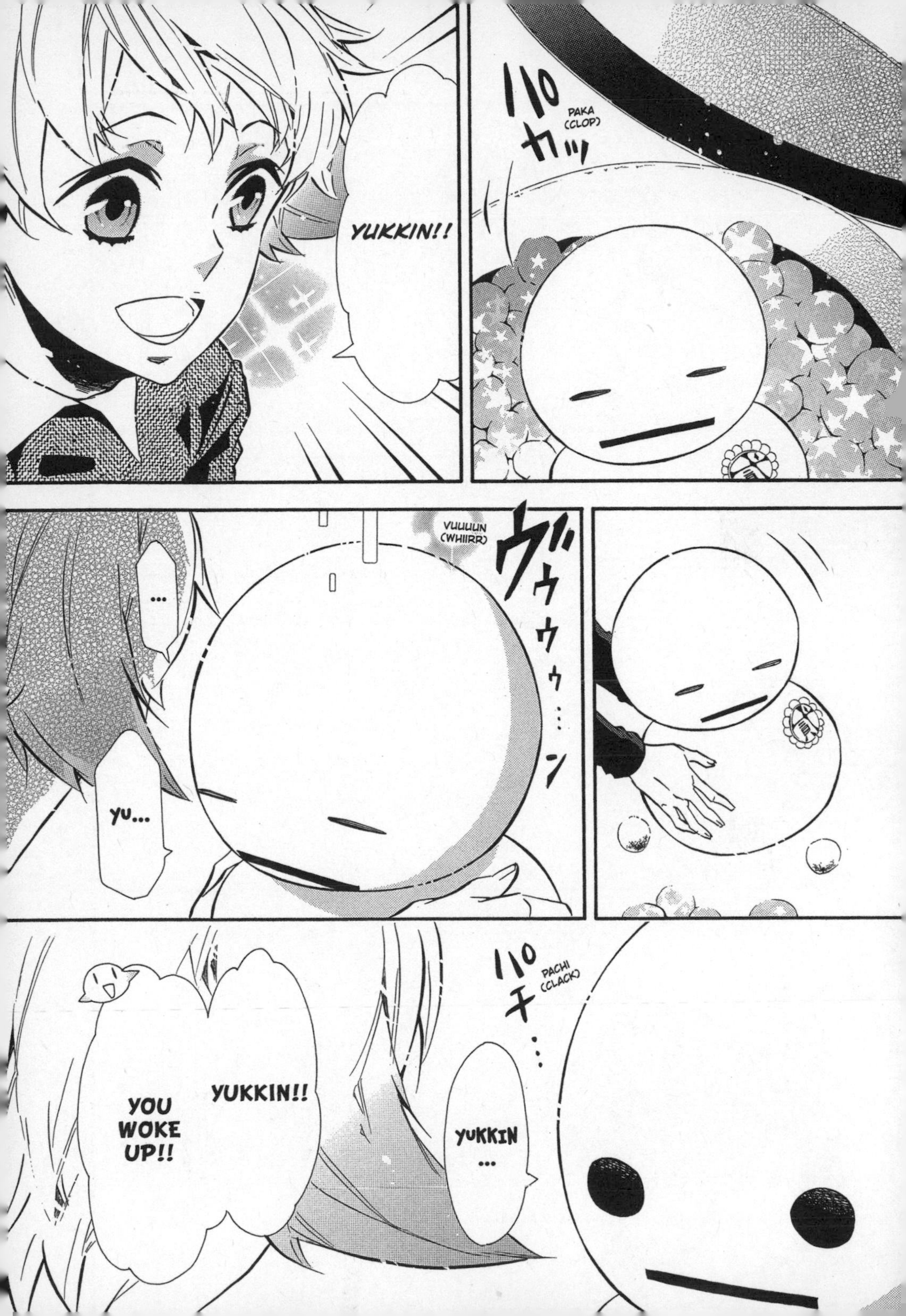
パカッ
PAKA (CLOP)
YUKKIN!!
ヴウウウ…ン
VUUUUN (WHIIRR)
...
YU...
パチ…
PACHI (CLACK)
YUKKIN ...
YUKKIN!!
YOU WOKE UP!!

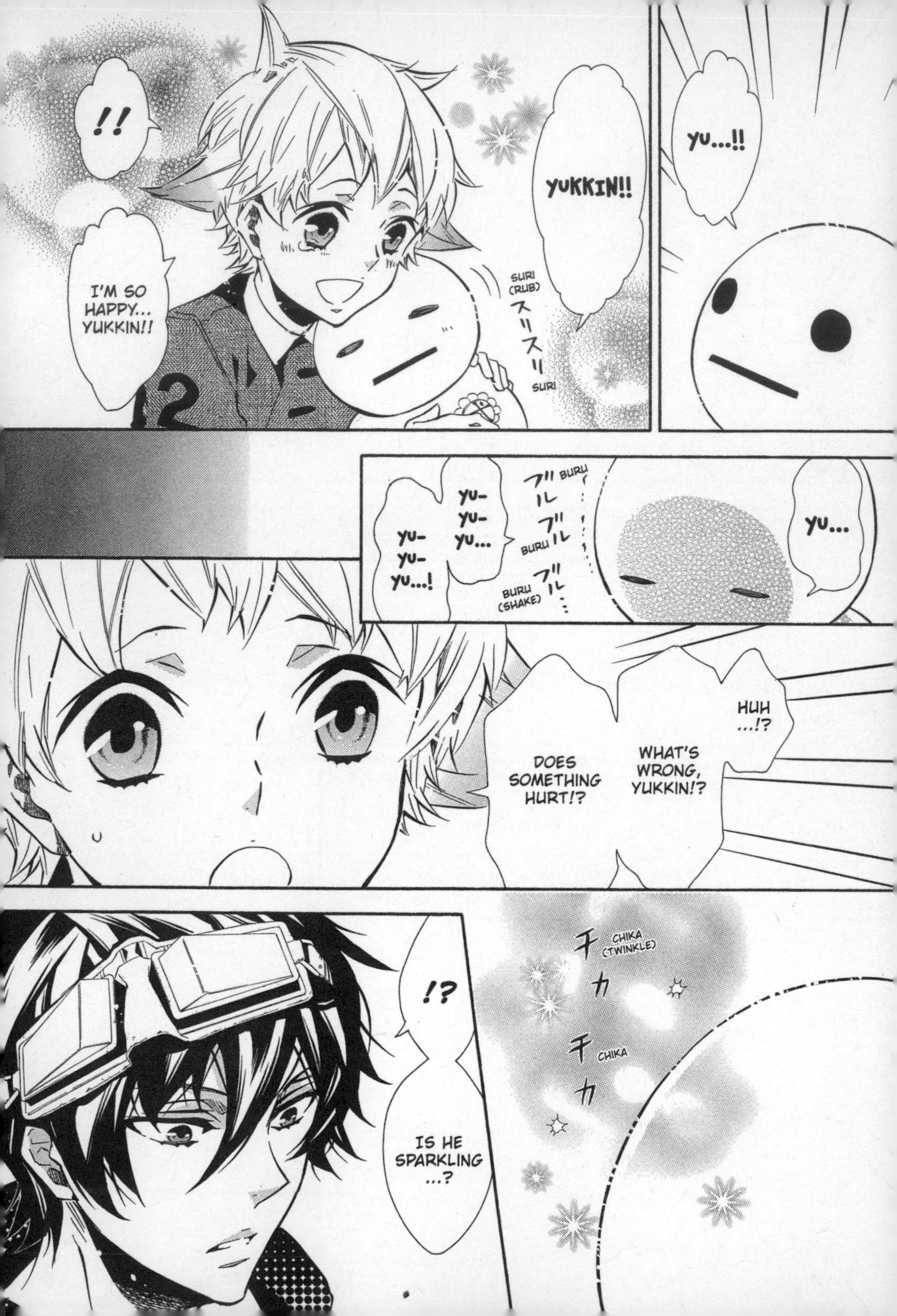
YU...!!
YUKKIN!!
SURI (RUB) スリスリ SURI
!!
I'M SO HAPPY... YUKKIN!!
YU...
BURU ブル BURU ブル BURU (SHAKE) ブル
YU-YU-YU...
YU-YU-YU...!
HUH ...!?
WHAT'S WRONG, YUKKIN!?
DOES SOMETHING HURT!?
CHIKA (TWINKLE) チカ CHIKA チカ
!?
IS HE SPARKLING ...?

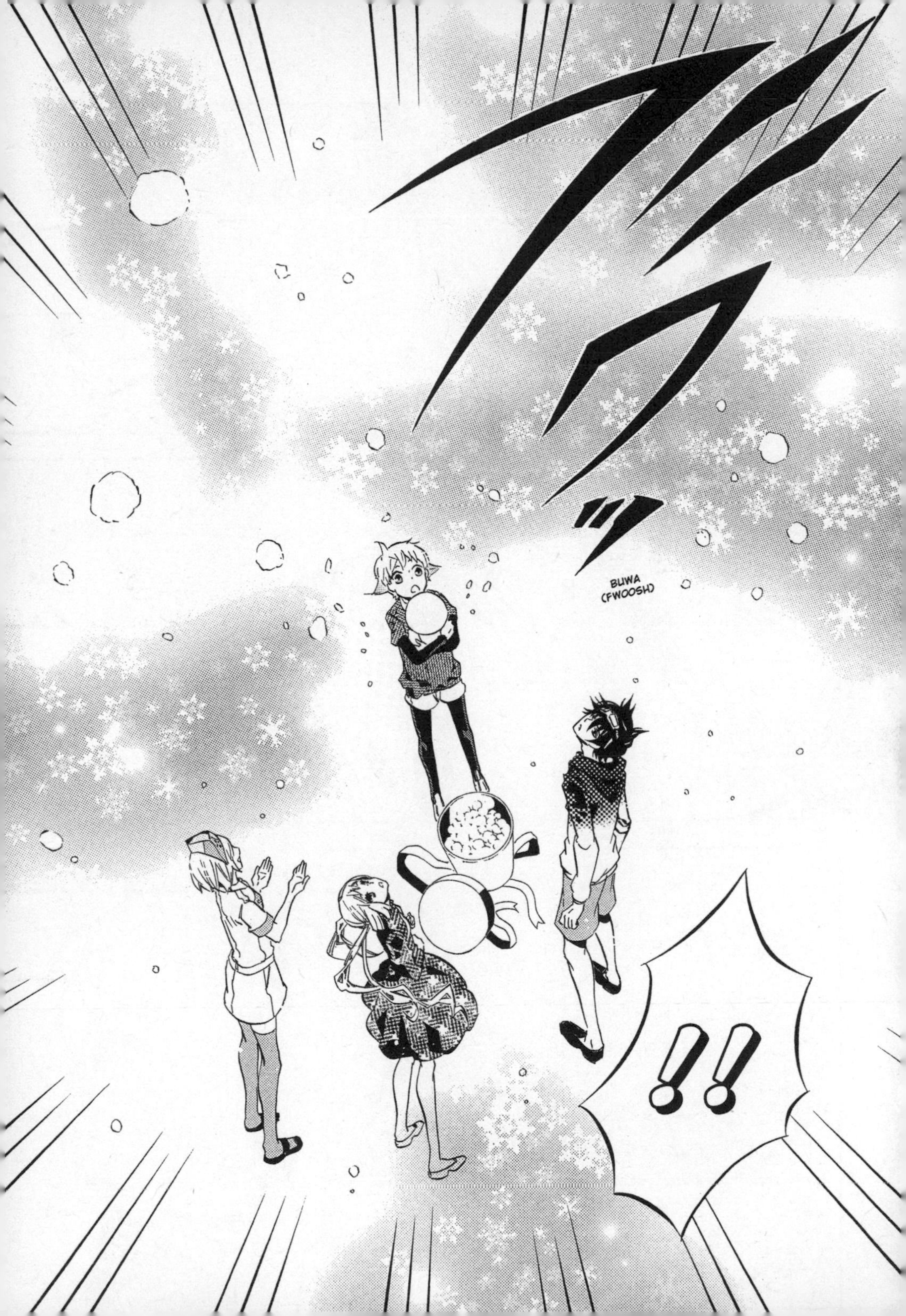
BUWA
(FWOOSH)
!!

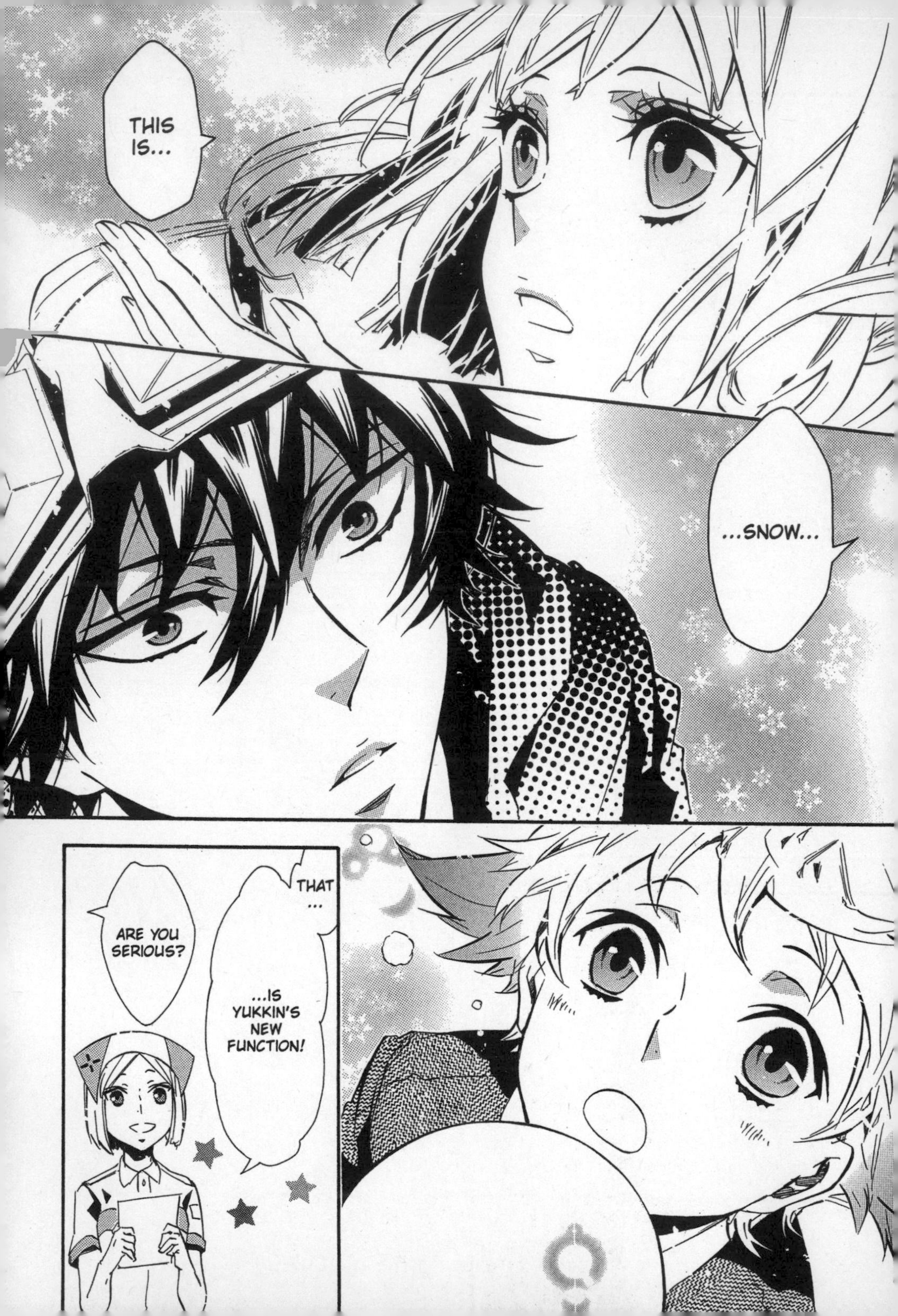
THIS IS...
...SNOW...
THAT ...
...IS YUKKIN'S NEW FUNCTION!
ARE YOU SERIOUS?

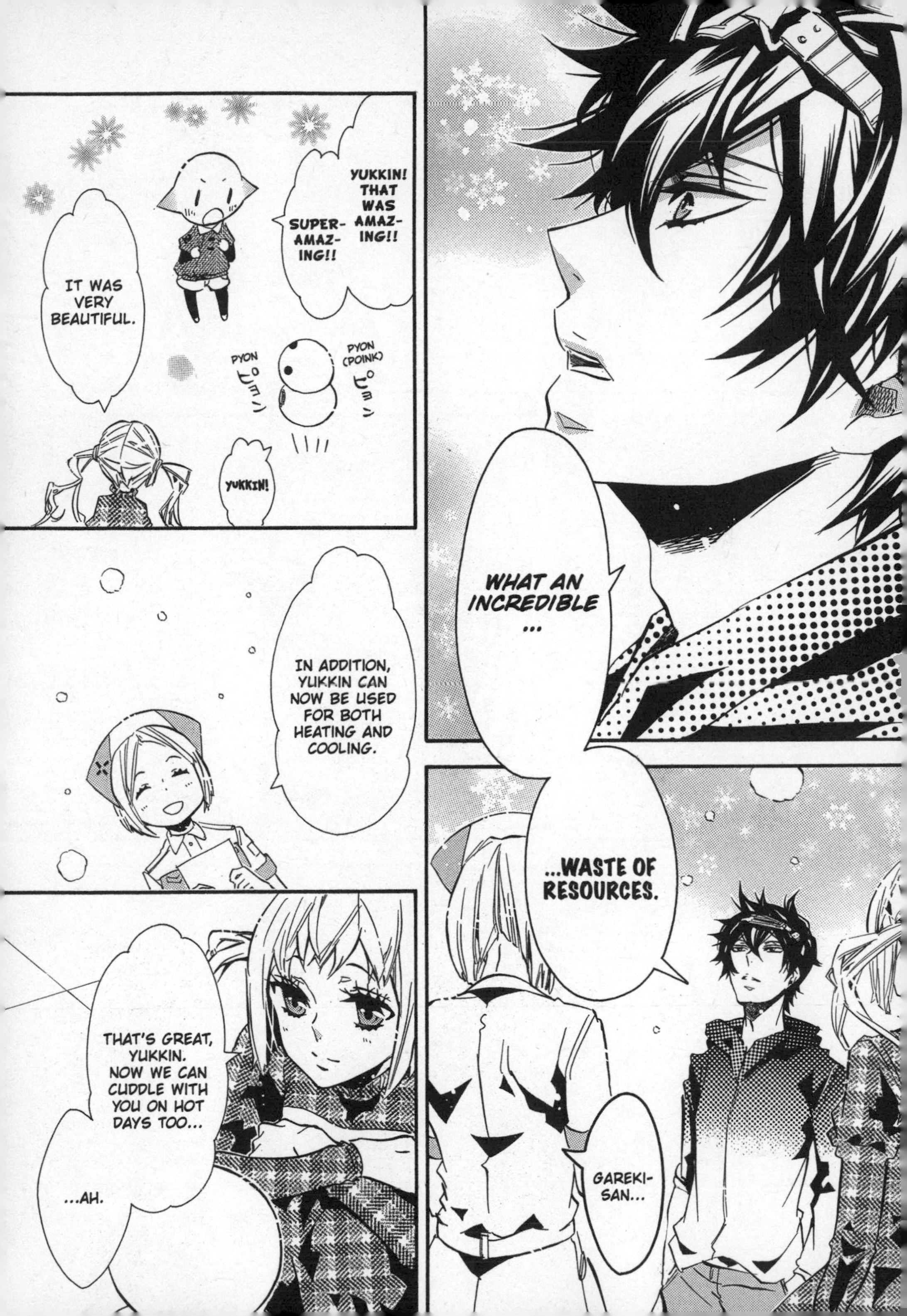
WHAT AN INCREDIBLE ...
...WASTE OF RESOURCES.
GAREKI-SAN...
YUKKIN! THAT WAS AMAZING!!
SUPER-AMAZING!!
IT WAS VERY BEAUTIFUL.
PYON (POINK) ぴょん
PYON ぴょん
YUKKIN!
IN ADDITION, YUKKIN CAN NOW BE USED FOR BOTH HEATING AND COOLING.
THAT'S GREAT, YUKKIN. NOW WE CAN CUDDLE WITH YOU ON HOT DAYS TOO...
...AH.

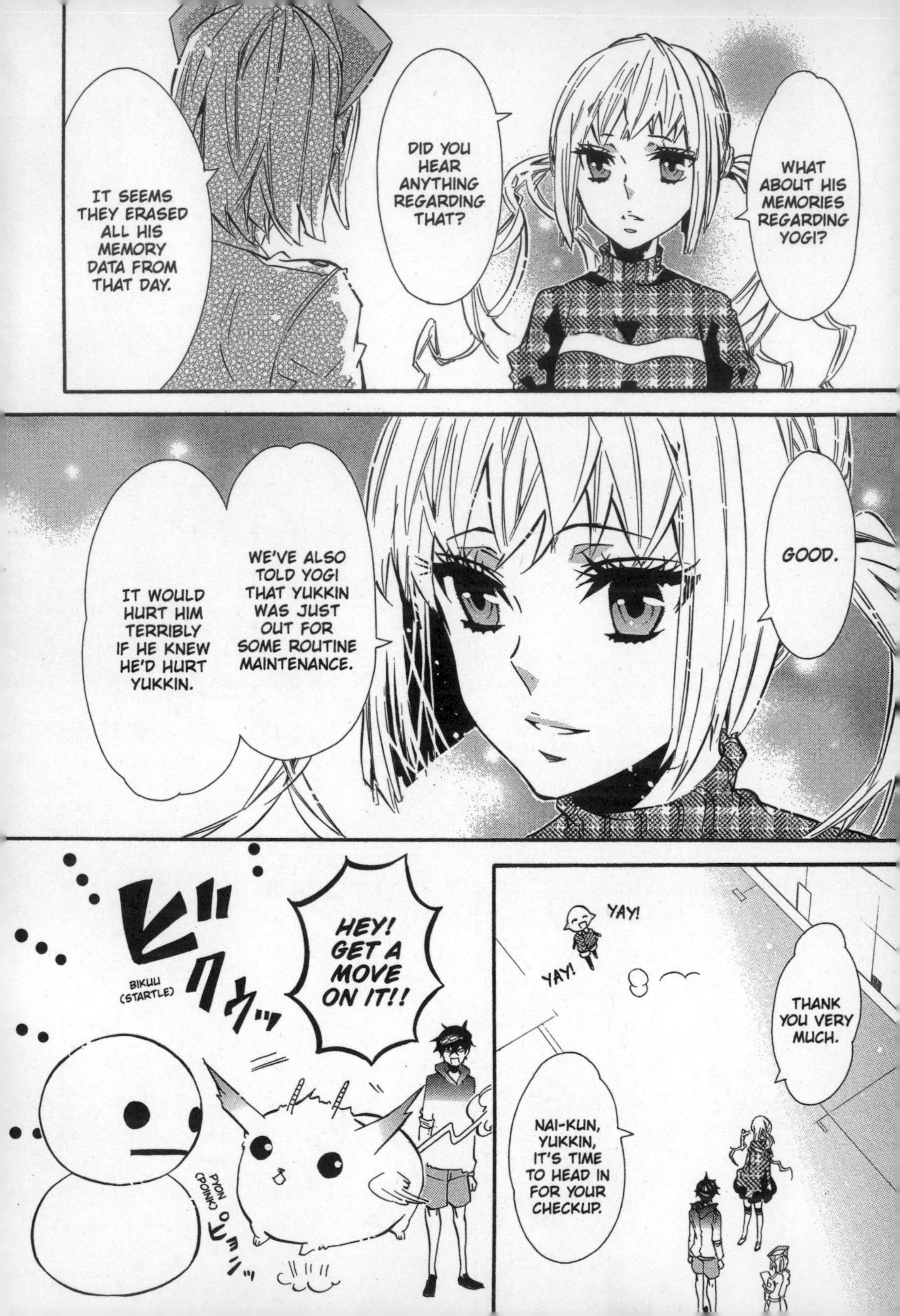
WHAT ABOUT HIS MEMORIES REGARDING YOGI?
DID YOU HEAR ANYTHING REGARDING THAT?
IT SEEMS THEY ERASED ALL HIS MEMORY DATA FROM THAT DAY.
GOOD.
WE'VE ALSO TOLD YOGI THAT YUKKIN WAS JUST OUT FOR SOME ROUTINE MAINTENANCE.
IT WOULD HURT HIM TERRIBLY IF HE KNEW HE'D HURT YUKKIN.
THANK YOU VERY MUCH.
YAY!
YAY!
NAI-KUN, YUKKIN, IT'S TIME TO HEAD IN FOR YOUR CHECKUP.
HEY! GET A MOVE ON IT!!
ビクゥッ
BIKUU (STARTLE)
PYON (BOING)

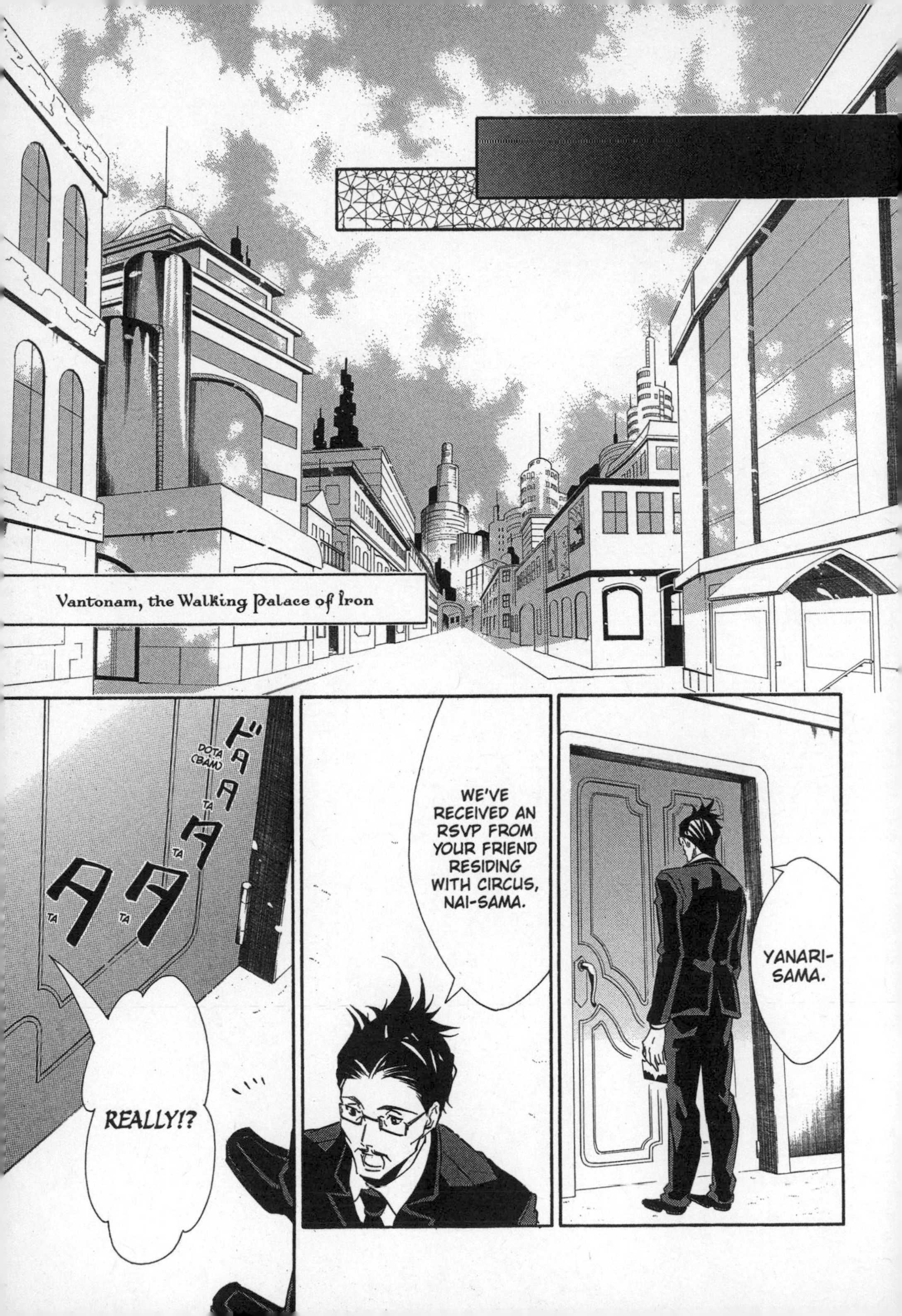
Vantonam, the Walking Palace of Iron
YANARI-SAMA.
WE'VE RECEIVED AN RSVP FROM YOUR FRIEND RESIDING WITH CIRCUS, NAI-SAMA.
ドタタタタ
DOTA (BAM) TA TA TA TA
REALLY!?

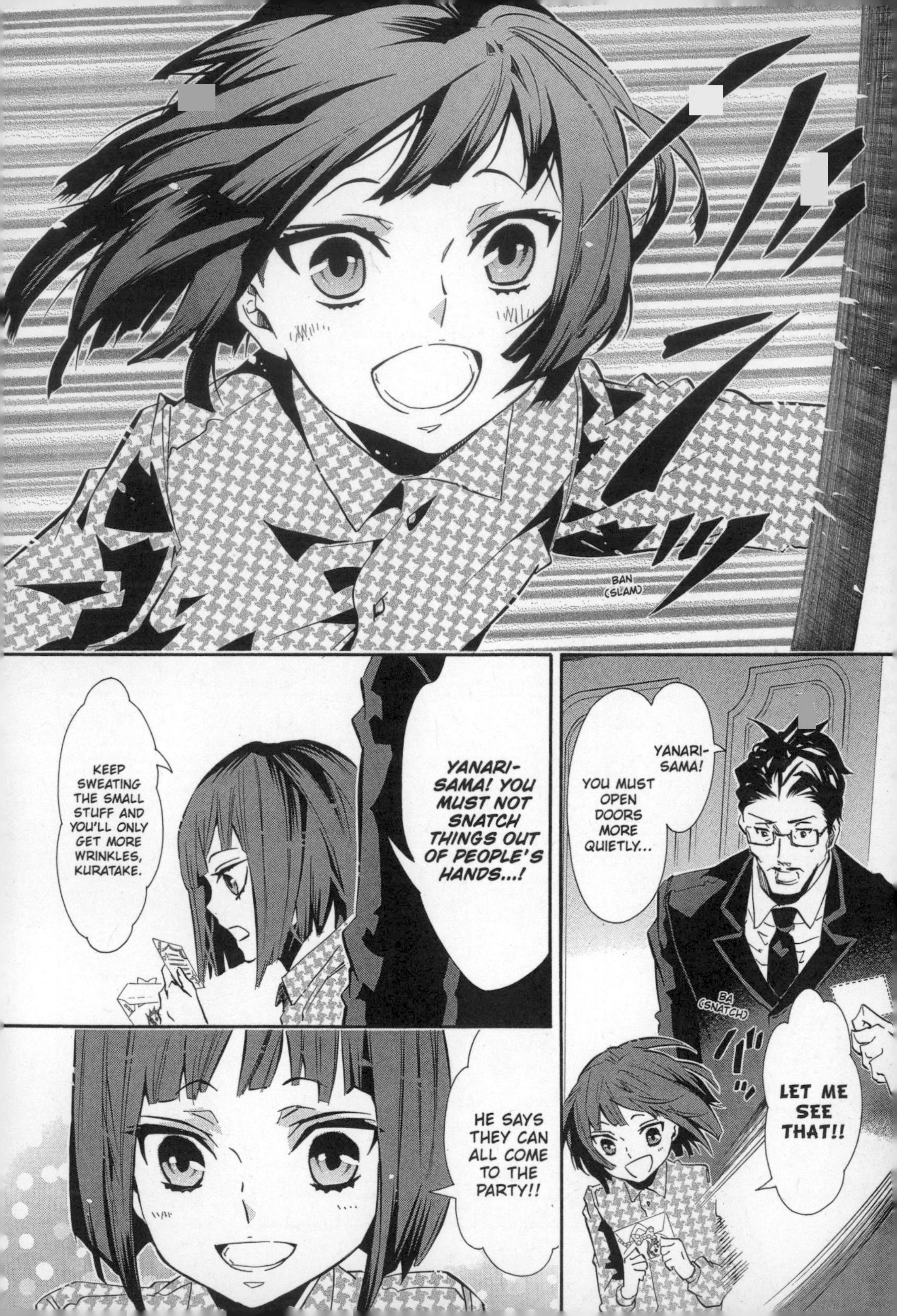
BAN (SLAM)
YANARI-SAMA!
YOU MUST OPEN DOORS MORE QUIETLY...
BA (SNATCH)
LET ME SEE THAT!!
YANARI-SAMA! YOU MUST NOT SNATCH THINGS OUT OF PEOPLE'S HANDS...!
KEEP SWEATING THE SMALL STUFF AND YOU'LL ONLY GET MORE WRINKLES, KURATAKE.
HE SAYS THEY CAN ALL COME TO THE PARTY!!

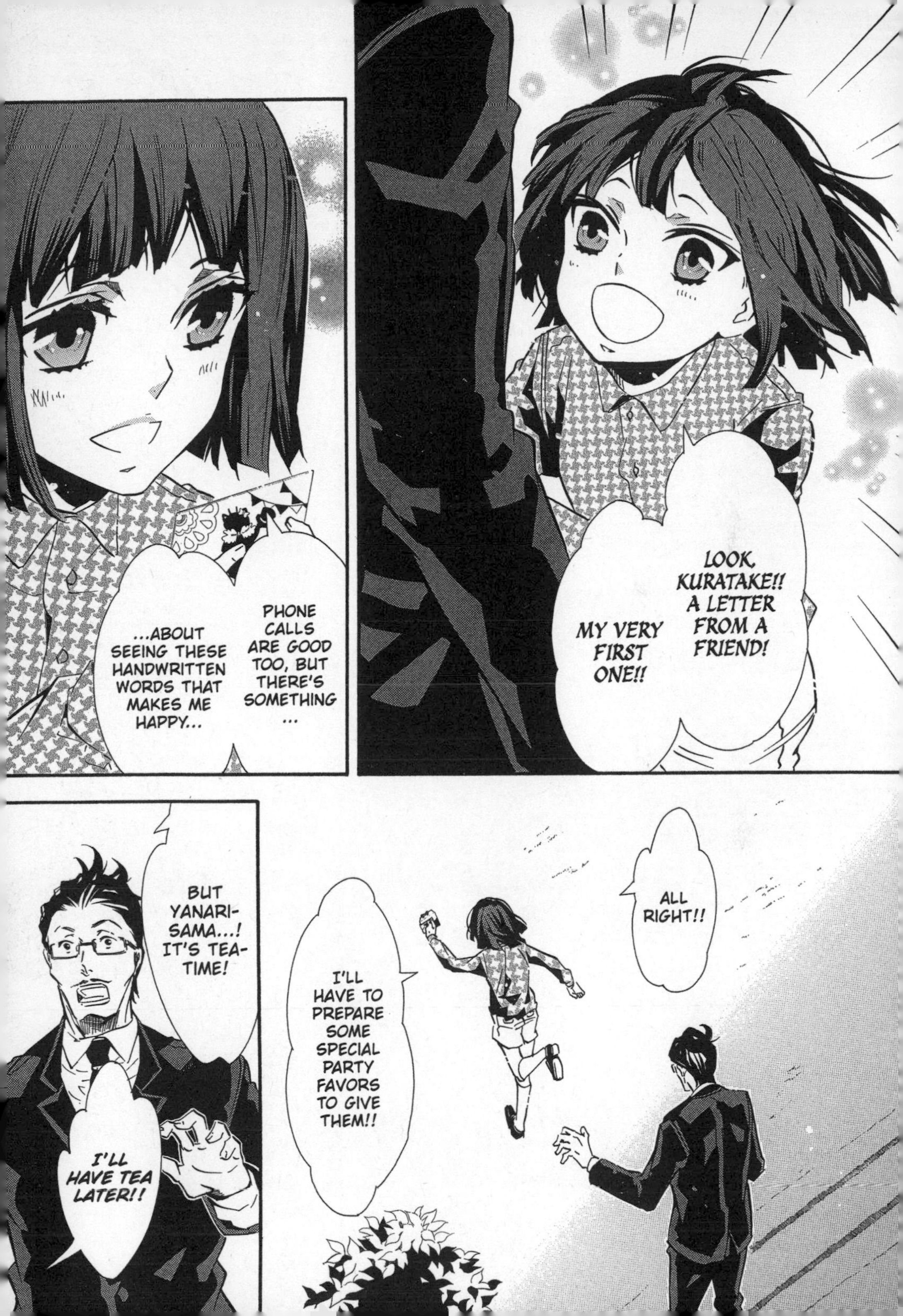
LOOK, KURATAKE!! A LETTER FROM A FRIEND!
MY VERY FIRST ONE!!
PHONE CALLS ARE GOOD TOO, BUT THERE'S SOMETHING ...
...ABOUT SEEING THESE HANDWRITTEN WORDS THAT MAKES ME HAPPY...
ALL RIGHT!!
I'LL HAVE TO PREPARE SOME SPECIAL PARTY FAVORS TO GIVE THEM!!
BUT YANARI-SAMA...! IT'S TEA-TIME!
I'LL HAVE TEA LATER!!

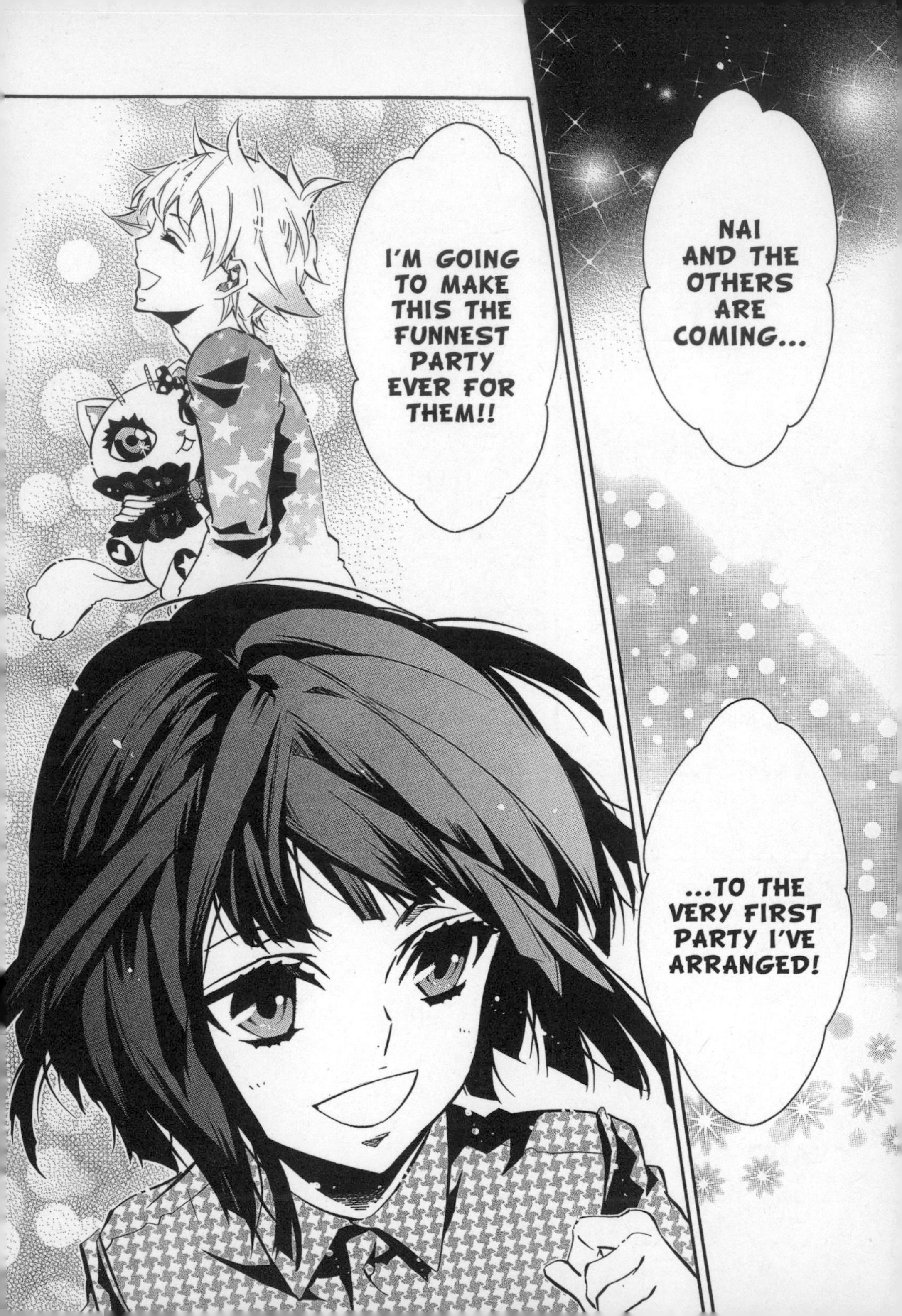
NAI AND THE OTHERS ARE COMING...
...TO THE VERY FIRST PARTY I'VE ARRANGED!
I'M GOING TO MAKE THIS THE FUNNEST PARTY EVER FOR THEM!!

KARNEVAL

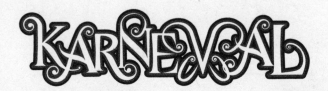

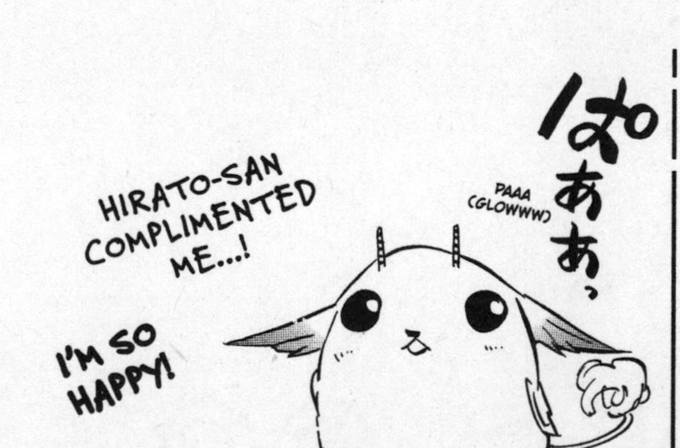

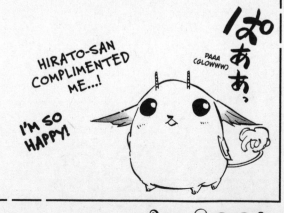

ぱあぁっ
PAAA (GLOWWW)
HIRATO-SAN COMPLIMENTED ME...!
I'M SO HAPPY!

KARNEVAL

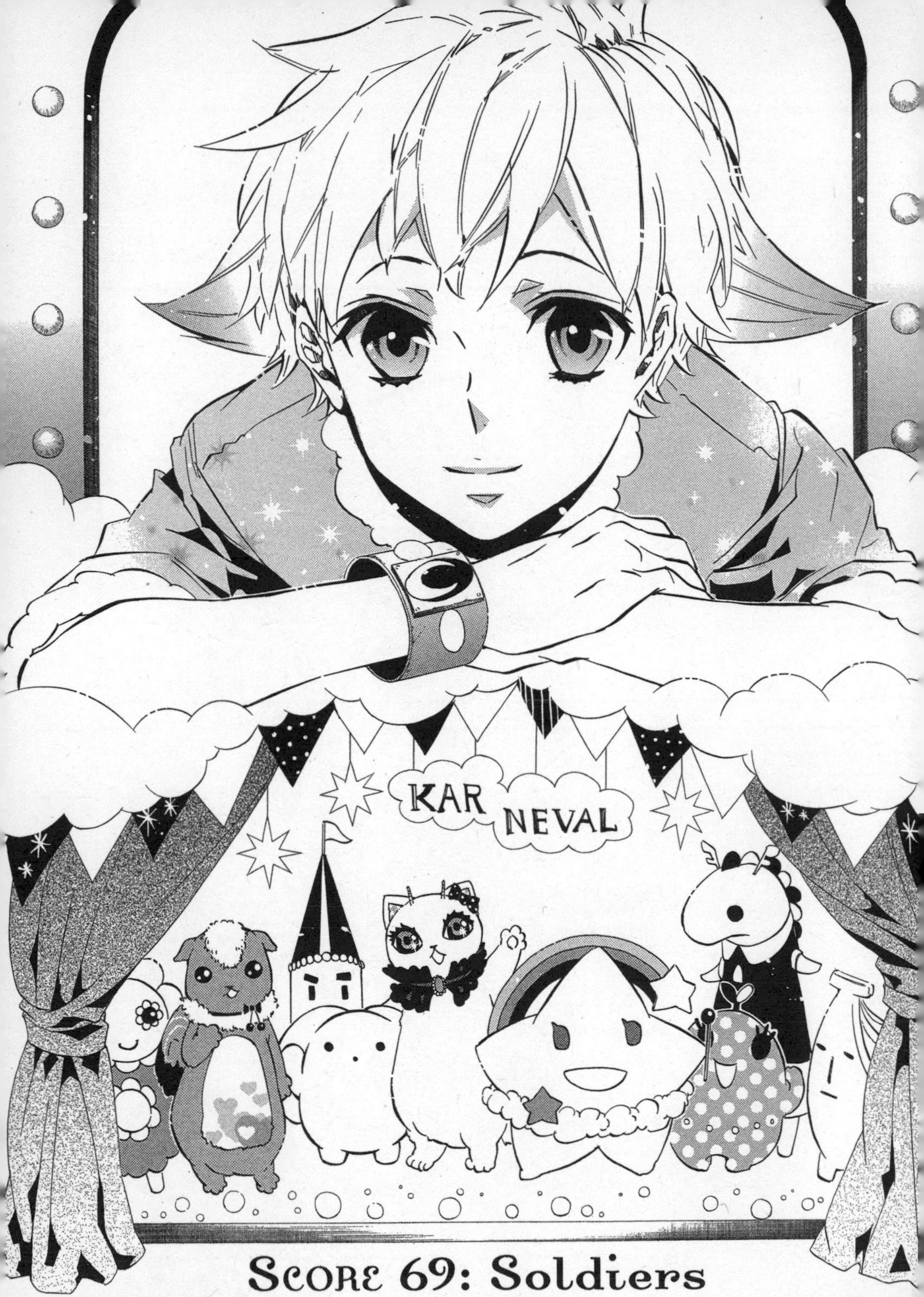
KAR NEVAL

Score 69: Soldiers

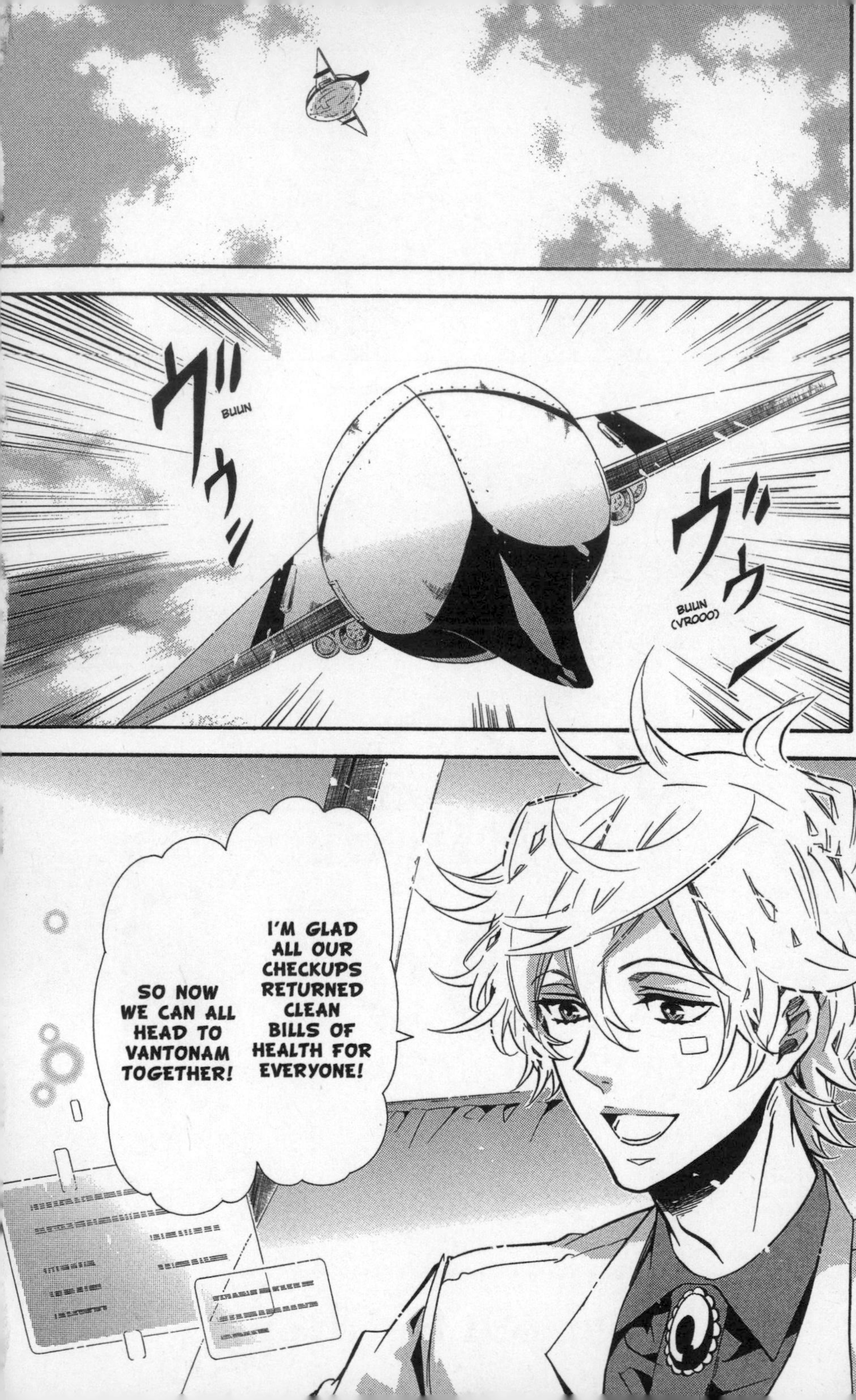
ヴゥン
BUUN (VROOO)
ヴゥン
BUUN
I'M GLAD ALL OUR CHECKUPS RETURNED CLEAN BILLS OF HEALTH FOR EVERYONE!
SO NOW WE CAN ALL HEAD TO VANTONAM TOGETHER!

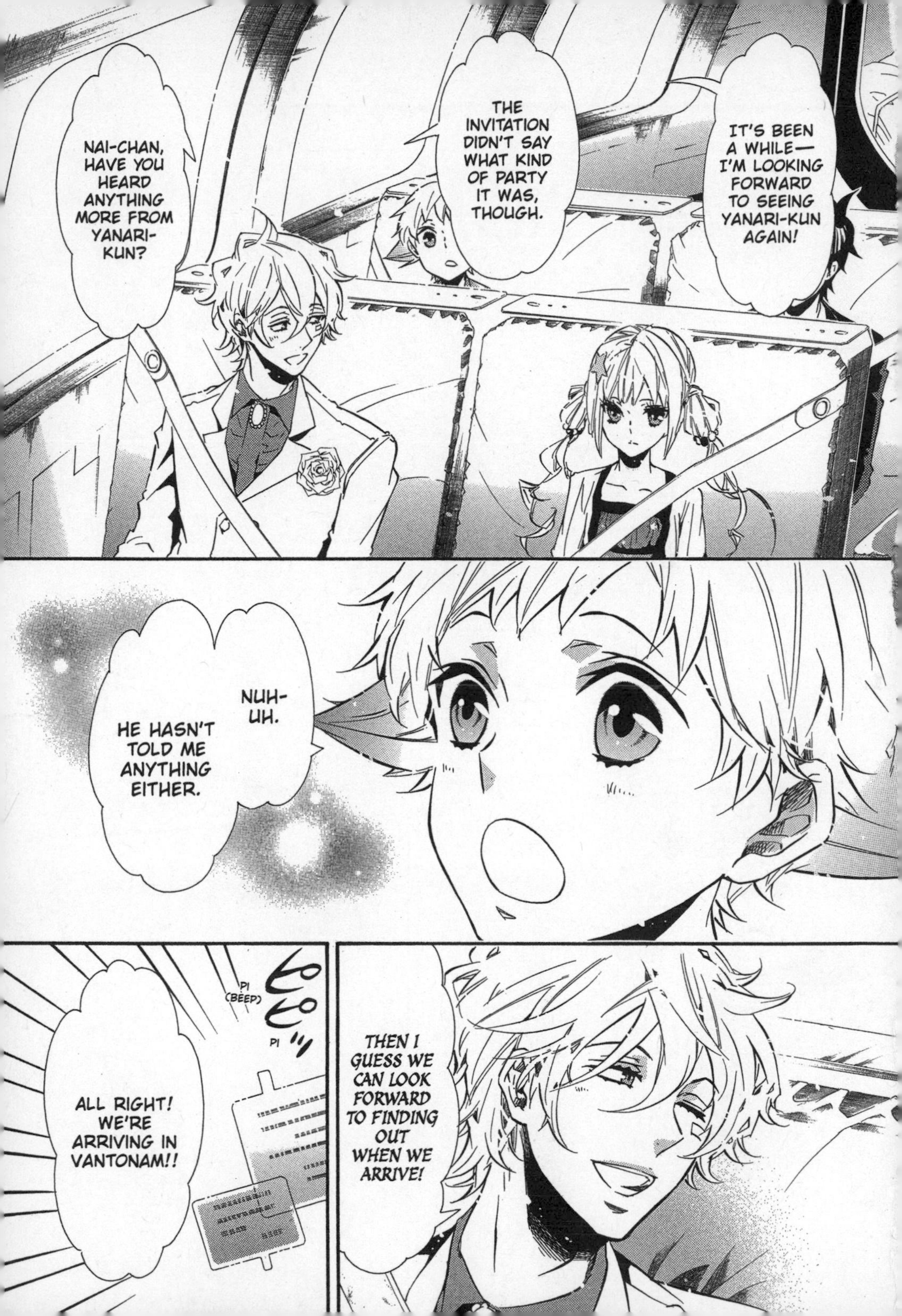
IT'S BEEN A WHILE—I'M LOOKING FORWARD TO SEEING YANARI-KUN AGAIN!
THE INVITATION DIDN'T SAY WHAT KIND OF PARTY IT WAS, THOUGH.
NAI-CHAN, HAVE YOU HEARD ANYTHING MORE FROM YANARI-KUN?
NUH-UH.
HE HASN'T TOLD ME ANYTHING EITHER.
THEN I GUESS WE CAN LOOK FORWARD TO FINDING OUT WHEN WE ARRIVE!
PI (BEEP) PI
ALL RIGHT! WE'RE ARRIVING IN VANTONAM!!

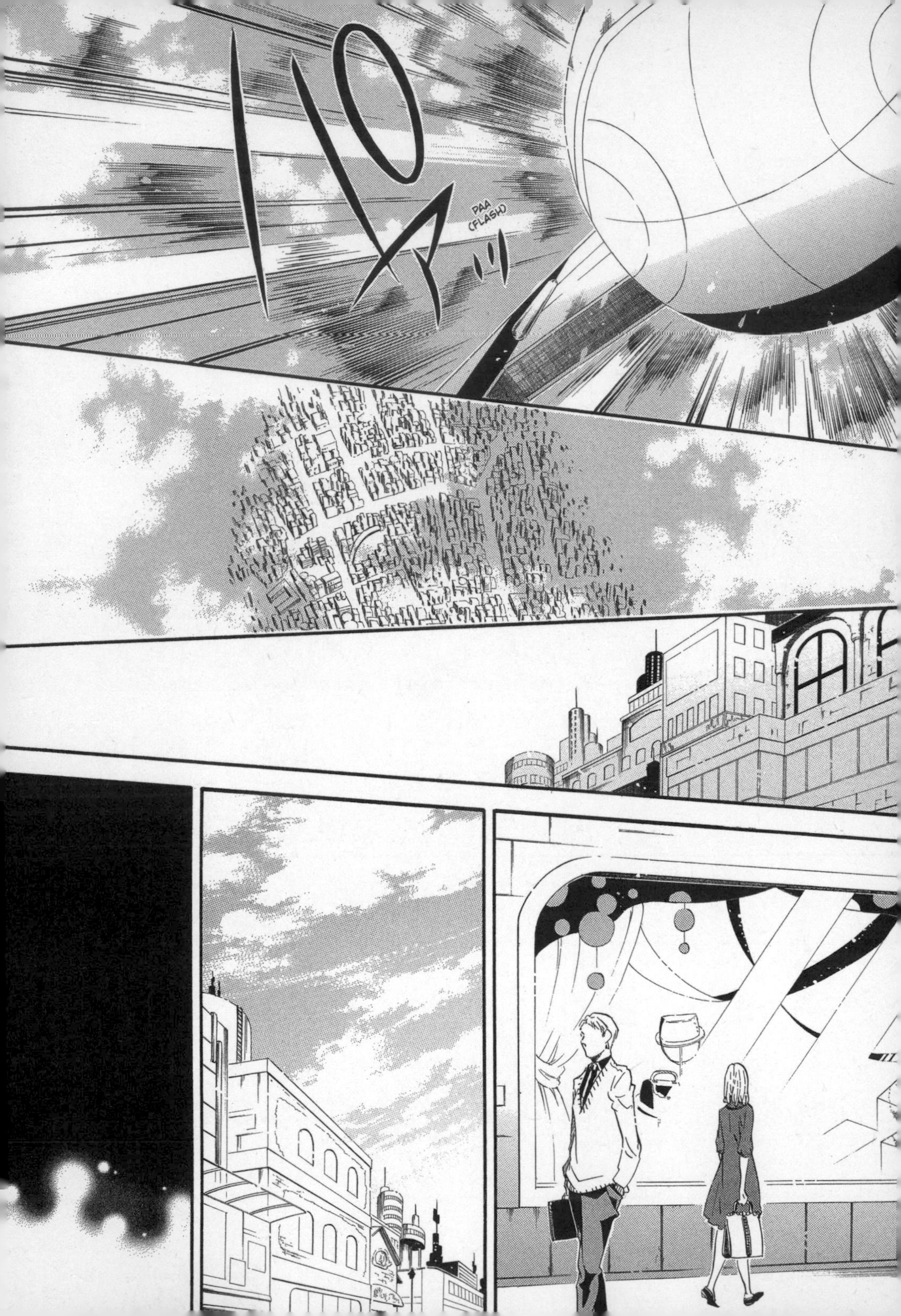
PAA
(FLASH)

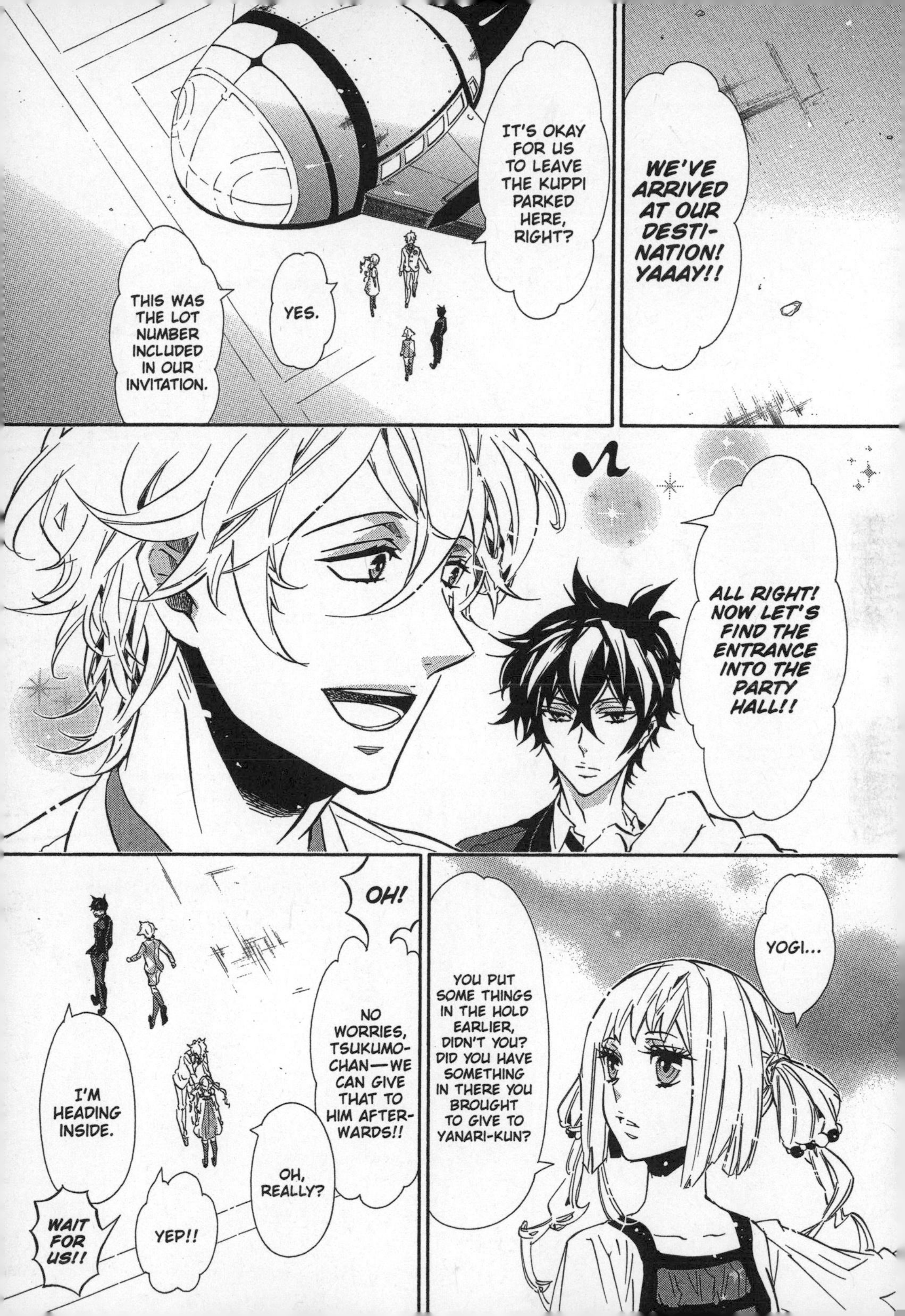
WE'VE ARRIVED AT OUR DESTI-NATION! YAAAY!!
IT'S OKAY FOR US TO LEAVE THE KUPPI PARKED HERE, RIGHT?
YES.
THIS WAS THE LOT NUMBER INCLUDED IN OUR INVITATION.
ALL RIGHT! NOW LET'S FIND THE ENTRANCE INTO THE PARTY HALL!!
YOGI...
YOU PUT SOME THINGS IN THE HOLD EARLIER, DIDN'T YOU? DID YOU HAVE SOMETHING IN THERE YOU BROUGHT TO GIVE TO YANARI-KUN?
OH!
NO WORRIES, TSUKUMO-CHAN—WE CAN GIVE THAT TO HIM AFTER-WARDS!!
OH, REALLY?
YEP!!
I'M HEADING INSIDE.
WAIT FOR US!!

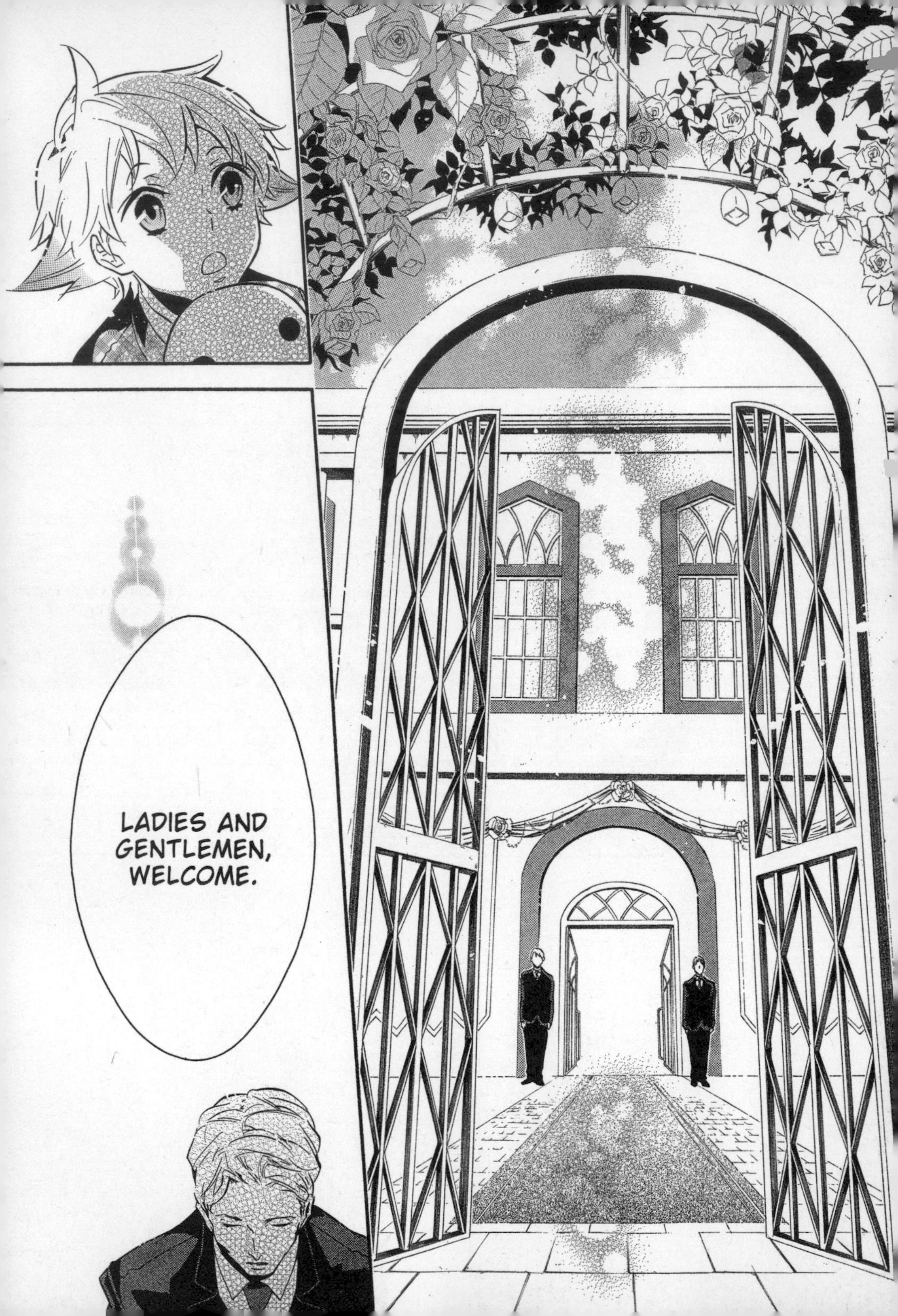
LADIES AND GENTLEMEN, WELCOME.

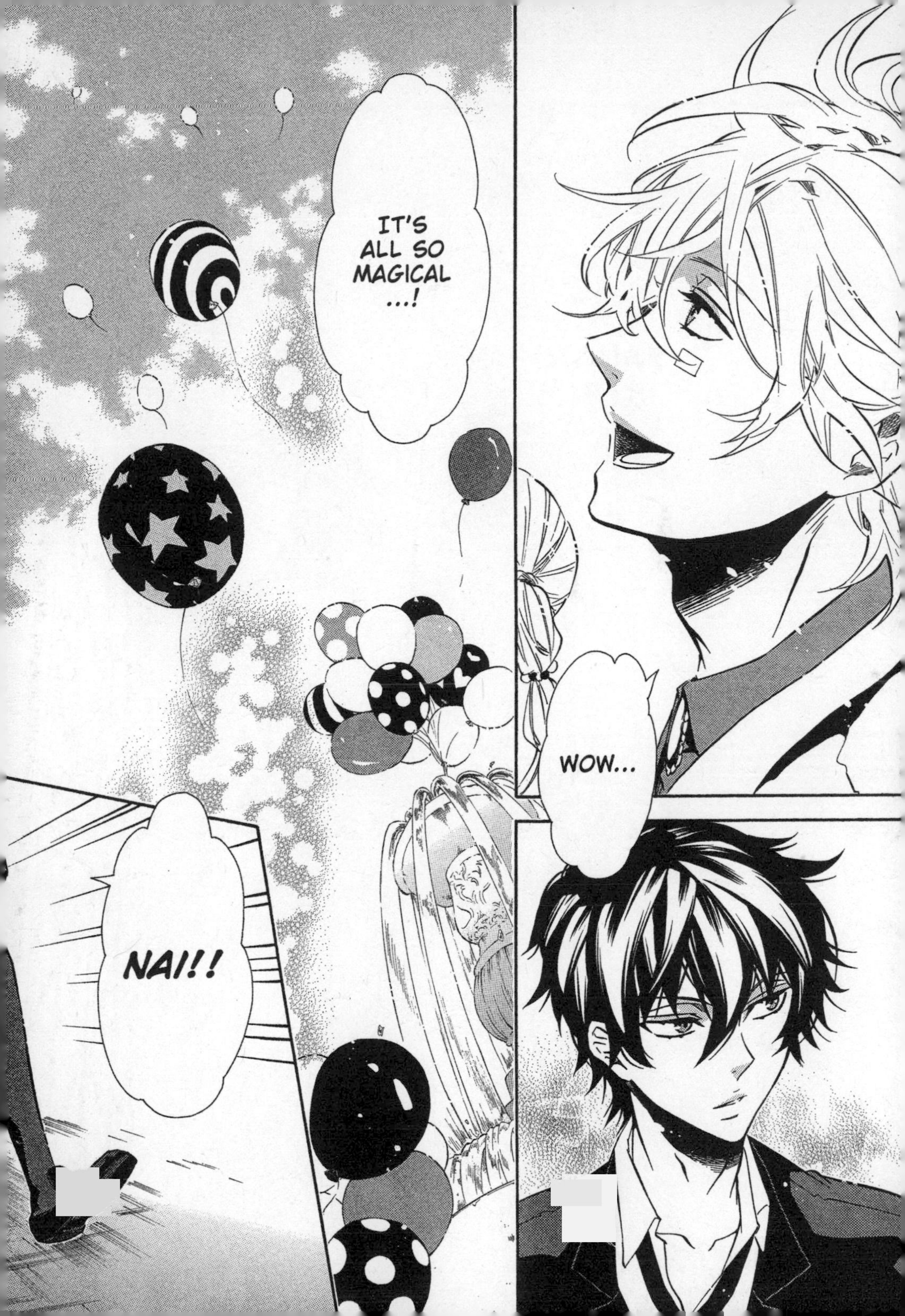
WOW...
IT'S ALL SO MAGICAL ...!
NAI!!

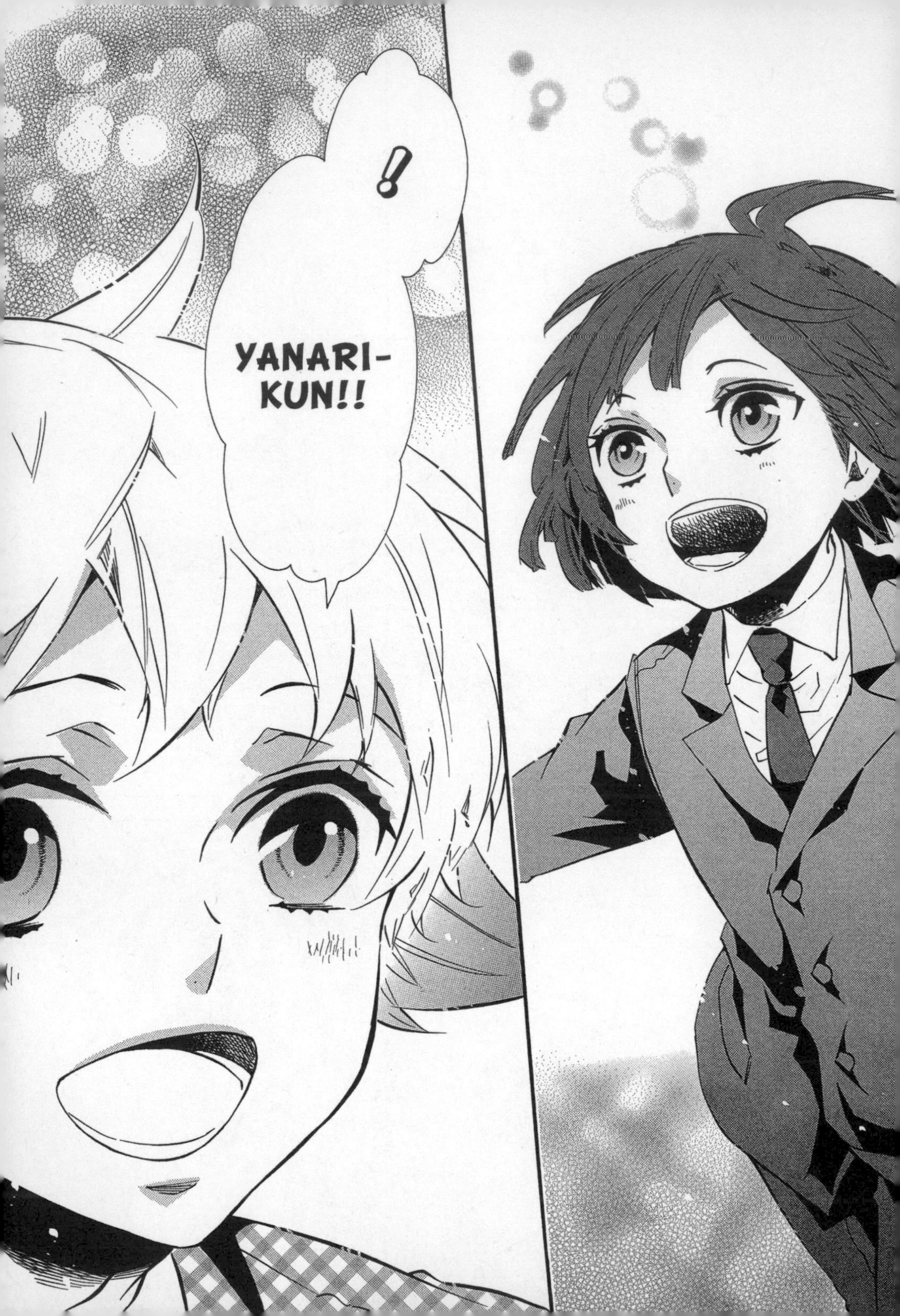
!
YANARI-KUN!!

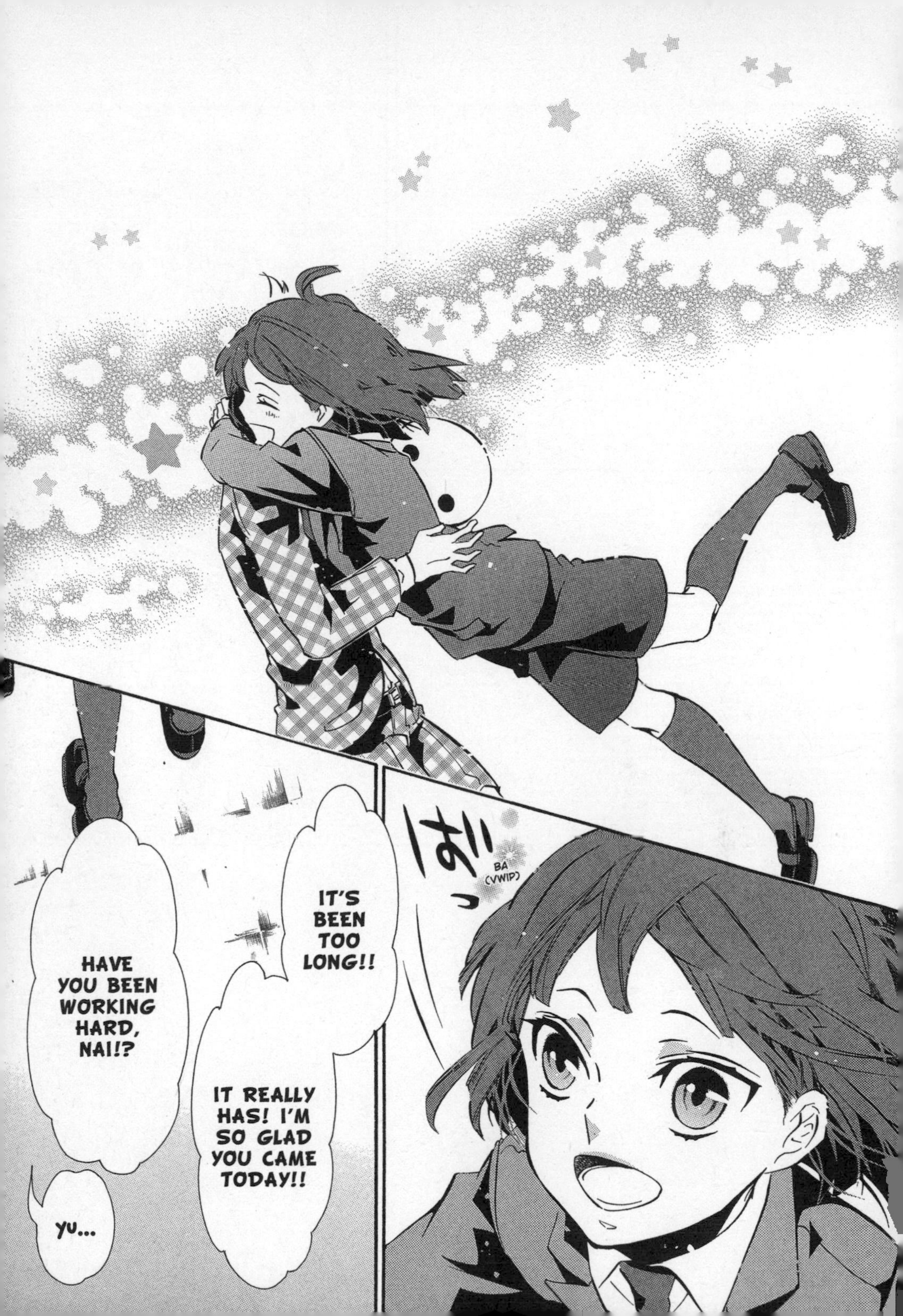
BA (VWIP)
IT'S BEEN TOO LONG!!
HAVE YOU BEEN WORKING HARD, NAI!?
IT REALLY HAS! I'M SO GLAD YOU CAME TODAY!!
YU...

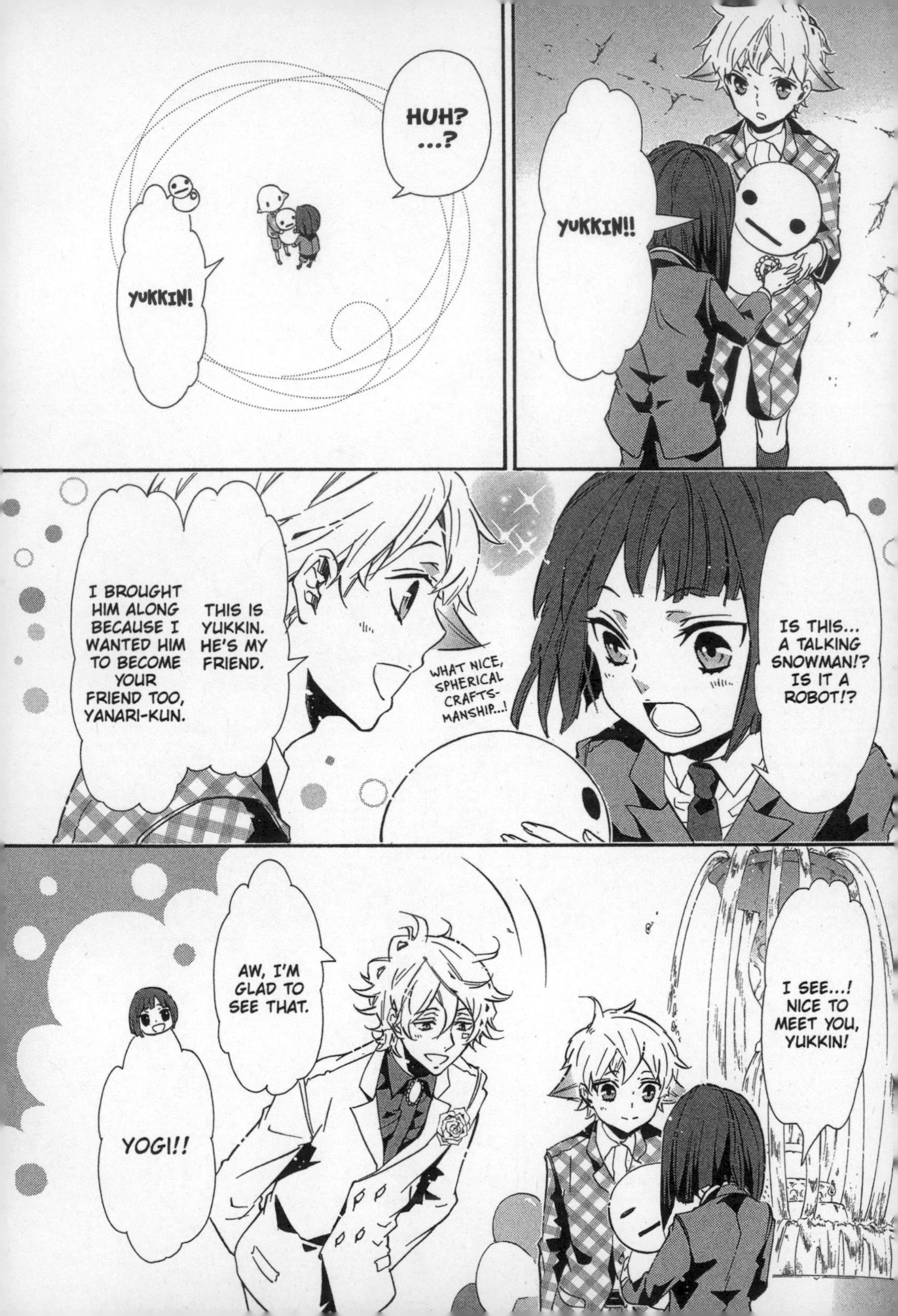
YUKKIN!!
HUH? ...?
YUKKIN!
IS THIS... A TALKING SNOWMAN!? IS IT A ROBOT!?
WHAT NICE, SPHERICAL CRAFTS-MANSHIP...!
THIS IS YUKKIN. HE'S MY FRIEND.
I BROUGHT HIM ALONG BECAUSE I WANTED HIM TO BECOME YOUR FRIEND TOO, YANARI-KUN.
I SEE...! NICE TO MEET YOU, YUKKIN!
AW, I'M GLAD TO SEE THAT.
YOGI!!

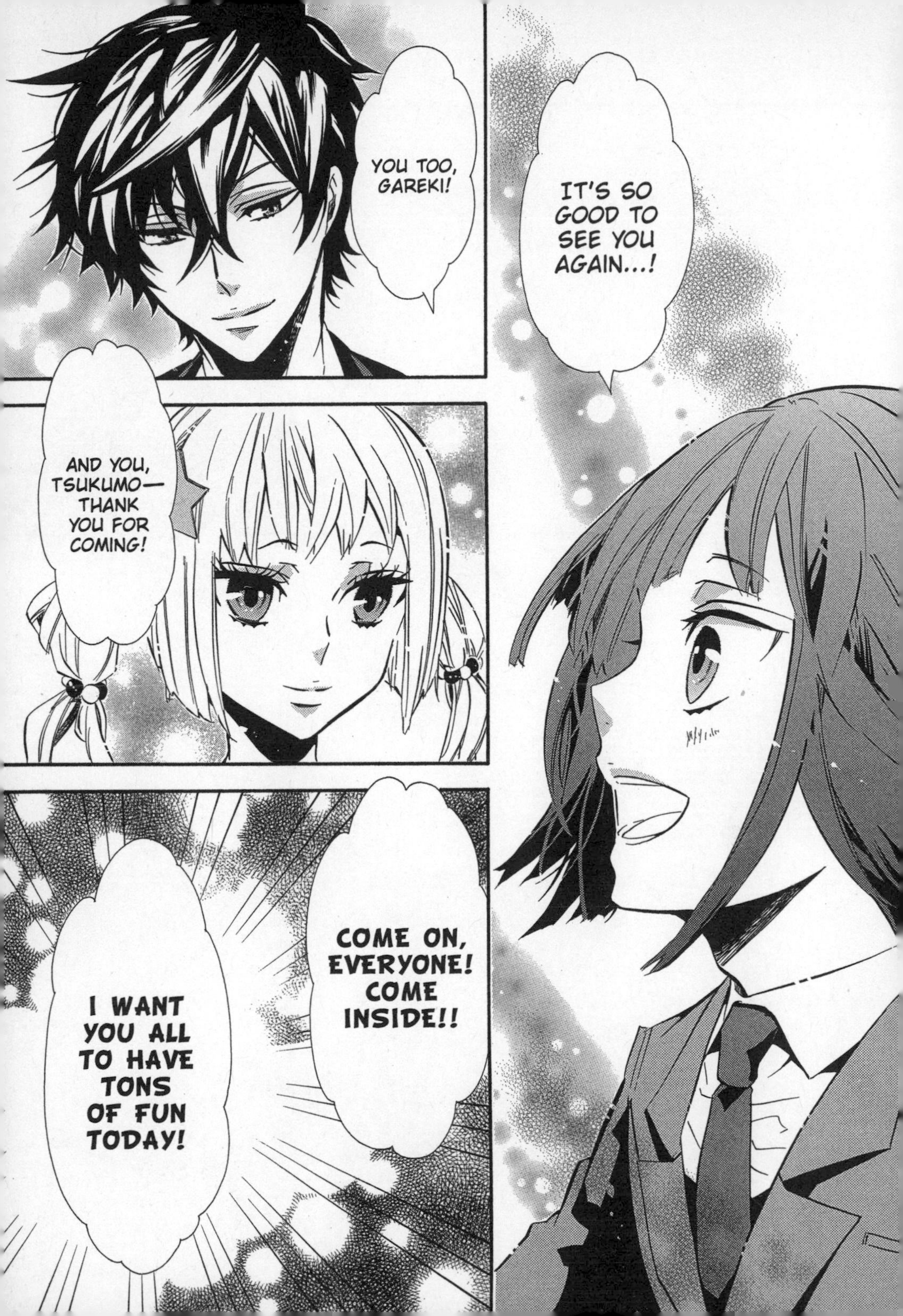
IT'S SO GOOD TO SEE YOU AGAIN...!
YOU TOO, GAREKI!
AND YOU, TSUKUMO—THANK YOU FOR COMING!
COME ON, EVERYONE! COME INSIDE!!
I WANT YOU ALL TO HAVE TONS OF FUN TODAY!

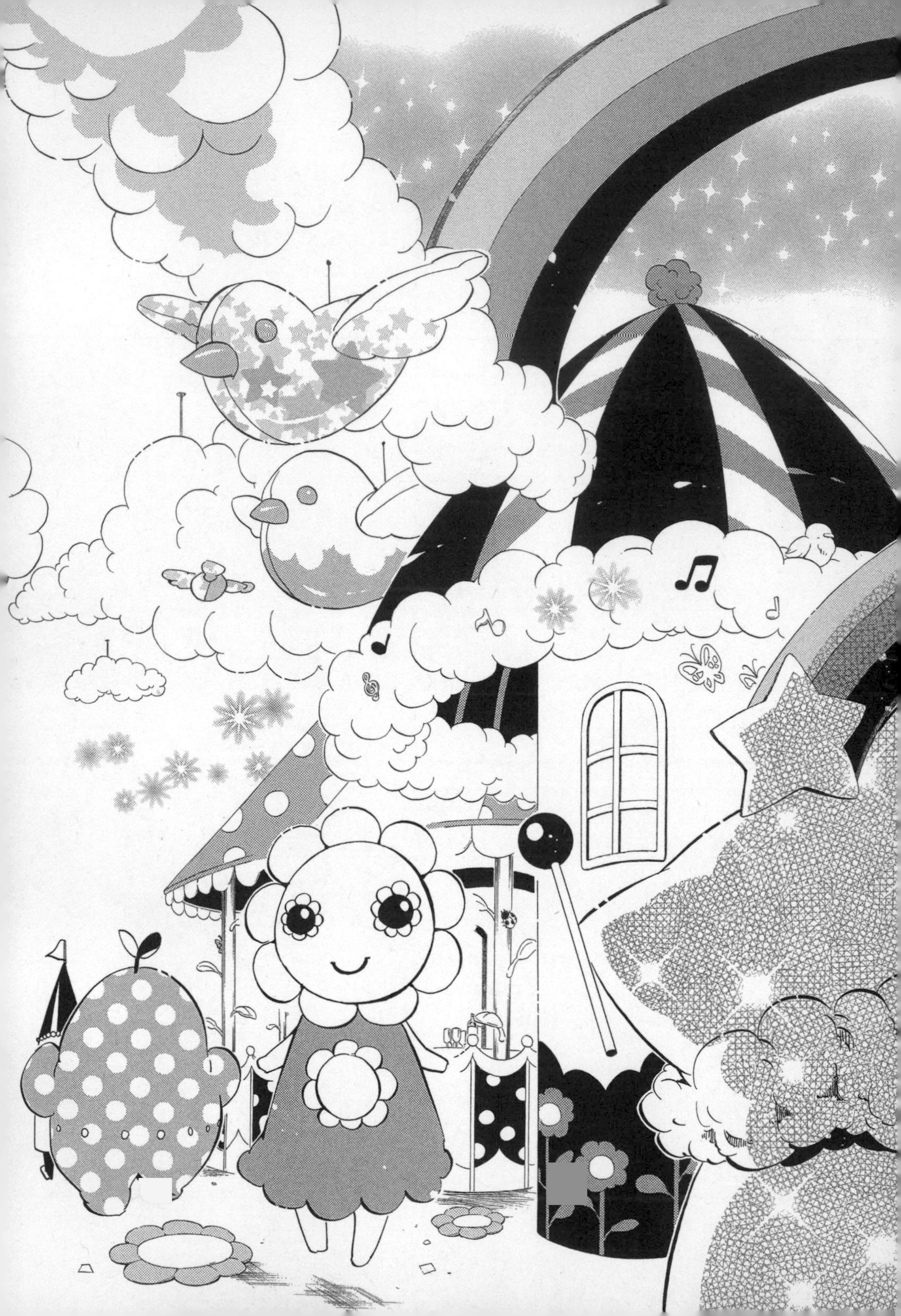

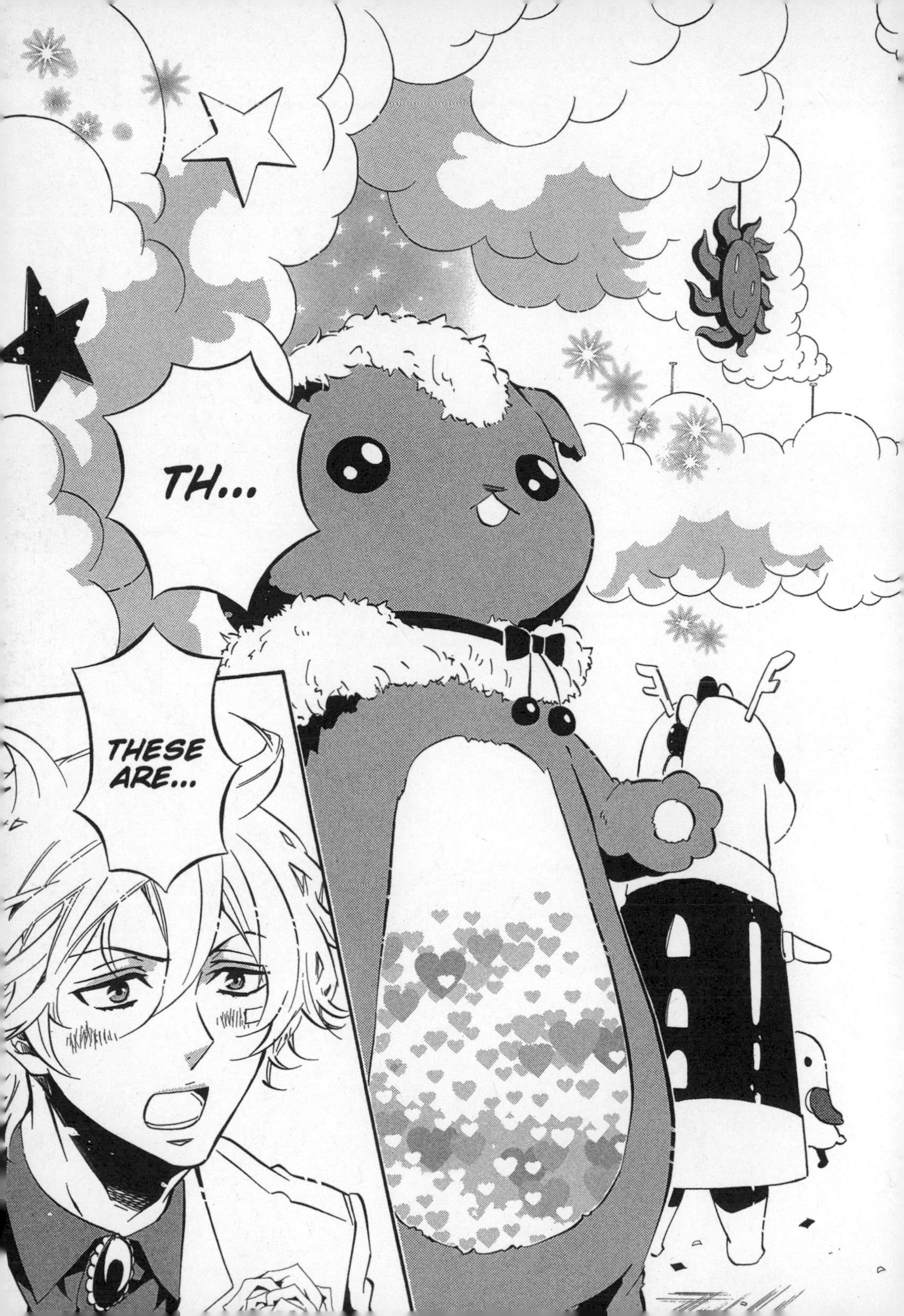
TH...
THESE ARE...

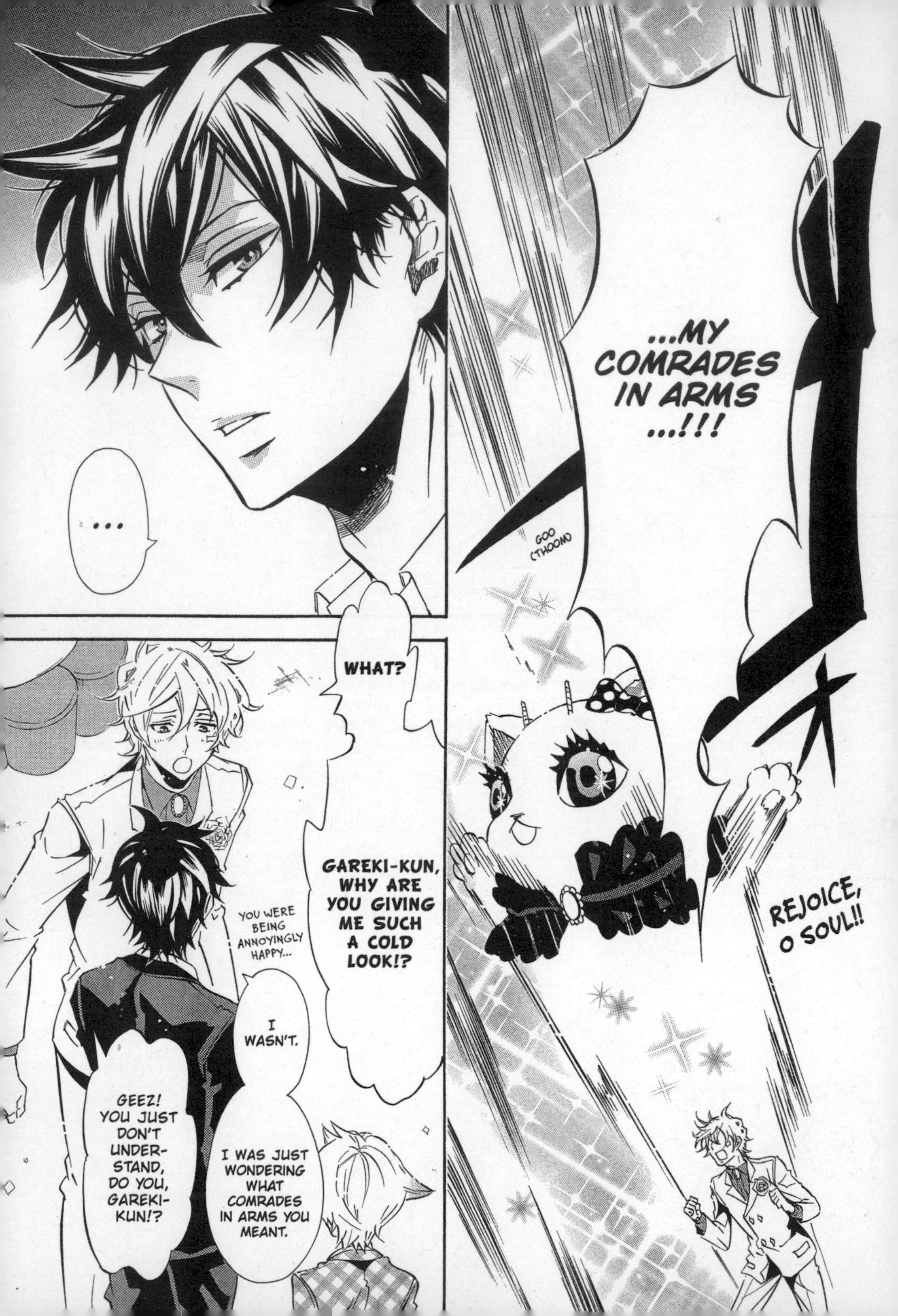
...MY COMRADES IN ARMS ...!!!
GOO (THOOM)
REJOICE, O SOUL!!
...
WHAT?
GAREKI-KUN, WHY ARE YOU GIVING ME SUCH A COLD LOOK!?
YOU WERE BEING ANNOYINGLY HAPPY...
I WASN'T.
I WAS JUST WONDERING WHAT COMRADES IN ARMS YOU MEANT.
GEEZ! YOU JUST DON'T UNDER-STAND, DO YOU, GAREKI-KUN!?

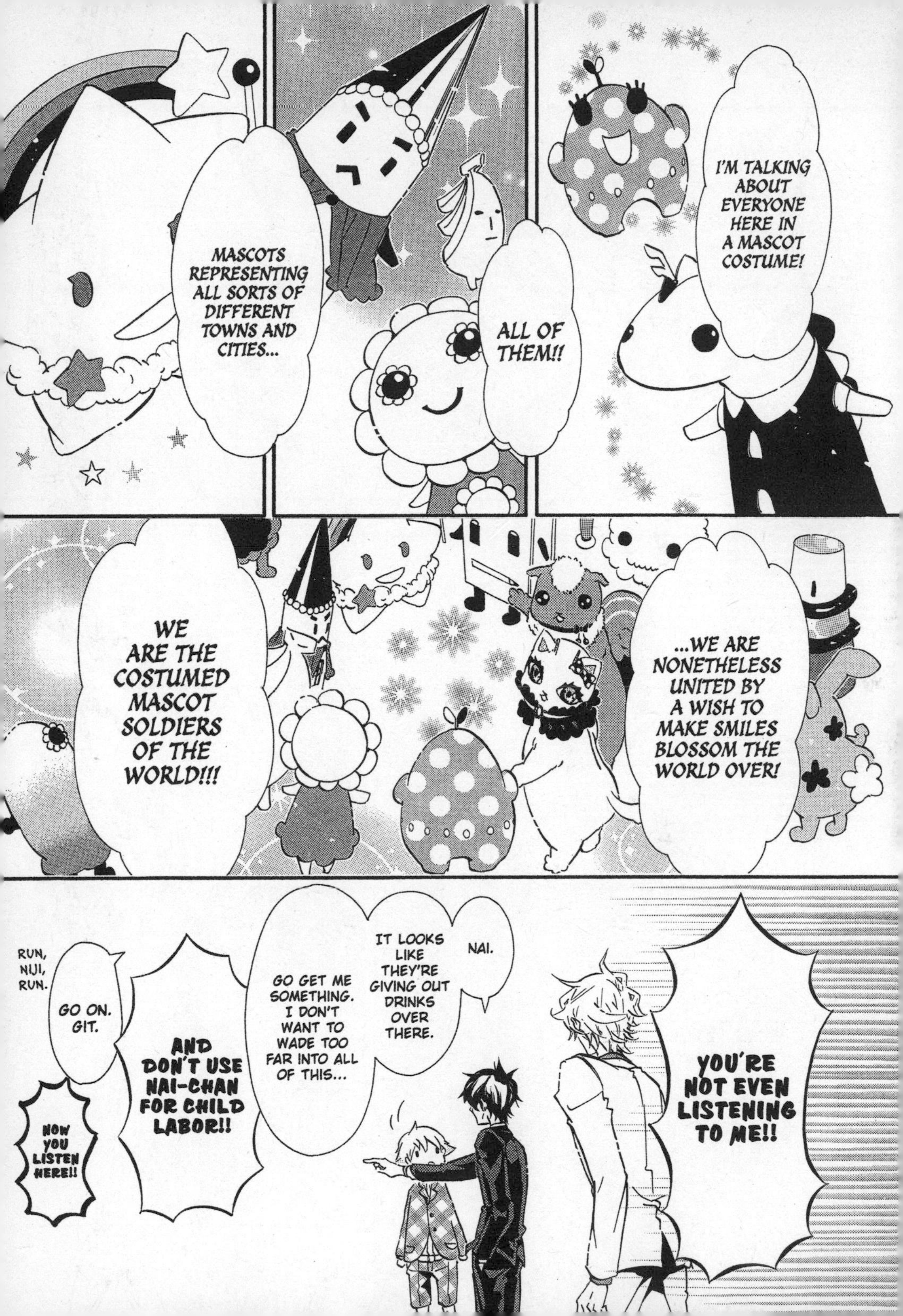
I'M TALKING ABOUT EVERYONE HERE IN A MASCOT COSTUME!
ALL OF THEM!!
MASCOTS REPRESENTING ALL SORTS OF DIFFERENT TOWNS AND CITIES...
...WE ARE NONETHELESS UNITED BY A WISH TO MAKE SMILES BLOSSOM THE WORLD OVER!
WE ARE THE COSTUMED MASCOT SOLDIERS OF THE WORLD!!!
YOU'RE NOT EVEN LISTENING TO ME!!
NAI.
IT LOOKS LIKE THEY'RE GIVING OUT DRINKS OVER THERE.
GO GET ME SOMETHING. I DON'T WANT TO WADE TOO FAR INTO ALL OF THIS...
AND DON'T USE NAI-CHAN FOR CHILD LABOR!!
GO ON. GIT.
RUN, NIJI, RUN.
NOW YOU LISTEN HERE!!

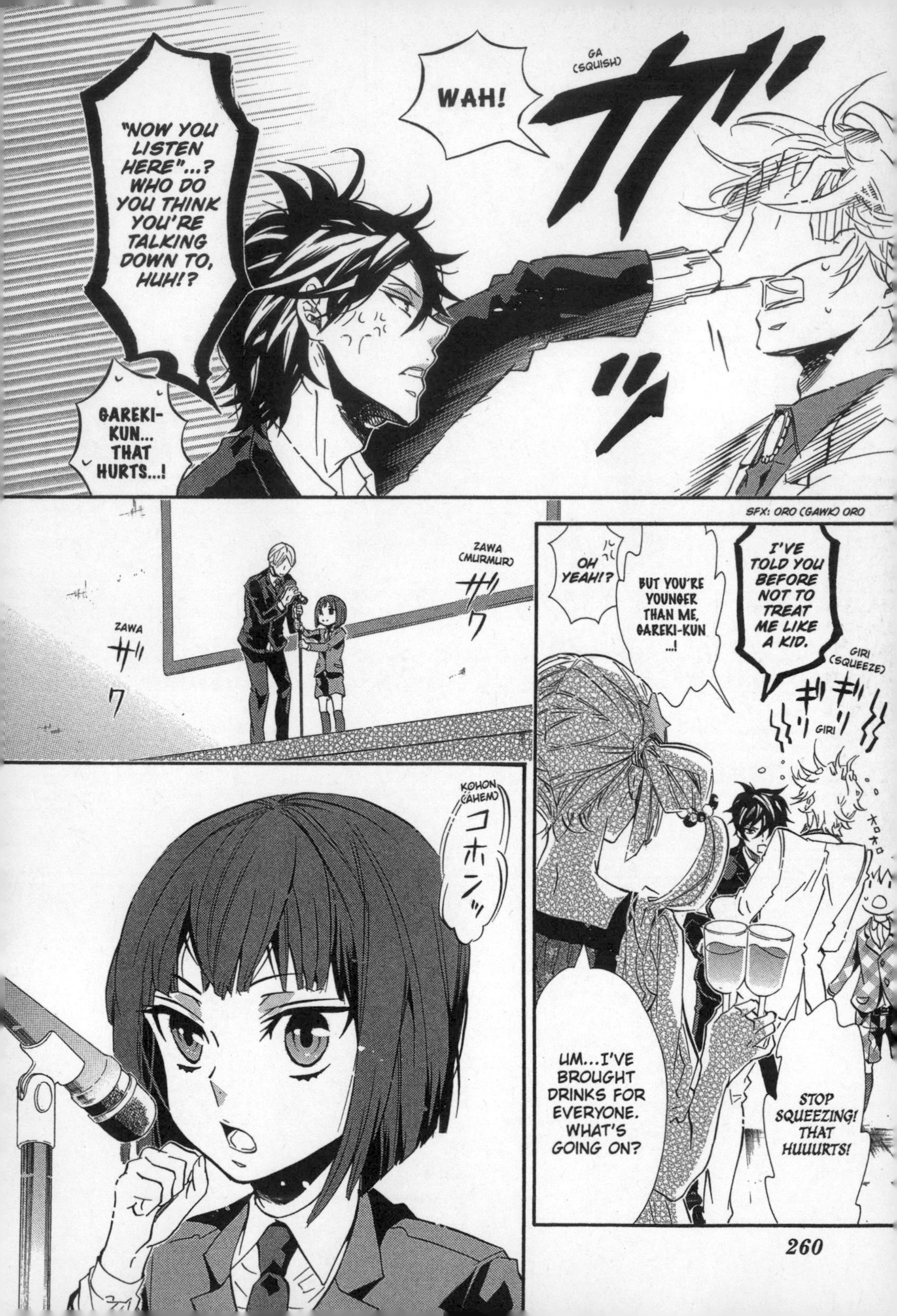
GA (SQUISH)
WAH!
"NOW YOU LISTEN HERE"...? WHO DO YOU THINK YOU'RE TALKING DOWN TO, HUH!?
GAREKI-KUN... THAT HURTS...!
SFX: ORO (GAWK) ORO
I'VE TOLD YOU BEFORE NOT TO TREAT ME LIKE A KID.
BUT YOU'RE YOUNGER THAN ME, GAREKI-KUN...!
OH YEAH!?
GIRI (SQUEEZE)
GIRI
STOP SQUEEZING! THAT HUUURTS!
UM...I'VE BROUGHT DRINKS FOR EVERYONE. WHAT'S GOING ON?
ZAWA (MURMUR)
ZAWA
KOHON (AHEM)

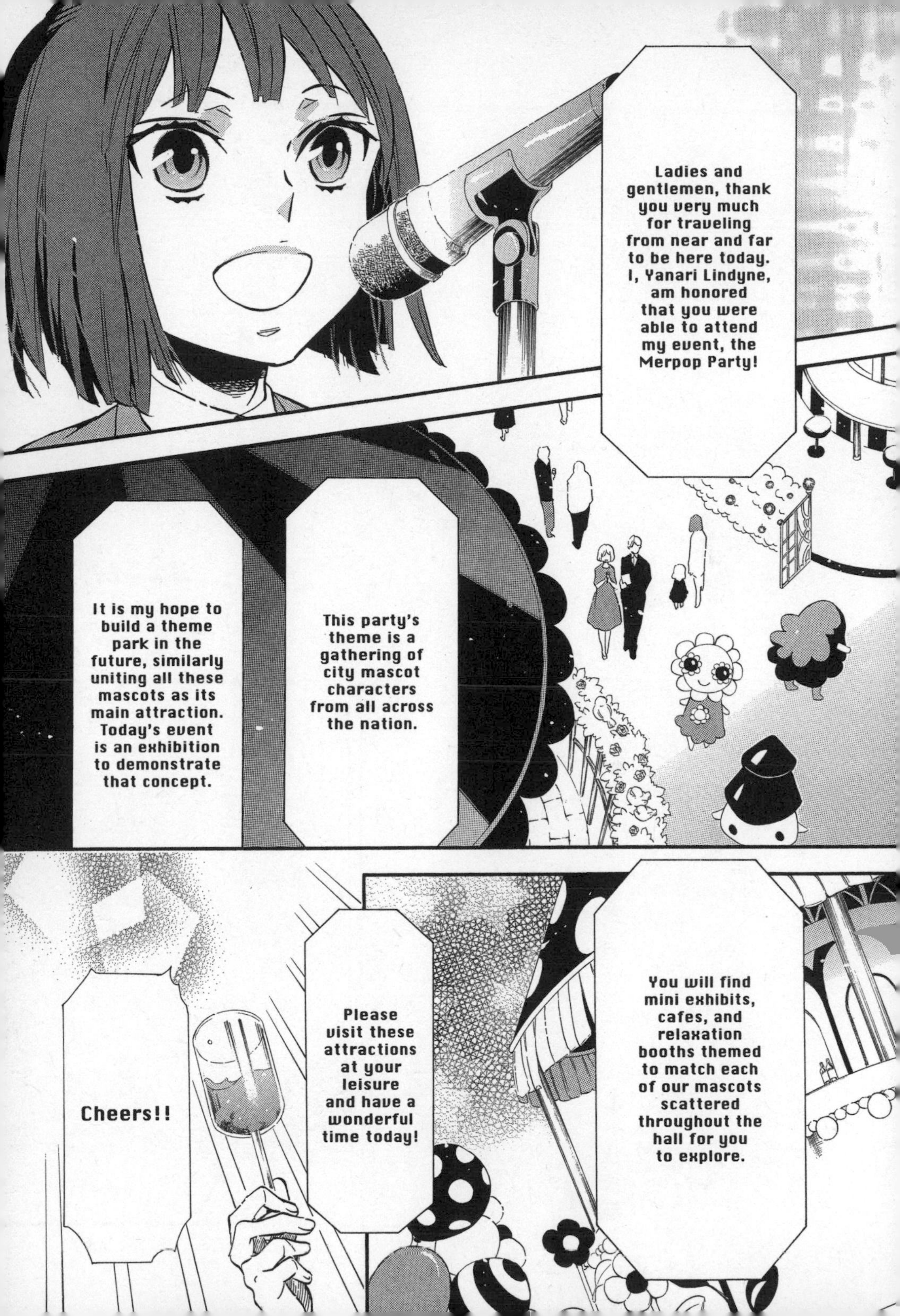
Ladies and gentlemen, thank you very much for traveling from near and far to be here today. I, Yanari Lindyne, am honored that you were able to attend my event, the Merpop Party!
This party's theme is a gathering of city mascot characters from all across the nation.
It is my hope to build a theme park in the future, similarly uniting all these mascots as its main attraction. Today's event is an exhibition to demonstrate that concept.
You will find mini exhibits, cafes, and relaxation booths themed to match each of our mascots scattered throughout the hall for you to explore.
Please visit these attractions at your leisure and have a wonderful time today!
Cheers!!

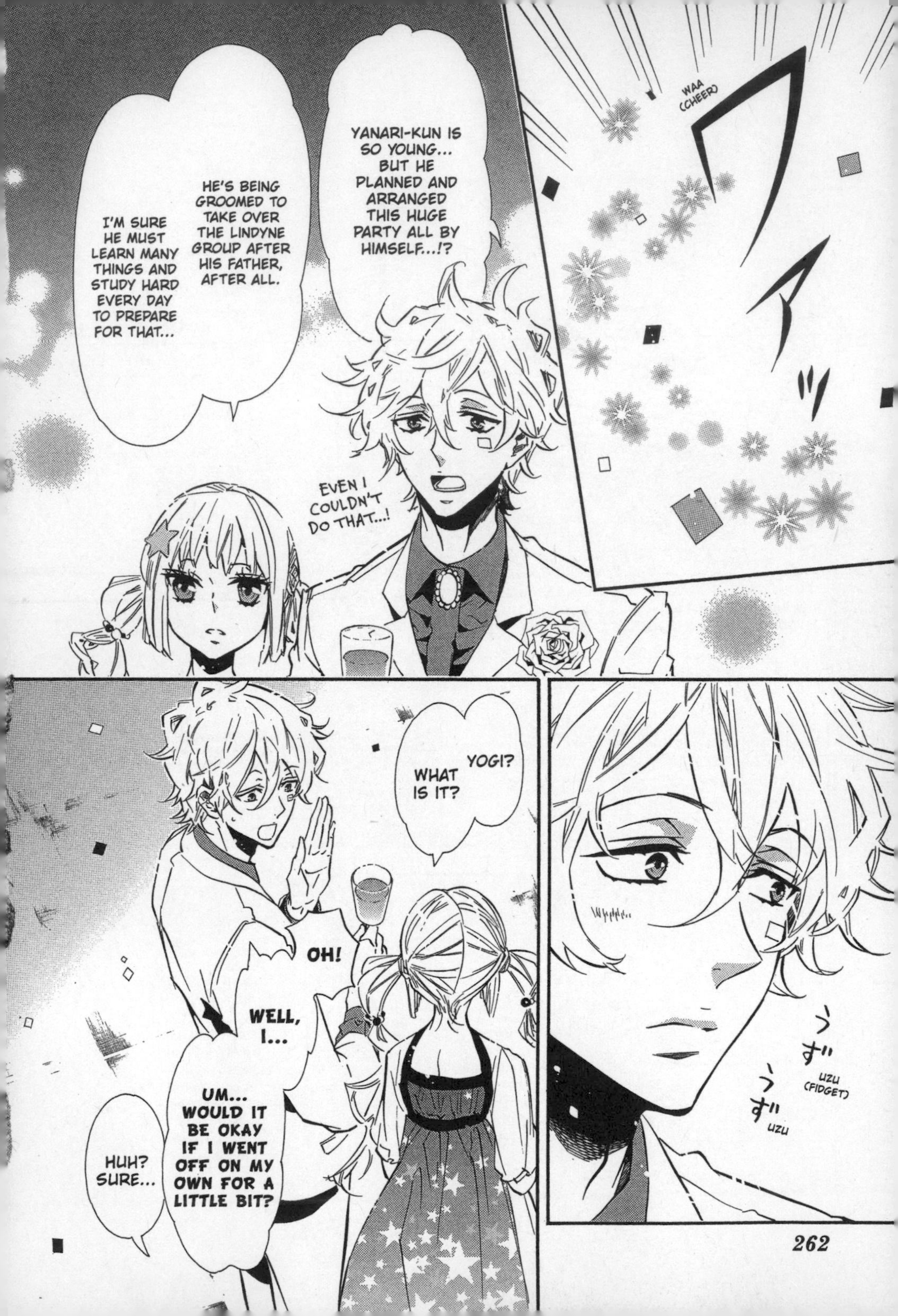

WAA (CHEER)
YANARI-KUN IS SO YOUNG... BUT HE PLANNED AND ARRANGED THIS HUGE PARTY ALL BY HIMSELF...!?
HE'S BEING GROOMED TO TAKE OVER THE LINDYNE GROUP AFTER HIS FATHER, AFTER ALL.
I'M SURE HE MUST LEARN MANY THINGS AND STUDY HARD EVERY DAY TO PREPARE FOR THAT...
EVEN I COULDN'T DO THAT...!
うず
UZU (FIDGET)
うず
UZU
YOGI? WHAT IS IT?
OH!
WELL, I...
UM... WOULD IT BE OKAY IF I WENT OFF ON MY OWN FOR A LITTLE BIT?
HUH? SURE...

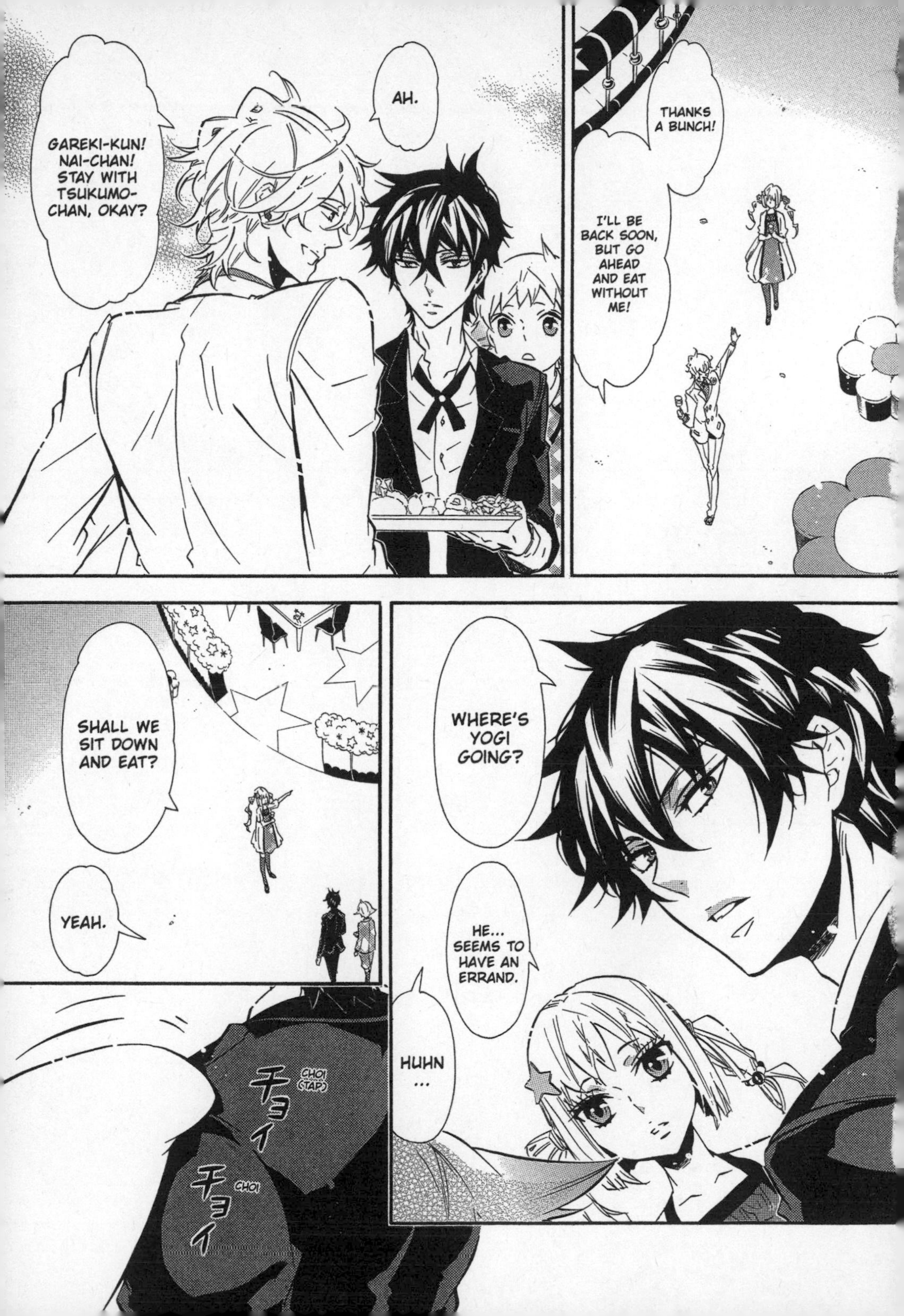
GAREKI-KUN! NAI-CHAN! STAY WITH TSUKUMO-CHAN, OKAY?
AH.
THANKS A BUNCH!
I'LL BE BACK SOON, BUT GO AHEAD AND EAT WITHOUT ME!
SHALL WE SIT DOWN AND EAT?
YEAH.
WHERE'S YOGI GOING?
HE... SEEMS TO HAVE AN ERRAND.
HUHN ...
チョイ
CHOI (TAP)
チョイ
CHOI

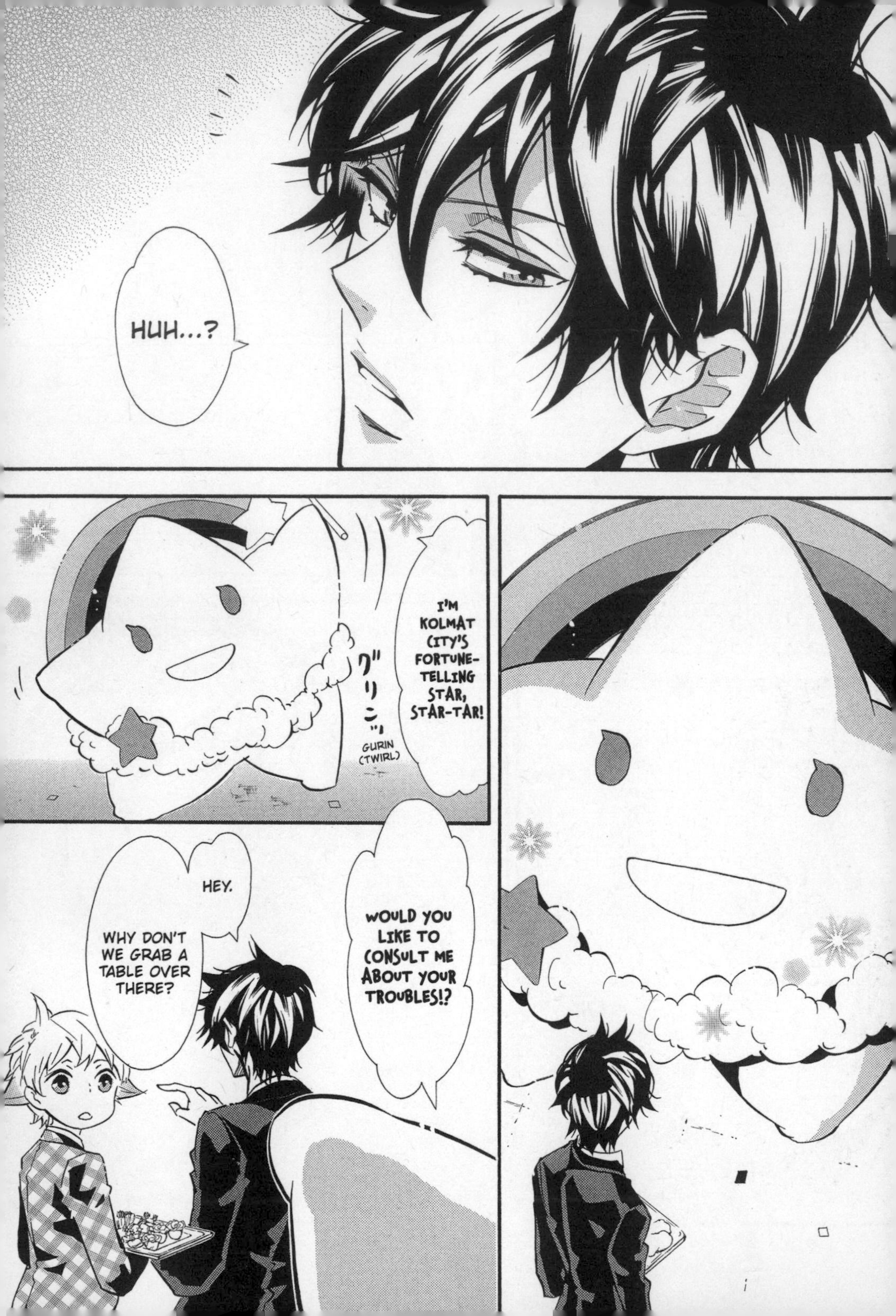
HUH...?
I'M KOLMAT CITY'S FORTUNE-TELLING STAR, STAR-TAR!
グリン
GURIN (TWIRL)
WOULD YOU LIKE TO CONSULT ME ABOUT YOUR TROUBLES!?
HEY.
WHY DON'T WE GRAB A TABLE OVER THERE?

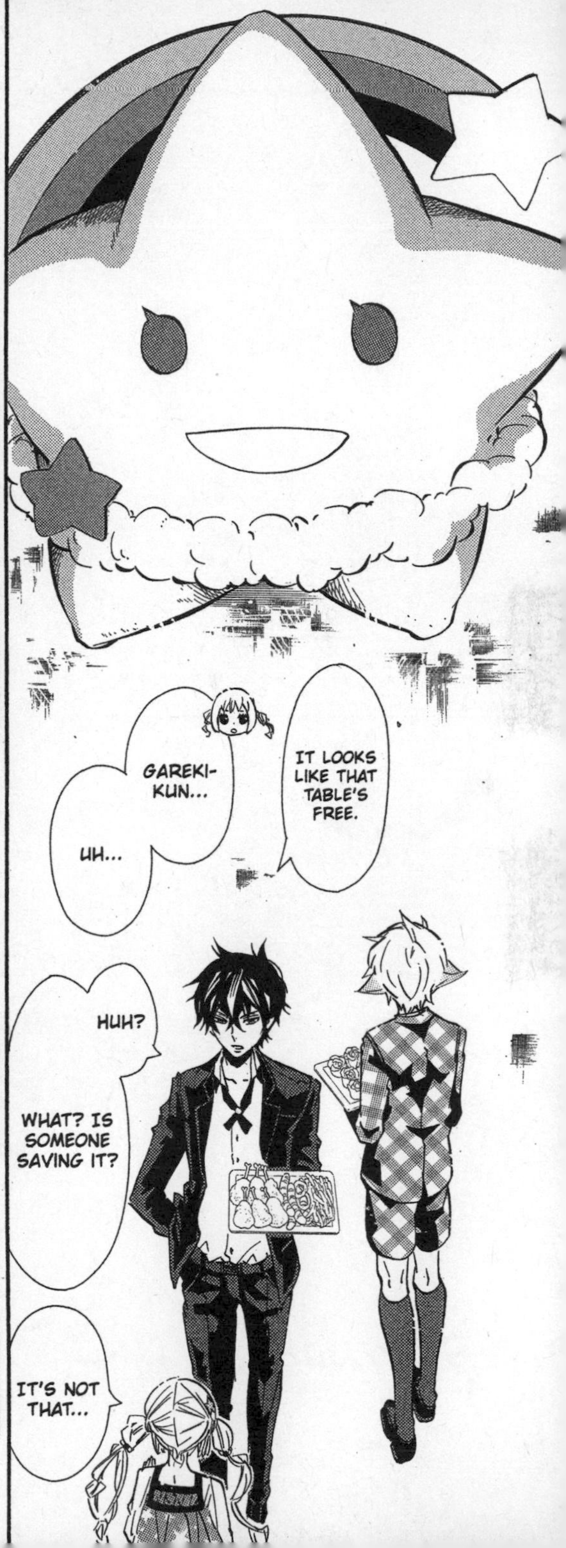
IT LOOKS LIKE THAT TABLE'S FREE.
GAREKI-KUN...
UH...
HUH?
WHAT? IS SOMEONE SAVING IT?
IT'S NOT THAT...

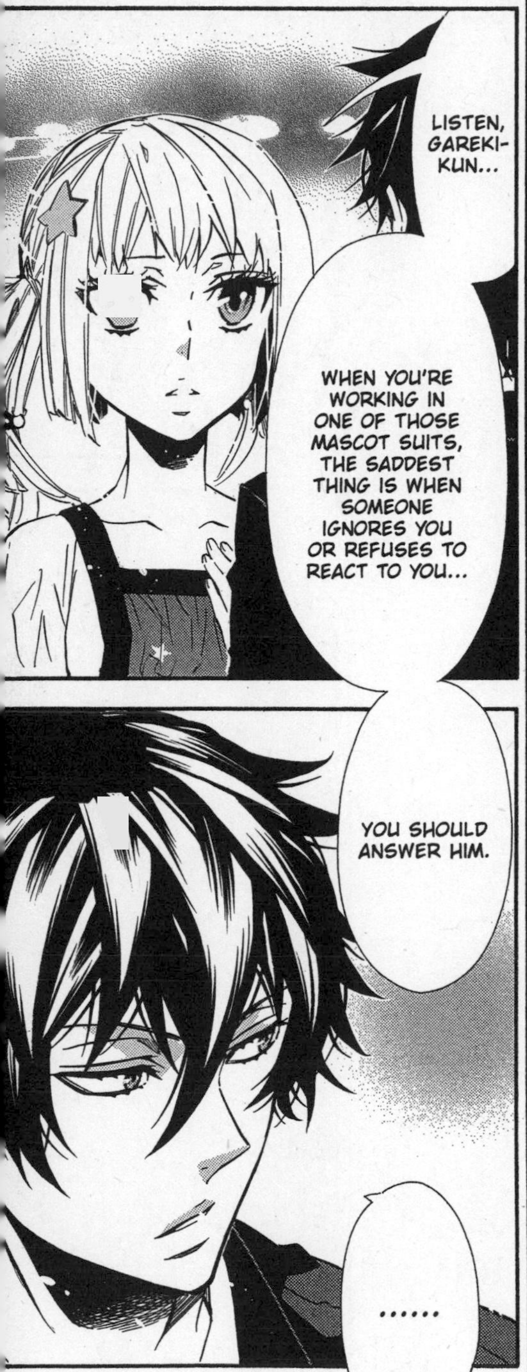
LISTEN, GAREKI-KUN...
WHEN YOU'RE WORKING IN ONE OF THOSE MASCOT SUITS, THE SADDEST THING IS WHEN SOMEONE IGNORES YOU OR REFUSES TO REACT TO YOU...
YOU SHOULD ANSWER HIM.
......

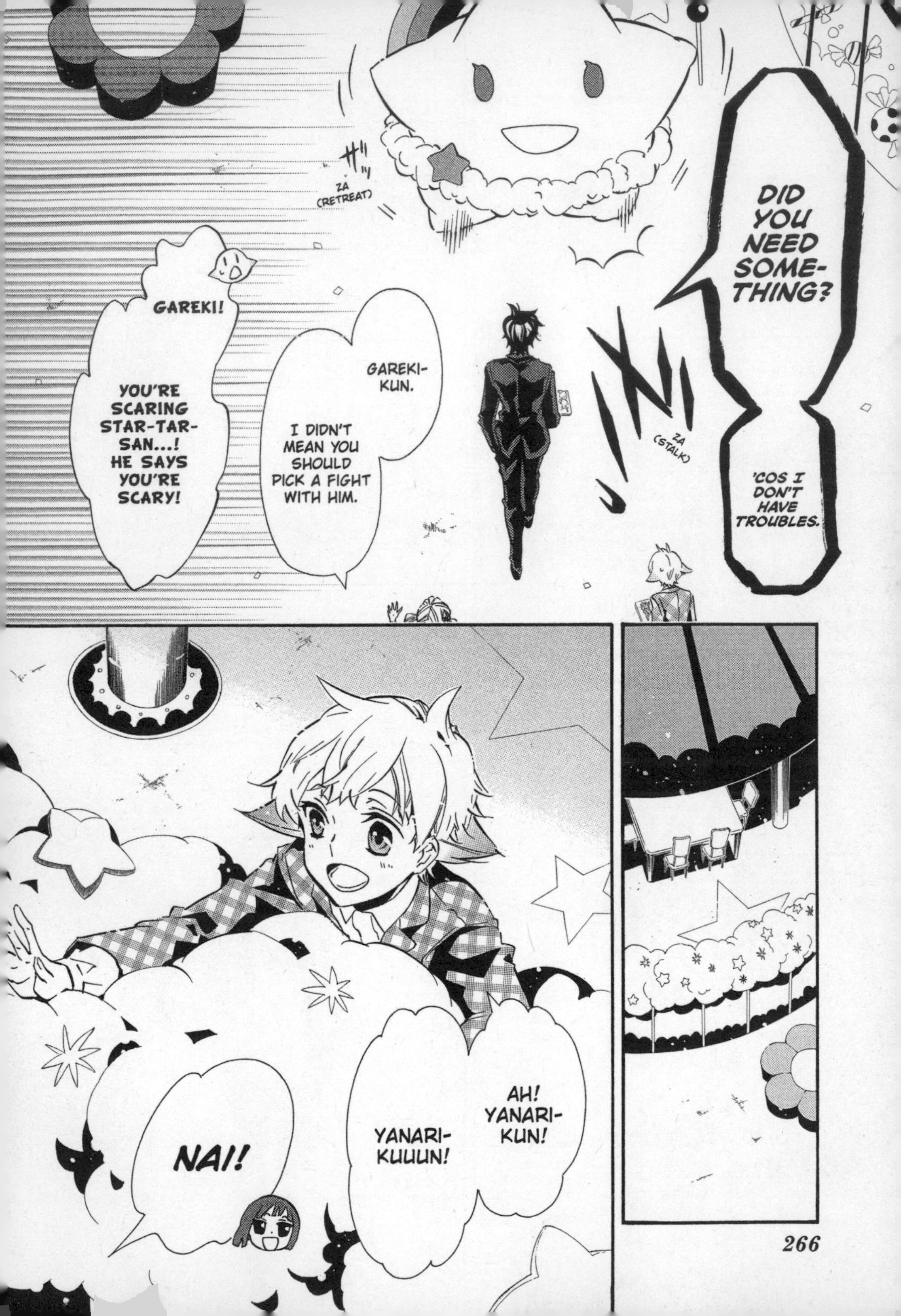
DID YOU NEED SOME-THING?
'COS I DON'T HAVE TROUBLES.
ZA (STALK)
ZA (RETREAT)
GAREKI-KUN.
I DIDN'T MEAN YOU SHOULD PICK A FIGHT WITH HIM.
GAREKI!
YOU'RE SCARING STAR-TAR-SAN...! HE SAYS YOU'RE SCARY!
AH! YANARI-KUN!
YANARI-KUUUN!
NAI!

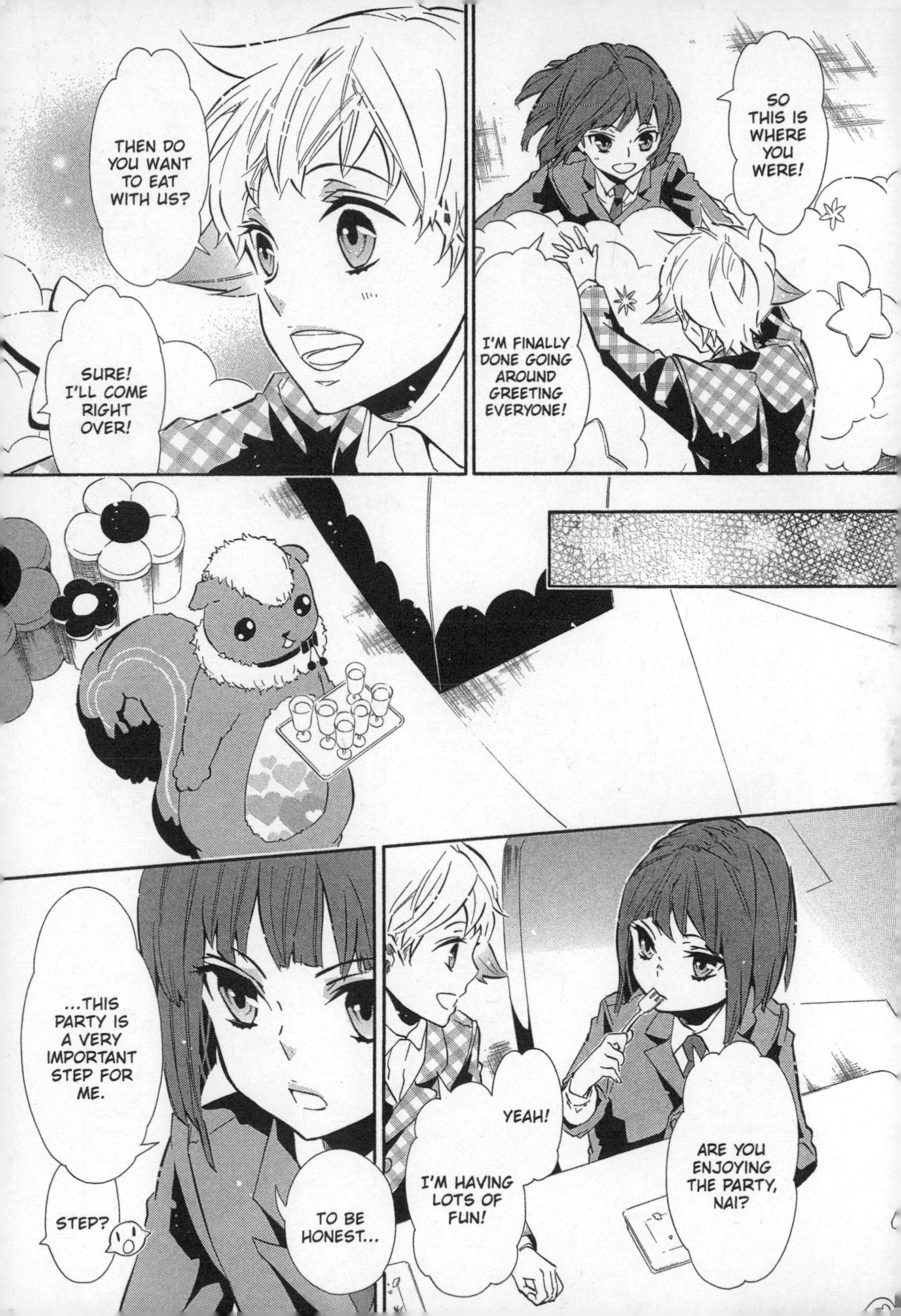
SO THIS IS WHERE YOU WERE!
I'M FINALLY DONE GOING AROUND GREETING EVERYONE!
THEN DO YOU WANT TO EAT WITH US?
SURE! I'LL COME RIGHT OVER!
ARE YOU ENJOYING THE PARTY, NAI?
YEAH!
I'M HAVING LOTS OF FUN!
TO BE HONEST...
...THIS PARTY IS A VERY IMPORTANT STEP FOR ME.
STEP?

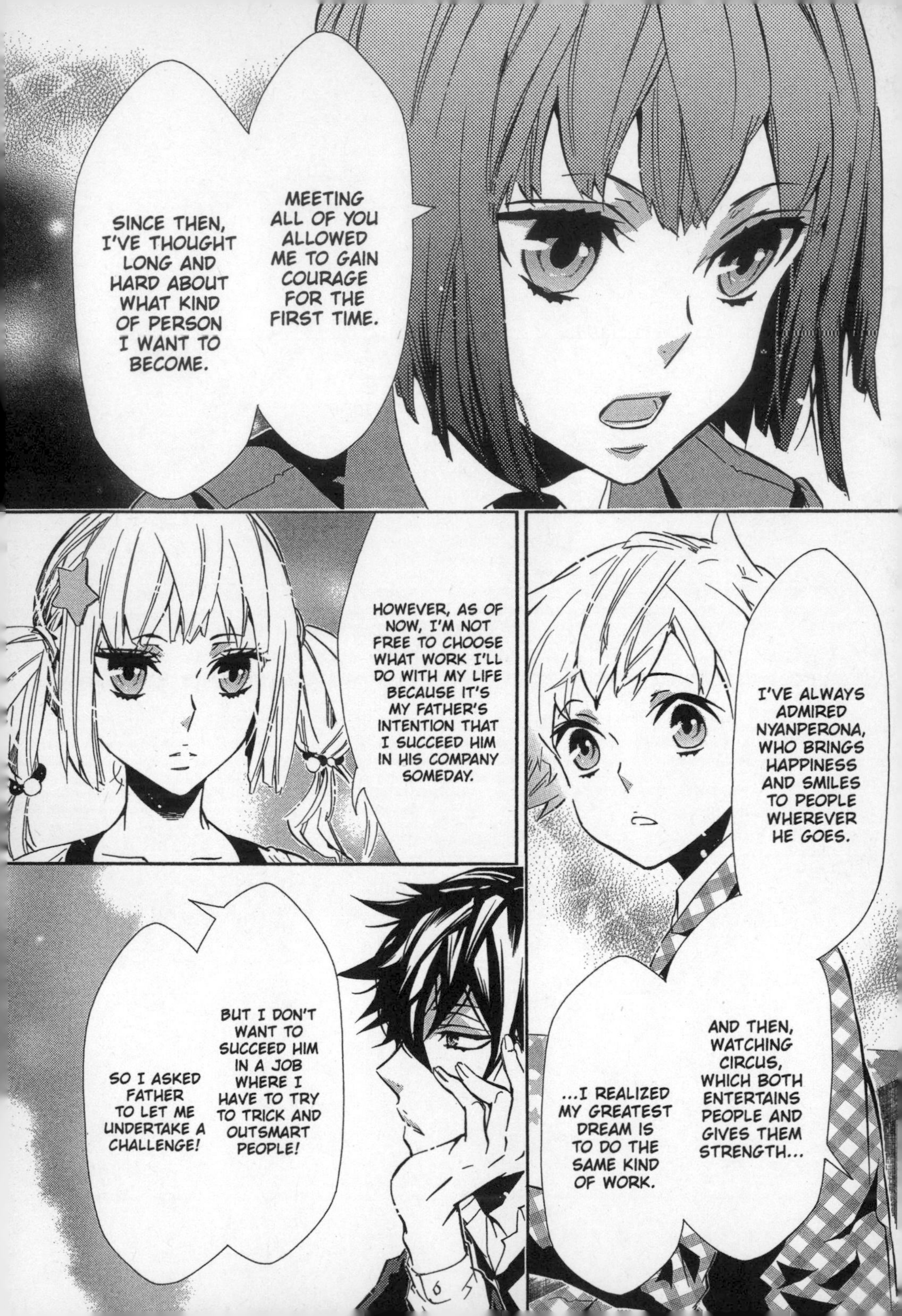
MEETING ALL OF YOU ALLOWED ME TO GAIN COURAGE FOR THE FIRST TIME.
SINCE THEN, I'VE THOUGHT LONG AND HARD ABOUT WHAT KIND OF PERSON I WANT TO BECOME.
I'VE ALWAYS ADMIRED NYANPERONA, WHO BRINGS HAPPINESS AND SMILES TO PEOPLE WHEREVER HE GOES.
AND THEN, WATCHING CIRCUS, WHICH BOTH ENTERTAINS PEOPLE AND GIVES THEM STRENGTH...
...I REALIZED MY GREATEST DREAM IS TO DO THE SAME KIND OF WORK.
HOWEVER, AS OF NOW, I'M NOT FREE TO CHOOSE WHAT WORK I'LL DO WITH MY LIFE BECAUSE IT'S MY FATHER'S INTENTION THAT I SUCCEED HIM IN HIS COMPANY SOMEDAY.
BUT I DON'T WANT TO SUCCEED HIM IN A JOB WHERE I HAVE TO TRY TO TRICK AND OUTSMART PEOPLE!
SO I ASKED FATHER TO LET ME UNDERTAKE A CHALLENGE!

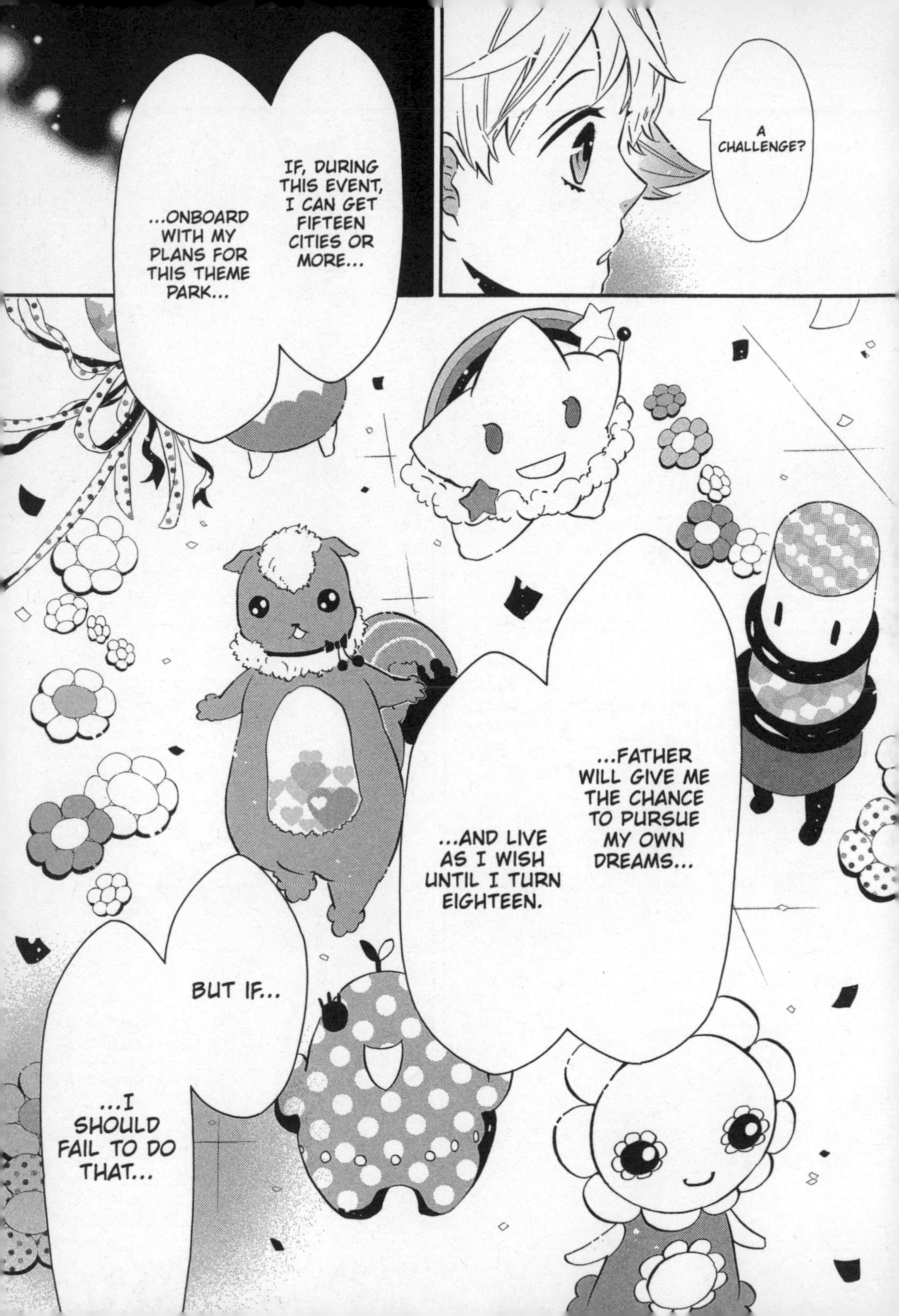
A CHALLENGE?
IF, DURING THIS EVENT, I CAN GET FIFTEEN CITIES OR MORE...
...ONBOARD WITH MY PLANS FOR THIS THEME PARK...
...FATHER WILL GIVE ME THE CHANCE TO PURSUE MY OWN DREAMS...
...AND LIVE AS I WISH UNTIL I TURN EIGHTEEN.
BUT IF...
...I SHOULD FAIL TO DO THAT...

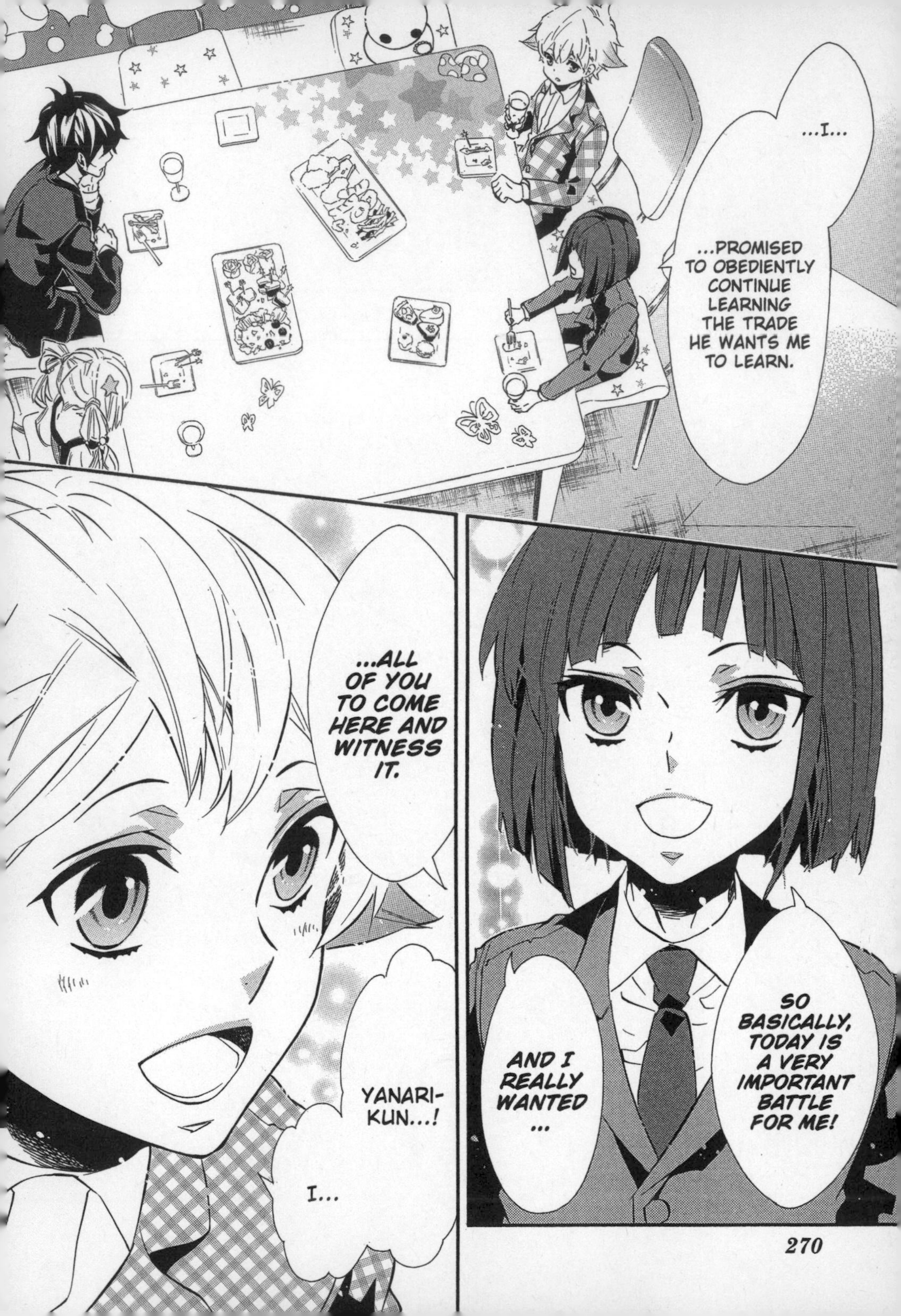

...I...
...PROMISED TO OBEDIENTLY CONTINUE LEARNING THE TRADE HE WANTS ME TO LEARN.
SO BASICALLY, TODAY IS A VERY IMPORTANT BATTLE FOR ME!
AND I REALLY WANTED ...
...ALL OF YOU TO COME HERE AND WITNESS IT.
YANARI-KUN...!
I...

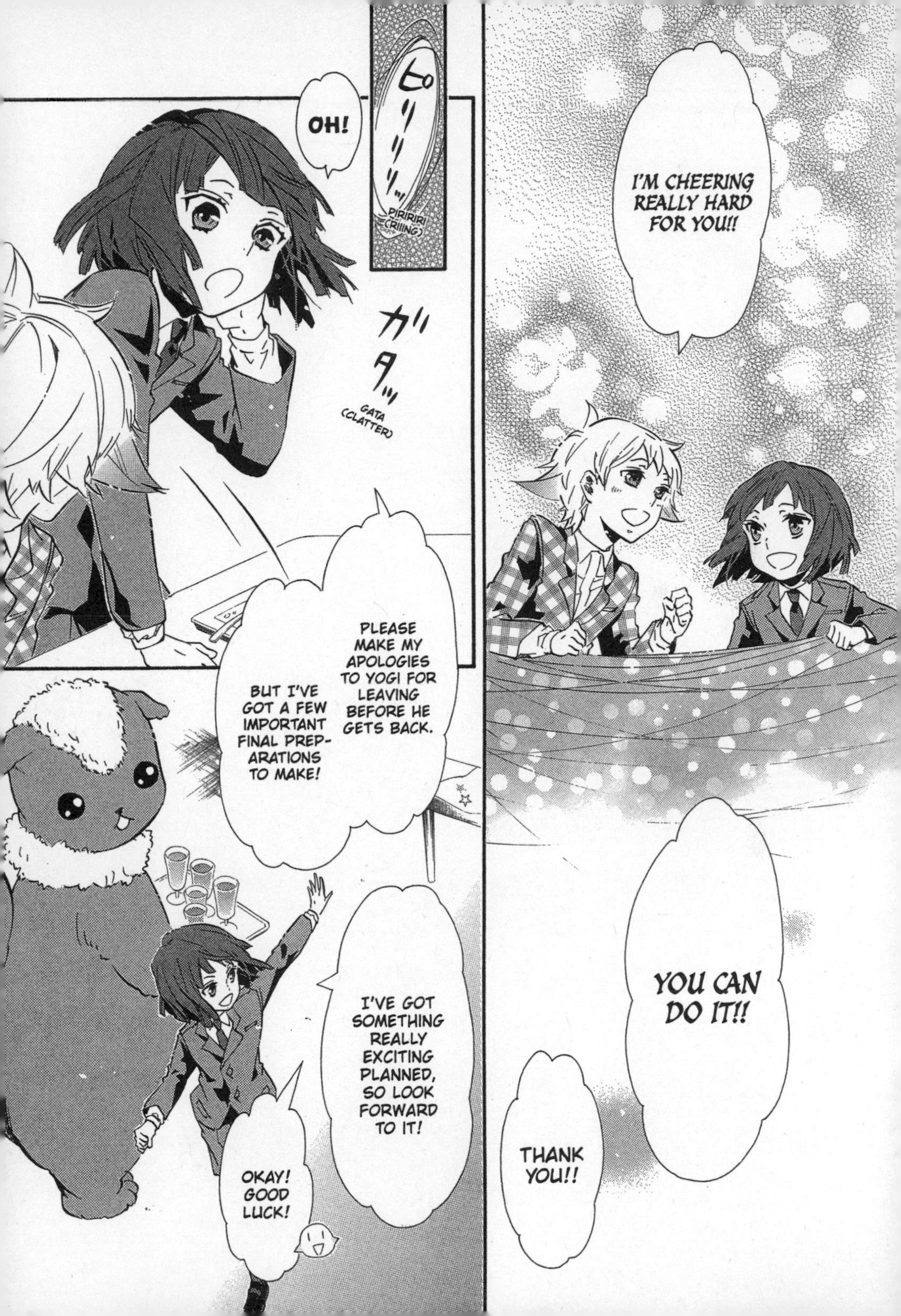
I'M CHEERING REALLY HARD FOR YOU!!
YOU CAN DO IT!!
THANK YOU!!
ピリリリッ
PIRIRIRI (RIIING)
OH!
ガタッ
GATA (CLATTER)
PLEASE MAKE MY APOLOGIES TO YOGI FOR LEAVING BEFORE HE GETS BACK.
BUT I'VE GOT A FEW IMPORTANT FINAL PREPARATIONS TO MAKE!
I'VE GOT SOMETHING REALLY EXCITING PLANNED, SO LOOK FORWARD TO IT!
OKAY! GOOD LUCK!

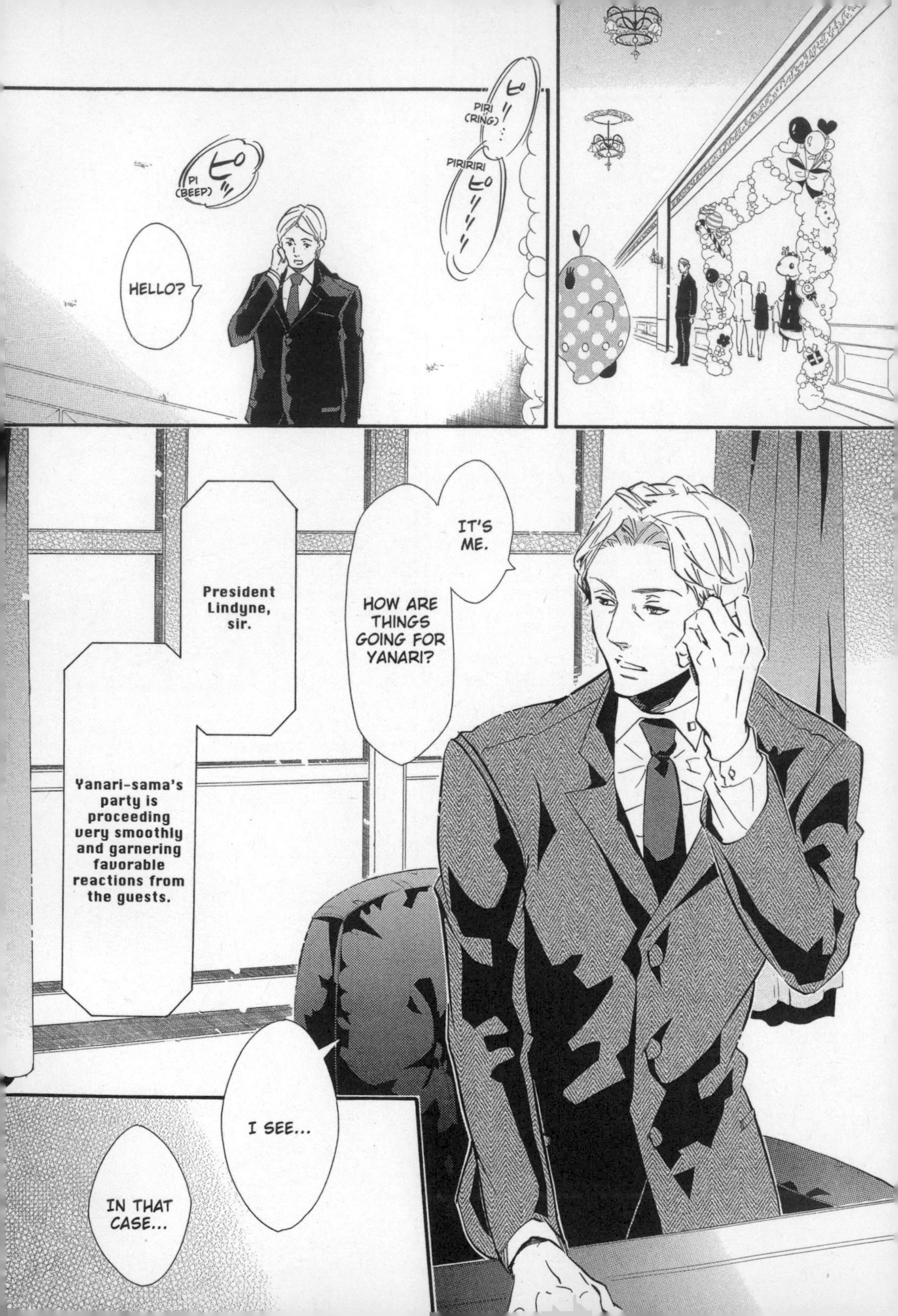
ピリッ…
PIRI (RING)
ピリリリリ
PIRIRIRI
ピッ
PI (BEEP)
HELLO?
IT'S ME.
HOW ARE THINGS GOING FOR YANARI?
President Lindyne, sir.
Yanari-sama's party is proceeding very smoothly and garnering favorable reactions from the guests.
I SEE...
IN THAT CASE...

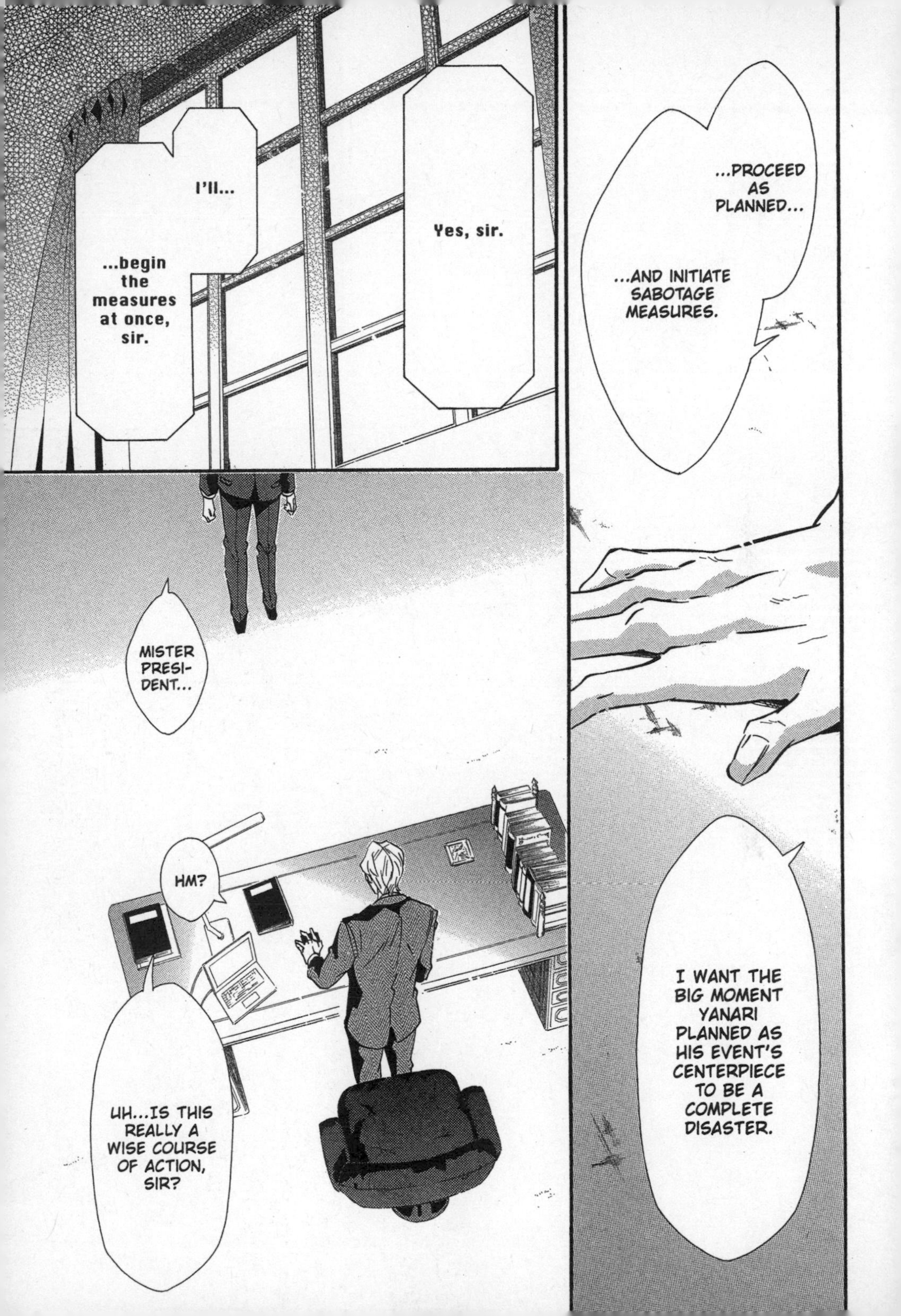
...PROCEED AS PLANNED...
...AND INITIATE SABOTAGE MEASURES.
I WANT THE BIG MOMENT YANARI PLANNED AS HIS EVENT'S CENTERPIECE TO BE A COMPLETE DISASTER.
Yes, sir.
I'll...
...begin the measures at once, sir.
MISTER PRESI-DENT...
HM?
UH...IS THIS REALLY A WISE COURSE OF ACTION, SIR?

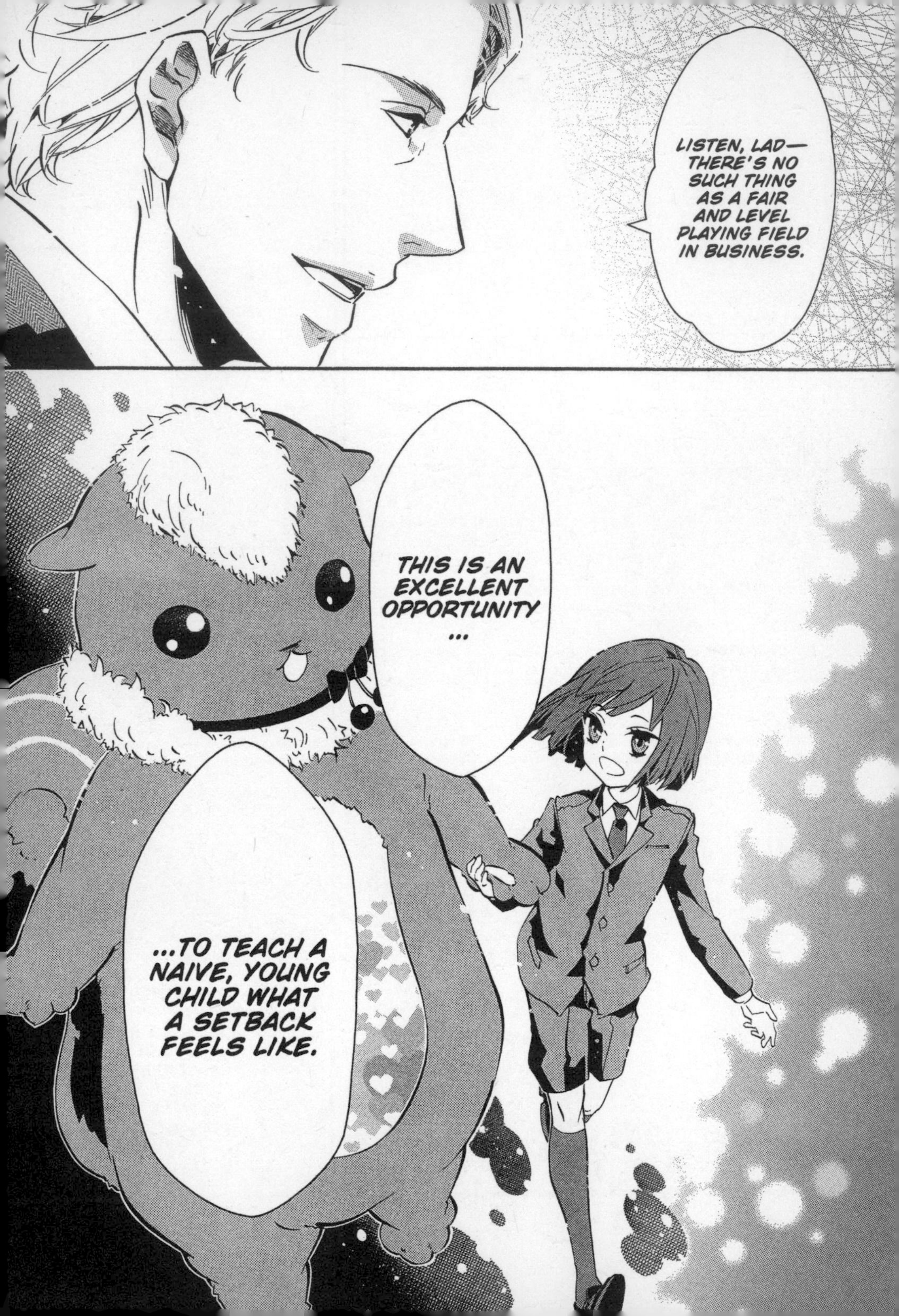
LISTEN, LAD—THERE'S NO SUCH THING AS A FAIR AND LEVEL PLAYING FIELD IN BUSINESS.
THIS IS AN EXCELLENT OPPORTUNITY ...
...TO TEACH A NAIVE, YOUNG CHILD WHAT A SETBACK FEELS LIKE.

KARNEVAL

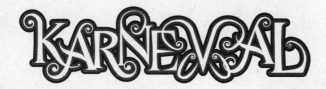

KARNEVAL

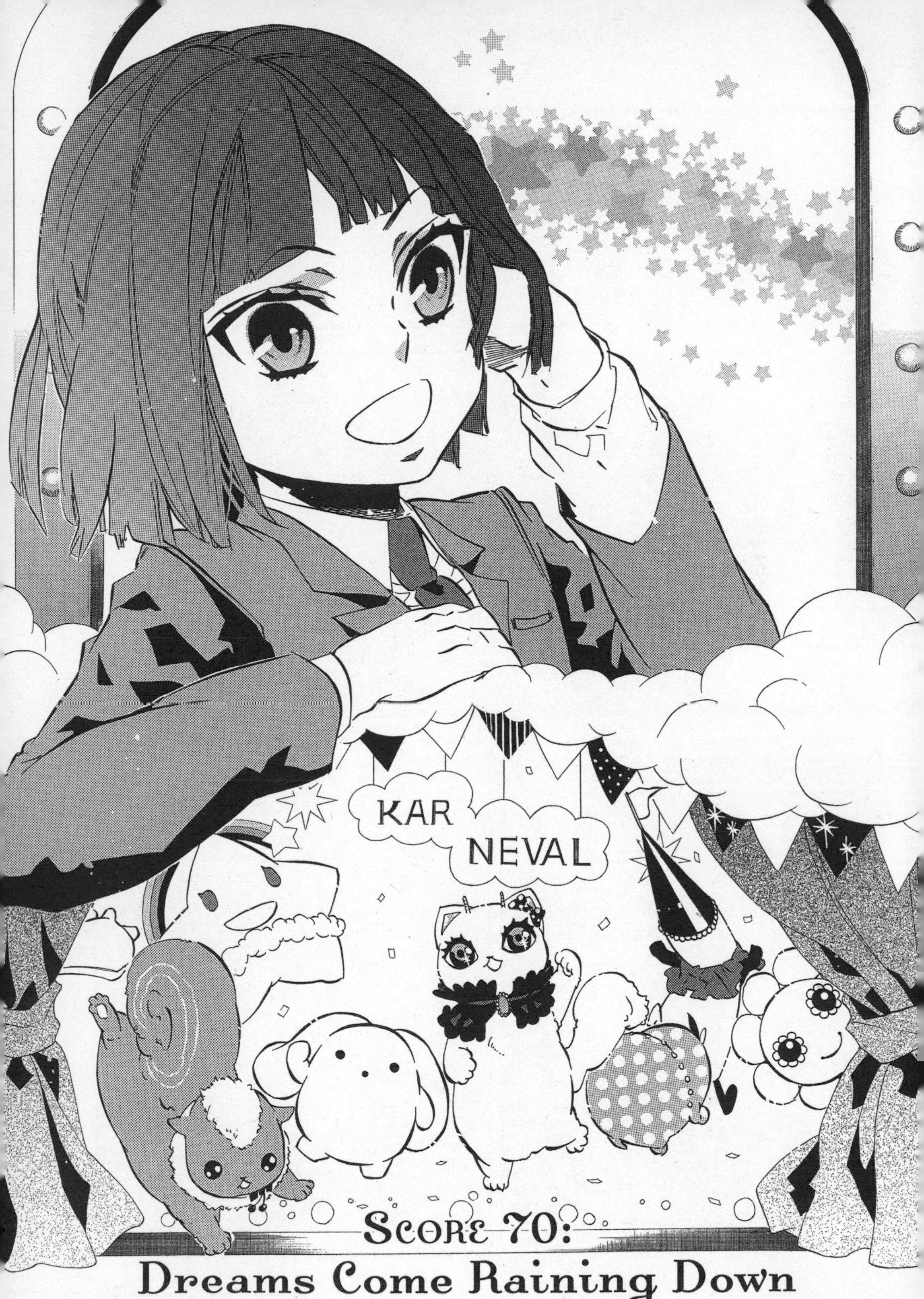
KAR
NEVAL

Score 70: Dreams Come Raining Down

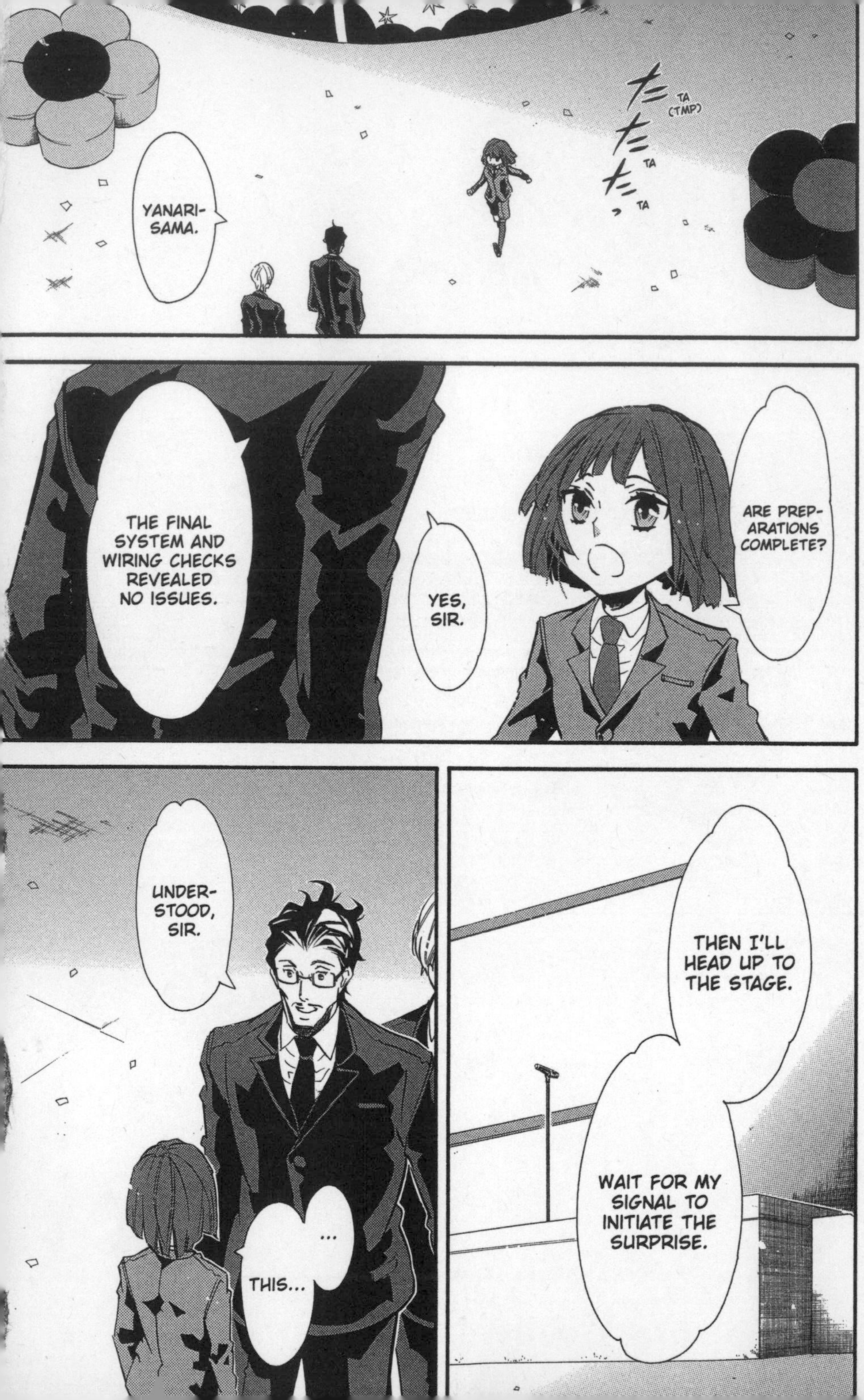
TA (TMP)
TA
TA
YANARI-SAMA.
ARE PREP-ARATIONS COMPLETE?
YES, SIR.
THE FINAL SYSTEM AND WIRING CHECKS REVEALED NO ISSUES.
THEN I'LL HEAD UP TO THE STAGE.
WAIT FOR MY SIGNAL TO INITIATE THE SURPRISE.
UNDERSTOOD, SIR.
...
THIS...

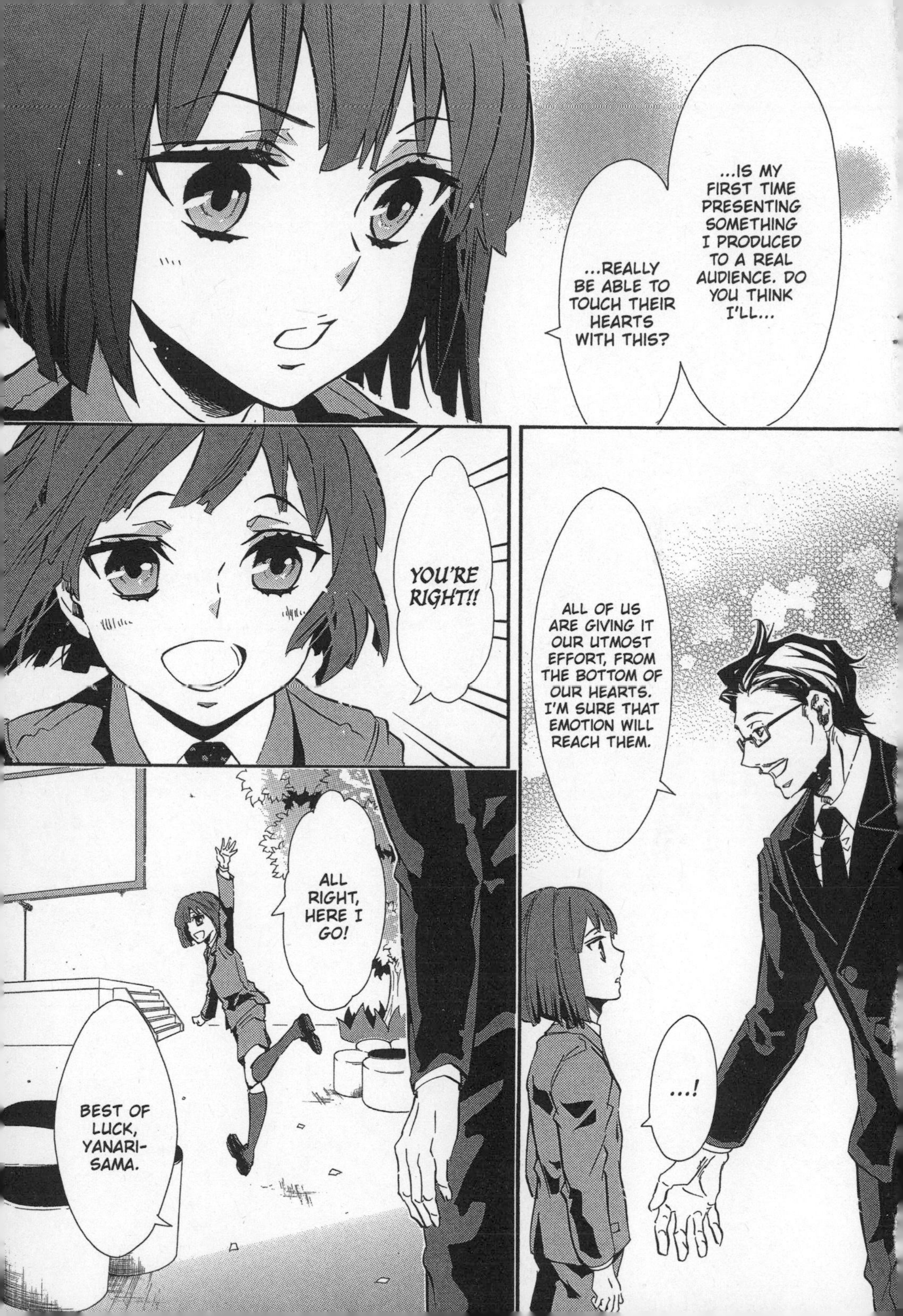
...IS MY FIRST TIME PRESENTING SOMETHING I PRODUCED TO A REAL AUDIENCE. DO YOU THINK I'LL...
...REALLY BE ABLE TO TOUCH THEIR HEARTS WITH THIS?
ALL OF US ARE GIVING IT OUR UTMOST EFFORT, FROM THE BOTTOM OF OUR HEARTS. I'M SURE THAT EMOTION WILL REACH THEM.
...!
YOU'RE RIGHT!!
ALL RIGHT, HERE I GO!
BEST OF LUCK, YANARI-SAMA.

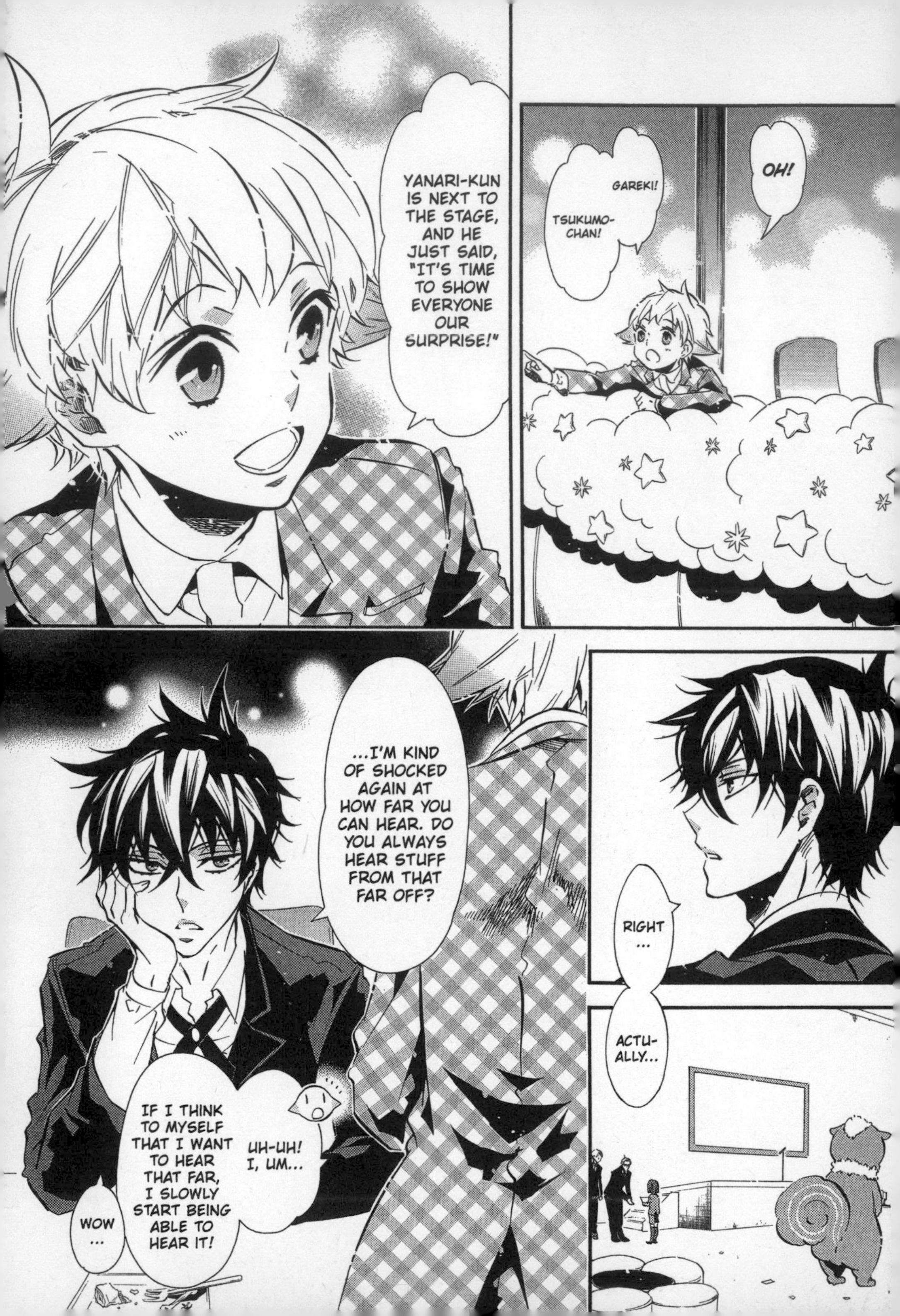
OH!
GAREKI!
TSUKUMO-CHAN!
YANARI-KUN IS NEXT TO THE STAGE, AND HE JUST SAID, "IT'S TIME TO SHOW EVERYONE OUR SURPRISE!"
RIGHT...
ACTU-ALLY...
...I'M KIND OF SHOCKED AGAIN AT HOW FAR YOU CAN HEAR. DO YOU ALWAYS HEAR STUFF FROM THAT FAR OFF?
UH-UH! I, UM...
IF I THINK TO MYSELF THAT I WANT TO HEAR THAT FAR, I SLOWLY START BEING ABLE TO HEAR IT!
WOW...

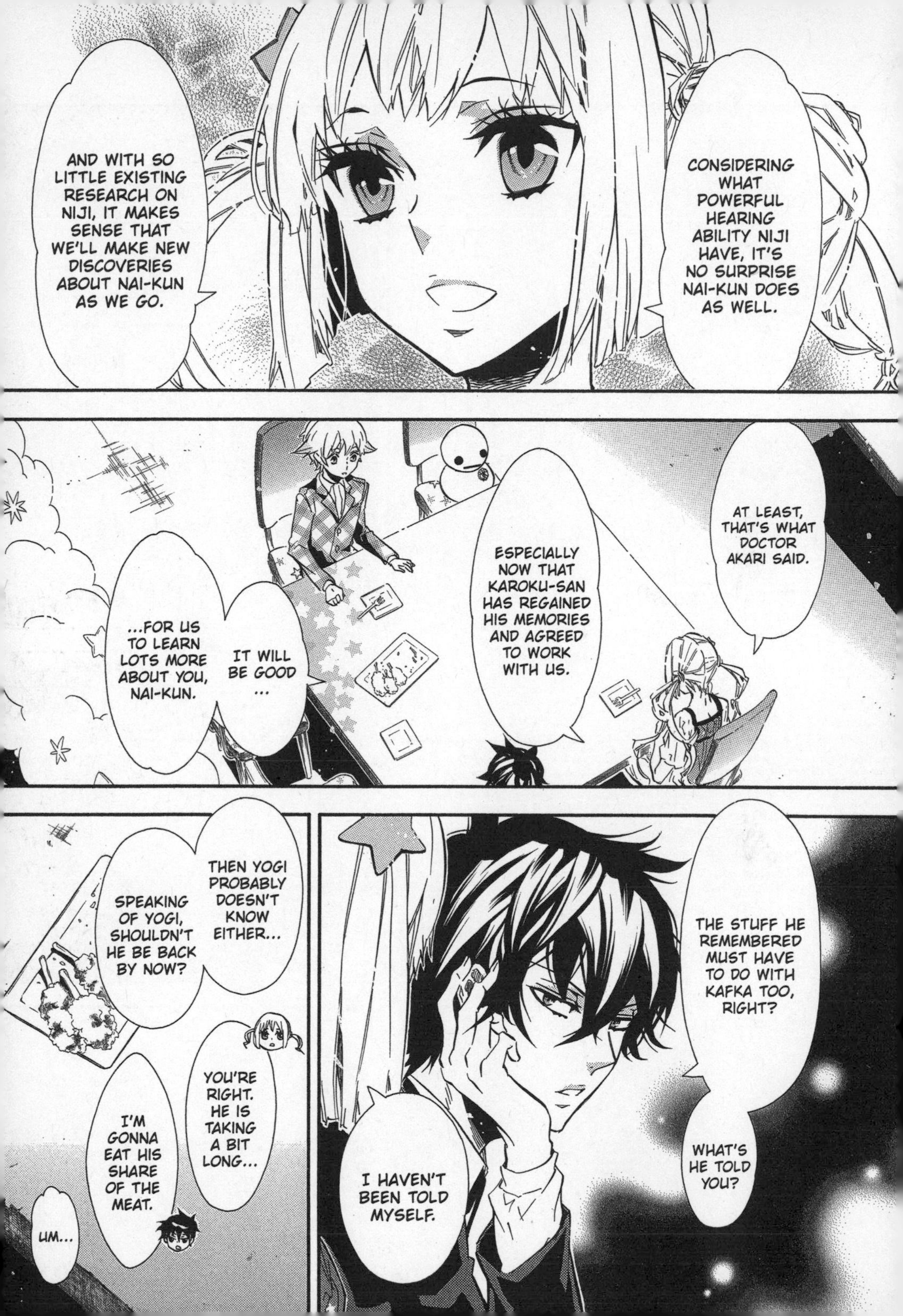
CONSIDERING WHAT POWERFUL HEARING ABILITY NIJI HAVE, IT'S NO SURPRISE NAI-KUN DOES AS WELL.
AND WITH SO LITTLE EXISTING RESEARCH ON NIJI, IT MAKES SENSE THAT WE'LL MAKE NEW DISCOVERIES ABOUT NAI-KUN AS WE GO.
AT LEAST, THAT'S WHAT DOCTOR AKARI SAID.
ESPECIALLY NOW THAT KAROKU-SAN HAS REGAINED HIS MEMORIES AND AGREED TO WORK WITH US.
IT WILL BE GOOD ...
...FOR US TO LEARN LOTS MORE ABOUT YOU, NAI-KUN.
THE STUFF HE REMEMBERED MUST HAVE TO DO WITH KAFKA TOO, RIGHT?
WHAT'S HE TOLD YOU?
I HAVEN'T BEEN TOLD MYSELF.
THEN YOGI PROBABLY DOESN'T KNOW EITHER...
SPEAKING OF YOGI, SHOULDN'T HE BE BACK BY NOW?
YOU'RE RIGHT. HE IS TAKING A BIT LONG...
I'M GONNA EAT HIS SHARE OF THE MEAT.
UM...

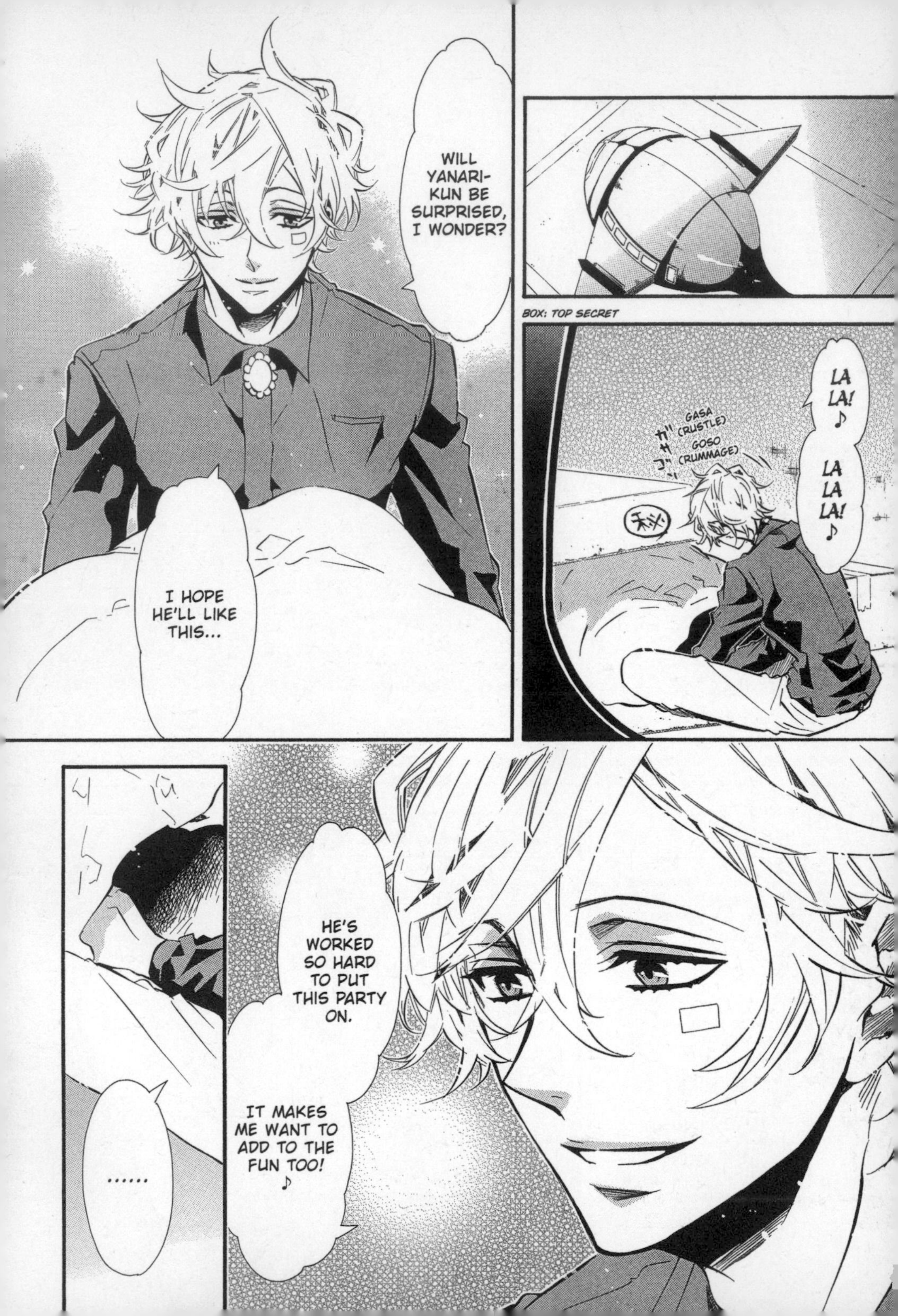
BOX: TOP SECRET
LA LA! ♪
GASA (RUSTLE)
GOSO (RUMMAGE)
LA LA LA! ♪
WILL YANARI-KUN BE SURPRISED, I WONDER?
I HOPE HE'LL LIKE THIS...
HE'S WORKED SO HARD TO PUT THIS PARTY ON.
IT MAKES ME WANT TO ADD TO THE FUN TOO! ♪
......

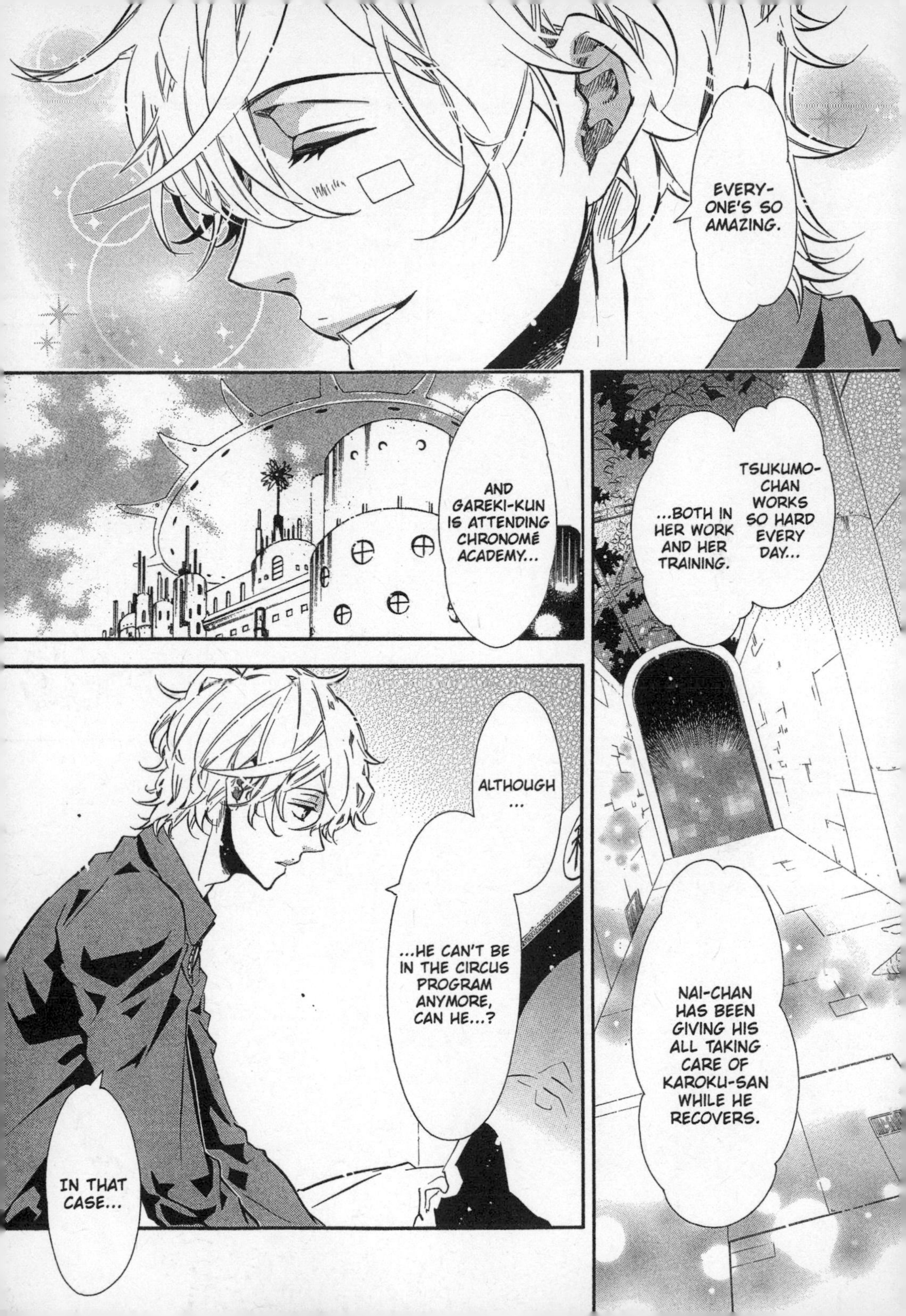
EVERY-ONE'S SO AMAZING.
TSUKUMO-CHAN WORKS SO HARD EVERY DAY...
...BOTH IN HER WORK AND HER TRAINING.
NAI-CHAN HAS BEEN GIVING HIS ALL TAKING CARE OF KAROKU-SAN WHILE HE RECOVERS.
AND GAREKI-KUN IS ATTENDING CHRONOMÉ ACADEMY...
ALTHOUGH...
...HE CAN'T BE IN THE CIRCUS PROGRAM ANYMORE, CAN HE...?
IN THAT CASE...

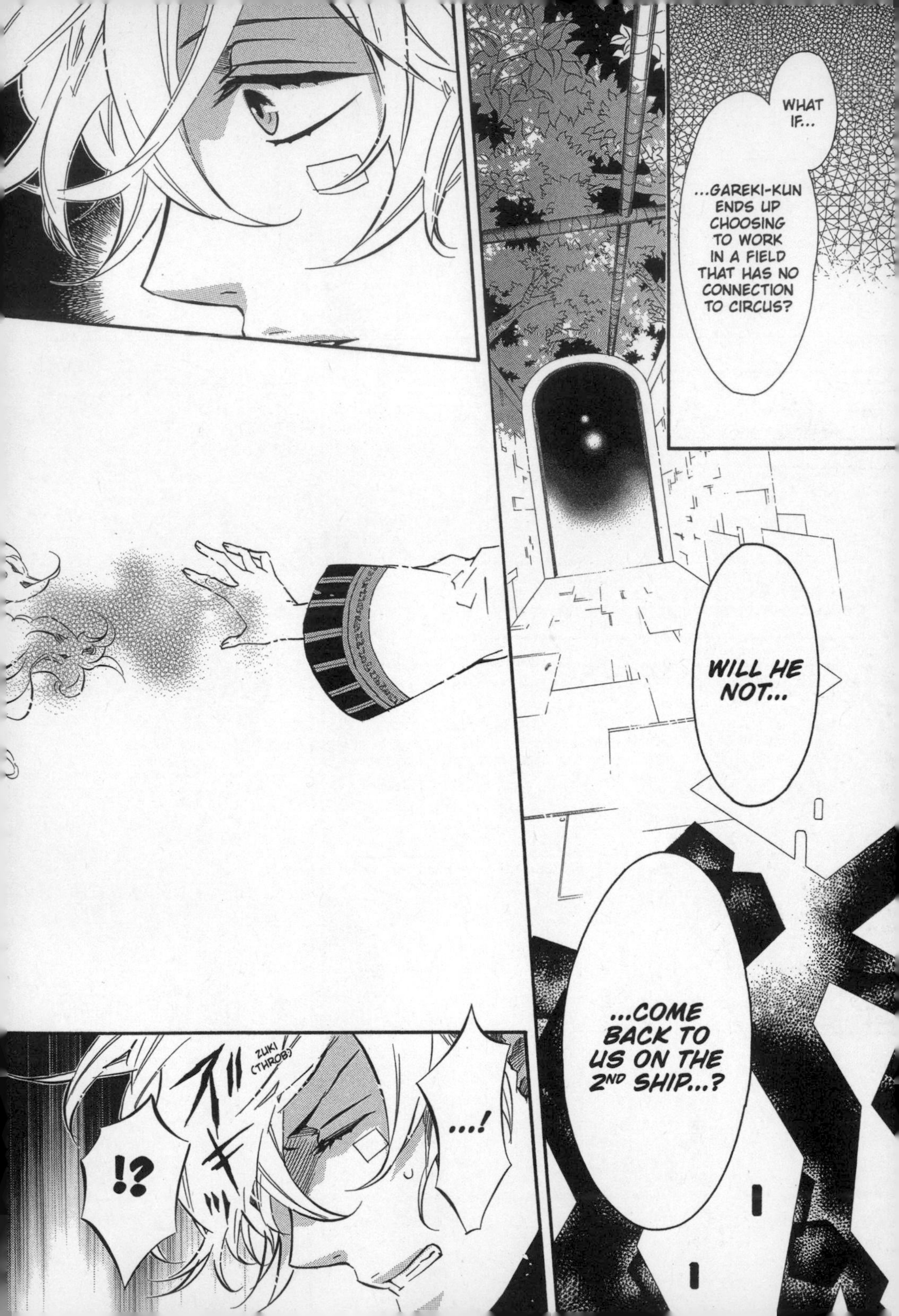
WHAT IF...
...GAREKI-KUN ENDS UP CHOOSING TO WORK IN A FIELD THAT HAS NO CONNECTION TO CIRCUS?
WILL HE NOT...
...COME BACK TO US ON THE 2ND SHIP...?
...!
ZUKI (THROB)
!?

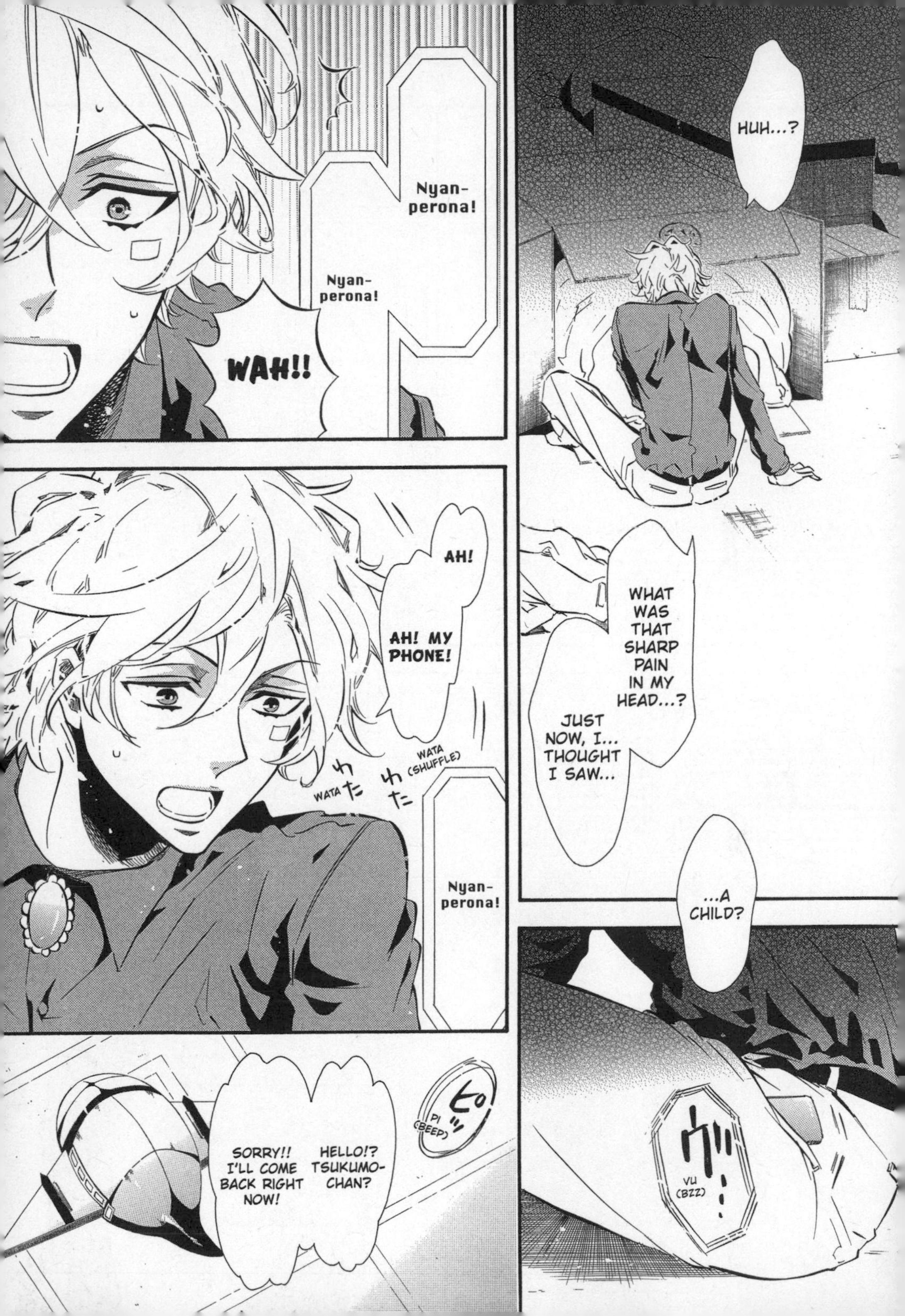
HUH...?
WHAT WAS THAT SHARP PAIN IN MY HEAD...?
JUST NOW, I... THOUGHT I SAW...
Nyan-perona!
Nyan-perona!
WAH!!
AH!
AH! MY PHONE!
WATA (SHUFFLE)
WATA
Nyan-perona!
...A CHILD?
VU (BZZ)
PI (BEEP)
HELLO!? TSUKUMO-CHAN?
SORRY!! I'LL COME BACK RIGHT NOW!

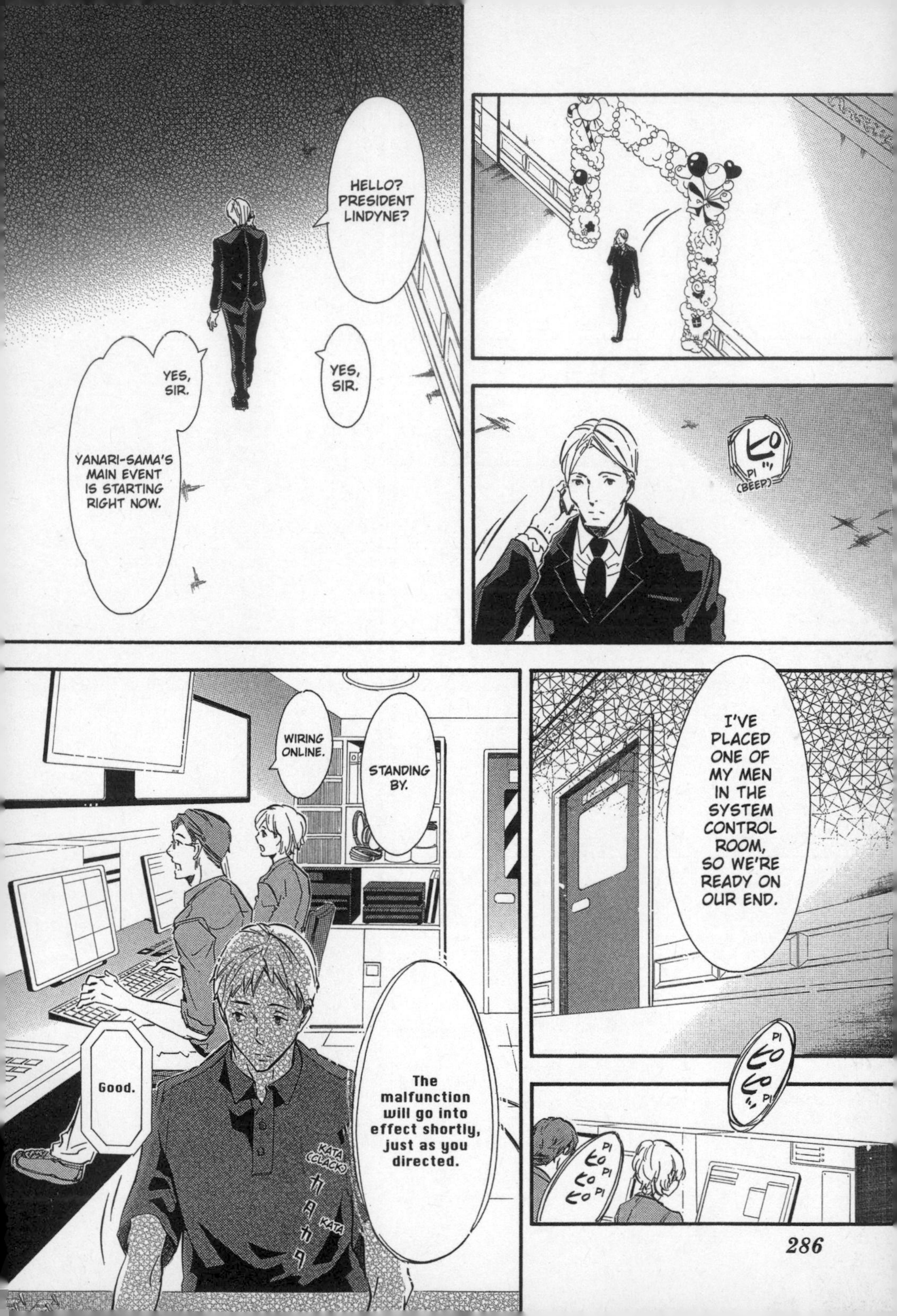
PI (BEEP)
HELLO? PRESIDENT LINDYNE?
YES, SIR.
YES, SIR.
YANARI-SAMA'S MAIN EVENT IS STARTING RIGHT NOW.
I'VE PLACED ONE OF MY MEN IN THE SYSTEM CONTROL ROOM, SO WE'RE READY ON OUR END.
PI PI
PI PI PI
STANDING BY.
WIRING ONLINE.
The malfunction will go into effect shortly, just as you directed.
Good.
KATA (CLACK) KATA

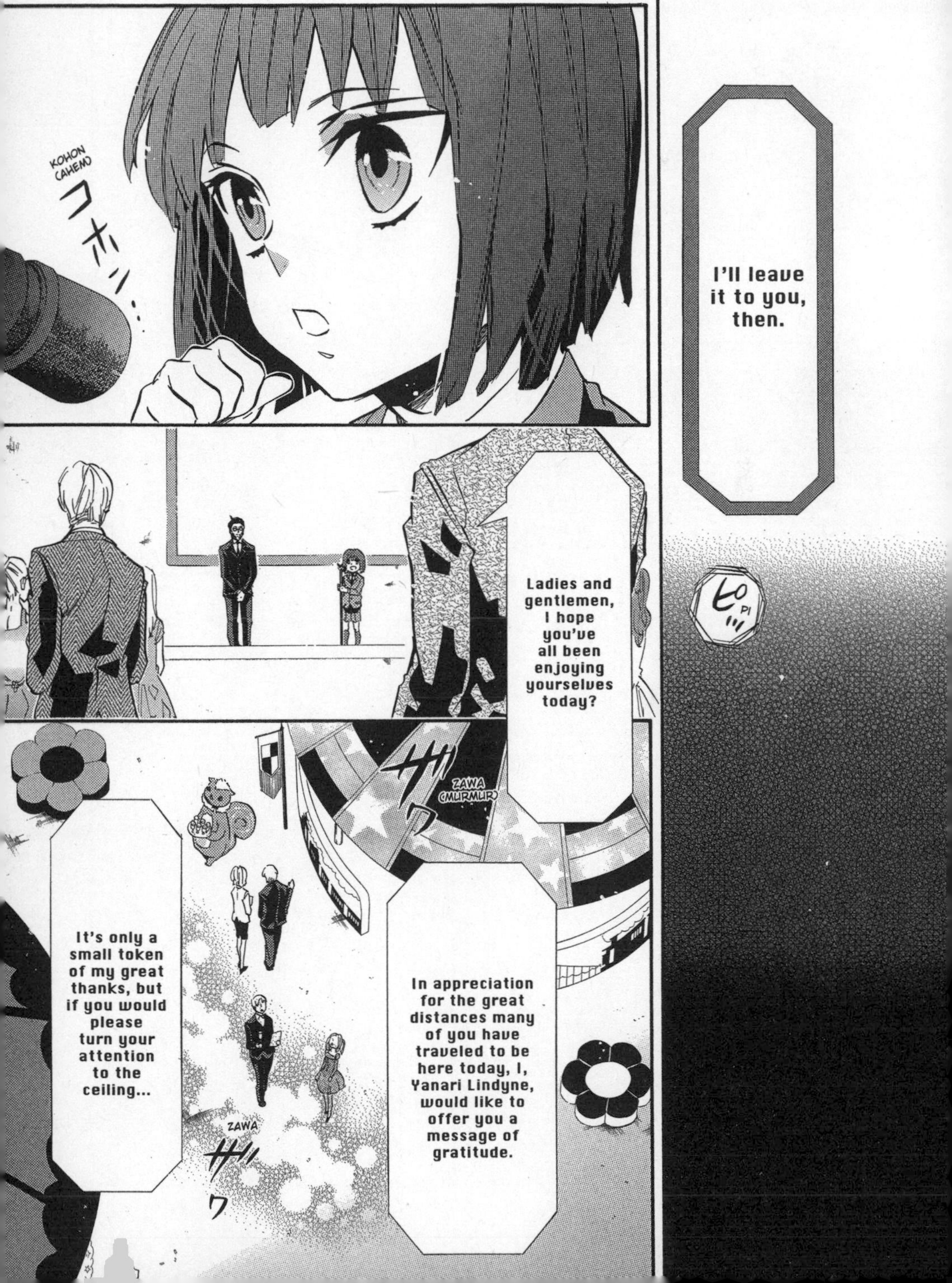
I'll leave it to you, then.
PI
KOHON (AHEM)
Ladies and gentlemen, I hope you've all been enjoying yourselves today?
ZAWA (MURMUR)
In appreciation for the great distances many of you have traveled to be here today, I, Yanari Lindyne, would like to offer you a message of gratitude.
It's only a small token of my great thanks, but if you would please turn your attention to the ceiling...
ZAWA

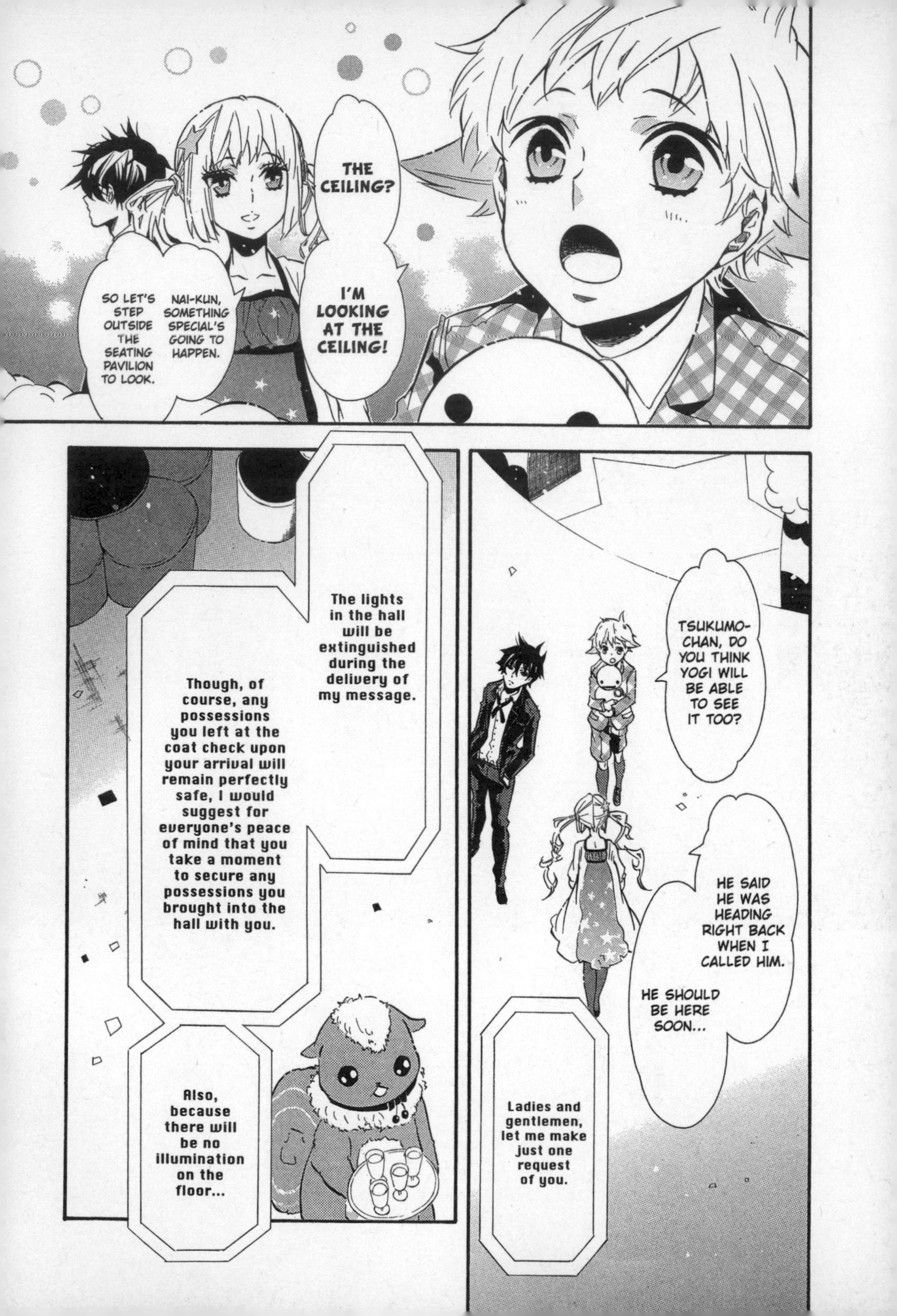
THE CEILING?
I'M LOOKING AT THE CEILING!
NAI-KUN, SOMETHING SPECIAL'S GOING TO HAPPEN.
SO LET'S STEP OUTSIDE THE SEATING PAVILION TO LOOK.
TSUKUMO-CHAN, DO YOU THINK YOGI WILL BE ABLE TO SEE IT TOO?
HE SAID HE WAS HEADING RIGHT BACK WHEN I CALLED HIM.
HE SHOULD BE HERE SOON...
Ladies and gentlemen, let me make just one request of you.
The lights in the hall will be extinguished during the delivery of my message.
Though, of course, any possessions you left at the coat check upon your arrival will remain perfectly safe, I would suggest for everyone's peace of mind that you take a moment to secure any possessions you brought into the hall with you.
Also, because there will be no illumination on the floor...

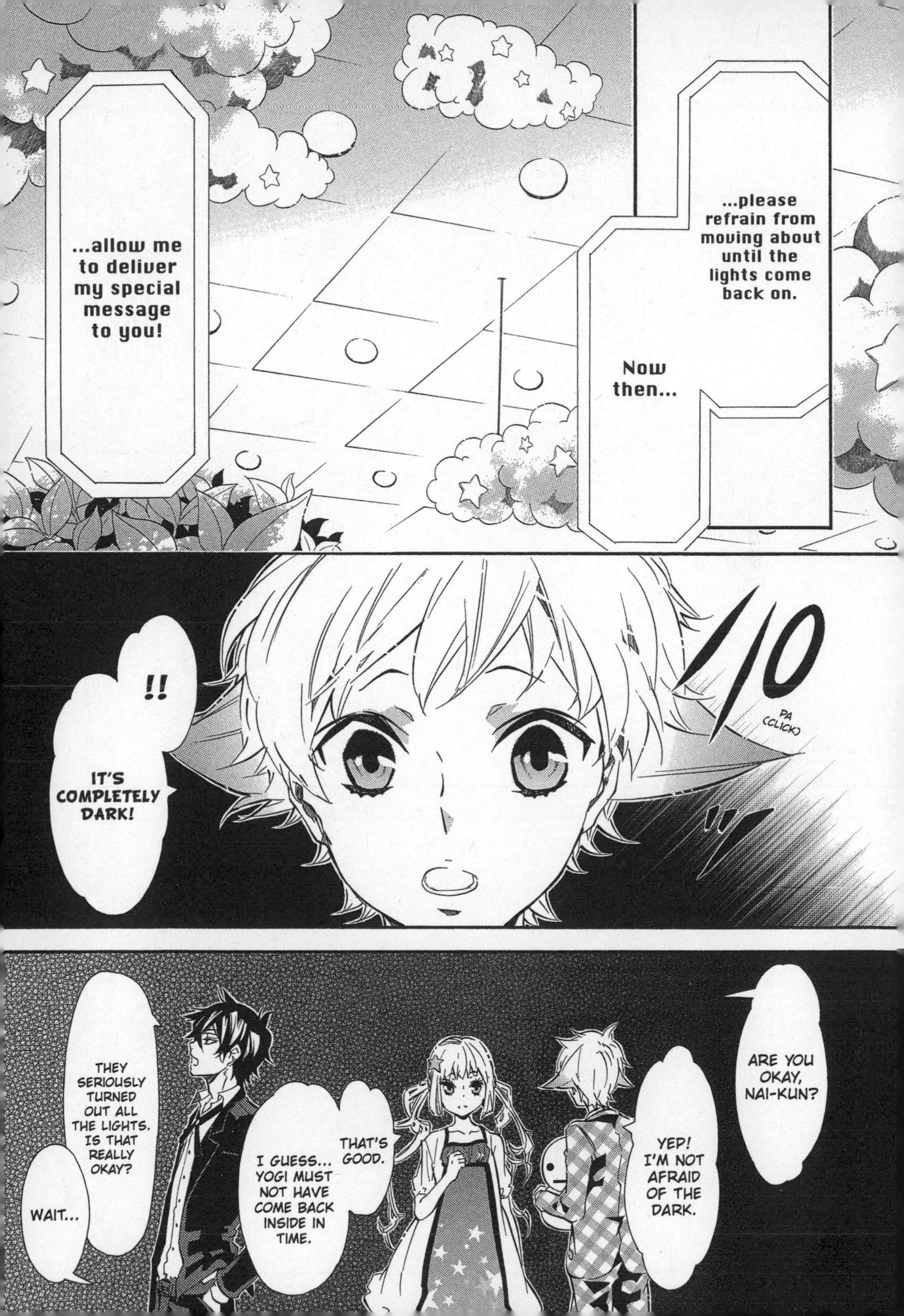
...please refrain from moving about until the lights come back on.
Now then...
...allow me to deliver my special message to you!
PA (CLICK)
!!
IT'S COMPLETELY DARK!
ARE YOU OKAY, NAI-KUN?
YEP! I'M NOT AFRAID OF THE DARK.
THAT'S GOOD.
I GUESS... YOGI MUST NOT HAVE COME BACK INSIDE IN TIME.
THEY SERIOUSLY TURNED OUT ALL THE LIGHTS. IS THAT REALLY OKAY?
WAIT...

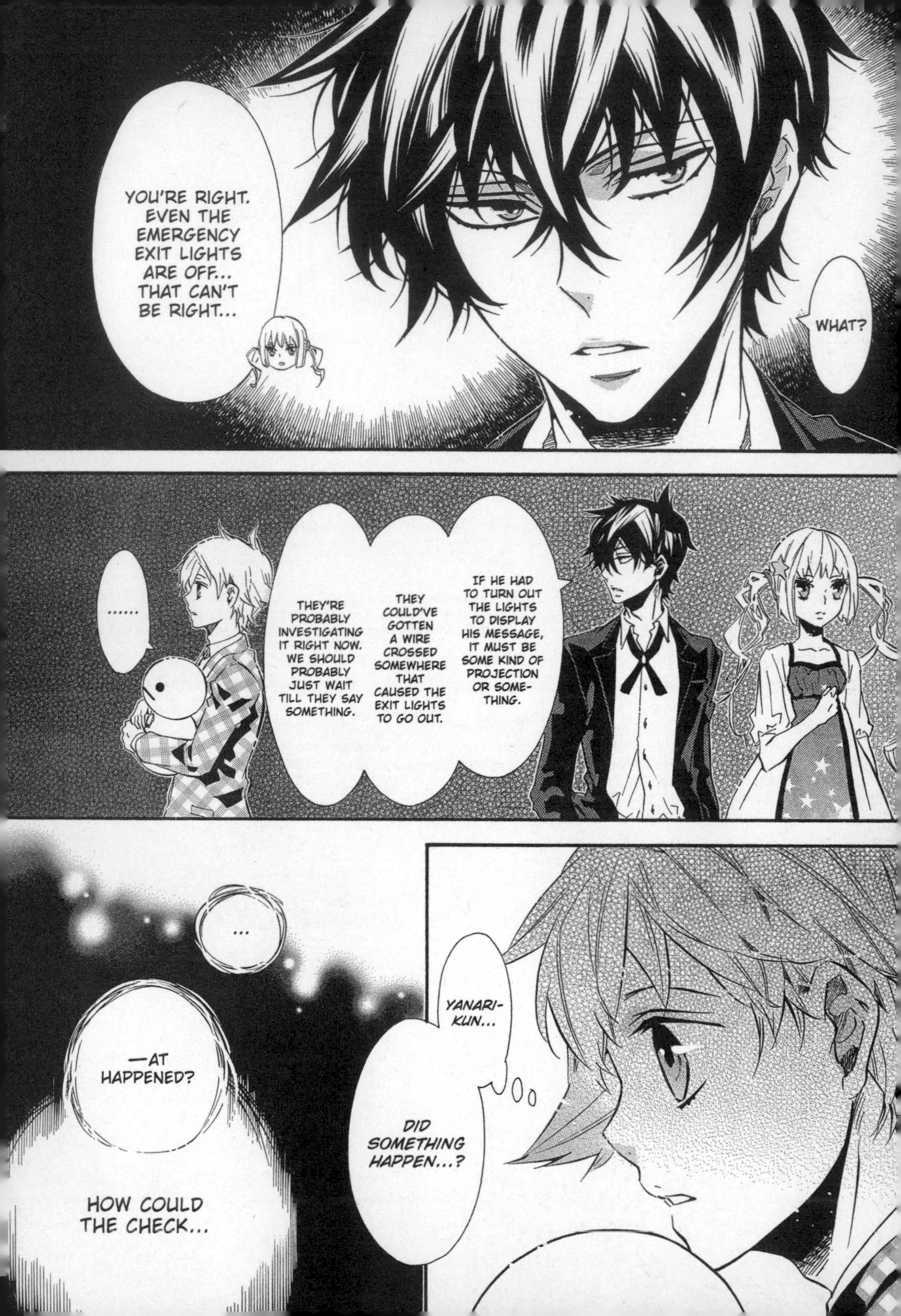
WHAT?
YOU'RE RIGHT. EVEN THE EMERGENCY EXIT LIGHTS ARE OFF... THAT CAN'T BE RIGHT...
IF HE HAD TO TURN OUT THE LIGHTS TO DISPLAY HIS MESSAGE, IT MUST BE SOME KIND OF PROJECTION OR SOME-THING.
THEY COULD'VE GOTTEN A WIRE CROSSED SOMEWHERE THAT CAUSED THE EXIT LIGHTS TO GO OUT.
THEY'RE PROBABLY INVESTIGATING IT RIGHT NOW. WE SHOULD PROBABLY JUST WAIT TILL THEY SAY SOMETHING.
......
YANARI-KUN...
DID SOMETHING HAPPEN...?
...
—AT HAPPENED?
HOW COULD THE CHECK...

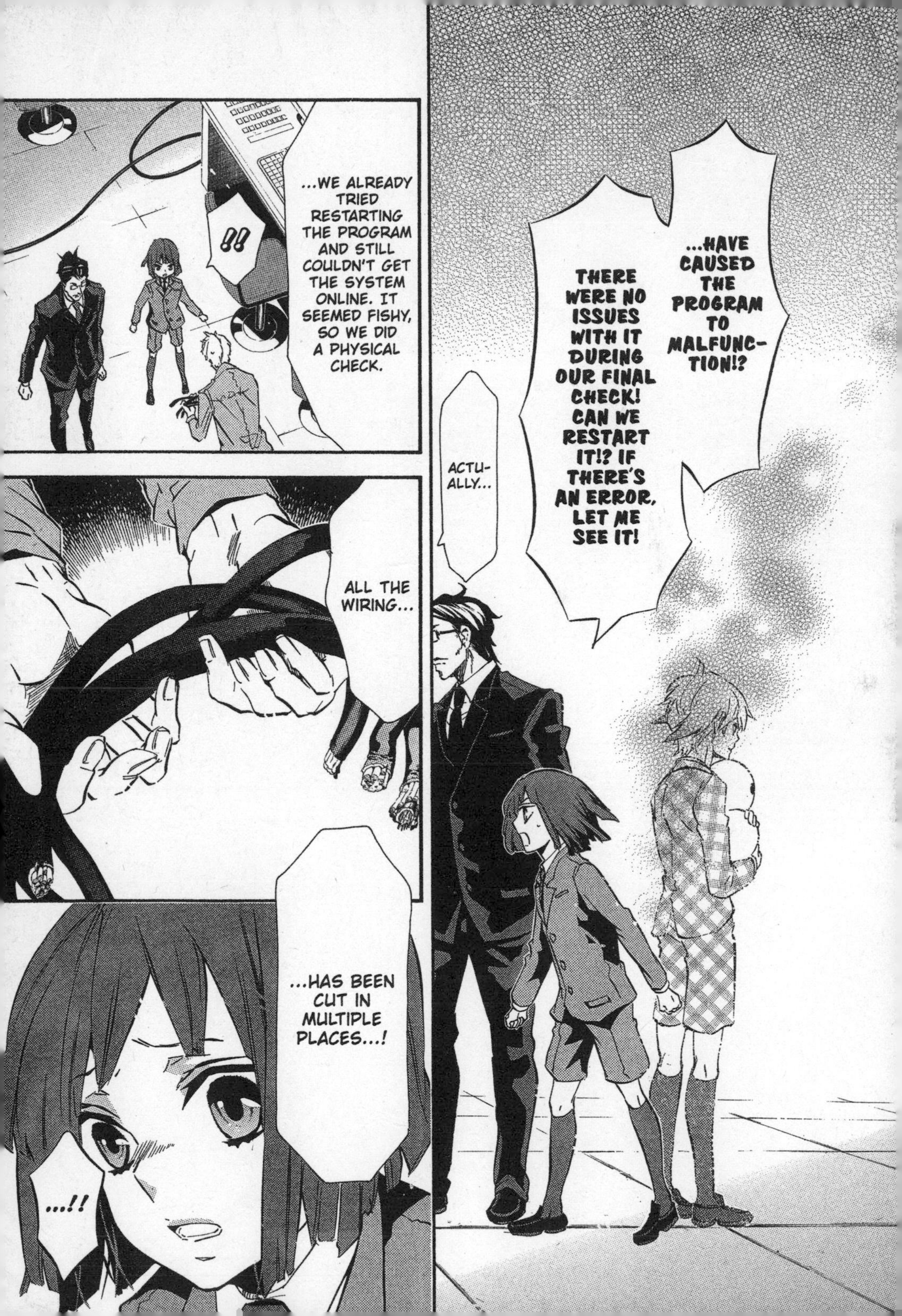
...HAVE CAUSED THE PROGRAM TO MALFUNCTION!?
THERE WERE NO ISSUES WITH IT DURING OUR FINAL CHECK! CAN WE RESTART IT!? IF THERE'S AN ERROR, LET ME SEE IT!
ACTUALLY...
...WE ALREADY TRIED RESTARTING THE PROGRAM AND STILL COULDN'T GET THE SYSTEM ONLINE. IT SEEMED FISHY, SO WE DID A PHYSICAL CHECK.
!!
ALL THE WIRING...
...HAS BEEN CUT IN MULTIPLE PLACES...!
...!!

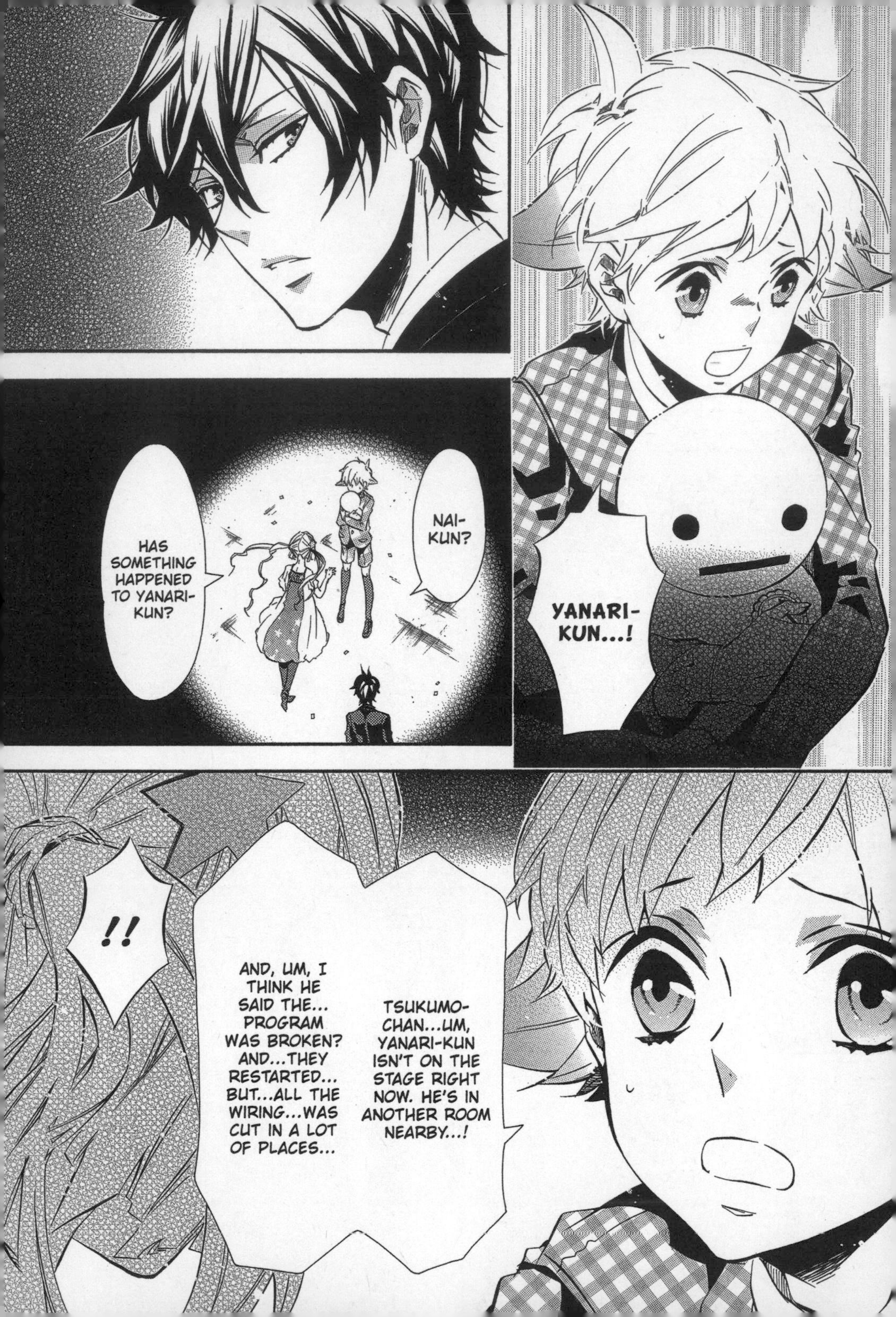
YANARI-KUN...!
NAI-KUN?
HAS SOMETHING HAPPENED TO YANARI-KUN?
TSUKUMO-CHAN...UM, YANARI-KUN ISN'T ON THE STAGE RIGHT NOW. HE'S IN ANOTHER ROOM NEARBY...!
AND, UM, I THINK HE SAID THE... PROGRAM WAS BROKEN? AND...THEY RESTARTED... BUT...ALL THE WIRING...WAS CUT IN A LOT OF PLACES...
!!

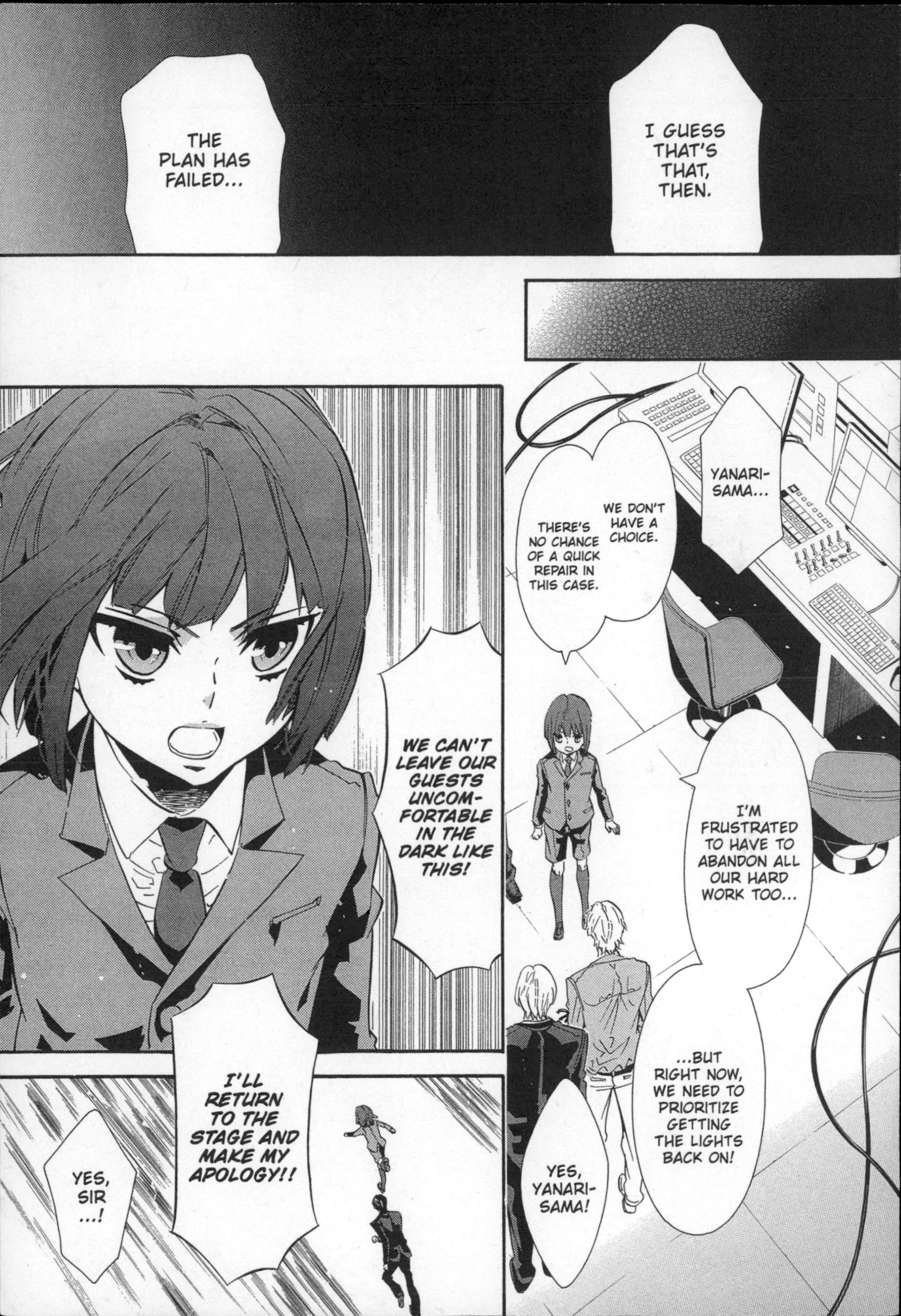
I GUESS THAT'S THAT, THEN.
THE PLAN HAS FAILED...
YANARI-SAMA...
WE DON'T HAVE A CHOICE.
THERE'S NO CHANCE OF A QUICK REPAIR IN THIS CASE.
I'M FRUSTRATED TO HAVE TO ABANDON ALL OUR HARD WORK TOO...
...BUT RIGHT NOW, WE NEED TO PRIORITIZE GETTING THE LIGHTS BACK ON!
YES, YANARI-SAMA!
WE CAN'T LEAVE OUR GUESTS UNCOMFORTABLE IN THE DARK LIKE THIS!
I'LL RETURN TO THE STAGE AND MAKE MY APOLOGY!!
YES, SIR ...!

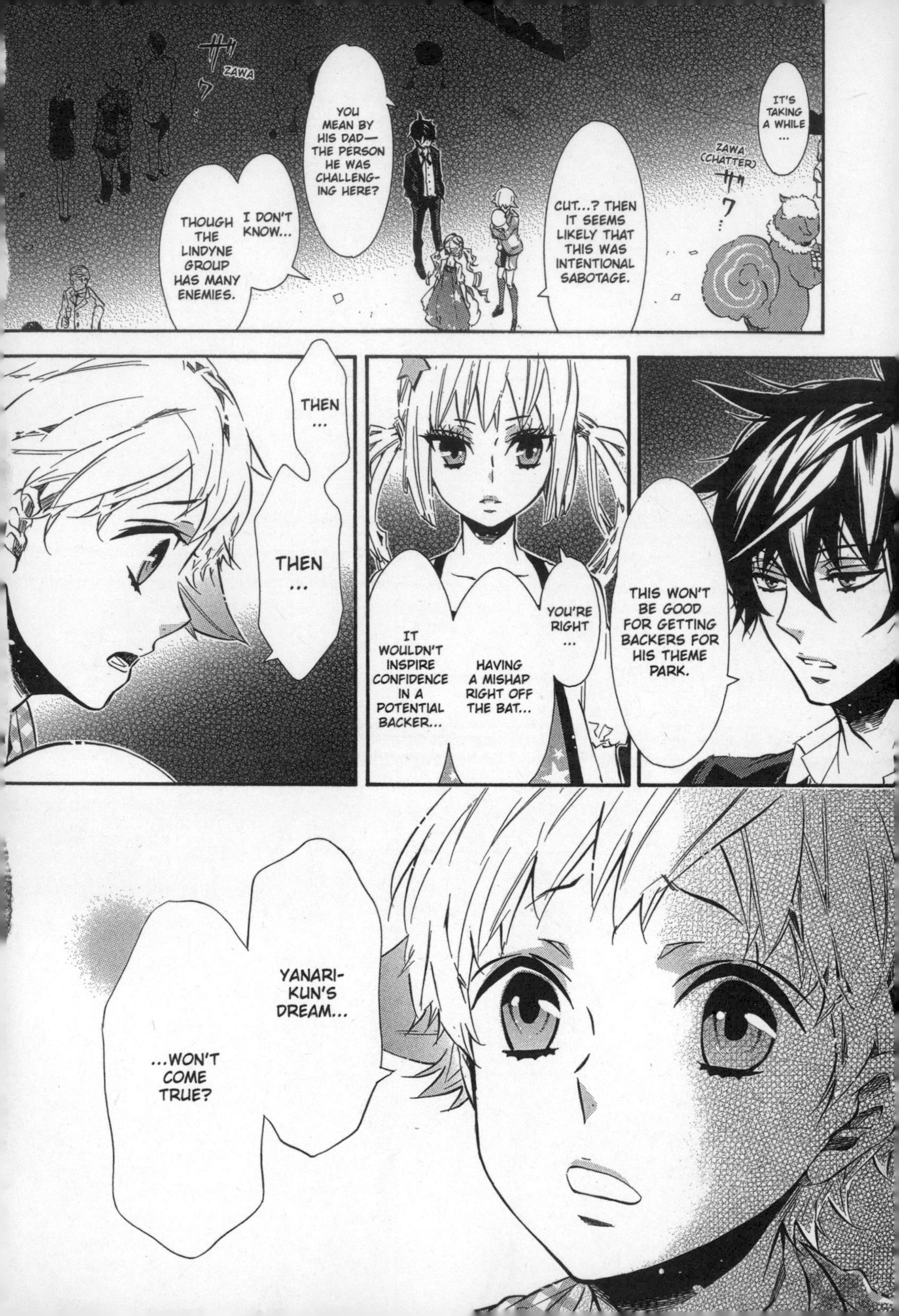
IT'S TAKING A WHILE...
ZAWA (CHATTER)
CUT...? THEN IT SEEMS LIKELY THAT THIS WAS INTENTIONAL SABOTAGE.
YOU MEAN BY HIS DAD—THE PERSON HE WAS CHALLENGING HERE?
I DON'T KNOW...
THOUGH THE LINDYNE GROUP HAS MANY ENEMIES.
ZAWA
THIS WON'T BE GOOD FOR GETTING BACKERS FOR HIS THEME PARK.
YOU'RE RIGHT...
HAVING A MISHAP RIGHT OFF THE BAT...
IT WOULDN'T INSPIRE CONFIDENCE IN A POTENTIAL BACKER...
THEN...
THEN...
YANARI-KUN'S DREAM...
...WON'T COME TRUE?

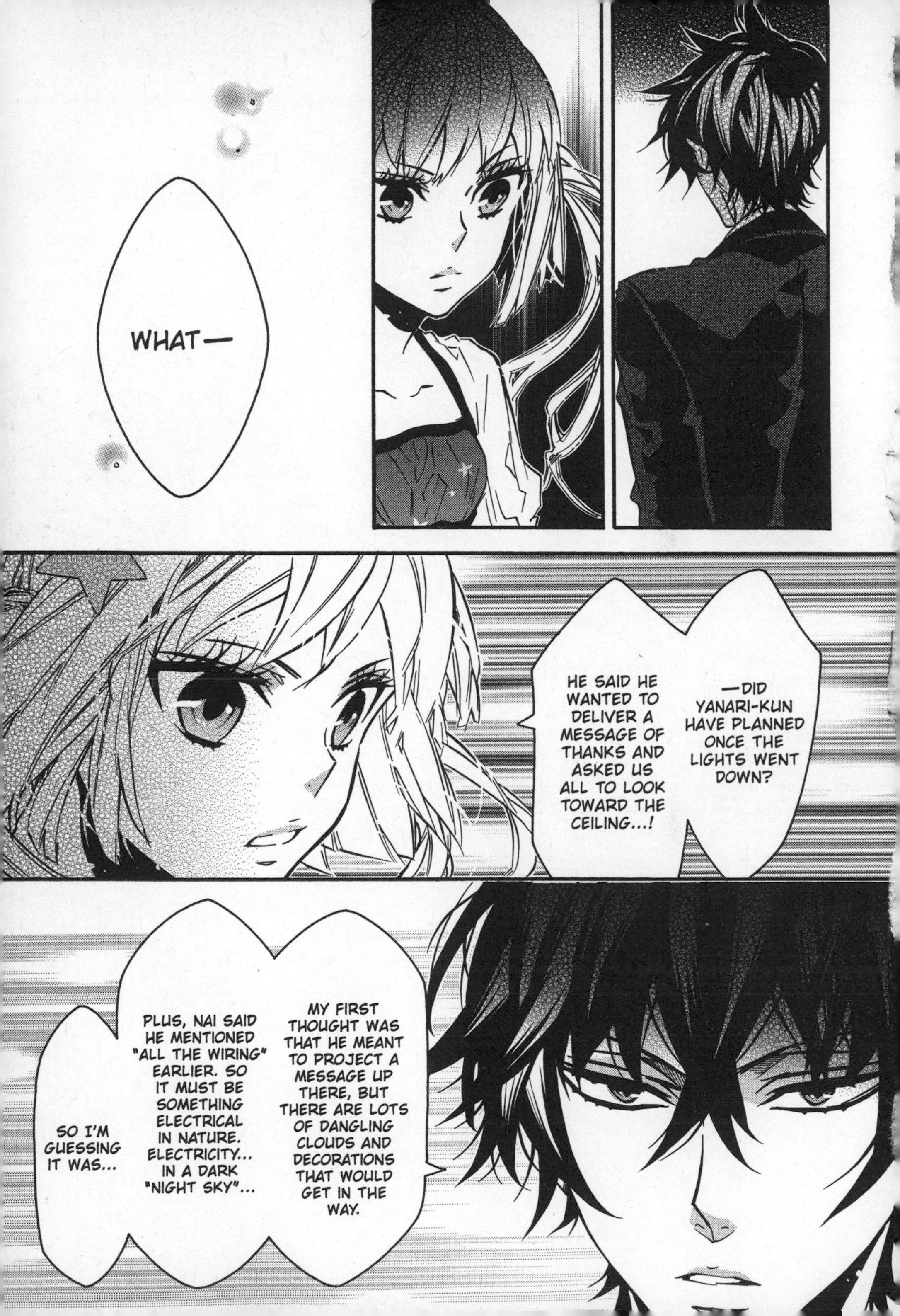
WHAT—
—DID YANARI-KUN HAVE PLANNED ONCE THE LIGHTS WENT DOWN?
HE SAID HE WANTED TO DELIVER A MESSAGE OF THANKS AND ASKED US ALL TO LOOK TOWARD THE CEILING...!
MY FIRST THOUGHT WAS THAT HE MEANT TO PROJECT A MESSAGE UP THERE, BUT THERE ARE LOTS OF DANGLING CLOUDS AND DECORATIONS THAT WOULD GET IN THE WAY.
PLUS, NAI SAID HE MENTIONED "ALL THE WIRING" EARLIER. SO IT MUST BE SOMETHING ELECTRICAL IN NATURE. ELECTRICITY... IN A DARK "NIGHT SKY"...
SO I'M GUESSING IT WAS...

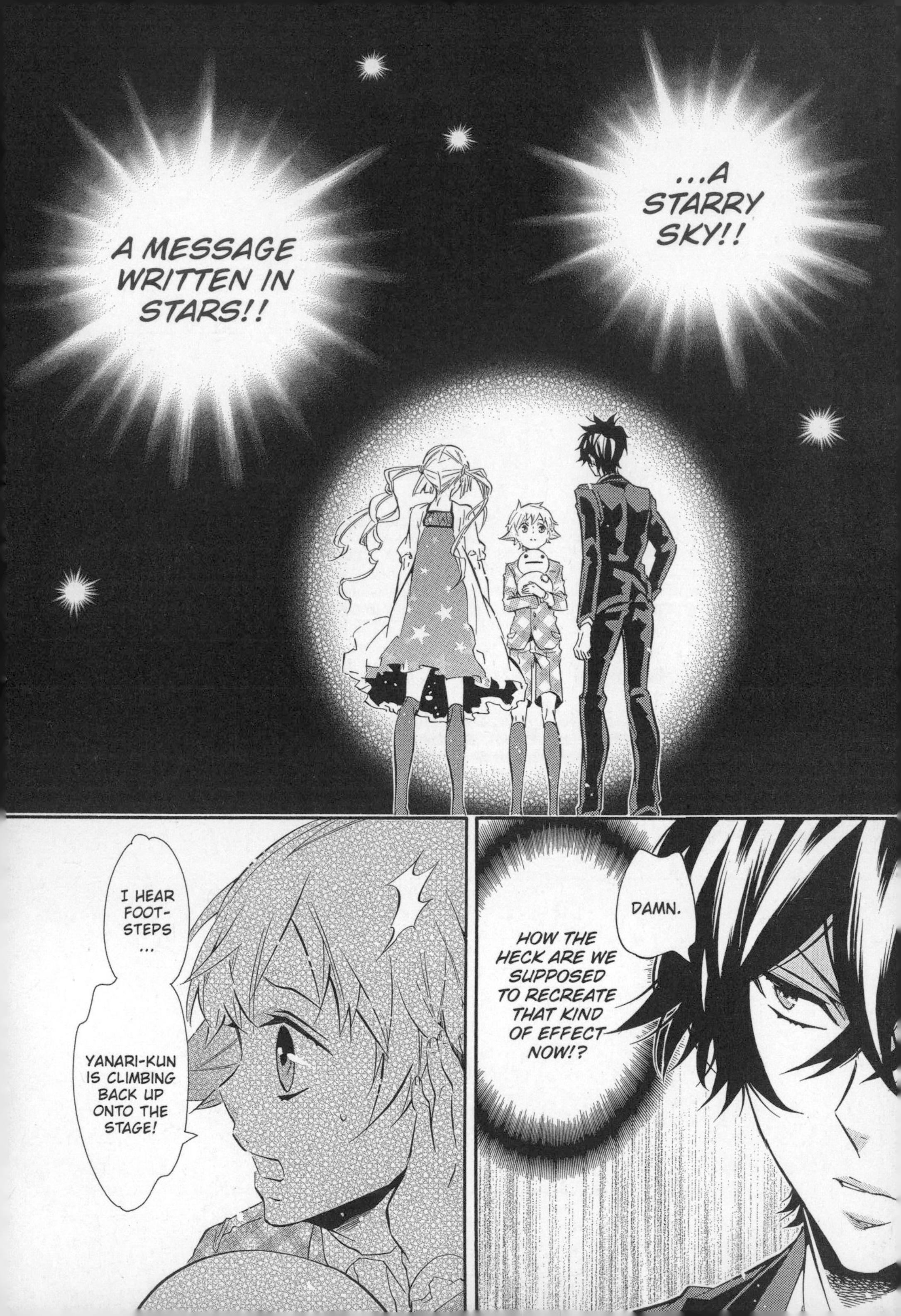
...A STARRY SKY!!
A MESSAGE WRITTEN IN STARS!!
DAMN.
HOW THE HECK ARE WE SUPPOSED TO RECREATE THAT KIND OF EFFECT NOW!?
I HEAR FOOT-STEPS...
YANARI-KUN IS CLIMBING BACK UP ONTO THE STAGE!

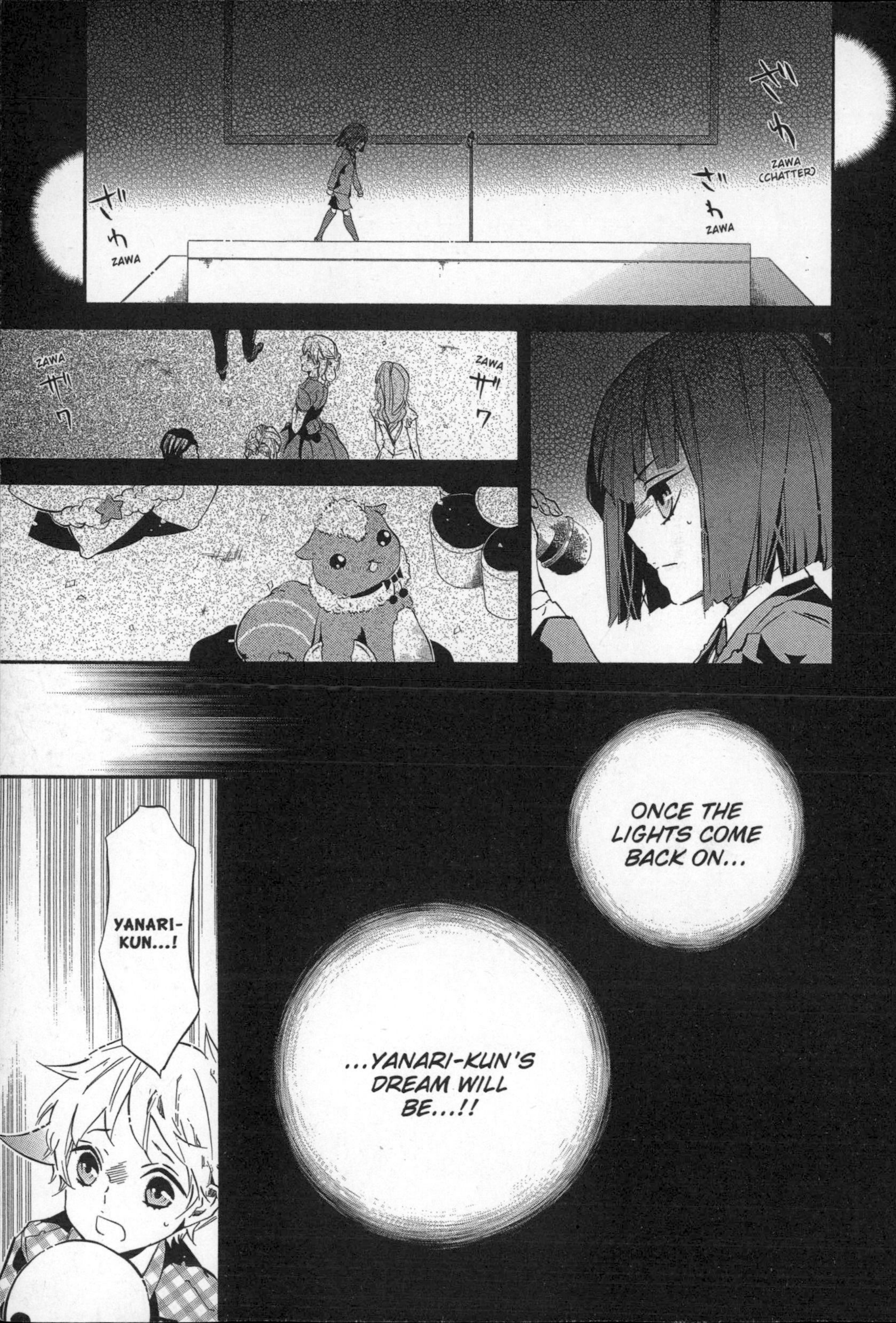
ZAWA (CHATTER)
ZAWA
ZAWA
ZAWA
ザワ
ZAWA
ザワ
ONCE THE LIGHTS COME BACK ON...
...YANARI-KUN'S DREAM WILL BE...!!
YANARI-KUN...!

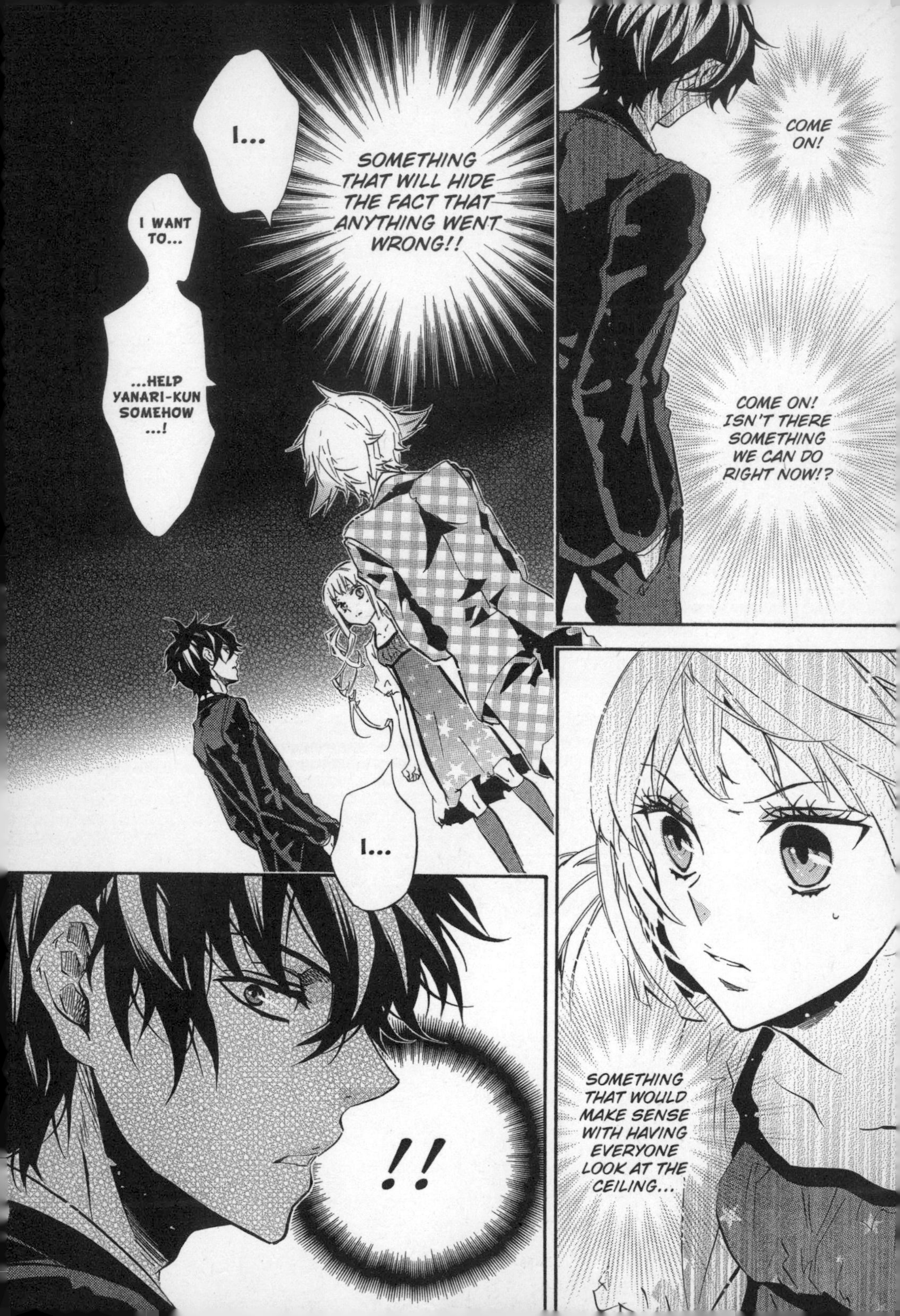
COME ON!
COME ON! ISN'T THERE SOMETHING WE CAN DO RIGHT NOW!?
SOMETHING THAT WILL HIDE THE FACT THAT ANYTHING WENT WRONG!!
I...
I WANT TO...
...HELP YANARI-KUN SOMEHOW ...!
I...
SOMETHING THAT WOULD MAKE SENSE WITH HAVING EVERYONE LOOK AT THE CEILING...
!!

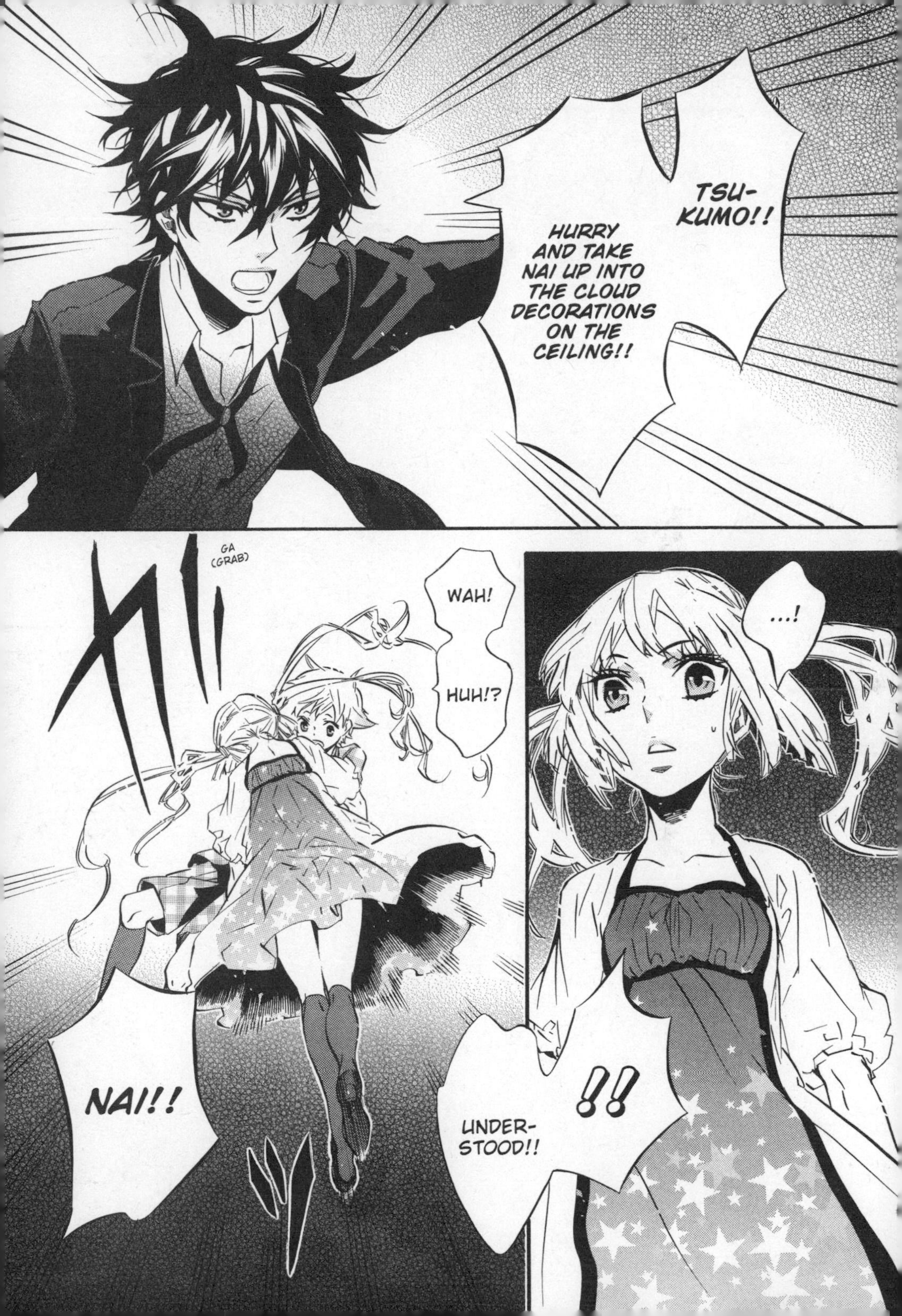
TSU-KUMO!!
HURRY AND TAKE NAI UP INTO THE CLOUD DECORATIONS ON THE CEILING!!
...!
!!
UNDERSTOOD!!
WAH!
HUH!?
GA (GRAB)
NAI!!

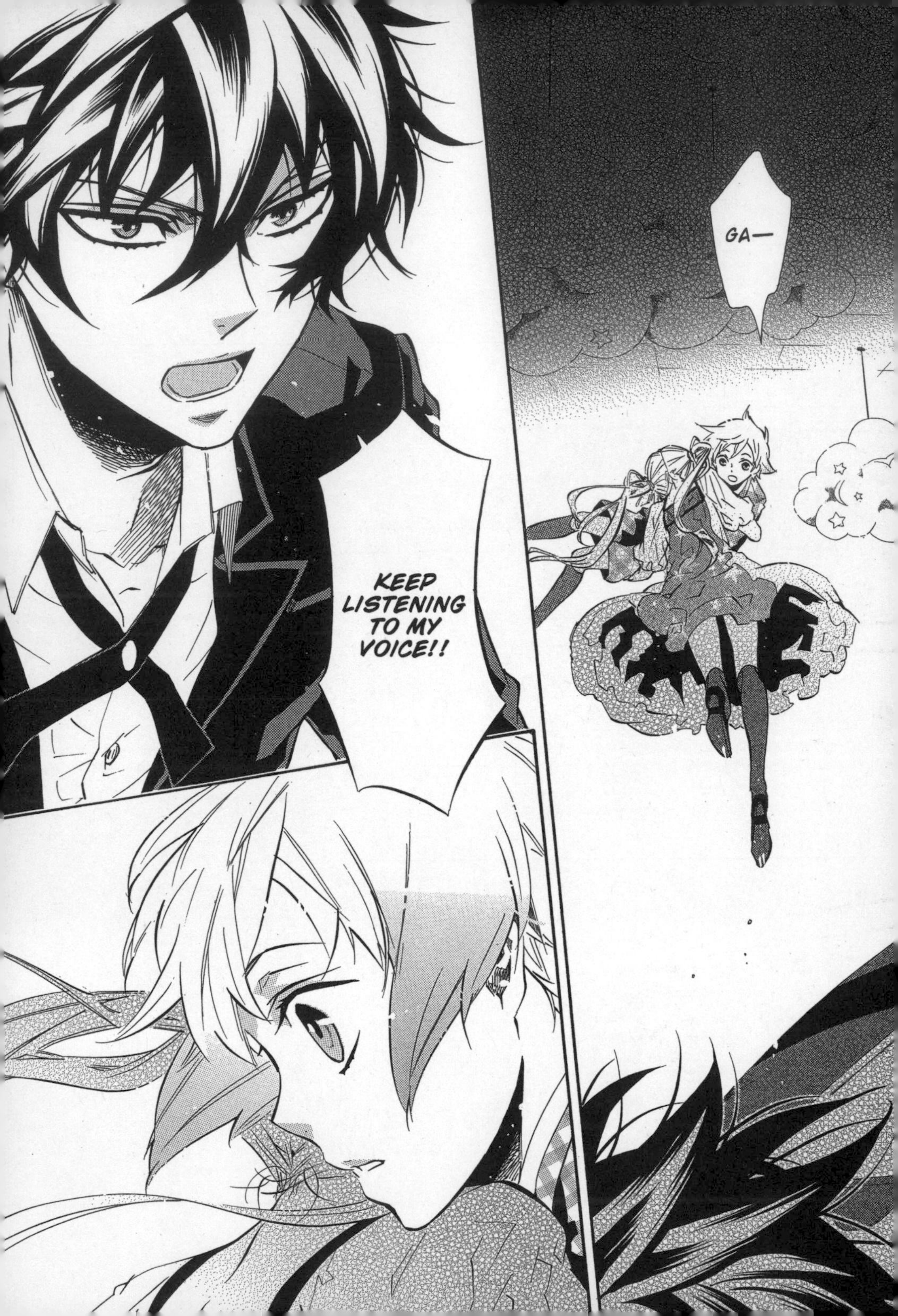
GA—
KEEP LISTENING TO MY VOICE!!

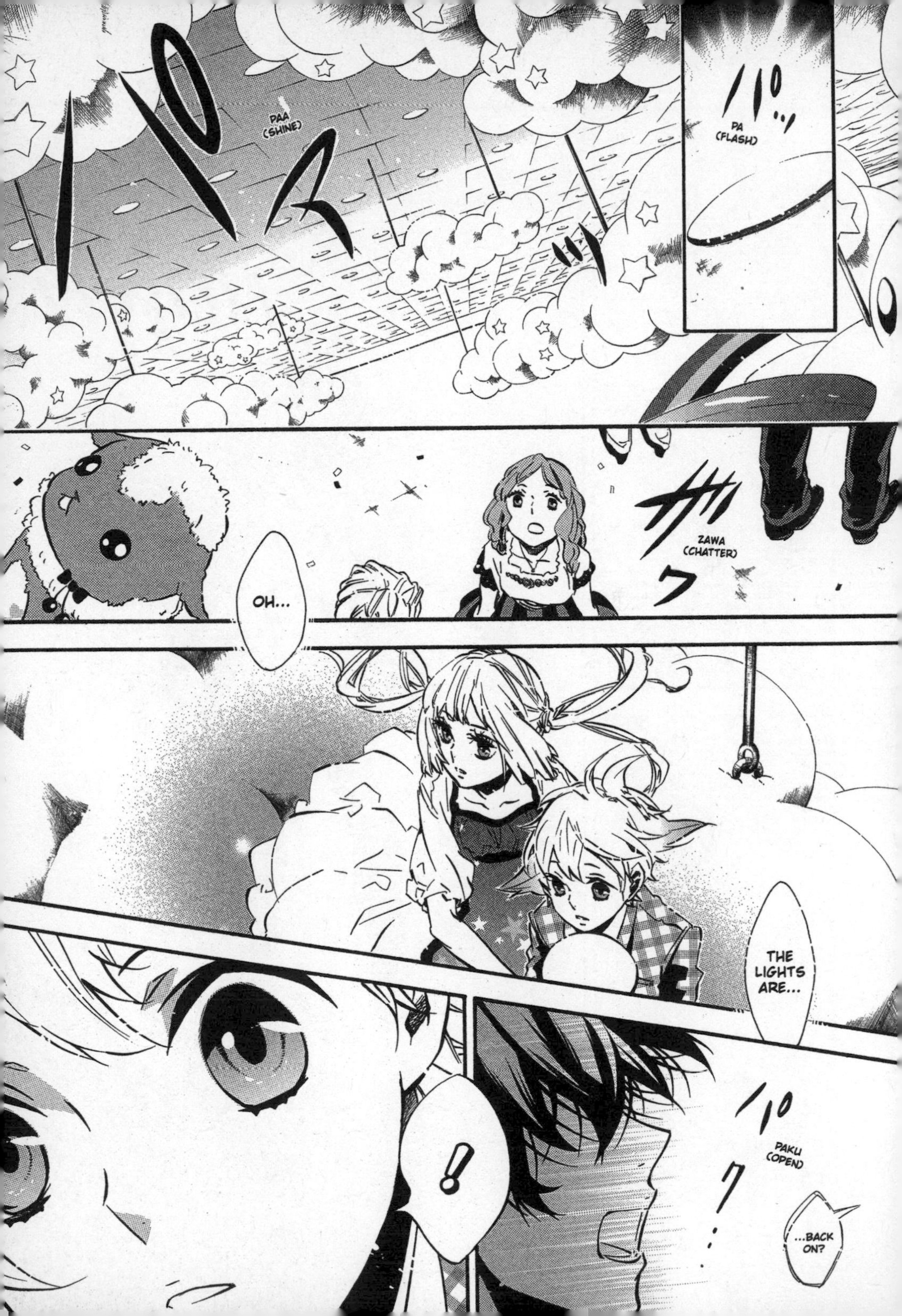
PA (FLASH)
PAA (SHINE)
ZAWA (CHATTER)
OH...
THE LIGHTS ARE...
PAKU (OPEN)
...BACK ON?
!

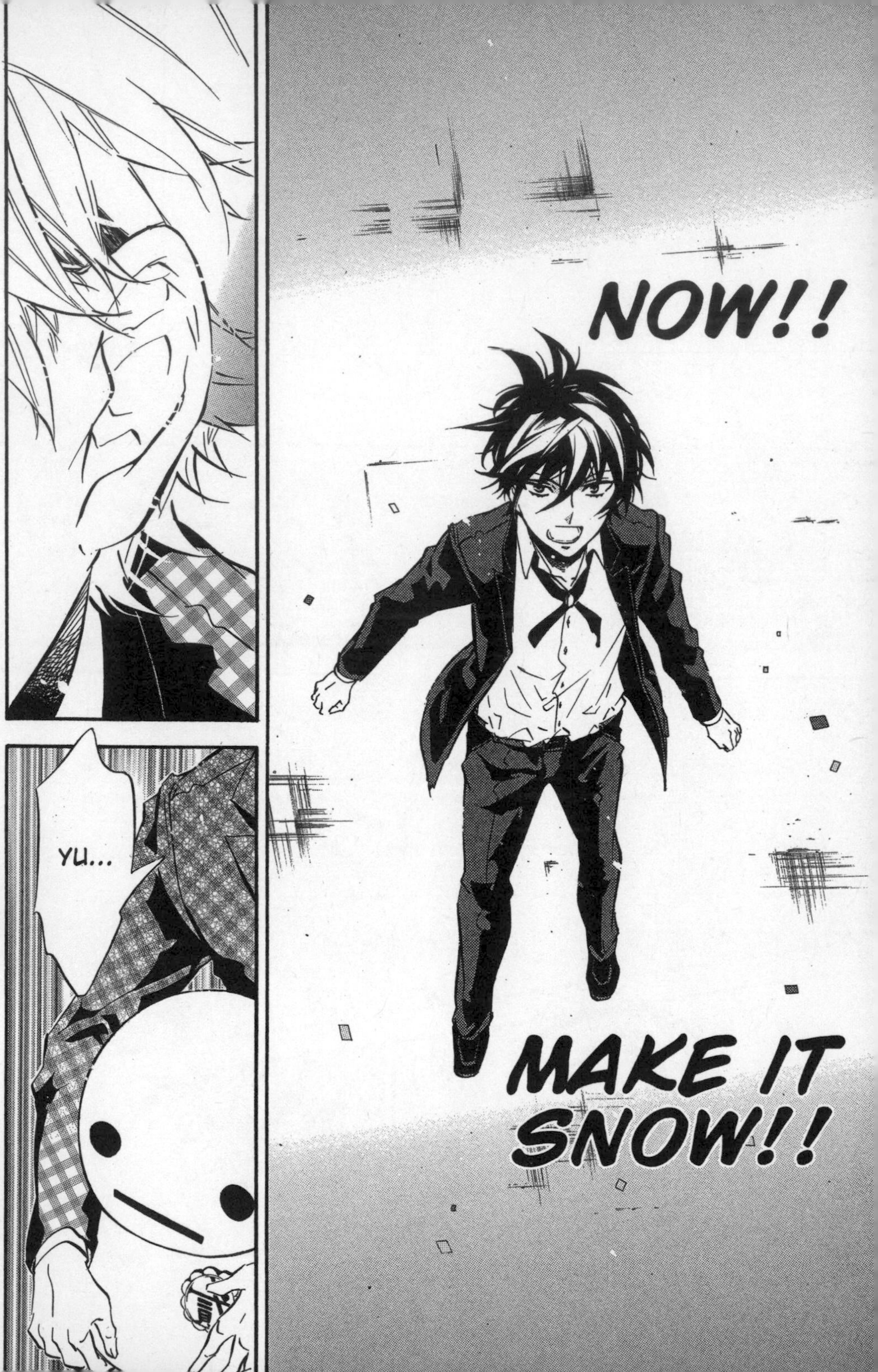
NOW!!
MAKE IT SNOW!!
YU...

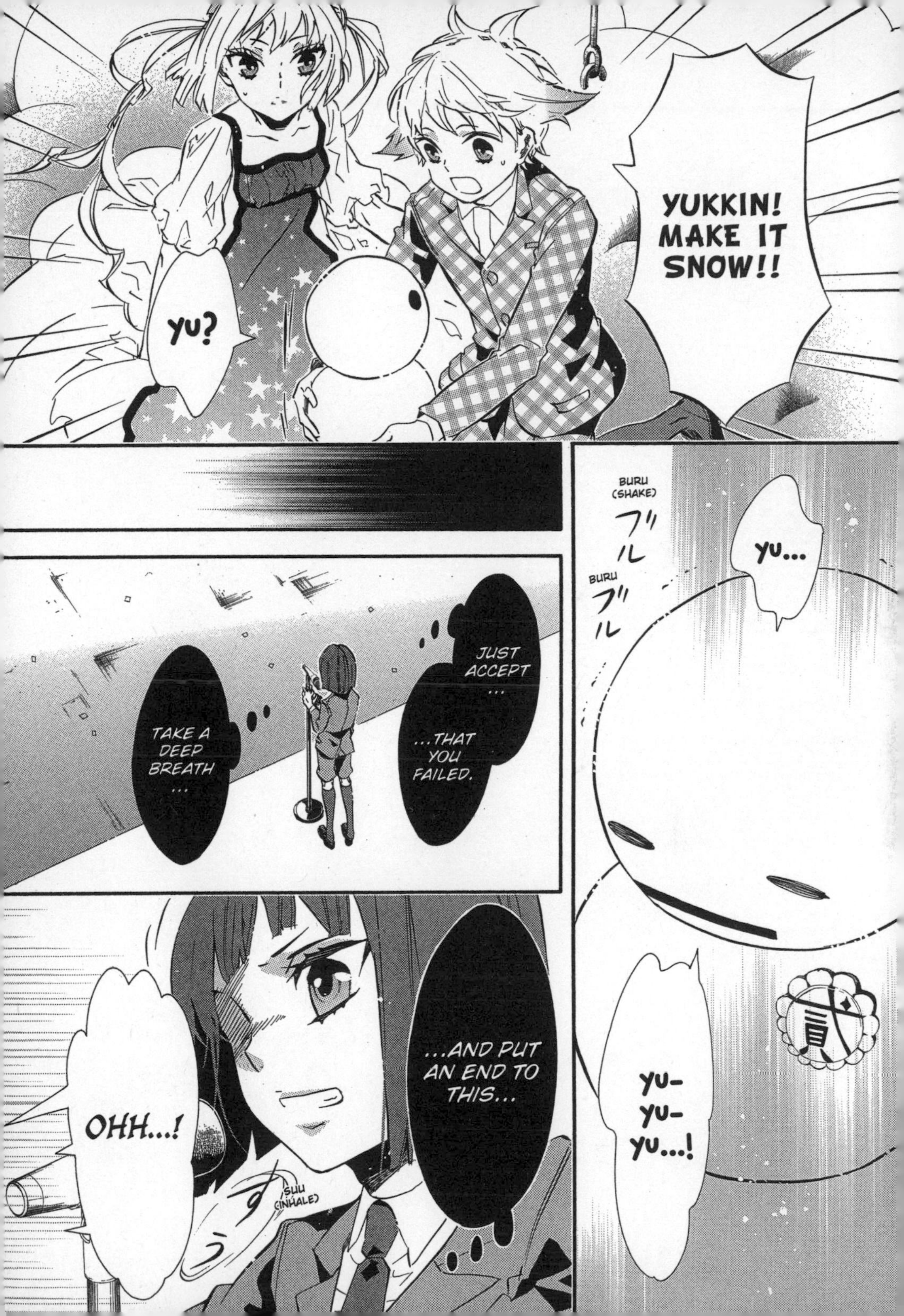
YUKKIN! MAKE IT SNOW!!
yu?
BURU (SHAKE)
ブル
BURU
ブル
YU...
YU-YU-YU...!
JUST ACCEPT...
...THAT YOU FAILED.
TAKE A DEEP BREATH...
...AND PUT AN END TO THIS...
SHU (INHALE)
OHH...!

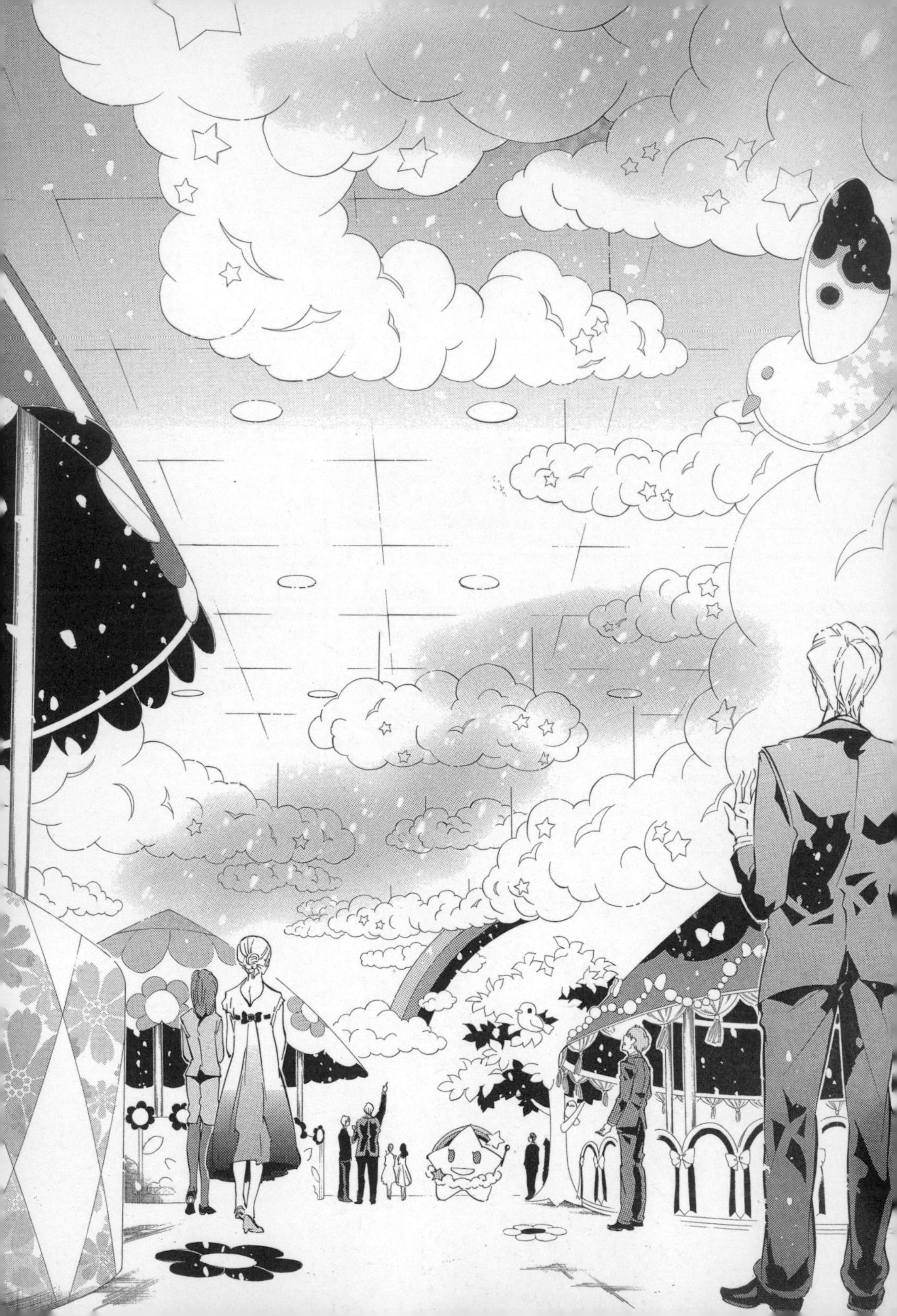

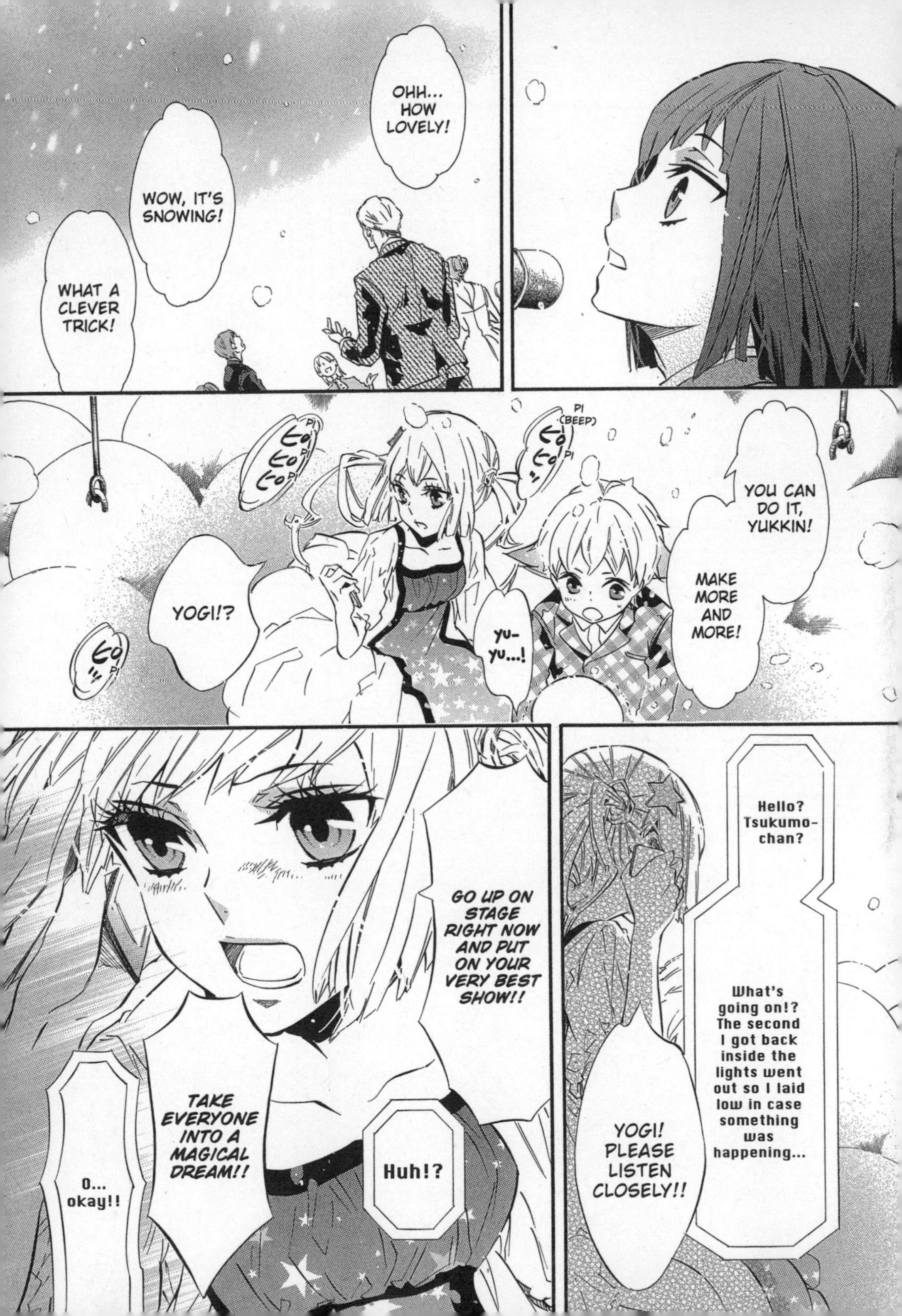
OHH... HOW LOVELY!
WOW, IT'S SNOWING!
WHAT A CLEVER TRICK!
YOU CAN DO IT, YUKKIN!
MAKE MORE AND MORE!
PI (BEEP)
yu-yu...!
YOGI!?
Hello? Tsukumo-chan?
What's going on!? The second I got back inside the lights went out so I laid low in case something was happening...
YOGI! PLEASE LISTEN CLOSELY!!
GO UP ON STAGE RIGHT NOW AND PUT ON YOUR VERY BEST SHOW!!
Huh!?
TAKE EVERYONE INTO A MAGICAL DREAM!!
O... okay!!

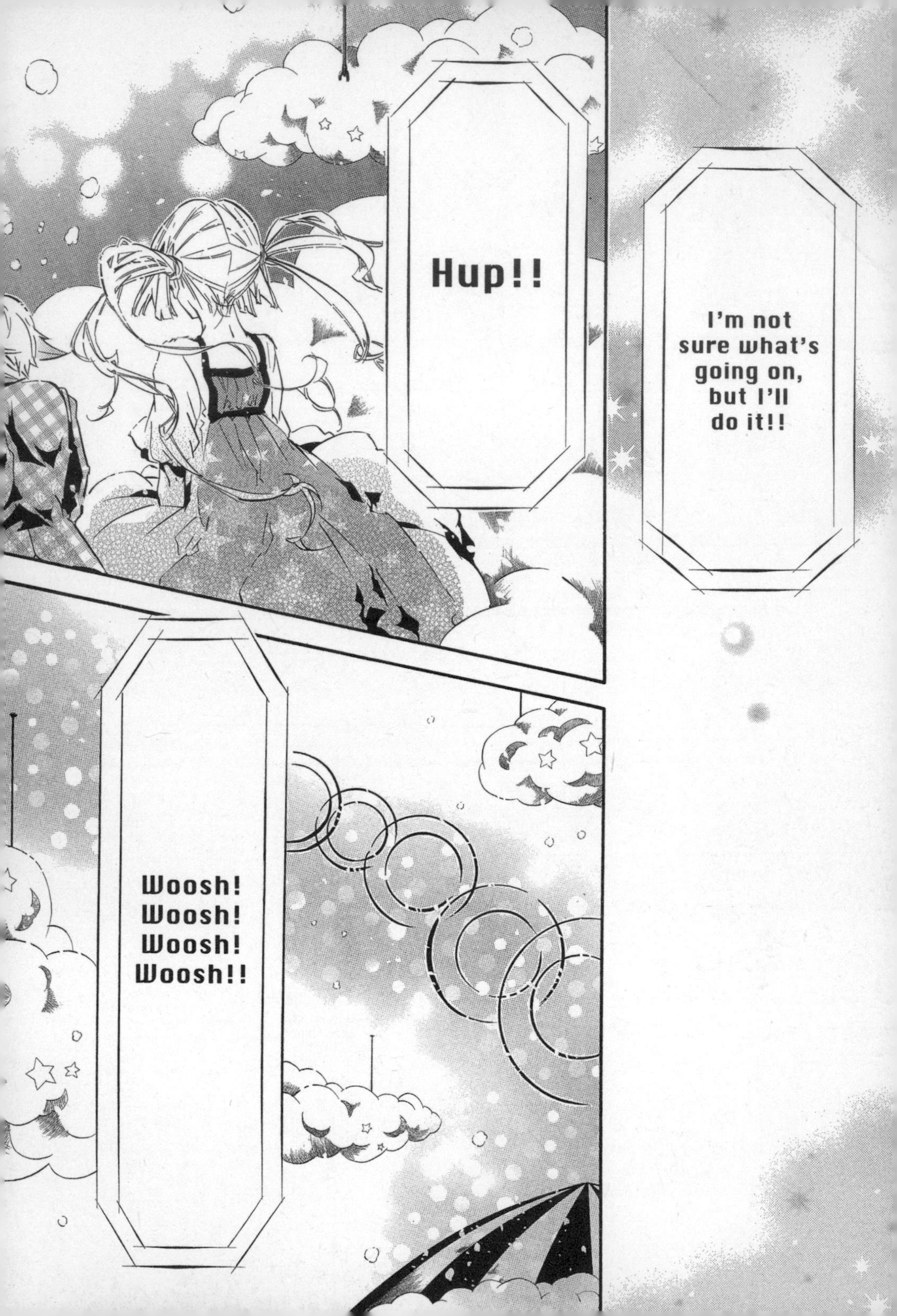
I'm not sure what's going on, but I'll do it!!
Hup!!
Woosh! Woosh! Woosh! Woosh!!

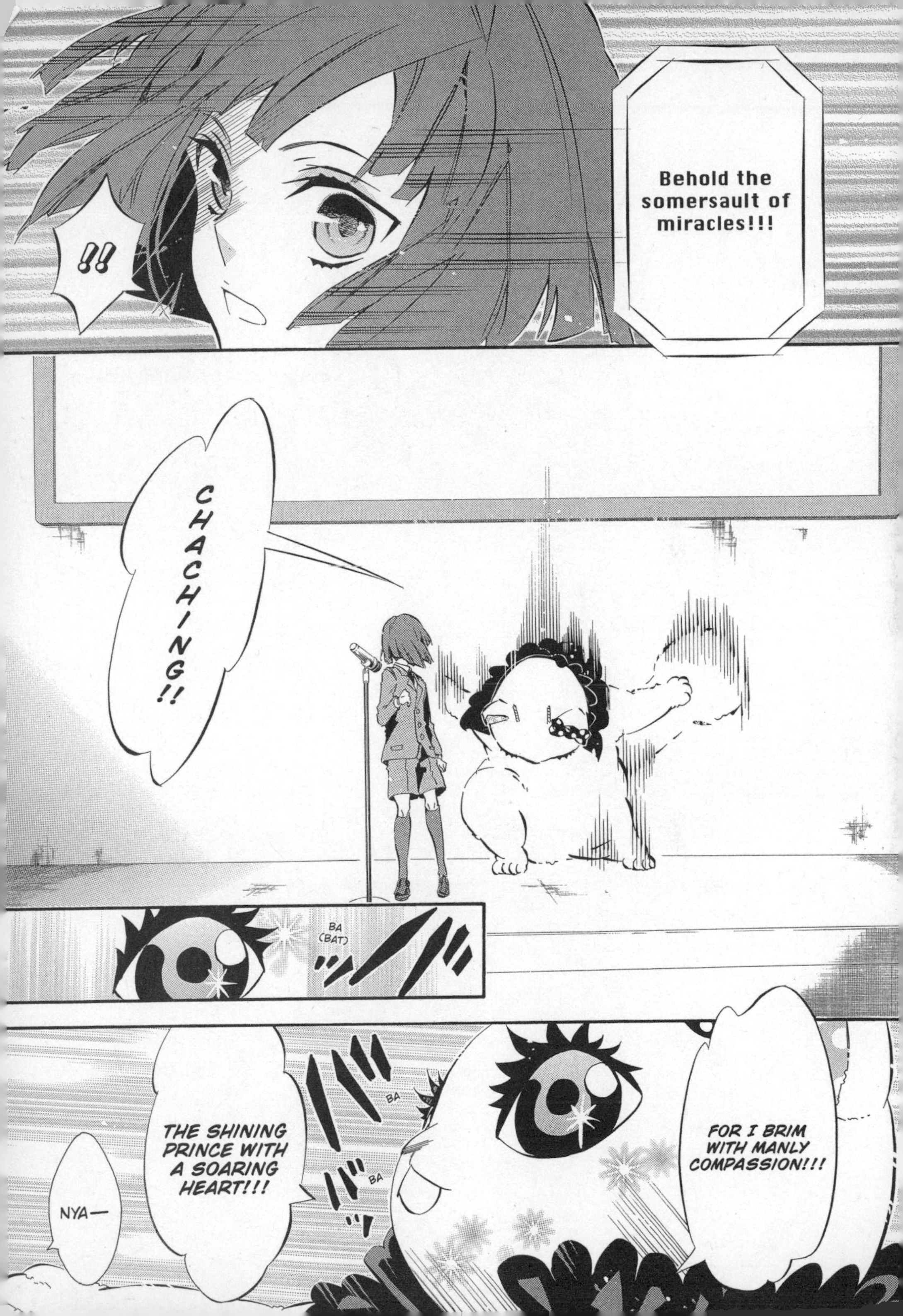

Behold the somersault of miracles!!!
!!
CHACHING!!
BA (BAT)
FOR I BRIM WITH MANLY COMPASSION!!!
BA
BA
THE SHINING PRINCE WITH A SOARING HEART!!!
NYA—

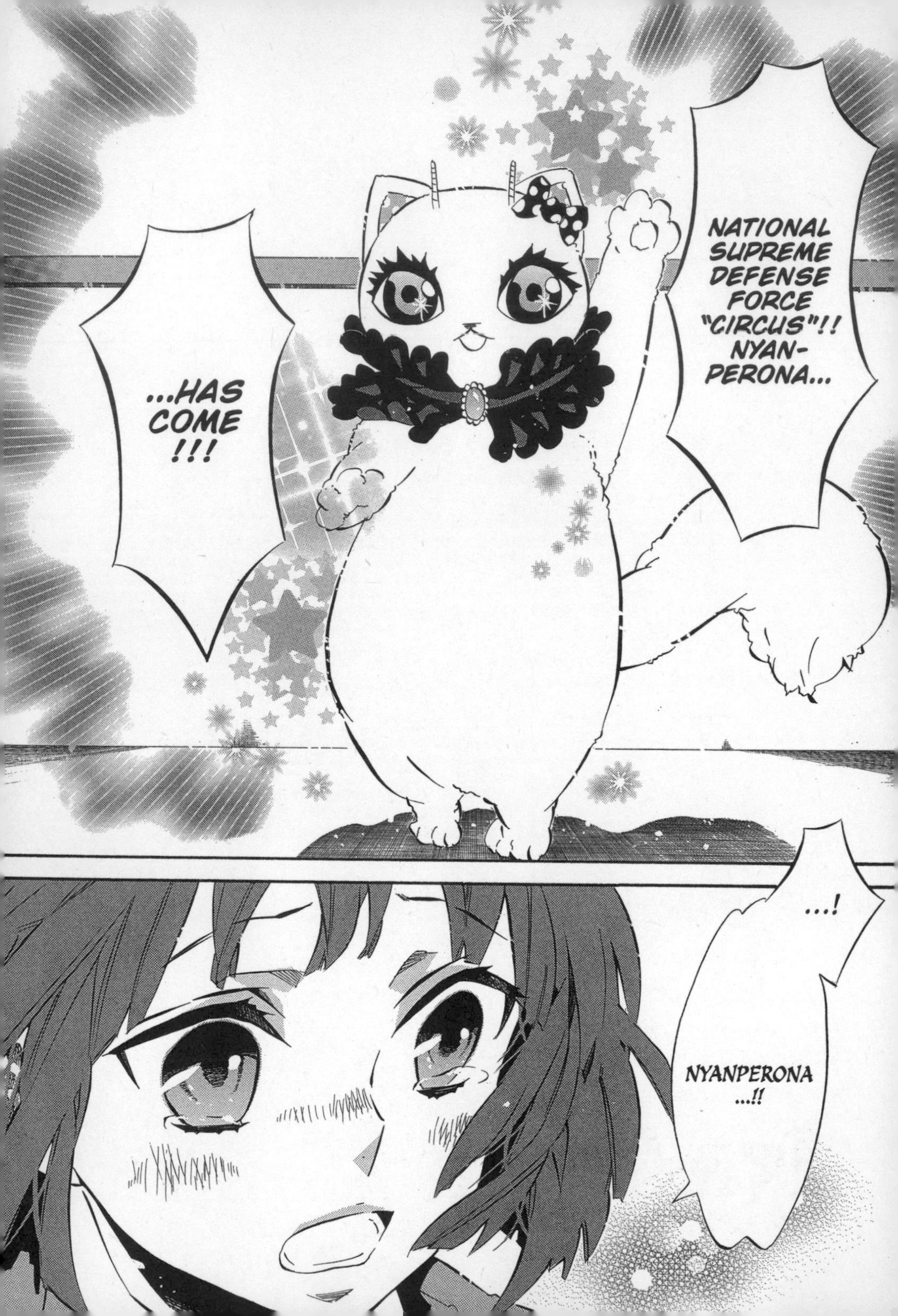
NATIONAL SUPREME DEFENSE FORCE "CIRCUS"!! NYAN-PERONA...
...HAS COME !!!
...!
NYANPERONA ...!!

KARNEVAL

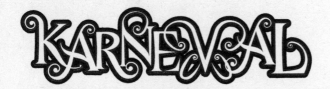

KARNEVAL

Score 71: Unmelting Snow

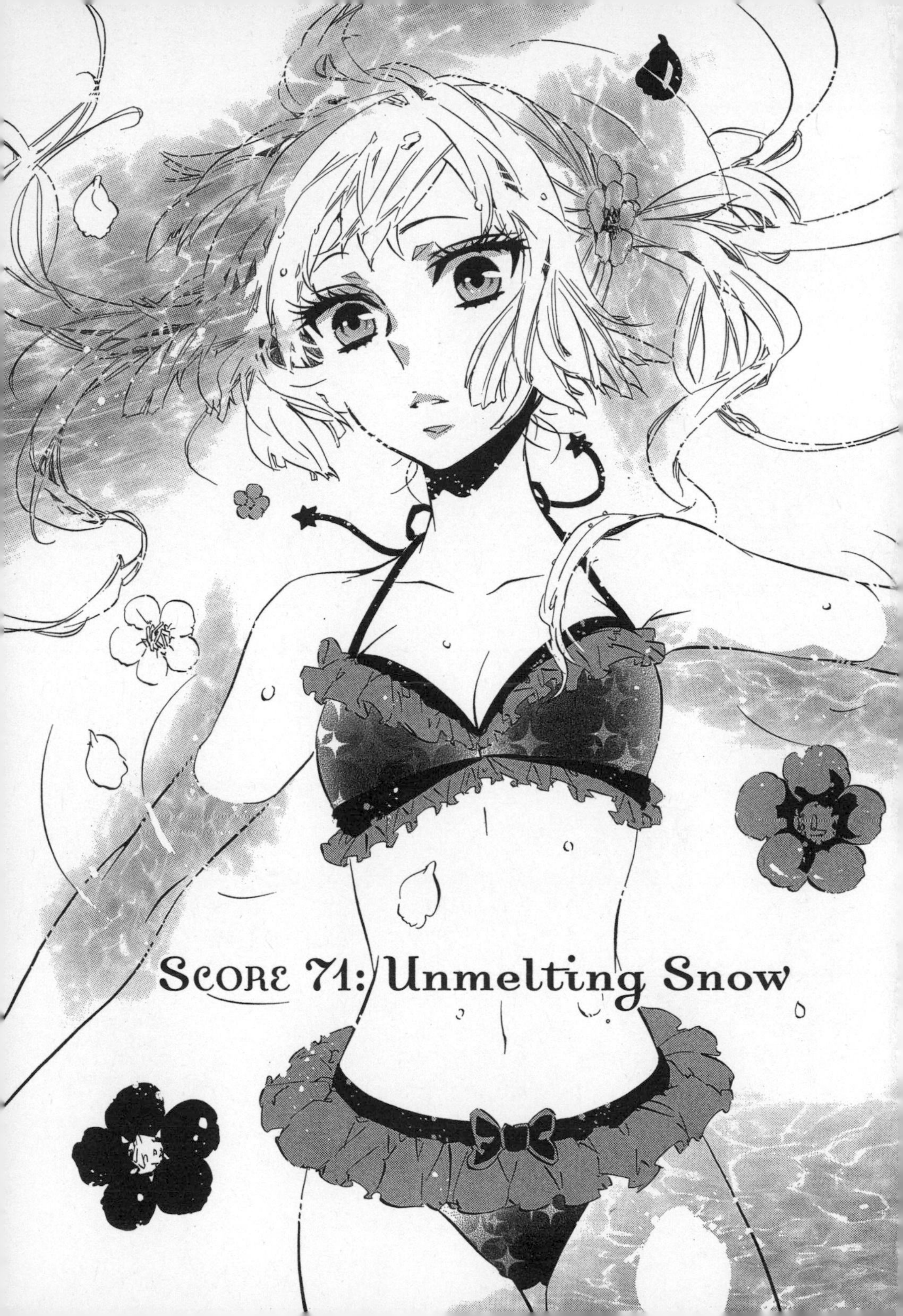

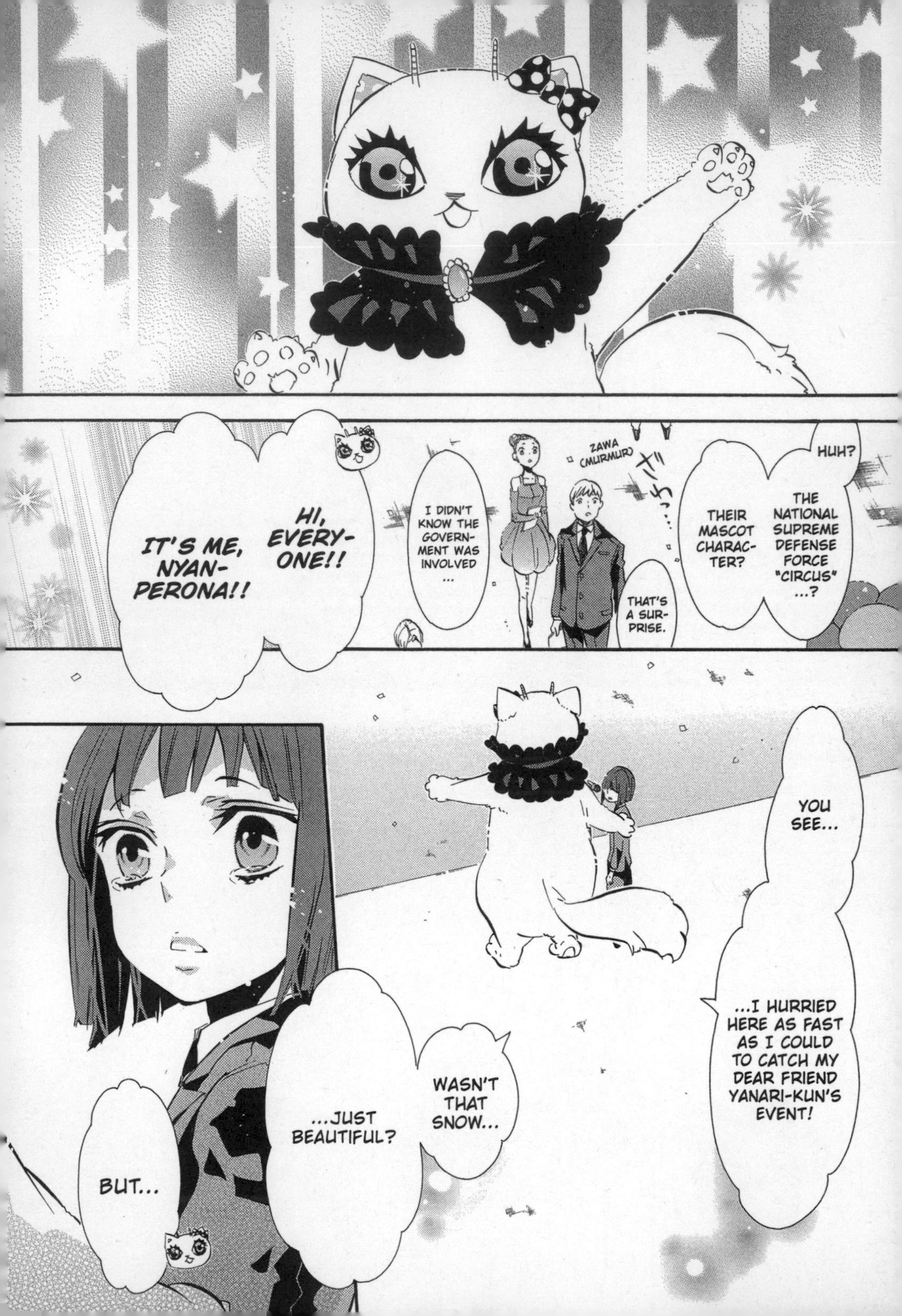
HUH?
THE NATIONAL SUPREME DEFENSE FORCE "CIRCUS" ...?
THEIR MASCOT CHARACTER?
ZAWA (MURMUR)
THAT'S A SURPRISE.
I DIDN'T KNOW THE GOVERNMENT WAS INVOLVED ...
HI, EVERYONE!!
IT'S ME, NYAN-PERONA!!
YOU SEE...
...I HURRIED HERE AS FAST AS I COULD TO CATCH MY DEAR FRIEND YANARI-KUN'S EVENT!
WASN'T THAT SNOW...
...JUST BEAUTIFUL?
BUT...

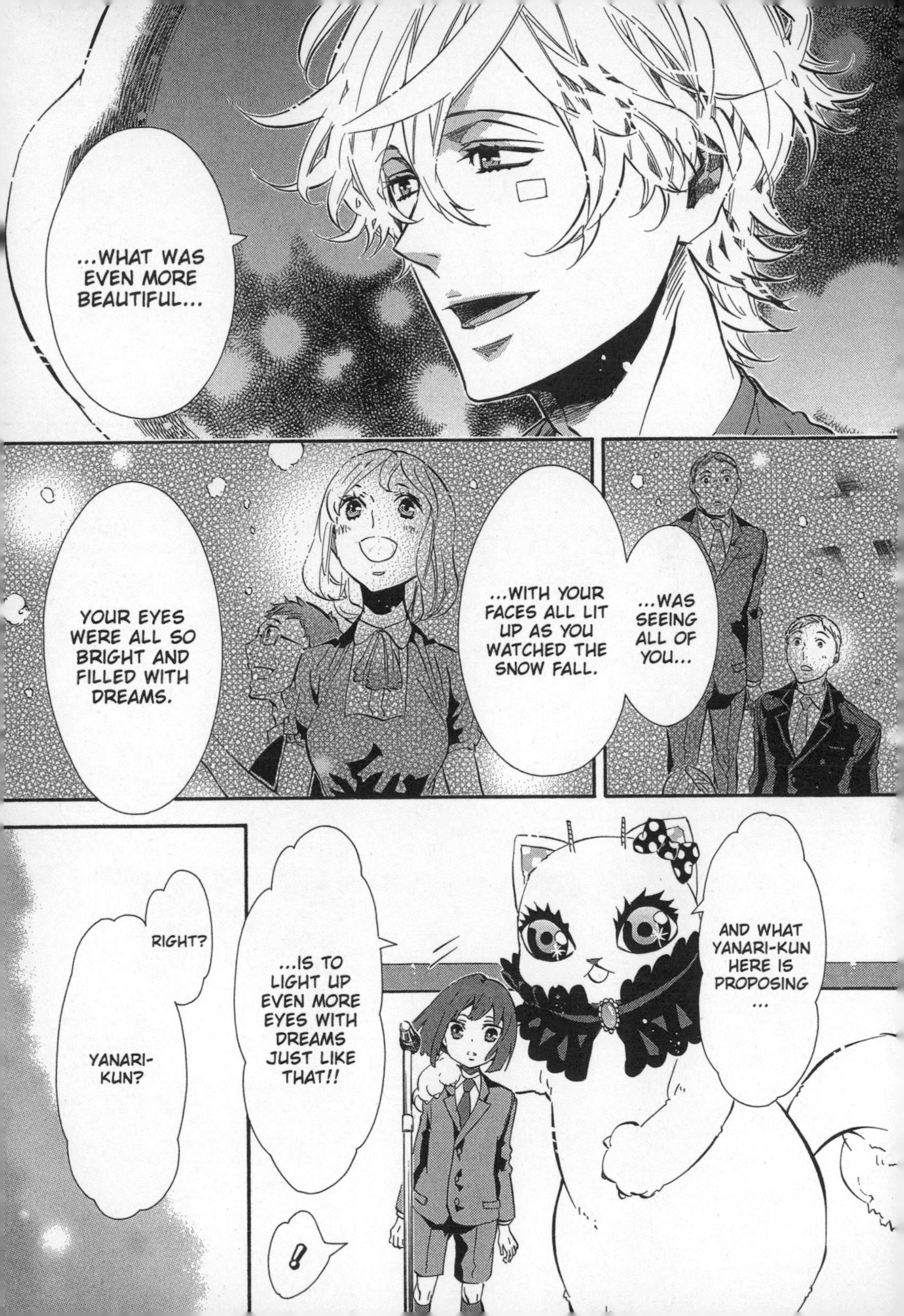
...WHAT WAS EVEN MORE BEAUTIFUL...
...WAS SEEING ALL OF YOU...
...WITH YOUR FACES ALL LIT UP AS YOU WATCHED THE SNOW FALL.
YOUR EYES WERE ALL SO BRIGHT AND FILLED WITH DREAMS.
AND WHAT YANARI-KUN HERE IS PROPOSING ...
...IS TO LIGHT UP EVEN MORE EYES WITH DREAMS JUST LIKE THAT!!
!
RIGHT?
YANARI-KUN?

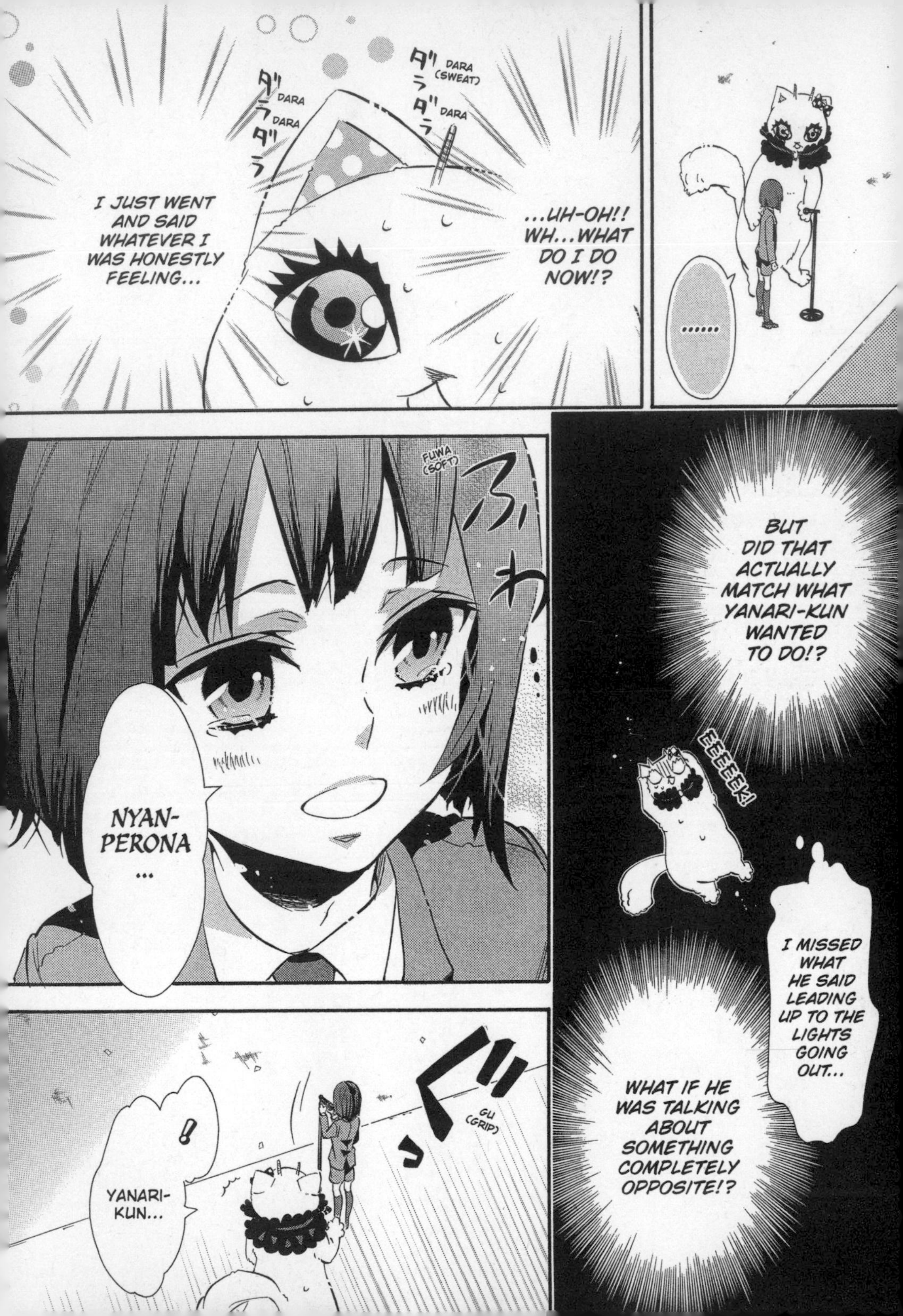
......
...UH-OH!! WH...WHAT DO I DO NOW!?
ダラ DARA (SWEAT)
ダラ DARA
ダラ DARA
ダラ DARA
I JUST WENT AND SAID WHATEVER I WAS HONESTLY FEELING...
BUT DID THAT ACTUALLY MATCH WHAT YANARI-KUN WANTED TO DO!?
EEEEEK!
I MISSED WHAT HE SAID LEADING UP TO THE LIGHTS GOING OUT...
WHAT IF HE WAS TALKING ABOUT SOMETHING COMPLETELY OPPOSITE!?
ふわ FUWA (SOFT)
NYAN-PERONA ...
ぐっ GU (GRIP)
!
YANARI-KUN...

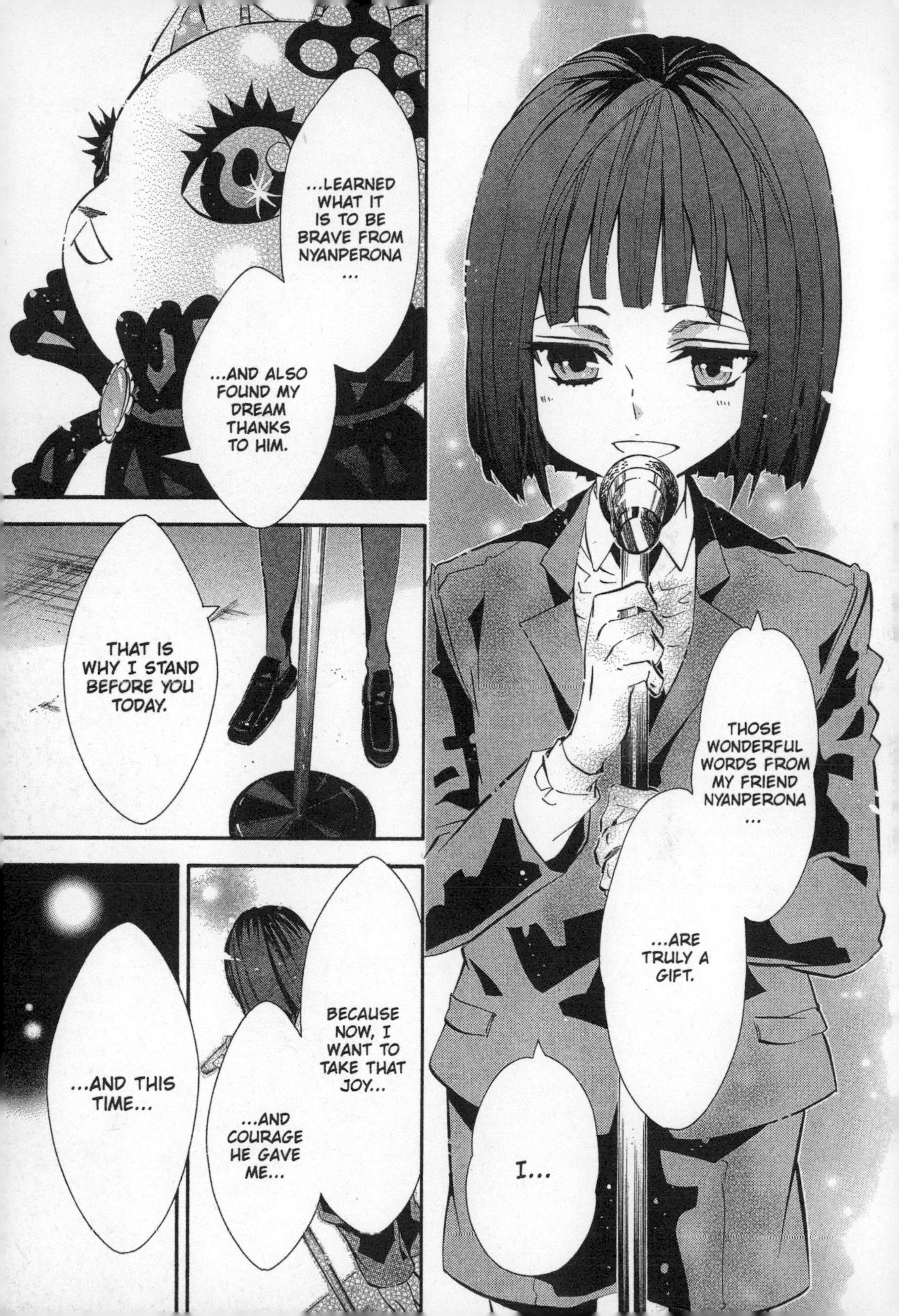
THOSE WONDERFUL WORDS FROM MY FRIEND NYANPERONA ...
...ARE TRULY A GIFT.
I...
...LEARNED WHAT IT IS TO BE BRAVE FROM NYANPERONA ...
...AND ALSO FOUND MY DREAM THANKS TO HIM.
THAT IS WHY I STAND BEFORE YOU TODAY.
BECAUSE NOW, I WANT TO TAKE THAT JOY...
...AND COURAGE HE GAVE ME...
...AND THIS TIME...

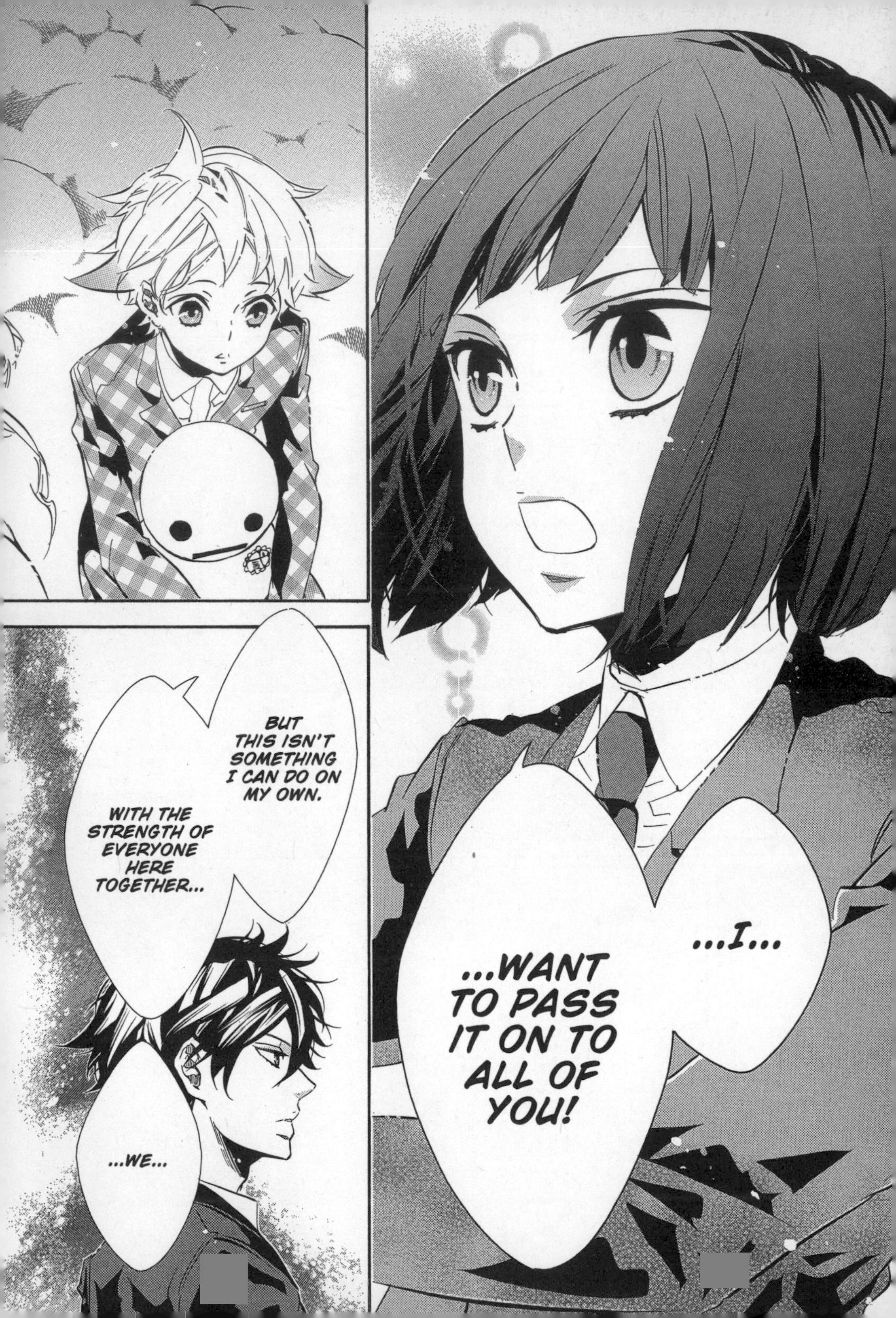
...I...
...WANT TO PASS IT ON TO ALL OF YOU!
BUT THIS ISN'T SOMETHING I CAN DO ON MY OWN.
WITH THE STRENGTH OF EVERYONE HERE TOGETHER...
...WE...

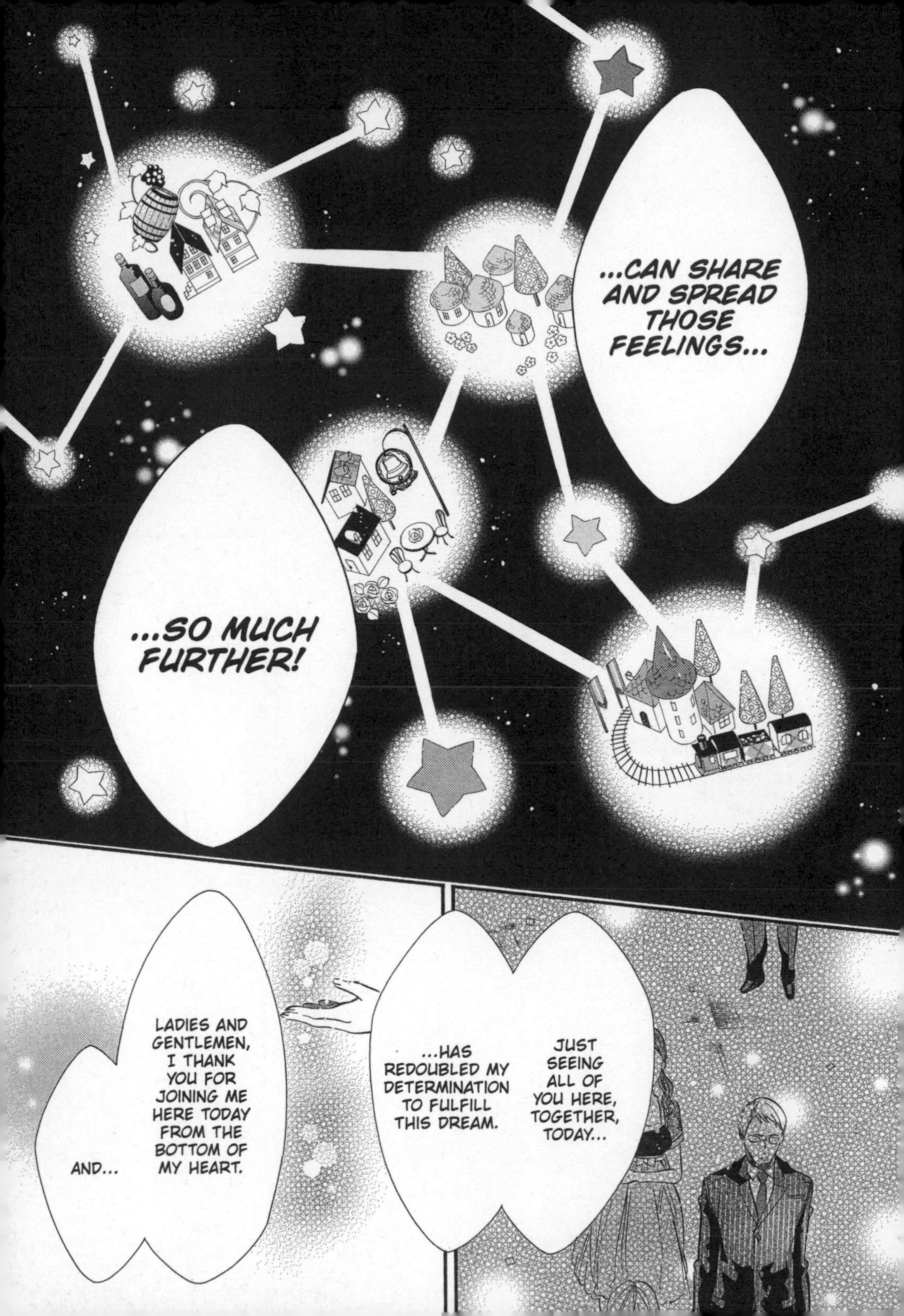
...CAN SHARE AND SPREAD THOSE FEELINGS...
...SO MUCH FURTHER!
JUST SEEING ALL OF YOU HERE, TOGETHER, TODAY...
...HAS REDOUBLED MY DETERMINATION TO FULFILL THIS DREAM.
LADIES AND GENTLEMEN, I THANK YOU FOR JOINING ME HERE TODAY FROM THE BOTTOM OF MY HEART.
AND...

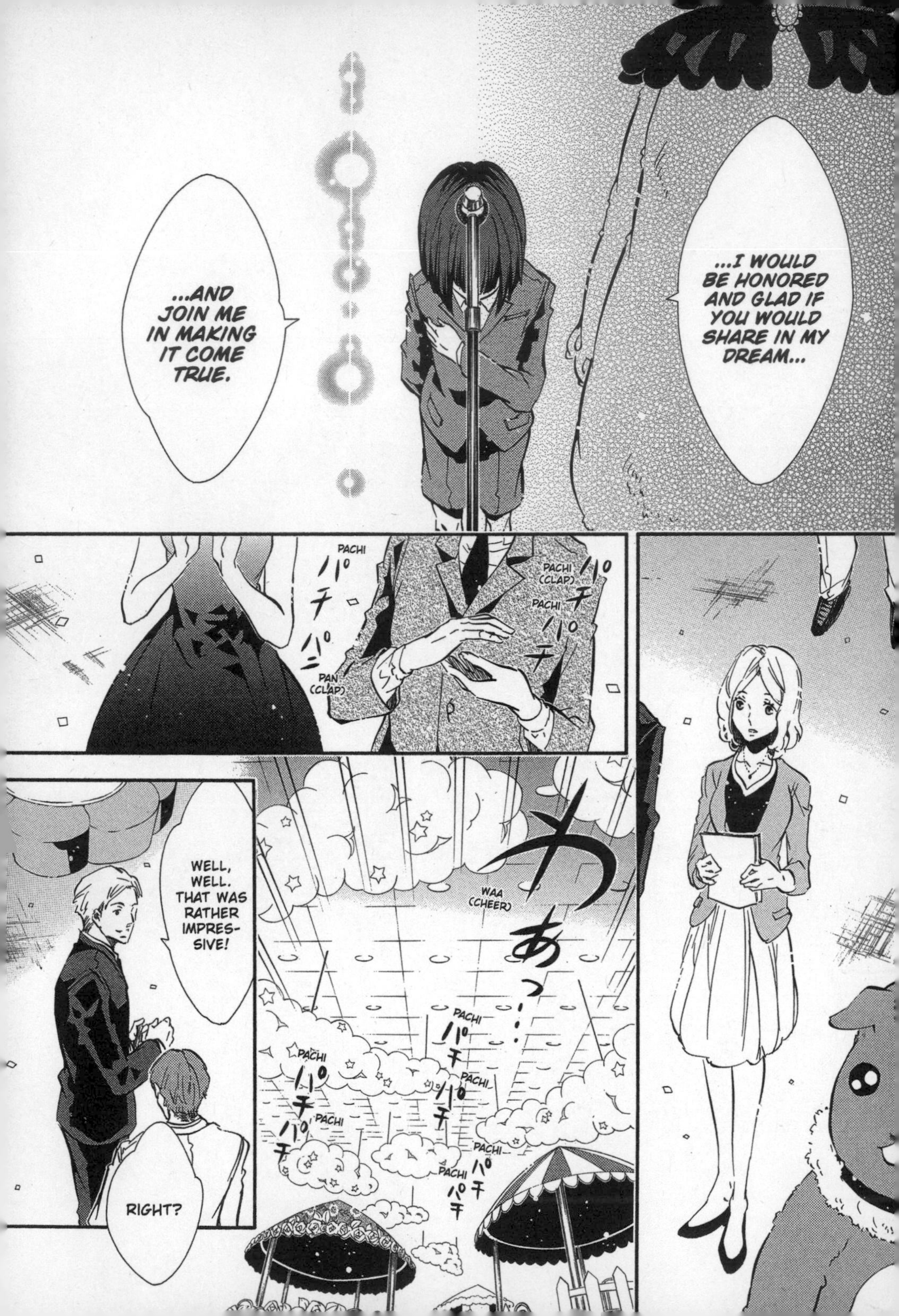
...I WOULD BE HONORED AND GLAD IF YOU WOULD SHARE IN MY DREAM...
...AND JOIN ME IN MAKING IT COME TRUE.
PACHI (CLAP) パチ
PACHI パチ
PACHI パチ
PAN (CLAP) パン
WAA (CHEER) わあっ…
PACHI パチ
PACHI パチ
PACHI パチ
PACHI パチ
PACHI パチ
PACHI パチ
WELL, WELL. THAT WAS RATHER IMPRES-SIVE!
RIGHT?

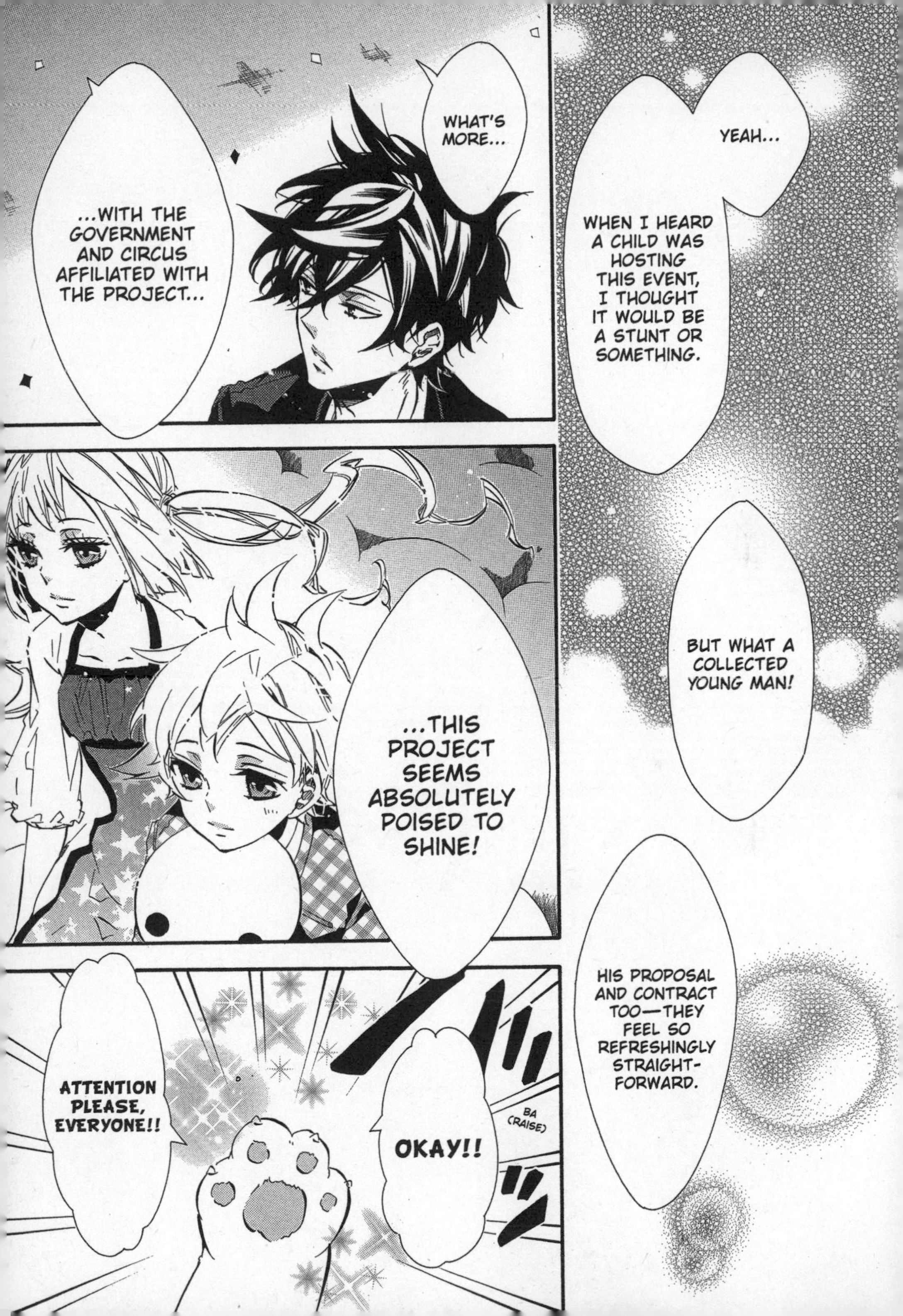
YEAH...
WHEN I HEARD A CHILD WAS HOSTING THIS EVENT, I THOUGHT IT WOULD BE A STUNT OR SOMETHING.
BUT WHAT A COLLECTED YOUNG MAN!
HIS PROPOSAL AND CONTRACT TOO—THEY FEEL SO REFRESHINGLY STRAIGHT-FORWARD.
WHAT'S MORE...
...WITH THE GOVERNMENT AND CIRCUS AFFILIATED WITH THE PROJECT...
...THIS PROJECT SEEMS ABSOLUTELY POISED TO SHINE!
OKAY!!
BA (RAISE)
ATTENTION PLEASE, EVERYONE!!

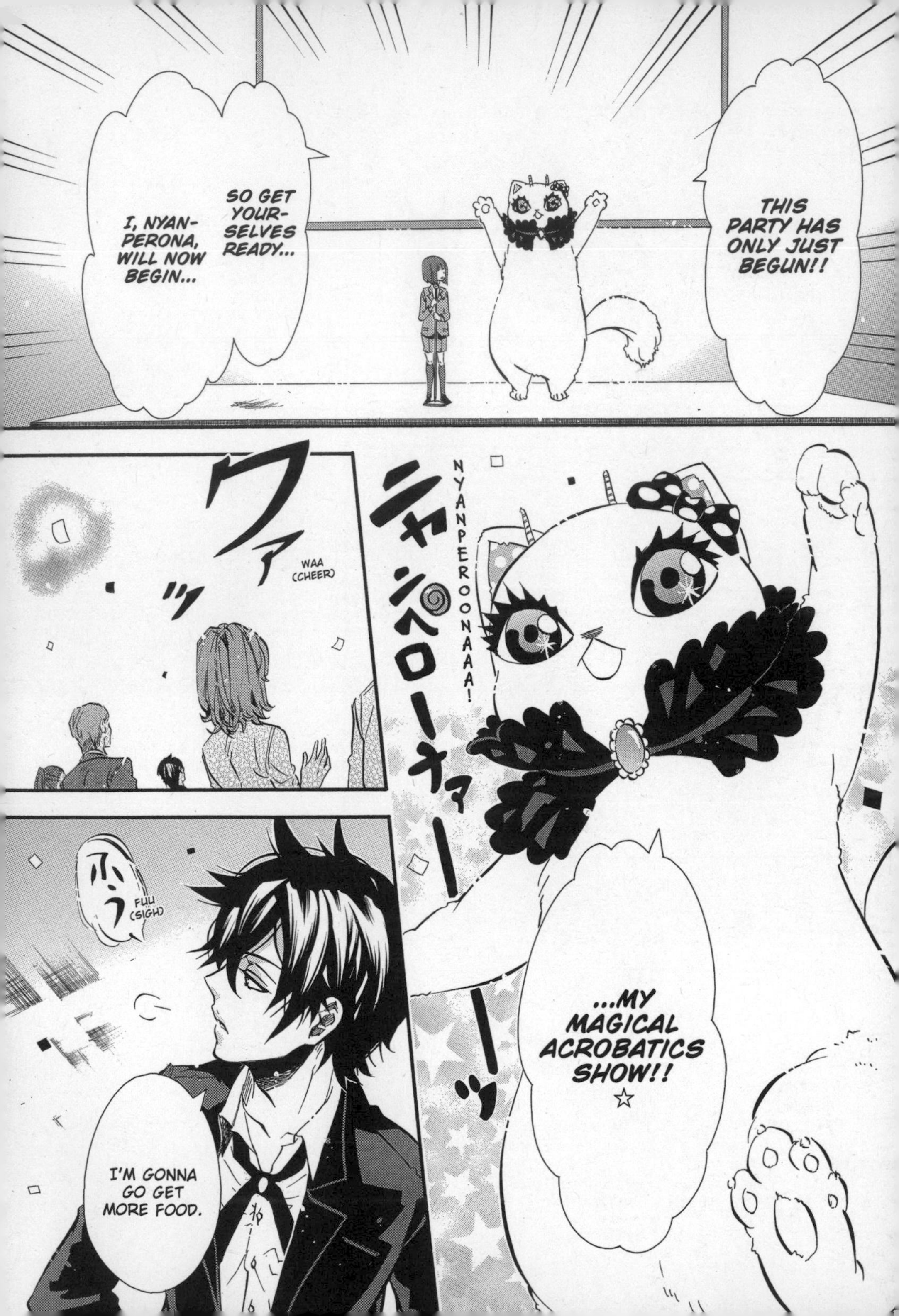

THIS PARTY HAS ONLY JUST BEGUN!!
SO GET YOURSELVES READY...
I, NYAN-PERONA, WILL NOW BEGIN...
ニャンペローナァーーッ
NYANPEROONAAA!
...MY MAGICAL ACROBATICS SHOW!! ☆
ワァッ
WAA (CHEER)
ふっ
FUU (SIGH)
I'M GONNA GO GET MORE FOOD.

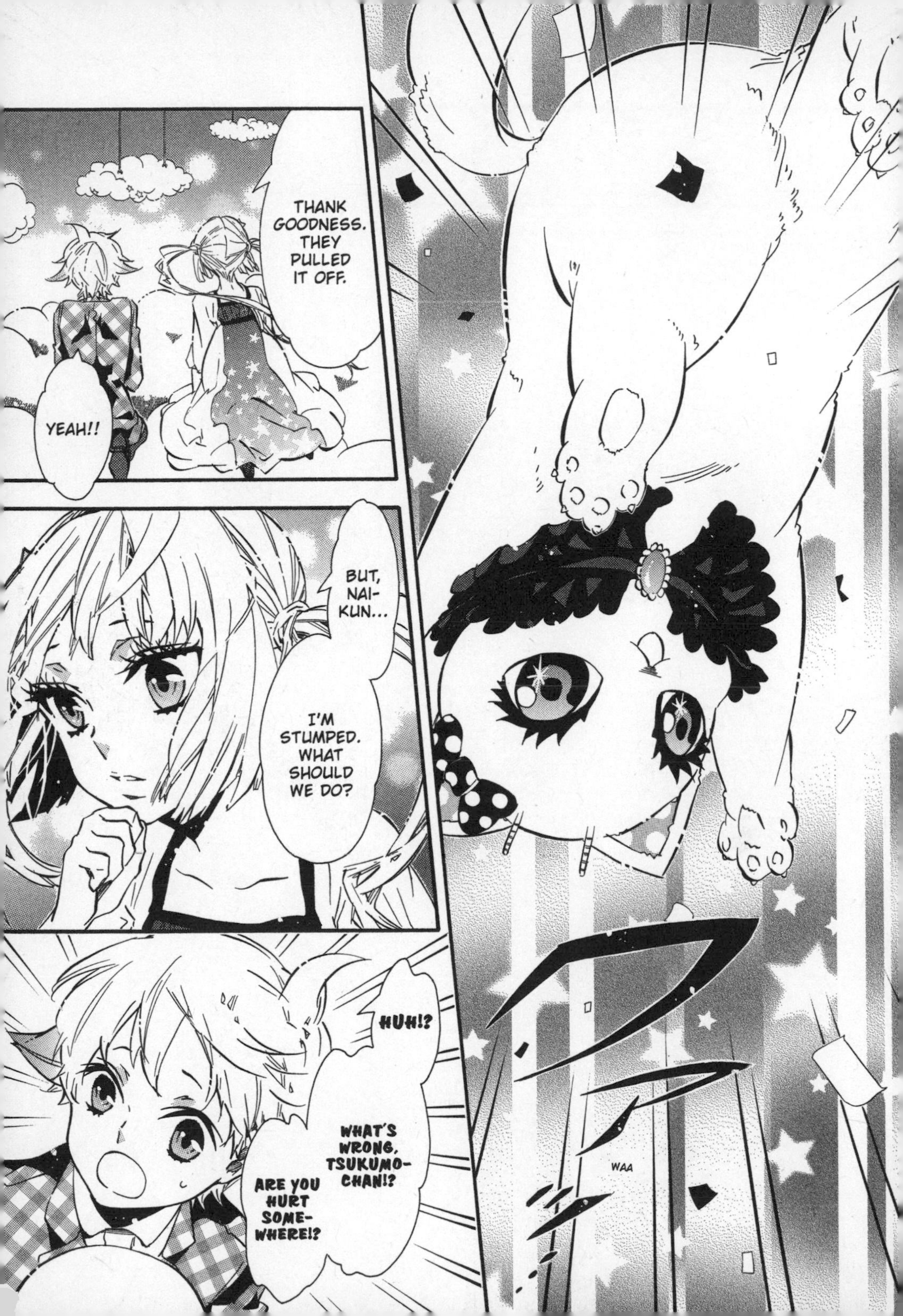
WAA
THANK GOODNESS. THEY PULLED IT OFF.
YEAH!!
BUT, NAI-KUN...
I'M STUMPED. WHAT SHOULD WE DO?
HUH!?
WHAT'S WRONG, TSUKUMO-CHAN!?
ARE YOU HURT SOME-WHERE!?

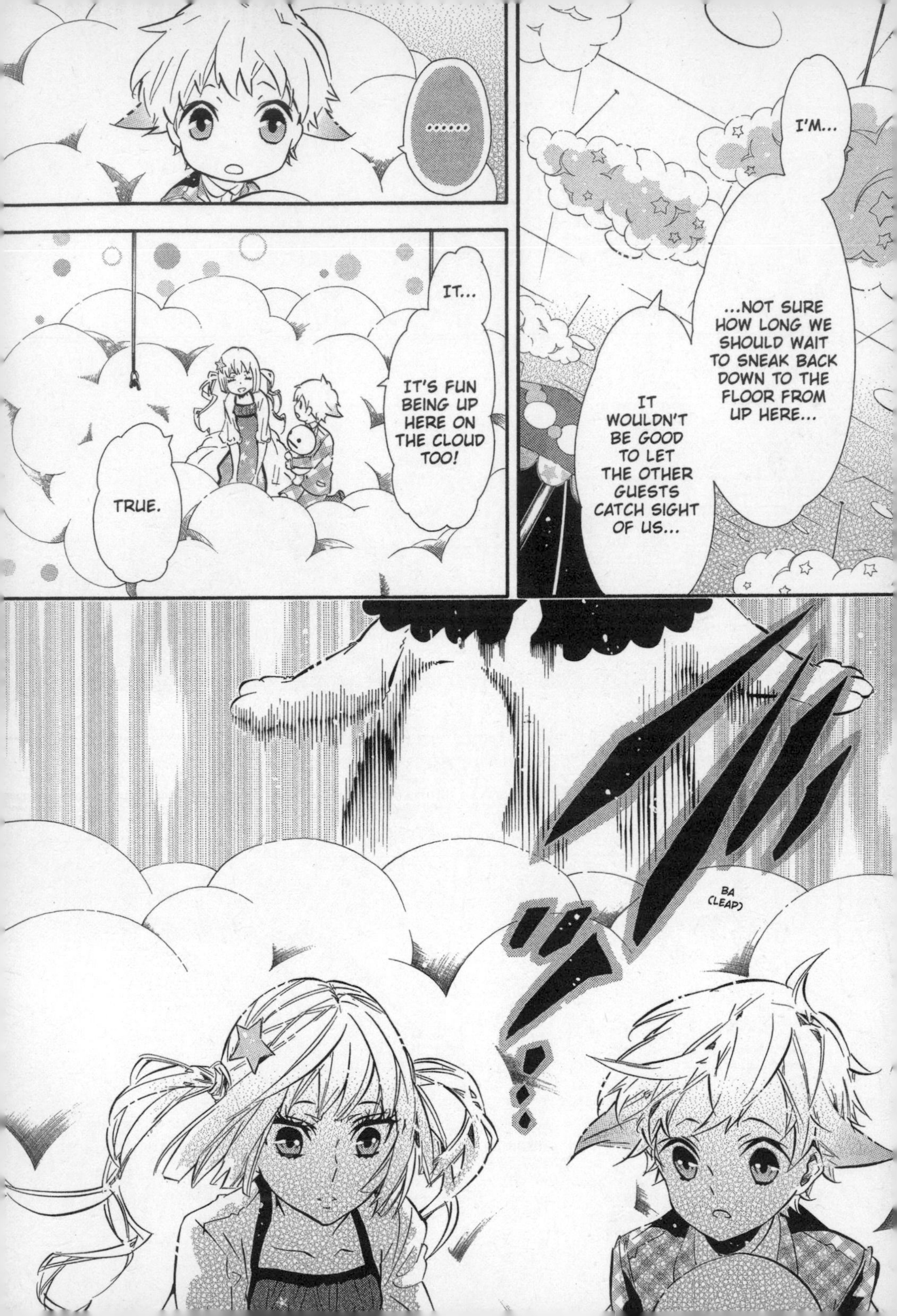
I'M...
...NOT SURE HOW LONG WE SHOULD WAIT TO SNEAK BACK DOWN TO THE FLOOR FROM UP HERE...
IT WOULDN'T BE GOOD TO LET THE OTHER GUESTS CATCH SIGHT OF US...
......
IT...
IT'S FUN BEING UP HERE ON THE CLOUD TOO!
TRUE.
BA (LEAP)

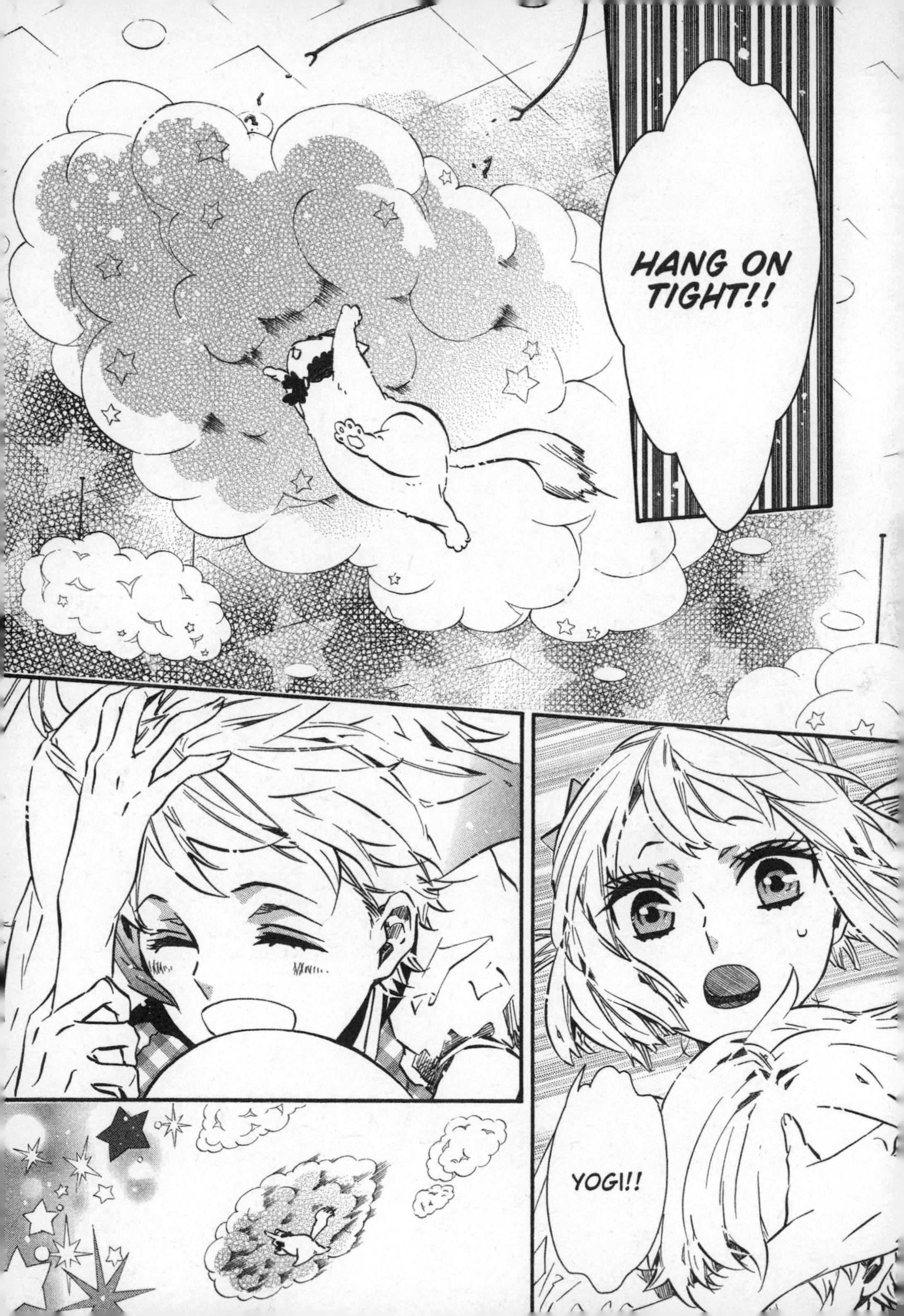
HANG ON TIGHT!!
YOGI!!

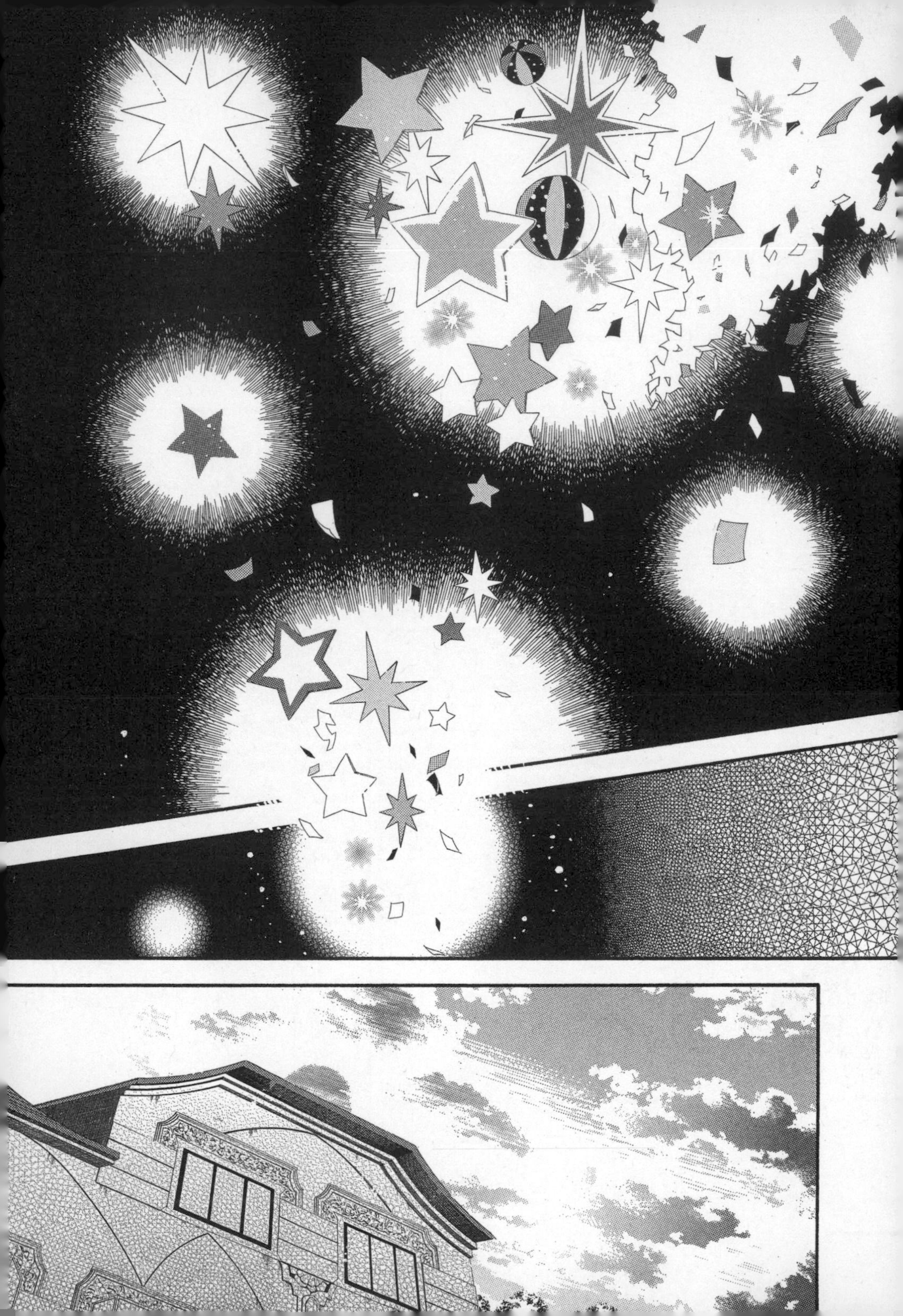

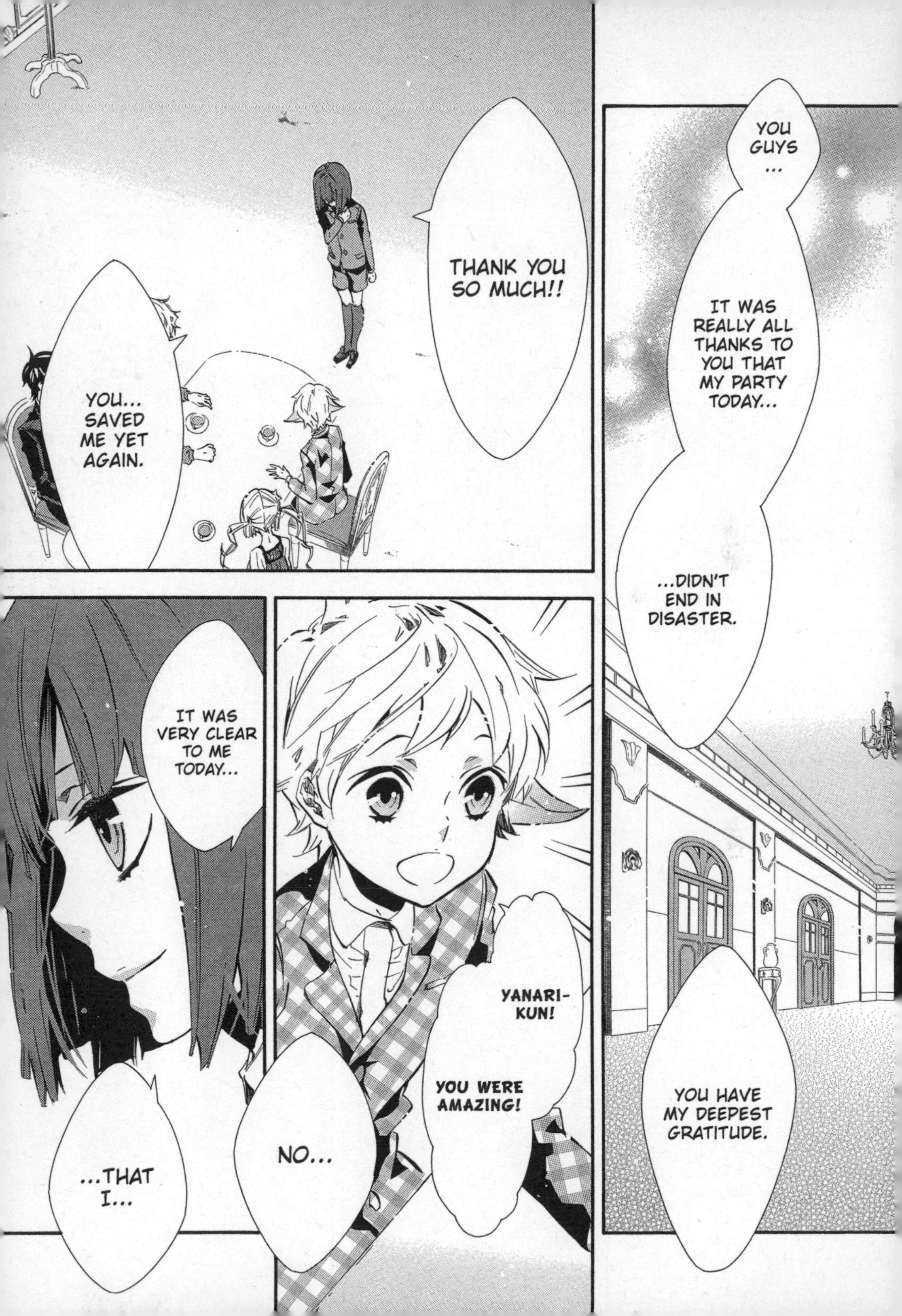
YOU GUYS ...
IT WAS REALLY ALL THANKS TO YOU THAT MY PARTY TODAY...
...DIDN'T END IN DISASTER.
YOU HAVE MY DEEPEST GRATITUDE.
THANK YOU SO MUCH!!
YOU... SAVED ME YET AGAIN.
YANARI-KUN!
YOU WERE AMAZING!
NO...
IT WAS VERY CLEAR TO ME TODAY...
...THAT I...

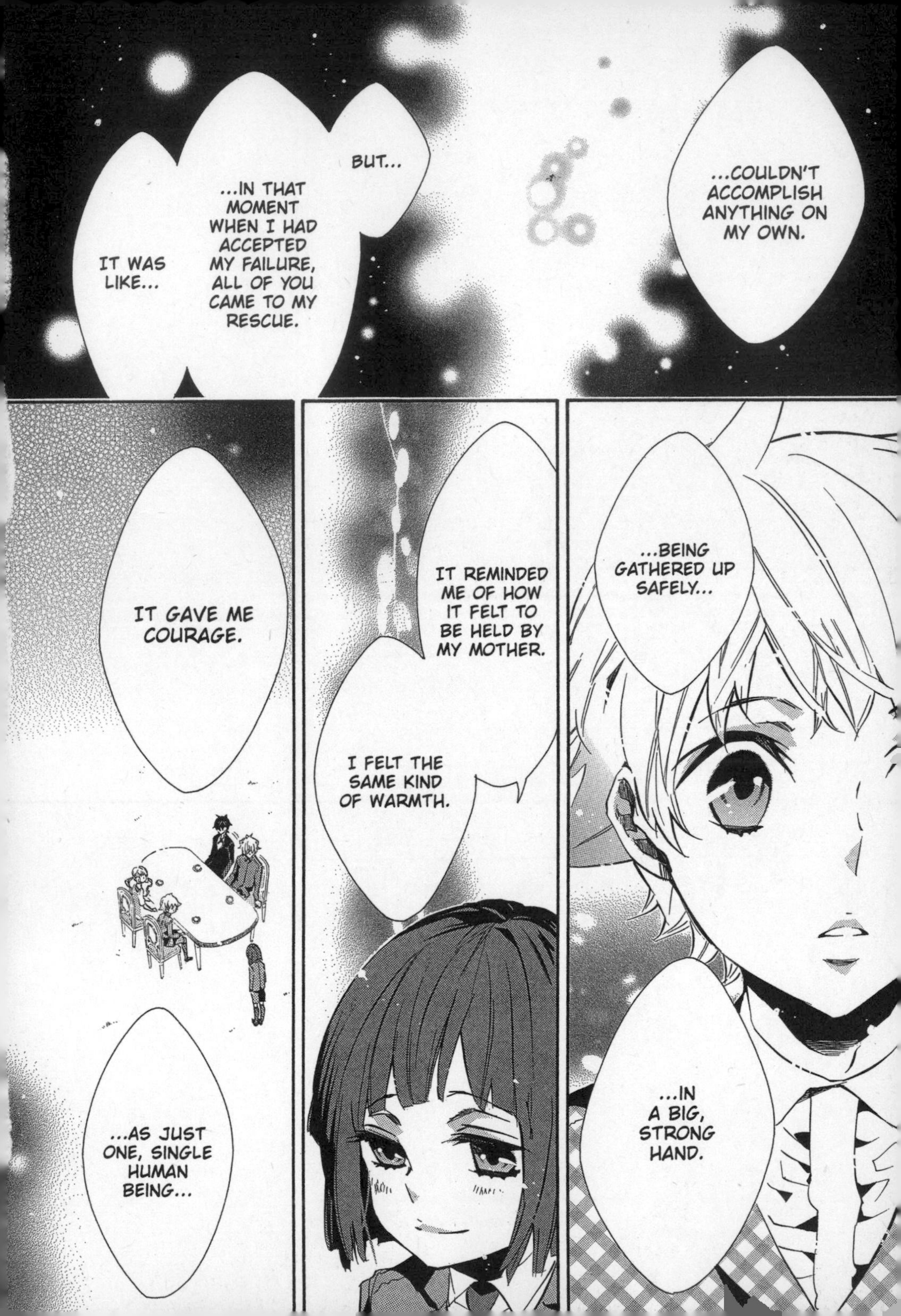
...COULDN'T ACCOMPLISH ANYTHING ON MY OWN.
BUT...
...IN THAT MOMENT WHEN I HAD ACCEPTED MY FAILURE, ALL OF YOU CAME TO MY RESCUE.
IT WAS LIKE...
...BEING GATHERED UP SAFELY...
...IN A BIG, STRONG HAND.
IT REMINDED ME OF HOW IT FELT TO BE HELD BY MY MOTHER.
I FELT THE SAME KIND OF WARMTH.
IT GAVE ME COURAGE.
...AS JUST ONE, SINGLE HUMAN BEING...

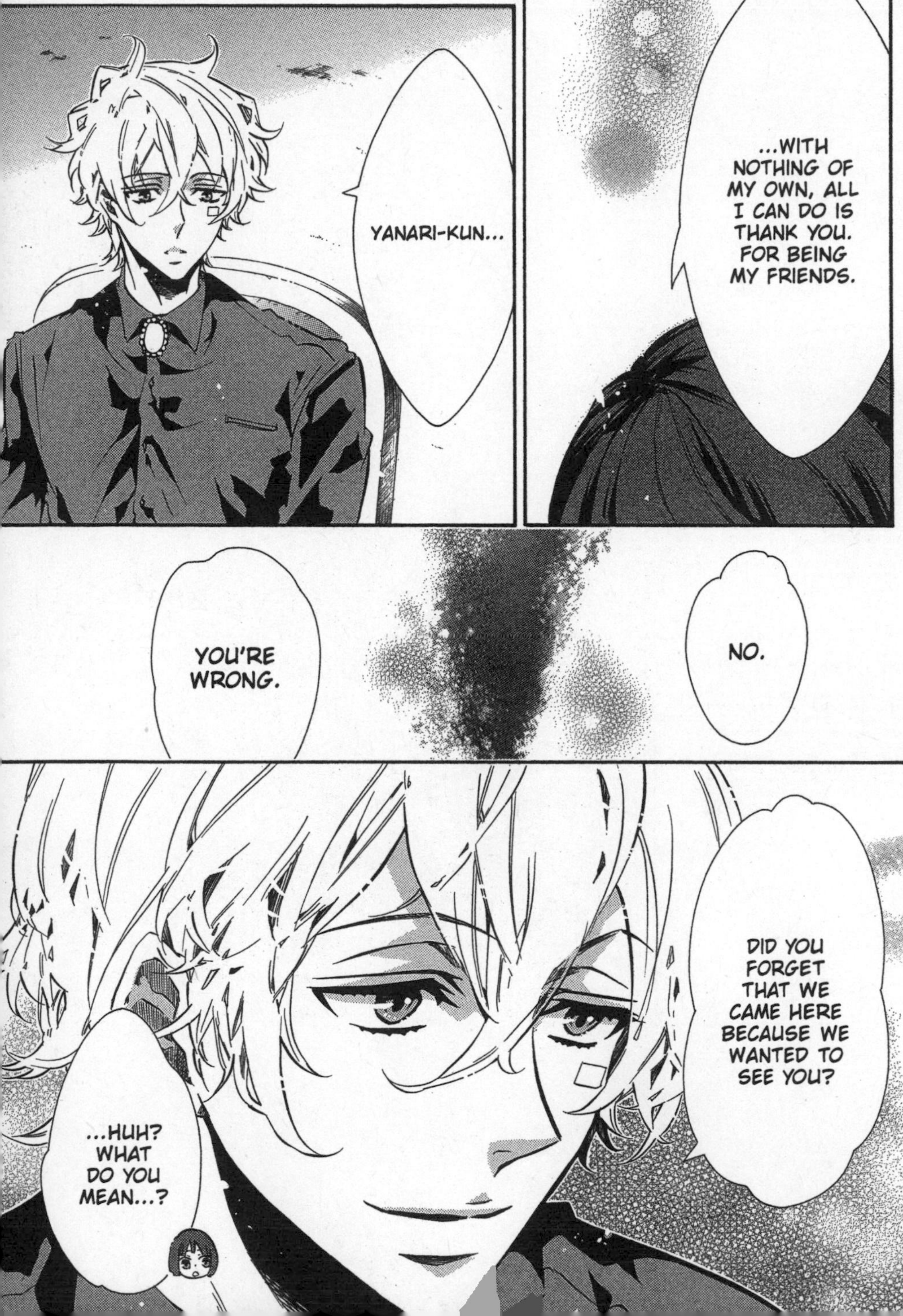
...WITH NOTHING OF MY OWN, ALL I CAN DO IS THANK YOU. FOR BEING MY FRIENDS.
YANARI-KUN...
NO.
YOU'RE WRONG.
DID YOU FORGET THAT WE CAME HERE BECAUSE WE WANTED TO SEE YOU?
...HUH? WHAT DO YOU MEAN...?

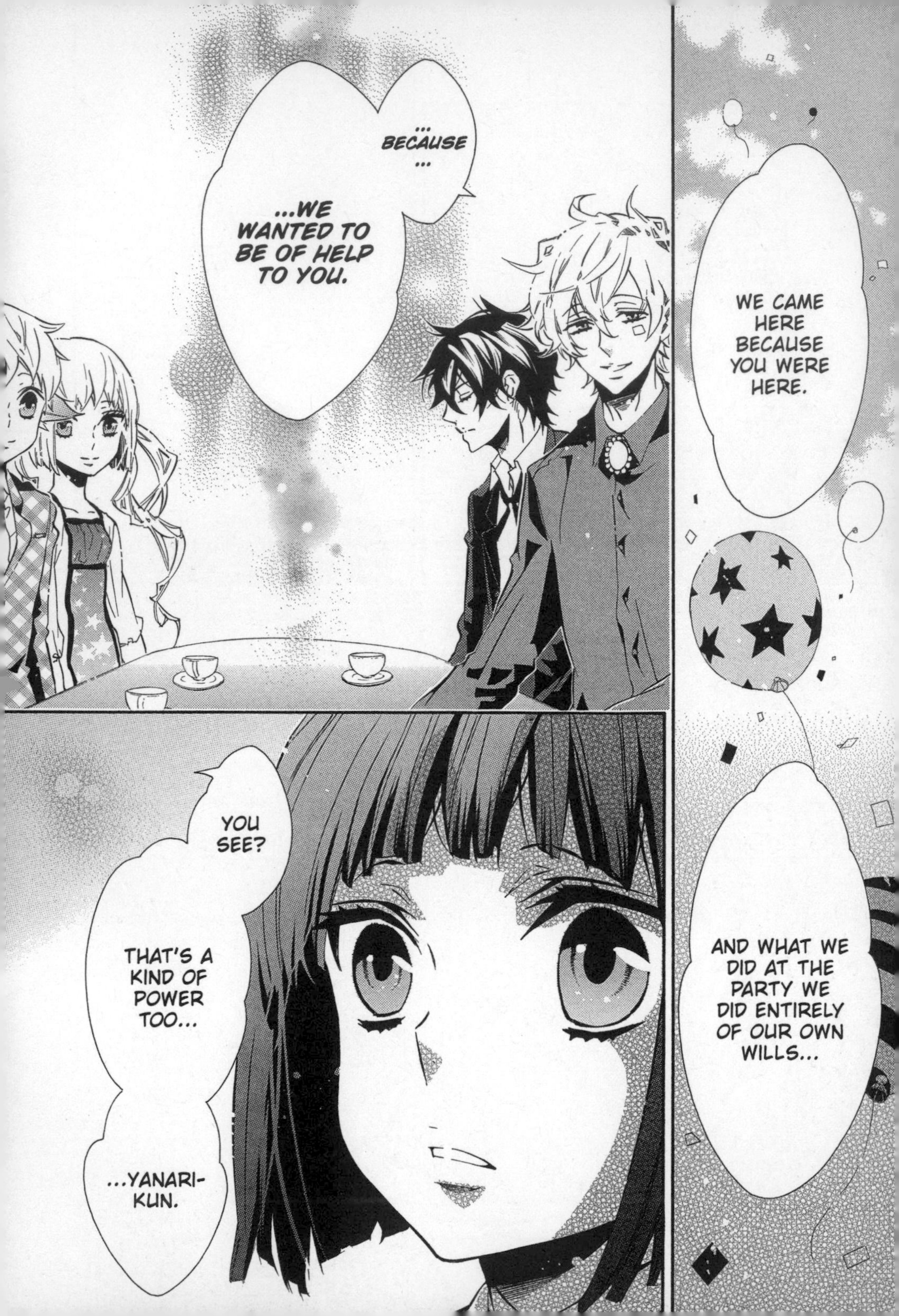
WE CAME HERE BECAUSE YOU WERE HERE.
AND WHAT WE DID AT THE PARTY WE DID ENTIRELY OF OUR OWN WILLS...
...BECAUSE...
...WE WANTED TO BE OF HELP TO YOU.
YOU SEE?
THAT'S A KIND OF POWER TOO...
...YANARI-KUN.

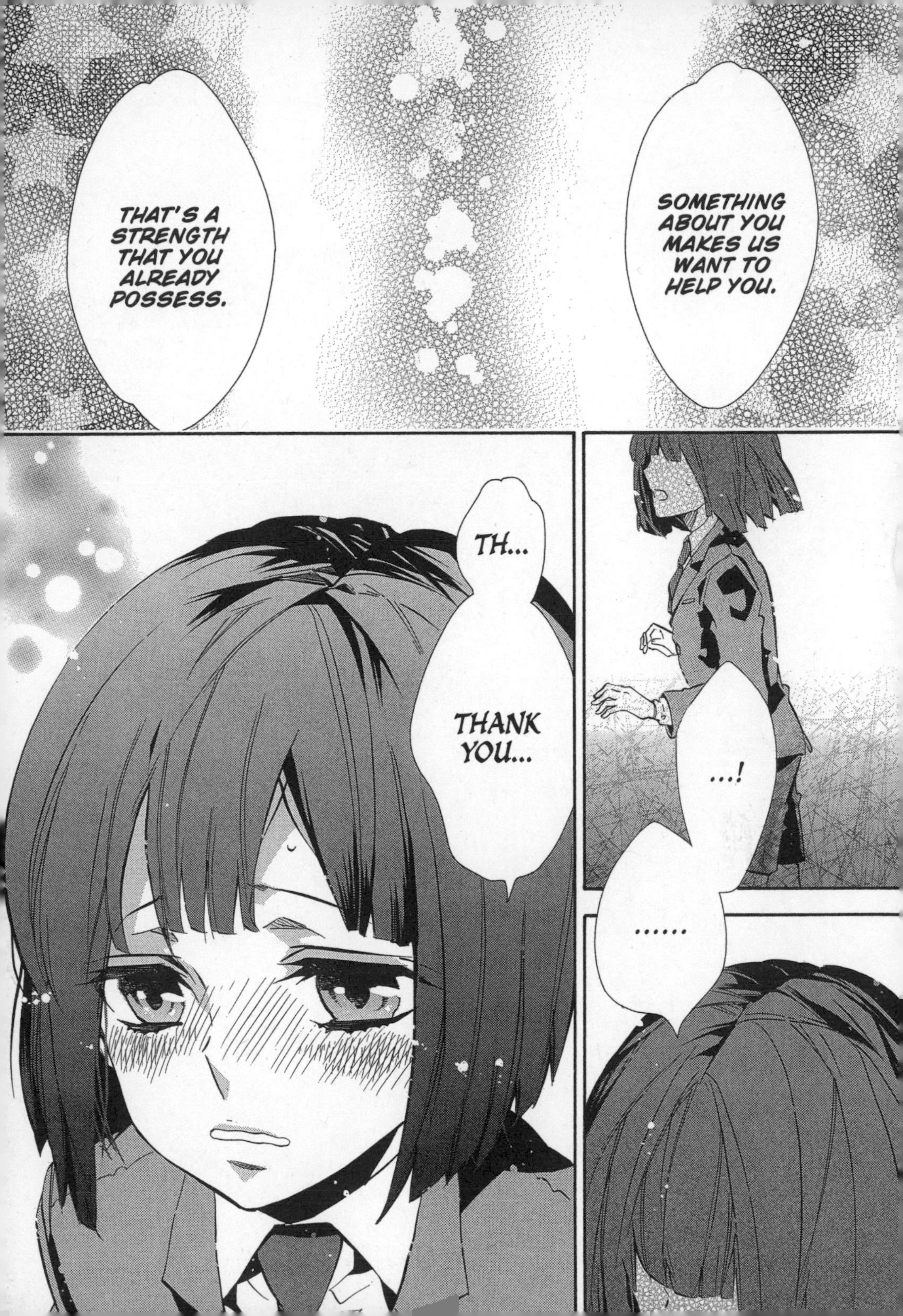
SOMETHING ABOUT YOU MAKES US WANT TO HELP YOU.
THAT'S A STRENGTH THAT YOU ALREADY POSSESS.
...!
......
TH...
THANK YOU...

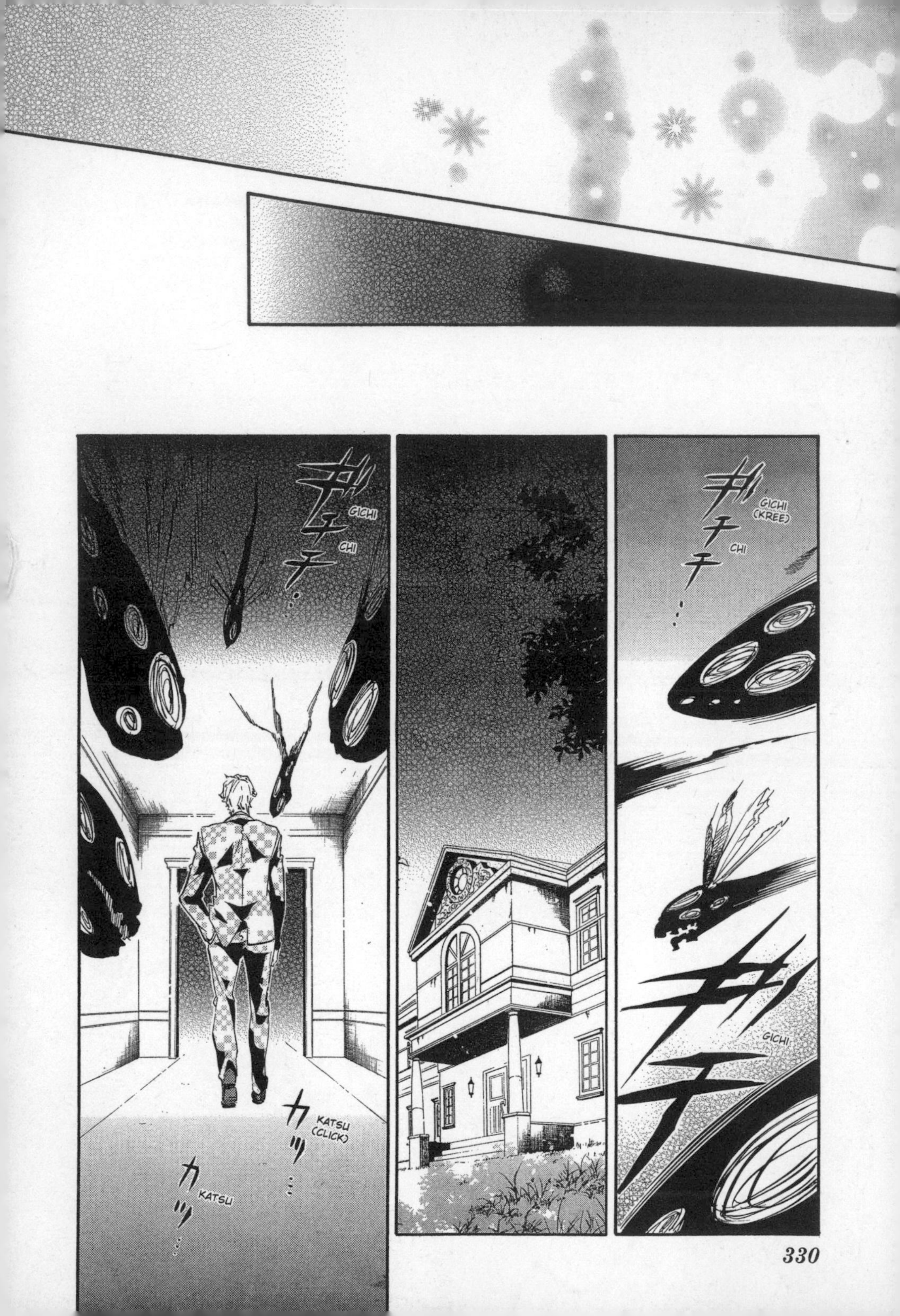
ギチチ…
GICHI (KREE)
CHI
ギチ
GICHI
ギチチ…
GICHI
CHI
カッ…
KATSU (CLICK)
カッ…
KATSU

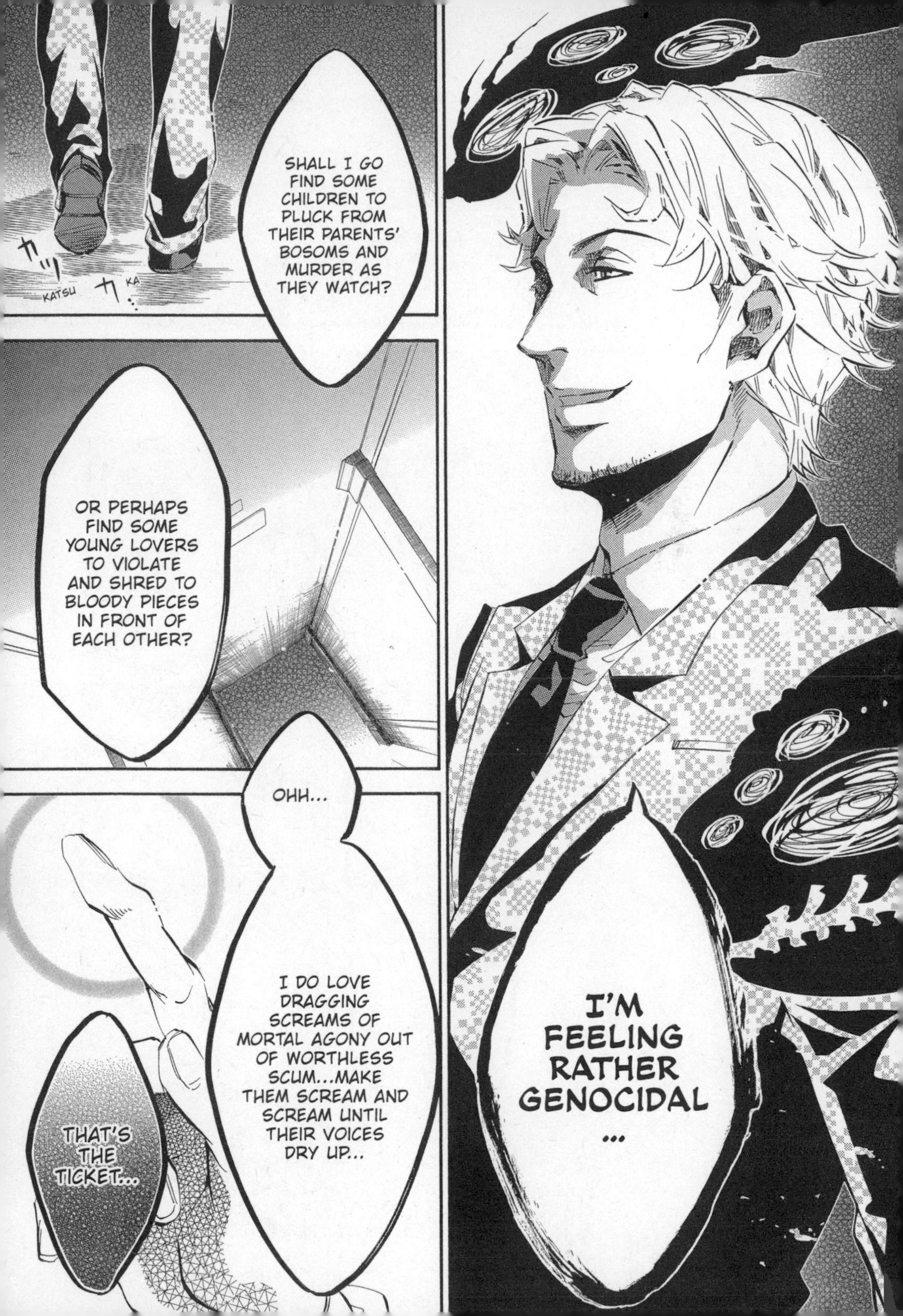
I'M FEELING RATHER GENOCIDAL ...
SHALL I GO FIND SOME CHILDREN TO PLUCK FROM THEIR PARENTS' BOSOMS AND MURDER AS THEY WATCH?
カツ
KATSU
カ
KA
OR PERHAPS FIND SOME YOUNG LOVERS TO VIOLATE AND SHRED TO BLOODY PIECES IN FRONT OF EACH OTHER?
OHH...
I DO LOVE DRAGGING SCREAMS OF MORTAL AGONY OUT OF WORTHLESS SCUM...MAKE THEM SCREAM AND SCREAM UNTIL THEIR VOICES DRY UP...
THAT'S THE TICKET...

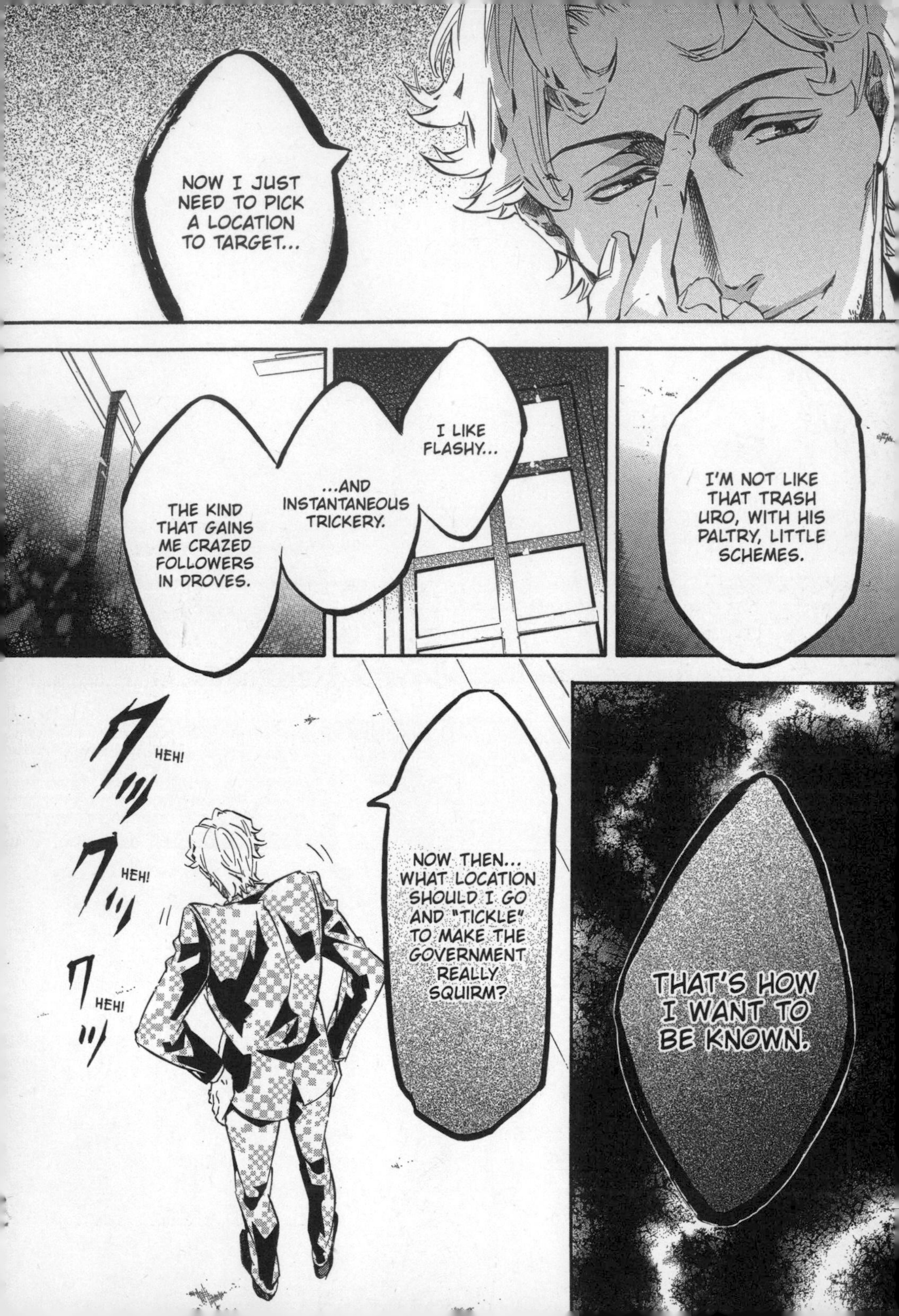

NOW I JUST NEED TO PICK A LOCATION TO TARGET...
I'M NOT LIKE THAT TRASH URO, WITH HIS PALTRY, LITTLE SCHEMES.
I LIKE FLASHY...
...AND INSTANTANEOUS TRICKERY.
THE KIND THAT GAINS ME CRAZED FOLLOWERS IN DROVES.
THAT'S HOW I WANT TO BE KNOWN.
NOW THEN... WHAT LOCATION SHOULD I GO AND "TICKLE" TO MAKE THE GOVERNMENT REALLY SQUIRM?
HEH!
HEH!
HEH!

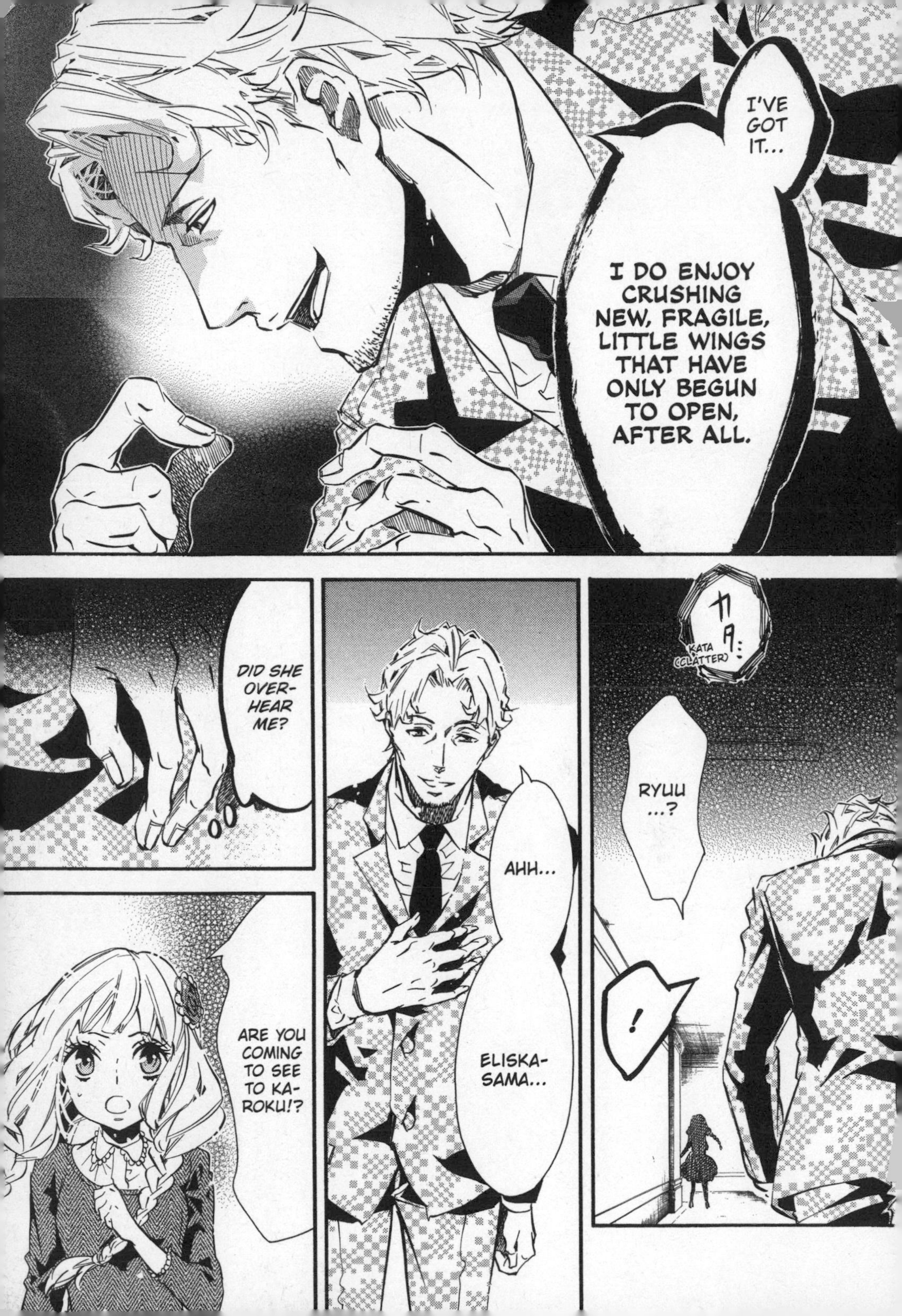
I'VE GOT IT...
I DO ENJOY CRUSHING NEW, FRAGILE, LITTLE WINGS THAT HAVE ONLY BEGUN TO OPEN, AFTER ALL.
カタ
KATA (CLATTER)
RYUU ...?
!
AHH...
ELISKA-SAMA...
DID SHE OVER-HEAR ME?
ARE YOU COMING TO SEE TO KA-ROKU!?

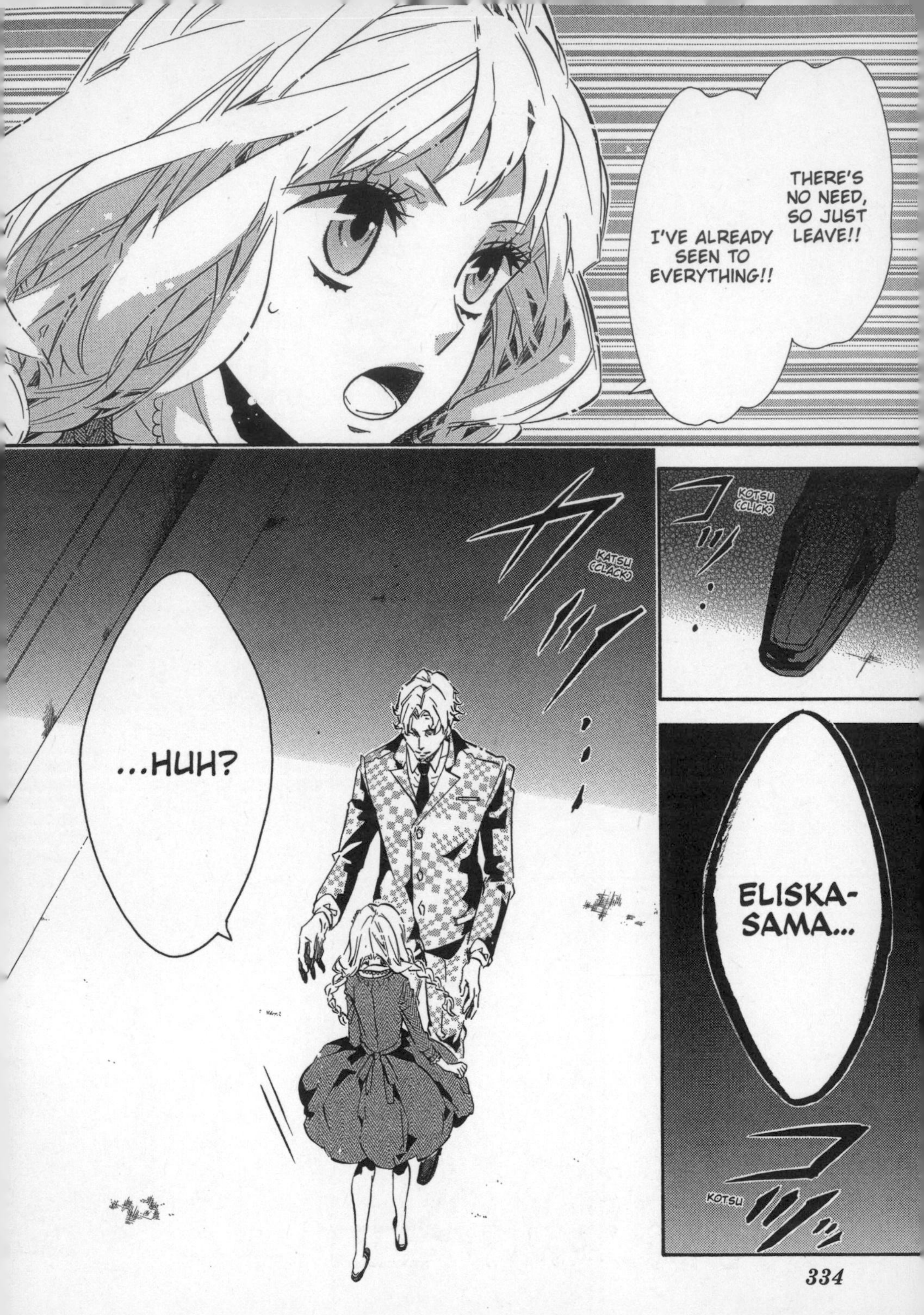
THERE'S NO NEED, SO JUST LEAVE!!
I'VE ALREADY SEEN TO EVERYTHING!!
KOTSU (CLICK)
ELISKA-SAMA...
KOTSU
KATSU (CLACK)
...HUH?

KARNEVAL

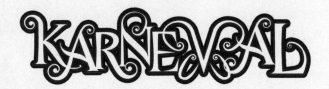

KARNEVAL

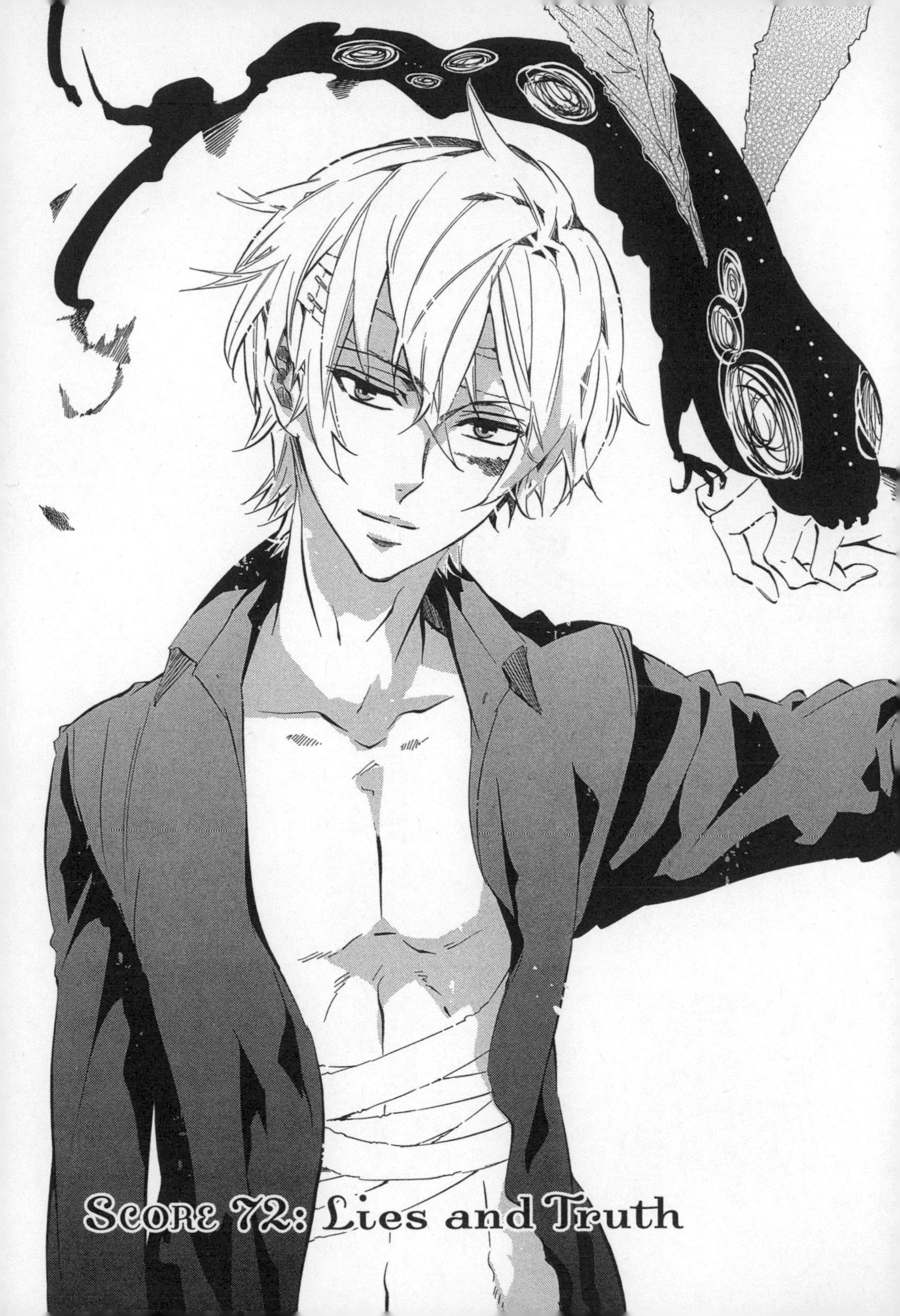
Score 72: Lies and Truth

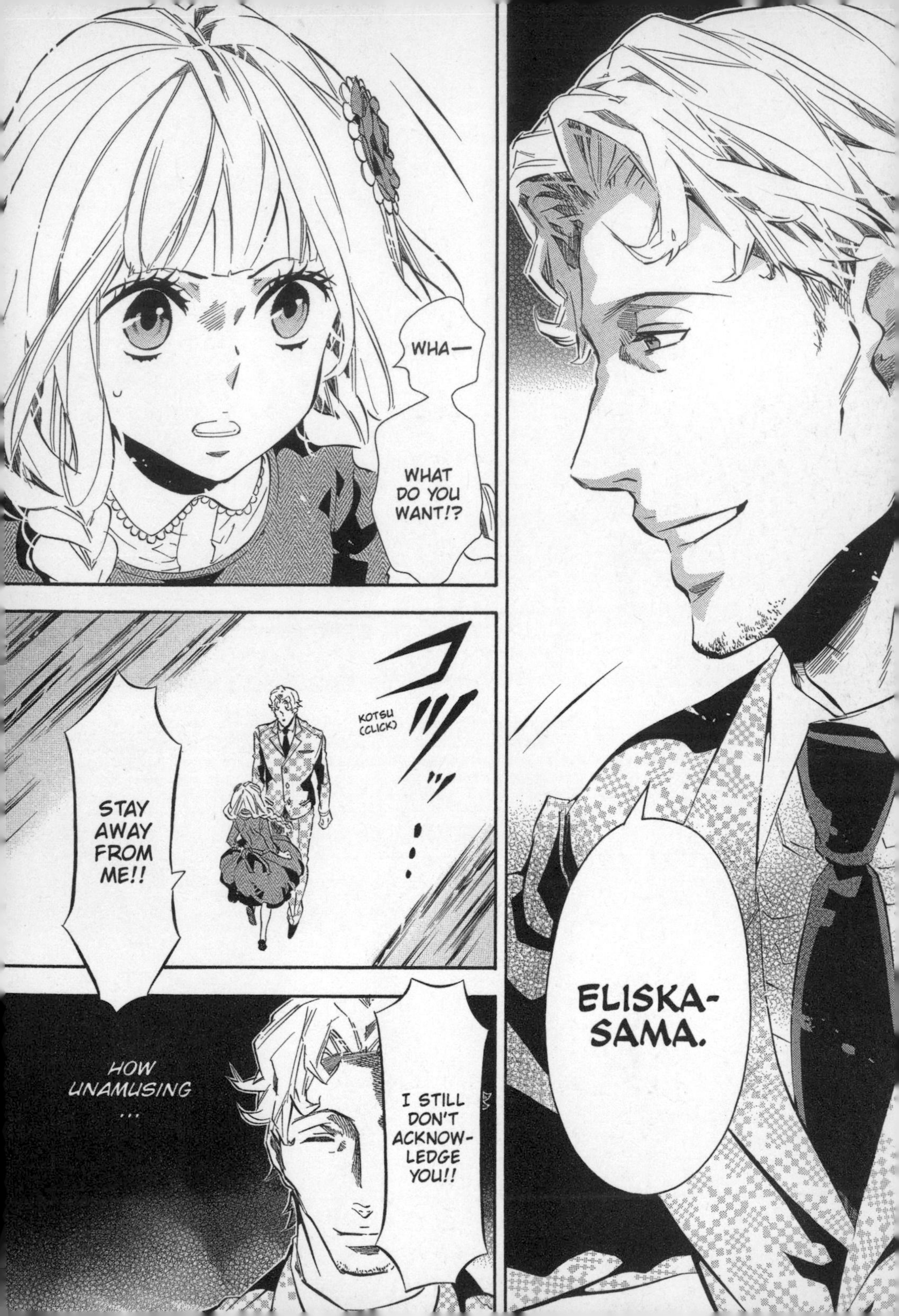
ELISKA-SAMA.
WHA—
WHAT DO YOU WANT!?
KOTSU (CLICK)
STAY AWAY FROM ME!!
I STILL DON'T ACKNOW-LEDGE YOU!!
HOW UNAMUSING ...

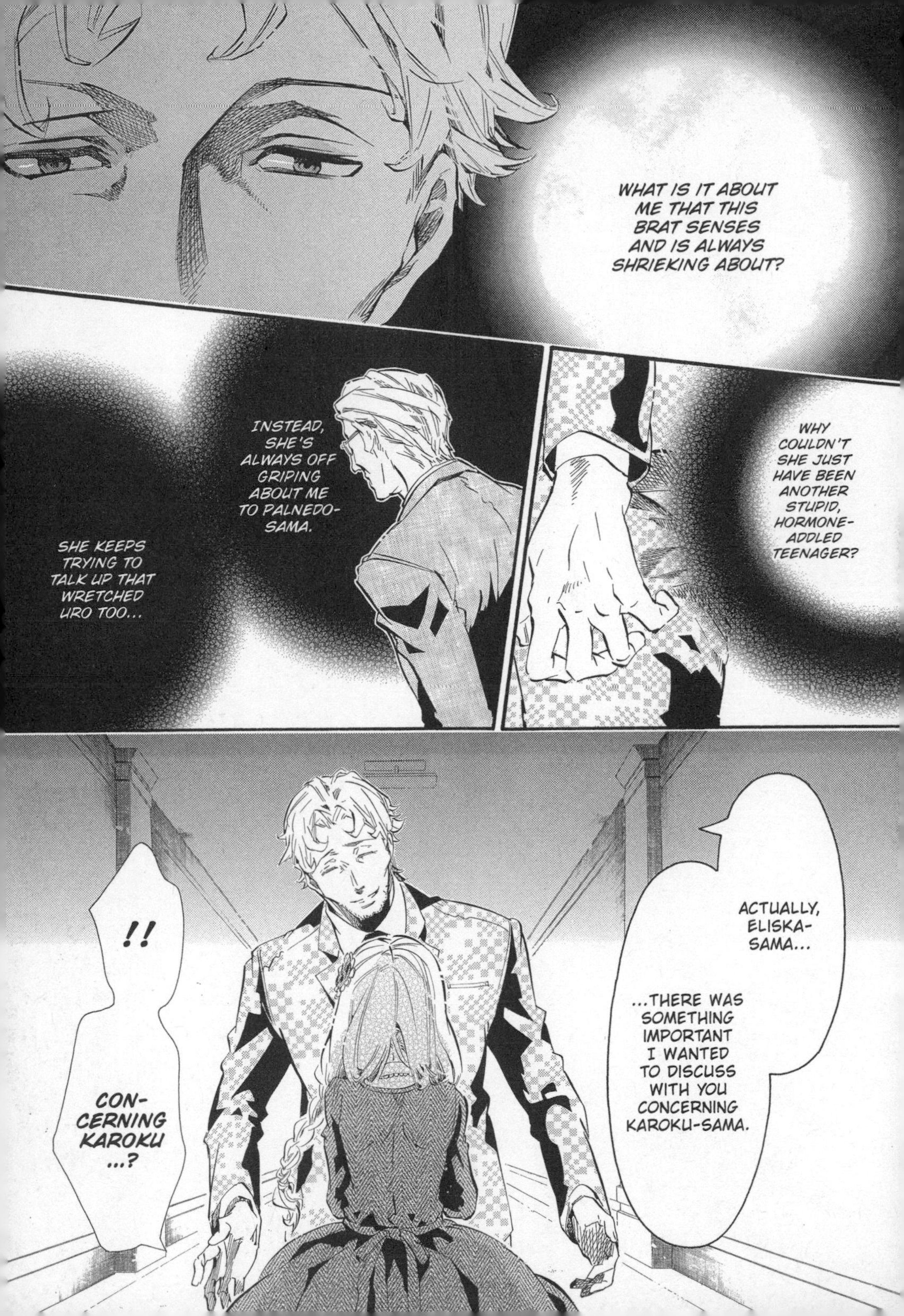
WHAT IS IT ABOUT ME THAT THIS BRAT SENSES AND IS ALWAYS SHRIEKING ABOUT?
WHY COULDN'T SHE JUST HAVE BEEN ANOTHER STUPID, HORMONE-ADDLED TEENAGER?
INSTEAD, SHE'S ALWAYS OFF GRIPING ABOUT ME TO PALNEDO-SAMA.
SHE KEEPS TRYING TO TALK UP THAT WRETCHED URO TOO...
ACTUALLY, ELISKA-SAMA...
...THERE WAS SOMETHING IMPORTANT I WANTED TO DISCUSS WITH YOU CONCERNING KAROKU-SAMA.
!!
CON-CERNING KAROKU...?

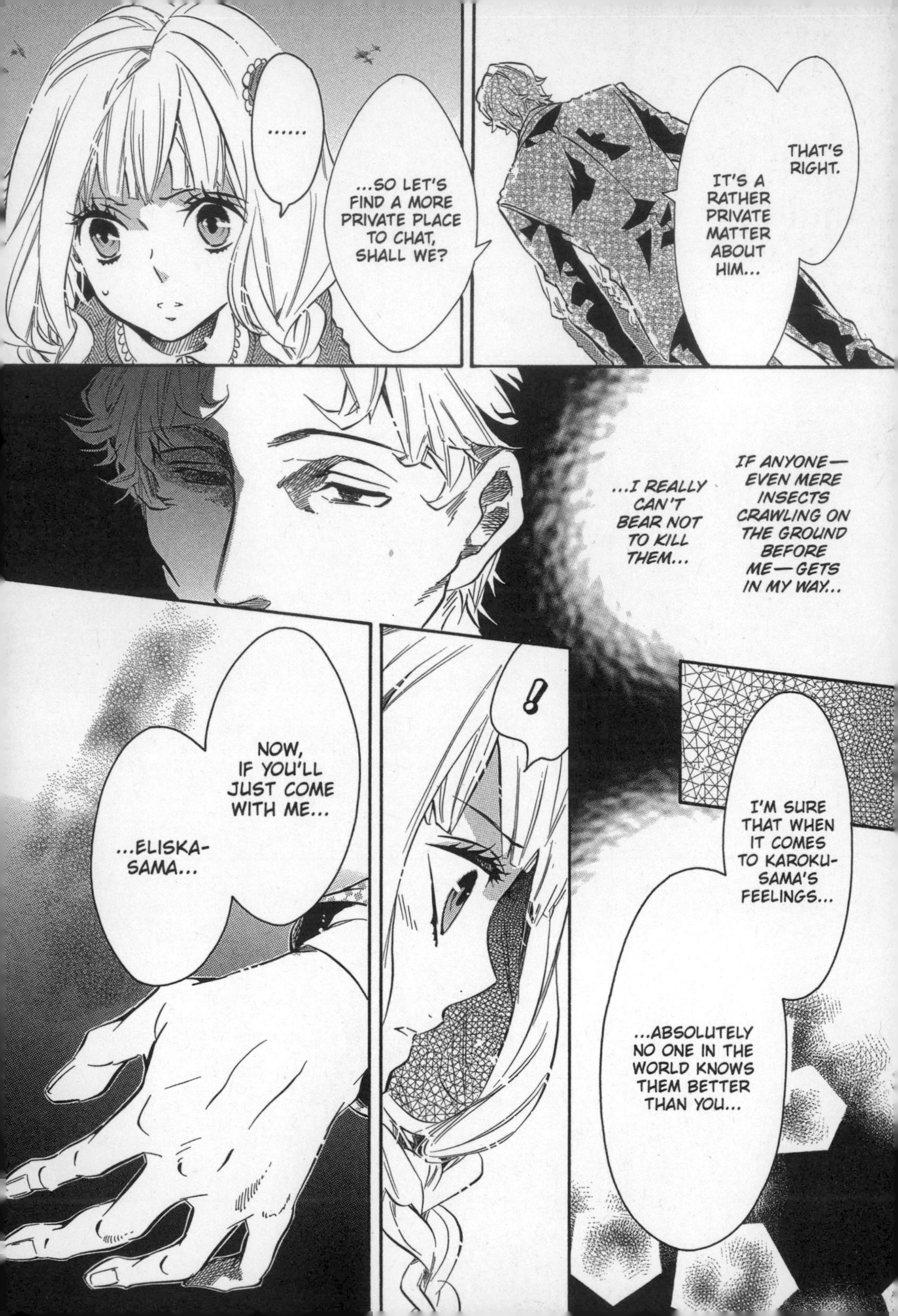
THAT'S RIGHT.
IT'S A RATHER PRIVATE MATTER ABOUT HIM...
...SO LET'S FIND A MORE PRIVATE PLACE TO CHAT, SHALL WE?
......
IF ANYONE—EVEN MERE INSECTS CRAWLING ON THE GROUND BEFORE ME—GETS IN MY WAY...
...I REALLY CAN'T BEAR NOT TO KILL THEM...
I'M SURE THAT WHEN IT COMES TO KAROKU-SAMA'S FEELINGS...
...ABSOLUTELY NO ONE IN THE WORLD KNOWS THEM BETTER THAN YOU...
!
NOW, IF YOU'LL JUST COME WITH ME...
...ELISKA-SAMA...

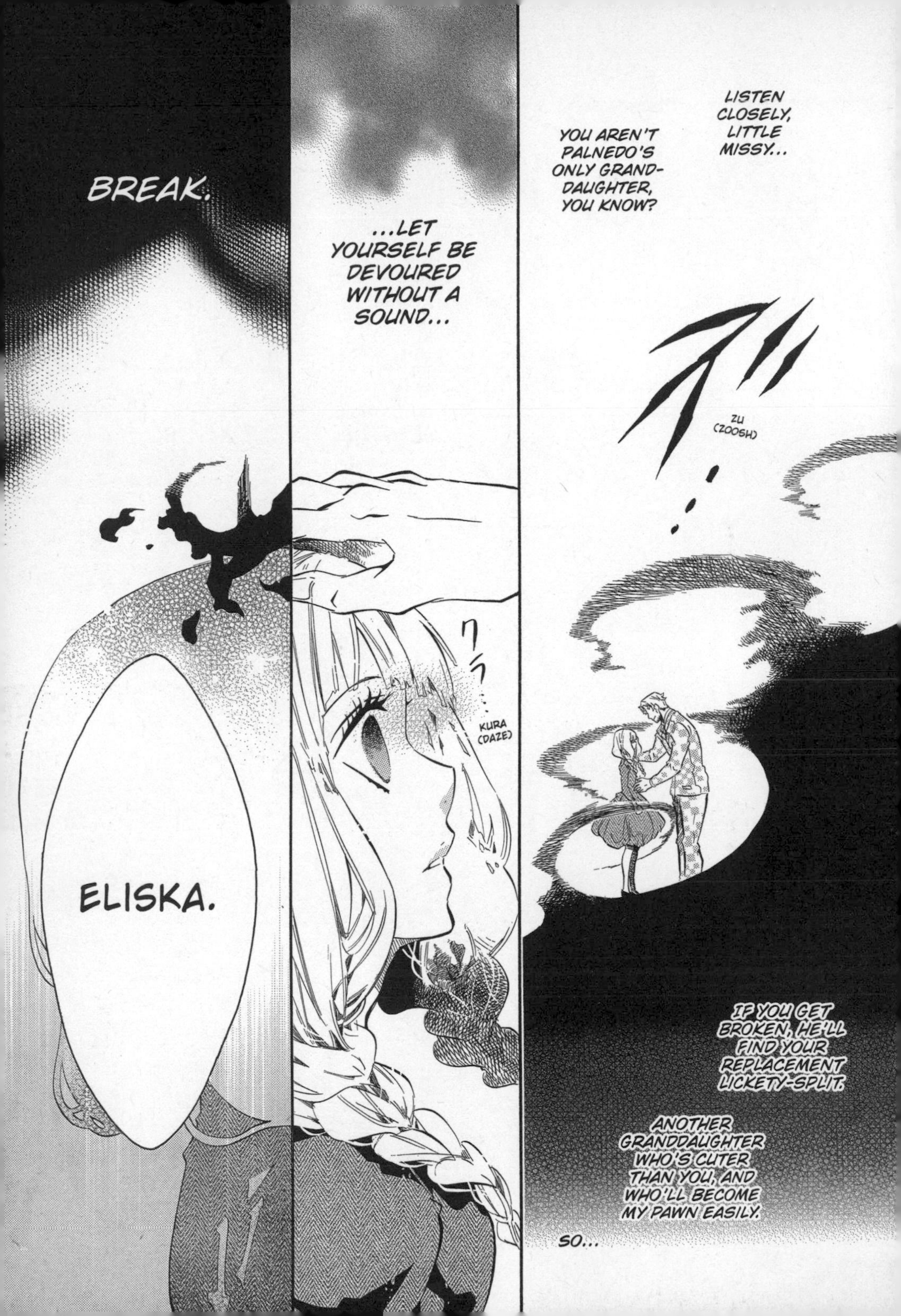
LISTEN CLOSELY, LITTLE MISSY...
YOU AREN'T PALNEDO'S ONLY GRAND-DAUGHTER, YOU KNOW?
ZU (ZOOSH)
IF YOU GET BROKEN, HE'LL FIND YOUR REPLACEMENT LICKETY-SPLIT.
ANOTHER GRANDDAUGHTER WHO'S CUTER THAN YOU, AND WHO'LL BECOME MY PAWN EASILY.
SO...
...LET YOURSELF BE DEVOURED WITHOUT A SOUND...
クラ
KURA (DAZE)
BREAK.
ELISKA.

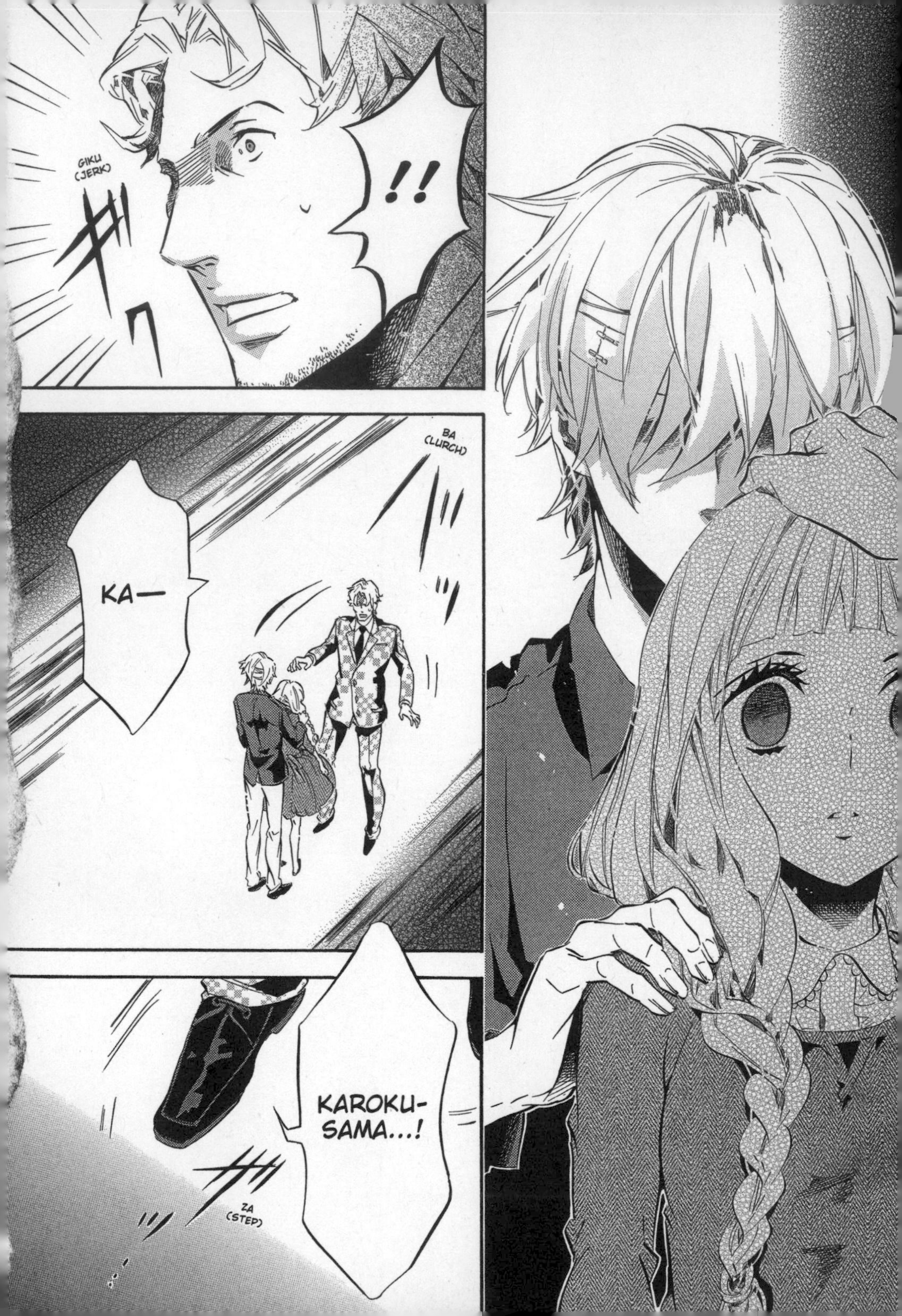
!!
GIKU (JERK)
BA (LURCH)
KA—
KAROKU-SAMA...!
ZA (STEP)

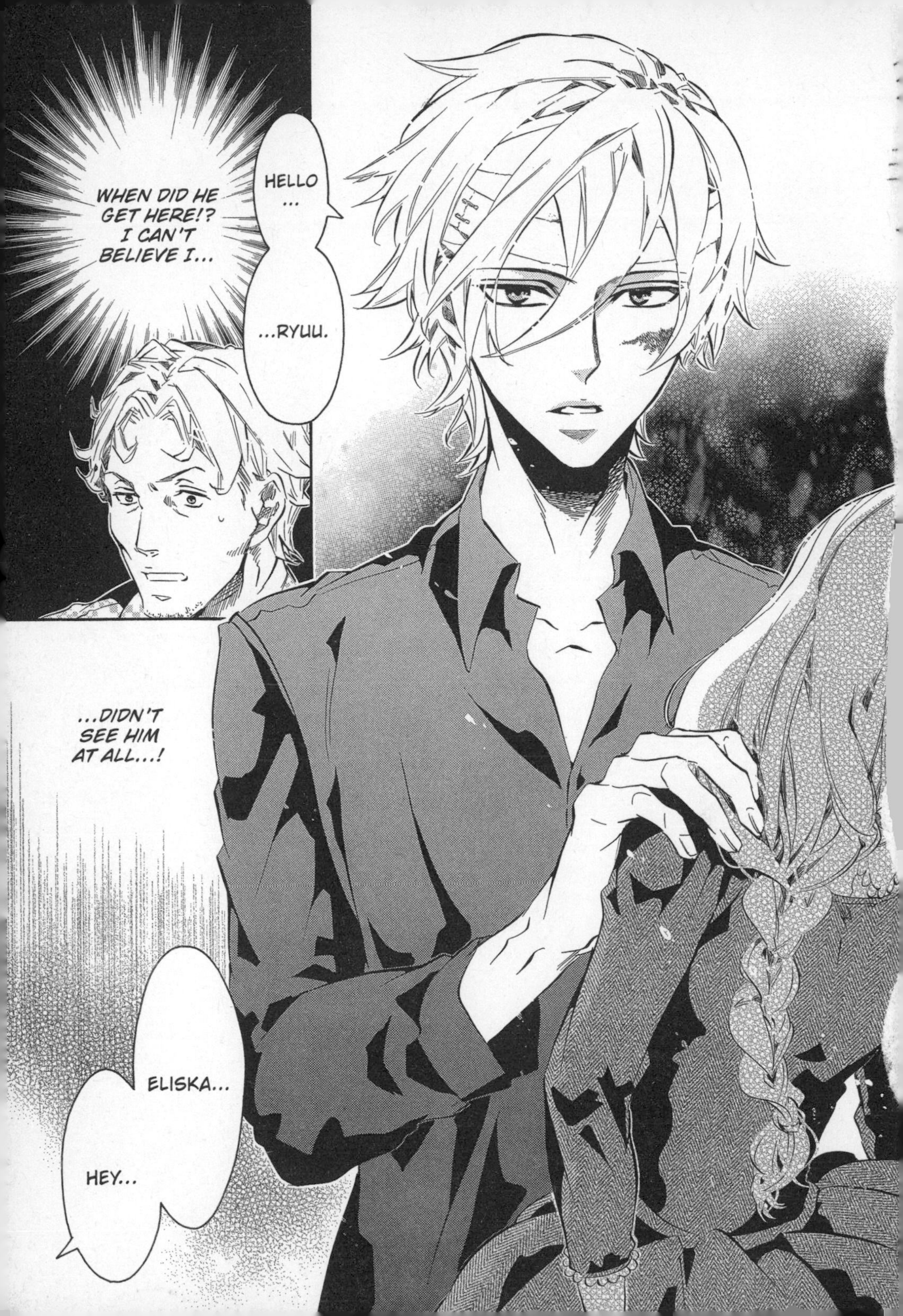
HELLO ...
...RYUU.
WHEN DID HE GET HERE!? I CAN'T BELIEVE I...
...DIDN'T SEE HIM AT ALL...!
ELISKA...
HEY...

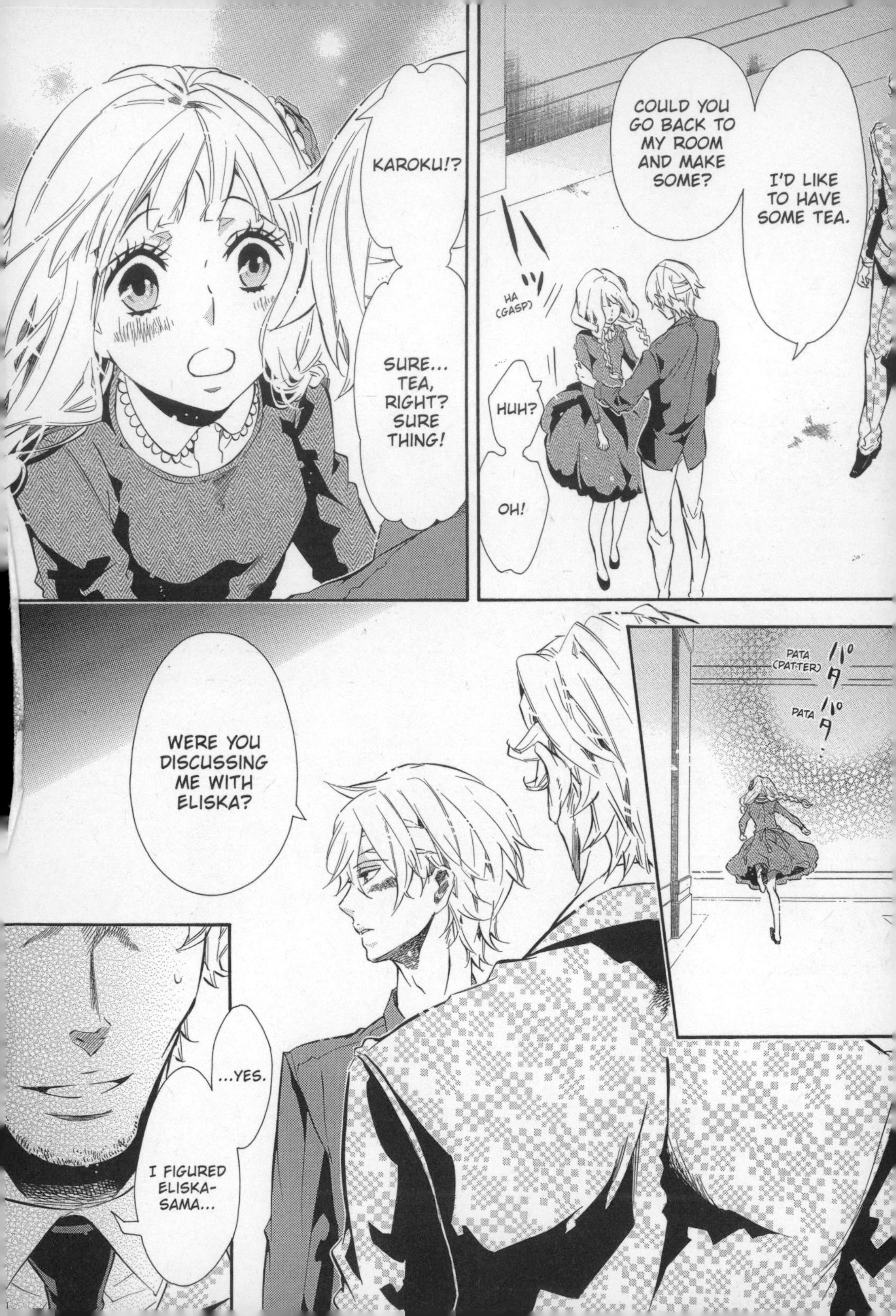
I'D LIKE TO HAVE SOME TEA.
COULD YOU GO BACK TO MY ROOM AND MAKE SOME?
HA (GASP)
HUH?
OH!
KAROKU!?
SURE... TEA, RIGHT? SURE THING!
パタ PATA (PAT-TER)
パタ PATA
WERE YOU DISCUSSING ME WITH ELISKA?
...YES.
I FIGURED ELISKA-SAMA...

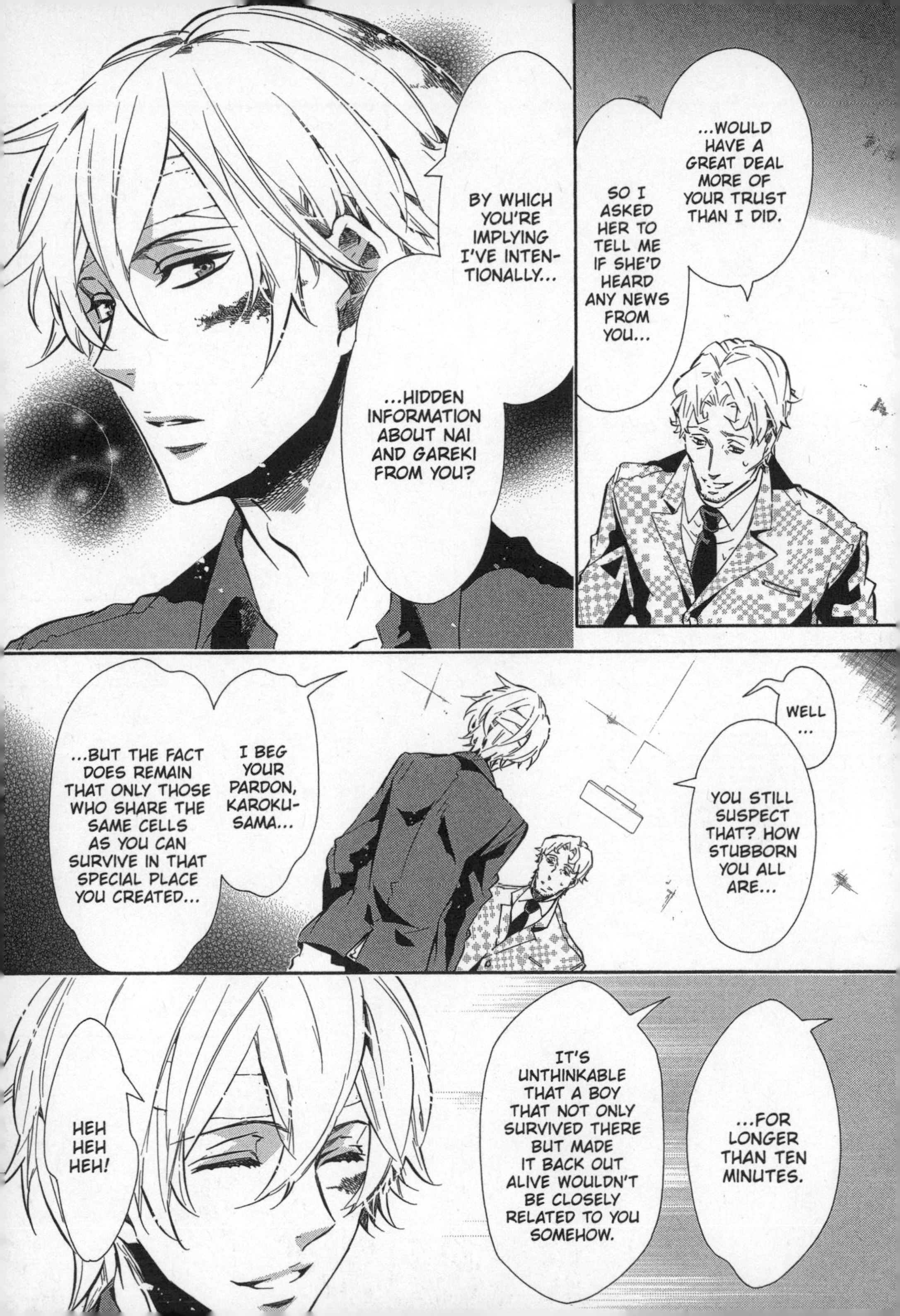
...WOULD HAVE A GREAT DEAL MORE OF YOUR TRUST THAN I DID.
SO I ASKED HER TO TELL ME IF SHE'D HEARD ANY NEWS FROM YOU...
BY WHICH YOU'RE IMPLYING I'VE INTEN-TIONALLY...
...HIDDEN INFORMATION ABOUT NAI AND GAREKI FROM YOU?
WELL...
YOU STILL SUSPECT THAT? HOW STUBBORN YOU ALL ARE...
I BEG YOUR PARDON, KAROKU-SAMA...
...BUT THE FACT DOES REMAIN THAT ONLY THOSE WHO SHARE THE SAME CELLS AS YOU CAN SURVIVE IN THAT SPECIAL PLACE YOU CREATED...
...FOR LONGER THAN TEN MINUTES.
IT'S UNTHINKABLE THAT A BOY THAT NOT ONLY SURVIVED THERE BUT MADE IT BACK OUT ALIVE WOULDN'T BE CLOSELY RELATED TO YOU SOMEHOW.
HEH HEH HEH!

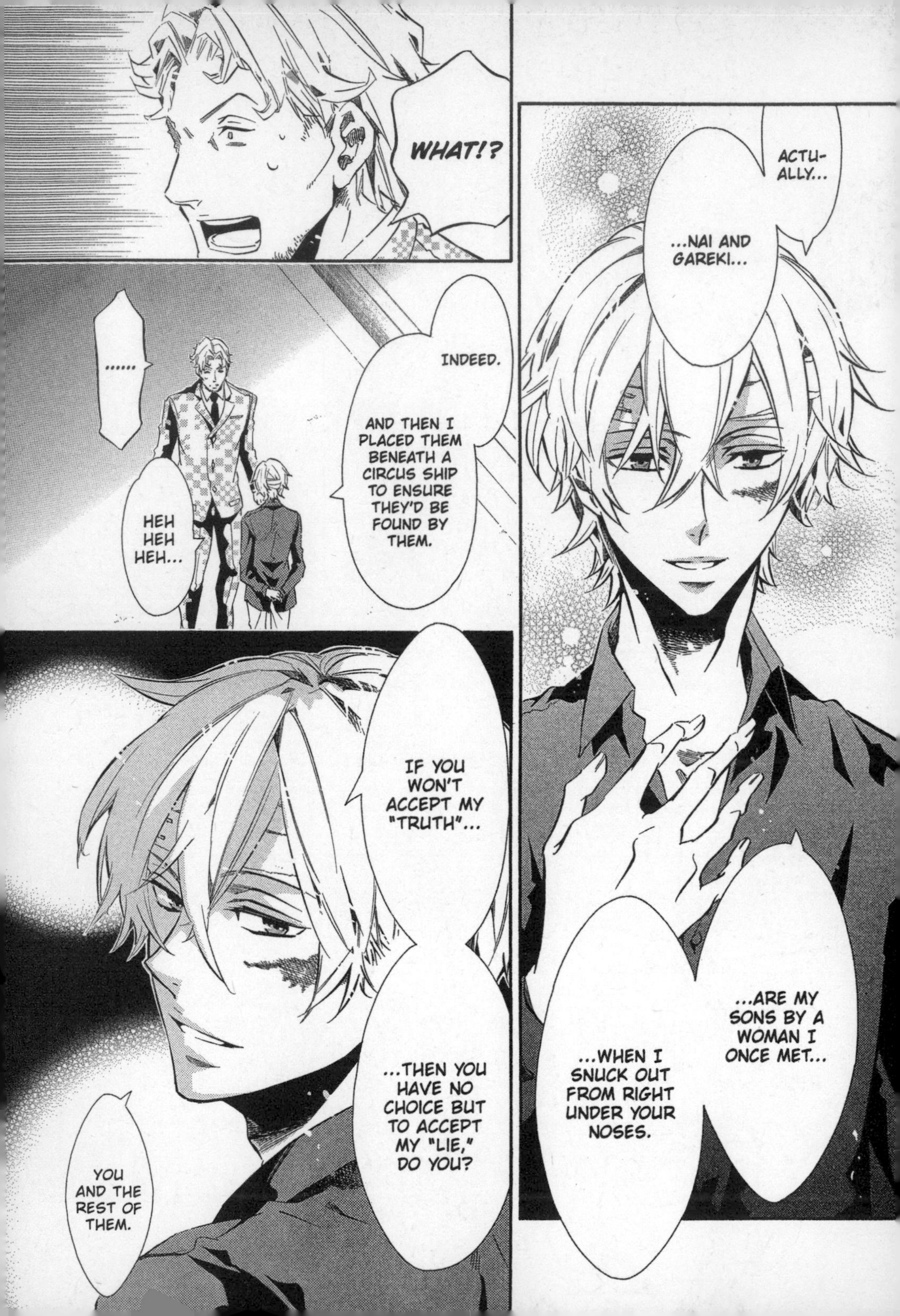
ACTU-ALLY...
...NAI AND GAREKI...
...ARE MY SONS BY A WOMAN I ONCE MET...
...WHEN I SNUCK OUT FROM RIGHT UNDER YOUR NOSES.
WHAT!?
INDEED.
......
AND THEN I PLACED THEM BENEATH A CIRCUS SHIP TO ENSURE THEY'D BE FOUND BY THEM.
HEH HEH HEH...
IF YOU WON'T ACCEPT MY "TRUTH"...
...THEN YOU HAVE NO CHOICE BUT TO ACCEPT MY "LIE," DO YOU?
YOU AND THE REST OF THEM.

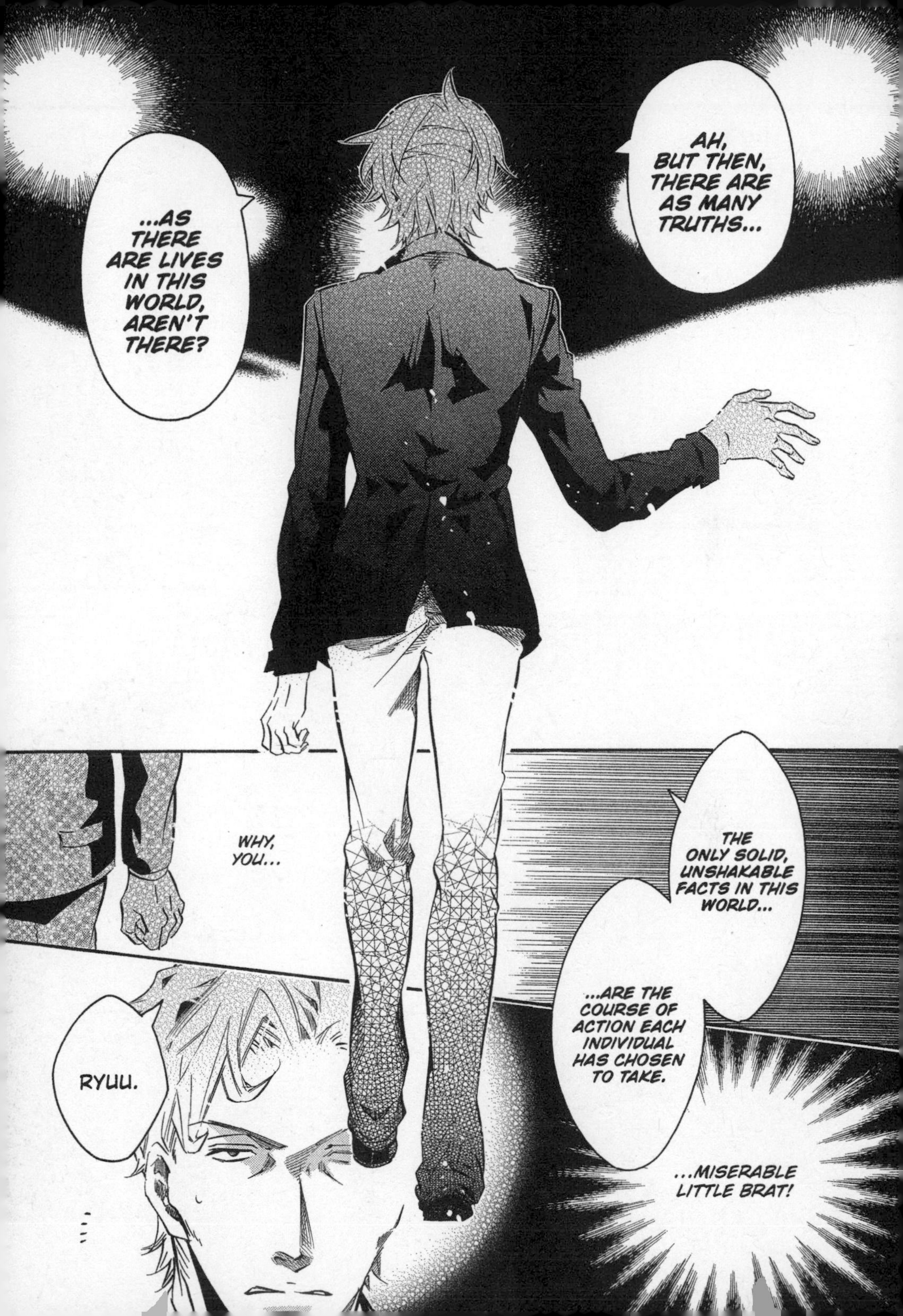

AH, BUT THEN, THERE ARE AS MANY TRUTHS...
...AS THERE ARE LIVES IN THIS WORLD, AREN'T THERE?
THE ONLY SOLID, UNSHAKABLE FACTS IN THIS WORLD...
WHY, YOU...
...ARE THE COURSE OF ACTION EACH INDIVIDUAL HAS CHOSEN TO TAKE.
RYUU.
...MISERABLE LITTLE BRAT!

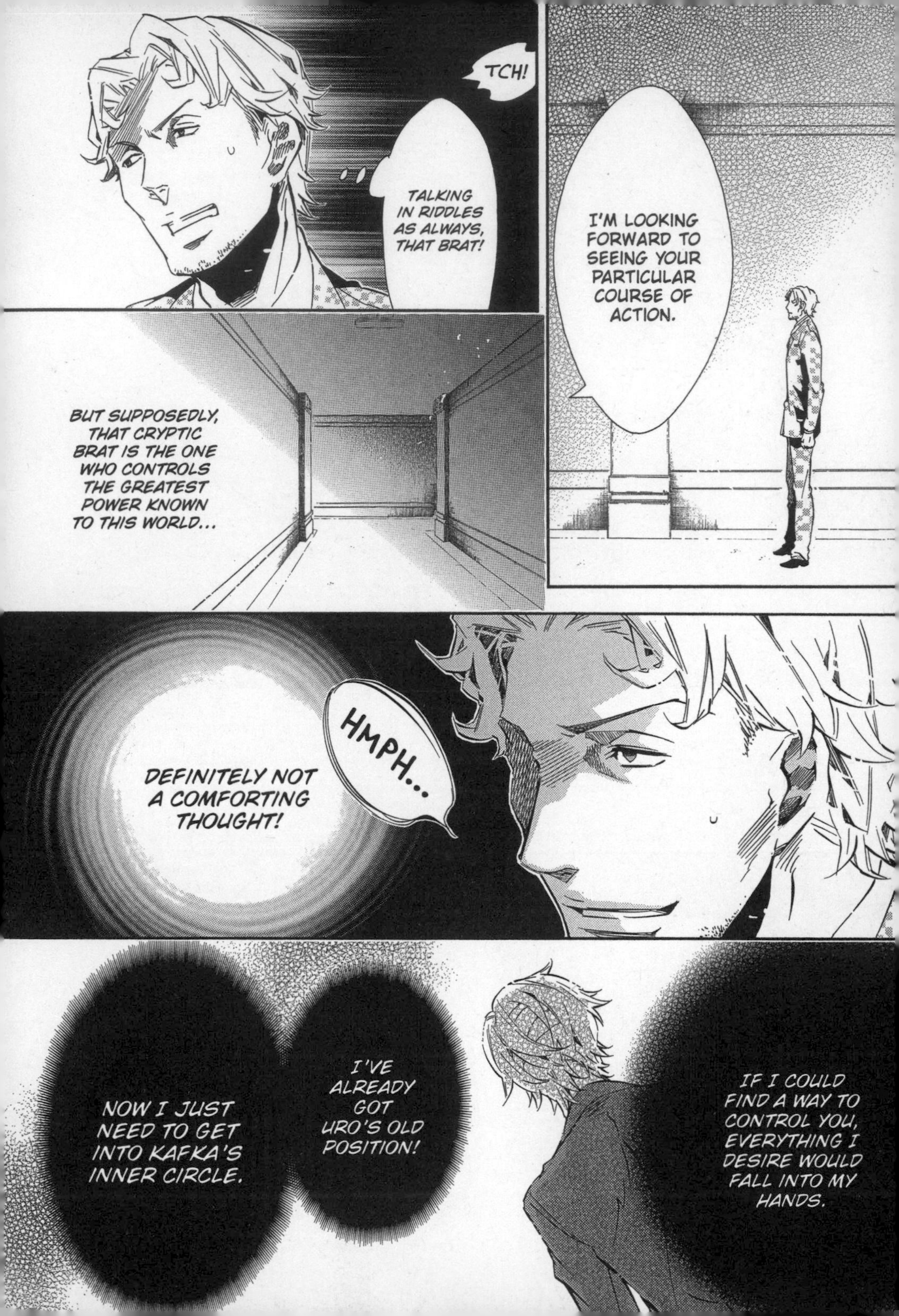
I'M LOOKING FORWARD TO SEEING YOUR PARTICULAR COURSE OF ACTION.
TCH!
TALKING IN RIDDLES AS ALWAYS, THAT BRAT!
BUT SUPPOSEDLY, THAT CRYPTIC BRAT IS THE ONE WHO CONTROLS THE GREATEST POWER KNOWN TO THIS WORLD...
HMPH...
DEFINITELY NOT A COMFORTING THOUGHT!
IF I COULD FIND A WAY TO CONTROL YOU, EVERYTHING I DESIRE WOULD FALL INTO MY HANDS.
I'VE ALREADY GOT URO'S OLD POSITION!
NOW I JUST NEED TO GET INTO KAFKA'S INNER CIRCLE.

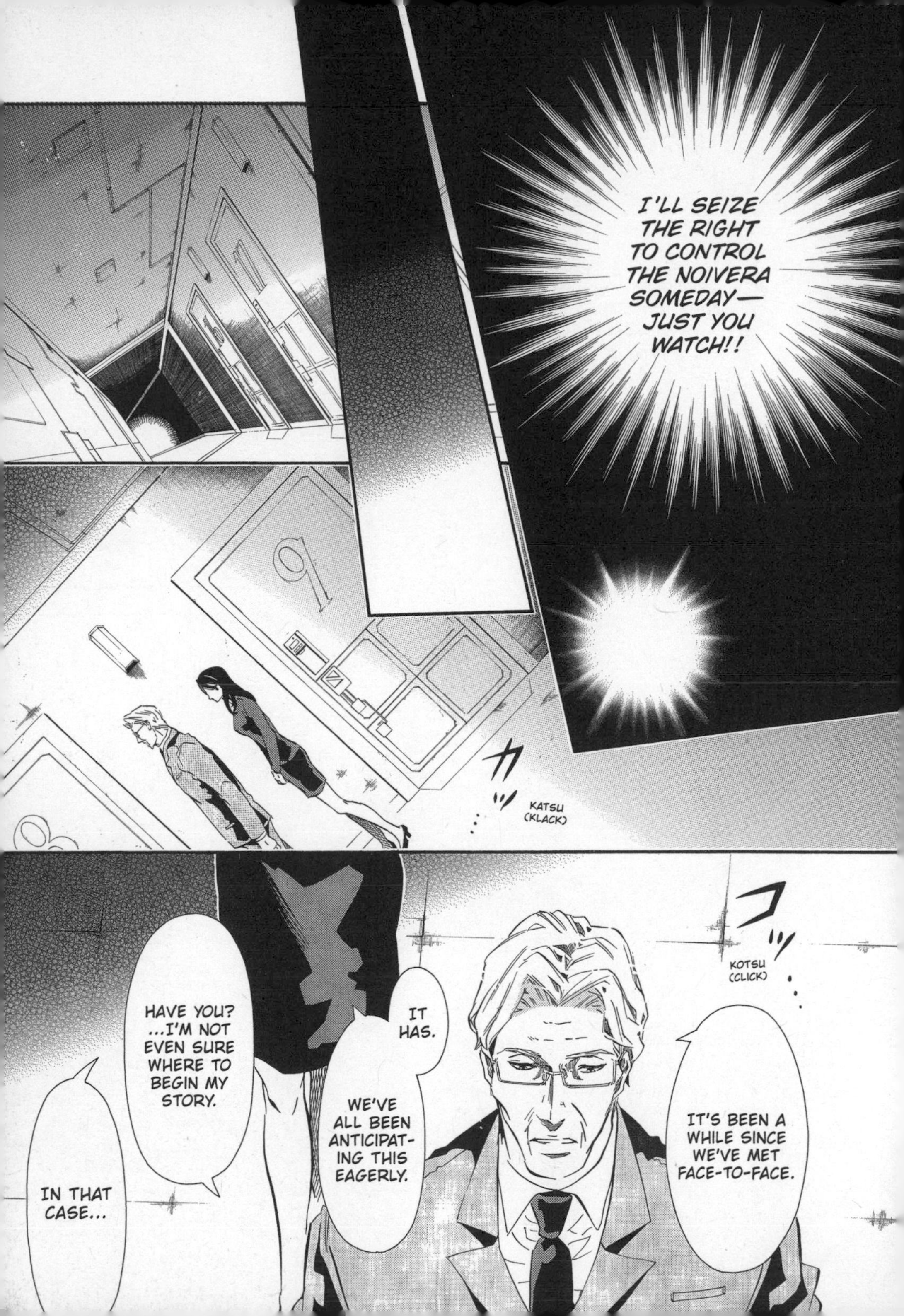
I'LL SEIZE THE RIGHT TO CONTROL THE NOIVERA SOMEDAY—JUST YOU WATCH!!
カッ
KATSU (KLACK)
コッ
KOTSU (CLICK)
IT'S BEEN A WHILE SINCE WE'VE MET FACE-TO-FACE.
IT HAS.
WE'VE ALL BEEN ANTICIPAT-ING THIS EAGERLY.
HAVE YOU? ...I'M NOT EVEN SURE WHERE TO BEGIN MY STORY.
IN THAT CASE...

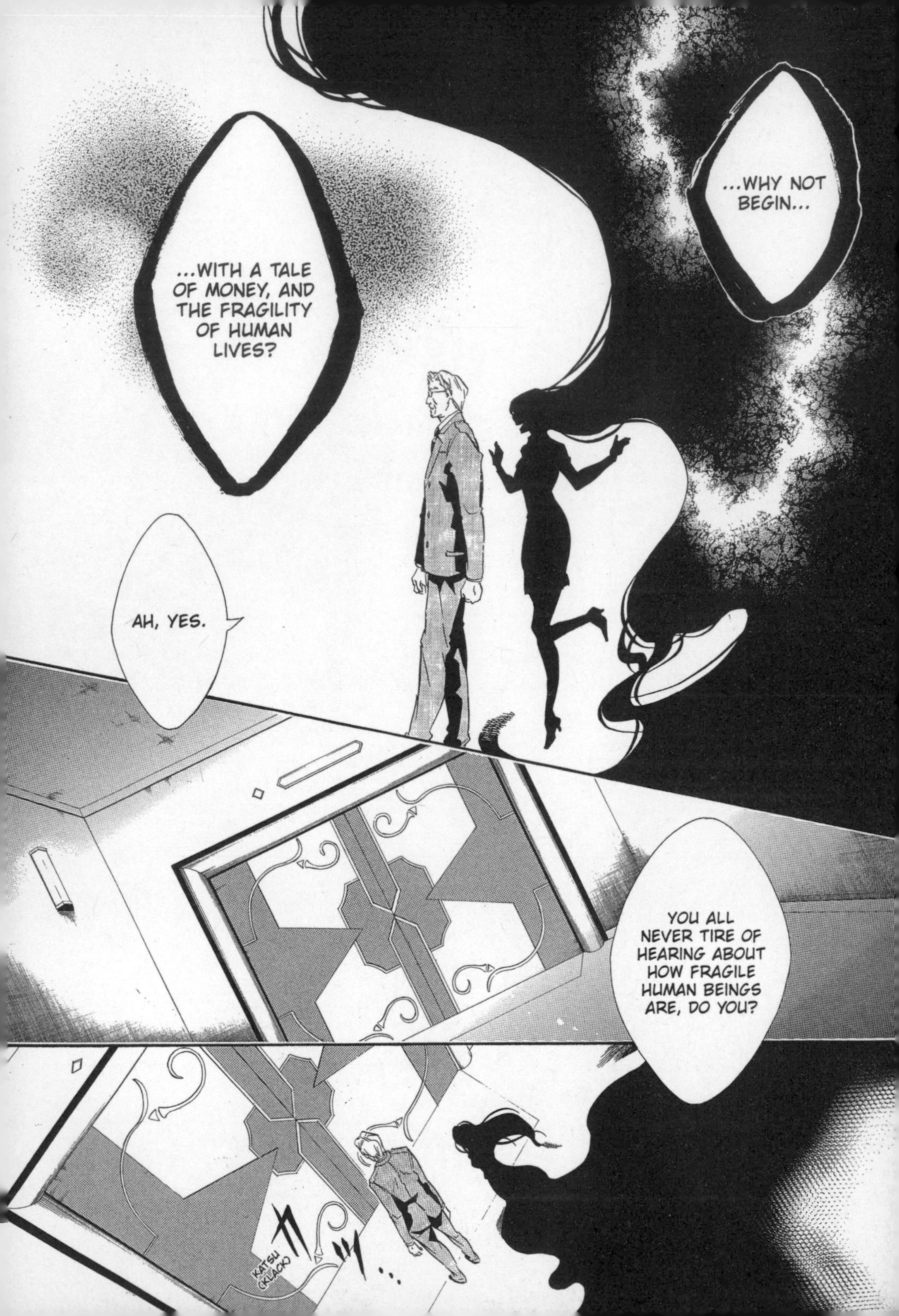
...WHY NOT BEGIN...
...WITH A TALE OF MONEY, AND THE FRAGILITY OF HUMAN LIVES?
AH, YES.
YOU ALL NEVER TIRE OF HEARING ABOUT HOW FRAGILE HUMAN BEINGS ARE, DO YOU?
KATSU (KLACK)
...

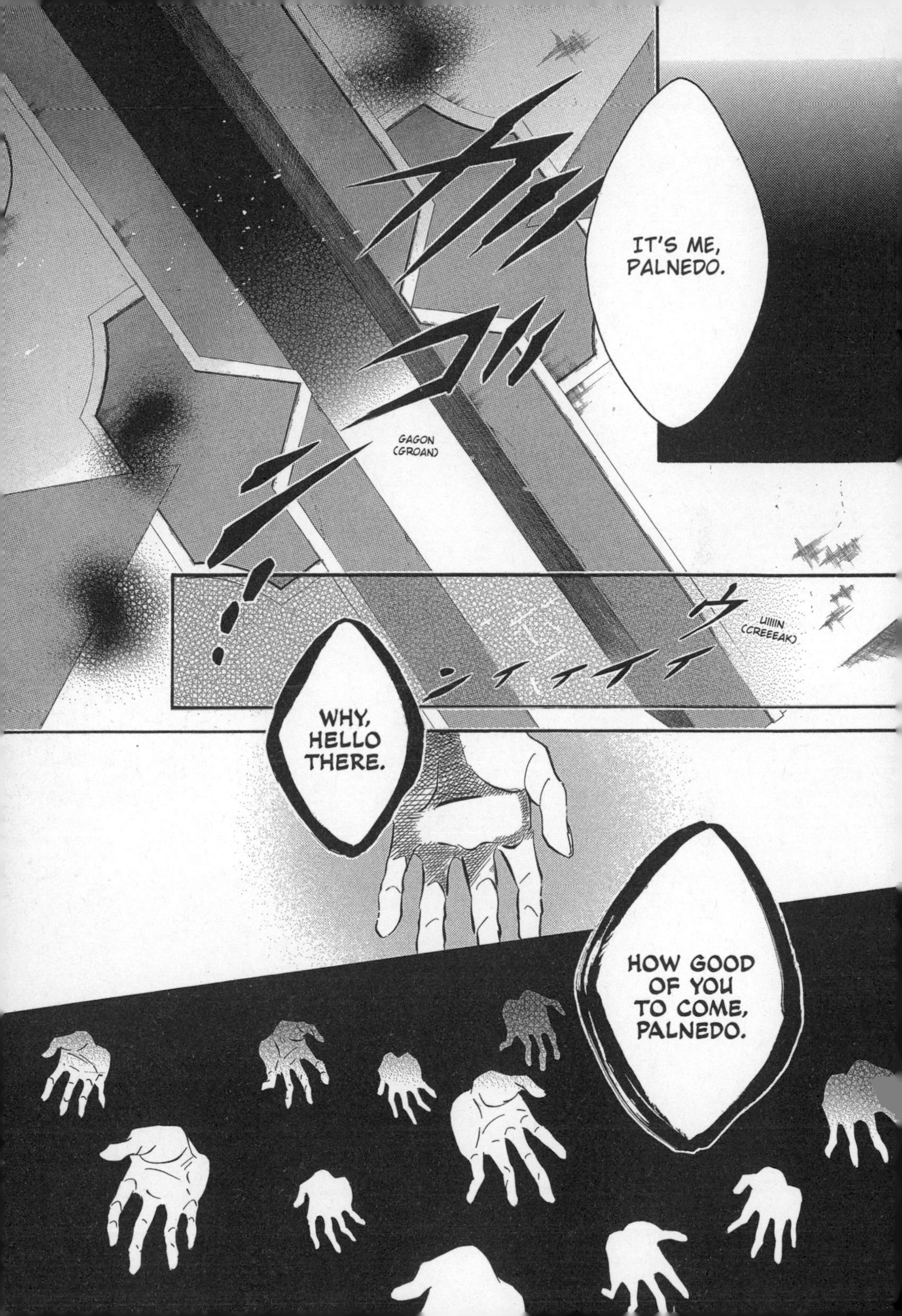
IT'S ME, PALNEDO.
GAGON (GROAN)
UIIIIN (CREEEAK)
WHY, HELLO THERE.
HOW GOOD OF YOU TO COME, PALNEDO.

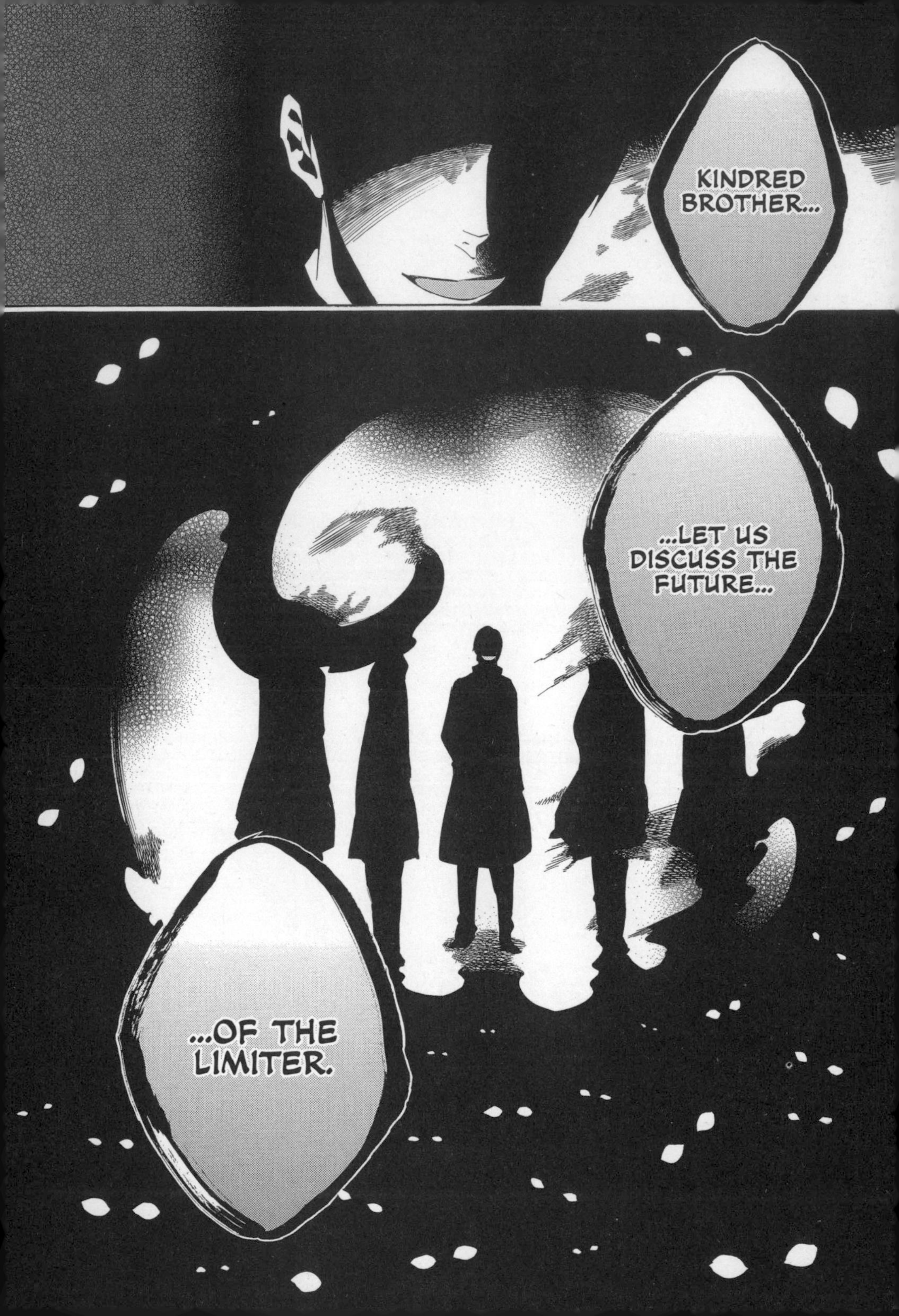
KINDRED BROTHER...
...LET US DISCUSS THE FUTURE...
...OF THE LIMITER.

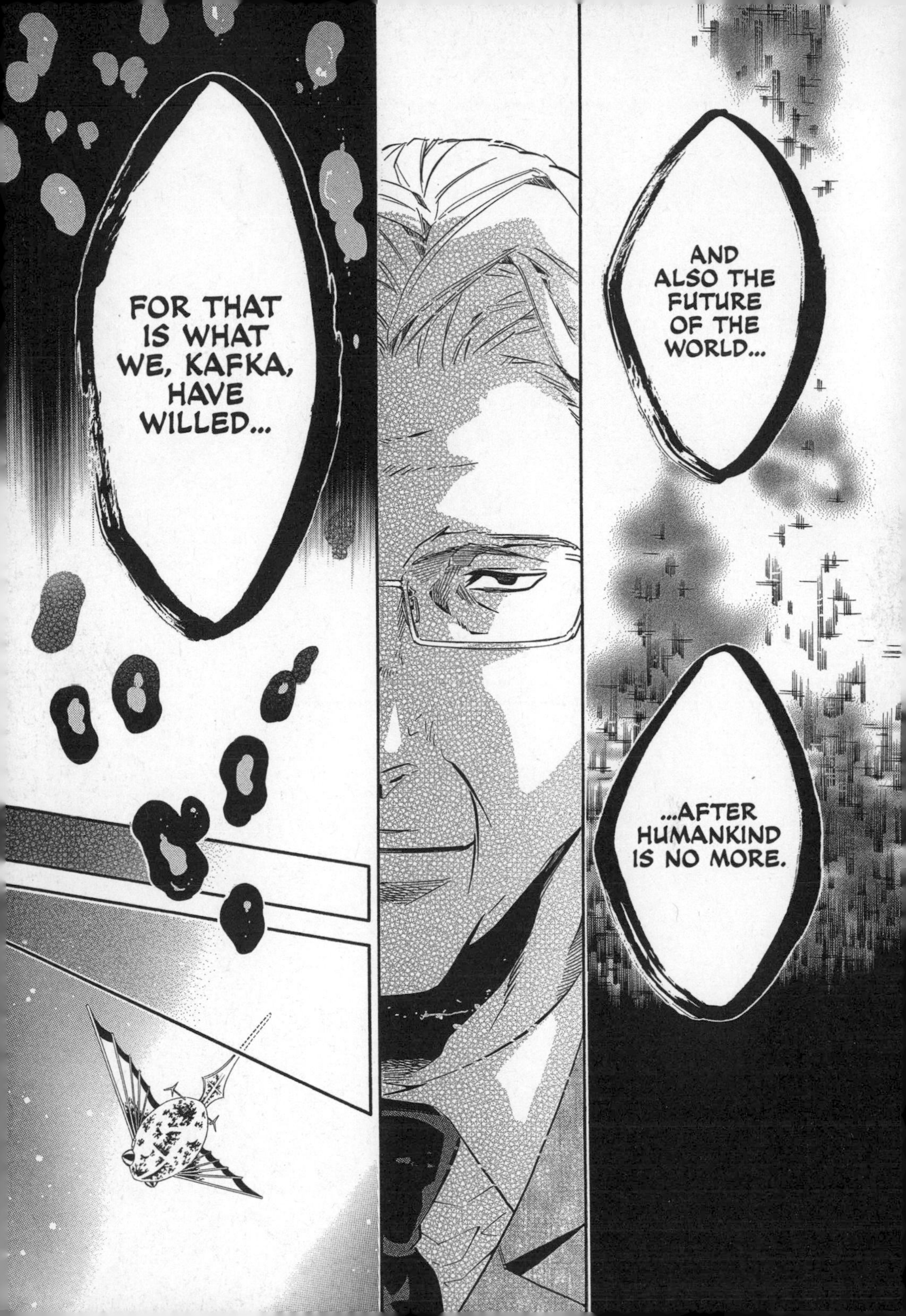
AND ALSO THE FUTURE OF THE WORLD...
...AFTER HUMANKIND IS NO MORE.
FOR THAT IS WHAT WE, KAFKA, HAVE WILLED...

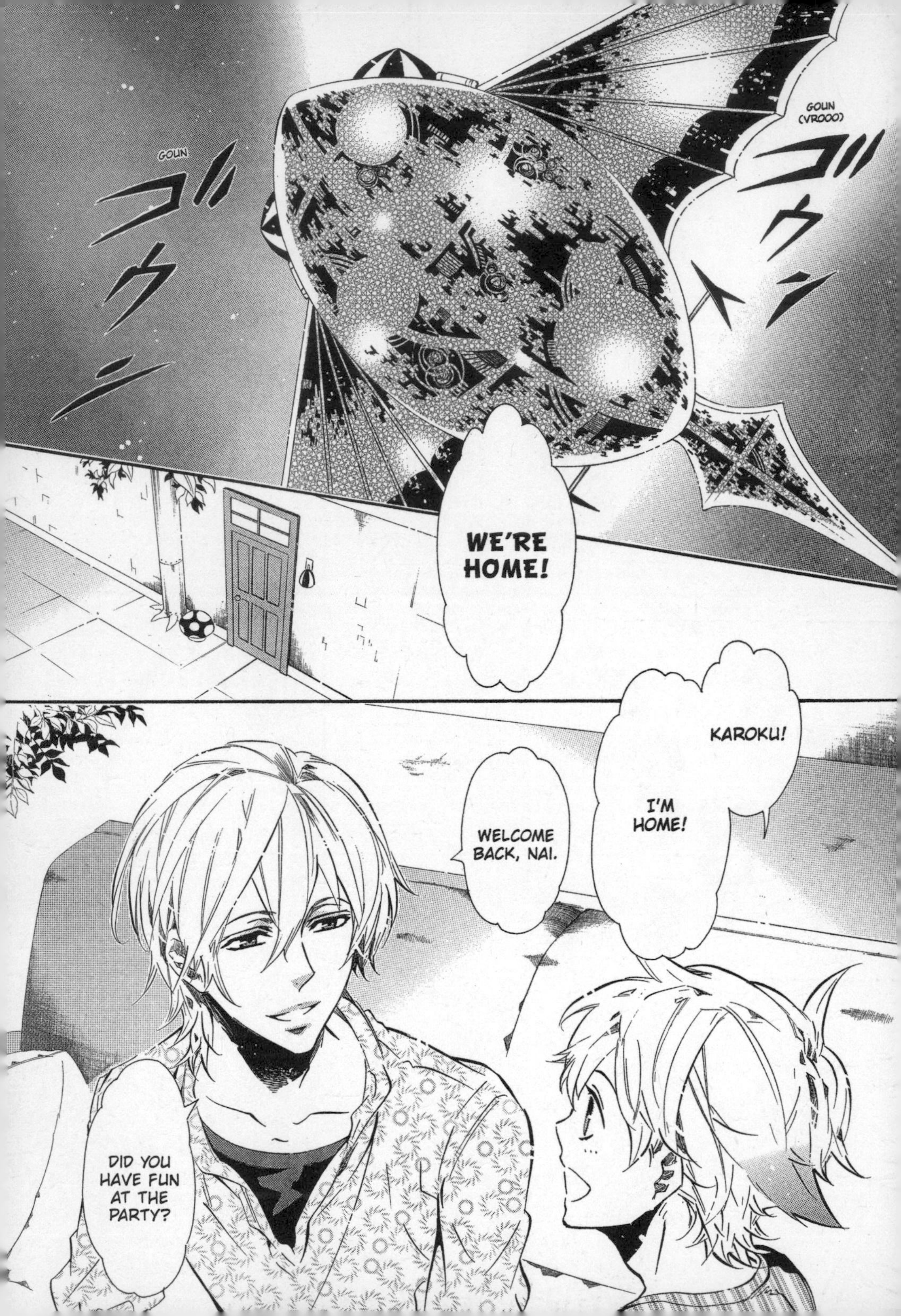

ゴウン
GOUN (VROOO)
ゴウン
GOUN
WE'RE HOME!
KAROKU!
I'M HOME!
WELCOME BACK, NAI.
DID YOU HAVE FUN AT THE PARTY?

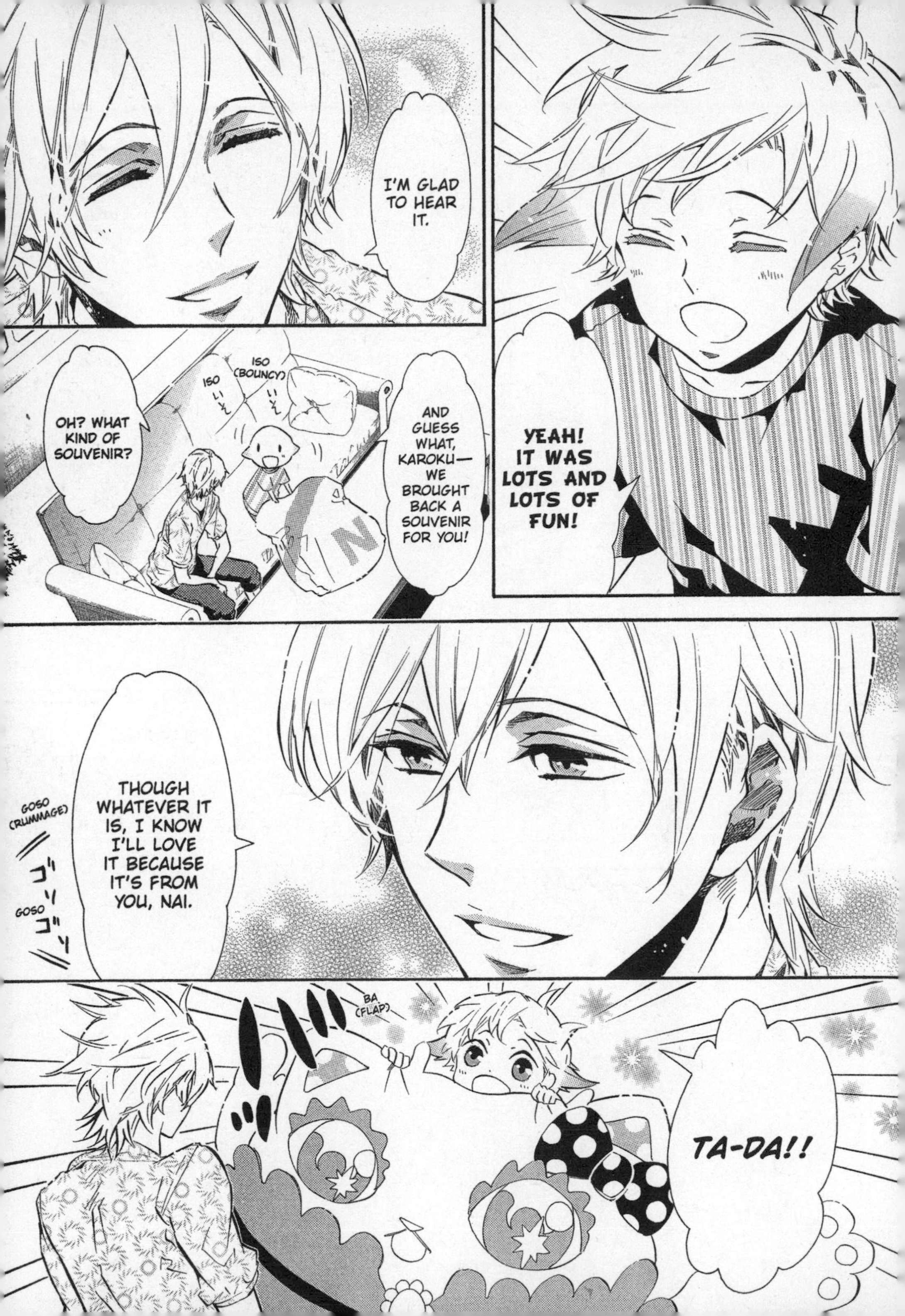
YEAH! IT WAS LOTS AND LOTS OF FUN!
I'M GLAD TO HEAR IT.
AND GUESS WHAT, KAROKU— WE BROUGHT BACK A SOUVENIR FOR YOU!
ISO (BOUNCY)
いそ
ISO
いそ
OH? WHAT KIND OF SOUVENIR?
THOUGH WHATEVER IT IS, I KNOW I'LL LOVE IT BECAUSE IT'S FROM YOU, NAI.
GOSO (RUMMAGE)
ゴソ
GOSO
ゴソ
TA-DA!!
BA (FLAP)

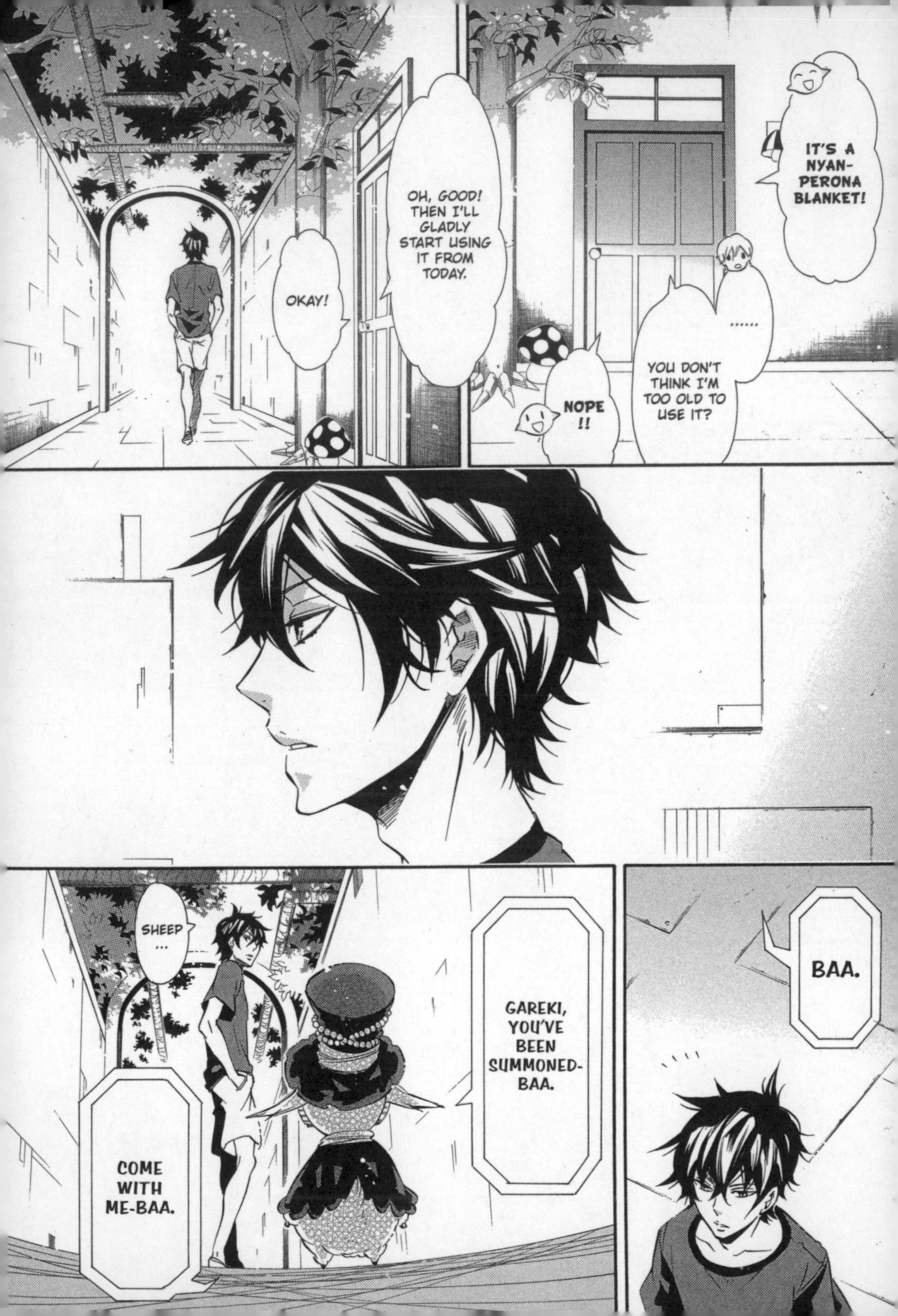
IT'S A NYAN-PERONA BLANKET!
......
YOU DON'T THINK I'M TOO OLD TO USE IT?
NOPE !!
OH, GOOD! THEN I'LL GLADLY START USING IT FROM TODAY.
OKAY!
BAA.
GAREKI, YOU'VE BEEN SUMMONED-BAA.
SHEEP ...
COME WITH ME-BAA.

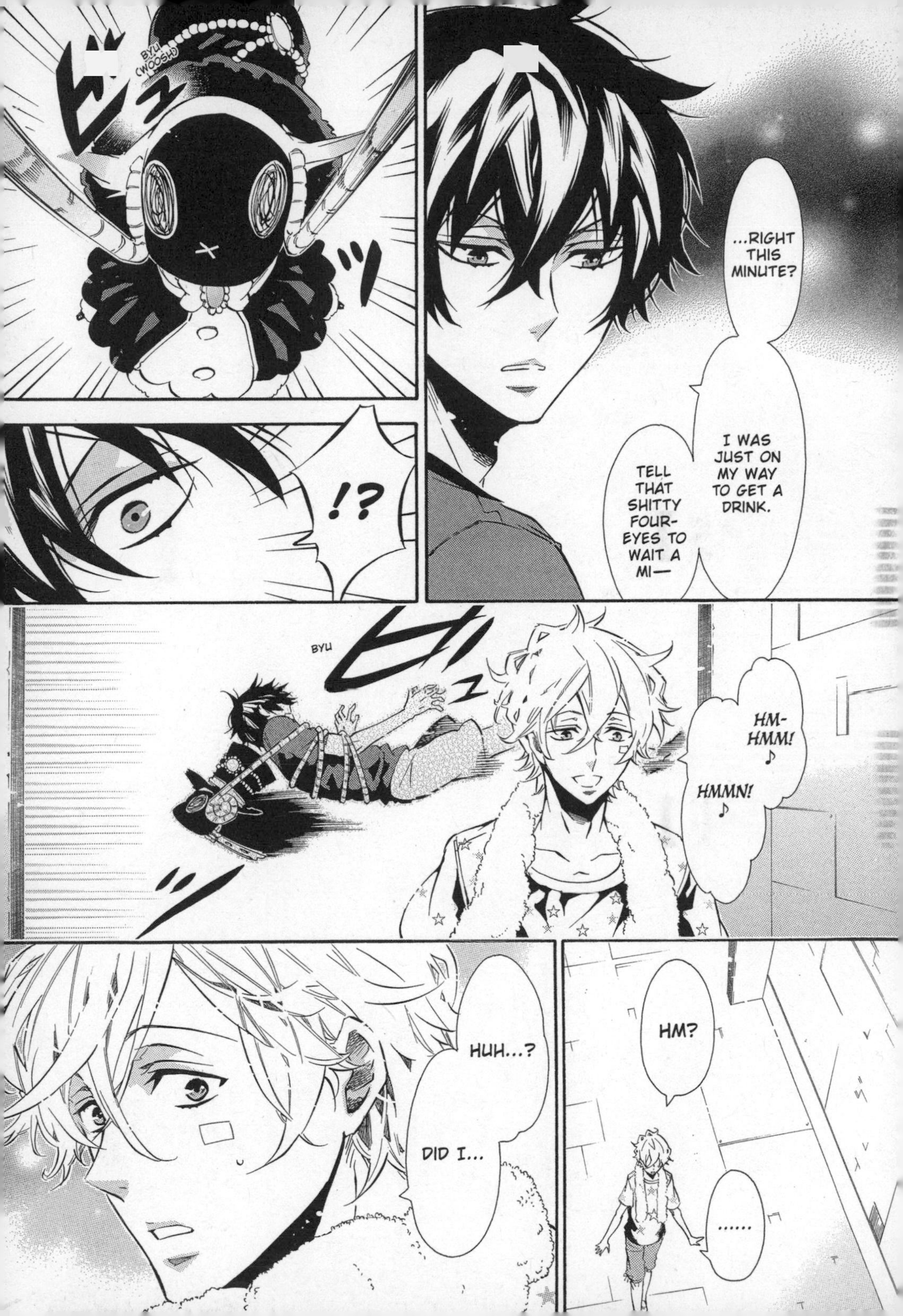
...RIGHT THIS MINUTE?
I WAS JUST ON MY WAY TO GET A DRINK.
TELL THAT SHITTY FOUR-EYES TO WAIT A MI—
BYU (WOOSH)
!?
HM-HMM! ♪
HMMN! ♪
BYU
HM?
......
HUH...?
DID I...

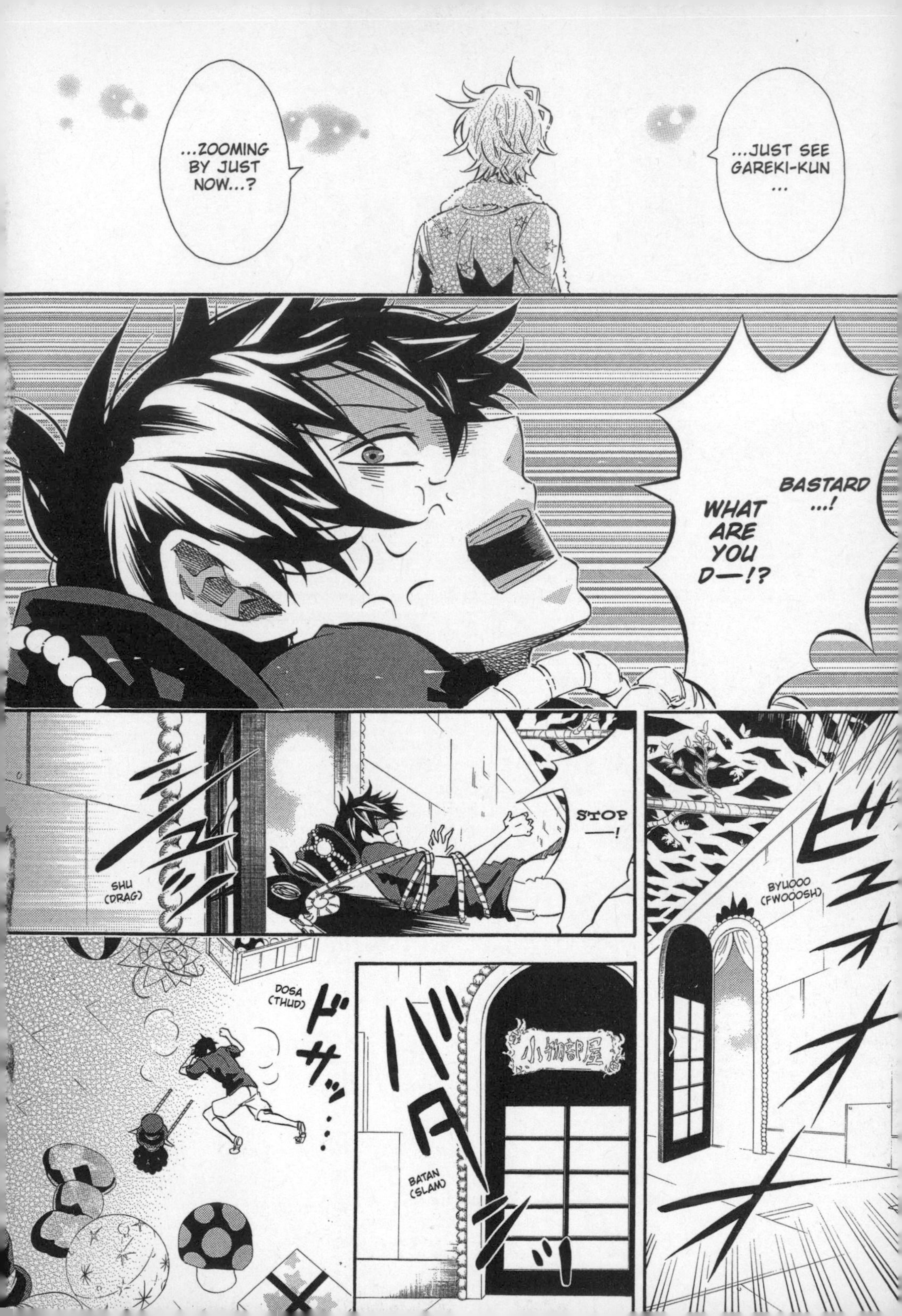
...JUST SEE GAREKI-KUN ...
...ZOOMING BY JUST NOW...?
BASTARD ...!
WHAT ARE YOU D—!?
BYUOOO (FWOOOSH)
STOP —!
SHU (DRAG)
小物部屋
BATAN (SLAM)
DOSA (THUD)

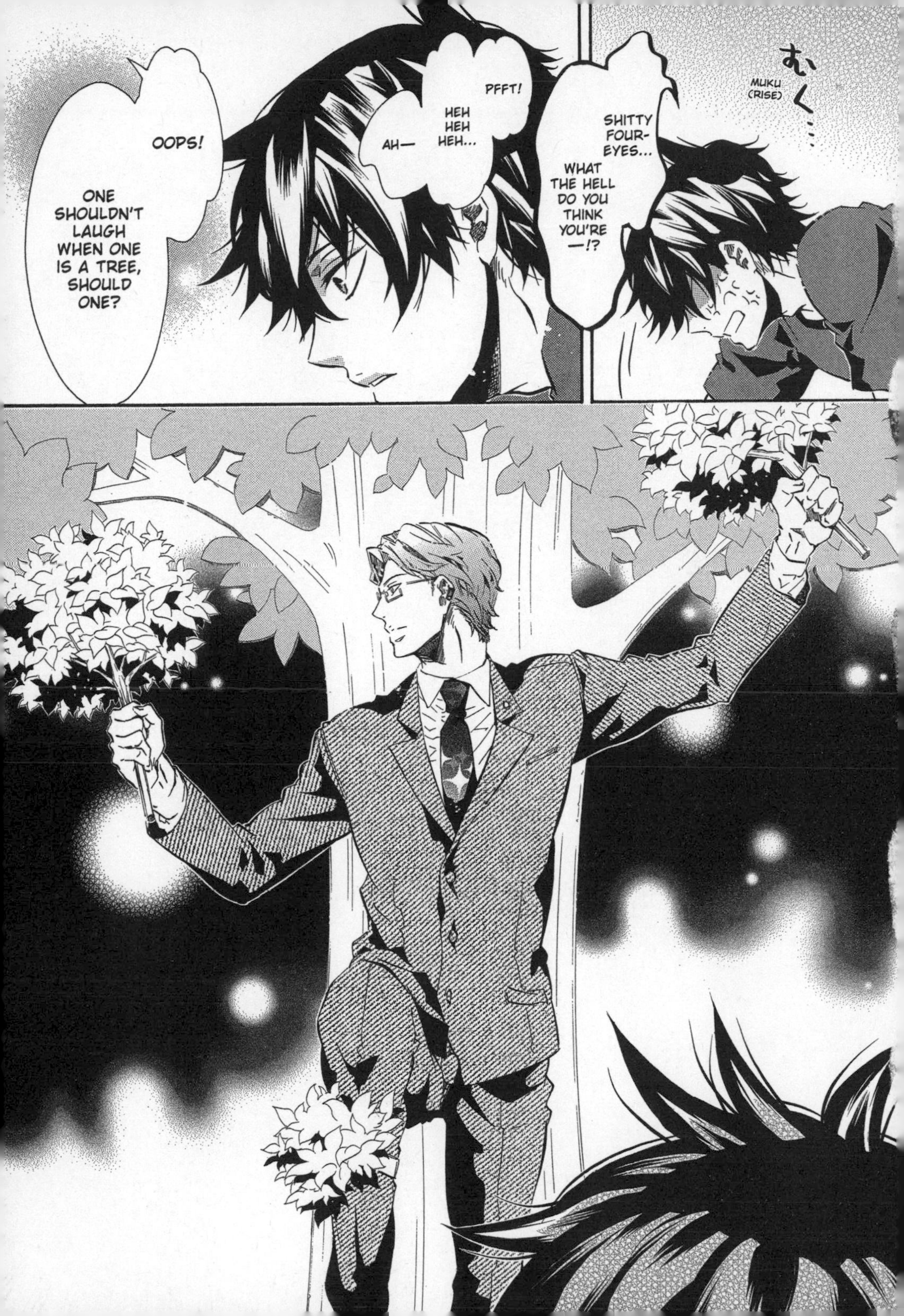
むく…
MUKU (RISE)
SHITTY FOUR-EYES... WHAT THE HELL DO YOU THINK YOU'RE—!?
PFFT!
HEH HEH HEH...
AH—
OOPS!
ONE SHOULDN'T LAUGH WHEN ONE IS A TREE, SHOULD ONE?

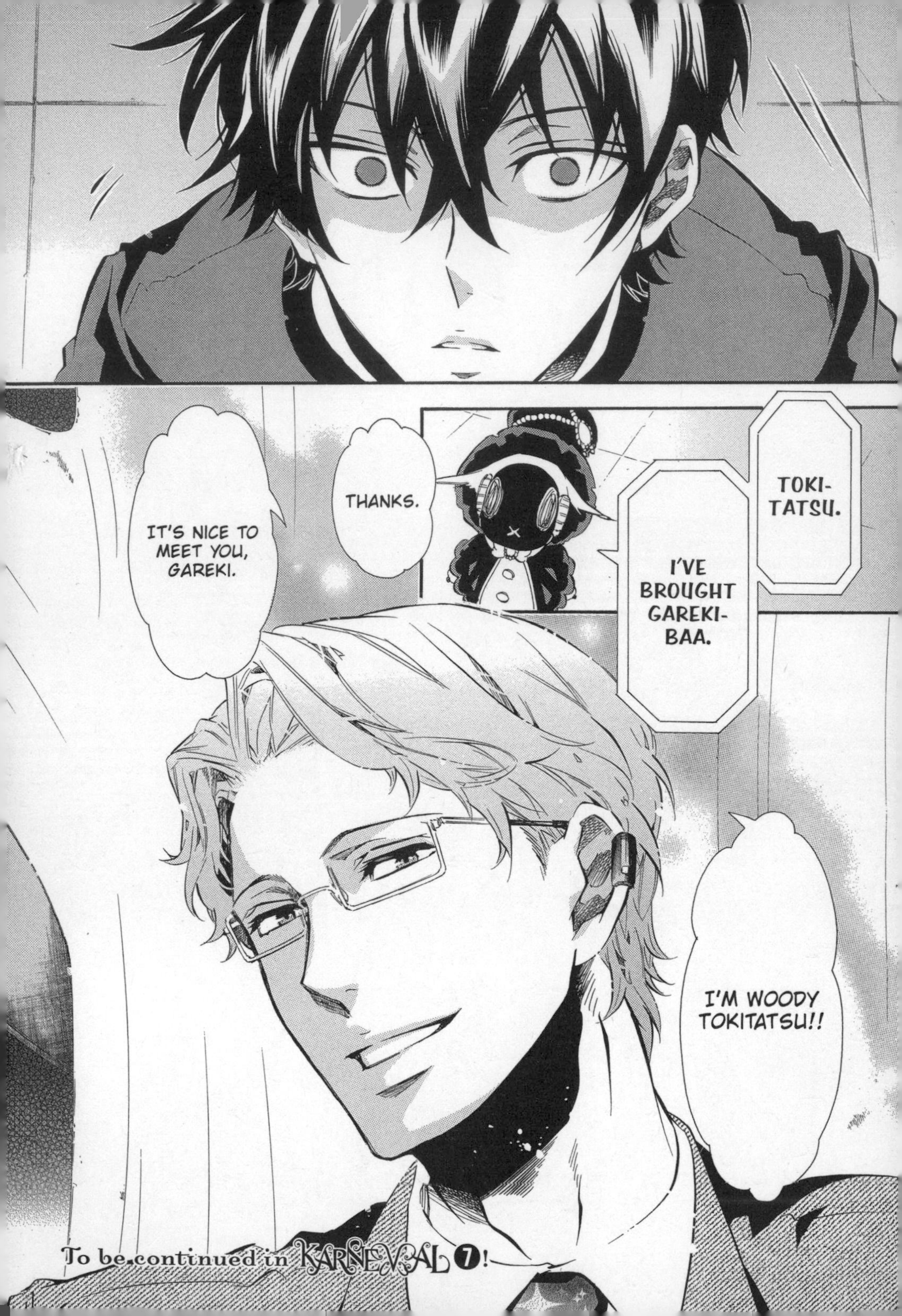
TOKI-TATSU.
I'VE BROUGHT GAREKI-BAA.
THANKS.
IT'S NICE TO MEET YOU, GAREKI.
I'M WOODY TOKITATSU!!
To be continued in KARNEVAL 7!

BA
(FLAP)

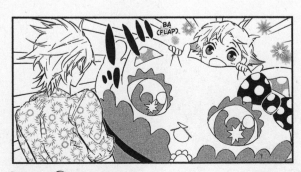

KARNEVAL

KARNEVAL

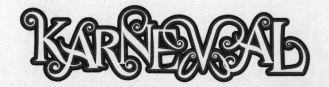

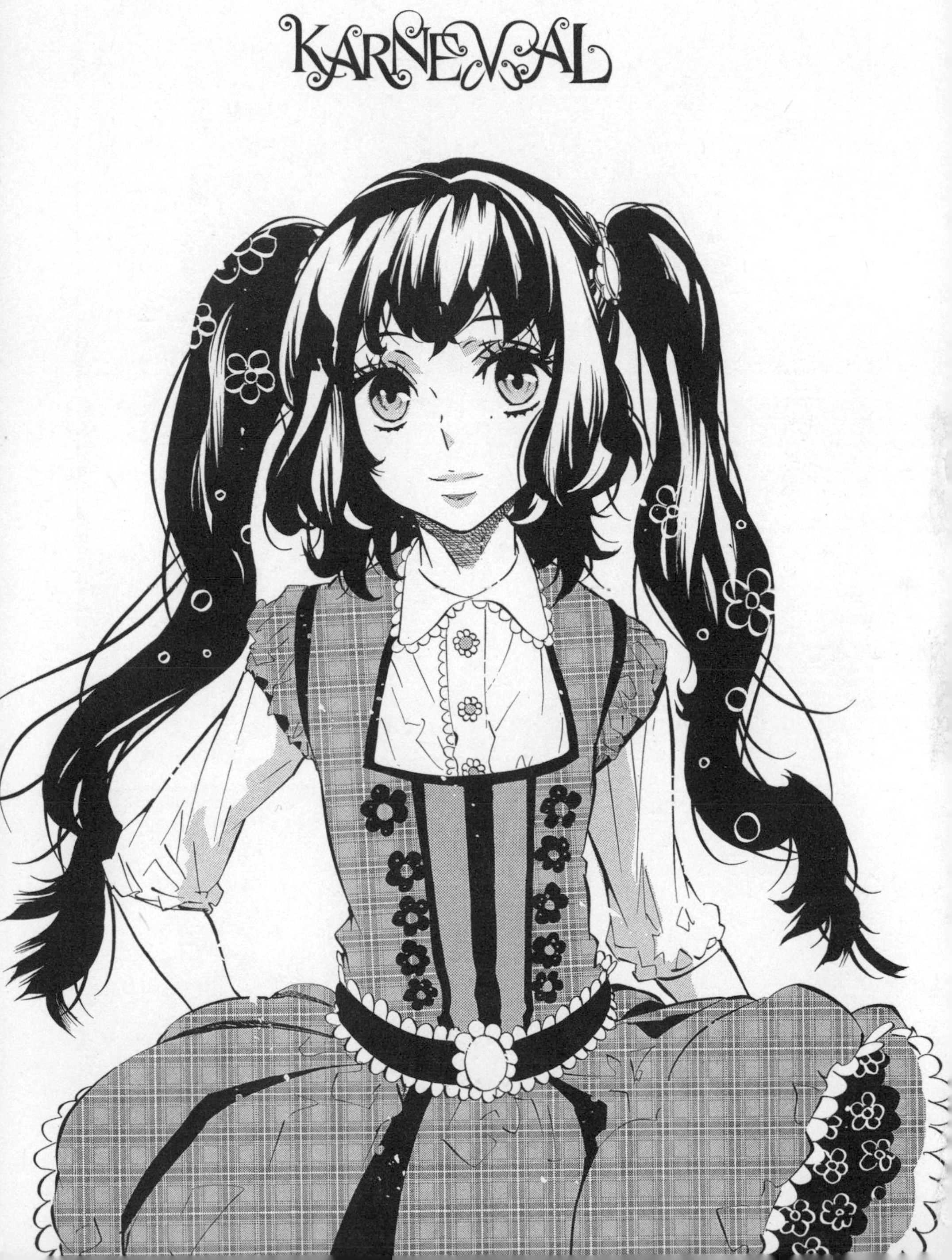
KARNEVAL

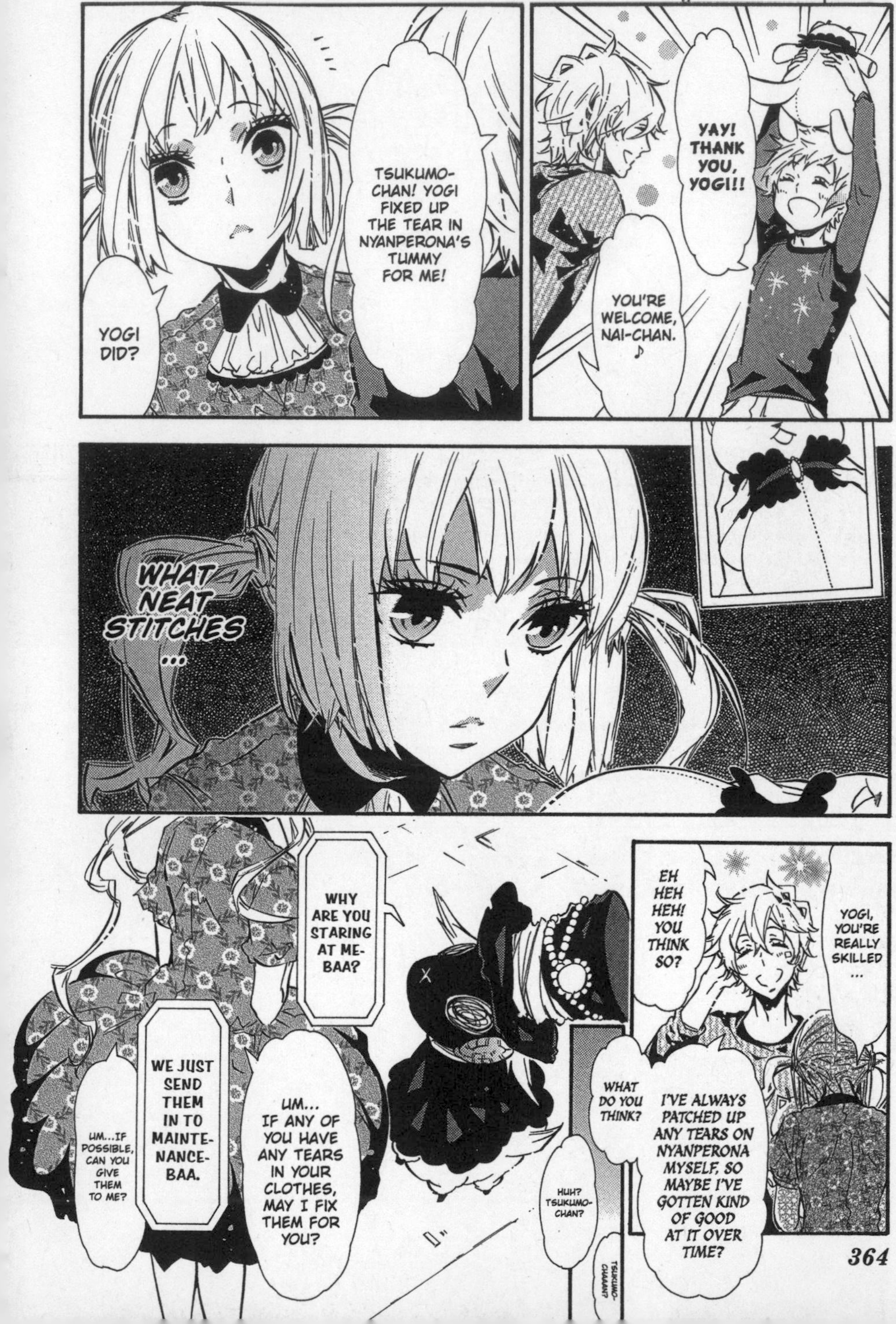
YAY! THANK YOU, YOGI!!
YOU'RE WELCOME, NAI-CHAN. ♪
TSUKUMO-CHAN! YOGI FIXED UP THE TEAR IN NYANPERONA'S TUMMY FOR ME!
YOGI DID?
WHAT NEAT STITCHES...
YOGI, YOU'RE REALLY SKILLED...
EH HEH HEH! YOU THINK SO?
I'VE ALWAYS PATCHED UP ANY TEARS ON NYANPERONA MYSELF, SO MAYBE I'VE GOTTEN KIND OF GOOD AT IT OVER TIME?
WHAT DO YOU THINK?
HUH? TSUKUMO-CHAN?
TSUKUMO-CHAAN!
WHY ARE YOU STARING AT ME-BAA?
UM... IF ANY OF YOU HAVE ANY TEARS IN YOUR CLOTHES, MAY I FIX THEM FOR YOU?
WE JUST SEND THEM IN TO MAINTENANCE-BAA.
UM...IF POSSIBLE, CAN YOU GIVE THEM TO ME?

Bonus Comic 2 - Here It Comes...!!

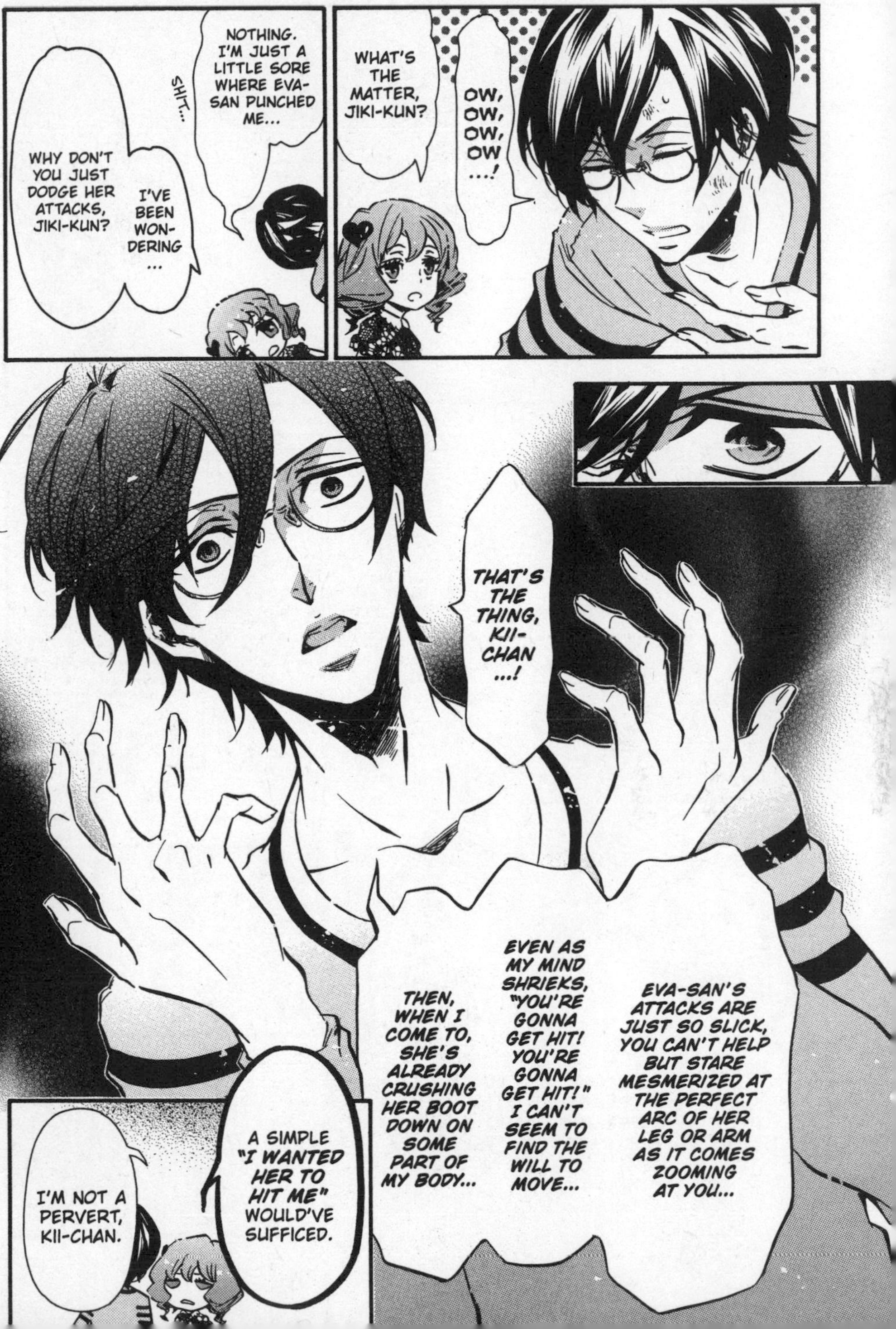
OW, OW, OW, OW ...!
WHAT'S THE MATTER, JIKI-KUN?
NOTHING. I'M JUST A LITTLE SORE WHERE EVA-SAN PUNCHED ME...
SHIT...
I'VE BEEN WONDERING ...
WHY DON'T YOU JUST DODGE HER ATTACKS, JIKI-KUN?
THAT'S THE THING, KII-CHAN ...!
EVA-SAN'S ATTACKS ARE JUST SO SLICK, YOU CAN'T HELP BUT STARE MESMERIZED AT THE PERFECT ARC OF HER LEG OR ARM AS IT COMES ZOOMING AT YOU...
EVEN AS MY MIND SHRIEKS, "YOU'RE GONNA GET HIT! YOU'RE GONNA GET HIT!" I CAN'T SEEM TO FIND THE WILL TO MOVE...
THEN, WHEN I COME TO, SHE'S ALREADY CRUSHING HER BOOT DOWN ON SOME PART OF MY BODY...
A SIMPLE "I WANTED HER TO HIT ME" WOULD'VE SUFFICED.
I'M NOT A PERVERT, KII-CHAN.

Bonus Comic 3 - Raising a Glass with a Friend at Journey's End

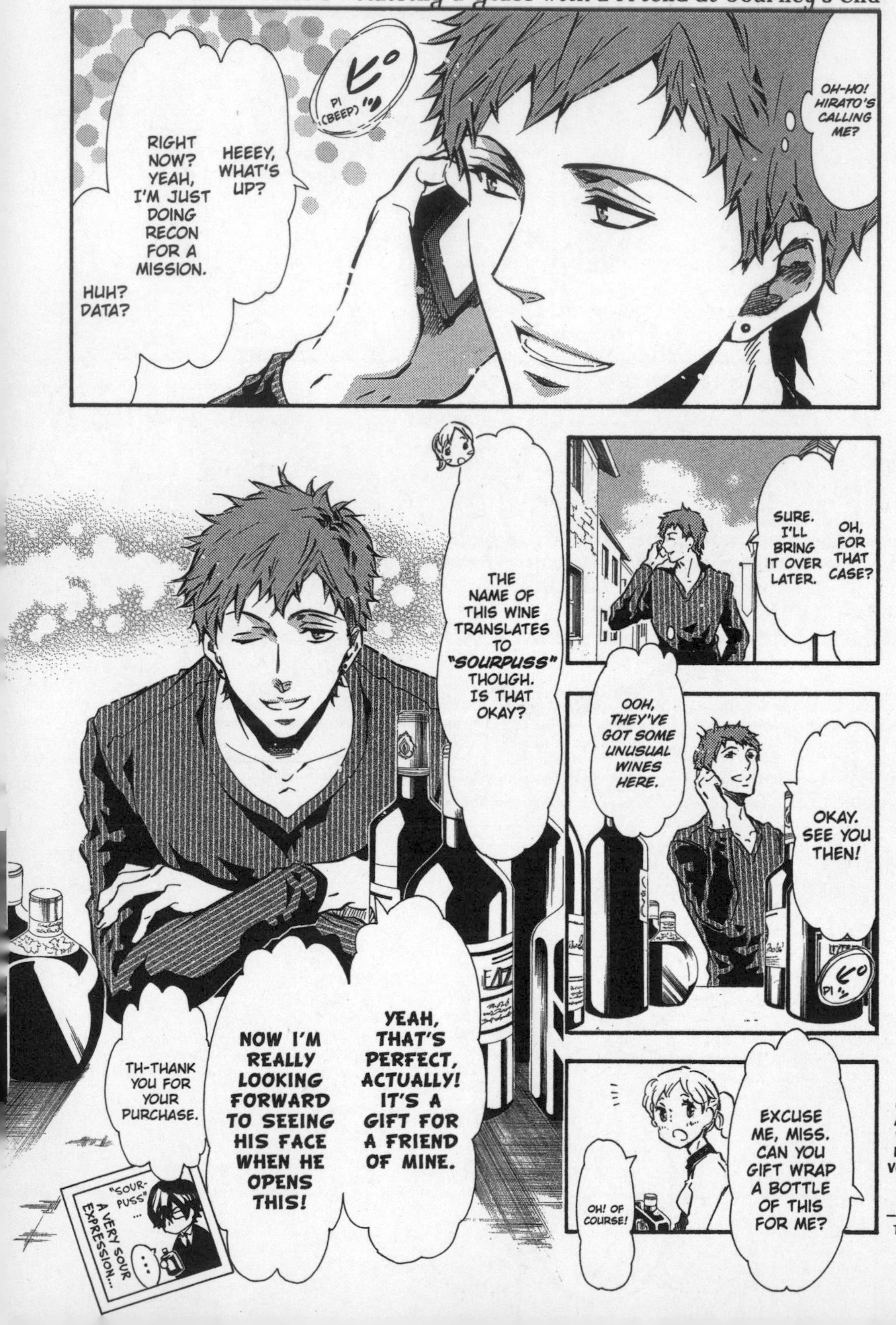
OH-HO! HIRATO'S CALLING ME?
PI (BEEP)
HEEEY, WHAT'S UP?
RIGHT NOW? YEAH, I'M JUST DOING RECON FOR A MISSION.
HUH? DATA?
OH, FOR THAT CASE?
SURE. I'LL BRING IT OVER LATER.
OKAY. SEE YOU THEN!
OOH, THEY'VE GOT SOME UNUSUAL WINES HERE.
PI
EXCUSE ME, MISS. CAN YOU GIFT WRAP A BOTTLE OF THIS FOR ME?
OH! OF COURSE!
THE NAME OF THIS WINE TRANSLATES TO "SOURPUSS" THOUGH. IS THAT OKAY?
YEAH, THAT'S PERFECT, ACTUALLY! IT'S A GIFT FOR A FRIEND OF MINE.
NOW I'M REALLY LOOKING FORWARD TO SEEING HIS FACE WHEN HE OPENS THIS!
TH-THANK YOU FOR YOUR PURCHASE.
"SOUR-PUSS"... A VERY SOUR EXPRESSION...
...

COME AWAY WITH ME TO VOLUME 6! ☆ —TSUKI-TACHI

THANK YOU SO MUCH FOR CONTINUING TO READ KARNEVAL! THE SERIES
WAS TURNED INTO AN ANIME THIS YEAR, AND BETWEEN THAT AND A
FEW OTHER THINGS IN MY LIFE, I CAN'T BELIEVE SIX MONTHS HAVE
GONE BY IN THE BLINK OF AN EYE! REALLY, 2013 HAS BEEN QUITE A
BUSY YEAR FOR ME. IT FEELS LIKE I'VE REALLY UNDERGONE A LOT OF
PERSONAL CHANGE IN MY LIFE. BUT I INTEND TO KEEP WORKING REALLY
HARD GOING FORWARD SO THAT I'LL ALWAYS BE ABLE TO CREATE
MANGA AND ARTWORK THAT I HOPE YOU WILL ALL CONTINUE TO ENJOY.
PLEASE CHEER ME ON MY WAY—THAT WOULD MAKE ME SO HAPPY!
I'M ABSOLUTELY THRILLED TO SEE HOW MANY NEW NYANPERONA
GOODS THERE ARE AVAILABLE NOW! ESPECIALLY THE ANI-KUJI A PRIZE
NYANPERONA STUFFED ANIMAL THAT'S FIFTY CENTIMETERS TALL—IT'S
SO BIG AND ADORABLE, I JUST ABSOLUTELY LOVE IT! SERIOUSLY, I CAN
HARDLY CONTAIN MYSELF. I REALLY ENJOYED THE ANIME'S CHARACTER
SONGS TOO! I ACTUALLY HAVE THEM ON ALL THE TIME WHILE I WORK.
THANK YOU TO EVERYONE WHO CONTRIBUTED TO THE FAN TALK
AS WELL! THOUGH I'M NOT ABLE TO SEND YOU ANSWERS, I'VE READ
EVERYTHING AND REALLY TREASURED IT ALL. IT ALSO MADE ME SO
HAPPY TO SEE EVERYONE ENJOYING THEMSELVES AT THE ANIME LAUNCH
EVENT AND THE SUMMER-PERONA SHOW. I WAS SO CRAZY ABOUT THE
NYANPERONA COSTUMED MASCOT THEY HAD THERE, I TOOK A TON OF
PHOTOS WITH HIM. HE WAS JUST SO CUTE AND SUCH A PERFECT IDOL!
I ALSO HAD FUN DOING THE COLLABORATION WITH WOOSER'S HAND-TO-
MOUTH LIFE! IN FACT, WOOSER-SAMA ACTUALLY SHOWS UP SOMEWHERE
IN THIS VOLUME OF KARNEVAL, SO PLEASE GO LOOK FOR HIM.

—TOUYA MIKANAGI

and
to you!

Special Thanks

o KANA-CHAN, -SAN
  MOTSU-SAN, SUAMA-SAN

o MY EDITOR, ABE-SAN

o EVERYONE AT ICHIJINSHA
  PUBLISHING

o ALL THE COLLABORATORS
  AND EVERYONE AT OUR
  AFFILIATED COMPANIES
  WHO'VE TAKEN CARE OF ME

o ALL THE TEACHERS AND
  FRIENDS WHO HAVE TAKEN
  CARE OF ME, TEN-CHAN,
  JUN-SAN, MY FAMILY, AND MY
  BELOVED OLDER SISTER

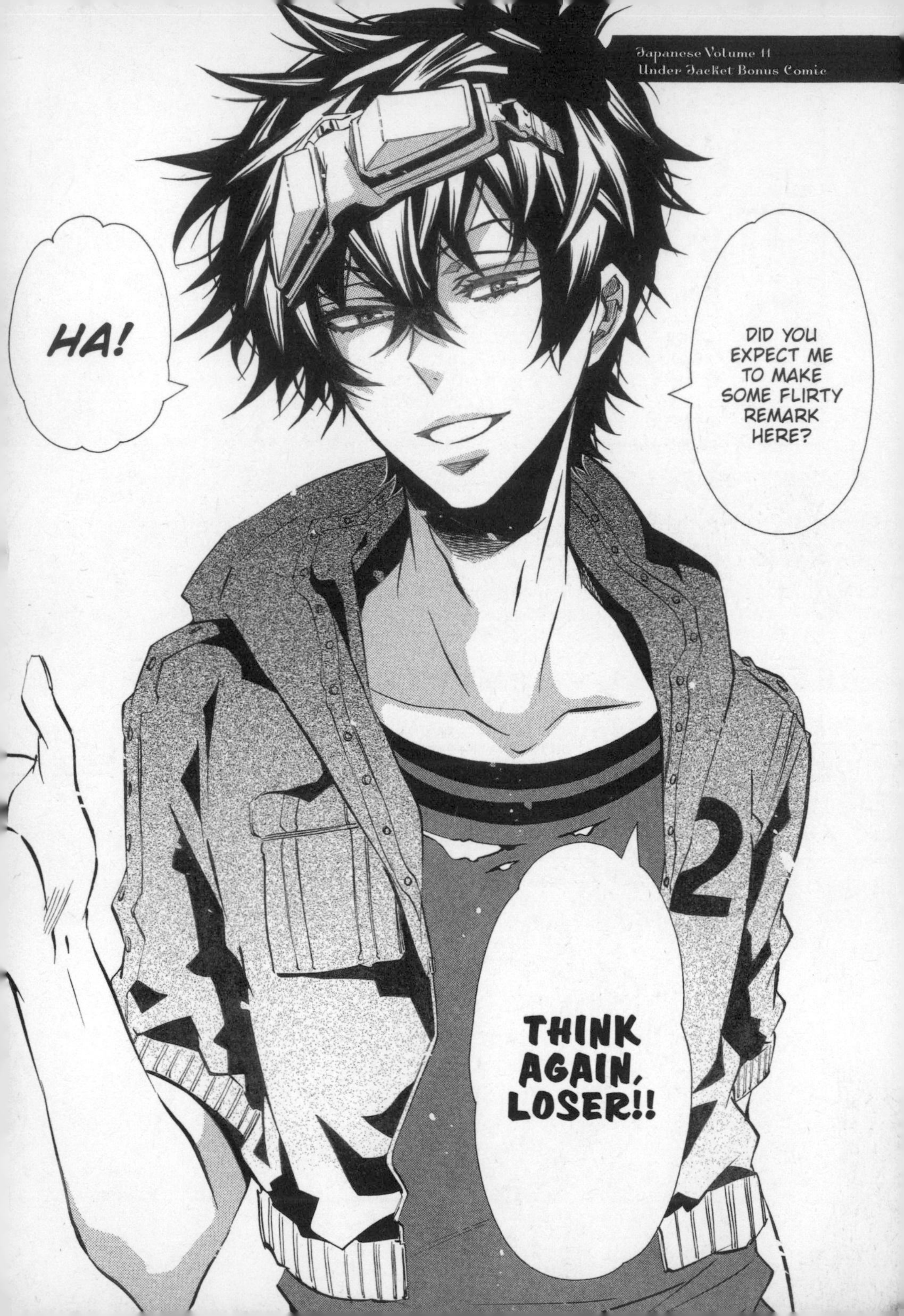
DID YOU EXPECT ME TO MAKE SOME FLIRTY REMARK HERE?
HA!
THINK AGAIN, LOSER!!

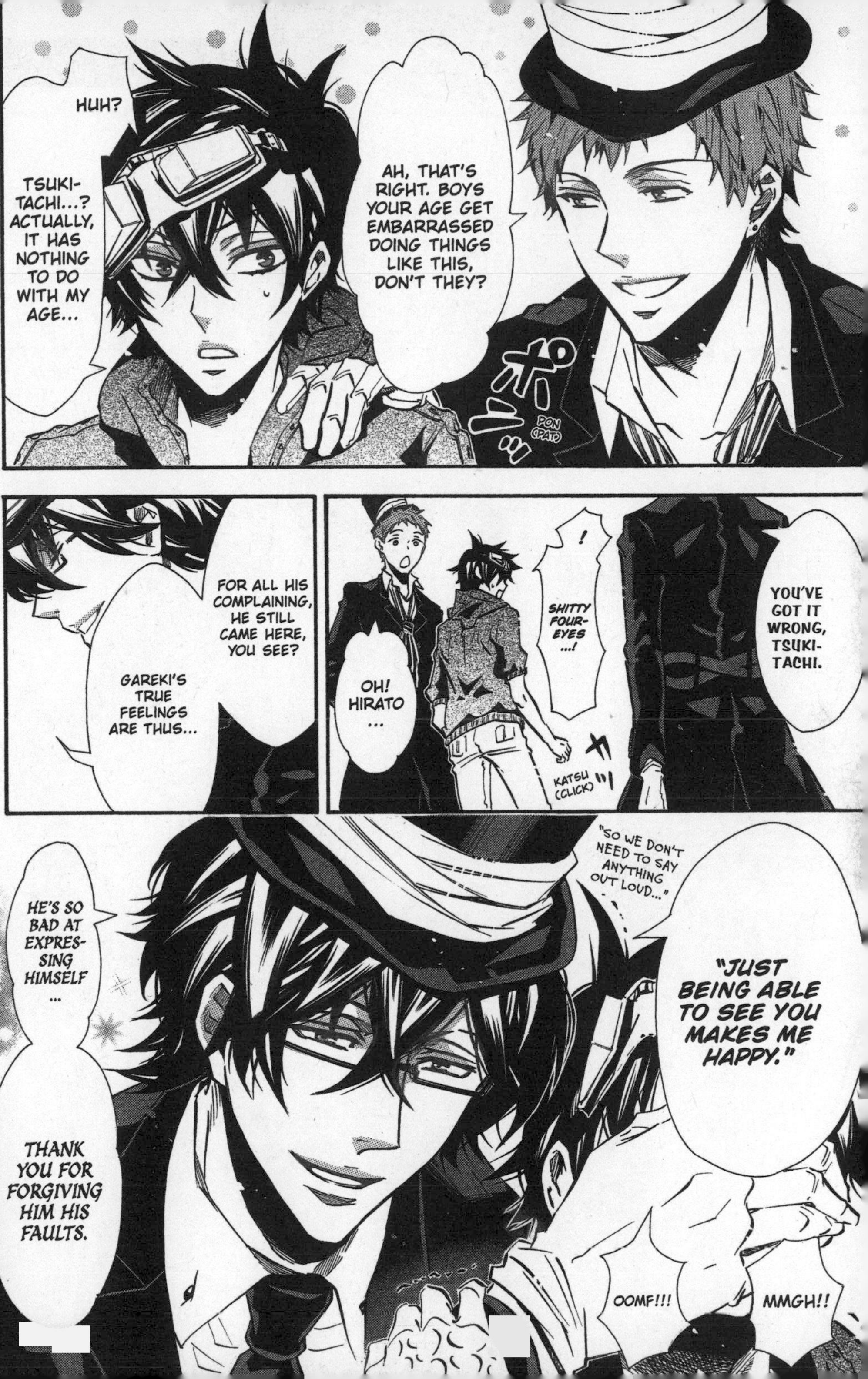
AH, THAT'S RIGHT. BOYS YOUR AGE GET EMBARRASSED DOING THINGS LIKE THIS, DON'T THEY?
PON (PAT)
HUH?
TSUKI-TACHI...? ACTUALLY, IT HAS NOTHING TO DO WITH MY AGE...
YOU'VE GOT IT WRONG, TSUKI-TACHI.
!
SHITTY FOUR-EYES ...!
OH! HIRATO ...
KATSU (CLICK)
FOR ALL HIS COMPLAINING, HE STILL CAME HERE, YOU SEE?
GAREKI'S TRUE FEELINGS ARE THUS...
"SO WE DON'T NEED TO SAY ANYTHING OUT LOUD..."
"JUST BEING ABLE TO SEE YOU MAKES ME HAPPY."
HE'S SO BAD AT EXPRES-SING HIMSELF ...
THANK YOU FOR FORGIVING HIM HIS FAULTS.
MMGH!!
OOMF!!!

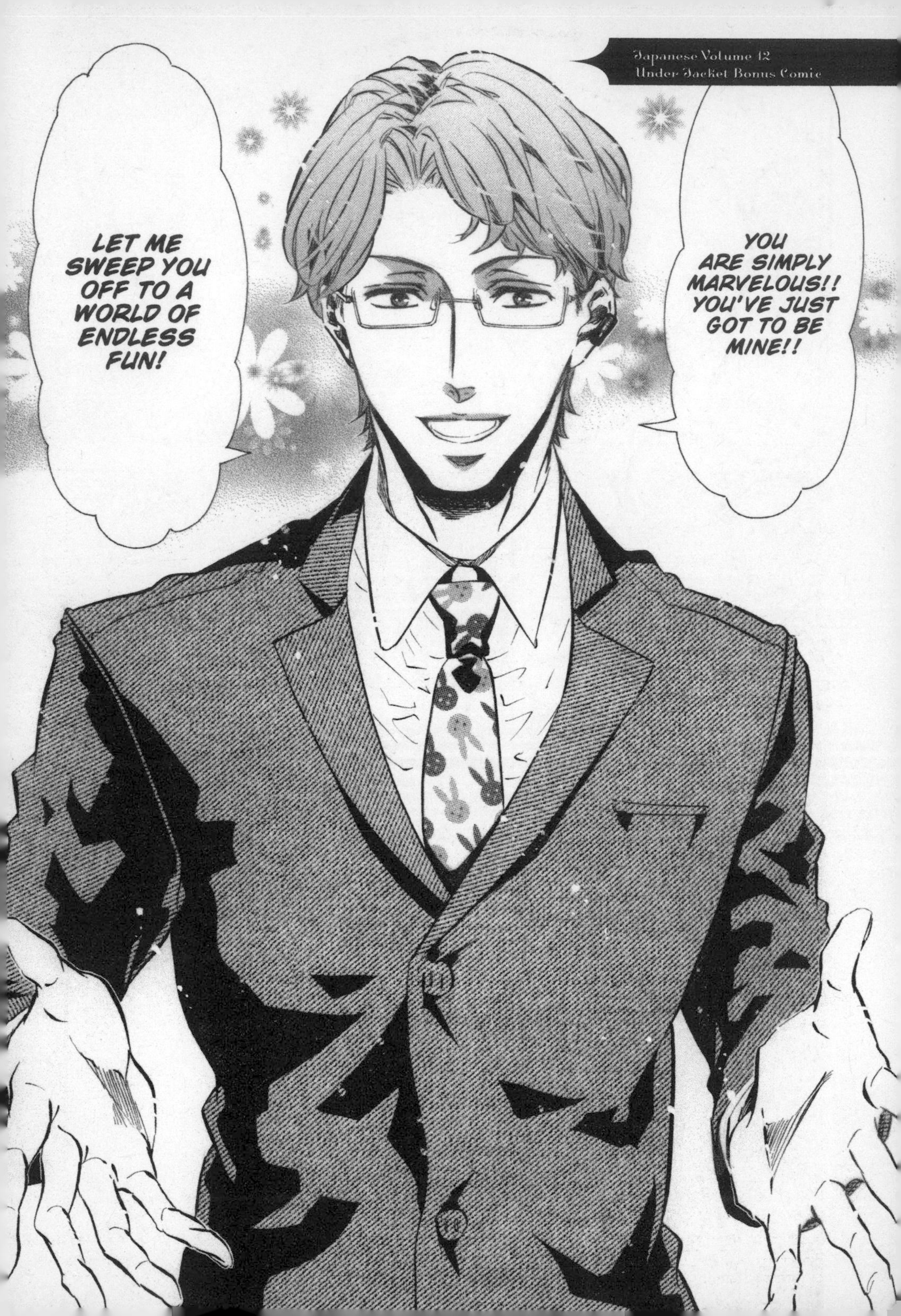
Japanese Volume 12 Under Jacket Bonus Comic
YOU ARE SIMPLY MARVELOUS!! YOU'VE JUST GOT TO BE MINE!!
LET ME SWEEP YOU OFF TO A WORLD OF ENDLESS FUN!

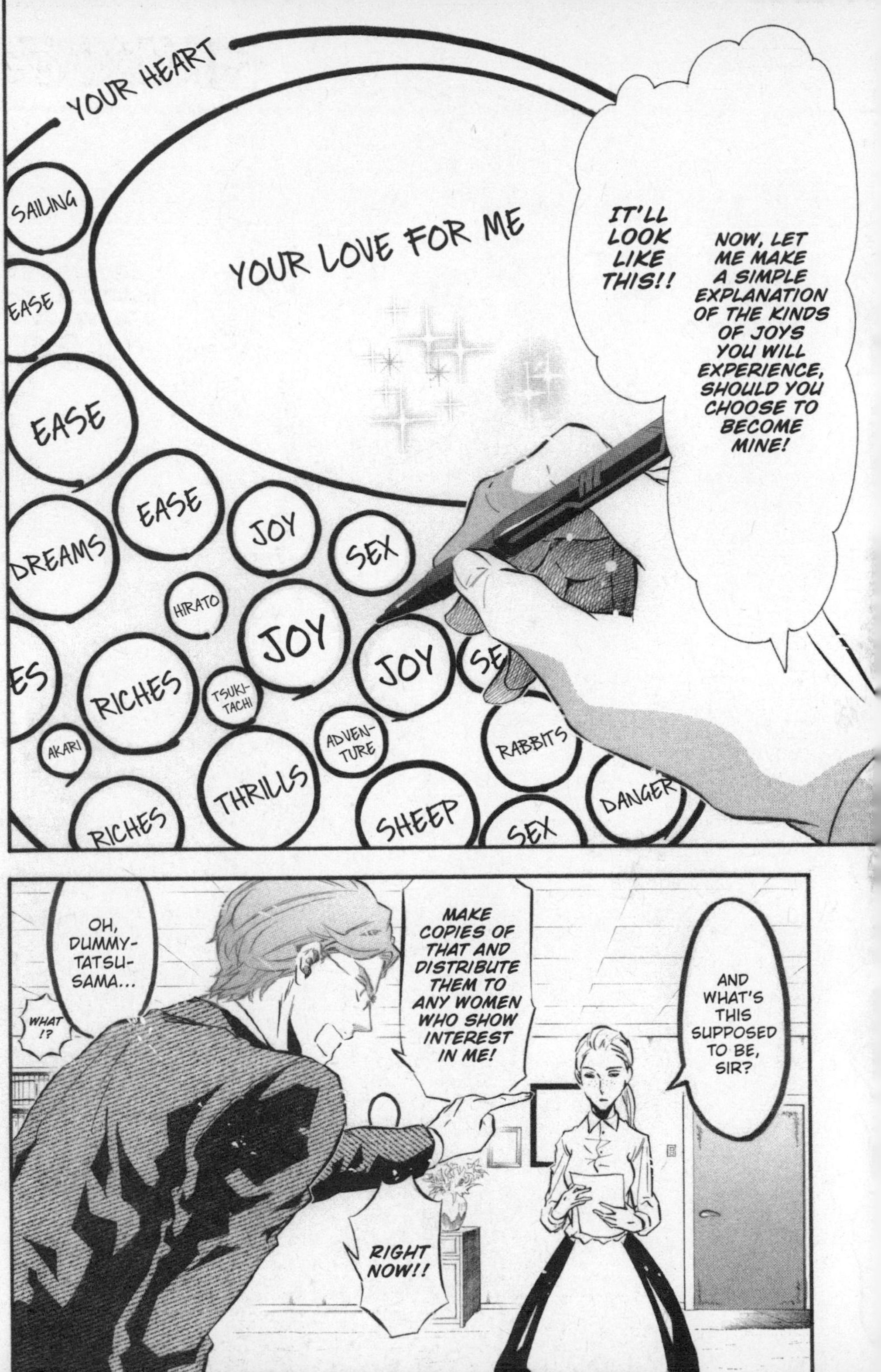
NOW, LET ME MAKE A SIMPLE EXPLANATION OF THE KINDS OF JOYS YOU WILL EXPERIENCE, SHOULD YOU CHOOSE TO BECOME MINE!
IT'LL LOOK LIKE THIS!!
YOUR HEART
YOUR LOVE FOR ME
SAILING
EASE
EASE
EASE
DREAMS
JOY
SEX
HIRATO
JOY
JOY
RICHES
TSUKI-TACHI
AKARI
ADVEN-TURE
RABBITS
THRILLS
RICHES
SHEEP
SEX
DANGER
AND WHAT'S THIS SUPPOSED TO BE, SIR?
MAKE COPIES OF THAT AND DISTRIBUTE THEM TO ANY WOMEN WHO SHOW INTEREST IN ME!
RIGHT NOW!!
OH, DUMMY-TATSU-SAMA...
WHAT!?

KARNEVAL

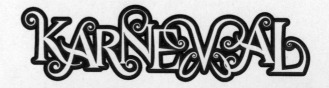

KARNEVAL 6

Touya Mikanagi

Translation: Su Mon Han   Lettering: Alexis Eckerman

Karneval vols. 11–12 © 2013 by Touya Mikanagi. All rights reserved. First published in Japan in 2013 by ICHIJINSHA. English translation rights arranged with ICHIJINSHA through Tuttle-Mori Agency, Inc., Tokyo.

English translation © 2016 by Yen Press, LLC

Yen Press
1290 Avenue of the Americas
New York, NY 10104

Visit us at yenpress.com • facebook.com/yenpress • twitter.com/yenpress • yenpress.tumblr.com • instagram.com/yenpress

First Yen Press Edition: November 2016

Yen Press is an imprint of Yen Press, LLC.
The Yen Press name and logo are trademarks of Yen Press, LLC.

The publisher is not responsible for websites (or their content) that are not owned by the publisher.

Library of Congress Control Number: 2016936531

ISBNs: 978-0-316-26353-5 (paperback)
978-0-316-26365-8 (ebook)

10 9 8 7 6 5 4 3 2 1

BVG

Printed in the United States of America